Nauvoo polygamy

UPDATED AND REVISED

Nauvoo polygamy

"... but we called it celestial marriage"

GEORGE D. SMITH

Signature Books
Salt Lake City • 2011

www.signaturebooks.com

The subtitle of *Nauvoo Polygamy* quotes the March 19, 1892, Temple Lot deposition of Emily Partridge, who described how Joseph Smith "taught me this principle of plural marriage that is called polygamy now, but we called it celestial marriage" (*Reorganized Church v. Church of Christ,* question 23).

Painting on jacket: *Sisters,* artist unknown, ca. 1840, oil on canvas, 18⅛ x 24 inches, courtesy National Gallery of Art, Washington, D.C., which received the painting as a gift from Edgar William and Bernice Chrysler Garbisch.

The text was composed in 11.25 pt. Janson.

Nauvoo Polygamy: "... but we called it celestial marriage" was printed on acid-free paper and was composed, printed, and bound in the United States of America.

2016 2015 2014 2013 2012 2011 6 5 4 3 2 1

LIBRARY OF CONGRESS CATALOGING-IN-PUBLICATION DATA

Smith, George D. (George Dempster), 1938-
Nauvoo polygamy : "... but we called it celestial marriage" / George D. Smith. — 2nd ed.
p. cm.
Includes bibliographical references and index.
ISBN 978-1-56085-207-0 (pbk : alk. paper) 1. Polygamy—Religious aspects—Church of Jesus Christ of Latter-day Saints. 2. Marriage—Religious aspects—Church of Jesus Christ of Latter-day Saints. 3. Polygamy—Religious aspects—Mormon Church. 4. Marriage—Religious aspects—Mormon Church. 5. Polygamy—Illinois—Nauvoo—History—19th century. 6. Nauvoo (Ill.)—Social conditions—19th century. I. Title.
BX8641.S633 2011
261.8'3584230882893—dc22

2010032062

To Libbie and Caroline,
who each married a sister's husband

how celestial is marriage
carriage to higher climes
spousal rhymes of double
treble images, shadows of
soft redundancy which night
might you be staying we
can negotiate but here you
are, rippling froth
cresting at day's end
a favor here to savor
savior, angel's warning sword
celestial kiss
in this Man's world a right
a privilege not to miss

Contents

Ilustrations

Tables

Preface to the Paperback Edition

Since publication of this book, I have been able to speak at a number of professional and other venues and to receive criticism from historians and general readers. I have appreciated the advice, complaints, and expressions of surprise from those unfamiliar with this history.

One reader, not a Mormon, discovered an ancestor in the chart at the end of the book along with several wives and children. This reader had known that he had Mormons deep in his family's past, and here they were in black and white. A Parley Pratt family historian contacted me and offered corrections, which I have included in this edition, while excluding unresolved name-and-date disputes among family historians.

I have amended the text and notes for accuracy and diction. A new table (3.3, p. 238), Joseph's Courtships and Emma's Pregnancies, illustrates ironies in their Smith marital chronology, such as Emma's conception just after Joseph's plural union with Louisa Beaman.

Although many readers have offered congratulations on the scope and message of the book, others have voiced concern about the book's tone where I related matter-of-factly what eyewitness sources reported. At one "author and critics" discussion, a fundamentalist Mormon—a wife in a polygamous family—said my book was a difficult read because of its implied criticism of polygamy and was not something she would recommend to friends, even though, as she also said, she encountered much in the book that she found to be informative and personally valuable.

By contrast, a feminist critic expressed curiosity and unease with the inelegant aspects of Nauvoo polygamy, for instance how Joseph Smith characterized his invitation to friends to take additional wives as "favors" and "privileges." This apparent commerce in women has been uncomfortable for some readers to accept. Resistance is understandable for those who were unaware of the nature of Nauvoo polygamy and whose view of a beloved church leader assumed present-day norms.

Another critic suggested that perhaps, based on what he considered to be the absence of evidence to the contrary, Joseph Smith may have had intimate relations only with single women but not with his plural wives who were already married. Of course, how would one know? Only a resulting child would prove a woman's intimacy with her prophet-husband; however, the absence of a child would not disprove a spousal relationship. Melissa Lott testified that she "roomed" with Smith "as his wife" but did not bear him children due to "lack of proper conditions … on my part probably."

However, the stated purpose of polygamy was to "raise righteous seed." Polygamy in the Old Testament was based on the command to be "fruitful and multiply." Similarly, the Book of Mormon allowed for the possibility of polygamy to produce children. The text gives conditional sanction to polygamy in the voice of the "Lord of hosts," to "raise up seed unto me" (Jacob 2:30). Condemned in the past, polygamy was a future option, but only for propagation.

Smith shared marital intimacy with his wives. He "ocupied the same room and bed with" Almera Johnson that he had previously occupied with Eliza Partridge, according to a statement by Almera's brother Benjamin. Smith's union with Sylvia Sessions may have resulted in a child, as she told her daughter, Josephine Lyon Fisher, that she was the prophet's daughter. Richard Van Wagoner (recently deceased) recognized the parental identification of Smith's plural child.

Although discussion over the nature of Smith's relationships continues, we return to the only reason given as a defense for plural marriage, the propagation of righteous offspring. From its inception in Nauvoo, this rationale implied marital intimacy.

George D. Smith
April 2011

Introduction

In 1792, Napoleon, then a young soldier in the French army, wrote to his "sweet and incomparable" Josephine of their first night together: "I have awakened full of you. The memory of last night has given my senses no rest ... What an effect you have on my heart! I send you thousands of kisses—but don't kiss me. Your kisses sear my blood."[1] The soldier's adventures had just begun.

Napoleon Bonaparte went on to conquer Austria, invade Egypt, and in 1804 crown himself Emperor of France. Although Josephine was not the only woman in his life, this alluring Creole from Martinique would marry her new lover and become Empress of France.[2]

A few decades later on the American frontier, another man of ambition, coincidentally inspired by what Napoleon had found in Egypt, wrote his own letter to a young woman. It was the summer of 1842 and the thirty-six-year-old prophet, Joseph Smith, hiding from the law down by the Mississippi River in Illinois, proposed a tryst with the appealing seventeen-year-old, Sarah Ann Whitney. "My feelings are so strong for you," he wrote. "Come and see me in this my lonely retreat ... now is the time to afford me succour ... I have a room intirely by myself, the whole matter can be attended to with most perfect saf[e]-ty, I know it is the will of God that you should comfort me."[3] Three

1. Daniel Meyerson, *The Linguist and the Emperor: Napoleon and Champollion's Quest to Decipher the Rosetta Stone* (New York: Ballantine Books, 2004), 26.

2. Robespierre had guillotined Josephine's former husband in the French Revolution.

3. Joseph Smith to "Brother and Sister, [Newel K.] Whitney, and &c. [Sarah Ann]," Nauvoo, Illinois, August 18, 1842, Joseph Smith Collections, The Church of Jesus Christ of Latter-day Saints (LDS), Salt Lake City, Utah.

weeks prior to this letter, Sarah Ann had secretly married the self-proclaimed seer and leader of the millennialist Latter-day Saints to become his sixteenth wife.

Historically, it has not been so unusual for the leader of a country or founder of a religion to take an interest in more than one woman. What *was* unusual in this instance was the further step Smith took, turning a predilection into a Christian obligation, institutionalizing polygamy. Curiously enough, the way Joseph did this was through his passion for ancient Egypt, derived from Napoleon's invasion of that country a few years before Smith's birth. Just as soulful kisses and succor appeased one desire in each of these two men, so both men had another inner stirring that was awakened by contact with a forgotten civilization. They showed a fascination with ancient Egypt, especially the hieroglyphic writing that was thought to hold the occult secrets of an unrivaled spiritual and temporal world power. The French adventurer's findings lit a fire in Smith that inspired even the language of his religious prose.

In 1798 Napoleon entered Egypt by way of the Nile. Following centuries of foreign occupation, he found stunning artifacts that at once consumed public attention. The pictographs appeared impossible to read. These enigmatic scripts enchanted Europeans, who decorated museums with them and designed articles of high fashion with Egyptian motifs. In America, towns named Memphis and Cairo emerged along the Mississippi in 1820 and 1837, not far downstream from where the Mormon capital of Nauvoo, Illinois, would be founded in 1839. It took the linguist Jean-François Champollion (1790-1832) more than twenty years to decipher the hieroglyphics inscribed on the Rosetta Stone and re-discover the social and religious life of a lost culture. His *Egyptian Grammar* was published posthumously in Paris in 1835-41; his *Dictionary*, in 1841-44.

Some thirty years after Napoleon unearthed the glyphs that turned out to hold the key to the ancient language, Champollion and other scholars were still hard at work decoding their meaning when Joseph Smith founded a religion based on what he said were his own translations of ancient Egyptian. While the early hieroglyphs were still indecipherable to most of the world, Smith told New York publisher James Arlington Bennet:

> The fact is, that by the power of God, I translated the Book of Mormon from hieroglyphics, the knowledge of which was lost to the world, in which wonderful event I stood alone, an unlearned youth, to combat the worldly wisdom and multiplied ignorance of eighteen centuries, with a new revelation, which would open the eyes of more than eight hundred millions of people ... God is my right hand man.[4]

Smith announced that he had found gold tablets buried in a hill, on which an ancient history was inscribed in "reformed Egyptian." By the power of God, he proclaimed that he was able to translate the hieroglyphics and in 1830 publish the story as the Book of Mormon.[5] This book explained the presence of Indians in the Americas, ascribing to them ancestors from ancient Israel, who were nevertheless not the rumored "lost tribes." A few years later, Smith published a variant of Genesis called the Book of Abraham, which he said was written on papyrus found in the funeral scrolls he purchased in 1835, complete with Egyptian mummies. Little did Napoleon dream that by unearthing the Egyptian past, he would provide the mystery language of a new religion.

It was in the Book of Mormon that the idea of plural marriage was first mentioned in Latter-day Saint references, an ironic source to justify polygamy since it was said to have been withheld from sixth-century BCE Hebrew tribes that had wandered to the Americas. Still, a man's right to have more than one wife would soon become Mormon doctrine, validating the many marriages Joseph had engaged in up to that point—his desire to wed the young Sarah Ann Whitney, for instance. Using Old Testament polygamy as a model, Smith's new

---

4. Smith to James Arlington Bennet, Nov. 13, 1843, in Joseph Smith et al., *History of the Church of Jesus Christ of Latter-day Saints,* ed. B. H. Roberts, 2nd ed. rev., 7 vols. (Salt Lake City: Deseret Book, 1963), 6:74, 78.

5. Moroni, son of Mormon, writes as he completes and buries the record of his father: "And now, behold, we have written this record ... in the characters which are called among us the reformed Egyptian" (Morm. 9:32, in Joseph Smith Jr., trans, *The Book of Mormon* [Salt Lake City: Church of Jesus Christ of Latter-day Saints, 1951], 475).

Church of Christ (ultimately renamed the Church of Jesus Christ of Latter-day Saints in 1838) revived the custom of the ancient patriarchs. The Mormon prophet introduced polygamy to the frontier, where his band of followers was preparing for the imminent "end of days" to descend upon the world.

The American frontier defined the Mormon Church as its members spent twenty years on the run from one state to the next, blazing new trails and founding new cities. As they were expelled by their neighbors from New York to Ohio, then to Missouri, during the 1830s, the homes of friends or converts along the way offered temporary refuge. This is where Smith became acquainted with the young women he would marry a decade later: they were the daughters of friends in the families where he stayed. In Illinois in the 1840s, he was betrothed to teenage women as young as fourteen. He made wedding vows with older women as well. Some of those he married already had husbands and children. However, if loyal to him, the wives and their polyandrous husbands were introduced into an inner circle which formed an aristocratic network of intermarried couples in the elite hierarchy. Beyond his quest for female companionship, Smith utilized plural marriage to create a byzantine structure of relationships intended for successive worlds.

What is also known is that Smith not only persuaded women to marry him, he convinced his closest male followers to expand their own families, adding more wives to their homes. This occurred within the last three years of Smith's life, ending tragically with an assassin's bullet after he was arrested for destroying a local press—which incidentally had disclosed the unannounced marriage practice. Over the next year and a half, under the direction of Brigham Young, plural marriages multiplied in Nauvoo so that by the time the Saints abandoned the city in 1846 there were about 200 male polygamists in the church with 700 plural wives added to their families.

Whether Joseph's wife, Emma, consented to any of these marriages remains a mystery. She was aware of at least five of her husband's wives whom she sent away from her household, yet she told her children the wives did not exist. Joseph's family—his mother, wife, and children—refused the leadership of Brigham Young and stayed in the midwest. The founding family remained there, free of polygamy, in a new Reorganized Church of Jesus Christ of Latter Day Saints (RLDS), established in 1853 and, by 1860, presided over by Joseph III, Joseph and Emma's oldest surviving son.

From the earliest whisperings of extramarital relationships in the 1830s to official records kept in the 1840s, Mormon authorities downplayed reports of polygamy as "anti-Mormon" rumors. However, an 1852 announcement in Utah led to a period of openness about plural wives. Then the polygamists retreated into the shadows again in 1890 when, for reasons of survival and statehood, the church withdrew its endorsement of plural marriage. Thereafter, the LDS Church in Utah tried to distance itself from its polygamous roots, just as the RLDS Church (recently renamed the Community of Christ) had already done. The two communities became united on one front: their mutual disavowal of a doctrine that was once said to be essential to salvation. Yet the memory of Mormon polygamy was kept alive, in part, by contemporary "fundamentalist" Mormon societies, primarily in Utah. Revulsion against their underage plural marriages today conveys a small sense of what the public outrage might have felt like in Illinois in the 1840s.

Smith's wives remain unacknowledged in the official *History of the Church of Jesus Christ of Latter-day Saints.* Even so, these women left their mark on the history of the American west. Aside from the thousands of Mormons who revered and emulated them, their participation in an experiment in a family oriented society has filled the Mormon consciousness for the better part of two centuries. Similarly, the primary characteristic of Mormons, according to outsiders, besides abstinence from coffee, tea, alcohol, and tobacco, is that the men at one time had multiple wives. However, today, in official Mormon circles, Smith's granting of favors to chosen followers, allowing them to take extra women into the home, is rarely mentioned.

The primary evidence for this arcane practice comes from diaries, letters, marriage records, and affidavits of those who lived in Nauvoo during the 1840s. The extant records constitute a secret chronicle, an addendum, if you will, to the carefully edited official history, from which any mention of the topic has been expurgated for the early period. After 1890, when polygamy went underground again, it became difficult to access records. Church leaders were less than pleased to find historians or journalists investigating this peculiar relic of the past, which had become an embarrassment and was considered a potential obstacle to missionary efforts. Historical items in the LDS Archives became unavailable to researchers. The cyclical nature of this suppression of information, first in Illinois and later in Utah, left a brief window in Mormon history from which most of the documentation has been recovered. During this period, following migration to the Great Salt Lake and until 1890, people collected oral histories and wrote reminiscences. The rest of the nation averted its eyes because its attention was trained on the Civil War and its aftermath. The benign neglect of the Territory of Utah was what Mormons had sought. However, because the history of polygamy in Nauvoo was never officially rewritten, even during the period of openness, Joseph Smith's initiation of the practice has remained in an historical penumbra to this day.

The story, as pieced together here, begins with Joseph Smith as a teenager in New York State, where he courted and eloped with his first wife, Emma, and published the Book of Mormon, which mentioned the possibility of polygamy. The topic was already on Joseph's mind, even in the 1820s. Chapter 1 traces Smith's "restoration" of biblical Christianity, although drawing as much from the Old Testament as the New. Plural marriage is anticipated: sometime before Smith met and courted his "celestial wives." The next chapter examines his initial marriages, beginning with Louisa Beaman in 1841. After marrying about sixteen wives by mid-1842, internal dissent drew Smith's actions into question, and plural weddings ceased during the summer and fall of 1842.

Chapter 3 details the resumption of polygamy after a six-month pause, culminating in the summer of 1843 when Joseph was ready to dictate the revelation which sanctioned plural marriages and required this practice for families intent on securing a place in heaven. In chapter 4, Joseph shares the "favor" of celestial marriage with dozens of other men in the community.

Chapter 5 tracks a surge in polygamy involving over thirty families and about two hundred wives, all during Smith's lifetime. One participant exulted, "I have six wives and am not afraid of another." After Joseph's death, the number of plural families swelled to almost two hundred, and after the journey to Utah began in 1846 these same polygamists continued marrying to the point that they had acquired an average of nearly six wives per family. This model became the blueprint for forty years of Utah polygamy.

Chapter 6 illustrates how a household with more than one wife functioned. When was the first wife told of a new courtship and how much was she told? Who determined what household responsibilities each wife would assume? What priorities did Mormon families have? What were the variations of age? How persistent were feelings of jealousy or other hard-to-reconcile problems?

The next two chapters, 7 and 8, look at the code of silence that prevailed in Nauvoo and how it fared against the inevitability of rumors. The suppressed history of a more or less insignificant river town was preserved though hundreds of extant documents—sources which somehow survived both neglect and contempt so that we are able to know both the facts of the matter and the behind-the-scenes human emotions that played a role in this extraordinary story.

Finally in chapter 9, antecedents to Mormon polygamy are presented from among other, centuries-old "latter-day" millennialists who similarly sought to restore a biblical model of society as they anticipated the end of the world. These predecessors to Mormonism are found in the side currents of Christian Europe, but they place Smith's innovations within a larger thematic social construct. For instance, three hundred years before the Mormons, a group of fervent Anabaptists in Münster, Germany, strived to restore primitive Christianity on European soil. In fact, descendants of the radical reformers of the sixteenth century settled in colonial America and helped preserve the memory of these older, millennialist offshoots of Protestantism. Through the Enlightenment period, social reformers took up the discussion of polygamy in the context of natural law and saw it as a way of bringing stability to family life. Some of these religious philosophers exported their ideas to America where they sought to create utopian societies.

The legacy of centuries of debate over marriage, which in the sixteenth century centered upon the question of whether marriage was a civil institution or a sacrament, which biblical model was most appropriate, and in the Mormon context, where a man had to be "sealed" to many wives, forms the continued political wrangling over what constitutes marriage. Headlined LDS separatists insist that polygamy is a sanctified form of marriage. This study concludes with some observations on the ambivalence mainstream Mormons exhibit toward a practice that their grandparents considered requisite for heaven. On the one hand, it is an honored history and part of their ancestral heritage; on the other hand, it now warrants harsh condemnation and dismissal from their long-since Americanized church. These events, which arose years ago on the banks of the Mississippi River, are part of an age-old discussion that can be seen as the confluence of two strains of thought: the attempt to adapt religion to human nature and, conversely, the attempt to conform human nature to accepted religious practice.

Acknowledgments

While editing William Clayton's journals, I came across his record of Joseph Smith's "celestial wives" in Nauvoo, Illinois, which raised questions about the extent of polygamy in this early "latter-day" community. An account of Smith's wives and the wives he allowed his inner circle of friends—about 160 polygamous husbands and wives, rising to about 900 by 1846—had not yet been published when I subsequently searched polygamy references in the New York Public Library. The library mentioned not only Mormon polygamy and a range of American millenniallist and utopian societies, it confirmed and delineated various marital practices, debated back through earlier centuries in different parts of the world.

Before polygamy was a Mormon template, the seventeenth-century English poet John Milton (known for his portrayal of Adam and Eve in *Paradise Lost*) advocated the practice in an unpublished essay that was rediscovered and reviewed in America in 1826. The review appeared the year before Joseph Smith began dictating to his newlywed wife, Emma, a text that would mention polygamy and become a scripture for a church he would soon found. The New York Public Library also provided the perspective of sixteenth-century "latter day saints" in Münster, Germany, where radical Christians formed a polygamous biblical community to await the end of the world.

In 1994 I visited the Stadtmuseum in Münster which displayed images of the Dutch Anabaptist prophet Jan van Leyden, assembled with his several "queens" for dinner. Among the German historians who directed me towards analyses of the Münster Anabaptist community were Dr. Karl-Heinz Kirchhoff, known for his ground-breaking source-critical examination of the 1534-35 experience, and Dr. Gerd Dethlefs of the Stadtmuseum. Dr. Dethlefs confirmed that the Münster Anabaptists imitated biblical models as they legitimized themselves as chosen of God and sought to remedy contemporary social problems of unmarried women by reenacting polygamous practices described in the Bible. Dethlefs highlighted primary source tracts from sixteenth-century Anabaptist preacher Bernhard Rothmann in Robert Stupperich, ed., *Die Schriften Bernhard Rothmanns.* Among other valuable sources were Ralf Klötzer, *Täuferherrschaft von Münster*, and Günther Bauer, *Anfänge täuferischer Gemeindebildungen in Franken.* Also important were Dr. Ernst Laubach's writings (Historisches Seminar, Westfälische Wilhelms-Universität in Münster), as well as George Huntston Williams's *Radical Reformation*, Cornelius Krahn's *Dutch Anabaptism*, and James M. Stayer's *Vielweiberei.*

Of invaluable assistance in translating many of the above texts and in facilitating my correspondence with German scholars was Professor of German Henry Lee Miner (University of Evansville, Indiana). I also benefited from the perusal of some German sources by Ron Priddis, not to mention his careful reading of the manuscript.

Along with New York and Münster, the University of California at Berkeley was a key source of European interest in polygamy. The Graduate Theological Union near the university houses the *Mennonite Quarterly Review*, which reflected the long Anabaptist effort at historical rediscovery. Other volumes defined the *Beichtrat* Protestant reformers granted Landgrave Philip of Hesse, who, like England's Henry VIII, wanted official permission to marry a second wife.

The Bancroft Library at Berkeley has an important Mormon collection which documents the American west and polygamy in Utah. Special thanks to Bancroft Director Charles B. Faulhaber, who guided me to Egyptian and Mormon source documents as well as read and helped to edit the manuscript. Berkeley's Doe Library has important sources which reflect centuries of marital debate in Europe concerning canon and natural law.

The primary records of Mormon polygamy are centered in and around Salt Lake City, Utah. The LDS Church Archives and Library in Salt Lake, administered by the Church of Jesus Christ of Latter-day Saints, contain letters, diaries, journals, and autobiographical reflections of key participants and eyewitnesses to celestial marriage as it unfolded in the 1840s along the banks of the Mississippi River in Nauvoo, Illinois. Thanks are due to a highly professional team of archivists led by H. Randall Dixon, William Slaughter, and Ronald Watt, among others. Collections at the Utah State Historical Society, the University of Utah Marriott Library, the Harold B. Lee Library at Brigham Young University (Provo) and the library at Utah State University (Logan) are important sources. I recall the helpful direction of Leonard J. Arrington (now deceased) who served both this university and acted as official LDS Church Historian during a period of expanding scholarly use of Church Archives. Special Collections Librarian Everett L. Cooley (now deceased) is remembered for his service to the University of Utah and for his assistance to me in research and writing efforts; Gregory C. Thompson continues Cooley's professional tradition at this library.

Important collections are found at the Huntington Library in San Marino, California, the Chicago Historical Society, the Illinois State Historical Society, the Beinecke Library at Yale University, and the

Community of Christ archives and library in Independence, Missouri.

I am also indebted to Gary James Bergera, Todd Compton, Lavina Fielding Anderson, Peter Boothe Wiley, H. Michael Marquardt, Maria H. Marquez, Peter McGuinness, Kathy E. Evans, and Camilla M. Smith for reading the manuscript and offering valuable editorial suggestions. Thanks also to Arnold W. Donald and Janet L. Visick for reviewing an early draft of this manuscript, and to Fawn M. Brodie, D. Michael Quinn, Richard S. Van Wagoner, Todd M. Compton, Lawrence Foster, Danel Bachman, Linda K. Newell, and Valeen T. Avery (now deceased) whose early research provoked interest in this story.

Thanks to Robert N. Evans and Jake Evans for data analysis and presentation of the some 200 Nauvoo plural families in Appendix B. Special thanks to Karen Lau for her skilled analysis of verbal and quantitative data which she brought into a coherent whole, applying access and cross-referencing systems to a cascade of historical events which compliment and frame years of research.

The record-keepers of former years should also be acknowledged for reporting contemporary events. Their decisions and labor to record what they witnessed are, of course, essential to our ability to look back into a prior age.

Thanks to Connie Disney for the design, and typesetting of this book; thanks also to Keiko Jones and Jani Fleet for their preparation and copy editing, to Tom Kimball for communications planning, and to Greg Jones for his role in production and distribution. Without the contributions of these many people this book could not have been completed. However, I alone am responsible for any errors or omissions.

I should also mention how patient my wife and children and friends have been while I have been consumed with this topic.

ONE.

Anticipation

"The restoration of all things"

On a spring afternoon in April 1841, a young woman wearing a man's hat and coat accompanied two men to a secluded spot near the banks of the Mississippi River. No one else knew what was about to take place. It was going to be momentous. The unmarried twenty-six-year-old Louisa Beaman was about to become the first plural wife of Joseph Smith, founder of the Church of Jesus Christ of Latter-day Saints.[1] Standing at his side, Louisa listened quietly as the church president told her brother-in-law, Joseph Bates Noble, what to say as he conducted the ceremony. Louisa may have harbored some doubts about marrying a married man. What did this farmer's daughter think of slipping out of town to this secluded spot for such a purpose? Had romance blossomed between her and the charismatic thirty-five-year-old prophet, or was this a religious calling she felt obliged to accept?[2]

Whatever the case, the handsome leader would persuade other

---

1. There is some evidence that Smith might have engaged in the practice prior to this, but this is the first documented marriage.

2. Louisa was one of four daughters of Alvah Beaman of Livonia, New York. On Mar. 15, 1834, Smith was "at Father Beamans" when "Brother Sidny [Rigdon] and Lyman [Wight] arrived at his house to [the] Joy of our Souls in Lyvona [Livonia]" (Scott Faulring, ed., *An American Prophet's Record: The Diaries of Joseph Smith* [Salt Lake City: Signature Books and Smith Research Associates, 1987], 24).

men's daughters, orphaned girls, middle-aged spinsters, and some men's wives to join him in matrimony over the next two and a half years. The women who married him ranged in age from fourteen to fifty-eight. He explained this and other invitations as a calling to restore an Old Testament practice, which he characterized as "celestial marriage," a heaven-inspired matrimony. Thousands of his adherents would follow in his footsteps beginning in Nauvoo, Illinois, in the 1840s, then across the Western frontier through the 1880s. After a church "Manifesto" publicly suspended the controversial and illegal practice in 1890, fervent believers, including a number of apostles, continued to form polygamous families while the practice died a slow death. A significant minority of people with Mormon roots persist in polygamy today despite risking criminal prosecution and excommunication from the mainstream LDS Church.

Early Mormon polygamy took root in the 1840s in Nauvoo, a bustling Mississippi River town with several thousand inhabitants. The Latter-day Saints had gathered there expecting the *parousia,* or Second Coming of Christ, in what they believed were the earth's last days. No one knew precisely when the final end would come, but they knew it was imminent. Their prophet had told them about the kingdom they would be called to administer when Jesus returned to rule.[3]

With an acquisitive eye on neighboring lands and the will to triumph over older settlers through political bloc voting, Joseph's behavior concerned some of the longtime Illinoisans who lived around the Saints. A few years earlier, the people in Missouri had gone to war to expel Mormons from their state. Now fear of their city-wide militia, use of local petitions of habeas corpus to dismiss state warrants, and rumors of a "plurality of wives" had put citizens on edge.

The Mormons had left their New York homes under uneasy circumstances. Moving ever further west, they felt compelled to leave Ohio and Missouri, just as they would soon be forced to depart from Illinois for what was then Mexican territory in the intermountain west. Inadvertently, the U.S. followed them in their westward march,

---

3. Dan Erickson, *"As a Thief in the Night": The Mormon Quest for Millennial Deliverance* (Salt Lake City: Signature Books, 1998), 6, 46, 59, 121, 123-48.

acquiring large tracts of territory in 1848 after the Mexican-American War, again embracing the Mormon problem. In 1857 the U.S. government decided to act forcefully to bring the Mormons to submission and to do something about the "barbarism" of polygamy.

So plural marriage was central to the broad sweep of LDS experience, especially in adding flame to the fire of their neighbors' contempt for half a century. Their peculiar marriage practices were not new. As "polygyny," where a man has several wives, and "polyandry," where a wife has several husbands, it had been known in ancient societies and continues today in Islamic countries and sub-Saharan Africa. Mormon polygamy had its own cultural antecedents in the interpretation of Old Testament accounts of Abraham, David, and Solomon. Despite the appeal to the Bible, the reality in the eighteen hundreds was that for centuries polygamy had been forbidden among Jews and Christians, both in America and Europe. It was illegal on that afternoon in 1841 when the Mormon prophet married Louisa Beaman.[4]

Conspicuously absent from the unannounced riverside wedding was Smith's first and legal wife, thirty-six-year-old Emma Hale. Nor were their children present: Joseph, eight; Frederick, four; Alexander, two; nor nine-year-old adopted daughter, Julia Murdock—not to mention Joseph's siblings or the bride's and groom's parents: their fathers were deceased, but both mothers lived in Nauvoo. In Emma's fourteen years of marriage to Joseph, which spanned temporary residences in New York, Pennsylvania, Ohio, Missouri, and finally Illinois, she had come to question and even confront her husband about the women he befriended. At their new home in Nauvoo in 1839-44, dozens of celestial wives would offend the moral sensibilities, not only of Emma, but of almost anyone who learned about Joseph's relationship to his young female tenants and neighbors.

It was in Nauvoo that the practice of "plurality of wives" became less forbidden, to the extent that Joseph chose some thirty-three men to share the "principle," men who would join him in denying its prac-

---

4. See the *Revised Laws of Illinois, 1833; Revised Statutes of the State of Illinois, 1845*, secs. 121, 122.

tice. This inner circle included three of the Smith family—his brothers Hyrum and William, and his Uncle John. It would lose one of its key members in 1842 when John C. Bennett quarreled with Smith and then left. In Joseph's final three years, to the age of thirty-eight, he would marry some thirty-seven women after Emma. This was done in the midst of internal opposition that erupted in mid-1843, in part due to the growing awareness and persistent rumors of polygamy. On June 27, 1844, vigilantes took Joseph's life, along with that of his brother Hyrum.

Two years later the Mormons were forced from Illinois. Before they left, a final surge of marriage ceremonies nearly overwhelmed the newly completed Nauvoo temple. Thereafter, a steady caravan of believers crossed the frozen Mississippi and wended its way across Iowa, the converts leaving behind their comfortable homes for the uncertainty of the west.[5] Smith's *de facto* successor, Brigham Young, took the institution of polygamy with him to the new territory, officially disclosing Mormon marriage practices for the first time in 1852, eight years after Smith was killed. He did it through a spokesperson, Orson Pratt, who was one of the Quorum of Twelve Apostles. Pratt delivered a forthright explication of Utah's family arrangements and affirmed on August 29 that "the Latter-day Saints had embraced the doctrine of a plurality of wives, as a part of their religious faith." His rationale was that it fulfilled the "promises made to Abraham, Isaac, and Jacob," whereby they would "become as numerous as the sand upon the seashore." God had extended this Hebraic promise to the Latter-day Saints, he said.[6] The response from the United States was shock. Even though people suspected that Mormons had ventured away from traditional marriage, the brazenness of Pratt's defense confirmed that the Latter-day Saints had departed from mainstream Christianity. From that day on, for the better part of half a century, the LDS Church

5. See Bernard De Voto, *The Year of Decision, 1846* (Boston: Little, Brown, and Company, 1943), for a description of the broader historical context in which the trek to Utah took place.

6. *Journal of Discourses,* 26 vols. (London: Latter-day Saints' Book Depot, 1854-86), 1:53-66.

would struggle with this, finally having to demonstrate to the U.S. Congress that it had ended the practice once and for all before Utah could be granted statehood in 1896. Those who continued to advocate polygamy regarded this accommodation as *prima facie* evidence of the church's apostasy, of an all-too convenient yielding to the secular government rather than to divine guidance.

Remarkably, Smith's role in introducing polygamy in Nauvoo has been largely excised from the official telling of LDS history. Neither the Mormon founder nor any of the Nauvoo Saints publicly acknowledged their multiple wives before Joseph's death. Smith's writings, such as his extant diaries and the official *History of the Church*, mostly edited after his death, fail to mention his marriage to Louisa Beaman in 1841 or any of his other thirty-plus wives. Official church texts have ignored polygamy's role in the death of the prophet and the westward migration that was forced upon the church.[7] In an entry on "plural marriage" in the *Encyclopedia of Mormonism,* Danel Bachman and Ronald K. Esplin, both LDS educators, briefly mention the "rumors" of plural marriage in the 1830s and 1840s but only obliquely refer to the "teaching [of] new marriage and family arrangements."[8]

Such revisionism continues today. When asked about polygamy on national television in 1998, LDS President Gordon B. Hinckley dismissed its historical importance, positing that "when our people came west [in 1846-47], they permitted [polygamy] on a restricted scale." He failed to acknowledge how important the "law of celestial marriage" had been for the church's founder and his followers. Particularly revealing was how the church president phrased his answer to exclude the entire pre-Utah period of church history. He made it clear he would not welcome any probing into the life of Joseph Smith and his wives or of Smith's requirement that others embrace the practice.[9]

---

7. *History of the Church of Jesus Christ of Latter-day Saints,* ed. B. H. Roberts, 2nd ed. rev., 7 vols. (Salt Lake City: Deseret Book, 1963).

8. *Encyclopedia of Mormonism,* ed. Daniel H. Ludlow (New York: MacMillan, 1992), 3:1,091-95. Although there was official church oversight of this publication, "its contents do not necessarily represent the official position of The Church of Jesus Christ of Latter-day Saints" (lxii).

9. Gordon B. Hinckley, interviewed by Larry King, CNN broadcast, Sept. 8,

Polygamy Restored

Polygamy shaped the culture of the Latter-day Saints from Illinois to the American west. Where there was resistance, the prophet inveighed against it, revealing God's rule that "no one can reject [polygamy] and enter into my glory" (D&C 132:51, 52, 54).[10] The rationale advanced for re-inaugurating this controversial, divisive practice was his insistence that all of the ancient religious practices found in the Bible, belonging to the "original true church," needed to be restored. This restoration would have to occur before the apocalyptic second coming of Jesus, which Smith said was "nigh at hand."[11] At General Conference in Nauvoo on April 6, 1843, Smith addressed the question of how soon Jesus would reappear: "Were I going to prophecy," he told Heber Kimball, Orson Pratt, Willard Richards, George A. Smith, Hyrum Smith, John Taylor, Brigham Young, Wilford Woodruff, and many others in an assembly of Saints, "I would prophecy the end will not come in 1844 or 5 or 6 or 40 years," quickly adding that "there are those of the rising generation who shall not taste of death till Christ comes." Refining his projection, he said "a voice" had declared to him, "My son, if thou livest till thou are 85 years of age, thou shalt see the face of the son of man." He clarified that this meant "48 years hence or about 1890" and said he had received this communication on April 2, 1843, at Ramus, Illinois. By coincidence, this was the same time and place where he was courting Almera Johnson, who was soon to become his plural wife.[12]

Witnessing advances in astronomy and the physical sciences

1998, qtd. in "On the Record: 'We Stand for Something,'" *Sunstone*, Dec. 1998, 70-72; "Hinckley Attacks Polygamy on National TV," *Salt Lake Tribune*, Sept. 9, 1998, A-1.

10. The Doctrine and Covenants of the Church of the Latter Day Saints (Kirtland, Ohio: F. G. Williams & Co., 1835); Doctrine and Covenants of the Church of Jesus Christ of Latter-day Saints (Salt Lake City: Church of Jesus Christ of Latter-day Saints, 1981). The Doctrine and Covenants (D&C) is recognized as canon by the LDS Church, Community of Christ, and most other Restoration churches. All references here are to the LDS edition. The current 1981 version, based on the 1876 edition, contains various amendments.

11. D&C 43:25-26.

12. Faulring, *American Prophet's Record*, 349; see also *History of the Church*, 5:336; D&C 130:14-15.

since the eighteenth century, Smith was eager to embrace new scientific findings, which he mixed with religion and folk magic. His theology posited the existence of deities on other planets: many deities, each with plural spouses, fathering an endless posterity in populating innumerable worlds. The secrets of the universe, as he understood them, included a continuous perfecting of those with the "keys" of transcendent knowledge and power. Smith was familiar with nineteenth-century writer Thomas Dick, who reasoned that since "no particle of matter is ever lost[,] … when the body is dissolved in death, the soul takes its ethereal flight into a *celestial* region" and "puts on immortality." Using terminology and concepts of an indestructible afterlife similar to Dick's celestial immortality, Smith's "celestial marriage" was designated for individuals bound for a Celestial (heaven-like) Kingdom, which Smith defined as the highest of three domains one could inherit in the afterlife, preceded by the Terrestrial (earth-like) and Telestial Kingdoms: the latter may have been inspired by the eighteenth-century term, "teleology," meaning the study of design in nature. Dick might have also inspired Smith's view of endless worlds when he projected that "if room were wanted for new creations, ten thousand additional worlds could be comprised within the limits of the solar system" and that "the immeasurable spaces … between our planetary system and the nearest stars would afford an ample range for the revolutions of millions of worlds."[13] On these many worlds, Joseph said, select men would take their families and progress eternally toward godhood and beyond. He had already proven his own mettle among God's elect when he mastered the use of magic stones and "translated" the Book of Mormon, which he said had been written in an inaccessible form of ancient Egyptian. As a prophet and seer, Smith was illuminating the way to perfection for innumerable other disciples by revelation received through the same mediums. Celestial marriage was just one aspect of the restoration of all an-

13. Thomas Dick, *The Philosophy of a Future State,* 2nd American ed. (Brookfield, Mass.: n.p., 1830), emphasis added, qtd. in the *LDS Messenger and Advocate* 3 (Dec. 1836): 423-25. Fawn Brodie references Dick, although for different passages, in *No Man Knows My History: The Life of Joseph Smith* (New York: Knopf, 1945), 171-72.

cient truth now coming to light but which had once comprised the gospel—truth which was needed for the commencement of the millennium.

For those of Smith's followers who saw New Testament events through an Old Testament lens, Jesus' original church had begun with Adam and Eve and continued through a succession of apostasies and new "dispensations." This dispensational concept recurs in Christian literature beginning with the writings of Barnabas and other apostolic fathers in the second century CE. It re-emerges among medieval mystics such as Joachim de Fiore. However, the underlying dispensational model existed at least as early as the sixth century BCE in Persia. Zoroaster described history as a struggle between good and evil in successive epochs lasting 3,000 years each. In the end, the forces of good were destined to be victorious and there would be a resurrection of the just and a last judgment, the Zoroastrians believed. In time, Hebrew and Christian theologians adopted these same concepts, including specific time periods and ending with the world's destruction. Reared on the Bible, Smith believed that Jesus had introduced the penultimate of seven dispensations. Smith also came to believe that the Christian dispensation had ended and that he himself was the prophet of the last days to inaugurate the epoch preceding the Last Judgment.[14] On January 23, 1845, seven months after Smith's death, Brigham Young and John Taylor designed a seal consisting of a crown over an all-seeing eye, encircled by the capital letters: PSTAPCJL SLDAOW, meaning "Private Seal of the Twelve Apostles, Priests of

---

14. In its theological sense, a dispensation is an ordering of events under divine authority through the administration of religious law. The apostle Paul justified his ministry "according to the dispensation of God" (Col. 1:25) and announced that it was "the dispensation of the fulness of times" (Eph. 1:10). Mormon theology conceives of seven dispensations under Adam, Enoch, Noah, Abraham, Moses, Jesus, and Joseph Smith—plus additional "stewardships" for Book of Mormon peoples and the lost tribes of Israel. Discussed by Mormon theologian B. H. Roberts, this view finds Paul's understanding to be wanting since his "were not the last days in any general sense at all, as there have been now some 2,000 years of days since then" (see Rand H. Packer, "Dispensation of the Fulness of Times," and Courtney J. Lasseter, "Dispensations of the Gospel," *Encyclopedia of Mormonism,* 1:387-90; *History of the Church,* 1:xxx-xxxi).

the Church of Jesus Christ of Latter-day Saints in the Last Dispensation All Over the World."[15]

In 1845, Joseph's mother voiced her confidence that "a dispensation of the Gospel was committed to [Joseph,] of which the starting bud had scarcely made its appearance" before her son's untimely death.[16] Not unlike today, the nineteenth-century public wanted to hear about prophecies foretelling earthquakes, storms, fire, disease, and war, which Smith preached as regularly as any other apocalyptic preacher of his day, quoting the horrors of Daniel and Revelation in his sermons and publications. The church's periodicals promoting this theology bore such telling names as the *Millennial Star* and *A Voice of Warning*. LDS Apostle Parley P. Pratt predicted that "lightnings shall strike from the east" and that "the voice of thunderings … of lightnings … of tempests … of earthquakes and great hailstorms, … famine and pestilences" would demonstrate when "the day has come" and "the cup of the wrath of my indignation is full."[17] Similarly, future church president Wilford Woodruff saw "signs in the Last Days." He wrote in August 1840 that the moon looked like someone had painted it red and that "while looking at it one part of it fell in peices & the appearance of a soldier was seen in the moon with a white feather in his cap."[18] Such portentous signs were as evident in the night sky as they were in the turmoil of nature and human events.

Although understandably hesitant to specify a precise date for the end of the world, Smith knew that "our redemption draweth near."[19] Visitors traveled long distances to share their apocalyptic beliefs with

---

15. Dean C. Jessee, ed., *John Taylor Nauvoo Journal* (Provo: Grandin Book, 1996), 38n132.

16. Lavina Fielding Anderson, ed., *Lucy's Book: A Critical Edition of Lucy Mack Smith's Family Memoir* (Salt Lake City: Signature Books, 2002), 452. Lucy dictated her narrative to Martha and Howard Coray. Anderson compares the preliminary draft of 1844-45, the Coray-edited version, and Orson Pratt's 1853 publication in Liverpool.

17. Parley P. Pratt, *A Voice of Warning and Instruction to All People* (1837; Liverpool: Brigham Young Jr., 1866), 64-65; *History of the Church*, 1:156.

18. Scott Kenney, ed., *Wilford Woodruff's Journal*, 9 vols. (Midvale, Utah: Signature Books, 1983), 1:478.

19. See Dean C. Jessee, ed., *The Personal Writings of Joseph Smith*, rev. ed. (Salt Lake City: Deseret Book, 2002), 306.

him. On November 9, 1835, "a man came in, and introduced himself to me, calling [himself] by the name of Joshua the Jewish minister." The visitor was actually Robert Matthews and was known by several epithets, including "Matthias." What was certain was that he was a mystic, as was apparent from his "sea-green frock coat, & pantaloons of the same." He also claimed to be "God the Father," although reincarnated as a "litteral descendant of Mathias the Apostle." Smith found him credible enough to converse with from 11:00 a.m. until evening, when Smith invited him to stay for dinner.

The message to later generations of Latter-day Saints was that Smith thought to tell his strange guest that at age fourteen, he himself had seen a vision of two "personages" and "many angels." At seventeen, Smith continued, he had experienced "another vision of angels," wherein he had learned that "the [American] Indians were the literal descendants of Abraham." Matthias told Smith about a previous prophesy he had made regarding the destruction of Albany, New York. The men continued on like this after dinner in discussing the visions of Daniel and events of "the latter days." Without objection from Smith, Matthias asserted: "The silence spoken of by John the Revelator which is to be in heaven for the space of half an hour, is between 1830 & 1851, during which time the judgments of God will be poured out; after that time there will be peace."[20]

On other occasions Smith contemplated "the rapidity with which the great and glorious day of the coming of the Son of Man advances."[21] He wrote in a letter that the Saints in Independence, Missouri, would survive destruction at the end of the world: "I verily know that [the Lord] will spedily deliver Zion [Independence] for I have his immutible covenant that this shall be the case[,] but god is pleased to keep it hid from mine eyes." He reiterated that "the means" or "exactly how" this would be done remained unknown. Even so, he instructed his followers to have faith in unseen forces that would re-

---

20. Dean C. Jessee, ed., *The Papers of Joseph Smith,* 2 vols. (Salt Lake City: Deseret Book, 1992), 2:68-73, 568-69; see Rev. 8:1. Here Smith recorded an account of his First Vision that mentioned "many angels"; although "another personage soon appear[e]d like unto the first," there is not an explicit reference to the "father and son."

21. See Jessee, *Personal Writings,* 326.

ward those who believed in what they did not understand. At the end of the world, he said, he expected to see the faithful inherit Missouri, that God would "permit me to settle on an inhe[r]itance on the land of Zion."[22]

It is probably significant that the Latter-day Saints emerged at a time and place when utopian enthusiasm had captured the interest of many people. Groups emerged that experimented with new forms of living, even touching on such taboos as marriage and property, among others. Matthews advocated what he called a "community of property, and of wives," in a more "spiritual generation."[23] Other groups, such as the Oneida Perfectionists, established "spiritual wifery" in which no male was entitled to any particular female. Historian Lawrence Foster has compared the Oneida, Mormon, and Shaker societies in a broad study of American social experiments.[24] Jacob Cochran's followers in Saco, Maine, the "Cochranites," defined female marriage partners as "spiritual wives."[25] Mormons avoided the idiom but not the practice, preferring the less obvious "celestial marriage," which was nevertheless synonymous with plural marriage. However, early LDS writings were sprinkled throughout with the "spiritual wife" term.[26] During the 1830s and 1840s, Mormon communal practices extended to property as well as to marriage. Property was said to be God's alone and was consecrated to the church through the "United Order of Enoch." Across the Atlantic, the communal experiment advocated by Marx and Engels appeared in London only a few years later in 1848.[27]

---

22. Ibid., 308-09.

23. "Memoirs of Matthias the Prophet Prepared for the *New York Sun*," Stanley S. Ivins Collection, USHS, quoted by Richard S. Van Wagoner, *Mormon Polygamy: A History* (Salt Lake City: Signature Books, 1989), 8.

24. See Lawrence Foster, *Religion and Sexuality: Three American Communal Experiments* (New York: Oxford University Press, 1981).

25. See the vast literature on nineteenth-century American utopian communities, including "Jacob Cochran," in Donald E. Pitzer, ed., *America's Communal Utopias* (Chapel Hill: University of North Carolina Press, 1997).

26. *Times and Seasons,* July 1, 1845; *Journal of Discourses,* 3:125; Nauvoo City Council Minutes, Jan. 3, 1844, LDS Archives, Salt Lake City.

27. Karl Marx and Friedrich Engels, *Communist Manifesto* (1848; New York: Bantam, 1992).

A Conditional Possibility

Polygamy was evidently on Smith's mind even before founding the Mormon Church, if that can be deduced from the marriage formula inscribed in the Book of Mormon. Joseph described the Book of Mormon as his translation of a hidden record, written in Egyptian, of early Hebrew tribes living in America before the time of Christ. Polygamy is mentioned in his work-in-progress, begun shortly after he eloped with Emma Hale in January 1827. Although the Hales were doubtful about the career and character of this young seer, Emma ignored her parents and accompanied Joseph on a night trip in a borrowed wagon to South Bainbridge, New York. On arrival, they stayed with Smith's employer, Josiah Stowell, and were married the next day in front of justice of the peace Zachariah Tarbell. Rather than return to Emma's home, the bride and groom headed 160 miles northwest to the Smith family home in Manchester, New York, west of the Palmyra residence the family had occupied from 1816 to 1823.

That fall, Smith began dictating the Book of Mormon, first to Emma, then to other scribes. At twenty-one, the farmer's son had not only married a Pennsylvania girl who was a year older than himself, he had completed a ritualized five-year search for the gold plates said to be buried near his Manchester home. Each year at the autumnal equinox, which according to rodsmen and seers was a favorable time to approach the spirits guarding buried treasures, Smith had gone to the hill where he sought after the plates.[28] With the protection and help of his seer stones and amulets, he found the proper spot and prayed. He began this ritual visit to what he called "the Hill Cumorah" late on a Sunday night, September 21, 1823.[29] An early believer, Smith's third cousin, Oliver Cowdery, explained that the annual visit to the hill oc-

---

28. See Jean-Louis Brau, Helen Weaver, and Allan Edmands, eds., *Larousse Encyclopedia of Astrology* (New York: McGraw-Hill, 1980), 194, 107; Ronald W. Walker, "Joseph Smith, the Palmyra Seer," *BYU Studies* 24 (Fall 1984): 461-72; Dan Vogel, ed., *Early Mormon Documents,* 5 vols. (Salt Lake City: Signature Books, 1996), 2:18, 27-28, 59-74; D. Michael Quinn, *Early Mormonism and the Magic World View* (Salt Lake City: Signature Books, 1987), 112-49.

29. As noted by Quinn, that day in September 1823 was ruled by Jupiter, Smith's ruling planet (*Early Mormonism and Magic,* 120-21).

curred each fall from 1823 to 1827, each time on the autumnal equinox; Joseph would "commune with some kind of messenger" there. Cowdery said Smith "had heard of the power of enchantment, and a thousand like stories, which held the hidden treasures of the earth."[30] Practitioners of magic claimed that the pull of a divining rod or the light in a translucent stone could lead them to treasures by transmitting important messages to guide them. What Joseph said he was doing on the hill was communing with an angel.

For one who lived in upstate New York, it was natural to be curious about the origin of American Indians. The mounds of ancient bones and other Native American artifacts near Palmyra were unavoidable and elicited speculation about their source. This was before archeologists would dig in age-specific strata to identify the Asian migrations over the Bering land bridge. Writers before Smith such as James Adair, Elias Boudinot, Josiah Priest, and Ethan Smith, had postulated that Native Americans had descended from the lost ten tribes of Israel.[31] Joseph Smith also promoted this attractive idea after communing for years with higher powers and then extracting from Cumorah the ancient record he said was inscribed on gold leaves. His translation of the narrative specifically prohibited polygamy among the migrant Hebrew peoples of 600-500 BCE: "There shall not any man among you have save it be one wife," followed immediately by grounds for exception: "For if I will, saith the Lord of Hosts, raise up seed unto me, I will command my people" (Jacob 2:27, 30).[32] Smith elaborated this idea to "raise up seed," that the signal

30. Oliver Cowdery to W. W. Phelps, *LDS Messenger and Advocate* 1 (Feb. 1835): 79; qtd. in Quinn, *Early Mormonism and Magic*, 125, 134. See also Dan Vogel, *Indian Origins and the Book of Mormon* (Salt Lake City: Signature Books, 1986), 14-15.

31. See George D. Smith, "'Is There No Way to Escape These Difficulties?' The Book of Mormon Studies of B. H. Roberts," *Dialogue: A Journal of Mormon Thought* 17 (Summer 1984): 97.

32. *The Book of Mormon, An Account Written by the Hand of Mormon upon Plates Taken from the Plates of Nephi, Translated by Joseph Smith, Jun.* (1830; Salt Lake City: The Church of Jesus Christ of Latter-day Saints, 1951), 111. This admonition of marital fidelity to the Nephites, a Hebrew tribe in America, continues in Jacob 3 in a context of curses and dark skins. While the Nephites' brothers, the Lamanites, suffer from "filthiness and the cursing which hath come upon their skins," they are nevertheless considered more righteous because they have kept the commandment that "they

might be given again and polygamy would be reintroduced, perhaps in the last days to increase the number of the righteous on earth prior to the Second Coming.

This conditional proposition required the young church founder to sacrifice traditional assumptions about marital fidelity. In a series of events, Smith published the Book of Mormon in March 1830, founded the "Church of Christ" the next month, and the next year sanctioned the first breach in marriage mores. It occurred in Smith's charge to missionaries to the Indians when he told single and married men alike that they should marry native women.[33] Polygamy may have been on his mind, since he and his scribe Oliver Cowdery had been working on their "inspired" revision of the Bible and had just read about the wives and concubines of David and Solomon. In any case, church editor W. W. Phelps reported on the prophet's instructions in all their antebellum racism. Through intermarriage, Smith said, the Indians would "become white, delightsome, and just" and fulfill the Book of Mormon prophecy that "the scales of darkness shall begin to fall from their eyes; and many generations shall not pass away among them, save they shall be a white [pure] and delightsome people."[34] A later LDS presi-

---

should have save it were one wife." The Nephites are told that "unless ye shall repent," the "Lamanites' skins" will be "whiter than yours" (Jacob 3:5, 8-9).

33. Known as the Church of Christ from 1830 to 1834, the name changed to the Church of the Latter Day Saints, then in 1836 to the Church of Christ of Latter Day Saints, and in 1838 to the Church of Jesus Christ of Latter-day Saints, sometimes known as LDS or Mormon. See D&C 20:1, 115:4; Susan Easton Black, "Name of the Church," *Encyclopedia of Mormonism,* 3:979.

34. See W. W. Phelps to Brigham Young, Aug. 12, 1861, LDS Archives. Smith's wording echoed 2 Ne. 30:6. The 1840 Book of Mormon substituted the word "pure" for "white," although the wording reverted back to "white" again in the English 1841 and later foreign editions, then became "pure" again in 1981. Even so, other passages in the Book of Mormon still refer to "white" as "delightsome" and a "skin of blackness" as a "curse" (2 Ne. 5; Jacob 3:5, 8-10; Alma 3:6-9; 3 Ne. 2:14-15; Morm. 5:15). Skin color was important in other LDS scriptures as well, and blacks of African ancestry were denied full participation in the church until 1978. Interestingly, the rhetoric underlying the theology may have resulted from 1830s Mormons trying to convince their neighbors in the slave state of Missouri that they were not abolitionists. See Douglas Campbell, "'White' or 'Pure': Five Vignettes," *Dialogue: A Journal of Mormon Thought* 29 (Winter 1996): 119-20; Lester E. Bush Jr. and Armand L. Mauss, *Neither White nor Black: Mormon Scholars Confront the Race Issue in a Universal Church* (Salt Lake City: Signature Books, 1984).

dent, Smith's nephew Joseph F. Smith, concluded that the principle of plural marriage must have been revealed to the founder already in 1831, based on these extraordinary instructions to missionaries. An early convert and later dissident, Ezra Booth, summed up the expressed goal of the mission as being to secure a "matrimonial alliance with the natives." However, the missionaries did not seem successful in this area.[35] Even so, the significance of this is that Smith introduced the possibility of polygamy in 1831. Later he would set a striking personal example and then invite others to follow.

According to Smith in 1843, the Old Testament patriarch Abraham had "received all things"; Smith would now "restore all things" (D&C 132:29, 40; see Appendix A). Abraham was promised that the "fruit of his loins" would continue eternally (v. 30). God told Smith "this promise is yours also" (v. 31). Smith would restore a gospel of numerous wives, numerous children, and numerous worlds. He invoked an imperative whereby worthy men would become gods and populate their own domain. "Then they shall be gods, because they have no end; therefore shall they be everlasting" (v. 20), according to the wording of Smith's revelation. This would be God's "new and everlasting covenant," revealed through Smith in the restoration of "all things."

One wonders when Emma Smith might have first suspected that her husband was contemplating plural marriage. Aside from the conditional mention of polygamy in the Book of Mormon and Smith's instructions to the Ohio missionaries in 1831, was there anything to suggest this outcome? As Emma regarded her handsome spouse, what in Joseph's youthful experiences may have suggested the unusual family arrangements that were to follow? We know Joseph often stayed overnight on visits with other families. Was Emma aware that later marriages would develop out of these family visits among their close friends? Could she have seen this coming—the injunction to enter into "celestial marriage?" An examination of Smith's adolescence from his personal writings reveals some patterns and events that might be significant in understanding what precipitated his polygamous incli-

---

35. See *Deseret News,* May 20, 1886; Ezra Booth letter, *Ohio Star,* Dec. 8, 1831.

nation. A decade later, Joseph married not only friends but also the children of his early acquaintances.

Joseph's Early Life

The vices and follies of youth

Joseph began keeping a personal diary in 1832 that would become the blueprint for a later history. He kept diaries, periodically dictating entries to scribes, from November 27, 1832, to almost the day of his assassination, June 27, 1844. He wanted "to keep a minute account of all things that come under my observation." He provided a few insights from his diaries into his early married life and regarding the time period when he introduced plural marriage, although without specifically addressing the topic of polygamy. For the years prior to 1832, information about his life and first marriage found its way into autobiographical statements, letters, and other contemporaneous accounts up to the years he and Emma spent in Kirtland, Ohio.

He seems to have written his earliest autobiographical sketch in 1832, the same year he began his diary. One of its most interesting characteristics is that it remains the only extant personal history, written at least partly in his own hand.[36] Here he tells us that in 1816, at age ten, his family moved from Vermont to New York to buy farmland in Palmyra. His father intended to grow wheat and sell it to buyers along the Susquehanna River, located near the New York-Pennsylvania border. Joseph was raised in the middle of nine children: Alvin, Hyrum, Sophronia, Joseph, Samuel, William, Katharine, Don Carlos, and Lucy: he lived in close quarters with his brothers and sisters.[37] "Indigent circumstances," he wrote, "obliged" them to "labour hard for the support" of each other, and they were therefore "deprived of the bennifit of an education[;] suffice it to say I was mearly instruct[e]d in reading ~~and~~ writing and the ground (rules) of Arithm[e]tic which constituted my whole literary acquirements."[38] His parents raised him

36. Jessee, *Papers of Joseph Smith,* 1:1.
37. Ibid., xlv.
38. Ibid., 5.

in an atmosphere which emphasized reading out of the Bible and engaging in religious discussions.

Did young Joseph experience the usual challenges and questions accompanying adolescence? Is there anything to suggest a coming-of-age struggle? A few passages from his autobiography indicate that two years after the family moved to New York State, he confronted some uncertain feelings he later termed "sinful." At a time when boys begin to experience puberty, "from the age of 12 years to 15," or 1817-21, he "became convicted [convinced] of my sins." Seeing his awakened emotions as "sinful" seems to have reflected parental admonitions prior to the age of fifteen or sixteen (1820-22), when he also sought divine assistance for his worries. "I cried unto the Lord for mercy ... in the 16th year of my age," he wrote. In response to his prayer, a personage he would later identify as Jesus confronted him and said: "Joseph my son thy sins are forgiven thee." Even so, he reported that he again "fell into transgression and sinned in many things ... there were many things that transpired that cannot be written." These cryptic words echo in his subsequent statements to friend and counselor Oliver Cowdery, leaving us to suspect that he was referring to the curious thoughts of an intense teenager. An elaboration might be found in the Book of Mormon expressions about "the will of the flesh and the evil which is therein," whereby "the devil" is given "power to captivate, to bring you down to hell" (2 Ne. 2:29).[39]

Two years after his initial autobiographical sketch, Smith addressed similar vaguely defined infractions of youth, including "vices and follies," he wrote. The contemporary definition of "vice" was "every act of intemperance, all falsehood, duplicity, deception, lewdness and the like," as well as "the excessive indulgence of passions and appetites which in themselves are innocent," according to Noah Webster's 1828 *American Dictionary*. "Folly" was defined as "an absurd act which is highly sinful; and conduct contrary to the laws of God or man; sin; scandalous crimes; that which violates moral precepts and

---

39. Joseph Smith Letter Book 1, 1-6, Joseph Smith Papers, LDS Archives; Jessee, *Papers of Joseph Smith*, 1:1-10. About half of this holographic work is in Smith's hand, the remainder in that of Frederick G. Williams, to whom Smith dictated entries.

dishonors the offender." In other words, "vices and follies" implied sins great and small, which conceivably involved sex but were not limited to it.[40] In a letter to Cowdery, now the "Second Elder" of the church, and reprinted in the December 1834 issue of the LDS *Messenger and Advocate,* Smith reiterated the circumstances of his birth in 1805 and his family's move eleven years later to Palmyra, then the short move to the adjacent town of Manchester in 1823, where he stayed until he was twenty-one.[41] Smith defended himself in the letter against unsavory remarks his in-laws and neighbors had made about him, which had followed him from Manchester to Harmony, Pennsylvania, and from there to Fayette, New York.[42] Wherever he and Emma settled, whether in Kirtland, Ohio, or the town of Far West, Missouri, in the early 1830s, it seems the family often found controversy.

In addition to Smith's diaries, and those of his acquaintances, Joseph's neighbors conveyed additional background about his youthful years. Doctor (his given name) P. Hurlbut joined the LDS Church in Kirtland in 1833. After becoming disaffected, he recorded interviews with those who had known the Smiths in New York, Pennsylvania, and Ohio. These interviews, presented as affidavits, were published by Eber D. Howe in his 1834 exposé, *Mormonism Unvailed.*[43] Hurlbut was just one of many who joined Smith's church in Kirtland in 1833 and

---

40. Noah Webster, *An American Dictionary of the English Language* (New York: S. Converse, 1828), s.v. *vice, folly.*

41. See Jessee, *Papers of Joseph Smith,* 1:13.

42. Joseph and Emma lived in Harmony for a while, near Emma's parents, during which time Joseph worked on the Book of Mormon. When they left again in June 1829, it was in duress and under a cloud of suspicion involving a young woman by the name of Eliza Winters, according to statements by Martin Harris and Levi Lewis (Dan Vogel, *Joseph Smith: The Making of a Prophet* [Salt Lake City: Signature Books, 2004], 178, 514).

43. The preferred spelling at the time was "vail," not "veil," as reflected in Webster, *American Dictionary,* 2:105-106.

On March 13, 1833, Hurlbut spoke with Smith about the Book of Mormon and became converted to it, although he said that if he found he had been tricked he would seek revenge. He was ordained an elder by Sidney Rigdon on March 18. For a brief period, Hurlbut's "license" was taken from him, then reinstated on June 21. Smith said Hurlbut had been guilty of "lude and adulterous" conduct. On March 31, 1834, Smith charged that Hurlbut had made threats against him, resulting in Hurlbut

then thought better of it—the dissension reaching 15 percent of the church membership by 1838. During his brief time in the church, Hurlbut was close enough to the hierarchy to court Lovina S. Williams, the "beautiful daughter" of Frederick G. Williams, patriarch of one of the leading families.[44] Hurlbut's subsequent rift and excommunication on June 23, 1833, prompted his interest in Joseph's background, which led him to conclude that the "vices" Joseph mentioned implied his involvement in sorcery.[45] In-law and neighbor comments tend to support this spiritualist interpretation of "vices."

One of the individuals interviewed was Peter Ingersoll, who asserted:

> In the month of August, 1827, I was hired by Joseph Smith, Jr., to go to Pennsylvania, to move his wife's household furniture up to Manchester, where his wife [Emma] then was. ... [W]e arrived at Mr. Hale's in Harmony, Pa., from which place (Mr. Hale) addressed Joseph, in a flood of tears: "You have stolen my daughter, and married her ... You spend your time in digging for money ... pretending to see in a stone, and thus try to deceive people." Joseph wept, and acknowledged he could not see in a stone now, nor never could; ... He then promised to give up his old habits of digging for money and looking into stones. Mr. Hale told Joseph, if he would move to Pennsylvania and work for a living, he would assist him in getting into business.[46]

Others, such as William Stafford, remembered "Joseph ... looking

---

being required to post a bond of $200 for six months to guarantee that he kept the peace (Jessee, *Papers of Joseph Smith,* 2:19n1, 27-29, 29n1; *Personal Writings,* 311.

Hurlbut's work was double-checked by RLDS Apostles William H. and E. L. Kelly (brothers), magazine editor Frederic G. Mather, and writer Arthur B. Deming, all of whom returned to Smith's neighborhoods and re-interviewed his friends and acquaintances. A comparison of the later interviews shows general agreement with Hurlbut's transcripts (Rodger I. Anderson, *Joseph Smith's New York Reputation Reexamined* [Salt Lake City: Signature Books, 1990], 113-16).

44. Richard S. Van Wagoner, *Sidney Rigdon: A Portrait of Religious Excess* (Salt Lake City: Signature Books, 1994), 187. Hurlbut also dated Electa Sherman, sister of Lyman R. Sherman who married Delcena Johnson (Dale R. Broadhurst, "Crisis at Kirtland," *Oliver Cowdery Memorial Home Page—D. P. Hurlbut,* online at http://oliver cowdery.com).

45. *History of the Church,* 1:355n; Vogel, *Early Mormon Documents,* 2:13-77.

46. Eber D. Howe, *Mormonism Unvailed* (1834; New York: AMS Press, 1977), 234-35.

in his glass" and seeing "spirits ... clothed in ancient dress" standing guard over treasures. Joseph cut "a sheep's throat [and] led [it] around a circle while bleeding," his former acquaintances remembered, to appease the evil spirit. When digging a well in 1822, Joseph "discover[ed] a singularly appearing stone" which he "put into his hat" for remote viewing. During this time, a spirit showed him where he could unearth an ancient book written "on plates of gold." In the meantime, Joseph "professed to tell people's fortunes" by gazing at a "stone which he used to put in his hat," by which he eventually also translated the text of the "golden plates" in Harmony, Pennsylvania.[47]

Joseph's father-in-law reported:

> I first became acquainted with Joseph Smith, Jr. in November, 1825. He was at that time in the employ of a set of men who were called "money diggers;" and his occupation was that of seeing, or pretending to see by means of a stone placed in his hat, and his hat closed over his face. In this way he pretended to discover minerals and hidden treasure. His appearance at this time, was that of a careless young man ... Smith, and his father, with several other money-diggers boarded at my house while they were employed in digging for a mine ... This took place about the 17th of November, 1825.[48]

In his own interpretation of "vice," Joseph explained in 1834 to Oliver Cowdery that in time he outgrew his childhood pleasures: "During this time [10-21 years of age], as is common to most, or all youths, I fell into many vices and folleys," including "a light, and too often vain mind, exhibiting a foolish and trifling conversation." He told Cowdery he wanted to make a "public confession of my former uncircumspect walk and unchaste conversation," adding that he had never "pretended to be any other than a man subject to passion, and liable ... to deviate from that perfect path."[49]

Throughout the rest of Joseph's life, he continued to periodically relate anecdotes about his early life in different contexts but in similarly brief fashion, omitting details or highlighting a certain aspect of

47. Vogel, *Early Mormon Documents,* 2:13-77.
48. Ibid., 4:281-90; see also Anderson, *Joseph Smith's Reputation Reexamined,* 126-27.
49. See Jessee, *Papers of Joseph Smith,* 1:11-14.

his life according to circumstances. In a March 1, 1842, letter to John Wentworth, editor of the weekly *Chicago Democrat,* he left out any reference to the sinful thoughts he had previously mentioned. He had come effectively to de-emphasize the feelings of sin and guilt he had once experienced.[50] Despite his ambiguity on these points, there is every indication that he took an interest in polygamy at an early period, beyond what we read in his autobiographies or in the Book of Mormon.

In his official six-volume *History of the Church* (a seventh volume was added after his death), Joseph Smith attempted to explain more fully his role in founding the Church of Christ. Two years after founding the church, he had attempted, without success, to write this story. At that time, he had narrated the nighttime admonitions of Moroni, the Book of Mormon prophet who visited him in 1823, and otherwise summarized events leading to publication of the Book of Mormon seven years later. In 1834 Smith made another statement about his background, which Cowdery published. And in 1838 he began again, this time sustaining his interest long enough to complete the text that would comprise volume 1 of the *History of the Church* (Manuscript History Book A-1), a draft of which he would revise in 1839 and then serialize in the Nauvoo *Times and Seasons* beginning in 1842. What was new about this latest account was that this time the 1823 angelic announcement was preceded by an 1820 "First Vision," which included not just "personages" or "angels" but a visitation by the God of heaven—"The Father and The Son."

A few months after Joseph was assassinated in Carthage jail in 1844, his mother dictated a history, published in 1853 as *Biographical Sketches.* She said little about Joseph's childhood prior to his encounter with an angel.[51] "I shall say nothing respecting him," she wrote, "until he arrived at the age of fourteen." She knew some readers would be "disappointed" that she had not related "remarkable incidents which attended his childhood; but, as nothing occurred during his early life" outside of common "trivial circumstances," she would "pass them in silence," she said.

---

50. *History of the Church,* 4:535-41; see also Jessee, *Personal Writings,* 241-48.
51. Anderson, *Lucy's Book,* 545.

Lucy may not have known how much she revealed about Joseph's personality in describing his negotiation with the angel guarding the gold plates. Coincidental with her son's annual rendevous with the angel, Lucy said, "in the course of our evening conversations[,] Joseph would give us some of the most ammusing recitals … [and] describe the ancient inhabitants of this [American] continent their dress their maner of traveling the animals which they rode."[52]

There is nothing in Lucy's account about women, wives, or early struggles with chastity, nor is there anything of that sort in Joseph's own retrospective writings begun in 1832, the same year he became head of the church in Kirtland. Yet, that same year, he had famously become involved with a sixteen-year-old carpenter's daughter named Fanny Alger, who eventually moved into the Smith home in about 1835. Lucy's editor speculated that the prophet's mother "probably did not know or want to know" about his plural wives, which was no doubt the case.[53] The comment was probably equally applicable to Joseph's father, who died in September 1840, six months prior to the prophet's marriage to Louisa Beaman. If his father had known about the relationship with Fanny Alger, he didn't say. As for Joseph's legal wife, Emma never indicated that her husband had told her anything specifically about his experiences prior to their marriage or the details of his involvement with other women, although she did know about Fanny Alger. Unfortunately, Emma did not leave a diary, and her letters do not mention anything about Joseph's adolescence or later experiences with women.

Whatever she may have known about Joseph before they married, it must have been a fascinating courtship, conducted as it was among unseen spirits and Joseph's unsettling conversations with angels. However, Joseph and Emma had been bound by treasure magic from their first meeting in 1825, because when Joseph and his father, Joseph Sr., arrived in Harmony, Pennsylvania, to help Josiah Stowell locate buried treasure, they boarded with Emma's father. Stowell had a farm across the Pennsylvania border in South Bainbridge, New York. Prior

52. Ibid., 329, 345.
53. Ibid., 784-85.

to hiring Joseph, he had traveled 160 miles to Palmyra to meet the younger Joseph. He did so because he had heard the young man "possessed certain keys by which he could discern things invisible to the natural eye," according to Lucy.[54] Emma's father, Isaac Hale, remembered that the activity involving buried treasure "took place about the 17th of November 1825."

Lodging with the Hales, Joseph soon noticed Isaac's twenty-one-year-old daughter, Emma. "After these occurrences," Hale observed, "young Smith made several visits at my house, and at length asked my consent to his marrying my daughter Emma." Confirming Ingersoll's recollection, Hale refused, partly because Smith "followed a business that I could not approve." Joseph "left the place," but "not long after this," in January 1827, he "returned, and while I was absent from home," Hale recounted, Joseph "carried off my daughter into the State of New York, where they were married without my approbation or consent."[55]

Treasure digging and marriage

It was in a mysterious atmosphere of imaginative lore and a mix of theology and magic that Joseph and Emma eloped. The treasure seeker presented himself as someone who had special knowledge that was beyond the woman's ken. She lived in the peaceful Susquehanna Valley, which had been settled in the seventeenth and eighteenth centuries by Mennonites and Quakers. By comparison, the region surrounding Joseph's hometown had experienced the religious excitement of the Great Awakening beginning around 1740 and a second awakening that engulfed the area from 1800 to around 1850. The intense interest in salvation was especially pronounced after the War of 1812 and gained momentum in the revivals held in 1826, 1831 (the year of the largest conversions), and 1835-37.[56] Not far from Palmyra, Rochester was the fastest growing community in the United States in

54. Ibid., 359-60; Vogel, *Early Mormon Documents,* 1:309-10.

55. See Vogel, *Early Mormon Documents,* 4:284.

56. Whitney R. Cross, *The Burned-over District: The Social and Intellectual History of Enthusiastic Religion in Western New York, 1800-1850* (Ithaca: Cornell University Press, 1950), 3-51, 66.

the 1820s. The commercialization of agriculture and waterways such as the Erie Canal were bringing industry and trade from coastal cities inward to new, westward-expanding towns.

When the Smiths visited Harmony, they came from an agricultural community astir with religious fervor. The famous evangelist Charles Finney preached in Rochester in 1830.[57] Migration roads, commerce, and religious excitement would eventually connect the Erie Canal region in central New York State with the Susquehanna River area. The revivalist atmosphere of upstate New York in the 1820s coincided with Joseph's reorientation from his commerce in seer stones and money digging toward a more orthodox expression of religion, although with many unique qualities, such as the millennialist emphasis, which had more in common with Anabaptist and other radical theological currents than with mainstream Protestantism.[58]

In 1838, Smith confirmed that a treasure-digging contract had first brought him into contact with Emma. He was in Missouri and, on April 30, began writing his long narrative of the church's founding. "Owing to the many reports [from] evil disposed and designing persons," he wrote, it was necessary for him to return to his early life in all its sparse detail. He explained that at age nineteen he had hired out on a treasure digging job in Pennsylvania, where he met Emma. His employer, Josiah Stowell, had arranged for him to "board with a Mr. Isaac Hale" in Harmony (now Oakland), Pennsylvania:

> In the month of October Eighteen hundred and twenty five I hired with an old Gentleman, by name of Josiah Stoal who lived in Chenango County, State of New York. He had heard something of a silver mine having been opened by the Spaniards in Harmony, Susquahana County, State of Pensylvania, and had previous to my hiring with him been digging in order if possible to discover the mine. After I went to live with him he took me among the rest of his hands to dig for the silver mine, at

57. See Paul E. Johnson, *A Shopkeeper's Millennium: Society and Revivals in Rochester, New York, 1815-1837* (New York: Hill and Wang, 1990), 4-8, 14-38.

58. See John L. Brooke, *The Refiner's Fire: The Making of Mormon Cosmology, 1644-1844* (Cambridge: Cambridge University Press, 1994), 149-94; George Huntston Williams, *The Radical Reformation*, 3rd ed. (Kirksville, Mo.: Truman State University Press, 2000).

> which I continued to work for nearly a month without success in our undertaking, and finally I prevailed with the old gentleman to cease digging after it. Hence arose the very prevalent story of my having been a money digger.[59]

What Joseph failed to explain in this version was the apparent continuum from treasure seeking to finding gold plates or the similar *modus operandi* in placing a "seer stone" in a hat and putting his face up to the hat to exclude light so he could gaze at the stone, whether searching for buried treasure or translating the Book of Mormon.[60]

It is also true that Joseph's career in money digging was much more extensive than he intimated in his 1838 narrative. The documents surrounding his arrest for being a "glass looker" and "disturbing the peace" confirm this. In the case of *People of the State of New York vs. Joseph Smith,* a hearing was held in Bainbridge on March 20, 1826, before Justice Albert Neeley. Stowell's nephew, Peter Bridgeman, had charged Joseph Smith with being "a disorderly person" and "imposter," arguing that Joseph had deceived Peter's uncle by saying he could locate buried treasure.[61] As for himself, Stowell was entirely satisfied with Smith's performance as a seer and believed that Smith had a genuine gift allowing him to see underground. At the trial, Abram W. Benton recorded this exchange with the witness:

> Did Smith ever tell you there was money hid in a certain place which he

59. See Jessee, *Personal Writings,* 238; *History of the Church,* 1:17. Treasure seeking persisted in Mormon culture. Wilford Woodruff's patriarchal blessing offered "access to the treasures hid in the sand" (Kenney, *Wilford Woodruff's Journal,* 1:143). In Nauvoo in 1845, Hosea Stout described a boy using a "peep stone" to locate money he "could see hid up in the ground" (Juanita Brooks, ed., *On the Mormon Frontier: The Diary of Hosea Stout, 1844-1861* [Salt Lake City: University of Utah Press andUtah State Historical Society, 1982], 1:62). In the 1870s-80s one of the church's original apostles, William E. McLellin, by then a critic of the church, still promoted seer stones (Stan Larson and Samuel J. Passey, eds., *The William E. McLellin Papers, 1854-1880* [Salt Lake City: Signature Books, 2007], 183-86, 300, 402, 405, 484; cf. 505-06). See also Quinn, *Early Mormonism,* 206-11.

60. Richard Van Wagoner and Steven Walker, "Joseph Smith: 'The Gift of Seeing,'" *Dialogue: A Journal of Mormon Thought* 15 (Summer 1982): 2:50; George D. Smith, "Joseph Smith and the Book of Mormon," *Free Inquiry* 4 (Winter 1983-84): 27n2.

61. *Fraser's Magazine,* Feb. 1873, 229, cited by H. Michael Marquardt, *The Rise of Mormonism: 1816-1844* (Longwood, Fla.: Xulon Press, 2005), 66-73.

> mentioned? [Stowell:] Yes. Did he tell you, you could find it by digging? [Stowell:] Yes. Did you dig? [Stowell:] Yes. Did you find any money? [Stowell:] No. Did he not lie to you then and deceive you? [Stowell:] No! the money was there, but we did not get quite to it! How do you know it was there? [Stowell:] Smith said it was![62]

Dogged in his pursuit of treasure, Stowell had encouraged Joseph and others to stay on and not give up. The *Elder's Journal* in Kirtland buttressed Smith's history by adding that money digging had never been "a very profitable job to him, as he only got fourteen dollars a month for it."[63] However, in a scene reminiscent of Daniel Thompson's 1835 story, *The Money Diggers: A Green Mountain Tale,* Joseph and his new bride visited the "Hill Cumorah" on September 22, 1827, around midnight, having traveled there in a borrowed wagon. Previous unsuccessful attempts to exhume the gold plates had ended in failure, but this time, with the help of his wife, Joseph was able to get them. Three months later, beginning in December, Emma and her brother Reuben recorded Smith's translation of the strange inscriptions said to be on the plates.[64]

In the ensuing time, Emma's parents had acquiesced to their daughter's circumstances and allowed her to briefly return home to recover her property—"clothing, furniture, cows &c." At the end of 1827, the newlyweds decided to move to Harmony and accept the Hales' offer to occupy a small house on the property behind the family residence. Isaac Hale went on in his 1834 affidavit to say that "Smith stated to me, that he had given up what he called 'glass-looking' and that he expected to work hard for a living." However, it became clear that they had brought a "wonderful box of Plates down with them,"

---

62. Wesley P. Walters, *Joseph Smith's Bainbridge, N.Y., Court Trials* (Salt Lake City: Modern Microfilm, n.d.), reprinted from *Westminster Theological Journal* 36 (Winter 1974): 128; see also H. Michael Marquardt and Wesley P. Walters, *Inventing Mormonism: Tradition and the Historical Record* (San Francisco: Smith Research Associates, 1994), 176-77.

63. *History of the Church,* 3:28-29, referencing the *Elders Journal,* 1:2, 28-29.

64. Anderson, *Lucy's Book,* 172-73; D[aniel] P. Thompson, *May Martin, or The Money Diggers: A Green Mountain Tale, 1835* (Montpelier, Vt.: E. P. Walton and Son, 1835), 86-87: "It was a dark night in July ... that the money diggers resumed their labours."

Isaac recorded—an artifact Isaac was "not allowed to look" at. Unimpressed by this clumsy subterfuge, Hale observed that "the manner in which he [Smith] pretended to read and interpret, was the same as when he looked for the money-diggers, with the stone in his hat, and his hat over his face, while the Book of Plates were at the same time hid in the woods!" Joseph kept his promise to change his employment but retained the same tools of the trade, applied to a different object. To his father-in-law, it was just more of the same. Eventually, Emma and Joseph had to leave Harmony for good. When they did, it marked the end of their relationship with Isaac and Elizabeth Hale, who thereafter had little contact with their daughter and son-in-law.

From what Isaac Hale had seen of money digging, which he believed was a pretense of sorcery, he was unable to look at the Book of Mormon favorably. "I conscientiously believe," he stated in 1834, "that the whole 'Book of Mormon' (so-called) is a silly fabrication of falsehood and wickedness, got up for speculation, and with a design to dupe the credulous and unwary—and in order that its fabricators might live upon the spoils of those who swallowed the deception."[65]

During this same time period, Smith's relationship with his treasure-hunting employer, Josiah Stowell, deepened. Smith had worked with Stowell for four years, 1825-29, and Stowell's conviction of Smith's mystical abilities had not diminished. When Smith visited him on October 4, 1829, having just completed his translation of the Book of Mormon, Stowell sold him a horse and then offered to buy a thousand copies of the forthcoming book. Writing to Cowdery, who was back in Manchester helping supervise publication of the Book of Mormon, Smith mentioned Stowell's loyalty, saying: "I have bought a horse of Mr. Stowell and want someone to come after it as soon as convenient[.] Mr. Stowell has a prospect of getting five or six hundred dollars. He does not know certain that he can get it but he is going to try and if he can get the money, he wants to pay it in immediately for books."[66]

---

65. See Vogel, *Early Mormon Documents,* 4:287-88; Howe, *Mormonism Unvailed,* 265-66; also "Mormonism," *Susquehanna Register and Northern Pennsylvanian,* May 1, 1834, 1.

66. See Jessee, *Personal Writings,* 251-52.

Joseph's personal charisma was working its effect where he needed to rely on others for help. He elicited sympathy and created a sense of urgency; his enterprises bore a strange significance. A talisman he is said to have worn while digging carried this inscription: "Confirm O god thy strength in us so that neither the adversary nor any Evil thing may cause us to fail."[67] In the latter half of 1832 at age twenty-six, Joseph recalled that eleven years earlier he had experienced a revelatory moment while pondering the "sittuation of the world." He would not speak openly of it for another eight years. He remembered a second experience that had occurred when he was seventeen years old.[68] Through all this, fortune seemed to smile upon him when he needed it most. For instance, just when his father-in-law was "about to turn me out of doors," he asked for heaven's help and ended up staying.[69] Looking back at the year 1827, he was satisfied that he had accomplished two great tasks which he seemed to equate: marrying Emma and finding the gold plates.

> I was married to Emma Hale Daughtr of Isaach Hale who lived in Harmony Susquehana County Pensylvania on the 18th [of] January AD. 1827, on the 22d day of Sept of this same year I obtained the plates.[70]

If his wife shared in his sense of triumph, she was nevertheless forbidden to see the plates herself.[71]

Married life was not easy. In fact, it was riddled with doubts, rumors, and deception from the start. There was, first of all, the business of seer stones and incantations, which created difficulties in the neighborhoods where the Smiths lived; second, Joseph was haunted by the suspicion, which followed him from place to place, that he crossed moral boundaries in his friendship with other women. For instance, rumors going back to 1828 circulated in Harmony about his involvement with a local girl named Eliza Winters, and in the early 1830s his

---

67. Quinn, *Early Mormonism and Magic,* 68; see also Van Wagoner and Walker, "Joseph Smith Gift," 2.

68. Jessee, *Personal Writings,* 9-14.

69. Van Wagoner and Walker, "Joseph Smith Gift," 49-68.

70. Joseph Smith, "History, 1832," in Jessee, *Personal Writings,* 13.

71. Van Wagoner and Walker, "Joseph Smith Gift," 50.

Kirtland neighbors talked about his relationship with Fanny Alger. There was also the inevitable gossip following his marriage to three dozen plural wives in the early 1840s.

First encounters

Emma's first son died in childbirth on June 15, 1828. While she was in mourning, her cousin Levi Lewis reportedly told Martin Harris that Joseph had tried to "seduce" one of Emma's friends, Eliza Winters. Lewis said the response from the Book of Mormon financier was that he did not care if Joseph *had* "attempt[ed] to seduce Eliza Winters &c.," thereby acknowledging the report. When Emma's mother, Elizabeth Hale, was asked about this in an interview forty-six years later, she declined to comment.[72] Whatever she might have known went with her to the grave in February 1842, three years after Emma's father died.

When the Smiths moved to Ohio in 1831, Joseph there met the majority of his future wives. Most of them were still adolescents—the children of close associates. Whenever the idea of polygamy became a realistic objective in Smith's mind, the theological foundations were established in Ohio long before a revelation formalized it in Illinois in 1843. In the revelation, Emma was promised annihilation if she failed to "abide this commandment." Curiously enough, the revelation did not invoke the Book of Mormon's justification for taking more wives—the call to raise a righteous seed.

Could the groundwork for polygamy have been laid as early as 1827? The same year he married Emma Hale, Joseph also probably had met Louisa Beaman, then only twelve years old. Her father, Alvah, had agreed to help the young scribe hide the gold plates. Apostle Parley P. Pratt said Smith knew the Beamans "long before the first organization of the [Mormon] church" and that Alvah had assisted Smith in 1827.[73] An interesting coincidence brought Joseph together with both

72. See Vogel, *Early Mormon Documents,* 4:296-97, 346-60; see also Frederick G. Mather, "The Early Mormons: Joe Smith Operates at Susquehanna," *Binghamton Republican,* July 29, 1880.

73. Parley P. Pratt Jr., ed., *Autobiography of Parley P. Pratt* (Salt Lake City: Deseret Book, 1961), 110; Jessee, *Papers of Joseph Smith,* 2:25. See other recollections of the

Emma and Louisa; in both instances, it was treasure digging. Alvah had not only helped Joseph hide the plates, he was a practitioner of the divining rod and had joined the Smiths in digging for treasure from 1822 to 1827. It was in 1822 that Joseph discovered a "seer stone" in a neighbor's well.[74]

Joseph made other acquaintances in his early life that presaged the plural marriages he would consummate in the 1840s. His relationships in Ohio with various families and their daughters—some quite youthful at the time—allowed him to invite the young women into his further confidence when they were older. In most cases, the women were adolescents or in their twenties when he met them. About ten were pre-teens, others already thirty or above. Most were with their families in Ohio, where Smith had sent missionaries from western New York in 1830. Then Smith issued a revelation in January 1831 ordering his followers to sell their property and trek 300 miles west to Kirtland, which he designated as a city of refuge for the church's converts. He became acquainted there with some twenty-seven of the women who would later become his mates, as will be discussed in chapter 2.

Several families in Kirtland offered to house the Smiths in February 1831. This was not pre-arranged but a spontaneous response when people encountered them on their arrival. For instance, when the Smiths visited a country store, its proprietor, Newel K. Whitney, was prompt to suggest temporary lodging at his home. Whitney's daughter Sarah Ann would become one of Joseph Smith's wives, although at the time she was only five years old. Whitney's business partner, Algernon Sidney Gilbert, was equally hospitable and invited Joseph and Emma to stay with him; but because he was already housing the John Porter

---

Smith-Beaman money digging period: Martin Harris, interviewed by Joel Tiffany, *Tiffany's Monthly*, Aug. 1859, 164; Mary A. Noble, Autobiography, in Vogel, *Early Mormon Documents*, 3:308-10; Anderson, *Lucy's Book*, 800; Joseph B. Noble, Affidavit, June 26, 1869, in "40 Affidavits on Celestial Marriage," 1869 (cf. Andrew Jenson's "Plural Marriage," *Historical Record* 6 [May 1887]: 221); Joseph Bates Noble, Journal, LDS Archives; Jessee, *Personal Writings*, 39; Dean Jessee, "Joseph Knight's Recollection of Early Mormon History," *BYU Studies* 17 (1976) 33-34; James H. Crockwell, *Pictures and Biographies of Brigham Young and His Wives* (Salt Lake City: Cannon & Sons, 1877), 20-21.

74. Faulring, *American Prophet's Record*, 24.

Rollins family, the Smiths accepted the Whitneys' offer. In any case, the Smiths would be in frequent contact with all three families. John Rollins's wife, Elizabeth, was a sister of Gilbert's wife, Keziah. John's twelve-year-old daughter, Mary Elizabeth, was a future wife of Joseph Smith. Mary had recently been baptized by Parley P. Pratt, himself a recent convert to Smith's Church of Christ and a former Campbellite Baptist preacher.

Mary remembered later that she felt "sealed" to the prophet from the time she first saw him. Her rhetorical embellishment should not be interpreted literally. The sealing would not occur for another decade. Yet she also asserted that polygamy "was given to" Smith "before he gave it to the Church."[75] An excitable and impressionable young woman who fully participated in the new millennial community, at age thirteen Mary had interpreted words spoken in tongues at Mormon gatherings in the fall of 1831 in Missouri.[76] In 1834, when she was sixteen, Smith is said to have received a commandment to marry her. If so, she nevertheless married Adam Lightner and became a mother at eighteen, while still remaining close to Smith through the 1830s.

It was eleven years after the Smiths roomed with the Whitneys that Joseph expressed a romantic interest in their daughter, as well. His 1842 letter to her and her parents remains extant even though Joseph instructed them to destroy it. Another future wife, Marinda Johnson, was fifteen when she met Smith in Ohio. She said when he looked into her eyes, she felt ashamed. At the time, the Smiths were living with Marinda's family and would continue to do so through 1832. On September 4, 1834, Marinda married Orson Hyde. The next year, Hyde became one of the Quorum of Twelve Apostles, though Marinda remained close to Smith up to the time of their plural marriage in early 1842. Another family that housed the Smiths in Ohio was that of Vinson and Martha Knight in 1834. Martha became

75. Mary Elizabeth Rollins Lightner, Remarks at Brigham Young University, Apr. 14, 1905, LDS Archives. For discussion, see Todd Compton, *In Sacred Loneliness: The Plural Wives of Joseph Smith* (Salt Lake City: Signature Books, 1997), 208.

76. Mary Elizabeth Rollins Lightner, Autobiography (typescript), 3, Utah State Historical Society, Salt Lake City, Utah.

Smith's plural wife eight years later. The seven-year-old daughter of Apostle Heber C. Kimball was still another future wife. Helen attended school next door to the Smiths in Kirtland in 1836. When she married Smith a few years later in Nauvoo at the age of fourteen, it was with her father's encouragement.

In 1837, while married to David Sessions, forty-two-year-old Patty Sessions met Smith in Kirtland, as did their nineteen-year-old daughter, Sylvia. Although Sylvia married Windsor P. Lyon the next year, both mother and daughter married Smith four years afterward in 1842. Almera Johnson was about twenty years old when she was baptized in the early 1830s and met Joseph through her older sister, Delcena, whose husband, Lyman Sherman, was a close friend of the prophet. Both sisters would marry Smith. Twenty-one-year-old Agnes Coolbrith met the prophet when he visited Boston in 1832. Her first marriage was to Joseph's youngest brother, Don Carlos,[77] in 1835. Don Carlos died in 1841. Soon thereafter, Agnes became one more of Joseph's wives. Another wife, Eliza Snow, was a twenty-seven-year-old when she and her family met the Smiths in Ohio. The Snows had been part of Sidney Rigdon's Campbellite following, which, like the Mormons, had anticipated a forthcoming millennium. Eliza was thirty-one in 1835 when she was baptized into Joseph's Church of Christ. Less than two months after she married the prophet in mid-1842, she moved in with the Smiths—as she had done once before in Kirtland when she taught school for the Smith children. So the arrangement may not have seemed unusual. However, her father became unhappy with the Mormons and took his family to Walnut Grove, Illinois, in 1842, leaving behind Eliza, her younger brother, Lorenzo (who was on a two-year mission to England), and their married sister, Leonora (who lived in Quincy and had two daughters).

This series of events raises a few questions. What was the nature

77. Named, apparently, for a member of Spanish royalty. Friedrich Schiller wrote a play in 1787 about Don Carlos of Spain, who attempted to free Flanders from the despotic grip of his father, King Phillip, that Giuseppe Verdi used in 1867 for his opera "Don Carlos." After the grandson of Holy Roman Emperor Charles V, several Spanish kings and princes were named Don Carlos.

of Smith's relationships with these young women from the time he first met them? How relevant is it that in many instances he had lived under the same roof as his future wife prior to marrying her? In some cases one or more of the parents became ill or died, providing an opportunity for Joseph and Emma to invite a girl to take up residence in the Smith household as a boarder or housekeeper. In 1834, Smith stayed for a short time with the Beaman household in Avon, New York, thirty miles southwest of Palmyra. Joseph was twenty-eight and Louisa was nineteen. In 1837 and 1840, respectively, Louisa's father and Joseph's father died, after which Joseph taught the principle of plural marriage to her brother-in-law, Joseph Noble, who performed a marriage ceremony for Joseph and Louisa less than a year later.

As has been seen, the opportunity to become closely associated with a future wife often occurred years before the marriage took place. Lucinda Pendleton and her husband, George W. Harris, were baptized in 1834 after hearing recent convert Orson Pratt deliver a fiery message in Indiana. They joined the Mormons in Missouri by 1836. Two years later as Smith traveled from Ohio to Missouri, when Lucinda was thirty-six, he stayed with the Harrises for two months. When the Mormons migrated to Nauvoo in 1839, Lucinda and George lived across the street from the Smiths. At an unspecified time, but probably by 1842, Lucinda became one more of the prophet's plural wives.

Sarah Kingsley met Smith about 1835 when she—but not her husband, John Cleveland—converted to Mormonism in Ohio. The next year they moved to Quincy, Illinois, and in 1839 Joseph and Emma stayed with the Clevelands on their way to Nauvoo. Sarah would marry Smith some three years later, also by 1842.

When the Smiths established their own home in Nauvoo, it was large enough that they were able to take in housekeepers and young women whose family lives were in flux. William and Zina Huntington converted in New York in 1835 and moved to Kirtland the next year, which is when their fifteen-year-old daughter, also named Zina, met Smith. That same year, 1836, their twenty-five-year-old daughter, Presendia, who had been married to Norman Buell since 1827, met Smith as well. When the Huntingtons moved to Nauvoo, mother

Huntington died and the young namesake, with her father and some of her siblings, moved in with the Smiths for a few weeks in August 1839. Both daughters, Zina and Presendia, each of whom was already married, became plural wives of Smith in late 1841.

After years of turmoil in Ohio and Missouri, the prophet achieved some stability for the Mormon community in Illinois. Occasionally he was still hunted by law officials for old offenses. Rather than submit to arrest, he opted to hide, once again necessitating the need to stay in the houses of his followers. This was the case when Smith lived with Ruth Vose and her husband, Edwin Sayers, in August 1842. Smith had met Vose ten years earlier when she was twenty-four and still several years away from being baptized. Evidently with her husband's acquiescence, she married the prophet sometime in February 1843.

Two more sets of sisters became boarders in the Smith mansion a year after the Huntington siblings took up residence there. Eliza and Emily Partridge had grown up near Kirtland. It was where their father was baptized in 1830. At age eleven in 1831, Eliza followed her father into baptism, as did Emily the next year at age eight. A year after their father died, in May 1840, seventeen-year-old Emily and twenty-one-year-old Eliza became maids in the Smith home. They both later married Joseph.

Sarah and Maria Lawrence were eleven and thirteen, respectively, when Smith visited Canada in 1837 and converted their parents. Three years later, after their father died, Smith was appointed their legal guardian and took the girls into his home from 1841 to 1842. The Lawrence sisters married the prophet in 1843, just after the Partridge sisters.

Lucy Walker was six when her father was baptized in 1832 in Kirtland and fifteen when she met Smith in Nauvoo in 1841. She lived in the Smith home, working for room and board—two years later marrying Joseph. Another girl, Elvira Cowles, lived near Palmyra and was seventeen when her family converted in 1830. She was baptized in 1835 at age twenty-two. She lived with the Smiths from 1840 to 1842 and married Joseph the next year. Desdemona Fullmer's family moved to Ohio from Pennsylvania in 1836. She was twenty-seven.

Desdemona was baptized the same year, then became a member of the Smith household in the spring of 1842, along with Elvira Cowles and the Partridge and Lawrence sisters, among others. She married Joseph in 1843. Melissa Lott, who also lived in Pennsylvania, was nine when her family converted to Mormonism. A decade later in 1843, when she was eighteen, she lived with the Smiths for a year before becoming Joseph's wife.

In other words, for over a decade prior to Smith's first plural marriages, he met and established relationships with those who would later become his wives. The approximate dates of their first meeting and of their marriage ceremonies in Nauvoo are summarized in the following table (1.1). For comparison, Emma was twenty-one when she met Joseph in 1825 and twenty-two when they married in early 1827.

The circumstance of the Smiths moving so often and staying with other families, and having others often stay with them, reflects the church's transient character during its migration through four states in the 1830s. The recurring westward movement was motivated in large measure by dissatisfaction and opportunity. In 1831 the community uprooted itself from the Erie Canal region of central New York and relocated to Ohio, where its numbers expanded with an influx of Baptist converts. The increase in membership made it possible to construct a large and elegant temple in Kirtland. Almost simultaneously with the move to Ohio, Mormons extended a branch of the church to Missouri, where a temple was also planned for Independence. During the 1837 recession, Smith's unchartered bank, called the Kirtland Safety Society Anti-banking Company, collapsed. Angry Ohioans could not be repaid for loans they had made to Mormon merchants and some church members lost their savings. A rebellion ensued. Many were so upset with Smith's financial mismanagement, at the same time that stories circulated about his relationship with a young female domestic worker, that previous restraint gave way to open criticism. In quick succession, several in the leadership were excommunicated, including Smith's second-in-command, Oliver Cowdery. Opposition to Smith coalesced in late 1837 when he was away in Far West, Missouri. The insurrection included Joseph Coe, John F. Boynton, Luke S. Johnson,

TABLE 1.1 Interval between first encounter and Nauvoo marriage

future wife	year met	age at meeting	age at marriage	year of marriage
Louisa Beaman	ca. 1827	12	26	1841
Zina Huntington	1836	15	20	"
Presendia Huntington	1836	25	31	"
Agnes Coolbrith	1832	21	30	1842
Lucinda Pendleton	1838	37	40	"
Mary Elizabeth Rollins	1831	12	23	"
Sylvia Sessions	1837	19	23	"
Patty Bartlett	1837	42	47	"
Sarah Kingsley	1835/39	47/51	53	"
Elizabeth Jane Davis	1831	40	50	"
Marinda Johnson	1831	16	26	"
Delcena Johnson	1832	26	35	"
Eliza Snow	1831-32	27	38	"
Sarah Rapson	–	49	–	"
Sarah Ann Whitney	1831	5	17	"
Martha McBride	1833	28	37	"
Ruth Vose	1832	24	35	1843
Flora Ann Woodworth	by 1841	14	16	"
Emily Partridge	1831	7	19	"
Eliza Partridge	1831	10	22	"
Almera Johnson	1832	19	29	"
Lucy Walker	1841	15	17	"
Sarah Lawrence	1837	11	16	"
Maria Lawrence	1837	13	19	"
Helen Mar Kimball	by 1836	8	14	"
Elvira Cowles	1835	22	29	"
Rhoda Richards	1843	58	58	"
Hannah Ells	by 1840	27	30	"
Mary Ann Frost	by 1837	28	34	"
Olive Frost	1843	26	27	"
Nancy Winchester	ca.1834	6	14	"
Desdemona Fullmer	1836	27	33	"
Melissa Lott	1836	12	19	"
Sarah Scott	–	25	–	"
Phebe Watrous	by 1841	36	38	"
Mary Huston	–	25	–	"
Fanny Young	1833	46	55	"

and Warren Parrish, who were said to have "united together for the overthrow of the Church." John Smith wrote to his son George A. Smith in 1838 that a total of twenty-eight "dissenters" had been "cut off" from their church affiliation. The *Elders Journal* claimed the "dissenting band" had "openly and publicly renounced the Church of Christ of Latter Day Saints … and set at naught Brother Joseph and the whole church, [and] denounced them as heretics."[78]

The trouble continued until Smith led those who were still loyal to him out of Kirtland in 1838, opting to settle in Far West. This would be a momentary stop rather than a permanent solution, as it turned out—a conduit for a successive migration to Illinois. Missourians were alarmed by the influx of Mormons, mostly New England yankees, and met to decide what to do about the intrusion. Sidney Rigdon warned that if they lifted their hand against the church, they would be "exterminated." In response to this incendiary speech, violence erupted on both sides, and Governor Lilburn Boggs soon declared in an echo of Rigdon's rhetoric that "the Mormons … must be exterminated," "treated as enemies," and "driven from the State if necessary" to protect "the public peace."[79]

In their peregrination over the span of less than a decade, Mormons found strife wherever they settled. In Missouri, this was true first in Jackson County, where Joseph had sent a vanguard to Independence, then to a succession of other counties: Clay to the north, Ray and Carroll to the northeast, and Caldwell north of Ray. The conflict reached a peak in Far West and Haun's Mill, Caldwell County settlements, and then spread to Daviess County, north of Caldwell. If the Mormons were to leave the state, it would shatter their hopes and plans to build the New Jerusalem there and hasten the millennium. Joseph had developed an affinity for Missouri and identified Jackson County as the place where the ancient Garden of Eden had been lo-

78. *Elders Journal,* July 1838, 36-37; cf. *History of the Church,* 2:528. See Max H. Parkin, "The Nature and Cause of Internal and External Conflict of the Mormons in Ohio between 1830 and 1838," M.A. thesis, Brigham Young University, 1966, 319.

79. *History of the Church,* 3:42, 175; for Christian societies claiming domain in America, see Michelle Goldberger, *Kingdom Coming: The Rise of Christian Nationalism* (New York: W. W. Norton, 2007).

cated. He also identified a place in Daviess County called Spring Hill, which he called "Adam-ondi-Ahman," where he said Adam and Eve had lived outside the Garden and "where Adam shall come to visit his people" when Christ returned.[80]

The Mormon leaders were apprehended and jailed by state and local militia, and their followers were expelled in November 1838. Early the next year, with the cooperation of their jailers, Smith and fellow inmates escaped to join their people in Illinois, where they proceeded to found a theocratic society. They remained there for seven years, 1839-46. Although Smith was assassinated in mid-1844, in part because of plural marriage, pressure continued for two more years to expel the Mormons from Illinois and from the United States altogether.

The Transition from Theory to Practice

Polygamy was not the exclusive prerogative of Joseph Smith. In his letters and other documents of the period, from his wedding to Emma in 1827 to his first recorded plural marriage in 1841, he committed himself to allow other men this form of concurrent matrimony. But at first, Joseph did not seek a formal wedding. About the time Joseph and Emma's oldest son, Joseph Smith III, was born in Kirtland in 1832, Joseph met the daughter of a carpenter, Samuel Alger, who had converted to Mormonism in October 1830 in Mayfield, about fifteen miles east of Cleveland and ten miles southwest of Kirtland. The fourteen-year-old Fanny Alger was the fourth of eleven children. As might be expected from a teenager from such a large family, she was looking for work, and Emma obliged by hiring her to help around the house. This made Fanny the first of many young women who would come to live with the Smiths as domestic workers. Before long, talk about Joseph echoed Fanny's name, maybe as early as 1832 but certainly from 1833 to 1835. The ensuing scandal contributed to the dissent and excommunication that swept the church in 1837-38, even after Fanny had left town and married someone else.[81]

---

80. Richard L. Bushman and Jed Woodworth, *Joseph Smith: Rough Stone Rolling* (New York: Alfred A. Knopf, 2005), 342-72. See also Stephen C. LeSueur, *The 1838 Mormon War in Missouri* (Columbia: University of Missouri Press, 1987); D&C 116-17.

81. Todd Compton has assembled the most complete documentation regarding

Joseph wrote in his journal on December 4, 1832: "Oh, Lord, deliver thy servant out of temtations and fill his heart with wisdom and understanding."[82] If this was not in reference to Fanny Alger, it coincided with the report of two of Joseph's scribes, Warren Parrish and Oliver Cowdery, that Joseph had been "found" in the hay with his housekeeper. Parrish said Joseph and Fanny were discovered together "as wife," while Cowdery called it a "dirty, nasty, filthy affair." As a result of having publicly discussed the incident, and for "seeking to destroy the character of President Joseph Smith jr by falsly insinuating that he was guilty of adultry &c.," Cowdery was expelled from the church.[83]

One of the apostles, William E. McLellin, assumed that this must have been the origin of celestial marriage because it was the "first well authenticated case of polygamy."[84] LDS leaders Heber C. Kimball and Joseph F. Smith also accepted as fact that Smith must have married Alger; furthermore, Chauncy Webb, Smith's grammar teacher, alleged more specifically that Joseph must have been "sealed secretly to Fanny Alger" in Kirtland.[85] Even the Assistant LDS Church Historian in Utah, Andrew Jenson, considered Alger to be "one of the first plural wives sealed to the Prophet."[86] Just to be sure, Alger was sealed to the deceased prophet by proxy in the Salt Lake Temple in 1899. At the

---

Joseph and Fanny's relationship (*Sacred Loneliness,* 25-42). However, I hesitate to concur with Compton's interpretation of their relationship as a marriage. In my view, Joseph Noble was correct when he said he had performed the first patriarchal marriage in this dispensation by sealing Louisa Beaman to Joseph Smith (Joseph Bates Noble, Autobiography [typescript], 30, L. Tom Perry Special Collections, Harold B. Lee Library, Brigham Young University, Provo, Utah).

82. Jessee, *Papers of Joseph Smith,* 2:5.

83. Donald Q. Cannon and Lyndon W. Cook, eds., *Far West Record: Minutes of the Church of Jesus Christ of Latter-day Saints, 1830-1844* (Salt Lake City: Deseret Book, 1983), 162-63; *History of the Church,* 3:16.

84. William E. McLellin to Joseph Smith III, July 1872, Community of Christ Library-Archives, Independence, Missouri (cf. Larson and Passey, *McLellin Papers,* 483-95); *Salt Lake Tribune,* Oct. 6, 1875; Van Wagoner, *Mormon Polygamy,* 5-12.

85. See W. Wyl (pseud. Wilhelm, Ritter von Wymetal), *Mormon Portraits or the Truth about the Mormon Leaders from 1830 to 1886* (Salt Lake City: Salt Lake Tribune, 1886), 57.

86. Jenson, "Plural Marriage," 233; see also Thomas M. Tinney, *The Royal Family of the Prophet Joseph Smith, Jr.* (Salt Lake City: Green Family Organization, 1973), 41.

end of the twentieth century, historians D. Michael Quinn and Todd Compton both came to the same conclusion about this, that Smith certainly must have been married to Alger, probably from about 1833.[87] Compton later clarified this deduction by admitting that the evidence for a "marriage" or a "sealing" implied hard-to-verify assumptions and uncertainties, and agreed that "late, second-hand reminiscences" may not be the best evidence.[88] In fact, the only thing that is well-attested about this relationship is that Joseph and Fanny were seen together in an intimate relationship. This evidence was weighed against subsequent patterns in Smith's life and superimposed on the earlier story, hence the assumption of a marriage.

In any case, McLellin shared information about the incident with Joseph III to convince him that his father had married more than one woman. In his letter of 1872, McLellin explained: "I was very intimate and familiar with your Father from Oct. 1831 until August 1836. I certainly knew him well, for he attended my High School during the winter of 1834, and the winter of 1835 we learned Hebrew together in the same class." McLellin noted that he "traveled with [Smith] hundreds of miles, [ate] with him, slept with him, etc. ... It seems to be but few men had better opportunities to know J. Smith for five years than I." After discussing the doctrinal issues in question, McLellin confided: "Now Joseph I will relate to you some history, and refer to your own dear Mother for the truth."

McLellin recalled a visit he paid to Emma in 1847, during which he mentioned "some stories" he had heard from Frederick G. Williams, a Kirtland printer.[89] Williams had been an early convert and counselor in the First Presidency from 1833 to 1837. When Joseph went to Missouri during the summer of 1832, Emma stayed with the Williamses in Ohio. She was pregnant with Joseph III at the time. Thinking her husband was away, she was startled at finding him *in flagrante delicto* "committ[ing] an act with a Miss Hill — a hired girl."[90]

---

87. D. Michael Quinn, *The Mormon Hierarchy: Extensions of Power* (Salt Lake City: Signature Books, 1997), 189; Compton, *Sacred Loneliness*, xxx.

88. See Todd Compton to editor, *Journal of Mormon History* 23 (Fall 1997), vi-vii.

89. *History of the Church*, 1:409.

90. As suggested by Linda King Newell and Valeen Tippetts Avery, *Mormon*

After Emma "saw him," Joseph tried to explain it away, but "Mrs. Smith refused to be satisfied." Therefore, Joseph "called in Dr. Williams, O. Cowdery, and S[idney] Rigdon to reconcile Emma," but Joseph "found he was caught" because "she told them just as the circumstances took place," and he finally "confessed humbly, and begged forgiveness. Emma and all forgave him." Emma confirmed this to McLellin. "Again I told her," McLellin continued," that the rumor in circulation was that she had "missed Joseph and Fanny Alger" one evening and "went to the barn and saw him and Fanny in the barn together alone. She looked through a crack [in the barn door] and saw the transaction!!!" According to McLellin, Emma told him "this story too was verily true." McLellin related these events so the prophet's son, now president of his own church, would know his father had not only believed polygamy to be of divine origin but that he "actually practiced it his individual self."[91]

Smith's relationship with Alger was also mentioned by Benjamin F. Johnson, Smith's brother-in-law through Smith's marriage to two of his sisters. In 1835, Alger was living with Delcena Sherman, Benjamin's married sister, when it was whispered that Alger enjoyed the attention of the prophet: "And I was afterw[a]rds told by Warren Parish That He himself & Oliver Cowdery did know that Joseph had Fanny Alger as wife for They were Spied upon & found togather." It might be important to mention that the testimony here and elsewhere regarding "[having] Fanny Alger as wife" employs a Victorian euphemism that should not be construed to imply that Fanny was actually

---

Enigma: Emma Hale Smith, Prophet's Wife, "Elect Lady," Polygamy's Foe, 1804-1879 (Garden City, N.Y.: Doubleday, 1984), 66, Fanny Alger may have been confused here with Fanny Hill from John Cleland's famous 1749 erotic novel, *Memoirs of a Woman of Pleasure.* On the other hand, Van Wagoner, *Mormon Polygamy,* 225n7, finds evidence for two separate girls: where McLellin says "again I told [Emma]," this could mean either that he repeated the same story or that he told a different one. Martin Harris placed the incident in about 1833. McLellin remembered it happening the year before, about the time of Joseph III's birth, 1832. However, Alger did not come to live with the Smiths until 1835. Compton, *Sacred Loneliness,* 33, 646, draws from a late reminiscence by Mosiah Hancock to suggest that Smith married Alger in early 1833. In any case, Emma discovered the girl with Joseph, and Oliver Cowdery and others were brought in to mediate.

91. McLellin to Smith, July 1872.

married to Joseph. This delicate wording may have later contributed to some of the misunderstanding about their marital status. If she had been sealed to him at the time, it was not mentioned and there is no record of it. Johnson knew that Jared Carter and others criticized the "doings of the Prophet" on the assumption that it was an affair, not a plural marriage.[92]

According to a third report about Fanny Alger, "Emma was furious, and drove the girl, who was unable to conceal the *consequences* of her celestial relation with the prophet, out of the house."[93] There is no evidence to corroborate the claim that Fanny was pregnant. Another contemporary wrote that in the spring of 1837, as she remembered it, "there was much excitement against the prophet [over] an unlawful intercourse between himself and a young orphan girl residing in his family, and under his protection."[94]

Benjamin Johnson said that Alger was with Smith for three years, but that they broke up before the social disruption of 1837-38. He added that the Algers moved to Indiana; although Fanny married a husband outside the Mormon community, she remained true to the church and the prophet, according to Johnson: "She did not turn from the Church nor from her friendship for the Prophet while She lived."[95] Historian Richard Van Wagoner has verified that Fanny married Solomon Custer of Dublin City, Indiana, on November 16, 1836, where they raised nine children.[96]

Five primary accounts narrated Smith's intimacy with Fanny Alger or a "Miss Hill" in Kirtland: (1) Scribes Oliver Cowdery and Warren Parrish, (2) Apostle William McLellin from Smith's Counselor Frederick G. Williams, (3) McLellin from Emma Smith, (4)

---

92. Benjamin F. Johnson to George F. Gibbs, Apr.-Oct. 1903, LDS Archives; published in Dean R. Zimmerman, ed., *I Knew the Prophets: An Analysis of the Letter of Benjamin F. Johnson to George F. Gibbs* (Bountiful, Utah: Horizon Publishers, 1976), 33.

93. See Wyl, *Mormon Portraits,* 57.

94. Fanny Brewer, Affidavit, Sept. 13, 1842, in John C. Bennett, *History of the Saints* (Boston: Leland & Whiting, 1842), 85-86.

95. See Zimmerman, *I Knew the Prophets,* 26-27.

96. Van Wagoner, *Mormon Polygamy,* 15n14.

Smith's brother-in-law Benjamin F. Johnson's report of Warren Parrish's familiarity, and (5) Fanny Brewer's affidavit.

Smith's revelations, compiled in the Doctrine and Covenants of the Church of the Latter Day Saints in 1835, included a statement on marriage that responded to a widespread claim that the church was guilty of "fornication, and polygamy." In its defense, the church asserted that its policy was "one wife … one husband" and explained that the wording of the statement was "selected from the revelations of God" and compiled by Oliver Cowdery and two other "Presiding Elders."[97] Whether intentionally or not, the statement tempered the Book of Mormon position that God might someday "command" his people to "raise up seed." Equally interesting was the fact that the presiding elders referred to were the same two men who had mediated Emma's complaint against Joseph and Fanny in 1832: Sidney Rigdon and Frederick Williams. A church conference approved the text of the Doctrine and Covenants in August 1835. Although Smith and Williams were out of town in Michigan, they had prepared the text for submission to the conference and must have concurred with this action.[98]

Did Smith's involvement with Alger embarrass the church in 1835 to the point that the church had to issue a statement rejecting polygamy? If so, the public reaction anticipated in a small way the rage that others in Nauvoo and throughout Illinois would express over the same issue in the 1840s. In 1835 the statement on marriage had to prohibit polygamy without qualification to reassure the public mind. If the prohibition was sincere, it was short-lived because by the early 1840s, Smith had begun *requiring* that other men in the hierarchy marry plural wives. This compulsion was based on the 1843 revelation, which would become Section 132 of the Doctrine and Covenants in 1876, thirty-two years after Smith's death. The same 1876 edition omitted for the first time the 1835 statement endorsing monogamous marriage. Section 132 remains part of the LDS canon and continues to authorize a man to marry additional women.

97. "On Marriage," D&C, 1835 edition, 251.

98. *History of the Church,* 2:243.

Already in the mid-to-late 1830s, the Mormons in Missouri were characterized as a "community of wives," as Smith noted when he wrote an open letter to church members in Caldwell County from his jail cell in neighboring Clay County in December 1838. He then acknowledged that people were saying the church had "not only dedicated our property but [also] our families … to the Lord, and [S]atan taking advantage of this has transfigured it into a lasciviousness such as a community of wives[,] which is an abomination in the sight of God."[99]

This denial confirmed the public view—one that ironically can probably be traced to Smith's own actions. For example, rumors may have been circulating already as early as 1832 that Smith had been familiar with fifteen-year-old Marinda Johnson, a member of the family with which Smith lived in Ohio and who would become one of Smith's plural wives in Illinois. Smith was dragged out of the house by, it was said, Marinda's brothers, who tarred and feathered him. No contemporary documentation explicitly attributes this violent act to an insult against the girl's virtue, but this was the explanation that was later given to it. Another possible source of rumors was Lucinda Harris's statement that she was Joseph's "mistress" four years before an 1842 conversation with Sarah Pratt, according to Pratt's later memory. Assuming Pratt remembered the statement accurately and that Lucinda might have made the same brag to anyone else as early as 1838, this also could have been a source of gossip.[100] Whether or not these are reliable accounts, something was no doubt said or done to trigger the rumors that circulated in Ohio.

---

99. Jessee, *Personal Writings,* 419. For context, see Edwin Brown Firmage and Richard Collin Mangrum, *Zion in the Courts: A Legal History of the Church of Jesus Christ of Latter-day Saints, 1830-1900* (Urbana: University of Illinois Press, 1988), 76, 402; *History of the Church,* 3:211, 230.

100. Wyl, *Mormon Portraits,* 60; D. Michael Quinn, *The Mormon Hierarchy: Origins of Power* (Salt Lake City: Signature Books and Smith Research Associates, 1994), 618. Van Wagoner (*Mormon Polygamy,* 4n4) and Compton (*Sacred Loneliness,* 220-22) argue that the mobsters (and if they included the Johnson brothers, two of them were future apostles) reacted to financial shenanigans, not to indiscretions with their sister. In defense of this position, Van Wagoner and Compton point to the fact that Sidney Rigdon was also tarred and feathered that night. Vogel (*Joseph Smith Making,* 514) cites other sources of early rumors of polygamy, all involving Smith.

No one knows exactly when Mormon polygamy began. It seems to have been on Smith's mind when he started to restore ancient Israel, as he put it. This "restoration of all things" became, in part, euphemistic for extending the "favor" of multiple wives to his selected associates. As already noted, the Book of Mormon anticipated the practice of plural marriage. As early as 1835 in Kirtland, Smith had developed doctrines that would pave the way for "celestial" marriage. Church members were being taught to recognize special meaning in such passages as where Paul says in 1 Corinthians that "man was not made … for the sake of woman, but woman for the sake of man. … Nevertheless, in the Lord woman is not independent of man or man independent of woman."[101]

As Gary James Bergera has detected in the theology surrounding plural marriage, it was introduced as part of Smith's concept of an eternal family. In immediate succession, "Smith introduced [church] members … to the ordinances of baptism for the dead (1840), eternal marriage (1841), and eternal proxy marriage (1842). … Baptism for the dead guaranteed deceased relatives (and friends) membership in Christ's church; eternal marriage united living husbands and wives after death; and proxy marriage linked spouses to their deceased partners." Later "adoption sealings would [add to] … an expanding web of eternally procreative relationships."[102] Nevertheless, the "first authorized marriage sealing," granting eternal marriage to a husband and wife, was not performed for two "civilly married spouses" but for "Smith and his first documented plural wife, Louisa Beaman. In fact, plural marriage—known among early participants as celestial marriage—represented the highest order, the *ne plus ultra,* of Smith's teachings on eternal or patriarchal marriage," superceding civil marriage, an outdated marriage contract which, church members came to understand, was as inefficacious as an improper baptism.[103]

---

101. Quinn, *Mormon Hierarchy Extensions,* 178; W. W. Phelps to Sally Phelps, Sept. 9, 1835, paraphrasing 1 Cor. 11:8, 9, 11, LDS Archives.

102. Gary James Bergera, "The Earliest Eternal Sealings for Civilly Married Couples Living and Dead," *Dialogue: A Journal of Mormon Thought* 35 (Fall 2002): 41-42.

103. Ibid., 45.

The precise date of Smith's plural marriage revelation is another issue that is open to some conjecture. LDS historian Dean Jessee argues for an 1831 revelation, which would justify Smith's extramarital relationships prior to Louisa Beaman.[104] Others propose an unspecified date prior to 1843 yet early enough to sanction the Smith-Beaman marriage. Still others suggest that Smith's words perhaps implied separate revelations received at different times, of which the culminating 1843 statement gave *ex post facto* validation to previous instances.[105]

Benjamin Johnson specifically addressed the issue of how early the prophet practiced polygamy:

> I will Say That the Revilation to the Church at Nauvoo July 12th, 1843 on the eternity of the Marriage Covenant and Law of plural Marriage was not the first Rivilation of that Law Received & Practiced by the Prophet[.] In 1835 at Kirtland I learned from my Sister [Delcena]'s Husband Lyman R Shirman, who was close to the Prophet and Recieved it from him[,] "That the ancient order of plural marriage was again to be practiced by the Church[."] This at the time did not impress my mind deeply[,] Altho there then lived with his Family a Neighbors daughter[,] Fanny Alger[,] A varry nice & Comly young woman about my own age[,] towards whoom not only mySelf but everyone Seemed partial for the ameability of her character and it was whispered eaven then that Joseph Loved her.[106]

This reported awareness of polygamy in 1835 could suggest that Smith was talking about it at that time. Dean Jessee has given a different interpretation to this. Noting the Fanny Alger incident, he has asserted that "Cowdery's accusation of adultery no doubt derived from his knowledge of the beginnings of plural marriage. There is evidence that the principle was revealed to Joseph Smith as early as 1831, that he had taken his first plural wife in Kirtland, and that rumors growing from this had contributed to the opposition against him."[107]

---

104. Dean C. Jessee, "A Comparative Study and Evaluation of Latter-day Saint and 'Fundamentalist' Views Pertaining to the Practice of Plural Marriage," M.A. thesis, Brigham Young University, 1959.

105. See Danel W. Bachman, "New Light on an Old Hypothesis: The Ohio Origins of the Revelation on Eternal Marriage," *Journal of Mormon History* 5 (1978): 19-32.

106. See Zimmerman, *I Knew the Prophets,* 37-38.

107. Jessee, *Papers of Joseph Smith,* 2:228n2.

There are more compelling references to plural marriage in 1840. In the fall of that year, Smith taught Joseph B. Noble "the principle of Celestial marriage or a 'plurality of wives,'" according to the latter's affidavit.[108] In another statement, Bathsheba Smith recalled that "in the year 1840, at a meeting held in Nauvoo, at which I was present, I heard the prophet Joseph Smith say that the ancient order would be restored as it was in the days of Abraham."[109] Restoring the "ancient order" was apparently already understood to imply polygamy. In that same year, on October 4, Smith gave a talk on priesthood, adding some clarity to the rather opaque thoughts he had expressed a year earlier regarding "keys" and "mysteries" of heaven. Then in July 1841, after several of his apostles began returning from a foreign mission, Smith spoke privately with all but a few of them about plural marriage.

Smith referred to polygamy as a "favor" that would come to be at some indeterminate point. The rhetoric aside, the year 1843 was when the doctrine officially arrived for a small, elite group of followers. Four of Smith's Nauvoo associates—James Allred, David Fullmer, Thomas Grover, and Aaron Johnson—testified that on August 12, 1843, "Hyrum Smith presented to the [Nauvoo Stake] High Council in his brick office at Nauvoo Assembled, the Revelation on Celestial Marriage, given to Joseph Smith, and written on the 12th day of July 1843."[110]

By the time Smith dictated the polygamy revelation, he had already spoken to at least twelve of the brethren, saying he expected them to participate in the so-called "principle." In July 1841, he invited Brigham Young to do so, making Young one of the first to be granted this honor. Other early invitations went to Reynolds Cahoon, Heber Kimball, and Vinson Knight. Smith explained to his personal secretary, William Clayton, in February 1843 that it was a favor Smith wanted to give him. That April, Smith spoke with Benjamin Johnson and Lorenzo Snow to make similar arrangements for them.

---

108. Noble, Affidavit, "40 Affidavits on Celestial Marriage," 1869.

109. Bathsheba Smith, Affidavit, Nov. 19, 1903, in "[Affidavits] Book No. 2," 1869-1870.

110. David Fullmer et al., Affidavit, Oct. 10, 1869, in ibid.

If there had been an earlier "revelation," it did not produce any material change in the teachings or customs of the community. Not until the prophet once more heard the Lord speak, as Clayton explained it. Clayton described the process of recording Joseph Smith's 1843 marriage revelation:

> I did write the revelation on Celestial marriage given through the Prophet Joseph Smith on the 12th day of July 1843. When the revelation was written there was no one present except the prophet Joseph, his brother Hyrum and myself. It was written in the small office upstairs in the rear of the brick store which stood on the banks of the Mississippi River. It took some three hours to write it. Joseph dictated sentence by sentence and I wrote it as he dictated. After the whole was written Joseph requested me to read it slowly and carefully which I did, and he then pronounced it correct. The same night a copy was taken by Bishop [Newel K.] Whitney which copy is now here [in the Historian's office] and which I know and testify is correct. The original was destroyed by Emma Smith.[111]

There are aspects of Smith's report of a revelation worth noting. In Smith's narrative, an otherworldly being Smith called "the Lord" defends polygamy against all critics, stating that "if any man espouse a virgin, and desire to espouse another ... he cannot commit adultery for they are given unto him." It was necessary for populating the earth in fulfillment of Abraham's promise. Not to miss the point, God again repeats that if a man has "ten virgins given unto him by this law, he cannot commit adultery, for they belong to him, and they are given unto him; therefore he is justified" (D&C 132:61-62).

The revelation contravenes the Book of Mormon passage where polygamy is said to be allowed under certain conditions but is likely an indication of wickedness, wherein men are sometimes inclined to claim privileges that are not theirs. In the Book of Mormon narrative published in 1830, the Lord reproached the people of Nephi for in-

---

111. William Clayton to Madison M. Scott, Nov. 11, 1871, William Clayton Letterbooks, Special Collections, J. Willard Marriott Library, University of Utah, Salt Lake City. See also George D. Smith, ed., *An Intimate Chronicle: The Journals of William Clayton* (Salt Lake City: Signature Books and Smith Research Associates, 1991), 110n42.

dulging in "wicked practices, such as like unto David of old, desiring many wives and concubines, and also Solomon, his son" (Jacob 1:15). Notice that the wording associates polygamy with concubinage: "Behold, David and Solomon truly had many wives and concubines, which thing was abominable before me, saith the Lord." However, Smith's 1843 revelation changes all this. Section 132 establishes polygamy as a virtuous higher law that is forever "true"—no longer a time-sensitive practice. According to the new message, Abraham received concubines "for his righteousness." This was also true for David and Moses because "in nothing did they sin" except in taking some wives without prior authorization (D&C 132:37-38).

In deference to the morality of early nineteenth-century America, the Book of Mormon placed explicit restraints on sexuality, characterizing adultery as the "most abominable above all sins, save it be the shedding of innocent blood or denying the Holy Ghost" (Alma 39:5). Another revelation, almost seeming to recall Smith's teenage concerns about sinful thoughts and behavior, reiterated this standard: "Thou shalt not commit adultery; and he that commiteth adultery, and repententh not, shall be cast out" (D&C 42:24). As the century advanced, societal views changed and even Brigham Young and other church leaders began speaking like social scientists, suggesting for instance that prostitution was a social ill that resulted from an unreasonable restraint on man's natural polygamous impulse. War and hardship, they said, created a surplus of marriageable females and a resulting inequity for which plural marriage was the natural solution—the means to a higher standard of morality for both men and women.

Perceiving that Mormons were different creatures than the clichés portrayed by most antagonists, Irish-born George Bernard Shaw wrote in 1933 that "nothing can be more ... frivolous, than to imagine that this polygamy had anything to do with personal licentiousness. If Joseph Smith had proposed to the Latter-day Saints that they should live licentious lives, they would have rushed on him and probably anticipated the pious neighbors who presently shot him."[112] Correct in

112. See Richard Vetterli, *Mormonism, Americanism, and Politics* (Salt Lake City: Ensign Publishing, 1961), 461-62.

his assessment of the solemnity with which Smith's associates approached marriage, Shaw was also right in characterizing the indignation people felt when they discovered that Smith had taken young girls and married women as wives. It was the discovery of what fellow church members considered to be abusive and promiscuous relationships that proved the final straw, piled on top of other accumulated complaints, and motivated a significant dissident faction to oppose him. In the wake of that conflict, irate Illinois residents assassinated him and drove his co-religionists from the state. The decision to promote polygamy had ignited a revolt that prefigured much of the additional trouble still to come.

Conclusion

Three years after Joseph Smith married Emma Hale, the Book of Mormon gave what amounted to conditional approval to the polygynous form of plural marriage. Eleven years later, in 1841, Joseph Smith and Louisa Beaman participated in the first formal ceremony to legitimize a plural coupling. Two years after that, a revelation authorizing plural marriage was brought to the attention of selected church leaders. In the interim Smith performed marriages for his close friends, family, and chief lieutenants to bind them to plural families and connect these designated upper-tier families into a dynastic hierarchy. He would marry dozens of women, and his male followers would collectively acquire tens of thousands of wives by the end of the nineteenth century. These followers would establish the Mormon kingdom as the most prominent polygamous Christian community ever (there had been others), from the Protestant Reformation to the present day.

Beyond the issue of having more than one wife, Smith engaged in even more perilous anti-social behavior by indulging in sexual relations with the daughters and wives of close friends, albeit mostly in marital and religious contexts. It is apparent that the prophet was successful in persuading many of his adherents to comply with these familial experiments. He acquired the tentative support of his own first wife, Emma, who gave tacit approval to the radical restructuring of their family, even though it was under some duress and with great reluctance. Smith convinced some thirty male colleagues to accept their "privileges" despite what they had been raised to believe about the sanctity of marriage to one chosen spouse. In the post-Smith Nauvoo years, the number of polygamists would quickly swell to about two hundred and then to thousands after Brigham Young transplanted Smith's celestial marriage concept to the American west.

In the century and a half since LDS leaders denied violating Illinois law, society has become less critical of variant social practices by religious minorities—to the point that some analysts have suggested that a court case might today recognize an adult woman's right to choose polygamy. Mitigating this liberal trend is the continued abusive coercion of underage girls in polygamous communities.[113] Although polygamy has been repeatedly condemned by the contemporary LDS Church, the Nauvoo beginnings of the practice remain in LDS scripture as Section 132 of the Doctrine and Covenants and in the church's temple sealings.

By the time the Latter-day Saints settled in Illinois, the young women Joseph once met as pre-teenagers had become old enough for him to marry. Several wives of his closest adherents were also willing to be sealed to him and then help introduce younger women to the principle. Nauvoo celestial marriage begun in the early 1840s previewed the nature of Mormon polygamy that would develop across the American west.

---

113. James Brook, "Utah Struggles with a Revival of Polygamy," *New York Times*, Aug. 23, 1998, 12; Ralph Blumenthal, "Fifty-two Girls Are Taken from Polygamist Sect's Ranch in Texas," "Additional Children Removed at Polygamist Ranch," ibid., Apr. 5, 6, 2008.

TWO.

Joseph's Wives

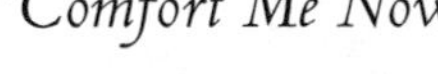

"Comfort Me Now"

"I think Emma wont come to night," Joseph Smith wrote anxiously in August of 1842. To be sure, he recommended that his friend, whose seventeen-year-old daughter he had just married, should "come a little a head, and nock … at the window." For when Emma "is not here," he wrote, "there is the most perfect saf[e]ty." The prophet then poured out his heart, writing to his newest wife: "My feelings are so strong for you … now is the time to afford me succour. … I know it is the will of God that you should comfort me now."[1]

He had been in hiding from Missouri sheriffs for ten days when he sent that urgent invitation to Sarah Ann Whitney and her parents. The Whitneys lived near the Smith family home on Water and Main streets in Nauvoo. Emma Hale, Joseph's wife of fifteen years, had left his side just twenty-four hours earlier. Now Joseph declared that he was "lonesome," and he pleaded with Sarah Ann to visit him under cover of darkness. After all, they had been married just three weeks earlier.

---

1. Smith, Letter to "Brother and Sister [Newel K.] Whitney, and &c.," Nauvoo, Illinois, Aug. 18, 1842, LDS Church Archives, Salt Lake City; photocopy in George Albert Smith Papers, Special Collections, J. Willard Marriott Library, University of Utah, Salt Lake City. See also Dean C. Jessee, ed., *The Personal Writings of Joseph Smith*, rev. ed. (Salt Lake City: Deseret Book, 2002), 566-69, validating the "handwriting of Joseph Smith"; *The Essential Joseph Smith* (Salt Lake City: Signature Books, 1995), 167.

Did Sarah Ann keep this rendezvous on that humid summer night? Unfortunately, the documentary record is silent. But she, or her parents, ignored Joseph's other request to "burn this letter as soon as you read it." As a result, the letter survives to illuminate the complexity of Smith's life in Nauvoo as church leader, politician, land dealer, mayor, and polygamist.

The story of Joseph Smith's documented marriages after wedding Emma in 1827 opens in April 1841 and ends some thirty-seven wives later with his marriage to Fanny Young in November 1843. His life during those two and a half years was dizzying as he juggled land purchases, religious appointments, speeches, meetings; armed and trained a town militia; welcomed settlers and immigrants to the new town; oversaw building projects; and assumed a prominent role in the nascent municipal government. All of this in addition to pronouncing revelations, avoiding arrest and extradition orders, and entering into matrimony with over three dozen women, which meant about one new wife a month. In spite of spending much of his time in hiding from legal officers, he maintained what seems to have been a relatively stable family life with Emma and their three children ranging from five to ten, and a twelve-year-old adopted daughter, in a household filled with relatives, extended family, friends, official guests, and hired girls. The household was full enough to require moving from their original homestead into a larger, more imposing Mansion House, as it was called. The Smith mansion still stands today in the restored Nauvoo, on a bluff overlooking the Mississippi River.

Woven throughout this fabric of daily public life is a concealed record of courtship and marriage that can be found in diaries, autobiographies, letters, affidavits, and sealing records which confirm these events. The unannounced marriages were kept out of public view and officially denied during Smith's lifetime, and for another eight years after his death. The arc of Smith's life, including his many wives, paralleled in important ways the heretical Anabaptist movement of sixteenth-century Germany, which also included polygamy as part of its biblical "restoration" (see chapter 9).

In his study of Smith's wives, classics scholar and historian Todd

Compton presented a series of individual biographies based on the lives of each woman Smith took in celestial marriage. Dr. Compton's work showed when Smith entered and exited the life of each woman and how she spent her years after his passing.[2] The present chapters, by contrast, focus on Smith's marriages within the context of his daily activities. What interested me most was how Smith went about courting and marrying these women, unseen amidst his public life as a religious and community leader who would even become a candidate for the U.S. presidency. This account should be read as contributing to a more complete narrative of Smith's life. It supplements the official record by shedding light on cryptic diary entries and other contemporary records that clarify what we find between the lines in the authorized history of the church he founded.

Polygamy marked the Latter-day Saints, becoming the most prominent theological principle of the religion. During the thirty-eight years of its public existence (1852 to 1890), practiced more than fifty years from its Nauvoo roots, it caused the LDS Church untold problems. When it was officially abandoned in 1890, what previously had been called "celestial marriage" was subtly redefined to specify something new: marriage performed in LDS temples for this life and for an expected eternal afterlife—marriage for "time and eternity." Plural marriage had been a key principle of Mormon exaltation; but by adaptation, celestial marriage was still said to be required, only now it meant monogamy rather than polygamy.

Joseph Smith's creativity helped in many ways to shape the climate in which plural marriage was introduced. He spoke in coded messages about the "privileges" he said were rightfully a man's. Despite his crowded daily schedule, the prophet interrupted other activities for secret liaisons with women and girls, whom he drew into his family network. He assured the women and their families that such unions were not only sanctioned but were demanded by heaven and fulfilled the ethereal principle of "restoration."

Joseph married women of various ages. Some were already mar-

---

2. Todd Compton, *In Sacred Loneliness: The Plural Wives of Joseph Smith* (Salt Lake City: Signature Books, 1997).

ried, some widowed; some were mothers or daughters. Several young women lived in Smith's own home. Some of Joseph's nearly forty "celestial marriages" lasted up to three years, all cut short by his sudden death after their discovery. There may have been even more wives and plural children. We might ask how Smith was able to share intimacy with so many women.

Louisa Beaman

wife number 2
an unmarried woman
April 1841

In the fall of 1840, Smith taught celestial marriage to Joseph Bates Noble, his soon-to-be plural brother-in-law.[3] He later asked Noble to assist in performing this first plural marriage. Smith had developed an interest in Louisa Beaman over several years. She was the sister of Mary Beaman, who had married Noble six years earlier on September 11, 1834. As Noble later remembered, Smith "taught it [plural marriage] in my house" in Montrose, Iowa, "right across the river opposite Nauvoo," introducing it "privately" there to "individuals in the church."

Noble (1810-1900), born in the Berkshire hills of Massachusetts, was a farmer and miller who also raised livestock. In 1832 he joined the Mormons in New York and in 1841 was appointed bishop of the Nauvoo 5th Ward. Occasionally he acted as one of Smith's bodyguards. After Smith's death, Noble crossed the Great Plains in 1847 and settled in Utah. From 1862 he raised peaches and apples on a ten-acre orchard in Bountiful, returning in 1872 on a proselytizing mission to "the states." He died near Bear Lake in Idaho, across the border from Utah.

Noble recalled Smith's first Nauvoo marriage when he faced ad-

3. B. H. Roberts wrote that "it was in the fall of 1840" when Smith took "steps" to introduce "plural marriages as a practice in the church"; in one of two affidavits in June 1869, Noble affirmed that Smith requested that he "assist him in carrying out the said principle" (Roberts, *A Comprehensive History of the Church of Jesus Christ of Latter-day Saints,* 6 vols. [Salt Lake City: LDS Church, 1930], 2:101).

versarial questioning by attorneys in the famous Temple Lot case, an 1892 suit over real estate Joseph Smith had designated in August 1831 as the site of a future temple in Independence, Missouri.[4] At the time of these proceedings over the ownership of Missouri property, plural marriage was a point of contention between the Utah LDS Church and the Midwestern RLDS Church in defining which organization was the legitimate heir of Joseph Smith's legacy.

The marriage Noble oversaw happened during a two-year gap in Smith's personal journal between October 15, 1839, and December 13, 1841. On the date he married Louisa, April 5, 1841, the official *History of the Church* chronicled a meeting in Manchester, England, but offered no news from the church's riverfront boomtown in Illinois.

For the next day, however, April 6, both the town weekly and the official history report a celebration at which the Nauvoo temple's cornerstones were laid, followed by a five-day conference with "scenes" of "intense" enjoyment.[5] On this twelfth anniversary of the church's founding, the paramilitary Nauvoo Legion paraded under the command of Major-General John Cook Bennett. Lieutenant-General Joseph Smith, with his guard, staff, and field officers, arrived at 9:30 a.m. "and were presented with a beautiful silk national flag by the ladies of Nauvoo." The reports do not specify whether Louisa was among the "ladies" who participated. While the history allocates six pages to this impressive celebration, it fails to mention the extraordinary event that had occurred the day before: the groundbreaking inauguration of plural marriage. Neither Smith nor Beaman left a personal account of their marriage (that has been found), but eleven other sources confirm that the ceremony did take place.

1. According to LDS Assistant Church Historian Andrew Jenson,

---

4. *Reorganized Church of Jesus Christ of Latter Day Saints v. Church of Christ of Independence Missouri, et al.* 60 F. 937 (W.D. Mo. 1894), deposition testimony (questions 38, 45-53, 642, 681-95), electronic copy prepared by Richard D. Ouellette; Andrew Jenson, "Jackson County, Missouri," *Historical Record* 7 (1888): 647-48.

5. See Joseph Smith et al., *History of the Church of Jesus Christ of Latter-day Saints,* ed. B. H. Roberts, 2nd ed. rev., 7 vols. (Salt Lake City: Deseret Book, 1963), 4:326-31, 336-43. See also "Laying the Cornerstone of the Temple. General Conference," *Times and Seasons,* Apr. 15, 1841, 375-83.

speaking at a stake conference on June 11, 1883, Smith "taught [Joseph Noble] the principle of plural marriage. … The girl [Louisa Beaman], after being convinced that the principle was true, consented to become the prophet's wife, and on 5 April 1841, she was married to him, Elder Noble officiating." Jenson added that Louisa's marriage was "the first plural marriage consummated" (by which Jenson probably meant to write "solemnized" or "consecrated").[6]

2. Recently converted and promptly named Assistant President of the LDS Church, John C. Bennett lived with the Smiths in April 1841. The prophet was pleased that Bennett had persuaded the Illinois legislature to pass the expansive Nauvoo city charter. However, the next year Bennett would dramatically fall out of Smith's favor and betray his confidence by reporting in the *Sangamo Journal* of Springfield, Illinois (Sangamon County), that the prophet secretly "married a Miss L***** B*****," encoded with the right number of asterisks for the letters that spell out Louisa's name. He did not provide details, but when he published his exposé, *History of the Saints,* that same year (1842), Bennett specified that Smith "went off to see Miss Louisa Beeman, at the house of Mrs. [Delcena] Sherman, and remained with her about two hours," implying an intimate visit. Bennett also designated "Elder Joseph Bates Noble" as the one who performed the ceremony with "Miss L***** B*****."[7] John C. Bennett was the first person to announce Joseph Smith's unspoken marriage to Louisa Beaman.

3. In 1869, eyewitness and participant in the Smith-Beaman wedding Joseph Noble himself affirmed under oath: "On the fifth day of April A.D. 1841, at the City of Nauvoo, County of Hancock, State of Illinois, he married or sealed Louisa Beaman, to Joseph Smith, President of the Church of Jesus Christ of Latter-day Saints, according to the order of Celestial Marriage revealed to the Said Joseph Smith."[8]

---

6. Andrew Jenson, "Plural Marriage," *Historical Record* 6 (May 1887): 232-33, 239.

7. John C. Bennett, *Sangamo Journal,* July 15, 1842; Bennett, *History of the Saints* (1842; Urbana: University of Illinois Press, 2000), 229, 256.

8. Joseph B. Noble, Affidavit, June 26, 1869, in "40 Affidavits on Celestial Marriage," 1869, a collection consisting of six folders compiled by Joseph F. Smith, LDS Archives. Resealed by proxy (B. Young) Sept. 19, 1844, Jan. 14, 1846 (Sealing Book A, 503-04; Cook, *Nauvoo Marriages,* 41).

Here Noble provided one of the first affidavits collected in 1869 by Apostle Joseph F. Smith to verify his Uncle Joseph's plural marriages.

4. Earlier that year, LDS Apostle Wilford Woodruff heard Joseph Noble talk about the marriage. Noble misremembered the date as May 6 instead of April 5, but he "said he performed the first Marriage Ceremony according to the Patriarchal order of Marriage ever performed in this dispensation By sealing Eliza [Louisa] Be[a]man to Joseph Smith on the 6 day of May 1841." The comment was made at a dinner engagement hosted by Jane Blackhurst on January 22, 1869.[9]

5. LDS Apostle Franklin D. Richards also recorded Noble's remarks at the Blackhurst dinner. According to Richards, Noble "related that he perform[ed] the first sealing ceremony in this dispensation in which he united sister Louisa Beaman to the prophet Joseph." This took place, he said, "during the evening under an Elm tree in Nauvoo. The Bride disguised in a [man's] coat and hat."[10]

6. LDS Apostle George A. Smith did not know about this marriage at the time, but based on subsequent testimony, including Noble's June 1869 affidavit collected by Joseph F. Smith, he wrote an October 1869 letter to Joseph Smith's oldest son, Joseph III, president of the RLDS Church: "On the 5th day of April, 1841, Louisa Beman was married to your father, Joseph Smith, for time and all eternity, by Joseph B. Nobles, a High Priest of the church. She remained true and faithful to him until the day of her death." He reported that she died six years after Joseph. George A. and Joseph III were first cousins (once removed).[11] The theological and political controversy about the origins of polygamy, waged in public debates and between missionaries of the two churches, was intensified by intra-family competition as Joseph III denied that his father would have been involved in "immoral" practices and the Utah branch of the family defended what they considered the founder's most significant theological principle. Ironically, Joseph III's denials prompted Brigham Young's administration to collect and

9. Scott Kenney, ed., *Wilford Woodruff's Journal,* 9 vols. (Midvale, Utah: Signature Books, 1983), 6:452.

10. Franklin D. Richards, Journal, Jan. 22, 1869, LDS Archives.

11. Joseph Jr. and George A. were sons of brothers Joseph Sr. and John Smith.

preserve some of the most conclusive evidence of the practice.

At the time he wrote to Joseph III, George A. Smith was LDS Church Historian and had been involved in documenting and defending polygamy. He stressed to young Joseph that polygamy explained why the prophet would have declared on April 5, 1844: 'You dont know me; you never knew my heart. No man knows my history. I cannot tell it; I shall never undertake it, I dont blame anyone for not believing my history. If I had not experienced what I have, I could not have believed it myself.'"[12]

7. Joseph Smith's personal secretary, William Clayton, recalled in an 1874 affidavit that in February 1843 Smith "gave me to understand that Eliza R. Snow, Louisa Beman, S[ylvia] P. Sessions, and Desdemona C. Fullmer, and others were his lawful wives in the sight of Heaven" even if they were kept from sight in Illinois. In his journals, Clayton went on to mention another eleven of Smith's "lawful, wedded wives, according to the celestial order."[13]

8. Ann Eliza Webb Young, formerly a plural wife of Brigham Young, added her own view of Noble's participation in the marriage as she heard it from her parents, possibly reinforced by Brigham's other wives, of whom Beaman herself had been number seven. In her 1875 exposé, written when she was thirty, Ann Eliza reported that Noble had been "among the earliest converts to the doctrine of plural wives" and that Smith had "advised Noble to seek a second wife for himself." In an embellishment on the historical record, she adds that "together the two men, with their chosen celestial brides, repaired one night to the banks of the Mississippi River, where Joseph sealed Noble to his

12. George A. Smith to Joseph Smith III, Oct. 9, 1869, Joseph Smith III Papers, Library-Archives, Community of Christ, Independence, Missouri; see also Journal History of the Church of Jesus Christ of Latter-day Saints, Oct. 9, 1869, LDS Church Archives. It was from Joseph Smith's April 7, 1844, sermon at the funeral of King Follett that Fawn M. Brodie formed the title to her 1945 biography *No Man Knows My History: The Life of Joseph Smith*, 2nd ed. (New York: Alfred A. Knopf, 1971). See *History of the Church*, 6:317.

13. William Clayton, Affidavit, Feb. 16, 1874, Salt Lake City, in "Affidavits [on Celestial Marriage], 1869-1915"; see also *Historical Record* 6 (May 1887): 224-26; George D. Smith, ed., *An Intimate Chronicle: The Journals of William Clayton* (Salt Lake City: Signature Books and Smith Research Associates, 1991), 557, 577, where Smith's wives are indexed.

first plural wife, and in return Noble performed the same office for The Prophet and [Noble's] sister[-in-law]."[14] In fact, Noble did not take a second wife until two years later.

9. Apostle Erastus Snow, an early Mormon convert from Vermont, who had married Louisa's sister, Artemisia Beaman, on December 13, 1838, in 1883 corroborated that his sister-in-law, Louisa, was "the first Woman that entered Plural Marriage in this last dispensation [with] Br Nobles officiating in a grove Near Main Street in the City of Nauvoo[,] The Prophet Joseph di[c]tating the ceremony and Br. Nobles repeating it after him."[15] Andrew Jenson also quoted Snow as saying: "The Prophet Joseph Smith first taught me the doctrine of celestial marriage, including a plurality of wives, in Nauvoo, Ill., in April, 1843. He also told me of those women he had taken t[w]o wives. My wife's sister, Louisa Beman, was his first plural wife, she being sealed to him by my brother-in-law, Joseph B. Noble, April 5, 1841."[16]

10. Almera Johnson, one of Smith's plural wives, was a reliable second-hand witness. In August 1883 she affirmed that she had married Joseph and lived with him. She further said, "I had many conversations with Eliza [Louisa] Beaman who was also a wife of Joseph Smith, and who was present when I was sealed to him, on the subject of plurality of wives, both before and after the performance of that ceremony."[17]

11. Joseph Noble's testimony in the Temple Lot hearings of 1892 was uniquely important because he gave it *after* the 1890 renunciation of polygamy. Noble emphasized that this first, precedent-setting plural marriage was more than a union in spirit. In his deposition he said he "performed the marriage ceremony giving him my wife's sister," or

---

14. Ann Eliza Young, *Wife Number Nineteen, or the Story of a Life in Bondage* (Hartford, Conn.: Dustin, Gilman & Co., 1875), 72, although Louisa died in 1850, eighteen years before Ann Eliza married Brigham.

15. See A. Karl Larson and Katharine Miles Larson, eds., *Diary of Charles Lowell Walker* (Logan: Utah State University Press, 1980), 610. In this published version, an error in the transcription described Louisa as the "first Mormon" instead of the "first Woman."

16. Jenson, "Plural Marriage," 232.

17. Almira W. Johnson Smith Barton, Affidavit, Aug. 1, 1883, in Joseph Fielding Smith, *Blood Atonement and the Origin of Plural Marriage: A Discussion* (Salt Lake City: Deseret News Press, 1905), 70-71.

"Louisa Beeman to the prophet," at a rented house in Nauvoo. Asked whether there was a honeymoon, he said, "I know it, for I saw him in bed with her," adding that "right straight across the river [from Iowa] at my house they slept together." Noble gave the prophet some "counsel" to "blow out the lights and get into bed, and you will be safer there." Smith "took my advice," he continued; then Noble laughed "heartily," according to the court reporter. Noble said the newlyweds "got into bed" soon after the ceremony between about 6:00 and 8:00 p.m. as Noble left the house. Noble recalled he knew they spent the night because Joseph later "told me he did."[18]

In four of the above accounts, Noble was the source, directly or indirectly. In addition to his own affidavit and Temple Lot testimony, his conversation at a dinner party was reported by two apostles. How reliable are these sources? They vary in some details but essentially portray a consistent picture, keeping in mind that one was an eyewitness participant and the others heard about it from the actual participants. All of the sources but Ann Eliza Young were close to Joseph Smith. From their memories, we can construct a believable account of what took place. We learn from Noble, Richards, and Young that the ceremony occurred in the evening. Four specify that it was in Nauvoo: Noble says it took place in a rented house "straight across the river" from Iowa; Snow says it was near Main Street "in a grove" that extended to the Mississippi; Richards says under an elm tree—perhaps corresponding with the grove; Ann Eliza Young places it "one night" along the "banks of the Mississippi River." Harmonizing these accounts, one could say the Smith-Beaman ceremony took place in Nauvoo on a Monday evening, April 5, 1841, in a grove or under a tree that was on or near the bank of the Mississippi River or close to Noble's house, which was near the river. As Richards stated it, Louisa wore a coat and hat, and Joseph dictated the words for Noble to say. There is some question about whether Noble actually saw Joseph and Louisa in bed together. He said so and then hedged, adding that Joseph told him as much. Several decades later, historian Stanley Ivins,

18. *Reorganized Church v. Church of Christ,* questions 688-90, 698, 702.

who initiated research in 1934, possibly unaware of all these accounts, concluded that the "plurality of wives" had begun in 1841 in Nauvoo in a "cornfield outside the city."[19]

In many ways Louisa was a typical wife of Joseph's. Like ten of the others, she was in her twenties when she married him. He had known most of them for at least a year, some for as long as eleven years. In other words, they were not women he had met the day before and compulsively married. Seventeen of them were single. Three of the teenaged wives and three of those in their twenties were orphaned or separated from their parents. Unlike Louisa, fourteen of the wives were already married and typically had children. At least three of the existing husbands had apparently consented to their wives' polyandrous co-marriages to the prophet. As will be seen, conjugal visits appear furtive and constantly shadowed by the threat of disclosure.

Louisa was also typical in that the wives rarely shared a home with Joseph. Even though six were hired girls who lived and worked in the Smith family home,[20] thirty-one lived elsewhere. Even if they had a room in the Smith household, it was considered Emma's home, not a place for thirty-eight wives to gather around the hearth. This is relevant to the wives not being acknowledged during Smith's lifetime, as they would have been had they set up home with him. For his married wives, their children by Smith, if any, would be assumed to have been sired by other husbands. Smith's untimely death in 1844 prevented any of these overlapping concurrent relationships from lasting longer than two and a half years.

How much Emma knew about these arrangements has been the subject of some discussion. She knew of at least several of the relationships. Even more puzzling, she seems to have accepted some of them, albeit briefly. At least one of her detractors suggests she was part of a plan to access the wealth of other families (see chapter 7). Nevertheless, she bristled whenever she learned about her husband's inti-

19. Stanley S. Ivins, "Notes on Mormon Polygamy," *Western Humanities Review* 10 (Summer 1956), 229-39, repr. in *The New Mormon History: Revisionist Essays on the Past*, ed. D. Michael Quinn (Salt Lake City: Signature Books, 1992), 169.

20. Emily and Eliza Partridge, Maria and Sarah Lawrence, Elvira Cowles, and Eliza Snow.

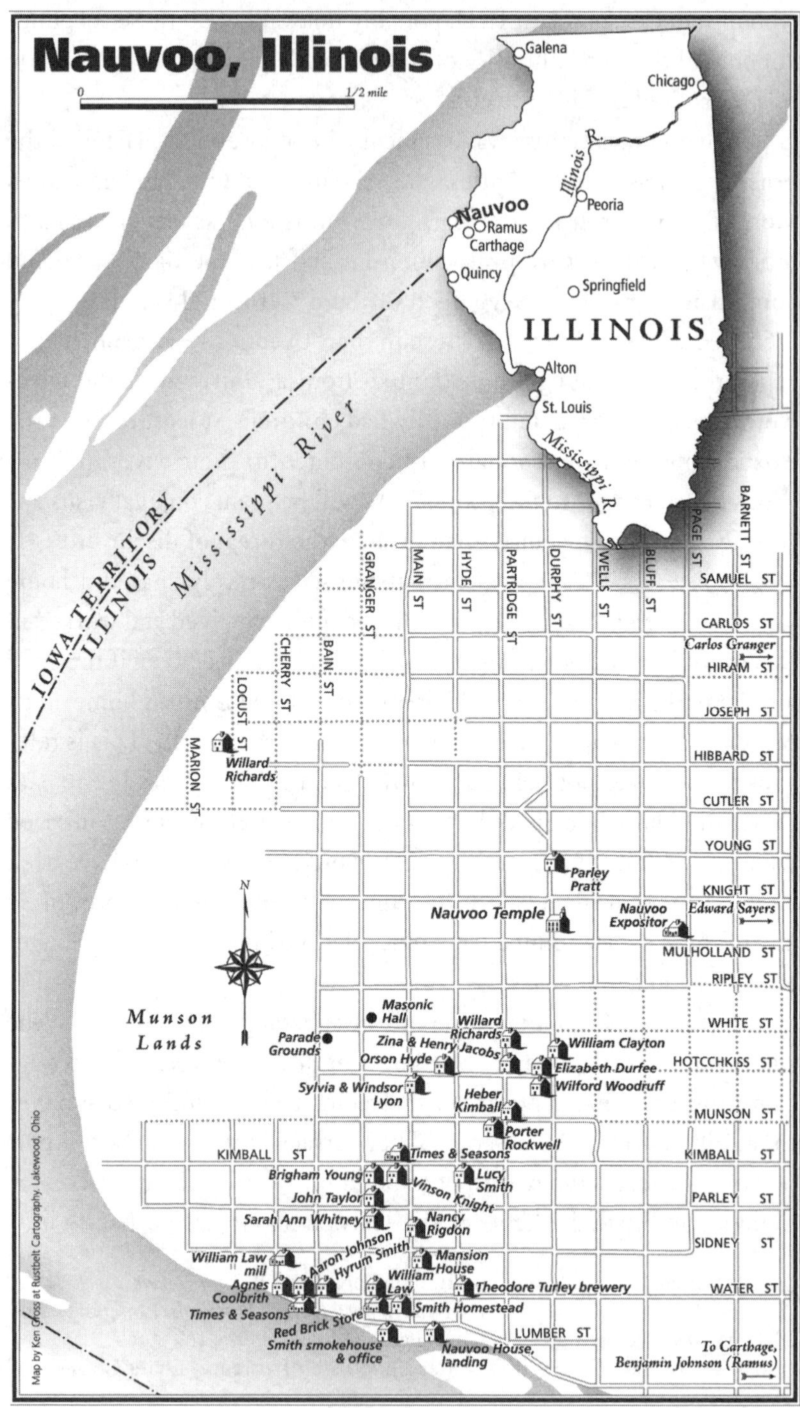

Nauvoo, Illinois
0
1/2 mile
Galena
Chicago
Illinois R.
Peoria
Nauvoo
Ramus
Carthage
Quincy
Springfield
ILLINOIS
Alton
St. Louis
Mississippi R.
Mississippi River
IOWA TERRITORY
ILLINOIS
GRANGER ST
MAIN ST
HYDE ST
PARTRIDGE ST
DURPHY ST
WELLS ST
BLUFF ST
PAGE ST
BARNETT ST
SAMUEL ST
CARLOS ST
Carlos Granger
HIRAM ST
JOSEPH ST
HIBBARD ST
CUTLER ST
YOUNG ST
KNIGHT ST
Edward Sayers
MULHOLLAND ST
RIPLEY ST
WHITE ST
HOTCCHKISS ST
MUNSON ST
KIMBALL ST
PARLEY ST
SIDNEY ST
WATER ST
LUMBER ST
CHERRY ST
BAIN ST
LOCUST ST
MARION ST
Willard Richards
Parley Pratt
Nauvoo Temple
Nauvoo Expositor
N
Munson Lands
Masonic Hall
Parade Grounds
Willard Richards
Zina & Henry Jacobs
William Clayton
Orson Hyde
Elizabeth Durfee
Sylvia & Windsor Lyon
Wilford Woodruff
Heber Kimball
Porter Rockwell
KIMBALL ST
Times & Seasons
Brigham Young
Lucy Smith
Vinson Knight
John Taylor
Sarah Ann Whitney
Nancy Rigdon
William Law mill
Aaron Johnson
Hyrum Smith
Mansion House
Agnes Coolbrith
William Law
Theodore Turley brewery
Times & Seasons
Smith Homestead
Red Brick Store
Smith smokehouse & office
Nauvoo House, landing
To Carthage, Benjamin Johnson (Ramus)
Map by Ken Gross at Rustbelt Cartography, Lakewood, Ohio

macies with other women, from Fanny Alger in Kirtland to the clandestine liaisons in Nauvoo. There appears to be no evidence to suggest she was aware of Louisa Beaman. When Joseph requested that Sarah Ann Whitney visit him and "nock at the window," he reassured his new young wife that Emma would not be there, telegraphing his fear of discovery if Emma happened upon his trysts. On three occasions when Emma learned her husband had married women who were staying in her home, she told them to leave.

John C. Bennett

One of the instrumental people in the inauguration of plural marriage was John Bennett, who in 1841 functioned as perhaps Joseph Smith's closest confidant. He was important, not only in being the earliest individual publicly to identify Louisa Beaman as Joseph's plural wife, but also for what his intimate association with Smith revealed about the origins of the practice. The prophet drew this entrepreneur into close friendship in 1840, inviting him into the Mormon community, sharing power with him. However, after nineteen months of daily interaction, their trusting relationship soured precipitously. In the spring of 1842, Bennett spoke out against Smith and was soon stripped of his offices and titles. Each accused the other of immoral behavior. Bennett—exiled from power, angry, and now an informed source on Smith's marriages—was willing to make his insider's knowledge public. While some of his claims may have been exaggerations, much of what he reported can be confirmed by other eyewitness accounts. Even though his statements must be weighed critically, he cannot be merely dismissed as an unfriendly source who fabricated scandal.[21]

John Cook Bennett was born in Fairhaven, Massachusetts, to John Bennett and Abigail Cook on August 3, 1804, a year before Smith. Bennett's parents were shipbuilders and shipowners; his father was a ship captain. They were early settlers in Marietta, Ohio, and profited from foreign trade along the Ohio River. Bennett's uncle, Dr. Sam-

21. See Andrew F. Smith, *The Saintly Scoundrel: The Life and Times of Dr. John Cook Bennett* (Urbana: University of Illinois Press, 1997), xi, 4, 8, 12, 13-33, 40-50, 54-77, 78-128; Gary James Bergera, "John C. Bennett, Joseph Smith, and the Beginnings of Mormon Plural Marriage in Nauvoo," *John Whitmer Historical Journal* 25 (2005): 52-92.

uel P. Hildreth, a physician and renowned natural scientist, encouraged young John to study medicine.[22] Bennett met Smith in January 1832 in Hiram, Ohio, through William McLellin, a recent convert whom Smith later called to his first Quorum of Twelve Apostles. Bennett was a member of the Disciples of Christ, the primitive restorationist church led by Alexander Campbell, and thus a believer in the perfectibility of human character. Despite Campbell's hostility to Smith, many of Smith's converts in Ohio were formally with Campbell.[23] Sidney Rigdon, Orson and Parley Pratt, Orson Hyde, and Edward Partridge converted from the Disciples to Smith's Church of Christ in Ohio a decade before Bennett. Bennett had an ambiguous but colorful background. He was a promoter of colleges, a doctor who had passed a medical exam and received a license to practice medicine in Ohio, a salesman of college diplomas, a militiaman, and a Mason. He wrote to Smith on July 25, 1840, informing him of his interest in moving to Nauvoo. Bennett may have already known something about Smith from Campbell's 1832 tract, *Delusions: An Analysis of the Book of Mormon,* and Eber D. Howe's 1834 book, *Mormonism Unvailed.* Howe was the editor of the *Painesville [Ohio] Telegraph* and had printed some of the diplomas Bennett marketed in the 1830s.[24]

Most importantly, Bennett and Smith shared interests and talents. Both had an ability with words, written or spoken, and achieved some success in promoting business and civic ventures: the development of land tracts, schools, militias, corporate structures. They both enjoyed pageantry. Sharing such interests, they may have been attracted to each other. Then, competing for leadership roles, they fell inevitably into disagreement over matters of authority and possibly even women. Writing on March 23, 1846, Bennett claimed to have

---

22. John C. Bennett, *History of the Saints* (Boston: Leland & Whiting, 1842), 10-18. Bergera, "John C. Bennett," 52-92, Smith, *Saintly Scoundrel,* 1-5.

23. This church was variously identified as the Christians, Christian Church, Christian Disciples, Disciples of Christ, or Campbellites and still exists as the Christian Church or Disciples of Christ (Smith, *Saintly Scoundrel,* 13).

24. Alexander Campbell, *Delusions: An Analysis of the Book of Mormon* (Boston: Benjamin H. Green, 1832), first published in the *Millennial Harbinger,* Feb. 1831, and Eber D. Howe, *Mormonism Unvailed: Or a Faithful Account of That Singular Imposition and Delusion* (Painesville, Ohio: By the author, 1834).

known "Joseph *better than any other man living* for at least fourteen months!"[25] Those fourteen months included nine when Bennett lived in Smith's home, from September 1840 to June 1841. Accepted almost immediately as a respected member of the Nauvoo community, Bennett was well positioned to know all about any behind-the-scenes transactions.

When he arrived in Nauvoo in early September 1840, Bennett was thirty-six, and Smith was about to turn thirty-five. Soon thereafter, on September 14, Smith's father died. The next day Missouri Governor Lilburn Boggs asked Illinois Governor Thomas Carlin to arrest Smith and extradite him as a fugitive from justice. It was not Boggs's first attempt to bring Smith to judgment.[26] That same fall, Smith had spoken to Joseph Noble about plural marriage. Six months later, Smith would acquire his first official plural wife. During the fall, the Mormon leader was confronted by the complexity of the legal problems and building projects he dealt with in Nauvoo, in addition to his family's bereavement—not to mention his extra-marital courtships. In this context, he must have welcomed Bennett's adept political skills and shared interest in a strong Nauvoo city charter, local land development, and military force. Bennett also filled a social vacuum created by the departure of Smith's apostles on two-year missions begun the previous year in August and September 1839.[27]

Bennett traveled to Springfield, the Illinois state capital, two months after arriving in Nauvoo, to lobby for the enabling charter needed to grant Nauvoo broad local powers. Mormons had nominally supported both major political parties, the Whigs and Democrats, which allowed Bennett to win support from both, ultimately giving the city expansive habeas corpus powers to resist arrest warrants for

---

25. See Smith, *Saintly Scoundrel,* 56; emphasis Bennett's.

26. *History of the Church,* 4:189-91, 198.

27. Nine of Smith's key men (Orson Hyde, Heber C. Kimball, brothers Parley and Orson Pratt, Willard Richards, George A. Smith, John Taylor, Wilford Woodruff, and Brigham Young) were away when he taught polygamy to Louisa Beaman and Joseph Noble. When three of the apostles (Kimball, Taylor, and Young) returned on July 1, 1841, Smith introduced them to plural marriage. On December 27, he unfolded "privileges" to the entire Twelve, according to Wilford Woodruff (Kenney, *Wilford Woodruff's Journal,* 2:144).

Smith later. At a Democratic state gubernatorial convention a year later (1841), Smith learned that Adam W. Snyder, a nominee for Illinois governor, and John Moore, running for lieutenant-governor, were "intimate friend[s] of General Bennett long before that gentleman became a member of our community." Feigning impartiality, Smith announced: "We care not a fig for a *Whig* or *Democrat*: they are both alike to us," then signaled his intention to influence the voting: "We shall go for our *friends*." Long before the Lincoln-Douglas debates, Smith had aligned the Mormon vote with Stephen A. Douglas, a Democrat.

Like Smith and Brigham Young, Stephen Douglas (1813-61) moved to Illinois from Vermont. He did so in 1833, six years before Smith would leave a Missouri jail and bring his followers to Nauvoo. Douglas opened a law office and was elected attorney general for the first judicial district, became a judge of the Illinois Supreme Court, and was appointed Illinois secretary of state in 1840. Three years later he was elected to the U.S. Congress. "Douglass is a Master Spirit," Smith announced in late 1841, "and his friends [are] our friends … Snyder, and Moore, are his friends—they are ours." Smith's speech was carried by the *Sangamo Journal*, which expressed concern that if "this letter was put forth as a sort of royal edict … commanding all his followers, and all of the same faith or persuasion with himself, to vote for the men whom he did signify," then Smith's followers might "suffer one man to shackle their free thoughts and opinions," making them "the very worst of slaves." The paper argued that "we wish to see our candidate elected by freemen—men who do not let others think and act for them."[28] So even before Bennett broke from Smith, the *Sangamo Journal* detected the undemocratic bloc voting that would become characteristic of Nauvoo. The upcoming religious split would further the *Journal*'s political case.

Following Bennett's success in enhancing Nauvoo's political strength, Smith presented a revelation on January 19, 1841, extolling Bennett, albeit conditioned with several "ifs":

> Again, let my servant John C. Bennett, help you in your labor, in sending

---

28. "Citizens of Illinois—Read and Consider!" *Sangamo Journal*, Jan. 21, 1842.

my word to the Kings and people of the earth, and stand by you, even you my servant Joseph Smith in the hour of affliction, and his reward shall not fail if he receive council; and for his love, he shall be great; for he shall be mine if he does this, saith the Lord. I have seen the work he hath done, which I accept, if he continue; and will crown him with blessings and great glory.[29]

Bennett was Smith's candidate for Nauvoo mayor. As such, he ran unopposed on February 1 and reaped praise from the church's official periodical in Nauvoo, the *Times and Seasons:* "Long acquainted with Dr. Bennett, both as a physician, and minister of the gospel," W. G. Goforth of Belleville, Illinois, was quoted in one article, "his present character in the military department of this State, is not inferior to any in existence, throughout the Union."[30]

A few shadows from Bennett's past followed him to Nauvoo. When LDS Bishop George Miller was commissioned to investigate troubling rumors regarding Bennett's credentials, Miller returned from Ohio on March 2 with what appears to have been a negative assessment. "Bennett," he said, "has the vanity to believe he is the smartest man in the nation."[31] Undeterred, Smith named Bennett Assistant President of the Church a month later at the church's spring general conference, three days after Smith married Beaman.[32] A day earlier, Bennett had participated in the conference by reading from the Book of the Law of the Lord, an early manuscript copy of Smith's revelations; enumerating what donations had been made for the Nauvoo temple; reviewing recent minutes of meetings; and reading some excerpts from Smith's journal. On April 8, Bennett was called to sup-

29. "Extracts from a Revelation Given to Joseph Smith, Jr., Jan. 19th 1841," *Times and Seasons,* June 1, 1841, 424; see also Smith, *Saintly Scoundrel,* 61-62; D&C 124:16-17.

30. Statement from *Belleville Advocate,* Mar. 22, 1841, in *Times and Seasons,* May 15, 1841, 419.

31. George Miller, "Letter to Dear Sir [Joseph Smith]," Mar. 2, 1841, later published, possibly with negative retrospective editing, in the *Times and Seasons,* July 1, 1842, 842.

32. Earlier, on September 14, 1840, Hyrum Smith had been ordained patriarch; Sidney Rigdon and William Law were Joseph's first and second counselors in the First Presidency. Rigdon suffered from what may have been manic-depressive illness. See Richard S. Van Wagoner, *Sidney Rigdon: A Portrait of Religious Excess* (Salt Lake City: Signature Books, 1994), 81, 117, 254, 279, 282.

port Joseph Smith "until President [Sidney] Rigdon's health should be restored."[33]

Smith and Bennett remained confidants until about March the next year (1842). Meanwhile, the *Times and Seasons* defended Bennett against attack by the *Warsaw Signal* for becoming a Mormon, "a creed in which no one believes he has any faith." The *Times and Seasons* continued to endorse Bennett's character "as a gentleman, an officer, a scholar, and physician [who] stands too high to need defending by us, suffice it to say, that he is in the confidence of the executive, holds the office of quartermaster general of this stage, and is well known to a large number of persons of the first respectability throughout the state. He has, likewise been favorably known for upwards of eight years by some of the authorities of this church, and has resided three years in this state."[34]

With such accolades, so also the responsibilities and titles multiplied. Bennett was named Chancellor of the University of the City of Nauvoo; Major General of the Nauvoo Legion, which grew to 5,000 men by 1844; and Secretary of Nauvoo's Masonic Lodge, which he helped establish. There seemed to be no office or honor within reach that Smith did not hasten to grant to Bennett. On May 6, the assistant president was appointed Master in Chancery for Hancock County, a position that carried with it the duties of an Illinois Supreme Court judge.[35] During the nearly two years Bennett was in Nauvoo, September 1840 to July 1842, he was undeniably one of the region's most prominent citizens.

About that time, Smith was courting several women, all while Bennett was still a guest in the Smith home and otherwise accompanied the prophet's every step. Even before Smith married Beaman, he had reportedly proposed to Zina Huntington, who married Henry Jacobs instead but then reconsidered seven months later in response to Joseph's restated interest. Joseph's autumn 1841 proposal presumed even more than usual—because Zina was pregnant at the time. Seem-

33. *History of the Church,* 4:341.
34. "The Warsaw Signal," *Times and Seasons,* June 1, 1841, 431-32.
35. See the *Times and Seasons,* May 15, 1841, 421; "The Warsaw Signal," 431.

ingly impatient, Joseph soon after married Zina's sister, Presendia, who was also already married. According to Bennett's 1842 account, he witnessed the uncertainties of these courtships, including some subsequent proposals that failed altogether. Demonstrating his access as a source for Smith's otherwise discreet relationships, he recorded the prophet's two-hour courtship visit with Louisa Beaman at the house of Delcena Sherman, a woman who had been a widow since 1839 and would herself marry Smith in the spring of 1842, a year after his first official plural marriage.[36]

Bennett alleged that during the summer and fall of 1841, Smith made unsuccessful advances toward Apostle Orson Pratt's wife, Sarah. Orson was then on a mission to England. Bennett said he was in their company and overheard Sarah's rebuff when Smith claimed "the Lord has given you to me as one of my spiritual wives." Bennett said Smith told her he had been granted the same rights to marry as Jacob and other holy men in the Old Testament. He confessed he had long looked upon her with "favor," and hoped she would "not deny" him. Sarah allegedly had no interest in the "blessings of Jacob," she believed in no "such revelations," and under no circumstances would she consent to such a proposal.

After Orson returned home in mid-July 1842, Joseph rekindled the former tension with Sarah by "approaching her and kissing her," according to Bennett. She relayed this to her husband, who "told Joe never to offer insult of the like again," Bennett wrote.[37] Whatever the accuracy of the quotes, the two men quarreled over Joseph's conduct with Orson's wife, a dispute which led to Orson's temporary suspension from the Quorum of the Twelve Apostles. After Brigham Young's own disputes with Pratt over unrelated matters, Young would use these few months of absence from the quorum to disqualify Pratt from the line of ascension to the church presidency.[38] In retrospect,

---

36. Bennett, *History of the Saints,* 229.

37. Bennett, "Further Mormon Developments!! Second Letter from Gen. Bennett," *Sangamo Journal,* July 15, 1842; Bennett, *History of the Saints,* 226-32.

38. See Gary James Bergera, *Conflict in the Quorum: Orson Pratt, Brigham Young, Joseph Smith* (Salt Lake City: Signature Books, 2002), 279-80.

the important aspect of this incident is that it tells us less about Bennett's motive in recalling this dispute and more about Orson's willingness to support his wife over his religious leader, enough to forfeit his standing in the church. Eventually Orson accepted Joseph's explanation that he merely wanted to test Sarah's obedience, and was not seriously courting this married woman. However, Joseph concluded that she had been wrong to reject him—and that she had failed the test. The defiance she exhibited ultimately led to alienation with her husband and marked her as an exception during Smith's 1841-42 courtships, a period in which he completed nearly two dozen marital unions with single and married women alike.

Meanwhile, Bennett seems to have followed his leader in courting several women himself. In addition to his legal wife, Mary Ann Barker, from whom he was divorced or separated in 1842, he appears to have married, or was intimate with, five other women in 1841 and 1842.[39] In their protracted argument following their initial 1842 rift, Smith and those loyal to him called Bennett a libertine whose "marriages" were illegitimate, while Smith's own marriages remained unannounced and, when challenged, were publicly denied. Bennett resigned from the church on May 17, 1842. In retaliation, church leaders apparently excommunicated him on May 25, an action Bennett claimed was postdated to May 11 to appear that it had occurred before his resignation.[40]

A year earlier, on June 5, 1841, Illinois Governor Thomas Carlin had arranged for Smith's extradition to Missouri. Nauvoo authorities nullified the warrant, but other Missouri officers returned in mid-1842 with a charge that Joseph had conspired to assassinate ex-Governor Boggs. The legal pressure brought to bear, along with Bennett's public avowal of Smith's entangled romantic relationships, surged to the top

39. These women were (1) a woman named Brown, (2) Catherine Warren, (3) Melissa Jane Schindle, (4) Margaret Nymans/Neyman, and (5) Matilda I. Nymans/Neyman. Bennett's "marriages" did not end when he left the Mormon town and faith. He married at least two more wives: (6) Sarah "Sally" Ryder and (7) Tamar F. Hartley. See Mary Audentia Smith Anderson, ed., *Joseph Smith III and the Restoration* (Independence, Mo.: Herald House, 1952), 32-33.

40. Smith, *Saintly Scoundrel*, 86-89.

of the news in Nauvoo. Smith's Nauvoo theocracy was falling apart; the center could not hold.[41]

So, after Bennett joined Smith in September 1840 and spoke at the church's fall general conference, Smith expressed his approval and announced a revelation on Bennett's behalf in January 1841.[42] Bennett was appointed mayor, commissioned to train the Nauvoo Legion, and was invited to reside with Joseph and Emma from the fall of 1840 to summer 1841. Up until early 1842, Smith and Bennett seemed to be on good terms. It is entirely plausible that Bennett was then privy to Smith's domestic matters. But in the spring of 1842, the two men quarreled and Smith had Bennett excommunicated, after which Bennett retaliated with revelations about Smith's multiple relationships, published first in eight issues of the *Sangamo Journal* beginning on July 15, then in his *History of the Saints,* published by Leland & Whiting in October 1842.

Zina Jacobs

wife number 3
a married woman
October 1841

Six months after marrying Louisa Beaman, Smith completed his courtship of the Huntington sisters: Zina Huntington Jacobs and Presendia Huntington Buell. Their parents, William and Zina Baker Huntington, had read the Book of Mormon and joined the LDS

41. Stephen A. Douglas decided in June 1841 that the writ of arrest was inoperable; he declined to examine the evidence since its admissibility depended on the "future conduct of the different states," specifically whether the Missouri governor would make a new demand (*History of the Church,* 4:364-71). After Boggs issued his infamous extermination order in October 1838, two years of official silence followed, then he requested Smith's extradition through Governor Carlin in September 1840. Smith was not arrested until June 5, 1841. The second attempt at arrest and extradition came after Boggs survived an assassination attempt on May 6, 1842 (Edwin Brown Firmage and Richard Collin Mangrum, *Zion in the Courts: A Legal History of the Church of Jesus Christ of Latter-day Saints, 1830-1900* [Urbana: University of Illinois Press, 1988], 93-101). For the famous line of verse, "Things fall apart; the centre cannot hold," see William Butler Yeats, "The Second Coming," in *The New Oxford Book of English Verse, 1250-1950,* ed. Helen Gardner (New York: Oxford University Press, 1984).

42. Doctrine and Covenants 124:16.

Church in April 1835. The next year in October, they left a prosperous farm near Watertown in upstate New York for Ohio. When they reached Kirtland, their fourth daughter and seventh child, Zina, was fifteen. Her older sister Presendia was twenty-six and married. In 1841, when they married Smith, both were adult women twenty and thirty-one years old respectively.

Zina began an autobiography in September 1840 that recalled her first meeting with the prophet when she and her family arrived in Kirtland: "I saw the Prophet's face for the first time[.] he was 6 feet[,] light aubern hair and a heavy nose[,] blue eyes[,] the [eye]ball[s] ful & round[,] rather long forehead[,] [and] when he was filled with the spirit of revilation or inspiration—to talk to the saints[—]his countenance would look clear & bright."[43] Her mother died on July 8, 1839. Her father, William, suffered financial losses because of Smith's failed Kirtland "anti-banking society" and the expulsion of Mormons from Missouri. Because of these hardships, Joseph and Emma, in the autumn of 1839, invited the Huntington girls into their home for an interim stay.[44]

Another of Smith's adherents, Henry Bailey Jacobs, turned his attention to Zina while she was living in the Smith home. In the history of her grandparents, Oa Jacobs Cannon wrote that Zina spoke frequently with Smith, who must have tutored her over the space of a year on the "principle of plural marriage" and eventually asked her to be his wife. "Joseph pressed Zina for an answer to his marriage proposal on at least three occasions in 1840," Cannon wrote, "but she avoided answering him."[45]

---

43. Martha Sonntag Bradley and Mary Brown Firmage Woodward, *Four Zinas: A Story of Mothers and Daughters on the Mormon Frontier* (Salt Lake City: Signature Books and Smith Research Associates, 2000), 74n19, citing Zina Young, Autobiography 1, Zina D. H. Young Collection, LDS Archives; Compton, *Sacred Loneliness*, 657, citing Zina Young, Autobiography 1, Zina Card Brown Collection, LDS Archives. There are several drafts of Zina Young's autobiography, as well as a variant typescript.

44. Oa Jacobs Cannon, "History of Henry Bailey Jacobs," 5, LDS Archives. Cannon cites (1) her mother, Emma R. Jacobs, who talked to Zina, and (2) an eighteen-year-old record of unspecified origin.

45. Bradley and Woodward, *Four Zinas*, 107, citing Zina Young, Autobiography 4, Zina D. H. Young Collection. Zina was eager to be counted among Joseph Smith's earliest plural wives, so her information must be read with caution (Bradley to author, May 1, 2004). In other statements, Zina said it was her brother Dimick who intro-

Instead, Zina married twenty-three-year-old Henry Jacobs on March 7, 1841. They asked Joseph to perform the ceremony, but he declined; neither would he agree to attend the wedding. John Bennett officiated instead. Within a few months, according to Cannon, Joseph insisted that "the Lord had made it known unto him that she [Zina] was to be his Celestial wife." Most remarkably, according to Cannon, Jacobs evidently accepted this on the assumption that "whatever the prophet did was right."[46] Thus the couple—husband as well as wife—were apparently willing to let the prophet insinuate himself into their marriage. On October 27, about six months pregnant with her first child, twenty-year-old Zina became the first Mormon woman to accept a polyandrous union.

In an autobiographical passage that conceals the sequence of her marriages, Zina is full of conviction regarding the rewards her family was going to receive in the next world at the price of honor in the here and now:

> [W]hen I heard that God had revealed the law of celestial marriag[e] [and] that we would have the privilege of associating in family relationships in the worlds to come[,] I search[ed] the scripture & b[y] humble prayer to my Heavenly Father I obtained a testimony for myself that God had required that order to be established in this church. I mad[e] a greater sacrifice than to give my li[f]e for I never anticipated again to be looked uppon as an honerable woman by those I dearly loved.

For Zina, religious convictions superceded any personal concern she might have for her reputation: "Could I compremise conscience [and] la[y] aside the sure testimony of the spiret of God for the Glory of this world after having been baptized by one having authority and covenanting at the waters edge to live the life of a saint[?]"[47]

According to Cannon, Jacobs "accepted each sacrifice that was

---

duced the prophet's teachings to her. See the brief discussion in Gary James Bergera, "Identifying the Earliest Mormon Polygamists, 1841-44," *Dialogue: A Journal of Mormon Thought* 38 (Fall 2005): 31-32.

46. Zina Young, Autobiography 4; Cannon, "History of Henry Jacobs," 5; Bradley and Woodward, *Four Zinas,* 108-15; Compton, *Sacred Loneliness,* 79-82. Each recounts the concurrent courtships and marriages of Zina and her two suitors.

47. Zina Young, Autobiography 2, Zina D. H. Young Collection, LDS Archives.

asked of him without complaint, even though his heart was breaking."[48] Less than two weeks after marrying Zina, Joseph addressed the Saints on November 7 on the subject of charity. In the context of having just married a pregnant wife, his words acquire added meaning: "If you will not accuse me, I will not accuse you," he offered. "If you will throw a cloak of charity over my sins, I will over yours—for charity covereth a multitude of sins. What many people call sin is not sin; I do many things to break down superstition, and I will break it down."[49] To emphasize how grave it would be to "accus[e] the brethren," he compared it to the biblical sin and "curse" that fell on Noah's son Ham after Ham mocked his father's drunkenness.[50]

Henry and Zina's first child, Zebulon, was born on January 2, 1842. Two weeks later, Smith sent Jacobs on a mission to Chicago, from which he returned the following March. Neither the Smith diary nor the official church history mentions Henry or Zina again; nor do these sources give any hint of conjugal contacts Smith might have had with this wife. In April 1843, Brigham Young and the Quorum of the Twelve called Jacobs to a mission to western New York for six months. Jacobs was one of 115 missionaries who were charged to "go forth into the vineyard to build up the churches" at that time.[51] In May 1844, Jacobs departed again, this time with about 200 church elders sent to campaign for Smith's candidacy for U.S. president.[52] When Jacobs returned in June, shortly before Smith's death, he found Zina accompanying Joseph to private meetings involving Masonic-like handshakes, oaths, and special clothing.[53]

---

48. Cannon, "History of Henry Jacobs," 6.

49. *History of the Church,* 4:445; cf. his letter to Nancy Rigdon discussed later in this chapter.

50. *History of the Church,* 4:526. Smith believed "the curse remains upon the posterity of Canaan ... until the present day" (4:445); that Canaan was the father of the Africans and a descendant of Ham; that the curse began with Cain, who was Ham's ancestor; cf. Smith's Book of Abraham (Abr. 1:24); Brigham Young's statements about descendants of "Cain and Ham" (*Diary of Charles Lowell Walker,* 154-55).

51. "Elders Conference," *Times and Seasons,* Apr. 1, 1843, 157.

52. See Henry Bailey Jacobs to G. W. Goforth, May 4, 1844, in Bradley and Woodward, *Four Zinas,* 125.

53. Zina D. H. Young, Journal, "June 5, 6, 7, 8, 9," 1844, Zina Card Brown Collection; see also Bradley and Woodward, *Four Zinas,* 124. Fifty years later in Utah, Zina

From the time of Joseph's marriage to Zina in 1841 to his death in 1844, a little over two and a half years, Zina continued to reside with Henry, although he was absent on missions a week after their son's birth in 1842, twice in 1843, and again in early 1844. Even though Zina was pregnant with Henry's child when she married Joseph, the theology of "sealing" meant that in the next life she and her children would be Joseph's "eternal possessions," unconnected to Henry.

On February 2, 1846, Brigham Young invited Zina, six months pregnant with Henry's second son, into the Nauvoo temple for a "second sealing" to the deceased Smith. According to Oa Cannon, "Brigham Young stood as a proxy and Henry as witness." Then Young sealed himself to Zina "for time,"[54] meaning for this world, as compared to her eternal sealing to Smith. Henry witnessed this marriage as well. Zina left Nauvoo the next month under Henry's protection. But on May 31, Brigham Young interrupted him at Mount Pisgah, Iowa, and sent him on another mission, this time to England. Some sources say Young advised him to find a wife who could be his eternal partner. While Henry was away, Zina, in her own words, "was welcomed by President Young into his family." She recorded that for "some of the girls [plural wives] it was the first time they had ever left their parents, but the Pres was so kind to us all, nothing but God could have taught him and others how to be so kindly to the[ir] large families [in] [t]his order [of marriage] ... not [having] be[en] on the Earth for 1800 years [and] with all our tradition like garments woven around us."[55]

---

minimized her relationship to Henry. Interviewed in October 1898, she stated: "I was married to Mr. Jacobs, but the marriage was unhappy and we parted" (John W. Wight, "Evidence from Zina D. Huntington-Young," *Saints' Herald*, Jan. 11, 1905, 28-30). On closer examination, Zina continued to live with Henry for several years after Joseph's death. Although Joseph had repeatedly sent Henry away on missions, Zina never completely "parted" from him in Nauvoo.

54. Cannon, "History of Henry Jacobs," 7. Oa was the daughter of Henry Chariton Jacobs. Todd Compton (*Sacred Loneliness*, 661), D. Michael Quinn (*The Mormon Hierarchy: Origins of Power* [Salt Lake City: Signature Books and Smith Research Associates, 1994], 607), and Lyndon W. Cook (*Nauvoo Marriages, Proxy Sealings, 1843-1846* [Provo: Grandin Book, 2004], 178-79) conclude that Brigham must have married Zina in September 1844, although in each case without providing evidence.

55. Zina Young, Autobiography 2. In 1852 William Hall said Brigham Young advised Jacobs that "it was time for men who were walking in other men's shoes to step

Until her death in 1901, Zina played an active role in the LDS Church. Henry obediently married another wife in 1846. Without a legally recognizable separation or divorce, Zina lived with Brigham and in 1850 bore him a daughter, Zina Presendia. Brigham explained that "if a woman can find a man holding the keys of the preisthood with higher powers and authority than her husband, and he is disposed to take her, he can do so, otherwise she has got to remain where she is. In either of these ways of sep[a]ration, you can discover, there is no need for a bill of divorcement."[56] Outliving Brigham by nine years, Henry died in Salt Lake City in 1886. Zina had gone her own way in reestablishing and leading the LDS Relief Society, a benevolent organization formed in Nauvoo in 1842, serving as its third president after the Nauvoo leaders Emma Smith and Eliza R. Snow. Zina attended feminist meetings, accepted interviews with journalists, publicly advocated plural marriage, and in 1893 represented Mormon women at the Chicago World's Fair.

When Oa Cannon first discovered the details of her forebear's marriage, she asked her mother, Zina's daughter-in-law, about the apparent ménage-à-trois and was told "it was not true" and that her daughter was "never to reveal it to anyone." Zina similarly felt that keeping the secret of her plural marriage was a paramount duty.[57] "It was something too sacred to be talked about; it was more to me than life or death. I never breathed it for years," she emphasized. "We hardly dared speak of it. The very walls had ears. We spoke of it only in whispers."[58] The "we" Zina referred to seems to imply her older sister, who was another of Smith's three dozen wives. Perhaps these matters which were unspoken circulated only among the other wives, all

---

out of them." Hall said Young added this: "Brother Jacobs, the woman you claim for a wife does not belong to you. She is the spiritual wife of Brother Joseph, sealed up to him. I am his proxy, and she, in this behalf, with her children, are my property. You can go where you please, and get another, but be sure to get one of your own kindred spirit." (William Hall, *Abominations of Mormonism Exposed* [Cincinnati: I. Hart & Co., 1852], 43-44, qtd. in Compton, *Sacred Loneliness,* 662n11.)

56. Brigham Young, "A few words of Doctrine," Oct. 8, 1861, LDS Archives; Bradley and Woodward, *Four Zinas,* 132; see also chapter 4.

57. Cannon, "History of Henry Jacobs," 12, 14.

58. See Wight, "Evidence from Zina Young."

of whom had stories that were ambiguous enough in the family records to leave their descendants perplexed for generations.

Despite the secrecy, Zina affirmed in May 1869 that on October 27, 1841, in Nauvoo she was indeed "married or Sealed to Joseph Smith" by her brother, Dimick B. Huntington, "in the presence of Fanny Maria Allen Huntington," Dimick's wife. Dimick corroborated this date, saying he "married or Sealed" Zina to Joseph, performing a similar ceremony a few weeks later for Joseph's marriage to Presendia Huntington, again witnessed by Dimick's wife.[59] LDS historian Andrew Jenson officially listed Zina among Smith's plural wives in 1887.[60]

Presendia Buell

wife number 4
a married woman
December 1841

Smith's affection for Zina's older sister, Presendia, goes back at least to the winter of 1838 when he was imprisoned in Missouri,[61] although they may have met as early as 1836 when Presendia and her husband of nine years, Norman Buell, arrived in Ohio from New York. They had converted to Joseph's church and were baptized that June when Presendia was twenty-five. In Ohio, she displayed an affinity for mystical religious experiences as one of the women who began speaking and singing in tongues at Mormon church services.

---

59. From "40 Affidavits on Celestial Marriage," 1869, we read that on October 27, 1841, "Zina Diantha Huntington Young ... was married or Sealed to Joseph Smith ... by Dimick B. Huntington ... in the presence of Fanny Maria Huntington" (fd. 5, p. 5) and that on December 11, "Presenda Lathrop Huntington Kimball ... was married or Sealed to Joseph Smith ... by Dimick B. Huntington ... in the presence of Fanny Maria Huntington" (p. 7). This information is repeated (p. 19), then Fanny Maria Huntington affirms that "she was present when Zina D. and Presendia L. Huntington were married or Sealed to Joseph Smith ... in the fall of 1841" (p. 21).

60. Jenson, "Plural Marriage," 233.

61. In her autobiography, Presendia spelled her name "Presendia." In her May 1, 1869, affidavit, she spelled it "Presenda." Her mother spelled it "Presendia," as did her younger brother, Oliver Boardman Huntington, in his "Diary and Reminiscences, 1843 June-1900 January," LDS Archives. Andrew Jenson used another variant, "Prescindia."

Norman appears to have been less drawn to religious excitement but was nevertheless ordained an elder. A year later the two moved to Far West, Missouri. It was a time of conflict between Mormons and their neighbors. Smith was arrested in November 1838. Three months later, a group of supporters, including Presendia, visited him at Liberty Jail. When she returned the next month, she was denied entry, probably because of two recent escape attempts. Around the time of Presendia's winter visits to the jail, Norman disengaged himself from the church.

On March 15, Joseph wrote to Presendia: "My heart rejoiced at the friendship you manifested in requesting to have a conversation with us." He said he regretted the jailer would not let the prisoners "converse with any one alone," something he had yearned for: "It would have gladdened my heart to have the privilege of conversing with you." He encouraged Presendia and his other followers to stand firm against those who had charged him with treason. However, in a climate of hostilities between the Mormons and Missourians, he advised Presendia that "it would be better for [her and her husband,] brother Buel[,] to leave and go [to Illinois] with the rest of the Brethren."[62] She did not take the prophet's advice prior to his permitted escape from jail on April 16. Nine months later, on January 31, 1840, she gave birth to a son, Oliver.[63] Later that year, Norman took Presendia to Lima, Illinois, where he operated a woolen mill twenty miles south of Nauvoo.

On December 11, 1841, almost three years after her prison visit,

---

62. Joseph Smith to Presendia Huntington Buell, Mar. 15, 1839, in Jessee, *Personal Writings*, 385-87. Cf. Smith's similarly affectionate 1842 letter to Jenetta Richards, ibid., 520.

63. Fawn Brodie pointed out that Oliver was born at least a year after Presendia's husband left the church and that Oliver had the angular features and high forehead of the Smith line (*No Man Knows*, 298ff, 301, 460). Compton considered it improbable that Joseph and Presendia would have found time together during the brief window of opportunity after his release from prison in Missouri (*Sacred Loneliness*, 670, 673). There is no DNA connection (Carrie A. Moore, "DNA tests rule out 2 as Smith's descendants: Scientific advances prove no genetic link," *Deseret News*, Nov. 10, 2007). Compton does find it "unlikely, though not impossible, that Joseph Smith was the actual father of" John Hiram, Presendia's seventh child during her marriage to Buell and born in November 1843 (*Sacred Loneliness*, 124, 670-71).

Presendia, now mother of two children (four had died), married Smith as his third plural wife just six weeks after Smith had married her pregnant sister, Zina—one week after God had warned another married woman, Marinda Hyde, to "hearken to ... Joseph in all things."[64] Emma was probably unaware of these marriages, as she joined her husband to organize the Female Relief Society in March 1842 and invited Presendia to join a month later. It may have been during Presendia's regular visits to Nauvoo for Relief Society that Joseph would have had opportunity to see her.

Presendia was similar to thirteen other wives who were already married when they married Smith. In the first two years of Nauvoo polygamy, Smith demonstrated a preference for married women. Why did he choose women who already had husbands and children? What began as a presumptuous "test" for some men—Joseph's asking for their wives—became a reality for others. Perhaps he considered that caring for a woman whose husband was away was a charitable act, at least within a society of his own making. On the other hand, Orson Pratt's reaction showed that such charity was unexpected and unwelcome—a reaction shared by other men. More practically, if there were children born to such an eternally sealed couple and the woman was already married to another spouse, no awkward departure or explanation would have been required. The child's paternity would not be questioned. Another consideration was that Smith had known and befriended these women as young girls. He watched Zina grow up and had met Presendia when she was a young housewife. In large part, these "girls" had been part of the early Mormon settlement of Kirtland, then Far West, and Nauvoo. In some cases, circumstances presented an opportunity where a woman had lost a husband or a girl had lost one or both parents. In other cases, the parents were devout acolytes who persuaded their daughters to participate in this new order of families. Occasionally, as King David did with Uriah the Hittite, Smith sent the husband away on a mission which provided the privacy needed for a plural relationship to flower. This applied to Zina but

64. *History of the Church*, 4:467.

not to Presendia, whose husband was miles away when she came to Nauvoo for meetings.

The *History of the Church* makes no mention of the second Huntington nuptial, only that on December 11, 1841, a Saturday, "late this evening while sitting in council with the twelve in my new store on Water Street," Smith directed Brigham Young to give instructions about donations for the Nauvoo temple, which was then under construction.[65] But John Bennett knew about the marriage that day and publicly identified the woman as "Mrs. B****."[66] As usual, he carefully marked the last name, Buell, with the correct number of asterisks, yet preserving her privacy. Moreover, Presendia's younger brother, Oliver, indirectly confirmed the marriage by recording on November 14, 1884 (two years after the anti-polygamy Edmunds Act was introduced to the U.S. Senate), that he "stood proxy" that day "for the Prophet Joseph Smith in havin[g] sealed or adopted to him a child of my sister Presendia, [which she] had while living with Norman Buell." The wording hints that it might have been Smith's child. Seventy-four years old and married for thirty-nine years to Heber C. Kimball, her third husband, Presendia may have chosen this occasion to acknowledge the child's paternity to a few select people. If so, it is not clear which of her children it might have been.[67]

Presendia had two living children when she married Smith: George, twelve, and Oliver, nearly two. She probably knew about Zina's polyandrous marriage six weeks earlier because their brother Dimick performed both weddings. It seems unlikely that these motherless girls would not have shared confidences, especially if their brother had spoken to one or both of them about his role in the other's wedding.

The marriage date is confirmed by Presendia's own statement on May 1, 1869, in Salt Lake City when she and Zina composed affidavits confirming their marriages to Smith. Presendia specified:

---

65. Ibid., 4:470.

66. Bennett, *History of the Saints,* 256.

67. Oliver Huntington, Journal, Nov. 14, 1884, Utah State Historical Society; see discussion in Compton, *Sacred Loneliness,* 140, 673.

> Be it remembered that on this first day of May A.D. 1869 personally appeared before me Elias Smith Probate Judge for Said [Salt Lake] County Presenda Lathrop Huntington Kimball who was by me sworn in due form of law and upon her oath saith, that on the eleventh day of December A.D. 1841, at the City of Nauvoo, County of Hancock[,] State of Illinois, She was married or Sealed to Joseph Smith, president of the Church of Jesus Christ of Latter Day Saints by Dimick B. Huntington, a High-Priest in Said Church, according to the laws of the same regulating marriage; in the presence of Fanny Maria Huntington.
>
> Presenda L. H. Kimball[68]

On the same day in 1869, Dimick swore his own affidavit that he had performed both ceremonies in 1841, for Zina on October 27 and Presendia on December 11. Dimick's wife Fanny Maria signed an affidavit as well to confirm that she had witnessed both weddings. In 1887, Andrew Jenson listed these two events as authentic early plural marriages.[69] In 1881, near the end of her life, Presendia wrote: "In 1841 I entered into the New and Everlasting Covenant—was sealed to Joseph Smith the Prophet and Seer, and to the best of my ability I have honored Plural Marriage, never speaking one word against the principle."[70]

After Smith's assassination, Presendia married his apostle Heber Kimball about September the following year to become Kimball's eighteenth wife. September 1845 was also when Brigham Young is thought to have married Zina. Brigham performed Heber's marriage to Presendia. Far from an honorary assignment, they considered this a real marriage. Presendia would soon bear Heber two children. On February 4, 1846, Presendia and Heber re-solemnized their marriage for time and her eternal marriage to Joseph Smith. It seems that she and Zina both fully expected to be sister wives to Smith in the celestial kingdom and to bear him children in the next world.

To sum up the year 1841, Joseph Smith introduced plural mar-

68. Presenda L. H. Kimball, Affidavit, May 1, 1869, Salt Lake City, in "40 Affidavits on Celestial Marriage," 1869.

69. Dimick B. Huntington, Affidavit, May 1, 1869, in "40 Affidavits on Celestial Marriage," 1869.

70. Presendia Lathrop Huntington Kimball, Autobiographical Sketch, 1881, LDS Archives.

riage by example. The importance of this for Mormon culture cannot be overstated, even though the change was not publicized. Smith courted five women and married three: Louisa Beaman in April, Zina Jacobs in October, and Presendia Buell in December. He made overtures to Sarah Pratt but was rebuffed. A week before marrying Presendia in December, he spoke in marriage-related terms to Marinda Hyde, inviting her to follow him "in all things"; she would delay her response until the spring of 1842. Four of these five women were already married. Sarah's and Marinda's husbands were apostles. Near the end of the year when the brethren on foreign missions had returned, "the Twelve or a part of them spent the day with Joseph the Seer & he unfolded unto them many glorious things of the kingdom of God[,] the privileges & blessings of the priesthood &c." These were coded terms for celestial marriage, confirming that Smith was beginning to unfold the privilege of more wives to his closest colleagues.[71]

He was engaged in these activities in September 1840 when John Bennett arrived and became Smith's confidant and housemate. The marriages and subsequent secret meetings went on in tandem with Smith and Bennett's organization of city government, establishment of a local militia, the founding of a university, and elaborations of doctrine. While the State of Illinois had smiled upon the Mormons by passing their city charter, the state cooperated with Missouri in processing the extradition request for Smith and involving itself in other legal disputes.

From the inception of plural marriage, Smith demanded confidentiality from those whom he taught the principle. On Sunday, December 19, 1841, eight days after his marriage to Presendia Buell, Wilford Woodruff recorded the prophet's comment that "the reason

71. Kenney, *Wilford Woodruff's Journal,* 2:144. Similar terminology appears in journals of Hosea Stout (Juanita Brooks, ed., *On the Mormon Frontier: The Diary of Hosea Stout, 1844-1861* [Salt Lake City: University of Utah Press and Utah State Historical Society, 1982], 22, 29) and William Clayton (Smith, *Intimate Chronicle,* 94). Linda King Newell and Valeen Tippetts Avery discuss "coded language" in *Mormon Enigma: Emma Hale Smith* (Garden City, N.Y.: Doubleday, 1984), 331-32n37; see also "patriarchal order" in *Journal of Discourses,* 26 vols. (London: Latter-day Saint's Book Depot, 1854-86), 2:13-14. Dean C. Jessee, ed., *John Taylor Nauvoo Journal* (Provo: Grandin Book, 1996), uses these terms without reference to polygamy (38n134).

we do not have the Secrets of the Lord revealed unto us, is because we do not keep them but reveal them; we do not keep our own secrets, but reveal our difficulties to the world, even to our enemies." Joseph added, "I can keep a secret till Doomsday."[72]

Coincident with plural marriage, a few Mormons began to embrace the equally covert society of Masons. A group of eighteen men, including John C. Bennett, William Felshaw, Heber C. Kimball, George Miller, and Newel K. Whitney, most of whom had been or would be granted the privilege of plural marriage within the next few years, met for the first time as an *ad hoc* association of Masons in Hyrum Smith's Nauvoo office in December, ten days after Smith had made an appeal to keeping confidences. Bennett was elected secretary. The next day, at the meeting of what was called the "Nauvoo Lodge," Willard Richards, Sidney Rigdon, Joseph Smith, John Taylor, Wilford Woodruff, Brigham Young, and others applied to the Standing Committee of Investigation (Bennett, Kimball, and Whitney) for admission.[73] Some were already Masons and had been when they moved to Nauvoo, although Joseph was not. At least part of the appeal of Masonry was the deep concealment with which its rites were shrouded.

During the next eight months, while other Freemasons in the state repudiated Nauvoo's seemingly runaway lodge, several hundred men were initiated in the upper room of Smith's red brick store, then in a newly constructed Masonic Hall. Several thousand Nauvoo citizens would later experience elements that Smith evidently adapted and redefined from the Masonic rituals and incorporated as part of the unfolding Mormon temple ceremonies. The vows of secrecy and threats of blood penalties intensified the mysterious rites of celestial marriage, which bestowed the privilege on select men in the hierarchy to receive more wives as part of the new and everlasting covenant.

Between January and August 1842, Joseph Smith would marry thirteen more women, almost two per month, but would also experi-

---

72. *History of the Church,* 4:479; *Wilford Woodruff's Journal,* 2:143.

73. Smith, *Saintly Scoundrel,* 75, quoting Joseph E. Morcombe, *History of the Grand Lodge of Iowa A. F. and A. M.,* 1910; David E. Miller and Della S. Miller, *Nauvoo: The City of Joseph* (Santa Barbara: Peregrine Smith, 1974), 101-07.

ence an increasing number of rejections.[74] Among his successful courtships were three widows, ten married women, and three single women. Smith continued to propound the doctrine to his apostles. Four of them would enter into their own plural marriages before long. However, Smith's marriage activity would suddenly cease from August 1842 through February 1843, even as the practice was about to spread further among his followers.

The reason is clear: Some of Smith's adherents had made his proposals public. In addition, his disenchanted compatriot John Bennett decided to broadcast details of several secret marriages as well as unsuccessful courtships during the summer and fall of 1842. Not only did these exposures embarrass the prophet, bigamy was a crime in Illinois. Missouri sheriffs already sought after Smith for the conspiracy to assassinate the former governor of Missouri, Lilburn W. Boggs, and now, possibly, for an added suspicion.

Agnes Smith

wife number 5
a widow
January 1842

On January 6, 1842, not quite a month after his union with Presendia Buell, Joseph Smith married his fourth plural wife, Agnes Moulton Coolbrith Smith, widow of his younger brother Don Carlos, who had died five months earlier in August 1841. As far as is known, Joseph married four other widows during his lifetime. Like many wives, Agnes left no personal record of her marriage to Smith. Her daughter Josephine, named in honor of Joseph but known throughout her life as "Ina" Coolbrith, became a prominent California writer and the subject of published interviews and commentary. She more or less concealed her Mormon background and made no known public reference to her mother's plural marriage. Whether she even knew about her mother's relationship with the prophet is unknown.[75]

---

74. Compton lists, but does not discuss, nineteen possible rejections (*Sacred Loneliness*, 2, 633-34).

75. Josephine DeWitt Rhodehamel and Raymund Francis Wood, *Ina Coolbrith:*

When Joseph and Agnes married, he had known her for nearly a decade. For the greater part of that time, as Joseph's sister-in-law, she belonged to his extended family. The daughter of Joseph and Mary Coolbrith, Agnes was born in 1811 near Portland, Maine. She first learned of Mormonism as a single adult working in Boston in 1832 when her landlady brought home a copy of the Book of Mormon. Not much later, she was baptized. Agnes may have met Joseph Smith when he and Newel Whitney visited Boston that fall.[76] When she moved to Kirtland in 1833, it was with Mary Bailey, another convert and close friend who lived in the same boarding house. In Kirtland Agnes and Mary lodged with the Smith family, which is how she came to know Don Carlos Smith, whom she married on July 30, 1835. Meanwhile, Mary Bailey had become acquainted with Don Carlos's brother, Samuel Harrison, whom she married. Although Don Carlos died about the time Joseph married Louisa Beaman, the younger brother apparently had opposed polygamy when rumors of its practice had begun to circulate. Ebenezer Robinson reported that while working with Don Carlos during the printing of the *Times and Seasons,* the latter had said: "Any man who will teach and practice the doctrine of spiritual wifery will go to hell; I don't care if it is my brother Joseph."[77] Don Carlos's evident awareness raises the question of what, if anything, Agnes, the mother of Don Carlos's three daughters, knew about polygamy at that time. What persuaded her, five months after becoming a widow, to marry her own brother-in-law in a transaction that, if known, would have been scandalous?

Brigham Young recorded the date of this levirate-like marriage in his diary.[78] In coded language, he wrote on January 6, 1842: "I was taken into the lodge[.] J[oseph] Smith *w.a.s.* [wed and sealed] Agness."[79]

Librarian and Laureate of California (Provo: Brigham Young University Press, 1973). Coolbrith was the State of California's first Poet Laureate.

76. *History of the Church,* 1:295.

77. Ebenezer Robinson, in *The Return,* June 1890, cited in Compton, *Sacred Loneliness,* 152. Josephine and Charlotte were the living daughters

78. So-called for the Old Testament reference to a brother-in-law (Latin: *levir*), who was obligated to father children for his brother's widow, to "take her to him to wife, and perform the duty of a husband's brother unto her" (Deut. 25:5-6).

79. Brigham Young, Diary, LDS Archives. On September 19, 1844, Young re-

There is no mention of the event in the *History of the Church.* In Smith's diary on that day, his clerk Willard Richards wrote for him that "truly this is a day long to be remembered ... a day in which the God in heaven has begun to restore the ancient <order> of his Kingdom ... the restitution of all things." Given the context, it is easy to see how Smith intended to memorialize the ancient marriage practice as part of the Latter-day Saint restoration.[80]

An additional confirmation comes, once again, from John Bennett, who left the Smith home before January 1842. However, he must have been well informed to write in his exposé that Smith married a "Mrs. A**** S*****" [Agnes Smith].[81] Mary Ann West, a friend of Agnes who had boarded with her in Nauvoo in 1843, would confirm this marriage fifty years later in her Temple Lot deposition.[82] She stated that when the two women lived together, Agnes "told me that she was married to Joseph Smith." She even asserted that Don Carlos had invited Agnes to marry his brother.[83]

Having left Missouri in February, in the summer of 1839 Agnes and her two daughters moved from a temporary residence in Macomb, Illinois, to join Don Carlos in Nauvoo in a room above the print shop he managed. In March 1841 her third daughter, Ina, was born. After Don Carlos succumbed to a fever that year, Agnes continued to maintain her own household and raise her children. However, there is a curious entry in Joseph Smith's diary for January 17, 1842, which

---

versed the code letters to "saw" (sealed and wedded) to record two marriages: Young's to "Louisa B[eaman] Smith" and Heber Kimball's to "Silv[i]a L[yon] Smith," the dates of the diary entries matching those of the sealing record (Compton, *Sacred Loneliness,* 153, 184). Young's code was deciphered in 1991 by Arturo de Hoyos (Timothy Rathbone, "Brigham Young's Masonic Connection and Nauvoo Plural Marriages," 1996, LDS Archives).

80. See Jessee, *Papers of Joseph Smith,* 2:352; *History of the Church,* 4:492-93. Richards was appointed secretary on December 13, 1841 (*History of the Church,* 4:470).

81. Bennett, *History of the Saints,* 256.

82. Mary Ann Covington was married and separated, though not divorced, from James Sheffield, then married William Smith briefly and separated, then married Joseph Stratton, who died in 1850. She then married Chauncey W. West, by whose name she was known in *Reorganized Church v. Church of Christ,* questions 75, 99-107, 114-24, 213-14, 681-83, 696-98.

83. Ibid., questions 677, 687, 697.

also appears in the *History of the Church* for that date, eleven days after Joseph and Agnes married. It reports that Joseph "and Brother Willard Richards dined with Sister Agnes M. Smith."[84] Richards's entry for the same date corroborates these entries: "Dined at sister Agness with Joseph and sister [Lucinda] Harris." Nothing about this report suggests anything out of the ordinary except that Emma was not present, even though the dinner was hosted by her sister-in-law, and Willard Richards's wife, Jennetta, was similarly absent. Instead, another of the women to marry Joseph, Lucinda Harris, was in attendance. A year later, Willard would marry his own first plural wife.

The Relief Society

Not quite two and a half months after Joseph and Agnes's marriage, the Nauvoo Female Relief Society, over which Emma Smith presided from its founding in March 1842, struggled with word of a scandalous relationship between Joseph and an unidentified woman. The issue was aired at the society's second, third, and fourth meetings, beginning on March 24 when Emma reported that one of Agnes's former lodgers, Clarissa Marvel, "was accus'd of telling scandalous falsehoods on the character of Prest. Joseph Smith without the least provocation." Emma called for "some plan to bring her to repentance." In Clarissa's defense, Agnes said the young woman was an orphan and had not given her any previous trouble. She had been a boarder "nearly a year"; Agnes "had seen nothing amiss of her." In what may have been a disingenuous effort to quash the investigation, Emma's second counselor, Sarah Cleveland, who was probably married to Joseph by that time, "proposed" at the March 30 meeting "that the rumor be trac'd out—and the innocent clear'd," then suggested a committee of two: Elizabeth Durfee, then a current or soon-to-be plural wife of Joseph Smith, and Elizabeth Warren, the wife of future polygamist James Allred. At this point, the Relief Society record did not yet implicate Agnes herself in rumors of misconduct.

On April 14 at the fourth Relief Society meeting, Cleveland reported that "the case of Clarissa M[arvel] had been satisfactorily set-

---

84. Jessee, *Papers of Joseph Smith,* 2:353; *History of the Church,* 4:494.

tled[,] ... that she had said no wrong &c." For the first time, Agnes Smith was identified in the record as the subject of these "scandalous falsehoods on the character of Prest. Joseph Smith." Clarissa had submitted a written statement dated "April 2th" that was read into the minutes of the September 28 meeting: "This is to certify that I never have at any time or place, seen or heard any thing improper or unvirtuous in the conduct or conversation of either President Smith or Mrs. Agnes Smith." Cleveland drew a moral from the investigation, "caution[ing] the Society against speaking evil of Prest. J. Smith and his companion," Emma, and saying that "the case of C[larissa] M[arvel] should be a warning, how we hear and how we speak ... [and that] the Lord would cut off those who will not take counsel &c."[85]

After Joseph's death in June 1844, now twice-widowed Agnes married George A. Smith on January 28, 1846. In the same ceremony that bound them together for mortality, Agnes was sealed to Don Carlos for eternity, George A. Smith acting as proxy for his deceased cousin. George A. had already acquired eight wives; when he trekked west with the pioneers in February 1846, he left Agnes in Nauvoo. Unhappy with this arrangement, she met William Pickett, a St. Louis printer with the *Missouri Republican* who had come to Nauvoo in the spring of 1846, perhaps to report on the aftermath of the Mormon departure. Agnes wrote at least two letters to her husband George, in June and November 1846, then with her two girls, Agnes and Ina, joined Pickett in St. Louis where, separated from George A. Smith, she married Pickett, probably in early 1847. On December 11, she gave birth to twin sons, Don Carlos and William, named for her first and fourth husbands. In 1852, Pickett took the family, including their twins and Agnes's two girls, to the California gold fields, stopping in Utah on the way, then on to Los Angeles three years later. In 1862 the family moved to San Francisco after Ina experienced an unpleasant divorce. Ina had already demonstrated a precocious talent as a poet. In 1870, Pickett left for Oregon, but his family declined to follow. At

85. "A Record of the Organization, and Proceedings of the Female Relief Society of Nauvoo," 12, 17-18, 21, 89, typescript; Female Relief Society of Nauvoo, Minutes, LDS Archives.

the time, they lived in San Francisco, and in 1873 they moved to Oakland, where Ina later became the first public librarian.

Agnes died in 1876 and was buried in an unmarked grave in an Oakland cemetery. In the next plot is her famous daughter, Ina, who after a literary social life with Brett Harte, Jack London, John Muir, Robert Louis Stevenson, and Mark Twain, breathed her last in 1928, never having re-married.[86]

Lucinda Harris

wife number 6
a married woman
by January 1842

Lucinda Pendleton's first husband was a famous Mason, William Morgan, who incurred the unappeasable wrath of his fraternity in 1826 when he wrote an exposé of Masonic rituals. At the time, they were living in Batavia, New York, about sixty miles from Joseph Smith's home in Palmyra. After William's book was published, he disappeared and was never seen again, presumably because he was abducted and murdered.

Widowed at twenty-five, Lucinda, "a petite blue-eyed blonde, pleasing to the eye,"[87] married George W. Harris, also a Mason, in 1830 in New York. They moved to Terre Haute, Indiana, and joined the Mormon Church in the fall of 1834. The couple moved to Far West, Missouri, two years later and purchased property there. George became an important figure in the LDS Church as a member of the High Council, which wielded more authority in those days than in

86. See Compton, *Sacred Loneliness,* 169; Daughters of the American Revolution Collection, 17:101, LDS Family History Library, Salt Lake City; Rhodehamel and Wood, *Ina Coolbrith,* 141-42, 370, 407; Marvin S. Hill, *Quest for Refuge* (Salt Lake City: Signature Books, 1989), 69-98. Agnes moved from 1302 Taylor Street (between Washington and Jackson streets) in San Francisco to Oakland on Fifteenth Street (between Jefferson and Clay streets). Four Coolbrith family members are listed in the cemetery records for that family site, but only Ina has a visible marker, placed in September 1986 by the Ina Coolbrith Circle.

87. Description by B. W. Richmond, *Deseret News,* Nov. 27, 1875; John E. Thompson, "The Mormon Baptism of William Morgan," *Mormon Temples,* online at www.lds-mormon.com/.

the current church. On March 14, 1838, when the Smiths arrived at Far West, they were "received under the hospitable roof of George W. Harris" and stayed there about two months.[88] After moving to Nauvoo in 1839, George and Lucinda, at Joseph's invitation, moved directly across the street from the Smiths near the corner of Water and Main streets. The precise date of Lucinda's marriage to Joseph Smith is not known. However, when Willard Richards wrote in his diary on January 17, 1842, that he "dined at sister Agness with Joseph and sister Harris,"[89] he suggests that Smith dined with a colleague and two plural wives.

Born on September 27, 1801, Lucinda would have been forty in January 1842. Interestingly enough, she was born in the small town of Washington, about twenty miles north of Smith's birthplace of Sharon, Vermont. Willard Richards began boarding with the Smiths on January 13, 1842, and was familiar with Joseph's affairs. Compton concludes with Fawn Brodie that Joseph and Lucinda established a connection as early as 1838 when the Smiths lodged with the Harrises in Far West and while George was away. There is no evidence of any specific marriage date, but Andrew Jenson listed her as "one of the first" plural wives. Sarah Pratt reported in 1886 that Lucinda had told her nearly forty-five years earlier in 1842: "Why[,] I am his [Smith's] mistress since four years,"[90] corresponding to 1838. LDS historian Glen Leonard concludes that an 1838 marriage between Joseph and Lucinda "cannot be proved" but was "possible," not as a sealing but as a plural wife prior to the time that "the Lord commanded it in Nauvoo."[91] Whatever the nature of Joseph and Lucinda's relationship in

88. Jessee, *Papers of Joseph Smith,* 2:213.

89. Willard Richards Diary, 1836-1852, 19 vols., LDS Archives, holograph 1490, microfilm 309.

90. See W. Wyl [Wilhelm Ritter von Wymetal], *Mormon Portraits: Or the Truth about the Mormon Leaders* (Salt Lake City: Tribune Printing and Publishing, 1886), 60; Michael S. Riggs and John E. Thompson, "Joseph Smith, Jr., and 'The Notorious Case of Aaron Lyon': Evidence of Earlier Doctrinal Development of Salvation for the Dead and a Trigger for the Practice of Polyandry?" *John Whitmer Historical Journal* 26 (2006): 101-19.

91. Glen M. Leonard, *Nauvoo: A Place of Peace, a People of Promise* (Salt Lake City: Deseret Book, 2002), 344, 717n12. The past tense seems intended to invalidate any plural relationship prior to when it was "commanded."

1838, the suggestion in Richards's diary, if correct, that they were officially connected by January 1842 conforms to Jenson's identification of Lucinda as "one of the first." Corroborating this somewhat hypothetical evidence is the fact that Lucinda was officially sealed to Joseph in the Nauvoo temple on January 22, 1846, at a time when previous plural marriages were re-solemnized and properly recorded. She was sealed to Joseph for eternity, with her civil husband George Harris acting as proxy for the deceased Smith.[92]

Lucinda and George stayed together in Kanesville, Iowa, where George assisted the Saints migrating west. By 1853, Lucinda had left George. Rob Morris, a Masonic historian, has written that Lucinda joined the Catholic Sisters of Charity at the outbreak of the Civil War.[93]

Mary Elizabeth Lightner

wife number 7
a married woman
February 1842

Among the women whom Smith had known during his early years in Ohio was Mary Elizabeth Rollins. By the time she wed the prophet, she was married to Adam Lightner, who was not a member of her faith, and she had given birth to two children. According to Mary's recollection seventy years later,[94] Smith reportedly had "made known to me that God had Commanded him in July 1834 to take me for a Wife, but he had not dared to make it known to me, for when he received the Revelation; I was in Missouri and when he did see me, I was Married."[95] She would not marry Joseph until late February 1842, the same month he became editor and publisher of the Nauvoo *Times and Seasons,* a task previously performed by his deceased brother, Don

92. Lyndon W. Cook, *Nauvoo Marriages,* 13, 110-11.

93. Rob Morris, *William Morgan: Or Political Anti-Masonry* (New York: Robert Macoy, 1883), 178-79, cited in Compton, *Sacred Loneliness,* 54.

94. Mary Elizabeth Rollins Lightner Smith to Emmeline B. Wells, summer 1905, Lightner Collection, 1865-1957, MS 753; Lightner Statement, Feb. 8, 1902, MS 752, LDS Archives.

95. Lightner, Autobiography, Utah State Historical Society Library, Salt Lake City.

Carlos. This would be an energetic and productive late winter for the prophet.

The sixth of his known plural wives, Mary was also the fourth of Smith's fourteen polyandrous wives. She was born on April 9, 1818, in Lima, Livingston County, New York, twenty miles from Palmyra. Her family moved to Ohio in 1828, where she was eventually baptized at age twelve with most of her family in November 1830. They then moved to Missouri in the fall of 1831 where, at thirteen, she began speaking in tongues in Smith's young church.

Mary left at least three accounts describing marital or quasi-marital encounters with Smith. In one, she claimed she was sealed to him the first time at age twelve or thirteen, suggesting that it was a "group-sealing" for eternal life rather than a marriage.[96] She was only fifteen or sixteen when Joseph later told her he had been "commanded" to marry her. Even while they were in different states, she, in turn, was attracted to him and dreamed that she was his wife. Nevertheless, in August 1835 at age seventeen, she married Adam Lightner, with whom she had ten children, six who survived infancy. She finally married Smith at the age of twenty-three in 1842. Sixty years later, she summed up this complicated youthful romance:

> I was Sealed to Joseph Smith the Prophet by commandment, in the Spring of 1831. The Savior appeared [and] commanded him to Seal me up to everlasting Life, gave me to Joseph to be with him in his Kingdom even as he is in the Father's Kingdom[.] in 1834 he was commanded to take me for a wife, I was a thousand miles from him, he got afraid. the Angel came to him three times the last time with a drawn Sword and threatened his life. I did not believe[.] if God told him So, why did he not come and tell me[?] the angel told him I should have a witness, and an Angel came to me, it went through me like lightning, I was afraid. Joseph said he came with more Revelation and knowledge than Joseph ever dare[d] reveal. Brigham Young Sealed me to him, for time & all Eternity[,] Feb 1842. Joseph Said I was his, before I came here. he Said all the Devils in Hell should never get me from him[.] I was Sealed to him in the masonic Hall over the Old brick Store, by Brigham Young in Feb 1842 and then

96. For the changing meaning of the word "sealing," see Gregory A. Prince, *Power from on High* (Salt Lake City: Signature Books, 1995), 155-72.

> again in the Nauvoo Temple by Heber C. Kimball [and] reconfirmed in St George Temple and the Manti Temple and Salt Lake Temple after I came to Utah. Etc.[97]

In a letter to the LDS *Woman's Exponent* in 1905, Mary repeated much of this same information, although now seeming to designate February 1842 as the exclusive date and simultaneously asserting that she "was the first woman God commanded [Joseph] to take as a plural wife." She said she would "never forget" Elizabeth Ann Whitney since "it was at her House that the Prophet Joseph first told me about his Great vision concerning me." Such a conversation may have occurred in the Whitney home in Kirtland in 1834 when Mary was fifteen or sixteen, or it may have been in Nauvoo when Mary was twenty-three. If it was in Nauvoo, then Joseph only proposed once, and the earlier dates represented some other kind of spiritual experience or reconstruction of Joseph's and Mary's later feelings. She repeated that Smith "was very much frightened" by the threatening angel until it "appeared to him three times" in 1842 and that "he was compelled to reveal it to me personally, by the Angel threatening him. I would not [ac]cept it until I had seen an immortal being myself." She re-confirmed the fact that in Nauvoo she "was sealed to Joseph Smith the Prophet by B[righam] Y[oung] in a room over the Old red brick store."[98]

In 1905, the same year Mary wrote to the *Woman's Exponent,* she told a Brigham Young University audience about her courtship and marriage to Joseph Smith. "I had been dreaming for a number of years I was his wife," she said. "I thought I was a great sinner. … I felt it was a sin; but when Joseph sent for me he told me all of these things." He told her "the angel came to [him] three times between the years of '34 and '42 and said [he] was to obey that principle or [the angel] would slay [him]." By 1842, Smith had told two other women, Zina Jacobs and Louisa Beaman, that the angel had threatened to destroy him; it was part of his marriage proposal.[99]

When Joseph worriedly asked if she "was going to be a traitor" and

97. Lightner statement, Feb. 8, 1902; see also Brodie, *No Man Knows,* 467.
98. Lightner to Wells, summer 1905.
99. An "angel and sword" motif is found in several of Smith's proposals.

disclose this intimate request, Mary reassured him, "I have never told a mortal and shall never tell a mortal that I had such a talk from a married man." Like other potential plural wives, Mary followed Smith's admonition to seek personal confirmation about the propriety of their relationship. In doing so, she became convinced that it was right and "went forward and was sealed to him. Brigham Young performed the sealing, and Heber C. Kimball the blessing."[100]

In addition to these statements, Andrew Jenson indicated in 1887 that Mary had become Smith's plural wife sometime "during the last three years of his life," which is compatible with an 1842 marriage date.[101] Mary's speech at Brigham Young University seemed ill-timed and conflicted with Mormon apostle Reed Smoot's (R-Utah) struggle to keep his U.S. Senate seat amidst charges that the LDS Church was secretly continuing plural marriage. At a time when polygamy was being de-emphasized and phased out after two "manifestos," 1890 and 1904, Smoot was advised to keep a low profile. By contrast, Mary stood before the BYU faculty and student body and supported the practice, affirming boldly that Joseph Smith had "preached polygamy[,] and he not only preached it but he practiced it." She presented herself as a "living witness" to the principle as one of "the first being[s] that the revelation was given to him for." She described the angelic visitation that confirmed her testimony. She said that "a few nights after" praying, "an angel of the Lord came to me" with eyes "like lightening. The angel leaned over me and the light was very great although it was night." Although the angel apparently did not speak, Mary interpreted her visual experience to mean she should marry Smith—this despite the fact that she "knew he had six wives" and "three children" by his plural wives. "They told me," she said. "I think two of them are living today, they are not known as his children as they go by other names."[102] None of Joseph's "plural children," if such existed, have been identified.

---

100. Mary E. Lightner, "Remarks" at Brigham Young University, Apr. 14, 1905, LDS Archives; see also "Mary E. Lightner's Testimony (As Delivered at Brigham Young University)," L. Tom Perry Special Collections, Brigham Young University.

101. Jenson, "Plural Marriage," 233-34.

102. Lightner, "Remarks."

In her letter to the *Woman's Exponent,* Mary complained of estrangement and neglect from the Smith family: "I feel as if I was not recognised by the Smith family. I have never had five minutes conversation with Joseph F. Smith in my life. I could tell him a great [number of] things about his Father [Hyrum Smith] that he does not know about the Early days of the Church, and in far west, but have never had the opportunity. I have received but very little council or advi[c]e since Joseph's death. I feel that I have been spiritualy neglected."[103]

No doubt, Mary derived satisfaction in her old age from corresponding with others and affirming her place in the elite circle of Smith's wives. Emily Partridge, who married Smith and then Brigham Young, wrote to Mary in 1886 about the deaths of some of Smith's wives: Eliza Partridge, Desdemona Fullmer, and Marinda Hyde. "All went pretty near together," she commented. "It seems as though Joseph was calling his family home."[104] Zina Jacobs Smith Young wrote to her co-wife, Mary Lightner, on the forty-second anniversary of their husband's assassination: "My Dear precious Sister … We remember this day, of all days to us. I went into Sister Eliza [Snow]'s. We talked over our past a little, then Sister E[liza] spoke a few words in tongues to comfort and cheer us, and how the vale was thinning as we advanced."[105]

There is no other contemporary record of Mary's early encounters with Joseph. In her 1902 and 1905 statements, she would have necessarily brought her later understanding of plural "sealings" to bear in recollecting what had happened. It was after her feelings of exclusion from the Smith family that her own admittedly selective memories solidified. Even so, as she described it, their marital history began more or less with an understanding in 1831 and this was better documented from 1834, followed by the more explicit commitment in 1842. How soon the union became an inevitability in Smith's mind and whether Mary's youthful attraction to the charismatic prophet

---

103. Lightner to Wells, summer 1905.

104. Emily P. Young to Mary Elizabeth Lightner, Apr. 28, 1886, Lightner Collection, 1865-1957; original at L. Tom Perry Special Collections.

105. Zina D. Young to Mary Elizabeth Lightner, June 27, 1886, in ibid.

was prompted or encouraged by Smith are difficult questions to answer. Despite her marriage to Adam Lightner, she was resealed to Smith in 1845 and 1846, Brigham Young standing in as proxy and simultaneously marrying himself to her "for time."[106] She remains one of the earliest and youngest objects of Smith's romantic attentions.

Sylvia Lyon

wife number 8
a married woman
February 1842

The winter of 1842 was particularly difficult for Emma. A year earlier, she and Joseph had lost an infant son, Don Carlos, named after Joseph's brother. On February 6 she gave birth to a stillborn child. Then her mother, Elizabeth, whom she had not seen since leaving Pennsylvania in 1830, died on February 16. Her father, Isaac, had died in 1839. Joseph had never fully repaired the estrangement from his in-laws. It was during this time of emotional difficulty that Joseph accelerated the pace of his marrying, apparently without Emma's permission.

Joseph's next plural wife was twenty-three-year-old Sylvia Porter Sessions Lyon, his fifth polyandrous wife. He married her on February 8, 1842, only a few weeks after he married Mary Elizabeth Lightner and only a few weeks before his marriage to Sylvia's mother, Patty Bartlett Sessions. The Sessionses converted to the LDS Church in Maine in 1834. They met Smith in Kirtland in mid-1837 and joined the Saints that fall in Missouri, where nineteen-year-old Sylvia wed Windsor Lyon in Far West on April 21, 1838. Ironically, according to her mother's diary, "Joseph Smith performed the wedding ceremony."[107] Windsor and Sylvia were among those who were exiled from Missouri in the winter of 1838-39 and reached Nauvoo in March. Windsor became a successful businessman there, retailing dry goods, drugs, and groceries. His drug store, which occupied a sec-

---

106. Cook, *Nauvoo Marriages,* 13, 52, 85.

107. Patty Sessions, Diary, excerpted in *Woman's Exponent,* 13 (Nov. 1, 1884): 86, cited in Compton, *Sacred Loneliness,* 177.

tion of his home, was a landmark at Main and Hotchkiss streets. He converted to the faith and became an officer in the Nauvoo Legion. Windsor and Sylvia had six children, although five died before adulthood. Only a daughter, Josephine, survived.

Sylvia secretly wed Joseph Smith three years after she had married Windsor. Years later, at about fifty, she initiated, but for some reason did not sign, an affidavit that read: "Cylvia Lyon, who was by me sworn in due formal law and upon her oath[,] that on the eighth day of February A.D. 1842, in the City of Nauvoo, County of Hancock[,] State of Illinois[,] She was married or Sealed to President Joseph Smith."[108] Andrew Jenson listed her as a plural wife in his *Historical Record*.[109]

As usual, the *History of the Church* made no mention of Sylvia on February 8, 1842. Two days earlier, Brigham Young and Heber Kimball went to La Harpe, Illinois, for two days. Smith stayed behind, "attending to the common vocations of life and my calling."[110] Tellingly, Sylvia began hosting gatherings for the upper echelon of the church leadership, including Joseph's other plural wives. She joined the Female Relief Society at its second meeting, held on March 24.[111] Joseph established the Holy Order, or Quorum of the Anointed, on May 4 to involve his most trusted followers in plural marriage; Sylvia was inducted in the winter of 1845. By that time, Sylvia and Windsor's home was already established as a center of Nauvoo social activity. On February 25, 1843, four of Smith's wives gathered there: Louisa, Marinda, Sylvia, and Patty. On April 15, Eliza Snow made note of a "very interesting and agreeable afternoon at Mr. Lyon's."[112]

Although Windsor was a member in good standing, he was reportedly not a fully active Latter-day Saint in February 1842. That fall, when he took Nauvoo Stake president William Marks to court for a

---

108. Affidavits on Celestial Marriage, 1869-1870, 62. The affidavit for Vienna "Jaques" similarly lacks a signature. Federal pressure and fear of public exposure may have frightened some women from signing.

109. Jenson, "Plural Marriage," 234.

110. *History of the Church*, 4:514.

111. "Record of the Organization," Mar. 24, 1842.

112. Compton, *Sacred Loneliness*, 182.

$3,000 debt, Marks retaliated by summoning Lyon before a church court for "instituting a suit at law against me on the 4th of November, and for other acts derogatory to the character of a Christian[,] Nauvoo Nov. 7th 1842." Lyon was excommunicated, although he continued to live in Nauvoo and was re-baptized four years later.[113]

During these years as Windsor's wife, Sylvia reportedly bore Smith a child in 1844. After the prophet's assassination, Sylvia married Heber Kimball for "time," Kimball acting as proxy for Sylvia's resealing "for eternity" to Smith on September 19, 1844. This was re-solemnized in the Nauvoo temple on January 26, 1846, Kimball again being acknowledged as husband and acting as Smith's proxy for the eternal sealing. All the while, Sylvia continued to bear Windsor's children from 1840 to 1848.

A child?

Of all the plural wives, Sylvia may be the best candidate to be the mother of a child fathered by Joseph Smith. Nothing as conclusive as genetic testing has been performed, but the documentary evidence is compelling.[114] Four months before Smith's assassination, Sylvia gave birth to Josephine Rosetta Lyon on February 8, 1844. Some thirty-eight years later, Sylvia told her daughter that she, Josephine, had been fathered by the prophet. When Josephine herself was advanced in age, she affirmed what her mother had told her in 1882.[115] Her affidavit reads:

> Fisher, Josephine Rosetta, a daughter of Sylvia Porter Sessions Lyon, was born in Nauvoo, Ill, Feb 8, 1844 ... [O]n the 24th of February 1915 elder Andrew Jenson, [Bountiful Stake] Pres. Joseph H. Grant and Irvin Frederich Fisher (son of Sister [Josephine] Fisher) visited Sister Fisher at her home at Bountiful, on which occasion she gave the following testimony: Just prior to my mothers death in 1882 she called me to her bedside and told me that her days on earth were about numbered and before she

113. Ibid., 180-81, 681-82.

114. See Ugo A. Perego, Natalie M. Myres, and Scott R. Woodward, "Reconstructing the Y-Chromosome of Joseph Smith Jr.: Genealogical Applications," *Journal of Mormon History* 31 (Summer 2005): 70-88.

115. See Compton, *Sacred Loneliness,* 180-81.

passed away from mortality she desired to tell me something which she had kept as an entire secret from me and from all others but which she now desired to communicate to me. She then told me that I was the daughter of the Prophet Joseph Smith, she having been sealed to the Prophet at the time that her husband Mr. Lyon was out of fellowship with the Church. She also told me that she was sealed to the Prophet about the same time that Zina D. Huntington and Eliza R. Snow were thus sealed. In conclusion, mother told me not to make her statement to me too public, as it might cause trouble and arouse unpleasant curiosity. I have followed her advice, and am relating the facts to-day practically the first time, responding to the request or desire of one of the assistant Church Historians.

Signed in the presence of — Josephine R. Fisher
Jos. H Grant[116] Andrew Jenson — Bountiful, Utah,
I[rvin] F. Fisher[117] — Feb[ruary] 24, 1915

It is significant that Josephine's statement was witnessed by one of the church's historians, Andrew Jenson; Josephine's stake president, Joseph Grant, who was a stepbrother of Apostle Heber J. Grant and nephew of Joseph B. Noble; and by her own son. Although Sylvia explained that she was sealed to Smith when her lawfully wedded husband was "out of fellowship with the Church," Windsor's November 1842 estrangement followed Sylvia's marriage to Smith by nine months. Windsor may have begun to offer private criticism before his disaffection became public. But it is more likely that Sylvia either put the circumstances in the best possible light or misremembered this sequence of events.

Four days after Josephine was born, which was recorded coinci-

---

116. Joseph H. Grant was Davis Stake president, son of Jedediah M. Grant and Susan F. Noble and a stepbrother of Heber J. Grant (Andrew Jenson, *Biographical Encyclopedia* [Salt Lake City: Andrew Jenson History Co., 1901], 4:64).

117. In Affidavits on Celestial Marriage, 1869-1870, fd. 1; Josephine F. Fisher to Andrew Jenson, Feb. 24, 1915, LDS Archives. Irvin Frederick Fisher was Josephine's son. Her husband, John Fisher, emigrated from Kent, England, to Utah in 1854, had been a Pony Express rider and stage coach driver, and became mayor of Bountiful, Justice of the Peace, and served in the Utah Territorial Legislature (Josephine E. Fisher, "Josephine Rosetta Lyon Fisher," at www.bountifulutah.gov/historicalcommission; Jenson, *Biographical Encyclopedia,* 1:447-48); www.xphomestation.com/fisher.html citing Raymond W. Settle and Mary Lund Settle, *Saddles and Spurs: The Pony Express Saga* (Reno: University of Nevada Press, 1972).

dentally as two years to the day after the date ascribed to Sylvia's marriage to Joseph, Patty Sessions reported that "Brother Joseph was at her [Sylvia's] house" and that "Mr Lyons, Sylvia's husband, lent him five hundred dollars."[118] Patty described other visits and said that after Josephine's birth, Joseph "visited at her [Sylvia's] house almost daily."[119]

In 1849, Windsor died in Iowa City. Sylvia had left Heber Kimball sometime prior to that or simply ignored her marriage to him altogether. Whatever the interpretation, her sealing to Kimball did not prevent her from marrying Ezekiel Clark (1817-98) on January 1, 1850, a year after Windsor's death. While she was with Ezekiel, she gave birth to three more children. But four years after their marriage, she grew unhappy with her husband's distance from her faith and journeyed to Utah with her brother Perrigrine, en route from his mission to England in 1854. Sylvia and her children resided in Bountiful, which had been called Sessions Settlement for years after Perrigrine's 1847 arrival, until her death twenty-eight years later in 1882.[120]

Josephine, based on her February 1844 birth, would have been conceived in about May 1843, when marriages were accelerating among Joseph's associates. Hyrum was about to support his brother in endorsing the principle, and in two months Joseph would present a revelation sanctioning new marriages, and even requiring them. Spring of 1843 was a watershed period leading to an optimistic surge in celestial marriages among Nauvoo's chosen men and the women they selected. Assuming Josephine was Joseph's daughter, the relationship between him and her mother lasted at least fifteen months from marriage to conception. During that time, Sylvia and Windsor lived about five blocks from Joseph and Emma's Nauvoo home (see map, p. 64).[121]

In addition to the three plural wives Smith acquired in 1841 and the four more in the first two months of 1842, he would now marry three March brides: Patty Sessions (Sylvia's mother), Sarah Cleve-

118. In "Patty Sessions," *Woman's Exponent,* 13 (Nov. 15, 1884): 95.

119. Ibid.

120. The name "Bountiful" was derived from a Book of Mormon city ("Bountiful," *Encyclopedia Britannica,* online at www. britannica.com).

121. Compton, *Sacred Loneliness,* 681.

land, and Elizabeth Durfee. By the end of the first quarter of 1842, Joseph had wedded ten wives in addition to Emma.

Patty Sessions

wife number 9
a married woman
March 1842

Just a month after Joseph married Sylvia Lyon, he married her mother, Patty, who was forty-seven. In 1866, Patty recorded: "I was sealed to Joseph Smith, by Willard Richards, March 9, 1842 in Newel K. Whitney's Chamber [two blocks north of Smith's office on Granger Street], Nauvoo, for time and all eternity ... Sylvia, my daughter, was presant when I was sealed to Joseph Smith."[122] Patty did not keep a diary at the time but included the preceding statement in a later journal. She was Smith's eighth plural and sixth polyandrous wife, and her husband David Sessions was a confidant of Joseph and belonged to his church. This was the first of what would be two mother-daughter marriages in Joseph's life, the other being Flora Woodworth and her mother, Phebe Watrous Woodworth. Typically, he never mentioned his marriage to Patty on paper, but his diary states that he spent that afternoon "with the Recorder," Willard Richards. That is significant because Richards happened to be the one who "sealed" Joseph to Patty that day. Smith effectively disguised his wedding within an afternoon ostensibly spent translating the Book of Abraham with Richards.[123]

As with many of Smith's plural wives, the dénouement of Patty's life after his death contained unexpected twists and turns. While her daughter Sylvia re-solemnized her marriage to Smith on completion of the Nauvoo temple in 1845-46, Patty neither referred to Sylvia's connection to Smith nor did she have herself resealed to Smith when other plural couples' marriages were being regularized and recorded.

122. Eula Fisher, notes on Patty Sessions diary, typescript, page following Dec. 31, 1866, entry, copied by Eva Jean Fisher Duke, 1953, copy in author's possession; see also Donna Toland Smart, ed., *Mormon Midwife: The 1846-1888 Diaries of Patty Bartlett Sessions* (Logan: Utah State University Press, 1997), 276-77, which includes a handwritten autobiographical statement.

123. Jessee, *Papers of Joseph Smith,* 2:367; see also *History of the Church,* 4:548.

Patty apparently waited until July 3, 1867, to be sealed to Joseph Smith. Joseph F. Smith acted as proxy for his uncle.[124] By that time, Patty's civil husband, David, had long since been dead.

Even though Patty was in a polyandrous union, she grieved when her own husband, David, took a second wife, Rosilla Cowen, on October 3, 1845. She complained that she had "seen many a lon[e]some hour" since David became acquainted with Rosilla. On August 2, 1846, "Mr Sessions took Rosilla across the river and left me on this side—Tuesday [September] 8 I feel bad again[;] he has been and talked with Rosilla and she fil[l]ed his ears full and when he came to my bed I was also quite chil[l]ed he was gone so long—he began to talk hard to me—and thre[a]tens me very hard of leaving me Oh may the Lord open his eyes and show him where he is deceived by listening to her false tales."[125]

In 1850, David married a third wife, Harriet Teeples Wixom, who at nineteen was thirty-five years younger than Patty. David died a few months later. The next year, Patty married John Parry, a widower who would become conductor of the Tabernacle Choir. When he died thirty years later, he was eulogized as the "Master Mason" of the LDS Logan temple.[126] Patty is best remembered as a pioneer midwife who delivered nearly four thousand babies and raised fruit trees in Salt Lake City and Bountiful. She died in 1892 at age ninety-seven.[127]

Sarah Cleveland

wife number 10
a married woman
by March 1842

No exact date has been established for Joseph's marriage to Sarah Cleveland, his seventh polyandrous wife, a woman seventeen years his senior. Born Sarah Kingsley in the Berkshire Mountains of Massachusetts in 1788, Sarah was an heiress who attended the Academy

124. Smart, *Mormon Midwife,* 20.
125. Ibid., 59-61.
126. Kenney, *Wilford Woodruff's Journal,* 8:101.
127. Smart, *Mormon Midwife,* 1-29.

for Girls in New Haven, Connecticut, near Yale College. At nineteen she married John Howe, a sea merchant who died eighteen years later; she also lost their only child, Edward. On March 16, 1826, she married "Judge" John Cleveland in Cincinnati. John became manager of the Howe estate near Quincy, Illinois, where he negotiated with tenant farmers and supervised the sale of crops and animals. He was a Swedenborgian, embracing a world view compatible with that of Mormons. Sarah was a revivalist Christian until she converted to Mormonism.[128]

The Clevelands, with their two children, moved to Quincy in about 1836, just a step ahead of the Mormons. They invited Emma Smith and her children into their spacious home when she immigrated there in 1839. Gaining freedom from a Missouri prison, Joseph joined Emma in Quincy and stayed with the Clevelands from April 22 to May 9. This may be when Sarah converted to Mormonism. In 1841, the Clevelands purchased a second home in Nauvoo attached to a store that John opened. The new Mormon capital was about forty miles from Quincy. Sarah was mentioned as having been baptized by proxy for the dead, a practice Smith introduced in 1840 to link family members together in an afterlife Mormon community.[129]

According to tax records, one of the two Cleveland houses was in Sarah's name. In the opinion of her Quincy neighbor, Mary Isabella Hales, this gave Sarah too much independence. Hales was originally from Kent County, England; she housed Joseph Smith when he visited Illinois Governor Thomas Carlin in Quincy in June 1841. In her autobiography, she said she later saw "the Prophet[,] with Sister Snyder," as they "called in his buggy upon Sister Cleaveland."[130] This observant neighbor could only guess at what she was seeing, but it may have

---

128. Biography of Sarah Maryetta Kingsley, LDS Archives.

129. See *History of the Church,* 4:206.

130. Mary Isabella Hales Horne, "Migration and Settlement of the Latter Day Saints," Salt Lake City, 1884, holograph, Bancroft Library, University of California, Berkeley; typescript, Utah Historical Society; time framed by *History of the Church,* 4:364. Mary was from Kentshire, England, and married a farmer in Toronto where, in 1836, Orson and Parley Pratt converted the couple. She was seventeen years old at her conversion.

been a courting visit. The "Sister Snyder" who accompanied Smith was likely Mary Heron Snider, listed by Compton as a possible wife of Joseph Smith.[131] Circumstantial evidence points to a March 1842 marriage for Sarah and Joseph. Andrew Jenson included their marriage in his 1887 listing but neglected to include a date. Compton deduced that she was Joseph's wife at least by June 29, 1842, when she witnessed his marriage to Eliza Snow. If she had not been already initiated into the secret, she would probably not have been privy to such an event.[132] Therefore, Compton concludes, Sarah "was converted to Joseph Smith's doctrine of celestial marriage … soon after moving to the Mormon city, if not before." He also posits that when Emma was "concerned about polygamy-related rumors proceeding from Clarissa Marvel" in March 1842, Cleveland was "probably a plural wife of Joseph Smith by this time."[133]

Within days of Sarah's sealing to Smith, Emma chose the accomplished and well situated Mrs. Cleveland to be her first counselor in the Female Relief Society. It was apparently a dissembling new plural wife who offered assistance in defending Joseph against rumors that would implicate herself if vigorously pursued. At the third meeting of the Relief Society on March 30, 1842, Sarah proposed an aggressive approach to trace the gossip, appointing Mrs. Allred and Elizabeth Durfee, Smith's next wife after Sarah, to the task.[134] On the assumption that it would have been difficult for Sarah to take charge of the inquiry in March and marry Joseph shortly thereafter, exposing herself to potential humiliation, she would have married him between the 1841 call in the buggy and the March 1842 inquiry. In her effort to protect Smith during this investigation, Sarah's appointment of Elizabeth Durfee, another of Smith's wives, is itself significant.

John Cleveland's Swedenborgian faith might have helped prepare Sarah for some of Joseph's teachings. Like Smith, followers of Emanuel Swedenborg conceived of a pre-existent life, "eternal mar-

131. Compton, *Sacred Loneliness*, 8, 9.
132. Ibid., 277.
133. Ibid., 261.
134. Female Relief Society minutes, 23-24.

riage" for couples who had a true "affinity" for each other, and a three-tiered heaven that required marriage for admission to the highest level.[135] Sarah's husband never joined the Mormons, but John's continued willingness to host LDS events indicated a likely compatibility of beliefs.

Like some of the other husbands of women who agreed to marry the prophet, John Cleveland nevertheless became "more and more bitter towards the Mormons."[136] When Smith died and Sarah was resealed to him in the temple on January 15, 1846, she used her maiden name, Kingsley. Joseph's uncle, John Smith, was proxy, and for his trouble was given Sarah as a wife for this life, at least on paper. Her daughter Augusta married John Smith's son, John Lyman Smith, and bore him children as he himself married a plural wife. Through all of this, Sarah and John Cleveland stayed together in Illinois and not only survived but lived in prosperity and comfort. Sarah died at the age of sixty-seven in 1856.

Elizabeth Durfee

wife number 11
a married woman
by March 1842

Smith's third putative marriage to an older woman was to fifty-year-old Elizabeth Davis Goldsmith Brackenbury Durfee, born in Riverhead on Long Island in 1791, one of a family of seven children. Her first husband, Gilbert Goldsmith, was a sailor who drowned. With her second husband, Joseph Brackenbury, she left New York for Ohio, where they met the Mormons and joined Joseph Smith's church in 1831. After her husband's death while on a church mission in 1832, Elizabeth followed the church migration to Missouri where, two years later, she married her third husband, Jabez Durfee, a carpenter from Rhode Island. Sampson Avard, the Mormon paramilitary leader

---

135. Emanuel Swedenborg, *Heaven and Hell,* trans. George F. Dole (West Chester, Pa.: Swedenborg Foundation, 2002), 18-32.

136. Sarah Cleveland to Augusta Lyman, 1847, John Lyman Smith Collection, L. Tom Perry Special Collections, cited by Compton, *Sacred Loneliness,* 284.

in Far West, identified Jabez as a fellow Danite insurgent.[137] The Danites were known for defending Mormon interests against both non-Mormon attacks and LDS dissenters. They often operated at night as guerrilla fighters. Their activities, and those of Missouri militias in the 1838 "Mormon War," were cited as a reason for the Mormons' expulsion from Missouri in 1838-39. With the rest of the faithful, Elizabeth and Jabez trekked to Nauvoo in 1839. After Joseph Smith's death in 1844, she separated from Jabez and married Cornelius Lott; then at some point she separated from him.

The evidence for her marriage to Smith comes from John Bennett and Sarah Pratt. In his *History of the Saints*, Bennett listed seven cases "where Joe Smith was privately married to his spiritual wives," including a "Mrs. D*****."[138] Presumably the marriage occurred before Bennett left Nauvoo in early July 1842. Sarah Pratt told Wilhelm Wymetal, a journalist who wrote under the pen name Wilhelm Wyl as he gathered stories about controversial aspects of polygamy: "There was an old woman called Durfee. She knew a great deal about the Prophet's amorous adventures and, to keep her quiet, he admitted her to the secret blessings of celestial bliss—she boasted here in Salt Lake of having been one of Joseph Smith's wives."[139] Elizabeth did not leave diaries or letters to confirm or deny this allegation.

However, Compton has documented Durfee's involvement in "facilitat[ing] Smith's marriages to younger wives."[140] Among the women she prepared to be his "spiritual wives" were Emily and Eliza Partridge, with whom she first spoke in the spring or summer of 1842 and then again in the winter of 1843. Both girls married Joseph Smith in March 1843. When "Mrs. Durf.— came to me one day," Emily later wrote, "and said Joseph would like an opportunity to talk with me, [I]" ended up marrying him that night.[141]

---

137. See Quinn, *Mormon Hierarchy Origins*, 479-81, 489.

138. Bennett, *History of the Saints*, 256.

139. Wyl, *Mormon Portraits*, 54.

140. Compton, *Sacred Loneliness*, 262.

141. Emily D. P. Young, handwritten pages, transcribed by Emily Hardy Blair, with Emily Young's "What I Remember" and "Incidents in the early life of Emily Dow Partridge," LDS Archives.

Durfee was prominent in the Nauvoo Female Relief Society, where she received assignments from Emma's two counselors. As the minutes indicate, she also took a leadership role in the meetings. She obviously knew and interacted with Emma and Joseph's other wives, such as Sarah Cleveland. She joined the Relief Society at its second meeting in Nauvoo on March 24, 1842. The next week, on March 30, she was appointed to contact Laura Jones and Hannah Burgess to ask them about the rumors they had heard from Clarissa Marvel.[142] Durfee took umbrage at this assignment, possibly realizing that if an investigation were undertaken, she herself could be implicated.[143] At the next meeting, she failed to provide a report. The only testimony, according to the minutes, was from Marvel, who sent a written denial of what she was alleged to have said.[144]

Durfee would eventually leave the LDS Church for Emma Smith's family-led Reorganized Latter Day Saint Church, moving with her sons to Kansas in 1868 and joining the RLDS Church the next year. Thus in 1869 when Joseph F. Smith (Hyrum's son) began collecting affidavits from Smith's surviving wives, Durfee lived in Kansas. She remained there with her sons until her death in 1876, sixteen years before the Temple Lot case that produced testimony from Joseph Noble and Emily Dow Partridge Young, among others.

Other religion-building events

March 1842 erupted with a flurry of marrying, history-telling, and doctrinal innovation. In addition to three plural marriages, Smith continued publishing installments of the history he had begun in Nauvoo in 1839 based on his autobiographical statements and diaries from 1832 in Kirtland.[145] With the benefit of John C. Bennett's intro-

---

142. "Record of the Organization," 17-18.

143. Compton portrays this shadow drama well (*Sacred Loneliness*, 261).

144. "Record of the Organization," 17-18.

145. See *Latter Day Saints Messenger and Advocate*, Dec. 1834, 40. By the time of Smith's death in June 1844, his official *History of the Church* had been completed to August 1838. The writing was then continued under the supervision of Church Historian Willard Richards. By June 1845, the manuscript had been completed only to February 1842. The events of March, including the formation of the Relief Society and Masonic Lodge, had not yet been included.

duction, he wrote to John Wentworth, editor of the *Chicago Democrat,* a "sketch" of his early history, also in March. It contained one of his first descriptions of his having seen two heavenly "personages" who advised him the existing churches were teaching "incorrect doctrines." Smith spoke of an unnamed angel who visited him three years later and told him about ancient records of "the Indians that now inhabit this country."[146] The "restoration" account Smith was in process of developing would soon provide a frame of reference for the patriarchal marriage practices in Nauvoo.

According to the *History of the Church,* Smith spent March 1 preparing illustrations for what would become a new Mormon scripture called the Book of Abraham, which he adapted from the papyrus scrolls and four Egyptian mummies he purchased from a traveling merchant along the Mississippi in 1835.[147] When Napoleon invaded Egypt in 1798 and exposed the world to then-indecipherable ancient writing, Europe and the United States became fascinated with Egyptian artifacts.[148] Egyptian hieroglyphics, like the origin of Native American tribes, were mysteries of the times, sometimes regarded as clues to Indian origins.[149] Smith identified the papyrus scrolls he had acquired as writings from the Old Testament patriarch Abraham.[150]

---

146. Bennett cultivated editors throughout the United States such as James Gordon Bennett, editor of the *New York Herald,* who published articles about the Mormons for a decade, and John Wentworth, editor of the weekly *Chicago Democrat,* who would be elected in 1843 to the U.S. House of Representatives and in 1857 as mayor of Chicago. See Smith, *Saintly Scoundrel,* 64-65; Jessee, *Personal Writings,* 212-20; *History of the Church,* 4:535-41.

147. As published in the *Times and Seasons,* Mar. 1, 15, 1842, 703-22, and later in *History of the Church,* 4:519-34, this new scripture was printed with the following explanation: "The Book of Abraham / Translated from the Papyrus, by Joseph Smith / A Translation of some Ancient Records that have fallen into our hands, from the Catacombs of Egypt, purporting to be the writings of Abraham, while he was in Egypt, called the Book of Abraham, written by his own hand upon papyrus."

148. See Richard G. Carrott, *The Egyptian Revival: Its Sources, Monuments, and Meaning, 1805-1858* (Berkeley: University of California Press, 1978), 1-2, 47-50.

149. In 1825, Ethan Smith wrote of "hieroglyphic books" and paintings among the Indians of Mexico in *A View of the Hebrews* (Poultney, Vt.: Smith & Shute, 1825), 182-85. See also Dan Vogel, *Indian Origins and the Book of Mormon* (Salt Lake City: Signature Books, 1986); Edward A. Kendall, "Account of the Writing Rock," *Memoirs of the American Academy of Arts & Sciences* 3 (1809): 165-91.

150. On July 3, 1835, Michael Chandler exhibited the mummies and papyri in

Joseph Smith had grown up in Vermont, New Hampshire, and New York during the time when public interest in the enigmatic Egyptians was burgeoning. The Manchester, New York, rental library, within five miles of the Smith family farm, had acquired a volume on Napoleon, published in 1815. This is not to suggest that Smith necessarily visited the library, but from the age of ten (mid-1816) to about age twenty-two (December 1827), when he began dictating the Book of Mormon, published accounts of Napoleon and his foray into Egypt would have been available in books, periodicals, and possibly tracts.[151] Orsamus Turner, a printer's apprentice in Palmyra from 1818 to 1822, recalled Joseph coming into the village of Palmyra to pick up his father's newspaper, *The Palmyra Register.* After moving to their Manchester farm in 1823, the Smiths subscribed to the successor newspaper, the *Wayne Sentinel.* Stories about Napoleon's 1798 invasion of Egypt and related speculation about the undeciphered glyphs would have reached the public in the Smith neighborhood through the *Register* and *Sentinel.*[152] When Joseph said he had heard from an other-worldly messenger about a buried hieroglyphic record not far from the family home in Palmyra, European scholars were simultaneously probing the

Kirtland, and "soon after this" the Saints purchased them for $2,400. With papyri in hand, Smith translated some of the hieroglyphics by means of his white seer stone (Quinn, *Mormon Hierarchy Origins,* 623, 633) to produce "an alphabet … [and] grammar of the Egyptian language" through July 1835 (*History of the Church,* 2:235-36, 238). Champollion's deciphering of the Rosetta Stone would not be published until 1841 in Paris and 1842 in London, according to the *New York Herald,* Dec. 28, 1842. Nevertheless, Joseph Smith found, to his joy, that the papyri in his possession contained the writings of Abraham from the Old Testament, which he translated for publication. Many years later—twelve years after Joseph's death and two weeks after his mother died—Emma Smith Bidamon sold the papyri, along with four Egyptian mummies, on May 26, 1856, to a Mr. Combs, who was thought to have taken them to Chicago. Until 1966 it was assumed the artifacts had perished in the Chicago fire of 1871, but it turned out that the New York Metropolitan Museum of Art had acquired them in 1947; later they were offered to the LDS Church, which accepted the offer. See Norman Tolk, Lynn Travers, George D. Smith, and F. Charles Graves, "The Facsimile Found: The Recovery of Joseph Smith's Papyrus Manuscripts," *Dialogue: A Journal of Mormon Thought* 2 (Winter 1967): 51-64.

151. See Robert Paul, "Joseph Smith and the Manchester (New York) Library," *BYU Studies* 22 (Summer 1982): 333-56.

152. H. Michael Marquardt and Wesley P. Walters, *Inventing Mormonism: Tradition and the Historical Record* (San Francisco: Smith Research Associates, 1994), 44.

significance of recently recovered language specimens from Egypt.

The very same year that Joseph first visited a hill to converse with the protector of the buried treasure, British scholar Thomas Young submitted an account to antiquities specialists of some recent discoveries.[153] These events unfolded in 1823, when Young noted that the Rosetta Stone, discovered after Napoleon invaded Egypt, would be the key to deciphering the ancient language based on parallel lines of modern script. He reported that the Rosetta Stone had been "safely and quietly deposited in the British Museum," that the Society of Antiquities had engraved and circulated a "correct copy" of its inscriptions to scholars. Young dismissed efforts to use "Indian" drawings to "illustrate the nature of hieroglyphical languages." He rightly concluded that these American symbols "appear to have had little or nothing in common with those of the Egyptians." Also in 1823, American author Ethan Smith (no known relation to Joseph) published his *View of the Hebrews,* seeking to connect Native Americans to ancient Hebrews by means of a supposed common hieroglyphic writing. In Ethan Smith's second edition in 1825, he added a subtitle to his book: *The Tribes of Israel in America.*

An Excursion on Egyptology: As we consider Joseph Smith's new religious texts in early 1842, we should review what was known of the language of ancient Egyptian, not only in 1823 when Smith began to anticipate the Book of Mormon's "reformed Egyptian records," but later in the 1830s and early 1840s when he prepared his second Egyptian scripture, the Book of Abraham. These were issues that figured as foundational assumptions for his new scripture in March 1842, the same month he evidently married Patty Sessions, Sarah Cleveland, and Elizabeth Durfee.

In 1830 the *North American Review* examined Harvard Professor Jacob Bigelow's 1829 *Elements of Technology,* in which Bigelow discussed the invention of letters, the Rosetta Stone, and "hints from the investi-

---

153. Thomas Young, *An Account of Some Recent Discoveries in Hieroglyphic Literature and Egyptian Antiquities* (London: John Murray, 1823). Thanks to Charles B. Faulhaber, director of The Bancroft Library, University of California, Berkeley, for locating books and articles reflecting the growing understanding of hieroglyphics after Champollion.

gations of Champollion [on] Egyptian hieroglyphics."[154] In an 1831 review of Greppo's *Essay on the Hieroglyphic System of M. Champollion, Jr.,* the reviewer noted that Champollion's works had not [yet] been translated into English, nor were foreign-language publications on the topic "of common occurrence in this country." They were, in fact "exceedingly rare in this country." Even so, the reviewer announced plans to compare Mayan picture writing and Egyptian hieroglyphics,[155] bringing to mind the connection Ethan Smith had implied in *View of the Hebrews,* as well as Joseph Smith's association of Native American pictographs with "reformed Egyptian." In 1843, the year after Joseph Smith published the Book of Abraham in the *Times and Seasons,* still another author grouped the antiquities of Egypt together with those of Central America.[156] Smith's association of these unrelated cultures simply reflected the prevailing misperceptions of the pre- to mid-nineteenth century.

The first ancient scripture Smith presented since the Book of Mormon was the Book of Abraham. The first installments, published on March 1 and 15, 1842, included a revision of the biblical Genesis story to produce a creation that was now effected by plural divinities: "And they (the Gods), said: let there be light … and the 'Gods' called the light day, and the darkness they called night."[157] This portrayal of multiple deities would reappear in the temple version of the creation story instituted by Smith on May 4, 1842.[158]

The formal installation of the Masonic Lodge in Nauvoo followed the gossip circulating in early 1842 about Joseph's marriage to Agnes Smith. John Bennett, still on good terms with Joseph, directed the ceremonies as the lodge's Grand Marshal. On March 15, Smith received the first three degrees of Masonry, which were simultaneously con-

---

154. *North American Review,* Apr. 1830, 344.

155. Ibid.

156. *Living Age* 3 (1844): 113, reviewing Charles Forster's 1843 *The Historical Geography of Arabia.*

157. *History of the Church,* 4:531. Smith's "translation" (revision) of the King James Version by July 2, 1833, in Kirtland, Ohio, altered over 3,400 verses but left the deities singular and in a Trinitarian format (Quinn, *Mormon Hierarchy Origins,* 620).

158. David John Buerger, *Mysteries of Godliness* (San Francisco: Smith Research Associates, 2002), 35-43.

ferred on Sidney Rigdon, his counselor in the First Presidency. This rapid ascent of the Masonic hierarchy generated great interest and concern about Nauvoo on the part of other Illinois lodges. Two months later, Masonic-influenced signs, oaths, dress, and symbolism would find their way into Smith's endowment ceremonies.[159] While accelerating his own celestial marrying and inviting other men to share in the privileges, the prophet coalesced astronomy, biblical mystery, ancient Egyptian writing, and Masonic ritual into portentous ceremony for his followers. Among the themes that emerged was a universe of multiple worlds with plural deities and plural wives. Each worthy man was offered a path to perfection, to manage his own planet with celestial wives and endless children. Along with this ambitious doctrinal expansion that spring, Smith also began to publish his history.

As doctrine formed, some would challenge Smith's leadership. The spring of 1842 was also the time when John C. Bennett began to separate himself from Smith and would soon leave Nauvoo entirely. Such disputes made the telling of history, which became public in 1842, an essential task. From the beginnings of the Church of Christ, official Latter-day Saint history assumed a defensive posture, perhaps initially due to Eber Howe's 1834 exposé, *Mormonism Unvailed.* Not surprisingly, then, Smith introduced his official life story, which he began writing in 1838 and published on March 15, 1842, with a defense of his reputation:

> Owing to the many reports which have been put in circulation by evil-disposed and designing persons, in relation to the rise and progress of the Church of Jesus Christ of Latter-day Saints, all of which have been designed by the authors thereof to militate against its character as a Church, and its progress in the world—I have been induced to write this history, to disabuse the public mind, and put all inquirers after truth into possession of the facts, as they have transpired, in relation both to myself and the Church, so far as I have such facts in possession.[160]

At about the same time, Smith presided at the Thursday, March

159. Ibid., 44-59.

160. *History of the Church,* 1:1; "History, 1838," begun April 30 of that year, in Dean C. Jessee, *Personal Writing,* 226-27.

17, organizational meeting of Nauvoo's Female Relief Society. Although he assisted in organizing it, the idea had arisen when a small group of women formed a sewing society to aid the temple construction workers. Meeting at Sarah Kimball's home, they sought the prophet's endorsement, and he proposed a charity and benevolence organization headed by a president and two counselors. Conceived at a time when Joseph had already wed eight plural wives and was about to wed eight more, it was ironic that the Relief Society developed into a moral tribunal, a watchdog society utilized to defend Joseph's public reputation against rumors of sexual indiscretion.[161]

As Smith continued to marry women secretly for the next twenty months, his wives included seven of the initial twenty-six members of the Relief Society. Over the next two years, the women met thirty-four times, with suspensions during the winter months. It is interesting that Smith addressed nine of those meetings, once by letter, all in the first year. When they first officially congregated, he admonished the women against gossiping. "Do not injure the character of anyone," he said. "If members of the Society shall conduct themselves improperly, deal with them, and keep all your doings within your own bosoms, and hold all characters sacred." At the third meeting, following the Marvel-Smith imbroglio, which had a direct bearing on his relations with Emma and his reputation within the community, Smith advised members to select women for membership "who will walk circumspectly."[162]

The women who defended Smith against charges of moral laxity were most often his own wives, many of them Emma's friends. As Emma presided over the Relief Society in the spring of 1842, she may not have realized the extent to which her colleagues were secretly marrying her husband. In the words of her biographers, "by late summer 1843 most of Emma's friends had either married Joseph or had given their daughters to him."[163] As concern about Joseph's presumed dalliances heated up within the ranks of the Relief Society and as John

161. "Record of the Organization," 1842 and 1843.

162. Ibid., 5, 16.

163. Newell and Avery, *Mormon Enigma,* 147.

Bennett was about to publicize the prophet's courtships—those that had flowered and those that had failed—the prophet sealed a courtship with Marinda Hyde in April. At the same time, he suffered some rebuffs. All of this would eventually disrupt the public calm and fracture the fraternity of Mormon leadership in Nauvoo, not to mention the close-knit society of women.

Joseph's three March wives had a common characteristic: all were his seniors by as much as seventeen years and all were currently married. They were older family women, respected members of the Relief Society, which may have improved Smith's ability to network with and influence the female body that would come to represent about half of Nauvoo's adult female church members. Elizabeth Durfee was instrumental in approaching potential new wives. These loyal, older women added eyes and ears to Joseph's ability to monitor reactions to new doctrines and rituals he was introducing. It is the older women for whom the strongest case may be made that theirs remained "spiritual" unions, although no documentary evidence has been adduced to support that hypothesis or its reverse.

Marinda Hyde

wife number 12
a married woman
April 1842

The sealing of Marinda Hyde in April 1842 consummated a relationship that had begun ten years earlier but had stalled the previous December. Between Smith's polyandrous marriages to the Huntington sisters in late autumn 1841, he courted Marinda Nancy Johnson Hyde, wife of the absent missionary Apostle Orson Hyde. Marinda may have been one of the "girls" who kept their marriage secret for a time, never mentioning Smith's courtship to friends. She met Joseph while he was retranslating the Bible with Sidney Rigdon in her parents' home in 1831. Sixteen years old, the ninth of fifteen children of John and Elsa Johnson of Hiram, Ohio, Marinda was the oldest daughter still at home. Joseph and Emma lived in the family's farmhouse from September 1831 until April 1832.

Three years later, in 1834, Marinda married Orson Hyde, who would become one of Joseph's twelve apostles.[164] After Orson's two six-month missions to the east and one-year mission to England, the Hydes migrated to Missouri in 1838, then on to Illinois in 1839. In April 1840, Orson went on a mission to England and then Jerusalem. In late 1841, when Marinda was twenty-six years old, Smith asked Ebenezer and Angeline Robinson if they would house Marinda and her three children until Orson returned. On that same day, Joseph instructed Marinda by revelation to obey "the counsel of my servant Joseph in all things,"[165] a euphemism usually tied to accepting the call to plural marriage. Marinda was close in age to her friend Louisa Beaman, Joseph's wife of eight months; Joseph had otherwise just married three other young women—Zina Jacobs, Mary Elizabeth Lightner, and Sylvia Lyon—all a few years younger than Marinda.

No precise marriage date has been ascertained, but Joseph's revelatory instruction to Marinda on December 2, 1841, effectively functioned as a courtship proposal. Her husband would be away for another year. Evidently the ceremony took place four months later, as indicated by a unique notation inscribed at the end of Smith's 1843 diary. Neither the diary nor the *History of the Church* explicitly mentions plural marriage, but the incautious reference to it at the end of the eighth diary is revealing. Most of the diary was written in the hand of Willard Richards; but on one of the leaves, the scribe, Thomas Bullock, added a list of eight marriages beginning with: "Apr 42 Marinda Johnson to Joseph Smith."[166]

A year following Smith's "hearken to Joseph in all things" revelation to Marinda, Orson Hyde returned from his two-and-a-half-year mission to Jerusalem, Europe, and Asia. His return was noted in Smith's diary on December 7, 1842, when Smith had dinner with the Hydes. Soon Joseph told Orson about plural marriage. Since Hyde

164. Quinn, *Mormon Hierarchy: Origins,* 552.

165. Uncanonized revelation, Dec. 2, 1841, in Jessee, *Papers of Joseph Smith,* 2:361; *History of the Church,* 4:467.

166. See Scott H. Faulring, ed., *An American Prophet's Record: The Diaries and Journals of Joseph Smith,* 2nd ed. (Salt Lake City: Signature Books and Smith Research Associates, 1989), 396.

was reportedly "furious"—perhaps accentuated by Joseph's attention to Marinda, now their mutual wife—his reaction to this new doctrine would have been anything but certain.[167] However, he eventually responded with enthusiasm and took two plural wives of his own in 1843, Martha Browett, twenty-four, and Mary Ann Price, twenty-six.

As it turned out, Marinda remained Orson's wife, at least for a while. When previous marriages were re-celebrated in the Nauvoo temple, Marinda chose on January 11, 1846, to be sealed for eternity to her legal husband rather than to the deceased prophet. According to a May 1869 affidavit in Salt Lake, her sealing to Smith had been re-celebrated in May 1843, so by 1846 she must have changed her mind. The officiator at the time, Brigham Young, told her she would live with Smith in the afterlife, along with the children Orson had fathered.

After the Nauvoo temple ceremony, Marinda and Orson stayed in Kanesville (Iowa) for a number of years, then followed the Saints to Utah. Orson married and had children with eight other wives. When he married two sixteen-year-olds, Ann Vickers and Helen Winters, in July 1857, Marinda once again changed her mind, now choosing to marry Smith for eternity and reversing her 1846 decision. This was about the time she conceived Zina Virginia, her tenth and last child with Orson, born in April 1858. In 1860, Brigham Young assigned Orson to develop Sanpete County in central Utah and Marinda decided to live apart from Orson, remaining in Salt Lake City with their children. Ten years later in 1870, after thirty-six years of marriage, Marinda and Orson divorced. She died at age seventy in 1886.

Rituals, a shooting, and polygamy gone public

If the spring of 1842 was a fruitful time for multiple marriages, it was also a time of creative development in terms of religious mystery and church protocol. After the April marriage to Marinda Hyde, Smith revealed what would become known as the LDS temple endowment: "the principles and order of the Priesthood, attending to washings, anointings, endowments, and the communication of keys

167. Ann Eliza Young, *Wife Number Nineteen,* 324-26.

pertaining to the Aaronic Priesthood, and so on to the highest order of the Melchisedek Priesthood."[168] Smith's personal secretary, William Clayton, described the temple ceremony as a ritualized drama of the creation, fall, and redemption of Adam, during which participants undergo a ritualized cleansing, take vows of obedience to church leaders, and present passwords and signs that allow them entrance into the celestial or highest kingdom of heaven.[169] On May 4, Joseph and Hyrum Smith shared these rituals with a select circle of seven men: James Adams, Heber C. Kimball, William Law, William Marks, George Miller, Newel K. Whitney, and Brigham Young. A day later, these seven bestowed the same rituals on the two primary Smith brothers.

The next day, May 6, an attempt was made on the life of Lilburn W. Boggs, ex-governor of Missouri. The assailant shot him in the head and neck, but Boggs survived. From his home in Independence, he accused Joseph Smith and Smith's close friend and bodyguard, Orrin Porter Rockwell, whom he accused Smith of sending to assassinate him. Boggs wanted Smith arrested as an accessory to attempted murder. When a sheriff attempted to detain Smith on August 8, the prophet went into hiding for most of the month. While he had now entered into enough plural marriages to tally nearly a dozen, he had also encountered some self-determined wives and daughters of church leaders, such as Sarah Pratt and Nancy Rigdon, who had rejected him, while Martha Brotherton had recently refused Brigham Young.

At the same time, in mid-May, tensions between Smith and Bennett reached a breaking point. Conceivably, a power struggle erupted over who had the authority to authorize plural marriages. Bennett had served in the First Presidency and had run much of Nauvoo. However, after his disagreement with Smith, the record of his celestial marriages was apparently expunged. On May 17 he resigned as mayor and withdrew his membership in the church. Smith told Bennett he could not withdraw from the church because he had been "disfellowshipped" two weeks before on May 11. This apparent backdating was an attempt to discredit Bennett. Two days after his resignation, Ben-

168. *History of the Church,* 5:1-2.

169. Smith, *Intimate Chronicle,* xxxvi, 203n10.

nett had publicly denied rumors that Smith had authorized him "to hold illicit intercourse with women,"[170] a courtesy Bennett would not have been likely to extend to Smith had he been summarily removed a week earlier.

Others than Bennett had begun connecting Smith to extraordinary relations with women. On May 20, the Nauvoo Stake High Council heard stinging testimonials from Sarah Miller and sisters Margaret and Matilda Neyman, who reported "iniquity" upon their "female virtue" by twenty-year-old Chauncey Higbee and others. Higbee was an official in the Nauvoo Legion and was later elected to the Illinois general assembly, state senate, and appellate court. According to the women, Higbee claimed Smith had "authorized him" to have "free intercourse with women if it was kept secret." Higbee evidently did not offer a defense and was subsequently expelled from the church.[171]

Sometime between May 13 and May 26, Emma Smith addressed the Relief Society. The minutes were kept by Eliza Snow, soon to become Smith's thirteenth plural wife: "'This day was an evil day.' She [Emma] said she 'would that this Society were pure before God,' that she 'was afraid that under existing circumstances the sisters were not careful enough to expose iniquity … that heinous sins were among us—that much of this iniquity was practiced by some in authority, pretending to be sanction'd by Pres[iden]t Smith.'"[172]

To forestall further talk about immoral activity, Joseph Smith told the sisters on May 26:

> Hold your tongues about things of no moment. [A] little tale will set the world on fire. At this time the truth on the guilty should not be told openly … Strange as this may seem, yet this is policy. We must use precaution in bringing sinners to justice lest in exposing these heinous sins,

170. *History of the Church,* 5:11-13; Smith, *Saintly Scoundrel,* 87; *Times and Seasons,* July 1, 1842, 841; see also Bergera, "John C. Bennett," 84-91.

171. Nauvoo High Council minutes, May 20, 24, 1842, LDS Archives; *History of the Church,* 5:18; see also Gary James Bergera, "'Illicit Intercourse,' Plural Marriage, and the Nauvoo Stake High Council, 1840-44," *John Whitmer Historical Journal* 23 (2003): 59-90, esp. 67-71.

172. "Record of the Organization," 45-46.

we draw the indignation of a gentile world upon us (and to their imagination justly too.) …

I am *advised by some* of the heads of the church to tell the Relief Society to be virtuous … but to save the Church from desolation and the sword beware[,] be still[,] be prudent. Repent, reform[,] but do it in a way to not destroy all around you. I do not want to cloak iniquity … all things contrary to the will of God should be cast from us, but dont do more hurt than good with your tongues.

Emma disagreed and said so plainly. "All idle rumors and idle talk must be laid aside yet sin must not be covered, especially those sins which are against the law of God and the laws of the country," she said, insisting that "all who walk [in a] disorderly [way] must reform, and any knowing of heinous sins against the law of God, and refuse to expose them, becomes the offender." She added that "she wanted none [to remain] in this Society who had violated the laws of virtue.[173]

Joseph seemed ambivalent about how to respond to this talk about offensive social behavior. In advising the Relief Society sisters to hold their tongues but bring sinners to justice, he was addressing the investigative body composed largely of his partners in marriage. When this *ad hoc* grand jury was directed to look into an alleged association with Sarah Cleveland, the inquiry no doubt would have seemed to Joseph to be reaching uncomfortably close to home.

Brigham Young married Lucy Ann Decker, his first plural wife, on June 14, 1842. In the wake of Bennett's disaffection, as Bennett's unions were denounced as adultery, Young's marriage would become the first that would recognize plural bonding beyond those of Joseph Smith's.[174] Subsequent marriages by Smith's associates will be discussed more fully in chapters 4 and 5.

Bennett left Nauvoo on July 1. Within the week, the *Sangamo Journal,* published eighty miles away in Springfield, Illinois (about half the distance to Chicago), printed the first of eight letters, one of which was written to the *St. Louis Bulletin,* in which Bennett publicly "de-

173. Ibid., 50.

174. Lucy Ann D. Young, Affidavit, July 10, 1869, in "40 Affidavits on Celestial Marriage," 1869.

nounce[d] Joe Smith as the seducer of single and married females."[175] Bennett also "pledge[d] himself to deliver up Joe Smith to the Governor of Missouri upon receiving legal authority."

letter	*composed*	*place*	*published*
1	June 27	Nauvoo, Illinois	July 8
2	July 2	Carthage, Illinois	July 15
3	July 4	"	"
4	July 15	St. Louis, Missouri	July 22
5	July 13	Carthage, Missouri	"
6	July 23	River steamer *Importer*	Aug. 19
7	Aug. 3	Canal boat *Nassau*	"
8	July 30	Cleveland, Ohio	Sept. 2

In Bennett's first letter, printed on July 8, he reported that Smith "attempted to seduce Miss Nancy Rigdon," a daughter of Sidney Rigdon, to "become one of his *clandestine* wives under the new dispensation." Bennett said Smith claimed authority to do so *"in the name of the Lord,* and by his authority and permission."[176]

In Bennett's second and third letters, published on July 15, he said that from autumn 1840 to mid-1842, Smith had "intended to make that amiable and accomplished lady [Sarah Pratt] one of his *spiritual wives,* for the Lord had given her to him." Bennett said he had accompanied Smith to the residence of John T. Barnett, "where Mrs. Pratt resided" while her husband was in England for the church, when Smith said:

> "Sister Pratt, the Lord has given you to me as one of my spiritual wives. I have the blessings of Jacob granted me, as he granted holy men of old, and I have long looked upon you with favor, and hope you will not deny me." She replied: "I care not for the blessings of Jacob, and I believe in no such revelations, neither will I consent under any circumstances. I have one good husband, and that is enough for me."[177]

175. See "Astounding Disclosures! Letters from Gen. Bennett," *Sangamo Journal,* July 8, 1842.

176. Bennett to *Sangamo Journal,* June 27, 1842, original emphasis.

177. *Sangamo Journal,* July 15, 1842, original emphasis.

Bennett said Smith "went off to see Miss _____ at the house of Mrs. Sherman." Probably a reference to Louisa Beaman, the name was omitted by the *Sangamo Journal's* editor in order not to "injure the feelings of individuals unnecessarily." Readers were informed they could see the missing names "in the original manuscript" at the newspaper office. Whoever the unnamed maiden was, Smith "remained with her an hour or two," Bennett said, "and then [Smith] returned to Barnett's, harnessed our horse[s], started for Ramus, and arrived at Carthage at early breakfast." That night they "put up at the house of Esq. Comer," and the next day they returned to Nauvoo.

In the meantime, Sarah Pratt had told the wife of Stephen H. Goddard she thought "Joseph was a corrupt man" because he had "made an attempt upon me." Continuing the story in his letter, Bennett wrote that

> three times afterwards he [Joseph] tried to convince Mrs. Pratt of the propriety of his doctrine, and she at last told him: "Joseph, if you ever attempt any thing of the kind with me again, I will tell Mr. Pratt on his return home. I will certainly do it." Joe replied, "Sister Pratt, I hope you will not expose me; if I am to suffer, all suffer; so do not expose me. Will you agree not to do so?" "If," said she, "you will never insult me again, I will not expose you unless strong circumstances require it." "Well, sister Pratt," says Joe, "as you have refused me; it becomes sin, unless sacrifice is offered;" and turning to me he said, "General, if you are my friend I wish you to procure a lamb, and have it slain, and sprinkle the door posts and the gate with its blood, and take the kidneys and entrails and offer them upon an altar of twelve stones that have not been touched with a hammer, as a burnt offering, and it will save me and my priesthood. Will you do it?" I will, I replied. So I procured the lamb from Captain John T. Barnett, and it was slain by Lieutenant Stephen H. Goddard, and I offered the kidneys and entrails in sacrifice for Joe as he desired; and Joe said, "all is now safe—the destroying angel will pass over, without harming any of us."

But "time passed," as Bennett wrote, and when Orson Pratt returned home, "Joe grossly insulted Mrs. Pratt again ... by approaching and kissing her. This highly offended her, and she told Mr. Pratt, who was much enraged and went and told Joe never to offer an insult of the like again." According to Bennett, Smith replied to his apostle that "Bennett made me do it!" To conclude his letter, Bennett wrote: "I now appeal to Mrs. Pratt if this is not true to the very letter. Just speak out boldly."

On July 15, Bennett sent the *Sangamo Journal* an affidavit by Martha Brotherton regarding Brigham Young's attempt to court her.[178] The incident with Brotherton and other early attempts by the hierarchy to acquire their first plural wives will be discussed in chapter 4.

Smith had anticipated Bennett's letters with strong charges of his own. On June 18, before Bennett had left Nauvoo, the church president convened a special meeting at which he "spoke his mind in great plainness concerning the in[i]quity and wickedness of Gen John Cook Bennet, & exposed him before the public," according to Wilford Woodruff's diary.[179] In doing so, Smith abandoned his previous course of speaking about Bennett in veiled allusions before the Relief Society. The crisis had grown to the point that it could not be managed with metaphors or admonitions to the women's auxiliary.

Five days later, Smith turned Bennett's charges back against him, drafting the following statement on the "conduct and character of Dr. John C. Bennett," which was published on July 1 in the *Times and Seasons:*

> [H]e went to some of the females in the city who knew nothing of him but as an honorable man, and began to teach them that promiscuous intercourse between the sexes was a doctrine believed in by the Latter-day Saints, and that there was no harm in it, but this failing, he had recourse to a more influential and desperately wicked course, and that was to persuade them that myself and others of the authorities of the Church, not only sanctioned but practiced the same wicked acts, and when asked why I publicly preached so much against it, said that it was because of the prejudice of the public, and that it would cause trouble in my own house. He was well aware of the consequence of such wilful and base falsehoods, if they should come to my knowledge, and consequently endeavored to persuade his dupes to keep it a matter of secrecy, persuading

178. "Miss Brotherton's Statement," St. Louis, July 13, 1842, in the *Sangamo Journal*, July 22, 1842.

179. Kenney, *Wilford Woodruff's Journal*, 2:179.

> them there would be no harm if they did not make it known. This proceeding on his part answered the desired end; he accomplished his wicked purposes; he seduced an innocent female by his lying, and subjected her character to public disgrace, should it ever be known.[180]

On July 22 a "mass meeting" was held in Nauvoo to show support for the prophet with the following resolution:

> Resolved, That having heard that John C. Bennett was circulating many base falsehoods respecting a number of the citizens of Nauvoo, and especially against our worthy and respected Mayor, Joseph Smith, we do hereby manifest to the world, that so far as we are acquainted with Joseph Smith, we know him to be a good, moral, virtuous, peaceable and patriotic man, and a firm supporter of law, justice and equal rights: that he at all times upholds and keeps inviolate the constitution of this state and the United States.[181]

The *Times and Seasons* reported the next day that the resolution passed, with only "two or three [who] voted in the negative." One of those who voted against it was Apostle Orson Pratt. But the *History of the Church* reported that the resolution was "adopted unanimously," thereby expunging the dissent of Pratt and others.[182] During these turbulent months, even as the Nauvoo press sought publicity to discredit Bennett's accusations, Smith married four more wives and officiated at Brigham Young's first plural marriage.

Delcena Sherman

wife number 13
a widow
June 1842

By the first of July 1842, Smith had married Delcena Diadamia Johnson Sherman, a thirty-five-year-old widow whose husband, Lyman Royal Sherman, had died in Missouri in 1839 and left her with six chil-

180. *History of the Church,* 5:36; "To the Church of Jesus Christ of Latter day Saints, and to all the Honorable Part of the Community," June 23, 1842 (*Times and Seasons,* July 1, 1842, 839-42).

181. *History of the Church,* 5:70.

182. *The Wasp,* July 23, 1842, 3; *History of the Church,* 5:70.

dren from one to nine years old. Delcena was raised in a family of sixteen children, one of whom was Benjamin Johnson. Not to be confused with the family of John and Elsa Johnson of Hiram, Ohio, and their daughter Marinda, Delcena's parents were Ezekiel and Julia Hills Johnson of western New York. Most adult members of the Johnson family joined the LDS Church in the fall of 1831. Two of them were baptized in Ohio and the rest in New York. In about 1832, Delcena and her husband moved to Kirtland, where Lyman was soon known to be "Joseph's right hand man." He worked on the Kirtland temple in 1834, studied Hebrew with Joseph in 1835, and at the end of the year was guaranteed salvation through a revelation to Smith: "Let your soul be at rest concerning your spiritual standing, and resist no more my voice … lo, I am with you to bless you and deliver you forever. Amen."[183] While Benjamin Johnson was visiting his brother-in-law, he recalled that "the spirit came upon" Lyman and he "opened his mouth in an unknown tongue." Lyman also sang in tongues in January 1837. With one foot in the spiritual realm and another in the physical world, Lyman served on two high councils, first in Ohio and then in Missouri.[184]

In 1903, Benjamin remembered the events of 1842, when he had returned from a mission to Canada to find on the "first of July" that Joseph had married Delcena. He wrote: "The marriage of my Eldest Sister to the Prophet was before my Return" to Ramus, Illinois, twenty miles from Nauvoo. He learned that Smith had talked to his mother about plural marriage and told her that "his first thought was to come and ask her for some of her daughters."[185] Delcena lived with Louisa

---

183. D&C 108:2, 8.

184. Benjamin F. Johnson, *My Life's Review* (1947; Mesa Ariz.: 21st Century Printing, 1992), 14-19, 52, 76, original in LDS Archives; "Lyman Sherman," *Mormon History 1830-1844,* online at www.saintswithouthalos.com; *History of the Church,* 2:345; "History of Willard Richards," 133, LDS Archives; Lyndon Cook, "Lyman Sherman—Man of God, Would-Be Apostle," *BYU Studies* 19 (Fall 1978): 121-24, cited by Compton, *Sacred Loneliness,* 707.

185. In Dean R. Zimmerman, ed., *I Knew the Prophets: An Analysis of the Letter of Benjamin F. Johnson to George F. Gibbs* (Bountiful, Utah: Horizon Publishers, 1976), 45; Johnson, *Life's Review,* 90, 94. Johnson remembers his return home to Ramus (renamed Macedonia) as "June—1842" in his letter to Gibbs (39) and as "first of July" in *Life's Review* (90). From there, he "soon visited Nauvoo." Perhaps using his *Life's Review,* Johnson, at age eighty-five, prepared his 1903 letter to Gibbs.

Beaman, and Smith was supporting both of them: "I Saw from apearances that they ware both in his Care and that he provided for there Comfort."[186] This placed the two women in the uncommon category of being directly supported by Smith, whereas nine of his other wives up to mid-1842 were married and had homes of their own with their first husbands. Louisa was single and Delcena a widow. Agnes Smith was a widow but had her own home. Counting Emma, Joseph was financially supporting three and perhaps four wives by mid-year 1842.

Johnson included his reminiscence in a letter to George F. Gibbs, secretary to the LDS First Presidency. He said he had learned about plural marriage "in 1835 at Kirtland" from Sherman, who died in 1839. Johnson was left with the impression that the marriage to his sister in 1842 had been approved by her first husband, although Sherman had not explicitly told him so. Curiously, when Johnson's reminiscence was published, his editor noted that the date "1835" had been written in pencil where an underscored blank in the original had been left to fill in later. The date was eventually supplied in the same hand as the earlier text. However, he specified "43" as the year God "gave us by command the high and holy law of plural marriage."[187]

On March 4, 1870, Johnson affirmed by affidavit that on "April 2, 1843," it was to his "great surprise" that Smith "commenced to offer to me the principle of plural or celestial marriage," a conversation perhaps intended to ease Smith's courtship of Johnson's second sister, Almera (see chapter 3).[188] It was then that twenty-four-year-old Benjamin Johnson discovered that his church president, already married to one sister was now courting another. Johnson's editor reasonably points out that if Johnson had in fact known about polygamy in 1835, "it would not have been the surprise of which he later testified."[189] Likewise, if he had known of Delcena's marriage to Joseph in 1842, the underlying doctrine should not have been so startling in 1843 when Joseph sought Almera.

---

186. Zimmerman, ed., *I Knew the Prophets*, 40.

187. Ibid., 38n26.

188. Benjamin F. Johnson, Affidavit, Mar. 4, 1870 in "[Affidavits] Book No. 2," 1869-1870.

189. Zimmerman, *I Knew the Prophets*, 37-40.

Perhaps the surprise was Johnson's realization that polygamy would be a favor, not just for the prophet, but expected of Johnson as well (see chapter 4). During the resealing ceremonies in the Nauvoo temple on January 11, 1846, Delcena chose to be wed for eternity to her first husband rather than to Smith. She was one of three early wives who opted to retain her first husband in the afterlife.[190]

Eliza Snow

wife number 14
an unmarried woman
June 1842

Smith married his thirteenth plural wife in a typically private ceremony. The bride was Emma's friend and secretary in the Relief Society, Eliza Roxcy Snow. The June 29 event was witnessed by Sarah Cleveland, another wife. Brigham Young performed the ceremony—two weeks after his own first plural marriage. This was two months after the Relief Society had concluded its investigation into Smith's "immoral" behavior with Agnes Smith. Snow and Cleveland were the two who closed the inquiry at the fourth Relief Society meeting on April 14.

Eliza cryptically began a Nauvoo journal on the same day as her unannounced marriage to Joseph. Perhaps referring to the prejudices and contempt for plural marriage she knew she would confront, and complying with the Nauvoo code of secrecy, she began judicially: "This is a day of much interest to my feelings," then without saying too much Eliza affirmed that she would "not fear."[191] Twenty-seven years later, she swore to the marriage date in an affidavit and added the detail that Brigham Young, to whom she would be sealed after Joseph's death, performed the ceremony. Six of Smith's marriages were performed by Young. For the narrative chronology in the *History of the Church*, all that is reported on the day of Smith's wedding to Eliza is

190. Delcena's and Agnes's first husbands were deceased. Marinda's first husband was living, away on a mission, when she married Smith. She was finally sealed to him.

191. Maureen Ursenbach Beecher, "Eliza R. Snow's Nauvoo Journal," *BYU Studies* 15 (Summer 1975): 391-416; see also Jessee, *Personal Writings*, 47-99.

that Smith "rode out in the City," simply "on business, with Brigham Young."[192] In yet a third treatment of her joyous but cautious moment with Joseph, Eliza felt at liberty, more than forty years after the fact, to mention the marriage in her autobiography which, six years after Emma's death, she signed "E. R. Snow Smith":

> In Nauvoo I first understood that the practice of plurality was to be introduced into the church. The subject was very repugnant to my feelings—so directly was it in opposition to my educated prepossessions, that it seemed as though all the prejudices of my ancestors for generations past congregated around me. But when I reflected that I was living in the Dispensation of the fullness of times, embracing all other Dispensations, surely Plural Marriage must necessarily be included, and I consoled myself with the idea that it was far in the distance, and beyond the period of my mortal existence. It was not long after, however, I received the first intimation before the announcement reached me that the "set time" had come—that God had commanded His servants to establish the order, by taking additional wives. ...
>
> As I increased in knowledge concerning the principle of Plural Marriage, I grew in love with it, and today esteem it a precious, sacred principle—necessary in the elevation and salvation of the human family—in redeeming woman from the curse, and the world from corruptions.
>
> I was sealed to the Prophet, Joseph Smith, for time and eternity, in accordance with the Celestial Law of Marriage which God has revealed.
>
> From personal knowledge I bear my testimony that Plural Celestial marriage is a pure and holy principle, not only tending to individual purity and elevation of character, but also instrumental in producing a more perfect type of manhood mentally and physically, as well as in restoring human life to its former longevity.[193]

Although she did not give a date for her plural marriage in her autobi-

---

192. Jessee, *Papers of Joseph Smith,* 2:395; Eliza R. Snow Smith, Affidavit, June 7, 1869, "40 Affidavits on Celestial Marriage," 1869; *History of the Church,* 5:49.

193. Eliza Roxcy Snow, "Sketch of My Life," Apr. 13, 1885, 13, 17, The Bancroft Library, Berkeley, California; also found in *The Personal Writings of Eliza Roxcy Snow,* ed. Maureen Ursenbach Beecher (Logan: Utah State University Press, 2000), 16. Snow likely refers to a "curse" upon women as a result of Eve giving Adam an apple in the Garden of Eden and to "corruption" as sexual relations outside of marriage, thus combining biblical and social justifications of polygamy. Cf. Eliza's 1884 *Deseret News* statement in chapter 4.

ography, begun in 1885 when the legal pressures on polygamy were mounting, she had earlier affirmed the 1842 date.

Eliza moved into the Smith household on August 18, six weeks after the marriage, and remained there until February 11, 1843. Whatever tension may have arisen from this shared occupancy, reports soon spread that Eliza had conceived Joseph's child and miscarried, that Emma had witnessed Joseph's affection for their houseguest and had angrily thrown her out. Questions cloud the story. The fragmented report of Eliza Snow's expulsion from the Smith home is based on late accounts that were recorded by individuals who heard the eyewitnesses speak rather than by the eyewitnesses themselves. Still, the secondary sources are convincing in their own right. An investigation into the topic was undertaken by LeRoi C. Snow (1876-1962) while he was employed by the LDS Church Historian's Office from 1926 to 1950, probably after hearing the story from his father, Apostle Lorenzo Snow, who was Eliza's brother. In the course of his research, LeRoi found a letter from Charles C. Rich to W. Aird Macdonald, dated August 11, 1944, in which Rich discussed the incident. Rich had been a close associate of Joseph Smith in Nauvoo.[194] Unfortunately, the original has been misplaced, so we have to rely on Snow's summary of it:

> Charles C. Rich called at the Mansion House, Nauvoo, to go with the Prophet on some appointment they had together. As he waited in the main lobby or parlor, he saw the Prophet and Emma come out of a room upstairs and walk together toward the stairway which apparently came down center. Almost at the same time, a door opposite opened and dainty, little, dark haired Eliza R. Snow (she was "heavy with child") came out and walked toward the center stairway. When Joseph saw her, he turned and kissed Emma goodbye, and she remained standing at the bannister. Joseph then walked on to the stairway, where he tenderly kissed Eliza, and then came on down stairs toward Brother Rich. Just as he reached the bottom step, there was a commotion on the stairway, and both Joseph and Brother Rich turned quickly to see Eliza come tumbling down the stairs. Emma had pushed her, in a fit of rage and jealousy; she

194. Macdonald served in the church's Southern States Mission, 1906-08, under Ben E. Rich, Charles Rich's son.

stood at the top of the stairs, glowering, her countenance a picture of hell. Joseph quickly picked up the little lady, and with her in his arms, he turned and looked up at Emma, who then burst into tears and ran [back] to her room. "Her hip was injured and that is why she always afterward favored that leg," said Charles C. Rich. "She lost the unborn babe."[195]

Eliza was typically cautious in her journal, but on December 12, 1842, she referred to what she called her "delicate constitution." As her biographers have noted, this was a nineteenth-century euphemism for pregnancy. Corroborating this, Joseph Smith's coachman, Solon Foster (1811-96), told Joseph Smith III in 1876 that he had watched one evening as young Joseph's angry mother, Emma, "turned Eliza R. Snow outdoors in her night clothes."[196] Joseph III "and all the family" "stood crying," Foster told him. Continuing, the coachman said: "I led you back to the house and took you to bed with me. You said, 'I wish mother wouldn't be so cruel to Aunt Eliza.'"[197]

We know of Foster's account because it was noted in Charles Walker's diary on December 17, 1876, and because Mary Audentia Smith included it in her 1952 biography, *Joseph Smith III and the Restoration.*[198] When Foster retold the anecdote in a church service in 1928, John R. Young (1837-1931), Brigham Young's nephew, was on hand and recorded it in his journal. Having gathered the salient points from these disparate accounts, historian Fawn M. Brodie thought the documentation was strong enough to include it in her biography of Smith. Brodie deduced that "Eliza conceived a child by Joseph in Nauvoo, and that Emma one day discovered her husband embracing Eliza in

---

195. See Maureen Ursenbach Beecher, Linda King Newell, and Valeen Tippetts Avery, "Emma and Eliza and the Stairs," *BYU Studies* 22 (Winter 1982): 90, 92.

196. John Ray Young, Scrapbook, 1928-30; John R. Young to Vesta P. Crawford, Apr. 1931, LDS Archives. See the discussion in Beecher et al., "Emma and Eliza," 91-92. Roger D. Launius dates Foster's visit with Joseph Smith III to 1885 on his second trip to Utah, about forty-two years after the event (*Joseph Smith III: Pragmatic Prophet* [Urbana: University of Illinois Press, 1988], 204-05).

197. Brodie documents that "Foster recounted this in a sermon in southern Utah that was heard by John R. Young. Young described it in a letter to Mrs. Vesta P. Crawford, who kindly consented to let me quote it here" (ibid., 471).

198. A. Karl Larson and Katharine Miles Larson, eds., *The Diary of Charles Lowell Walker* (Logan: Utah State University Press, 1980), 438; cf. Launius, *Joseph Smith III,* 205; Anderson, *Joseph Smith III and Restoration.*

the hall outside their bedrooms and in a rage flung her downstairs," resulting in a miscarriage. The drama was observed by "Solon Foster, coachman for the prophet, [who] was present in the Mansion House when the incident occurred."[199]

A more hostile account, at least in tone, comes from Brigham Young's former wife Ann Eliza Webb Young, as reported by Wilhelm Wyl: "'Miss' Eliza R. Snow, one of the most curious figures in the history of Mormondom … is the very prototype of what is called 'female roosters' in Zion, always ready to enslave and drag men and women into polygamy. She was one of the first (willing) victims of Joseph in Nauvoo. She used to be much at the prophet's house and 'Sister Emma' treated her as a confidential friend." In his book, *Mormon Portraits,* Wyl quoted Chauncey Webb's report that Joseph "made her [Eliza] one of his celestial brides" and that as a result, "feeling outraged as a wife and betrayed as a friend, Emma is currently reported as having had recourse to a vulgar broomstick as an instrument of revenge; and the harsh treatment received at Emma's hands is said to have destroyed Eliza's hopes of becoming the mother of a prophet's son." Webb told Wyl that Thomas Bullock and "other intimate friends of the prophet knew very well that he was proud of … the conquest of Eliza."[200]

Another account by a Mrs. Aidah Clements, who had worked in the Smith household, recalled that "once when she was at her work Emma went up stairs [and] pulled Eliza R. Snow down stairs by the hair of her head as she was staying there."[201] There could be other accounts. Some sources are more credible than others. Setting aside the question of primary versus secondary documentation, what of the story itself? Are the basic elements of the story believable? For instance, it had been seven months since Eliza's marriage, so she could have been visibly pregnant, as the narratives suggest. But if she was,

199. Brodie, *No Man Knows,* 470-71: "This tradition was stated to me as fact by Eliza's nephew, LeRoi C. Snow, in the Church Historian's office, Salt Lake City."

200. Wyl, *Mormon Portraits,* 57-58.

201. Newell and Avery, *Mormon Enigma,* 134, citing "The Testimony of Aidah Clements" (crossed out, then: "but I give this as rum[o]r only") from the patriarchal blessings and family histories of Mary Ann and John Boice, LDS Archives.

would it not have drawn undue attention and embarrassment to herself and the Smiths, especially within the circles of Relief Society women? Maybe she was not yet showing and the kiss was all that sparked Emma's jealousy, the "heavy with child" detail a later embellishment.

There are other questions that relate to circumstances. The witnesses seem to have the Mansion House in mind in referring to multiple rooms, a spacious staircase, and a second-floor hallway. It has traditionally been thought that the family moved to the mansion on August 31, six months too late for the scenario in question. Their previous house was modest. Joseph III described their initial "homestead" as a "double house with a half-story above," making it a "two-room house—to which Joseph and Emma added a living room with a fireplace on the back, thereafter using the two original rooms as bedrooms."[202] It would have been barely large enough for the Smiths and their four children, let alone allowing for guest rooms.

Another possibility is that Eliza might have moved into the uncompleted Mansion House about the time Joseph situated his office there in November 1842. Historian Maureen Beecher has found evidence that the Smiths may have begun moving into the mansion much earlier than previously thought.[203] At the other end of the time line, what other plausible reason could have impelled Eliza's departure? Joseph's diary explains that he was "changing the furniture in the house to receive Mother Smith in the family" on February 11, 1843.[204] For the same date, the *History of the Church* reports that "Mother came to my house to live."[205] The coincidence of his mother moving in might have been reason enough for Snow to leave—that is, if they had not already situated themselves in the more spacious Mansion House.[206]

Among the various reports, the two purported eyewitnesses,

---

202. See Lavina Fielding Anderson, *Lucy's Book: A Critical Edition of Lucy Mack Smith's Family Memoir* (Salt Lake City: Signature Books, 2001), 702n26.

203. *History of the Church*, 5:183, 5:556, 6:33; Ursenbach, "Eliza Snow's Nauvoo Journal," 402, citing the entry for Feb. 11, 1843; Beecher et al., "Emma and Eliza," 92n13.

204. Faulring, *American Prophet's Record*, 303.

205. *History of the Church*, 5:271.

206. Cf. Beecher et al., "Emma and Eliza," 92.

Charles Rich and Solon Foster, were both intimately involved in the Smiths' lives and had reason to observe what happened. Rich's account is corroborated by Foster's statement, which is attested to by several individuals. Taken together, these separate tellings may comprise a more or less credible report. This was Brodie's conclusion when she included the incident in her 1945 biography. Most convincing of all is to think that these stories were circulating widely and Eliza never bothered to clarify or refute them.[207]

If the story is accepted, even without the circumstantial details, it would constitute the first time Emma is suspected of having directly confronted one of her husband's plural wives. In that sense, it complements the discussion of what Emma knew, when she knew it, and how she responded. The rumors, denials, and sermons in the Relief Society about "virtue" would therefore be open to new interpretation. If she knew about Eliza, one might ask how she felt about the ordeal, since she had already confronted something similar to this in the 1830s when she found her husband involved with a hired girl.[208] Here she faced another breach of marital fidelity, this time with her friend and confidant Eliza Snow, an event which must have divided the two women and alerted Emma, in a deep and personal way, to her husband's ambiguous commitment to her, even if she viewed it within the context of a new religious order.

Following the February incident, Emma discovered that her husband was involved with yet another Eliza, this time Eliza Partridge, who worked alongside her sister, Emily, in the Smith household (see below). There is little question that at some point during the winter and spring of 1843, Emma had to confront the re-emerging issue of marital fidelity, or polygamy, within her home and within her own conscience. Whether or not she ever consented to the practice, she appeared to be unable to stop it or even slow it down.

---

207. Noted by Richard and Pamela Price, "Joseph Smith Fought Polygamy," *Restoration Bookstore*, online at http:/restorationbookstore.org/.

208. The basic Alger references come from Benjamin F. Johnson, William McLellin, and Ann Eliza Webb Young and are discussed in chapter 1. See also Compton, *Sacred Loneliness*, 26-36.

Sarah Poulterer

wife number 15
a married woman
by July 1842

Before Bennett's departure from Nauvoo in early July 1842, Smith apparently married Sarah Poulterer, whose maiden name was Davis or Rapson ("R," not "B"). Sarah had married Thomas Poulterer in 1814.[209] When Bennett referred to one of Smith's wives as Miss B*****, this led to speculation about her identity. Later chroniclers seem to have conflated these names to produce "Sarah Bapson." In an apparent reliance on Bennett, the LDS Church accepted the existence of a "Sarah Bapson" who appears in the sealing records for April 4, 1899, alongside eight other women thought to have been married to Joseph Smith during his lifetime but for whom no contemporary records existed. LDS President Lorenzo Snow ruled that Bapson's marriage to Smith was certain enough that a sealing should be performed posthumously "in order that a record might exist."[210] When Sarah Davis/ Rapson Poulterer died in 1879, the *Deseret Evening News* published an obituary which said that "she was in Nauvoo in early days, and was intimately acquainted with the prophet Joseph.[211] It may be assumed that because

---

209. Sarah Davis/Rapson was born October 7, 1794, in East Molesey, Surrey, England, most likely to William Davis and Ann Leonard Rapson Davis. She had two siblings or step-siblings, Elizabeth Davis and Maria Rapson. She married Thomas Poulter/Poulterer on September 26, 1814, in Ealing, Middlesex, England. She was baptized by proxy in Nauvoo in 1843 for her mother, father or step-father, husband, and siblings or step-siblings. See Susan Easton Black, *Annotated Record of Baptisms for the Dead, 1840-1845* (Provo: Brigham Young University Press, 2002), 5:2948-49. Sarah Rapson Poulterer, identified as having been born on March 7, 1791, is mentioned elsewhere as having received a patriarchal blessing in Nauvoo on June 28, 1843, from Hyrum Smith (Patriarchal Blessings, 3:131, LDS Archives); cf. note 211 below.

210. Bennett, *History of the Saints*, 256; Brodie, *No Man Knows*, 469. For the sealing, see Salt Lake Temple Sealing Records, Book D, 243, GS Film 184, 590, Family History Library, Salt Lake City, cited by Thomas Milton Tinney, *Royal Family of the Prophet Joseph Smith Jr.* (Salt Lake City: Tinney-Green Family Organization, 1973), 41, 63.

211. "Mother Poulterer Dead," *Deseret Evening News*, Aug. 20, 1879, 3. Her birthdate is given as March 27, 1793. She was buried in the Salt Lake City Cemetery ("Cemetery Burials Database," *Utah State History*, online at http://history.utah.gov. The 1870 census shows a seventy-six-year-old, British-born "Sarah Poulter" keeping house in Salt Lake City, while the 1860 census shows a sixty-six-year-old "Sarah Poulterer"

of Bennett's awareness of the woman, Joseph's interest in her would have most likely, although not necessarily, occurred before Bennett left Illinois. If so, that would make hers one of the last weddings of 1842. Historians have not found any information about Sarah Rapson or Thomas Poulterer outside of their names on census records.

Sarah Ann Whitney

wife number 16
an unmarried woman
July 1842

Joseph Smith had known Sarah Ann Whitney, his fifteenth plural wife, since she was six, probably since visiting her father's store on first arrival in Kirtland. She was the second of seven surviving children of Newel K. and Elizabeth Ann Whitney.[212] When Smith sought her hand in marriage, she was still seventeen, but "the first woman ever given in plural marriage by or with the consent of both parents," according to her mother. In a published reminiscence, her mother voiced her high regard for celestial marriage, about which she said the "most profound secresy [had to] be maintained."[213] The ceremony was performed by Sarah Ann's father in her mother's presence in Nauvoo on Monday, July 27, 1842.[214]

The wedding day was discreetly chosen to coincide with Emma's trip out of town to plead Joseph's case before Illinois Governor Tom Carlin.[215] Smith's own journal on that day says only that he "attended meeting at the Grove and listened to the Electioneering Candidates,

---

in Salt Lake City, born in Pennsylvania ("United States Federal Census") *Ancestry* (www.ancestry.com).

212. Whitney family tradition recounted by Roberts, *Comprehensive History,* 1:145-46n.

213. See Carol Cornwall Madsen, *In Their Own Words: Women and the Story of Nauvoo* (Salt Lake City: Deseret Book, 1994), 201-02, citing Elizabeth Ann Whitney, "A Leaf from an Autobiography," *Woman's Exponent* 7 (Dec. 15, 1878): 105.

214. Sarah A. [Whitney] Kimball, Affidavit, June 19, 1869, in Affidavits on Celestial Marriage, 1869-1870, 36; E[lizabeth] A. Whitney, Aug. 30, 1869, ibid., 72. Smith appointed Whitney bishop in Kirtland on December 4, 1831 (*History of the Church,* 1:239-41), and Nauvoo on March 1, 1842 (5:120n).

215. See Smith's letter to Carlin in *History of the Church,* 5:83.

and spoke at the close of the meeting." The *History of the Church* reports the day's activities in the same way without a hint of a wedding.[216]

Did Sarah Ann know she was the fifteenth plural wife? Perhaps not. She would learn soon enough as she came to know Joseph's other wives, some of them already familiar faces. Her childhood friend, Helen Mar Kimball, would also soon marry Joseph Smith. The Whitney and Kimball families were close. After Smith's death, Helen would marry Sarah's brother, Horace (see chapter 4). A decade earlier, when Sarah's father was a merchant at the crossroads of Markell and Chillicothe Roads in Kirtland, Smith appointed him to become the first bishop in the new church.[217] Whitney was preparing to move his family to Missouri when the conflict in that state became explosive. They ended up staying in Kirtland for a time, then joined the Smiths in Nauvoo in June 1840.

Like Smith's other wives, Sarah Ann was married to one of the apostles after Smith was killed in mid-1844. In March 1845, she wed Heber Kimball, with whom she lived until he died in 1868 in Salt Lake City. She continued to live five more years until September 1873.

Beyond Sarah Ann's parents, few people knew that she had wedded the prophet that day in the Mormon capital, which had now grown to about 10,000 inhabitants.[218] Five days earlier, on July 22, the

216. Faulring, *American Prophet's Record,* 245; *History of the Church,* 5:82.

217. Newel K. Whitney was baptized in Kirtland in the fall of 1830 and in 1832 entered into a business partnership known as the United Order or United Firm—or simply the Firm—which provided for common ownership of property and consolidated business activity for the benefit of the church. Because he was an agent of the firm, various branches carried the Whitney name. The Missouri branch was Gilbert, Whitney & Company and the Ohio branch was Newel K. Whitney & Company. See Joseph Smith to Emma Smith, June 6, Oct. 13, 1832, in Jessee, *Personal Writings,* 263-65, 277-80.

218. According to Joseph Smith, in December 1840 there were about 3,000 inhabitants of Nauvoo, a town which grew to about 15,000 or more by 1846 (Joseph Smith to the Twelve, Dec. 15, 1840). From 1837 to the time the Council of Twelve returned from England in 1841, the church had attracted about 8,000 converts, a large portion of whom migrated to Illinois (James B. Allen and Malcolm R. Thorp, "The Mission of the Twelve to England, 1840-41: Mormon Apostles and the Working Classes," *BYU Studies* 15 [Summer 1975]: 499-526; Jessee, *Personal Writings,* 515, 518). By the time Joseph Smith began marrying plural wives in 1841, Nauvoo had become the second largest city in Illinois, with a population approaching 7,000 (Van Wagoner, *Sidney Rigdon,* 311). An 1845 census indicated that Nauvoo had reached 11,036 residents, half the pop-

Nauvoo Relief Society had drawn "up a petition affirming, among other things, the 'virtue' of Joseph Smith."[219] There were only two polygamist men in the church at the time that we know of: Smith and Young. Three others, Reynolds Cahoon, Heber Kimball, and Joseph Knight, were about to join that fraternity.

Three weeks after the wedding, Joseph took steps to spend some time with his newest bride. Emma had returned to Nauvoo, but Joseph was in hiding; a Missouri sheriff was prowling the streets with a writ for Joseph's arrest as an accessory to the attempted murder on May 6 of former Missouri Governor Lilburn W. Boggs. The prophet and his bodyguard, Orrin Porter Rockwell, had been arrested once just ten days earlier under a warrant from Governor Carlin, which honored Boggs's accusation. In point of fact, Rockwell had been in Boggs's hometown of Independence the day of the shooting and had fled to Illinois after the incident. Smith was in Nauvoo during the time, but Boggs believed that, if Smith had not explicitly ordered the shooting, he had at least suggested it by prophesying that Boggs would die a violent death, then saying the prophecy "needs must be fulfilled."[220]

On August 5, Smith married Martha Knight (see below). Three days later, Smith and Rockwell were arrested by an Illinois deputy, then released by the Nauvoo Municipal Court on a writ of habeas corpus, meaning that the court was unable to find sufficient evidence to support the arrest. Outmaneuvered, the arresting officers left for Quincy, where Governor Carlin was spending a few days, with the intent to return to Nauvoo armed with more authority. However, since they had not left a writ of arrest with the Nauvoo city marshal, the prisoners were freed. Smith promptly decamped, so that by the time the sheriff re-appeared, he was nowhere to be found.[221]

---

ulation of Hancock County (Robert B. Flanders, *Nauvoo: Kingdom on the Mississippi* [Urbana: University of Illinois Press, 1975], 16); Bradley and Woodward, *Four Zinas,* 107.

219. *History of the Church,* 5:71.

220. Ibid., 5:50. In saying it "must needs be" fulfilled, if that was his wording (Carlin inverted the word order), Smith drew from the King James Bible (Gen. 17:13; 2 Sam. 14:14; Jer. 10:7; Matt. 18:7; Luke 24:7; Rom. 13:5); the phrase is also in the Book of Mormon (2 Ne. 2:11; Alma 32:28) and D&C (38:39; 82:21; 98:12; 103:15-20; 104:14-16).

221. See *History of the Church,* 5:67, 86, and 89.

To stay in touch with matters at hand, the prophet did not go far but frequently changed his place of hiding. Emma wrote to him often, sometimes in a practical tone,[222] and visited often. She and other trusted associates were the conduits through which the prophet-mayor issued instructions to his people and sent appeals to Illinois authorities for help. He could not be sure of his legal position even if local officials were prepared to release him again. In an extraordinary move, the Nauvoo City Council issued an ordinance limiting the power of state courts and claiming the right to review and dismiss future writs.[223]

Rockwell fled the state. Smith stayed out of sight for nearly four months, from August to December. After a new governor, Thomas Ford, was inaugurated on December 8, 1842, Smith gave himself up in Springfield to test the legality of the Missouri writ. It was declared invalid since Smith had not been in Missouri when the shooting occurred and therefore could not be accused of fleeing the state. Hoping somehow to benefit from the ruling even though he might have been in Missouri, Rockwell apparently allowed himself to be arrested in St. Louis three months later on his return to Nauvoo. He spent nine months in a St. Louis jail, until Christmas 1843.[224]

When Joseph was first arrested and released on Monday, August 8, 1842, he fled to his paternal uncle and aunt, John and Clarissa Smith,[225] who lived in the primarily Mormon town of Zarahemla on the Iowa side of the Mississippi River. On Thursday evening, August 11, he and two companions boated to an island between Nauvoo and Montrose, Iowa, where Emma soon joined them. Later that night, Smith rowed upriver to the home of Edward Sayers, north of Nauvoo

---

222. In one of her letters, she suggested Joseph might want to buy land that General James Adams was offering at $2 an acre and a $1,400 mortgage (*History of the Church,* 5:110).

223. Roberts, *Comprehensive History,* 2:468-69, citing Thomas Gregg, *History of Hancock, Illinois;* Leonard, *Nauvoo,* 467. The ordinance was not overturned until January 24, 1845 (*History of the Church,* 5:370-71).

224. See Miller and Miller, *Nauvoo: City of Joseph,* 50, 51.

225. "Uncle" John Smith, brother to Joseph Smith Sr., was one of eleven siblings: Jesse, Priscilla, Joseph Sr., Asael Jr., Mary, Samuel, Silas, John, Susanna, Stephen, and Sarah. Only four of them—Joseph Sr., Asael Jr., John, and Silas—converted to Mormonism.

on the Illinois side. Six months later Smith would marry Sayers's wife, Ruth, in a polyandrous union. On Friday, Emma Smith and Wilson Law sent a messenger to Smith's lawyer, Stephen Powers, whose office was downriver in Keokuk, Iowa, asking him to determine if Governor Carlin still sought to arrest the prophet. On Saturday, August 13, Emma arrived by carriage at Sayers's homestead and spent the night with Joseph. The next morning, Joseph and Emma "talked in the forenoon" and "read history" together. The Smiths used these meetings for more than family reunions; they also discussed land transactions and legal options. Joseph wrote to Lieutenant General Wilson Law of the Nauvoo Legion, outlining his plans to avoid arrest. Emma, escorted by Smith's secretary, William Clayton, and tailor, Erastus H. Derby, returned to Nauvoo with the letter to Wilson at six o'clock Sunday evening. During Emma's absence on Sunday, but clearly with her consent, Eliza Snow moved into the Smith home in Nauvoo. Almost certainly Emma did not yet know that Eliza had married her husband six weeks earlier.

On Monday morning, August 15, Law answered Joseph's letter, urging him not to turn himself over to the Missouri sheriffs and promising that the 1,500-man Nauvoo Legion would defend him. That same day, Edwin Woolley, who would later become a prominent Salt Lake City bishop, brought news from Carthage, Illinois, that the sheriffs were searching for Smith in both Nauvoo and Quincy. As a result, William Law, Amasa Lyman, George Miller, John Parker, Hyrum Smith, Newel K. Whitney, and by a separate path William Clayton brought the news to Smith at his hiding place at Sayers's home. In the new issue of the weekly *Times and Seasons,* Smith could read that Boggs had charged him with being an "accessory before the fact to an assault with intent to kill." As if in justification of such an assault, the paper noted that in 1838 Boggs had issued an "extermination order" against the Mormons in Missouri. Readers of the Mormon paper were recurrently urged to imagine a similar expulsion from their new Illinois home.[226]

---

226. "Persecution," *Times and Seasons,* Aug. 15, 1842, 886-89. The article failed to mention that in an intemperate Fourth of July oration in 1838, Smith's counselor

On Tuesday, August 16, Smith wrote a warm note of "sincere thanks" to Emma "for the two interesting and consoling visits that you have made me during my almost exile situation. Tongue cannot express the gratitude of my heart, for the warm and true-hearted friendship you have manifested in these things toward me." He signed the letter, "your affectionate husband until death, through all eternity; for evermore." As Erastus Derby took this and a letter for Wilson Law and headed toward Nauvoo, Smith recorded some tender thoughts in his journal about his first wife: "With what unspeakable delight, and what transports of joy swelled my bosom, when I took by the hand on that night [August 11] my beloved Emma, that she was my wife, even the wife of my youth and the choice of my heart ... again she is here, even in the seventh trouble, undaunted, firm and unwavering, unchangeable, affectionate Emma."[227] At nightfall, Derby returned, bringing a note from Emma to Joseph offering to come to him that evening, teasing affectionately, "there are more ways than one to take care of you."[228] However, she apparently did not visit that evening.

On that same Tuesday, James Arlington Bennet of New York City wrote to Smith, warning him that John C. Bennett (no relation) was going to publish "an exposition of Mormon secrets and practices." In fact, Bennett was going to turn the tables and accuse Smith of using the same approach with women of which Smith was accusing Bennett,

---

Sidney Rigdon had said: "It shall be between us and them [the Missourians] a war of *extermination,* for we will follow them, till the last drop of their blood is spilled, or else they will have to *exterminate* us" (Quinn, *Mormon Hierarchy Origins,* 96, 336n73, emphasis in original); see Boggs's statement of October 27 that Mormons were in "defiance of the laws" and, "having made war upon the people of the state," should "be exterminated, or driven from the state, if necessary for the public peace" ("Trial of Joseph Smith," *Times and Seasons,* July 15, 1843, 257; see also Stephen C. LeSueur, *The 1838 Mormon War in Missouri* [Colombia: University of Missouri Press, 1987], 37-41, 49-52, 150-53; Richard L. Bushman, *Joseph Smith and the Beginnings of Mormonism* [Urbana: University of Illinois Press, 1984], 354-55). The order was not revoked until 1976 ("The Ex-termination Order and How It Was Rescinded," *John Whitmer Historical Association,* online at www.jwha.info/mmff/exorder.htm).

227. See Jessee, *Papers of Joseph Smith,* 2:415-16; also *History of the Church,* 5:107. "Seventh trouble" may echo the apocalyptic seven angels, seven-headed beast, and seven thunders which some Christians expect at the end of the world (Rev. 10:4, 13:1, 16:17-18).

228. *History of the Church,* 5:110.

and even of having propositioned some of the same women. Bennett was in New York that month on a speaking tour.[229]

On Wednesday, August 17, Emma wrote to Carlin pleading that he spare her husband, while the Relief Society sent the governor a separate petition. Then, under cover of darkness, "Emma came to see me," Joseph recorded. Emma was uneasy, fearing they would be discovered. Her husband had been at the Sayers home six consecutive days; she urged him to move to Carlos Granger's farmhouse, northeast of Nauvoo. It was advice he took. In his diary, repeated in the *History of the Church*, Joseph said he "departed in company with Emma and brother Derby, and went to Carlos Granger's." Emma may have accompanied him the entire distance and stayed the night because Joseph added that "*we* were kindly received and well treated."[230] He neglected to record any events for Thursday, August 18, so there is no indication of exactly when Emma may have left. She likely traveled early Thursday morning in Derby's company, perhaps before first light to avoid being noticed.

It was the ninth night of Joseph's concealment, and Emma had visited him three times, written him several letters, and penned at least one letter on his behalf. She no doubt passed along messages, either written or verbal, from trusted associates. For his part, Joseph's private note about his love for Emma was so endearing it found its way into the official church history. In it, he vowed to be hers "for evermore." Yet within this context of reassurance and intimacy, a few hours later the same day, even while Joseph was still in grave danger and when secrecy was of the utmost urgency, he made complicated arrangements for a visit from his fifteenth plural wife, Sarah Ann Whitney.

On Thursday, August 18, just after Emma's departure, writing in his own hand, Smith urged his seventeen-year-old bride to "come to night" and "comfort" him—but only if Emma had not returned. It is not clear who the courier was—presumably not Emma—but Joseph judiciously addressed the letter to "Brother, and Sister, Whitney, and

229. See Smith, *Saintly Scoundrel*, 65, 108.

230. Jessee, *Papers of Joseph Smith*, 2:418; *History of the Church*, 5:118, emphasis added.

&c." The letter itself leaves no doubt who "&c." was. This extraordinary letter deserves to be reproduced in its entirety:[231]

> Nauvoo August 18th 1842
> Dear, and Beloved, Brother and Sister, Whitney, and &c.—
> I take this oppertunity to communi[c]ate, some of my feelings, privetely at this time, which I want you three Eternaly to keep in your own bosams; for my feelings are so strong for you since what has pased lately between us, that the time of my abscence from you seems so long, and dreary, that it seems, as if I could not live long in this way: and if you three would come and see me in this my lonely retreat, it would afford me great relief, of mind[.] if those with whom I am alied, do love me, now is the time to afford me succour, in the days of exile, for you know I foretold you of these things. I am now at Carlos Graingers, Just back of Brother Hyrams farm[.] it is only one mile from town, the nights are very pleasant, indeed, [and] all three of you can come and See me in the fore part of the night[.] let Brother Whitney come a little a head, and nock at the south East corner of the house at the window; it is next to the cornfield; I have a room intirely by myself, the whole matter can be attended to with most perfect saf[e]ty[.] I know it is the will of God that you should comfort me now in this time of affliction, or not at [a]ll[.] now is the time or never, but I hav[e] no kneed of saying any such thing, to you, for I know the goodness of your hearts, and that you will do the will of the Lord, when it is made known to you; the only thing to be careful of; is to find out when Emma comes [because] then you cannot be safe, but when she is not here, there is the most perfect saf[e]ty: only be careful to escape observation, as much as possible[.] I know it is a heroick undertakeing; but so much the greater frendship, and the more Joy[.] when I see you I will tell you all my plans[.] I cannot write them on paper, burn this letter as soon as you read it; keep all locked up in your breasts, my life depends upon it. one thing I want to see you for is to git the fulness of my blessings sealed upon our heads, &c. You will pardon me for my earnestness on this subject[.] when you consider how lonesome I must be, your good feelings know how to make every allowance for me[.] I close my letter[.] I think Emma wont come to night[.] if she dont[,] dont fail to come to night. I subscribe myself your most obedient, and affectionate, companion, and friend.
> Joseph Smith

231. Smith to Brother and Sister Whitney, and &c., Aug. 18, 1842.

Nauvoo August 18th 1842

Dear, and Beloved, Brother and Sister, Whitney, and &c.—

I take this opportunity to communicate some of my feelings, privately at this time, which I want you three Eternaly to keep in your own bosams; for my feelings are so strong for you since what has pased lately between us, that the time of my absence from you seems so long, and dreary, that it seems, as if I could not live long in this way: and if you three would come and see me in this my lonely retreat, it would afford me great relief, of mind, if those with whom I am alied, do love me, now is the time to afford me succour, in the days of exile, for you know I foretold you of these things. I am now at Carlos Graingers, Just back of Brother Hyrams farm, it is only one mile from town, the nights are very pleasant indeed, all three of you can come and see me in the fore part of the night, let Brother Whitney come a little a head, and nock at the south East corner of the house at the window; it is next to the cornfield; I have a room intirely by myself, the whole matter can be attended to with most perfect safty, I know it is the will of God that you should comfort me now in this time of affliction, or not at all now is the

Joseph Smith invited his newest wife, seventeen-year-old Sarah Ann Whitney, to join him, with her parents' help, in a nighttime visit. The holograph is preserved by LDS Church Archives, Salt Lake City.

time or means, but I have no need of saying
any such thing, to you, for I know the
goodness of your hearts, and that you
will do the will of the Lord, when it is
made known to you; the only thing
to be careful of, is to find out when
Emma comes then you cannot be
safe, but when she is not here, there
is the most perfect safty: only be
careful to escape observation, as
much as possible, I know it is a
heroick undertakeing; but so much
the greater friendship, and the more
Joy, when I see you I will tell you all
my plans, I cannot write them on
paper, burn this letter as soon as you
read it; keep all locked up in
your breasts, my life depends upon it. one thing I want to see you
for is to get the fulness of my blessings
sealed upon our heads, &c. you
will pardon me for my earnest-
ness on this subject when you consider how
lonesome I must be, your good
feelings know how to make every allowance for me, I close my letter,
I think Emma wont come tonight
if she dont dont fail to come to
night, I subscribe myself your
most obedient, and affectionate,
companion, and friend.

Joseph Smith

Twenty-seven years later, on August 13, 1869, Elizabeth Ann Whitney and her daughter Sarah Ann affirmed before James Jack, a notary public and future secretary to the LDS First Presidency, that they had on that day "deposited said letter in the [LDS] Historian's Office in the County and City of Salt Lake." A copy of the letter, which itself became part of this affidavit, was "upon their oath … a true copy of a letter written at Carlos Granger's by President Joseph Smith, dated, Nauvoo August 18th, 1842, to Newel K. and Elizabeth Ann Whitney and their daughter Sarah Ann Smith, who was married or Sealed to President Smith, July 27-1842."[232] Besides confirming the provenance of the letter and accuracy of the copy, Sarah Ann, who identified herself as "Sarah Ann Smith Kimball," affirmed on June 19 that she had been "married or sealed" to Joseph Smith, and in order to leave no stone unturned her mother returned on August 30 and swore to the same.[233]

The summer of 1842 had been an especially tumultuous three months for Joseph Smith and his family, as well as for Latter-day Saints generally—also for a growing assemblage of spouses who wanted to keep their plural marriages confidential, even as their numbers swelled. Smith's calendar between June 29 and his urgent plea for Sarah Ann's "comfort" on August 18 illustrates how compressed his time was.

The Summer of 1842: Joseph's Calendar

Wed., June 29	Marries Eliza Snow.
Wed., July 27	Marries Sarah Ann Whitney while Emma visits governor.
Sat., July 30	Thanks Governor Carlin for seeing Emma.

232. Elizabeth and Sarah A. Whitney, Affidavit, Aug. 13, 1869, in "[Affidavits] Book No. 2," 1869-1870. Danel W. Bachman wrote in 1975 that "on August 13, 1869, Elizabeth and Sarah Ann Whitney brought the letter to Joseph F. Smith" at church headquarters in Salt Lake City. Sarah's father, Newel Whitney, had died in 1849. Elder Smith "copied it into [the Joseph Smith Affidavit] books 2:25-27 and 3:25-27." The copies remained available for researchers but "the location of the original affidavit is unknown at present," Bachman noted ("A Study of the Mormon Practice of Plural Marriage before the Death of Joseph Smith," M.A. thesis, Purdue University, 1975, 162).

233. The 1869 affidavits are excerpted in Smith, *Blood Atonement,* 73, 74.

Fri., Aug. 5	Marries Martha Knight about this time.
Mon., Aug. 8	Is arrested, then released, for May 6 shooting of ex-Missouri Governor Lilburn Boggs.
Wed., Aug. 10	Hides out at Uncle John Smith's house in Zarahemla, Iowa.
Thurs., Aug. 11	Receives Emma on island in Mississippi River; later rows upriver to home of Edward and Ruth Sayers.
Fri., Aug. 12	Emma and Wilson Law write to lawyer to see if Illinois governor intends to pursue arrest.
Sat., Aug. 13	Receives Emma at Sayers home.
Sun., Aug. 14	Reads history with Emma; gives Emma letter to transport to Nauvoo; Eliza Snow moves into Smith home.
Mon., Aug. 15	Wilson Law receives letter regarding Joseph's plans to avoid arrest; Edwin Woolley tells Nauvoo leaders sheriffs want Joseph; William Clayton brings news to Sayers home.
Tues., Aug. 16	Writes love letter to Emma, confides affection for her in diary; she offers to visit him again; James Arlington Bennet writes about John Bennett's forthcoming exposé.
Wed., Aug. 17	Receives Emma again at Sayers home; Emma writes to Illinois governor; Joseph moves to Granger farm with Emma and Derby, who depart about Thursday morning.
Thurs., Aug. 18	Invites Whitneys, including Sarah Ann, to visit, "comfort me," if Emma not there. Offer accepted.

Nancy Rigdon rejects Joseph

As Joseph looked for a way to spend time with his recent wife, the summer of 1842 was not only a time of new beginnings but also a bitter harvest. Among the information John Bennett included in his July and August letters to local newspapers was that Nancy Rigdon, the daughter of one of Smith's counselors in the First Presidency, had refused to marry the prophet that April. Even after failing to convince Martha Brotherton to marry Brigham Young, Smith had continued undeterred in his efforts to persuade young women to accept plural marriage. According to Bennett, the contact with Nancy took place shortly after the funeral of Ephraim Marks on April 9, 1842, two days after Joseph's brother Hyrum had vehemently denied allegations concerning Brotherton that "a sister had been shut in a room for several days" to "induce her to believe in [a man] having two wives" (see chapters 3, 4). Bennett himself had been asked to help "in procuring Nancy as one of my [Joseph's] plural wives." Smith then asked Marinda Hyde, whom he had probably recently married, to arrange for the nineteen-year-old girl to meet him at Marinda's living quarters.[234]

Nancy was born December 8, 1822, to Sidney and Phebe Rigdon, the second of twelve children from 1821 to 1841. Named for her paternal grandmother, this eldest unmarried daughter, a "beautiful girl" of "moral excellence and superior intellectual endowments," as Bennett described her, held a special place in the Rigdon household. In 1819, Sidney had moved from Pennsylvania to Ohio and had given up farming to become a Baptist preacher. He joined the reformed Baptist followers of Alexander Campbell, later designated the Disciples of Christ. When the Mormons entered Ohio in 1830, another one-time Campbellite preacher, Parley Pratt, converted Sidney and Phebe to Joseph Smith's church in November. Rigdon brought with him his own followers to more than double the size of Smith's church. Twelve years older than Smith, Rigdon was an experienced preacher who immediately impressed the twenty-five-year-old prophet. Rigdon was named Smith's first counselor (1833-44), placing him second in rank within the now 200-member "Church of Christ." Oliver Cowdery, once second only to Joseph Smith, left Smith's church in 1837. Another high-ranking member, David Whitmer, declared that as a "scholar," "orator," and Smith's "private counsellor," Rigdon had more influence over Smith than any other man.[235]

Nancy was nearly eight years old when she met the prophet whom her parents had chosen to follow. At nineteen, she nearly became one

---

234. See *History of the Church,* 4:585-86; Bennett, *History of the Saints,* 241-43.

235. David Whitmer, *An Address to All Believers in Christ* (Richmond, Mo.: By the author, 1887), 35. Jesse Gause, a Quaker, was first counselor in 1832. Quinn, *Mormon Hierarchy Origins,* 465.

of Smith's wives, which would have made her the thirteenth wife, including the go-between, Marinda Hyde. The marriage proposal came within a year after Nancy's mother gave birth to her last child. Nancy's father was in many ways a mentor to Joseph—a venerable older man who was an experienced and educated clergyman—and not someone Joseph felt comfortable approaching to ask for his daughter's hand in polygamy. So Joseph appealed to the young woman directly.

On Saturday, April 9, 1842, at the funeral of Ephraim R. Marks, son of Nauvoo Stake President William Marks, Marinda Hyde arranged for Nancy to come to the printing office where Marinda was staying on the corner of Bain and Water streets. The previous year, Smith had arranged for Marinda to live in the first-floor space of the *Times and Seasons* office while her husband was on his mission. She lived with the family of printer Ebenezer Robinson until late January 1842 when the Council of the Twelve purchased the building and told the Robinson family to vacate. For some reason, Marinda stayed and Apostle Willard Richards, whose wife, Jennetta, was in Massachusetts, moved in around February.[236] Although the two may have lived in separate parts of the building, which was three blocks from the Rigdon home and two blocks from the Smiths, their living arrangements seemed to be an open scandal.

From this point on, the accounts vary in some details, although not in essence. Nancy's brother-in-law, George W. Robinson, wrote in a letter to an eastern correspondent on July 27 that "Smith and Bennett have always been on friendly terms, and were together a great deal, and I have no doubt but that Bennett was Smith's confidante in nearly all things." Robinson reported that "Smith sent for Miss Rigdon to come to the house of Mrs. Hyde, who lived in the under rooms of the printing-office." All Nancy knew was that "Smith wanted to see her." When she arrived, he "took her into another room, and locked the door, and then stated to her that he had had an affection for her for

236. *History of the Church,* 4:467, Bennett, *History of the Saints,* 241; Ebenezer Robinson, *The Return,* Oct. 1890, 347. Joseph Smith wrote to Jenetta Richards on June 23, 1842, to tell her that when she saw her husband, "he will be able to teach you many things which you have never heard; you may have implicit confidence in the same" (*History of the Church,* 5: 40).

several years and wished that she should be his." Smith assured her that he had "got a revelation on the subject" and that there was "no sin in it whatever; but, if she had any scruples of conscience about the matter, he would marry her privately, and enjoined her to secrecy." Displeased with the suggestion, Nancy "repulsed him, and was about to raise the neighbors if he did not unlock the door and let her out; and she left him with disgust, and came home." Eventually, she "told her father of the transaction."[237]

According to Nancy's younger brother John, when Joseph was sent for and confronted with what he had done, he "attempted to deny it." Nancy told the family he was not telling the truth. Addressing him directly, she said: "You did make such a proposition to me and you know it."[238] "She told the tale in the presence of all the family, and to Smith's face," Robinson said, adding: "I was present. Smith attempted to deny it at first, and face her down with the lie; but she told the facts with so much earnestness, and the fact of a letter being present, which he had caused to be written to her, on the same subject, the day after the attempt made on her virtue," that he could not persist with his prevarication. He had perhaps "fondly hoped" that the letter had been destroyed; instead, "all came with such force that he could not withstand the testimony." He "then and there acknowledged that every word of Miss Rigdon's testimony was true." Robinson explained that he had "reason to believe General Bennett's … disclosures of Smith's rascality." Robinson recognized that he was "not a witness to all of the facts, yet I am to some."[239]

In an affidavit in Salt Lake City on July 28, 1905, Nancy's brother John told a slightly different story. He was seventy-five years of age by then. The main point was the same: Smith had "made a proposition to my sister, Nancy Rigdon, to become his wife." In his memory, so long after the fact, he thought the year had been 1843 rather than 1842 and that the invitation for Nancy to visit had been extended at a church

237. George W. Robinson to James Arlington Bennet, July 27, 1842, LDS Archives; Bennett, *History of the Saints,* 245-47.

238. John Wyckliffe Rigdon, "The Life Story of Sidney Rigdon," 166, cited in Van Wagoner, *Sidney Rigdon,* 296.

239. Robinson to Bennett, July 27, 1842.

service rather than a funeral. It was an "old lady friend who lived alone," he recalled.[240] But if John Wyckliffe Rigdon remembered anything clearly, it was his sister's indignation: "Nancy flatly refused him, saying if she ever got married she would marry a single man or none at all, and thereupon took her bonnet and went home, leaving Joseph at the old lady's house." He said "the story got out and it became the talk of the town," also that their father was "wild with fury."[241]

If Bennett's April 9 date for the proposition is correct, then it places the following carefully phrased letter from Joseph to Nancy, written about April 10, in an intriguing context.[242]

> Happiness is the object and design of our existence; and will be the end thereof, if we pursue the path that leads to it; and this path is virtue, uprightness, faithfulness, holiness, and keeping all the commandments of God. But we cannot keep all the commandments without first knowing them, and we cannot expect to know all, or more than we now know unless we comply with or keep those we have already received. *That which is wrong under one circumstance, may be, and often is, right under another.*
>
> God said, "Thou shalt not kill;" at another time He said "Thou shalt

240. This friend does not sound like Marinda Hyde. Although Nancy was only nineteen and Marinda was twenty-six, Nancy probably would not have described her as an "old lady." Smith's older wives who acted as courtship go-betweens were Patty Sessions, age forty-seven, Elizabeth Durfee, age fifty-one, and Sarah Cleveland, age fifty-four, but none of them lived alone. Nevertheless, considering the proximity in time of Bennett's attribution of the invitation to Marinda Hyde, she is evidently the person he had in mind.

241. John W. Rigdon, Affidavit, July 28, 1905, in "Affidavits [on Celestial Marriage], 1869-1915." George F. Gibbs explained that Rigdon gave two statements, one of which was published in Smith, *Blood Atonement,* 81-85.

242. Smith's letter followed his April 9 request for a meeting with Nancy but preceded his June 28 visit to the Rigdons. Robinson dates it to "the day after the attempt was made on her virtue" (Robinson to Bennett, July 27, 1842; Bennett, *History of the Saints,* 246). John C. Bennett wrote that it was "in a day or two [that] Dr. [Willard] Richards … handed her the following letter from the Prophet Joe, (written by Richards, by Joe's dictation,) and requested her to burn it after reading" (*History of the Saints,* 242-43). On September 10, John F. Olney confirmed that "the letter published purporting to be from Smith to Miss Rigdon, was not in Smith's hand-writing, but in the hand-writing of Dr. Willard Richards—who did say that he wrote the letter as dictated by Joseph Smith" (*Sangamo Journal,* Sept. 14, 1842; Bennett, *History of the Saints,* 249-51). Church Historian B. H. Roberts accepted the letter as authentic (*History of the Church,* 5:134n).

utterly destroy." This is the principle on which the government of heaven is conducted—by revelation adapted to the circumstances in which the children of the kingdom are placed. *Whatever God requires is right, no matter what it is, although we may not see the reason thereof till long after the events transpire.* If we seek first the kingdom of God, all good things will be added. So with Solomon: first he asked wisdom, and God gave it him, and with it every desire of his heart, even things which might be considered abominable to all who understand the order of heaven only in part, but which in reality were right because God gave and sanctioned by special revelation.

A parent may whip a child, and justly, too, because he stole an apple; whereas if the child had asked for the apple, and the parent had given it, the child would have eaten it with a better appetite; there would have been no stripes; all the pleasure of the apple would have been secured, all the misery of stealing lost.

This principle will justly apply to all of God's dealings with His children. Everything that God gives us is lawful and right; and it is proper that we should enjoy His gifts and blessings whenever and wherever He is disposed to bestow; but if we should seize upon those same blessings and enjoyments without law, without revelation, without commandment, those blessings and enjoyments would prove cursings and vexations in the end, and we should have to lie down in sorrow and wailings of everlasting regret. But in obedience there is joy and peace unspotted, unalloyed; and as God has designed our happiness—and the happiness of all His creatures, he never has—He never will institute an ordinance or give a commandment to His people that is not calculated in its nature to promote that happiness which He has designed, and which will not end in the greatest amount of good and glory to those who become the recipients of his law and ordinances. Blessings offered, but rejected, are no longer blessings, but become like the talent hid in the earth by the wicked and slothful servant; the proffered good returns to the giver; the blessing is bestowed on those who will receive and occupy; for unto him that hath shall be given, and he shall have abundantly, but unto him that hath not or will not receive, shall be taken away that which he hath, or might have had.

> Be wise today; 'tis madness to defer:
> Next day the fatal precedent may plead.
> Thus on till wisdom is pushed out of time
> Into eternity.

> Our heavenly Father is more liberal in His views, and boundless in His mercies and blessings, than we are ready to believe or receive; and, at the same time, is more terrible to the workers of iniquity, more awful in the executions of His punishments, and more ready to detect every false way, than we are apt to suppose Him to be. He will be inquired of by His children. He says: "Ask and ye shall receive, seek and ye shall find;" but, if you will take that which is not your own, or which I have not given you, you shall be rewarded according to your deeds; but no good thing will I withhold from them who walk uprightly before me, and do my will in all things—who will listen to my voice and to the voice of my servant whom I have sent; for I delight in those who seek diligently to know my precepts, and abide by the law of my kingdom; for all things shall be made known unto them in mine own due time, and in the end they shall have joy.[243]

In addition to his confession to members of the immediate Rigdon family, Smith also acknowledged to Rigdon's cousin, Samuel James, that "he had approached Nancy Rigdon and asked her to become his spiritual wife." According to James's telling, Smith complained that Nancy "had to go and blab it."[244] As Sidney Rigdon's biographer wrote, the letter made its way from Nancy to "her suitor Frances Higbee, twenty-three-year-old son of Elias Higbee. Higbee passed it on to John C. Bennett, who published it in his book."[245] After publishing the letter, Bennett reported that "the original, of which the above is a literal copy, in the hand-writing of Dr. [Willard] Richards, is now in my possession. It was handed me by Colonel F[rancis] M. Higbee, in the presence of General George W. Robinson."[246]

---

243. *Sangamo Journal,* Aug. 19, 1842; *Essential Joseph Smith,* 158-59; Bennett, *History of the Saints,* 243-45; *History of the Church,* 5:134-36, emphasis added.

244. See Rigdon, "Life Story," 169.

245. Van Wagoner, *Sidney Rigdon,* 307n46. See also the discussion of Nancy Rigdon and Francis Higbee in Gary James Bergera, "Buckeye's Laments: Two Early Insider Exposés of Mormon Polygamy and Their Authorship," *Journal of the Illinois State Historical Society* 95 (Winter 2003): 350-90.

246. Bennett, *History of the Saints,* 245. Bennett published Smith's letter to Rigdon in the *Sangamo Journal* on August 19, 1842, leading B. H. Roberts to conclude the "essay" was written about that time (*History of the Church,* 5:134-36). Curiously, Roberts connected "happiness" with a "plurality of wives," even though it would be another year before the revelation authorizing plural marriages would be received. Roberts apparently felt no scruples over seeing the maxim, that "whatever God requires is right,"

Nancy married Robert Ellis Jr. in September 1846, gave birth to nine children from 1847-65, and died in November 1887 in Pittsburgh. Her father had died a decade earlier in Friendship, Allegheny County, New York.

It is significant to note the coincident timing of Smith's failed endeavors to court a wife for himself and a wife for Brigham Young: Both occurred about the first of April 1842. At that time, and apparently under Smith's direction, both Nancy and Martha were approached by several elders in a building apart from public access; each young woman was isolated in a locked room during the persuasive effort. These measures signaled an urgency in the spring of 1842 to convince new plural wives. What would have precipitated such urgency? Smith married three women in March and one in April; initiated the Female Relief Society on March 17; established a Masonic Lodge that month; published his "Book of Abraham" translations on March 1-15; and on May 4 in the upper room of his red brick store initiated what he declared were the complete temple endowment ceremonies.[247] It was in this highly innovative period that he also decided to advance plural marriage for his followers as well as for himself.

If ever there was a time when Smith's daily events seemed to careen haphazardly, thrusting him into the center of controversy, it was with the approach of summer 1842. If his claim to heavenly revelation did not arouse enough public curiosity and outcry, rumors of plural marriage did. His private life was under attack, as he had to endure the public fusillade of John Bennett. Those who defended Joseph in 1842—William Law and others—would be alerted to the seriousness of the problem through Joseph's 1843 revelation, validating what Joseph continued to deny in public.

---

applied to plural marriage. Contrary to Rigdon, Bennett said Joseph wrote the "letter" "a day or two" following the Thursday meeting, about Friday, April 15. On May 12-13, Smith spoke to Sidney Rigdon about "certain difficulties or surmises" on the part of the Rigdons and "certain evil reports—about some of Elder Rigdon's family." The prophet was clearly concerned about the Rigdons' reaction to his propositioning Nancy.

247. See Buerger, *Mysteries of Godliness,* 59.

Martha Knight

wife number 17
a widow
August 1842

As if Sarah Ann Whitney's liaison were not enough, or that of Sarah Poulterer, another marriage took place early in August 1842, this time to Martha Knight. As a McBride, Martha had grown up the youngest of nine children in New York State. Her parents were Campbellite Baptists. In 1826, at age twenty-one, she married a farmer and livestock man, Vinson Knight.

Smith met the Knights in 1833, seven years after they married. One year later, in 1834, after Joseph had resided in their house near Buffalo, Vinson and Martha joined his church. They lived close to him, building a house in Nauvoo on the corner of Kimball and Main streets; when Vinson died, Martha supported herself by renting out the downstairs portion of the house. Interestingly, Vinson was one of the earliest of Smith's followers to enter plural marriage. In mid-1842, he married Philinda Merrick. According to Martha's affidavit, sworn on July 8, 1869, she agreed to marry Smith shortly after Vinson's July 31, 1842, death.

> Be it remembered that on this eighth day of July, A.D. 1869, personally appeared before me[,] Edward Partridge, Probate Judge in and for said county, Martha McBride Kimball, who was by me sworn[,] in due form of law, and upon her oath saith that sometime in the summer of the year 1842, at the city of Nauvoo, county of Hancock, state of Illinois, she was married or sealed to Joseph Smith, President of the Church of Jesus Christ of Latter-day Saints, by Heber C. Kimball, one of the Twelve Apostles in said Church, according to the laws of the same [in] regulating marriage.

After her death in November 1901, Martha's obituary further specified that she had been sealed to Joseph "in August, 1842."[248] She had been about the same age as Joseph. The marriage probably occurred between Vinson's death at the end of July and Joseph's arrest

248. Compton cites Martha McBride Knight's obituary in a discussion of marriage dating (*Sacred Loneliness*, 724).

TABLE 2.1 Three seasons, fifteen marriages

season	name	age	status of polygamy	
winter, 1841-42	Zina Jacobs	20	polygyny /	polyandry
"	Presendia Buell	31	"	"
"	Agnes Smith	30	"	
"	Lucinda Harris	40	"	"
"	Mary Elizabeth Lightner	23	"	"
"	Sylvia Lyon	23	"	"
"	Patty Sessions	47	"	"
spring, 1842	Sarah Cleveland	53	"	"
"	Elizabeth Durfee	50	"	"
"	Marinda Hyde	26	"	"
"	Delcena Sherman	35	"	
summer, 1842	Eliza Snow	38	"	
"	Sarah Poulterer	49	"	"
"	Sarah Ann Whitney	17	"	
"	Martha Knight	37	"	

on August 8. During the following period of time, Smith was fully occupied in defending himself against Bennett's accusations of plural marriage, seduction, and religious rationalization, all of which the prophet still denied.[249]

It may be that Joseph married Martha on Friday, August 5, when his diary says he was "engaged in a variety of business" prior to a city council meeting at 6:00 p.m. On Saturday he attended a Masonic Lodge installation in Montrose, Iowa. On Sunday he was "at home all day." On Monday he was arrested.[250] If this was the window of opportunity, it means that Martha would have been a widow less than a week before she re-married. This would be similar to the circumstances surrounding Delcena Sherman and Agnes Smith, both of whom were recently widowed when they married Smith.

Two years later, when Martha was widowed again by Joseph's death, she became Heber Kimball's twelfth plural wife on October 12, 1844. On January 26, 1846, she re-solemnized her marriage to Smith

249. Ibid., 371.
250. Jessee, *Papers of Joseph Smith,* 2:401-02; *History of the Church,* 5:84-86.

for eternity and to Kimball as a companion for time, leaving Vinson in limbo. Following Kimball to Utah, she lived in the west until age ninety-six, often with her own children rather than with Kimball or his family.

During the winter of 1841-42, Smith married a total of six women, followed by four more in the spring of 1842 and five more in the summer. In three short seasons, he had solemnized fifteen of his thirty-seven plural marriages. Ten of these women were already married, three were widows, and two were single; they ranged in age from seventeen to fifty-three, with a mean age of thirty-five.

An interesting aspect of the marriages (see Table 3.3, Joseph's courtships and Emma's pregnancies, p. 238) is that they overlap Joseph's marital involvement with Emma, who conceived an unnamed son in May 1841, just after the April ceremony between Joseph and his first plural wife, Louisa Beaman. Emma conceived Joseph's last child, David Hyrum, in February 1844, the same month Joseph's professed daughter, Josephine Rosetta Lyon, was born to his plural wife, Sylvia Sessions Lyon. This table in chapter 3 concludes a discussion of all of Joseph's wives as we consider *Emma's dilemma* in evaluating her marriage with Joseph.

THREE.

A Pause, More Wives, and a Revelation

"Ten virgins . . . given by this law"

For about six months between August 1842 and February 1843, Joseph Smith may have courted but, according to available records, did not marry additional wives. Even so, he taught "the principle" to his apostles who had returned from their missions to England through the latter half of 1841. By year-end 1842, and likely before the six-month pause, four of Smith's associates had married additional women.

On August 19, eleven days after Smith's brief arrest for the Boggs shooting, John Bennett published the prophet's letter to Nancy Rigdon in the *Sangamo Journal.* Ten days later, on August 29, 1842—a month after Smith tried to defame Nancy Rigdon in a *Wasp Extra* and several days after Orson Pratt, Sidney Rigdon, and George W. Robinson declined to affirm Smith's good character—Smith assailed his critics: "I have the whole plan of the kingdom before me, and no other person has. And as to all that Orson Pratt, Sidney Rigdon, and George W. Robinson can do to prevent me, I can kick them off my heels, as many as you can name; I know what will become of them."[1]

1. Joseph Smith et al., *History of the Church of Jesus Christ of Latter-day Saints,* ed. B. H. Roberts, 2nd ed. rev., 7 vols. (Salt Lake City: Deseret Book, 1963), 5:124, 139. The *Times and Seasons,* Aug. 1, 1842, 869, confirms a negative vote of "two or three" on Smith's character, explaining Smith's assault the next month on three naysayers: Pratt,

On the last day of August, Smith addressed the Relief Society, as recorded in the *History of the Church,* in a manner reminiscent of his defensive letter to Nancy Rigdon. "Altho' I do wrong, I do not the wrongs that I am charg'd with doing," he told the Relief Society. "The wrong that I do is thro' the frailty of human nature like other men. No man lives without fault. Do you think that even Jesus, if he were here[,] would be without fault in your eyes? … If you know anything, hold your tongues, and the least harm will be done."[2]

The next day, the *Times and Seasons* reprinted the following conference resolution dismissing polygamy:

> All legal contracts of marriage made before a person is baptized into this church, should be held sacred and fulfilled. Inasmuch as this church of Christ has been reproached with the crime of fornication, and polygamy: we declare that we believe, that one man should have one wife; and one woman, but one husband.[3]

Like the anxious month of August, the next month was similarly filled with threats, charges, and refutations. On the first Saturday, Smith received a note at his office telling him to escape "out of the back door" because Missouri marshals were waiting for him out front.[4] The following Monday, September 5, the Relief Society sent a petition to Governor Carlin asking for protection for Smith, claiming that John Bennett's accusations were "bare-faced, unblushing falsehoods."[5] Two days later, Carlin replied: "I … must express my surprise at the extraordinary assumption of power by the [Nauvoo] board of alderm[e]n" in claiming authority to "release persons held in custody under the authority of writs issued by the courts or the executive of the state." He found this to be "most absurd and ridiculous" and stated that it was a "gross usurpation of power that cannot be tolerated."[6]

Rigdon, and Robinson; the *History of the Church* asserts that "almost every hand was raised and no opposite vote was called for."

2. "A Book of Records Containing the Proceedings of the Female Relief Society of Nauvoo," Aug. 21, 1842, 80-81, in *History of the Church,* 5:139.
3. Doctrine and Covenants (1835) 101:4, in *Times and Seasons,* Sept. 1, 1842, 909.
4. *History of the Church,* 5:144-46.
5. Ibid., 5:146-48.
6. Ibid., 5:153-55.

The Nauvoo charter, which was the basis for this presumption of independence from state jurisdiction, would in fact be repealed about seven months after Smith's death.[7]

Beset by internal unrest and at the same time afraid of arrest from outside, Smith denounced Bennett's forthcoming book as a "curse" to all who might touch it. On September 9 he sent Heber Kimball, Amasa Lyman, Charles Rich, George A. Smith, and Brigham Young to preach against Bennett throughout the entire state of Illinois.[8] The following Monday, the feared author completed his manuscript for the *History of the Saints;* it would be quickly published in less than two months in Boston. In the interim, James Arlington Bennet wrote to Smith advising him to let the author "depart in peace." But it was too late, because John had already left Nauvoo, although not in peace. Putting the best possible face on it, James Bennet, himself a Long Island publisher, predicted that the book would add "notoriety" to Smith's reputation and thereby draw new converts to Nauvoo.[9]

For October 1, the only report in the *History of the Church* was that construction on the Nauvoo temple was continuing. But in the adjacent state, storm clouds were forming. The next day, as the official history reports, Missouri Governor Thomas Reynolds offered a $300 reward for the capture of Smith and Rockwell. Sidney Rigdon warned Smith four days later that Carlin was planning to lure Smith to Carthage, Illinois, with an illegal writ Smith knew would be declared void so officers standing by could serve a legal arrest warrant and "bear him away to Missouri."[10] A week later, the official church history shows Nauvoo leaders again consumed with practical matters, such as the cost of 90,000 board feet of Wisconsin lumber for the temple and a new hotel called the Nauvoo House. During this time of apparent tranquility, someone with the improbable name of Udney Hay Jacob published a pamphlet called *The Peace Maker,* a thirty-seven-page defense of polygamy. Larry Foster has cited this October 1842 publi-

7. See chapter 2.
8. *History of the Church,* 5:157-60.
9. Ibid., 5:162-64.
10. Ibid., 5:168.

cation as the "only explicit defense of polygamy" published under Mormon auspices before the public announcement in Utah nearly ten years later. The presumed author, who was in fact a real person, was said to be a non-Mormon, although the title page identified him as "a shepherd of Israel" and gave "J. Smith" as the "printer." It is interesting that the pamphlet appeared during the hiatus in the erstwhile marriage frenzy of 1842 and while Smith's apostles were traveling the countryside to counter Bennett's words and deny polygamy. The Jacobs publication also appeared just as some of Smith's lieutenants were cautiously entering polygamy and the same month Bennett's *History of the Saints* appeared. Nauvoo leaders continued to deny Bennett's lurid revelations, which were nevertheless confirmed by women who had spurned Smith's romantic proposals.[11] The day after publication of the polygamy defense, on Saturday, October 29, Smith greeted church members arriving from Long Island, New York. News of any impending turmoil would pierce the normalcy of ongoing construction projects and the settling of immigrants.[12]

Without specifying polygamy, the official record hinted that Smith may have been courting new plural wives on Tuesday, November 1, when he and his secretary, William Clayton, rode out to the farm Smith owned and that was managed by Melissa Lott's father. They presumably saw the eighteen-year-old girl, whom Smith would marry withing a year.[13] A week later, Smith called on Windsor P. Lyon, whose wife, Sylvia Sessions, had married Smith the previous winter.[14] Was the prophet visiting a recent bride? In the *Times and Seasons* for December 1, he denied he was personally "sanctioning a community of wives and goods, with polygamy."[15]

As he withstood such pressure bearing down on his Camelot from all sides, he employed church spokesmen to deny polygamy. He himself continued to exchange insults with Bennett as he tried to deflect

---

11. Lawrence Foster, "A Little-Known Defense of Polygamy from the Mormon Press in 1842," *Dialogue: A Journal of Mormon Thought* 9 (Winter 1974): 21-34.

12. *History of the Church,* 5:181.

13. Ibid., 5:182. Was it a visit to another Lott daughter? See 223n202.

14. Ibid., 5:184.

15. "Mormons, or Latter Day Saints," *Times and Seasons,* Dec. 1, 1842, 27-28.

any tangible charges of immorality. This program of disinformation was only partly successful. When Gustavus Hills was brought before the Nauvoo Stake High Council on September 3 for "illicit intercourse with a certain woman by the name of Mary Clift," his defense was that he had not done anything the church leaders had not done.[16] He was disfellowshipped.[17]

This struggle to define orthodoxy while punishing heresy made it all the more difficult for Joseph and his fellow polygamists to go about their days unobserved. Bennett's confirmation of Smith's wives already had meant that a strategy of simply denying the practice was running thin. As it turned out, Smith had only two years left before further exposure would come through the independent newspaper, the *Nauvoo Expositor.* Two years thereafter, the entire Mormon community would be expelled from Illinois, primarily because of the dominant sense they betrayed public trust. The real question was how far the church leadership would take things before they were forced to leave Illinois. It turned out that in the remaining years in Nauvoo, Smith would take measures further to ratchet up the tension and isolate the city from the state by antagonizing non-Mormons, including the multiplication of wives—from a few score married to a handful of men in early 1843 to the better part of a thousand with over a hundred husbands. With so many people involved, polygamy became the city's least kept secret.

The six-month breather that divided Smith's known marriages up to August 1842 from those that began again in February 1843 was mostly due to Bennett's unwanted publicity. However, the scandal began to fade into the background, leaving Smith feeling emboldened in 1843 to add eight more women to his entourage of thirteen. Other privileged men of Nauvoo married even more. In addition, six further marriages for which the evidence is less definite have to be placed in the autumn of 1843.

---

16. Nauvoo Stake High Council Minutes, Sept. 3, 1842, LDS Archives, Salt Lake City.

17. See discussion of Theodore Turley in chapter 5; see also Gary James Bergera, "'Illicit Intercourse,' Plural Marriage, and the Nauvoo Stake High Council, 1840-44," *John Whitmer Historical Journal* 23 (2003): 75-77.

Three other men joined Smith's inner circle of plurality in January and February 1843: his scribe Willard Richards, his secret brother-in-law William Huntington (brother of Zina and Presendia Huntington), and Apostle Orson Hyde, whose wife, Marinda, Smith had married the previous April while Orson was on a mission. By February, a total of seven men had joined Smith in marrying extra wives (see chapters 4 and 5).

In the growing company of other men and their plural families—soon totaling twenty polygamous men—Joseph's fervor was re-ignited and perhaps even augmented by the growing political opposition. Midway through the year, he would convince his most faithful adherents that all was proceeding according to God's will. He would do so by dictating a revelation on the subject. This would prove faith-shattering to those who had assumed that the accusations of polygamy were based on vicious rumors. In fact, the surge in new wives after the 1843 revelation would fan the sparks of internal revolt that would eventually leave Nauvoo in flames.

Ruth Sayers

wife number 18
a married woman
February 1843

Thirty-five-year-old Ruth Vose and husband, Edward Sayers, had concealed Smith from a Missouri sheriff in August 1842. Now she would become Smith's first known wife of the subsequent year— his seventeenth plural and eleventh polyandrous wife. At this point, Joseph and Emma had been married sixteen years and had four children, ages eleven (Julia), nine (Joseph III), six (Frederick), and four (Alexander).

Joseph most likely met Ruth eleven years earlier in Boston when he was there prior to returning to Kirtland in the wake of his oldest son's birth on November 6, 1832.[18] Ruth was born near Boston in February 1808 and had worked in the upholstery business with her "Aunt

18. *History of the Church*, 1:295.

Polly," Mary Vose. Polly converted to Mormonism in July 1832, along with several other Boston women who accepted the missionaries' preaching. Among them were a future Joseph Smith bride, Agnes Coolbrith; a possible future wife, Vienna Jacques; and Mary Bailey, who married Joseph's brother Samuel. Agnes was four years older than Joseph, who was thirty-seven when they married. Mary was four years younger than Samuel. Jacques, by comparison, was eighteen years older than Smith.

In January 1841 at age thirty-two, Ruth married the "horticulturist and florist" Edward Sayers, and the couple moved to Nauvoo that same year.[19] Smith took refuge in the Sayers's home for seven days in August 1842 and spent some time there with Emma before moving to the Granger farm.

Ruth confirmed by affidavit on May 1, 1869, in Salt Lake City that in February 1843 she "was married or sealed to Joseph Smith[,] President of the Church of Jesus Christ of Latter Day Saints, by Hyrum Smith, Presiding Patriarch." Ruth and Edward continued to live together in Nauvoo until 1844 and then returned to Boston for a few years. There is a possible problem with the sealing date, however, since Hyrum apparently did not seem to accept his brother's teachings on plural marriage until May 1843 (see chapter 5). Ruth may be mistaken about the exact date or whether Hyrum was involved, although a plural marriage between Sayers and Smith certainly took place about this time.[20]

19. Emmeline Wells, "Ruth Sayers," *Woman's Exponent* 13 (Sept. 15, 1884): 61, in Todd Compton, *In Sacred Loneliness: The Plural Wives of Joseph Smith* (Salt Lake City: Signature Books, 1997), 383. Frontier florists were few and far between. Wilford Woodruff commented on Sayers's ornamental plants in Utah (Scott G. Kenney, ed., *Wilford Woodruff's Journal,* 9 vols. [Midvale, Utah: Signature Books, 1983], 5:66), saying "he had a fine lot of Black & yellow wild Cu- from Boston & Nauvoo bottoms." The handwriting is difficult, but Woodruff may have meant the popular garden plant for the time, the "black coleus," with two-color leaves. Cornelia Woodcock Ferris, *The Mormons at Home* (New York: Dix & Edwards, 1856), 185-86, was delighted by Sayers's garden, "a jewel in a swine's snout"; Sayers himself "an extravagant lover of flowers" with everything showing "neatness and taste." For Sayers's occupation in Nauvoo, where he laid out gardens and pruned trees, see Robert Bruce Flanders, *Nauvoo: Kingdom on the Mississippi* (Urbana: University of Illinois Press, 1965), 52.

20. "40 Affidavits on Celestial Marriage," 1869, a collection of six folders compiled by Joseph F. Smith, Joseph F. Smith Collection, LDS Archives. See also Gary

It is not known whether Ruth was actually intimate with Joseph—or for that matter with Edward, because she apparently did not have children; but after Joseph's death, she was one of the few wives who declined to be resealed to him. In 1849 the Sayerses moved to Salt Lake City, where she died thirty-five years later. It is difficult to imagine what Joseph and Ruth's brief married life was like. Whatever continuity they found in their relationship, her husband indulged his wife's involvement with the Saints. Known as "Brother Sayers," he was nevertheless not a member of the church and may not have known the full nature of his wife's association with Smith.

Even as history was being made in early 1843, Joseph was carving out time to record his own version of his life story. At the close of 1842, he wrote that he "read and revised my history with Secy [Willard] Richards."[21] Although he had returned a salvo of charges against John Bennett, he found his adversary still to be very much in the game. On January 10, 1843, Bennett wrote to Sidney Rigdon and Orson Pratt that Smith would again be arrested for the attempted assassination of Boggs and that new proceedings would be brought on the old charges: "Although Smith thinks he is now safe, the enemy is near, even at the door. He has awoke the wrong passenger."[22]

Joseph seemed undeterred. The same month he married Sayers, he was re-elected mayor of Nauvoo on February 6.[23] He seemed to have the unchallenged last word in all matters of church and state. In February 1843, he used a homely metaphor with temple workmen to emphasize the point: "There is a great deal of murmuring in the Church about me; but I don't care anything about it. I like to hear it thunder, and I like to hear the Saints grumble; for the growling dog gets the sorest head. … If any are hungry or naked … come and tell me, and I will divide with them to the last morsel; and then if the man is not satisfied, I will kick his backside."[24]

James Bergera, "Identifying the Earliest Mormon Polygamists, 1841-44," *Dialogue: A Journal of Mormon Thought* 38 (Fall 2005): 31-32.

21. *History of the Church,* 5:207.
22. Ibid., 5:250-51.
23. Ibid., 5:264. Smith replaced Bennett as mayor on May 19, 1842 (5:12).
24. Ibid., 5:285-86.

In the same speech, Smith addressed Bennett's specific charge that "Joe Smith" or any eminent leader had married women of the Relief Society, the "Mormon seraglio" as Bennett called it. The Relief Society was said to be having difficulty investigating moral lapses because the women never knew if one of their sisters had (1) fallen from virtue "without the sanction or knowledge of the Prophet"; (2) indulged their "sensual propensities" by "express permission of the Prophet"; or (3) had been given to a man to satisfy his affection for a woman, whether or not she was already married, and received as his "spiritual wife."[25]

The charge that Smith had married a good number of Relief Society sisters was proven true by LDS Apostle Joseph F. Smith in 1869 when he collected affidavits from the women who were involved in the formative period of the organization. At the time Bennett had made the accusation of licentiousness, the prophet had simply turned Bennett's charge back on the Relief Society itself:

> There is a great noise in the city, and many are saying there cannot be so much smoke without some fire. Well, be it so. If the stories about Joe Smith are true, then the stories of John C. Bennett are true about the ladies of Nauvoo; and he says that the Ladies' Relief Society are all organized of those who are to be the wives of Joe Smith. Ladies, you know whether this is true or not. It is no use living among hogs without a snout. This biting and devouring each other … For God's sake, stop it.[26]

The metaphor of smoke was apt: that if smoke implied fire, then when they implicated him they implicated themselves. It was a warning rather than a denial, followed by a threat:

> 'Tis right, politically, for a man who has influence to use it, … The pagans, Roman Catholics, Methodists and Baptists shall have place in Nauvoo—only they must be ground in Joe Smith's mill. I have been in their mill. I was ground in Ohio and York States, in a Presbyterian smut machine [that separated wheat from dust], … I have been through the

---

25. John C. Bennett, *History of the Saints* (1842; Urbana: University of Illinois Press, 2000), 220-23.

26. *History of the Church,* 5:286.

> Illinois smut machine; and those who come here must go through my smut machine, and that is my tongue.[27]

Flora Ann Woodworth

wife number 19
an unmarried woman
March 1843

Lucien Woodworth was one of the many migrants who found work in upstate New York at the completion of the canals. In Vermont he had been an architect and stone mason. After settling in Otsego County, New York, he met and married his wife, Phebe Watrous. She gave birth to their first child, Flora, in November 1826. Six years later they followed the Susquehanna River southwest into Pennsylvania, where they met the Mormons and were baptized. Flora was about six years old at the time. They moved with the church to Missouri, then to Illinois, where Lucien worked on Joseph Smith's hotel, the Nauvoo House, and on the Nauvoo temple. On March 4, 1843, sixteen-year-old Flora Ann married the thirty-seven-year-old prophet.[28]

Smith's secretary, William Clayton, stated in his 1874 affidavit that the ceremony occurred in the season of the May 1843 marriage to Lucy Walker: "During this period the Prophet Joseph took several other wives," Clayton wrote, including Helen Kimball, Eliza and Emily Partridge, Sarah Ann Whitney, and Flora Woodworth. Smith told him that "these all … were his lawful, wedded wives, according to the celestial order" and that "his wife Emma was cognizant of the fact of some, if not all, of these being his wives, and she generally treated them very kindly."[29]

The secrecy to which the women pledged themselves was poignantly illustrated when a young man, Orange Lysander Wight, tried to date Flora, a seemingly single young woman. Sometime in June 1843,

27. Ibid., 5:286-87.

28. See Compton, *Sacred Loneliness*, 389-91, 728. See *Nauvoo Polygamy* App. B, 651n367.

29. Clayton affidavit, Feb. 16, 1874, in *An Intimate Chronicle: The Journals of William Clayton*, ed. George D. Smith (Salt Lake City: Signature Books and Smith Research Associates, 1991), 557.

Wight returned to Nauvoo from New York and Pennsylvania, where he had been a missionary, and "concluded to lo[o]k about and try to pick up one or more of the young Ladies before they were all Gone ... [S]o I commenced keeping company with Flora Woodworth ... Daughter of Lucien Woodworth." One day as Wight was walking Flora down the street, Smith passed in a carriage and offered to take them for a ride:

> He opend the doore for us and when we were seated oposite to him he told the driver to drive on[.] [W]e went to the [Nauvoo] Temple lot and many other places during the Afternoon and then he drove to the Woodworth house and we got out and went in ... After we got in the house[,] sister Woodworth [Flora's mother] took me in an other room and told me that Flora was one of Joseph's wives, I was awar[e] or believed that Eliza R. Snow and the two Pa[r]trage Girls were his wives but was not informed about Flora[.] But now Sister Woodworth gave me all the information ness[ec]ary, so I knew Joseph Believed and practiced Poligamy ... Now as a matter of corse I at once after giving her [Flora] a mild lecture left her and looked for a companion in other places and where I could be more sure.[30]

The nineteen-year-old Orange, son of Lyman Wight, did not hold an ecclesiastic or civic position and was therefore not allowed into the inner social circle in the church town. Yet if a young man like Wight, not fully aware of the interconnections of the polygamous network, realized that Eliza Snow and the Partridge sisters had married Smith, it would seem that celestial marriage was a poorly concealed secret in Nauvoo. Emma may have known all too clearly about such relationships, including Flora's. On the other hand, it is difficult to know to what extent Orange's recollection might have been colored by later disclosures.

George A. Smith told Joseph Smith III about polygamy in an October 9, 1869, letter. Despite having been "intimately acquainted" with Joseph III's father, George A. wrote, he was nevertheless "greatly

30. Orange Lysander Wight, Untitled Reminiscence, 1903, LDS Archives. See also Jeremy Benton Wight, *The Wild Ram of the Mountain: The Story of Lyman Wight* (Bedford, Wyo.: Star Valley Llama, 1996), 211-12.

astonished at hearing from [Joseph Smith's] lips" in 1843 the text of the revelation on "patriarchal marriage." George A. named nine of Joseph's wives and the dates of their marriages, demonstrating his familiarity with the details from the time he first heard of the practice.[31] Such informed sources, augmented by collected affidavits from the network of wives, suggest that by 1843-44 more people in Nauvoo than just a few close advisors were aware of Smith's marriages.

Clayton recorded Smith's visits to Flora. "Joseph rode out today with Flora W," he wrote on May 2, 1843. "President Joseph told me that he had difficulty with E[mma] yesterday," Clayton explained on August 23. "She rode up to Woodworth's with him and called while he came to the Temple. When he returned she was demanding the gold watch of F[lora] ... On their return home, she abused him much." Just a few days later, Clayton wrote that "Hyrum and I rode up to my house and Joseph met Mrs. W[oo]d[wor]th and F[lora] and conversed sometime."[32]

It seems clear that Joseph was married to Flora by this time. Additionally, a shorthand notation in Smith's journal for March 4 reads "woodsworth," also pointing to a spring 1843 wedding. The timing explains later references to Woodworth in Clayton's journal and 1874 affidavit.[33] This also explains the tension with Emma in the fall.

Flora's mother, Phebe Watrous Woodworth, supported her daughter's marriage. Not only did she benefit socially from her daughter's connection to the societal leader, she and Flora were the second most likely mother-daughter marriage to Smith after Patty and Sylvia Sessions in 1842.

Not only was Phebe close to Joseph in August 1843 when "President Joseph met M[r]s. W[oo]d[wor]th at my [Clayton's] house," she

31. George A. Smith to Joseph Smith III, Oct. 9, 1869, Joseph Smith III Papers, Library-Archives of the Community of Christ, Independence, Missouri; see also Journal History of the Church of Jesus Christ of Latter-day Saints, Oct. 9, 1869.

32. Smith, *Intimate Chronicle*, 100, 118-19.

33. Scott H. Faulring, ed., *An American Prophet's Record: The Diaries and Journals of Joseph Smith*, 2nd ed. (Salt Lake City: Signature Books and Smith Research Associates, 1989), 327; Compton, *Sacred Loneliness*, 389-90; Smith, *Intimate Chronicle*, 100, 118-19, 557.

and her husband were admitted into the Quorum of the Anointed in October, which was a singular honor. Their membership in this elite group implied acceptance of plural marriage. On October 29, Brigham Young wrote in his diary that "Sisters Cahoon Cutler & Woodworth was taken into the order of the priesthood."[34] On January 17, 1846, Phebe would be sealed to Smith in preference to Lucien, and within the week Lucien would marry four additional wives himself.

Todd Compton cautions that Phebe's marriage to Joseph is not certain[35] and that without "definitive evidence linking Phebe to Joseph during his lifetime," she is left in the "category of posthumous wives."[36] D. Michael Quinn likewise considers it "only a possibility" that she married Smith prior to his death.[37] Lyndon Cook, on the other hand, concluded differently, that "although the precise date is unknown," the conclusion seems unavoidable that "Smith and Phebe Watrous Woodworth were sealed husband and wife during the prophet's lifetime."[38] Compton realized the implication of the mother's sealing to Smith in the Nauvoo temple was that she may well have married him at about the same time her daughter did in 1843.[39]

While we know that Flora married Joseph, the evidence for Phebe's wedding is tenuous but strongly suggests a marriage to Smith while he was alive.

When Smith died, Flora became a widow at eighteen. She soon married Carlos Gove, a one-time schoolmate from Nauvoo who was not a Mormon. Atypically, she did not have her marriage to Smith re-solemnized in 1846, perhaps as a reaction against her youth and coercion in her first marriage, perhaps out of devotion to her new husband. It may have been a negative reaction against her mother's decision to be sealed to Joseph over Flora's father, Lucien. Whatever the

---

34. Brigham Young, Diary, Oct. 29, 1843, LDS Archives.

35. Compton, *Sacred Loneliness*, 171, 391.

36. Ibid., 419.

37. D. Michael Quinn, *The Mormon Hierarchy: Origins of Power* (Salt Lake City: Signature Books and Smith Research Associates, 1994), 399.

38. Lyndon W. Cook, *Nauvoo Marriages, Proxy Sealings: 1843-1846* (Provo, Utah: Grandin Book, 2004), 85n3.

39. Compton, *Sacred Loneliness*, 390.

case, not much else is known about Flora except that she had two or three children and died in Kanesville, Iowa, en route to Salt Lake City. She was about twenty-five years of age.

After her death, her mother and father traveled to Utah, then to California to live in San Bernardino. Lucien died in 1867, at which time Phebe returned to Utah. Compton traced her role as a proxy wife for others of Joseph Smith's plural spouses into the 1870s, when she represented several deceased women at the altar. She died in October 1887 at age eighty-two.

Emily and Eliza Partridge

wives number 20 and 21
unmarried women
March 1843

In March 1843, while plural marriage was spreading among his closest male followers, Smith took two more plural wives, another pair of sisters who worked in his household. He married one of them, nineteen-year-old Emily Dow Partridge, on March 4, the same day he married sixteen-year-old Flora Woodworth. Emily's twenty-two-year-old sister, Eliza Maria Partridge, was added to his coterie of wives four days later on March 8. Emily was the primary recorder of these events.

The two young women had known Smith since 1831, after he baptized their father, Edward Partridge, in December 1830. Edward was soon called to be the first Mormon bishop. After selling their prosperous homestead on Lake Erie in Painesville, Ohio, the Partridges moved to Kirtland, about ten miles away. In doing so, Edward lost his "thriving business as a hatter" and "his property was sold at a great sacrifice."[40] Emily wrote that after joining the Mormons their family fell into "the depths of poverty."

In the Kirtland and Missouri settlements, Partridge and his family were known by just about everyone in the early church. In 1831, in re-

40. Emily Dow Partridge Young, "Diary and Reminiscences, 1874-1899," 5, L. Tom Perry Special Collections, Harold B. Lee Library, Brigham Young University, Provo, Utah.

sponse to a revelation from Joseph Smith to him, Edward joined those who tried to establish the church in Missouri.[41] This was even more difficult a transition than they had experienced years before when they had left their comfortable New England home in Pittsfield, Massachusetts, for their home on the Great Lakes. Missouri settlers drove the Partridges and other Mormons from county to county for eight years until they evicted them from the state in 1839. Edward died in Nauvoo in May 1840, and his wife Lydia married William Huntington,[42] a widower and father of Joseph's other pair of sister wives, Zina and Presendia.

Eliza wrote in her autobiography that she and her sister Emily "went to live in the family of the Prophet Joseph Smith. We lived there about three years."[43] She confirmed in a letter that she was "an inmate" there, as she described it, "for about three years."[44] The girls tended the Smith children, helped with the housework, and increasingly came to the attention of their benefactor from 1840 to 1843.

Other autobiographical writings, diaries and letters from 1874, and depositions during the 1892 Temple Lot hearings allow a personality sketch of the Partridge sisters. They were not just witnesses but were, in fact, right at the heart of the land dispute. It derived from confusion surrounding a lot their father bought in 1831 in Independence, Missouri, in trust for the LDS Church. Smith identified the particular area as "Zion" and said it was where Adam and Eve and their family had once lived and where Jesus was going to return to inaugurate a thousand-year reign. His intent was to construct a temple on the lot, but because the Saints were expelled from the area in 1833, these plans were delayed and politicized. As heirs of the Edward Partridge estate, his widow and daughters Eliza, Emily, and Caroline sold the Temple Lot to James Pool of Jackson County, Missouri, in May 1848. At that point, the heirs were in Pottawattamie County, Iowa, en route

41. D&C 58:14.

42. *Times and Seasons,* Oct. 1840, indicates William Huntington married Lydia Partridge on Sept. 27, 1840.

43. Eliza Maria Partridge Lyman, "Autobiography and Diary of Eliza Maria Partridge (Smith) Lyman," 1846-1885, 7, LDS Archives.

44. Emily Dow Partridge Young to Mr. W. Collins, Jan. 27, 1899, LDS Archives.

to the Salt Lake Valley. The Reorganized Church of Jesus Christ of Latter Day Saints, which subsequently bought the lot, sued in 1892 to enforce its rights, while the Church of Christ-Temple Lot claimed that Emily had had no right to sell the property in the first place. The issue then became a question of who the rightful successor to Joseph Smith was. Which of the various churches could claim the assets of the church Smith founded? This involved further questions about plural marriage, a practice the LDS Church had officially renounced some two years before the hearings. Even though the hearings seemed untimely and ironic, the witnesses who testified during the trial, including Emily Partridge (Young), helped to document the elusive record of Nauvoo celestial marriage.[45]

According to Emily, "times were hard" and they did not know "which way to turn" until they thought of hiring out as helpers in someone's household.[46] Eliza did not testify but wrote that at the time of her father's death, the Partridges were "in very poor circumstances." The family's property had become subsumed in the church's assets.[47] Several times the family had been forced to sell in order to quickly relocate elsewhere. Each time they did so, their property had been "sold at great sacrifice."[48]

About this situation, Emily wrote in a biographical sketch in 1877 that "Emma sent for me to come and live with her and [tend] her baby." Don Carlos Smith had been born on June 13, 1840, and his brothers, Alexander and Frederick, were still toddlers at two and four. "Tending babies was my delight, and about the only thing I knew how to do well," Emily wrote. She said her sister "came to live there also in a short time. Emma was very kind to us and I believe she was a good and noble woman until polygamy upset her. I feel very charitable towards her notwithstanding all she had done."[49] In her 1892 testimony,

---

45. Andrew Jenson, "The Temple Lot," *Historical Record* 7 (Dec. 1888): 647-48.

46. Emily Dow Young, "Incidents in the Life of a Mormon Girl," 176, MS 5220, folders 1-2 and on microfilm, LDS Archives.

47. Lyman, "Autobiography and Diary," 7.

48. Emily Dow Partridge Young, "What I Remember," Apr. 7, 1884, 4, LDS Archives.

49. Young, "Incidents," 177.

Emily gave more details about her living conditions: "I went there as a nurse girl," she said, for they had "a young baby and wanted me to tend it for them." Asked if she was paid for her services, Emily answered: "I never received any wages, while I was there but I just lived as one of the family."[50] One of the perquisites she was given was the "privilege of going to school."[51] In Emily's 1884 reminiscence, she recalled being comfortable and content: "As a general thing I was very happy going to parties and singing schools, and riding horseback. One day Emma said, as we had been to so many parties, we ought to have one and invite the young people in return. Of course that pleased us very much. We had an excellent time playing games" such as "poor puss wants a corner" and "dancing."[52]

These feelings of communal warmth diminished in the spring of 1842. While in April the sisters were accepted into the Nauvoo Relief Society, indicating their coming of age in the community, Smith complicated the camaraderie they enjoyed in his household when he set his sights on them as potential celestial mates. About thirty years later, Emily began a "Diary and Reminiscences" in which she told how Smith approached her and Eliza for marriage. She rehearsed the story again in her 1892 Temple Lot deposition. Emily recalled that she was "living at his house at the time," and a while after her father's death, "he came there into the room where I was one day, when I was in the room alone, and he asked me if I could keep a secret. I was about eighteen years of age."[53]

"Joseph said to me," she continued, "'Emily, if you will not betray me, I will tell you something for your benefit.' Of course I would keep his secret," she said, "but no opportunity offered for some time, to say anything to me. As I was passing through the room where he sat alone,

50. *Reorganized Church of Jesus Christ of Latter Day Saints v. Church of Christ of Independence, Missouri, et al.* 60 F. 937 (W.D. Mo. 1894), deposition questions 126-27, from the electronic copy prepared by Richard D. Ouellette.

51. Young, "Incidents," 178.

52. Young, "What I Remember," 28. "Pussy-wants-a-corner" is the U.S. version of the British "Puss in the corner," a children's game in which one player in the center tries to capture one of the other player's spots as they change bases.

53. *Reorganized Church v. Church of Christ,* questions 21-22.

he asked me [if] I would burn it if he would write me a letter. As I felt very anxious to know what he had to tell me, I promised to do as he wished, and left the room. I began to think that was not the proper thing for me to do … I went back and watched my opportunity to say I could not take a private letter from him. He asked me if I wished the matter ended. I said I did, and it rested for some time."[54]

It is important to keep in mind that Emily and Eliza had moved into the Smith household in about the fall of 1840. Emily, born on February 28, 1824, was sixteen. She said she was eighteen when asked if she could keep a secret and confirmed that "Joseph had tried to make these things known to me—I think, in the spring or summer of '42, but I had shut him up so quick that he said no more to me until the 28th of Feb, 1843, (my nineteenth birth day)."[55]

Emily said that "before he told me about it himself, there was reports around … that gave me an idea of what it was he wanted to say to me. … There was so many reports flying around there in Nauvoo … then I found out that the reports I had heard were connected with what he had to tell me."[56] Then "Mrs. Durfee," a fifty-one-year-old plural wife and intermediary of Joseph Smith (see chapter 2), "came to me one day, and said Joseph would like an opportunity to talk with me. I asked her if she knew what he wanted. She said she thought he wanted me for a wife." Emily reflected, "I think I was thoroughly prepared for anything." This conversation would have taken place during the winter of 1842-43.

To conclude this two-year courtship, Joseph called on a second intermediary for assistance, his close friend and apostle Heber C. Kimball. Durfee instructed Emily that she was to go "in the evening [to] Brother Kimball's," the father of a young friend of Emily's, the fourteen-year-old soon-to-be wife of Smith, Helen Mar Kimball. She said that Smith would also be there. "I had been helping with wash all day," Emily explained,

---

54. Young, "Diary and Reminiscences," 1.
55. Young, "Incidents," 185.
56. *Reorganized Church v. Church of Christ,* questions 218, 221.

> and I was so afraid somebody would mistrust where I was going, that I dare[d] not change my wash dress, so I threw a large cloak over me, and said I was going to run over to see mother; which I did, but did not stay long, and started out as if going back, but went to the place appointed instead. When I got there nobody was at home but [two of the children,] William and Helen Kimball. I don't know what they thought to see me there at that hour. I did not wait long before brother Kimball and Joseph came in. Brother Heber told his children they had better go in to one of the neighbors, as there would be a council that evening at their house and said to me, "Vilate is not at home, and you had better call another time," so I started out with Wm. and Helen and bid them goodbye. I started for home as fast as I could, so as to get beyond being called back, for I still dreaded the interview. However, I soon heard Brother Kimball call, "Emily, Emily" rather low—but loud enough for me to hear[.] I thought at first I would not go back, and took no notice of his calling, but he kept calling, and was about to overtake me, so I stopped and went back with him.[57]

In what might be considered a proposal hinted at earlier, Joseph Smith "told me then what he wanted to say to me, and he taught me this principle of plural marriage that is called *polygamy* now, but we called it *celestial marriage*, and he told me that this principle had been revealed to him, and he wanted to know if I would consent to a marriage, and I consented."[58] Emily then summarized: "Well, I was married there and then. ... Joseph went home his way, and I going my way alone" but to the same residence. "A strange way of getting married, wasn't it?" she remarked. "Brother Kimball married us, the 4th of March 1843."[59] When asked during the Temple Lot hearings what she would tell someone who doubted Smith's involvement in plural marriage, she stressed that "he taught it to me with his own lips."[60]

Her courtship and marriage are interwoven with those of her sister Eliza. Although Eliza gave fewer details, her story can be pieced together, at least partly, from what Emily said. In the spring or summer of 1842, the two girls spent an afternoon with Mrs. Durfee, who

---

57. Young, "Diary and Reminiscences," 1. Six-foot Heber outpaced Emily.
58. *Reorganized Church v. Church of Christ*, question 23, emphasis added.
59. Young, "Diary and Reminiscences," 1.
60. *Reorganized Church v. Church of Christ*, question 18.

asked them what they thought of the rumors circulating about "*spiritual wives* as they called it in those days." Emily thought she "could tell her something that would make her open her eyes if I chose, but I did not choose to, so I kept my own council and said nothing, but going home I felt impressed to tell Eliza. I knew she would not betray me. She felt very bad indeed for a short time, but it served to prepare her to receive the principles that were revealed to her soon after." Emily "learned afterwards that Mrs. Durfee was a friend to plurality and knew all about it and took that means to test me and draw me out, if I was disposed."[61]

Eliza wrote simply that while she and Emily lived with the Smiths, "he taught to us the plan of Celestial marriage and asked us to enter into that Order with him." It was "truly a great trial for me, but I had the most implicit confidence in him," she remembered, and this led her to "accept of the privilege of being sealed to him as a wife for time and all eternity."[62] She also married Smith in March 1843.[63]

Although it was never clear how much and when Emma Smith knew about her husband's plural marriages, by May 1843 she and Joseph had at least engaged in conversation about what Joseph called the "the restoration of all things," including ancient forms of marriage. During the spring of 1843 Emma was reportedly willing to accept the doctrine. Two months after Emily's marriage, "sometime in the first part of May," Emily recalled, "Emma told Joseph she would give him two wives if he would let her choose them for him. She chose my sister and I, and help[ed] explain the principles to us." Anticipating the turbulence that followed, the young girls were careful not to "make too much trouble, but were sealed in her presence with her full and free consent,"[64] this being after their initial marriages to Joseph. Emma's moment of self-abnegation would end rather abruptly. "From

61. Young, "Diary and Reminiscences," 1-2.

62. Eliza Maria Partridge Lyman, "Life and Journal of Eliza Maria Partridge (Smith) Lyman," 1877, 7, Special Collections, J. Willard Marriott Library, University of Utah.

63. Eliza Maria (Partridge) Lyman, Affidavit, July 1, 1869, Willard County, Utah, in "[Affidavits] Book No. 2," 1869-1870.

64. Young, "Diary and Reminiscences," 2.

that very hour," continued Emily, "Emma was our bitter enemy. We remained in the family several months after this, but things went from bad to worse."[65]

In her 1877 autobiography, Emily elaborated: "The ceremony was done over again in [Emma's] presence, on the 11th of May 1843." As their relationship with Emma deteriorated, Emily wondered why Joseph's first wife had given them to him "unless she thought we were where she could watch us better than some others outside of the house."[66] But "before the day was over," Emma "turned around, or repented of what she had done and kept Joseph up till very late in the night talking to him."[67]

Between March and May 1843, matters must have been difficult for the surreptitious teenage brides. Then, after their marriages were reenacted in front of Emma, it was even worse: "She kept close watch of us. If we were missing for a few minutes, and Joseph was not at home, the house was searched from top to bottom and from one end to the other, and if [we] were not found, the neighborhood was searched until we were found."[68] On May 23, Clayton learned that the president had experienced "a little trouble with Sister E.," meaning Emma. He was asking Eliza about the behavior of a Nauvoo man during Joseph's absence when "E came upstairs" and Joseph "shut [to] the door not knowing who it was and held it. [Emma] came to the door and called Eliza 4 times and tried to force open the door. President opened it and told her the cause &c. She seemed much irritated."[69] Clearly,

---

65. Ibid., 6.

66. Young, "Incidents," 185. The date of the May marriages is controversial. Smith's clerk, Willard Richards, dated the remarriage to May 23, 1843 (Diary, 1836-1852, 19 vols., LDS Archives), as does Quinn, *Mormon Hierarchy Origins,* 494. James Adams arrived from his Springfield home on May 22; early on May 23 Joseph was "in conversation with Judge Adams and others" (*History of the Church,* 5:403-04). On Saturday, March 14, 1892, as a Temple Lot respondent, Emily acknowledged she "may be mistaken in the date" since the questioner quoted the *Millennial Star* having Emma going to Quincy that day, making it difficult for her to witness a marriage between her husband and the Partridge girls. *Reorganized Church v. Church of Christ,* questions 373-79, 750.

67. Young, "Diary and Reminiscences," 2.

68. Ibid.

69. Smith, *Intimate Chronicle,* 105-06.

Emma was less than pleased to find her husband in a locked room, perhaps her own bedroom, with a teenage girl she had allowed him to become connected to in what Emma may have considered to be a symbolic marriage.

Everyone in this celestial *ménage-à-quatre* probably knew it could not continue. It should have been especially apparent to the husband, but he seemed either oblivious or overly hopeful. Emily described how Emma asserted her rights as Joseph's legal wife, leading to an open break. "She sent for us one day to come to her room. Joseph was present, looking like a martyr." In her dominant role, "Emma said some very hard things—Joseph should give us up or blood should flow." She added that "such interviews were [becoming] quite common" and that she wanted Joseph to stand up to his wife: "The last time she called us to her room, I felt quite indignant, and was determined it should be the last, for it was becoming monotonous, and I am ashamed to say, I felt indignant towards Joseph for submitting to Emma, but I see now he could do no different."[70]

Emma wanted the plural marriages terminated and the Partridge sisters to find other husbands. "She wanted us immediately divorced." The girls resisted her. "She seemed to think that she only had to say the word, and it was done. But we thought different. We looked upon the covenants we had made as sacred."[71] In another account, Emily portrayed Joseph as hapless: "When we went in[,] Joseph was there. His countenance was the perfect picture of despair—she [Emma] insisted that we should promise to break our covenants … [and then] Joseph asked her[,] if we made her the promises she required, if she would cease to trouble us, and not persist in our marrying some one else." The resolution signaled Emma's victory: "She made the promise. Joseph came to us and shook hands with us, and the understanding was that all had ended between us." Emily acknowledged that "I for one meant to keep the promise I was forced to make," but that Emma had "sought to annoy us in various ways." On one occasion, she said, Emma suggested to a young man that he ask Eliza out and then break

70. Ibid.

71. Young, "Incidents," 185.

the date, to "give her the mitten," as the saying went. "The young man would not consent to it."[72]

"After our interview was over," Emily recalled their quick divorce over a handshake, they

> went down stairs. Joseph soon came into the room where I was. Said, "how do you feel Emily?" My heart being still hard, I answered him rather short "that I expect I felt as anybody would under the circumstances." He said, "you know my hands are tied" and he looked as if he would sink into the earth. I knew he spoke truly, and my heart was melted. All my hard feelings was gone in a moment, (towards him) but I had no time to speak for he was gone.

Then Emily defended Joseph against his wife, saying that "Emma was on his track, and came in as he went out. [Emma] said 'Emily, what did Joseph say to you?' I answered, 'He asked me how I felt.' She said, 'you might as well tell me, for I am determined that a stop shall be put to these things, and I want you to tell me what he says to you.'"

Here, at least in her recollection, Emily spoke up to Emma: "I replied 'I shall not tell you, he can say what he pleases to me, and I shall not report it to you, there has been mischief enough made, by doing that. I am as sick of these things as you can be.' I said it in a tone that she knew I meant it." Emily reaffirmed she "was not sick of Polygamy—but I was sick of her abuse." Emily said she "did not know what effect my words might have, but learned afterwards that she gloried in my spunk."[73]

When asked by Temple Lot attorneys in 1892 if her marriage went beyond an "eternal sealing" and involved sexual relations, Emily affirmed that she had "slept" with Joseph after their first marriage on March 4 and "roomed" with him the day of their second marriage, May 11. She was not able to "live with him" after that because of Emma's close surveillance. She could not say how many times they had "carnal intercourse," only that she had been to bed with him several times after their wedding. She pointedly emphasized that she had

72. Young, "Diary and Reminiscences," 2.
73. Ibid.

not had "carnal intercourse" with a married man and father of three until after she had married him in March.[74]

Joseph's proposal to Emily began as a secret to be kept between them. The doctrine had been "revealed to him" but was "not generally known."[75] After the four ceremonies involving the Partridges—the one performed by Heber Kimball on the evening of March 4 after supper at Kimball's house; the second ceremony a few days later, March 8, also in the Kimball home, "sealed in 1843 by H[eber]. C. K[imball] in [the] presence of witnesses";[76] and the repeat ceremonies performed in May by James Adams at his residence (Adams was a patriarch, Mason, judge, and respected Smith family friend)—the sisters found themselves in a celestial netherworld. Although married, they were not recognized as such.

Emily testified "it was not generally known that we were married to him." Asked about a marriage record, she said she had never seen one. She seemed unfamiliar with the requirement that a county clerk had to record a marriage. In court, when asked if twelve-year-old Joseph III had been present at the ceremonies, Emily sounded surprised at the question and observed that "such young children did not know anything about these things." After all, "why should they tell [Joseph III] anything about it." He was not only too young to understand, it would not have been "very likely that they would take children into their confidence in a thing of that kind that was being kept secret" from adults. In response to another question about whether Joseph ever took her out publicly, even to a church meeting, Emily was clear: "No sir he never went with me."[77]

In her recollection of 1883, Emily explained that "in the days of Nauvoo the holy order of Celestial marriage was in its infancy; it was not taught publicly, consequently the people did not generally know of it."[78] She wrote that in 1843 "the principles of Celestial Marriage

74. *Reorganized Church v. Church of Christ,* questions 310-11, 480-84, 747-62.
75. Ibid., question 23.
76. *Life and Journal of Eliza Maria Partridge Lyman,* holograph, 13, LDS Archives.
77. *Reorganized Church v. Church of Christ,* questions 408, 850-51, 859.
78. Young, "Diary and Reminiscences," 73.

were being taught to [just] a few, that *everything was so secret.*"[79] Her sister, Eliza, confirmed that in Nauvoo, "a woman living in polygamy dare[d] not let it be known."[80]

When the Temple Lot attorney asked why Emily and Eliza were willing to marry a man whose wife had employed them to care for his children, Emily said she trusted him. Even without having seen a written revelation, "he told me it was all right and I just took his word for it."[81] By 1892 the Latter-day Saints justified plural marriage with the revelation of July 12, 1843, which later became canonized as official scripture. Emily felt that she had been married to Smith "under a revelation," even though it was not the revelation of July 1843: "I don't see how I could be married in March under a revelation given in the July following," she reasoned with undeniable logic.[82] When asked about the previous revelation prohibiting plural marriage ("one man should have one wife; and one woman, but one husband"), she said she was not familiar with it.[83] In Eliza's autobiographical sketch, she expressed the same sentiment regarding "the most implicit confidence" she had in the prophet and that it was a "privilege of being sealed to him as a wife for time and all eternity."[84]

Besides brushing aside questions about the official church policy of the day, Emily was equally indifferent regarding the dissimulation of the Nauvoo leadership who well knew about the existing church law of having only one wife. "Well, we agreed to be each other's companions—husband and wife," she responded. Did this mean "keeping yourselves for each other, and wholly from all others?" In her case, yes. In his case? "I think not, for he could have other wives."[85]

The sisters continued to live in the Mansion House for some time after their agreement to divorce the prophet but were not residing

79. Young, "Incidents," 185 (emphasis added).

80. Lyman, "Autobiography and Diary," 13.

81. *Reorganized Church v. Church of Christ,* question 225.

82. Ibid., questions 735-38.

83. "On Marriage," D&C 101, 1835 edition (rpt. *Times and Seasons,* Oct. 1, 1842, 939), "to show that Dr. J. C. Bennett's 'secret wife system' is a creature of his own make"; *Reorganized Church v. Church of Christ,* question 583.

84. Lyman, "Autobiography and Diary," 7.

85. *Reorganized Church v. Church of Christ,* questions 823-27.

there when he was martyred. Emily related that Emma "afterwards gave Sarah and Maria Lawrence to [Joseph] and they lived in the house as his wives. I knew this, but my sister and I were cast off."[86] "Emma could not rest till she had us out of the house," Emily wrote, "and then she was not satisfied, but wanted us to leave the city. ... I got a place, or Joseph did, for me with a respectable family. ... I do not remember seeing Joseph but once to speak to after I left the Mansion House."[87] Neither Emily nor Eliza gave a date for their departure. Emily remembered staying "several months," bringing us to the time in mid-August when Clayton recorded that Joseph told Emma "he would relinquish all for her sake." Clayton explained that Joseph knew if he continued to see the Partridges, Emma "would pitch on him and obtain a divorce and leave him. He however told me he should not relinquish anything."[88] Compton quotes a poem that Eliza Snow wrote to Eliza Partridge on October 19, alluding to her "submission" to the existing circumstances.[89]

Despite this turbulent time of courtship, marriage, and expulsion, Emily's feelings for Joseph remained strong. Writing in 1897, she confessed that "many times my heart has ached for him. ... He was all that the word 'gentleman' would imply—how long must we wait before we are permitted to enjoy his society again."[90] She averred that she had "never heard" her father "teach or preach polygamy" and doubted it was known by even the most stalwart Saints until after her father's death in May 1840.[91]

Eliza and sister Caroline married Apostle Amasa Lyman in September 1844 and Emily married Brigham Young about the same time[92] in marriages accompanied by resealings to Smith, their new earthly husbands acting as proxies for Smith. Emily traveled to Salt

86. Young, "Incidents," 185-86.

87. Young, "Diary and Reminiscences," 3.

88. *Reorganized Church v. Church of Christ,* question 360; Smith, *Intimate Chronicle,* 117.

89. Compton, *Sacred Loneliness,* 411.

90. Emily Dow Partridge to Lula Clawson Young, June 27, 1897, LDS Archives.

91. *Reorganized Church v. Church of Christ,* question 108.

92. Ibid., questions 277, 283.

Lake City and lived for a while at the Lion House with Young's other wives, then at his forest farm where produce was grown for the Lion House. After Young died, Emily lived in various homes, wrote and dreamed of Smith, and died at age seventy-five in 1899.

Eliza stayed in Salt Lake while Amasa went on an extended mission with Caroline to Southern California. Eventually Amasa took his other wives to live in Fillmore in central Utah. When Amasa was subsequently excommunicated for apostasy, it must have dissolved the rationale for his plural marriage to Eliza. Despite his abandonment and Eliza's new status as a single woman, she continued to defend polygamy until her death in 1886, four years before church president Wilford Woodruff called for an end to the practice.

Smith's marriage to the Partridges culminated a two-year quest to gain their approval. Its successful completion in the spring of 1843 and Emma's compliance made the season a high point in Smith's relationship with women. His summer 1842 call for an intimate visit from Sarah Ann Whitney and Emily Partridge's autobiographical writings vividly substantiate the intimate relationships he was involved in during those two years.

However, the *History of the Church* predictably gives no notice of these weddings. On Emily's wedding date, Smith is said only to have spoken with Benjamin Johnson about the doctrine of "blood atonement," under consideration by the Nauvoo City Council.[93] On the date of Eliza's wedding, the *History* tells of a "crowded" meeting at Kimball's home where the wedding took place but does not disclose what happened there that day.[94]

After the Partridge sisters became emotionally involved with Smith, the period of courtship and marriage lasted three or four years, the longest for which we have evidence. Surprisingly, Smith married the Lawrence sisters two months later, apparently on the same day as his re-marriage to the Partridge sisters. This timetable

93. On his wedding day with Emily, Joseph declared: "I was opposed to hanging, even if a man kill another, I will shoot him, or cut off his head, spill his blood on the ground, and let the smoke thereof ascend up to God; and if ever I have the privilege of making a law on that subject, I will have it so" (*History of the Church,* 5:296).

94. Ibid., 5:299; Young, "Diary and Reminiscences," 1.

raises a number of questions. Did these ceremonies escape Emma's attention? Does it suggest that Emma was aware of her husband's marriages to both pairs of sisters, and that by May 1843 she was actually helping Joseph choose wives? Moreover, between Smith's marriage and re-marriage to the Partridge girls, and during his courtship of the Lawrence girls, he acquired two other wives as well: Almera Johnson and Lucy Walker. Was Emma aware of these nuptials? Interestingly, one of the witnesses to the Walker wedding was Eliza Partridge.

Almera Johnson

wife number 22
an unmarried woman
April 1843

Almera Woodward Johnson's marriage to Smith in the spring of 1843 was another well-documented relationship. Smith had married Delcena a year earlier, and now two more of the Johnson sisters were on his mind. Almera, six years younger than Delcena, was another child of Ezekiel and Julia Johnson, farmers of western New York.

Probably the first time their brother Benjamin learned about polygamy was when Joseph married Delcena in 1842. Benjamin's careful record of conversations showed that he was later aware of Joseph's conjugal visits with Almera. Even before marrying Delcena and Almera, Joseph had hired Benjamin to serve as his real estate agent in Macedonia (Ramus), Illinois. After marrying the sisters, Smith allowed their brother the "privilege" of acquiring his own plural wives. In later years, after the prohibition of polygamy in 1890 and 1904, Benjamin would become a revered progenitor of fundamentalist Mormons who continued to practice plural marriage.[95]

On April 1, 1843, William Clayton recorded Smith's visit to the Johnson home in Macedonia. After privately outlining the favors and

95. Anne Wilde, "Fundamentalist Mormonism: Its History, Diversity and Stereotypes, 1886-Present," in *Scattering of the Saints: Schism within Mormonism,* eds. Newell G. Bringhurst and John C. Hamer (Independence, Mo.: John Whitmer Books, 2007), 258-89; Verlan M. LeBaron, *The LeBaron Story* (Lubbock, Tex.: Keels & Co., 1981), 1-28.

privileges of the ancient order of marriage to Benjamin, Joseph explained that he had previously wanted to approach his mother, Julia Johnson, "for Some of her daughters."[96] In their conversation, as they sat upon a log by the edge of the woods, Benjamin recalled that since Smith was

> Required of the Lord to take more wives, he had Come now to ask me for my Sister Almera ... His words astonished me and almost *took* my *breath* ... I Sat for a time amazed and finally almost Ready to burst with emotion I looked him Straight in the Face & Said "Brother Joseph This is Something I did not Expect & I do not understand it ... You know whether it is Right. I do not. I want to do just as you tell me, and I will try. But if I [come to] know that you do this to Dishonor & debauch my Sister I will kill you as Shure as the Lord lives["]— [A]nd while his eye did not move from mine He Said with a Smile and in a Soft tone "but Benjamin you will never *know that.* But you will know the principle is true & will greatly Rejoice in what it will bring to you." But how[,] I asked. Can I teach my Sister what I mySelf do not understand or *Show* her what I do not mySelf See? "But you will See & underStand it" he Said[.] ["A]nd when you open your mouth to talk to your Sister light will come to you & your mouth will be full & your toung loose.["][97]

Convinced, Benjamin approached Almera at first, acting as a family intermediary for Joseph. Only later would Hyrum and Joseph talk to her, right before the wedding. According to Benjamin, Joseph's proposal met with limited success. Almera's "heart was not yet won by the prophet."[98] Benjamin agreed to bring her to Nauvoo, perhaps around mid-April: "Within a few days of this period my Sister acompanied me to Nauvoo, where at our sister Delcenas we Soon met the prophet with his *Bro* Hyrum and Wm Clayton as his private *Sec* who always accompanied him."[99] Hyrum assured Benjamin that the new doctrine was "all Right" and reaffirmed "that Joseph was Comanded to take more wives and he waited untill an Angel with drawn Sword Stood

---

96. Dean R. Zimmerman, ed., *I Knew the Prophets* ... (Bountiful, Utah: Horizon Publishers, 1976), 41.

97. Ibid., 41-42.

98. Benjamin F. Johnson, *My Life's Review,* 2nd ed. (Mesa, Ariz.: 21st Century Printing, 1992), 95.

99. Zimmerman, *I Knew the Prophets,* 43.

before him and declared that if he longer delayed fulfilling that Command he would Slay him."[100]

Hyrum had previously opposed his brother's doctrine, as Benjamin knew, and now pleaded Joseph's case. "The Lord has revealed the principle of plural marriage to me and I know for myself that it is true," he told Almera. "I will have you for a sister, and you shall be blest."[101] Almera did not leave a journal account of this April courtship, but she affirmed before a Notary Public that

> in the years 1842 and 1843, I resided most of the time at Macedonia, ... sometimes with my sister [Delcena] who was the wife of Almon W. Babbit, and sometimes with my brother Benjamin F. Johnson. During that time the Prophet Joseph Smith taught me the principle of Celestial Marriage including plurality of wives and asked me to become his wife. He first spoke to me on this subject at the house of my brother Benjamin F. I also lived a portion of the time at Brother Joseph Smith's, in Nauvoo, when many conversations passed between him and myself on this subject. On a certain occasion in the spring of the year 1843, the exact date of which I do not now recollect, I went from Macedonia to Nauvoo to visit another of my sisters, the one who was the widow of Lyman R. Sherman, deceased, at which time I was sealed to the Prophet Joseph Smith.

Almera recalled that Hyrum "said I need not be afraid." She agreed to be married, and "after this time I lived with the Prophet Joseph as his wife, and he visited me at the home of my brother Benjamin F. at Macedonia."[102] Louisa Beaman had evidently also urged Almera to say yes[103] because Benjamin mentioned that "Louisa Beeman and my Sister Delcena had it agreeably aranged," adding that "after a little instruction, [Almera] Stood by the Prophets Side & was Sealed to him as a wife by Brother Clayton. After which the Prophet

100. Ibid. Again, as with Smith's sealing to Ruth Sayers, there is some question about the timing of Hyrum Smith's involvement in his brother's marriage to Almera. See Bergera, "Identifying Earliest Polygamists," 32-33.

101. Andrew Jenson, "Plural Marriage," *Historical Record* 6 (May 1887): 236.

102. Almera W. Johnson Smith Barton, Affidavit, Aug. 1, 1883, LDS Archives; Joseph Fielding Smith, *Blood Atonement and the Origin of Plural Marriage: A Discussion* (Salt Lake City: Deseret News Press, 1905), 70-71.

103. Ibid.

asked me [Benjamin] to take my Sister to ocupy Room No 10 in his Mansion Home dureing her Stay in the City."[104]

They returned to Macedonia on April 23. Three weeks later, according to Benjamin, "the Prophet again Came and at my house ocupied the Same Room & Bed with my Sister that the month previous he had ocupied with the Daughter of the Late Bishop Partridge as his wife."[105] Clayton recorded that they were joined on another trip to Macedonia by George Miller, Eliza Partridge and her mother Lydia (now Mrs. William Huntington), and one other person. Historians have known that some of Smith's wives, such as Beaman and the Partridges, aided him in his bridal acquisitions; but it appears they also accompanied him on marital visits, if this example is representative. The group stayed in Macedonia two days and nights, May 16-18.[106] Smith and Clayton would return to Macedonia and, as Benjamin recorded, stay "at my house again." This time, Benjamin wrote, Smith "asked me for my youngest sister, Esther," for a wife. Benjamin deflected this interest in his fifteen-year-old sister by telling his brother-in-law and business partner she was already "promised in marriage to my wife's brother."[107]

Following Smith's death, Almera married and had five children with Reuben Barton, from whom she separated in 1860. She then traveled west and lived in southern Utah. On August 1, 1883, she confirmed her marriage to Joseph Smith. She died in Parowan, Utah, in March 1896 at age eighty-two.[108]

A professed husband for Sarah Ann Whitney

On April 29, the same month as Almera's wedding, Smith approached Joseph Corrodon Kingsbury and asked him to marry Sarah Ann Whitney as a cover. Kingsbury "agread to stand by Sarah Ann Whitney as supposed to be her husband," he later wrote, "& had a pretended marriage for the purpose of bringing about the purposes of

104. Zimmerman, *I Knew the Prophets,* 43-44.
105. Compton, *Sacred Loneliness,* 298.
106. Smith, *Intimate Chronicle,* 101-04.
107. Autobiography of Benjamin Johnson, 96; Smith, *Intimate Chronicle,* 122.
108. Johnson, *Life's Review,* 384.

God in these last days."[109] His first wife, Caroline Whitney Kingsbury, Sarah Ann's paternal aunt, had died six months earlier. This indicates that at the same time Joseph was courting and marrying the Partridge sisters and adding Almera Johnson to some twenty plural wives, he was evidently maintaining his year-old marital relationship with Sarah Ann Whitney. The pretended marriage discouraged suitors and could have been a precaution against possible pregnancy. In recognition of Kingsbury's cooperation, Smith sealed him to his deceased wife, Caroline. Immediately after the marriage charade, Kingsbury moved in with Sarah Ann and her parents. After Smith was killed in 1844, Sarah Ann was claimed by Heber Kimball, who became "her husband for time as of March 17, 1845."[110] Kingsbury later married his own plural wives, one of whom was Eliza Partridge.[111] Altogether, Sarah Ann wed three men in Nauvoo in 1842, 1843, and 1845. In each instance, the marriages furthered the institution of polygamy but not a union of two people intent on sharing their lives together.

Lucy Walker

wife number 23
an unmarried woman
May 1843

Just days after his marriage to Almera and the arrangement of a feigned marriage for Sarah Ann, the most married man in Nauvoo acquired his twenty-second plural wife. Lucy Walker had been raised on a farm in Smith's home state of Vermont, about fifty miles east of Burlington. When Lucy was six years old, her father converted to the Mormons' teachings; her mother joined three years later after they had moved 100 miles west of Burlington to the St. Lawrence River in

109. Joseph C. Kingsbury, Autobiography, 1812-1864, Special Collections, Marriott Library; see also ref. to 1846-64 journal in Lyndon W. Cook, *Joseph C. Kingsbury: A Biography* (Provo: Grandin Book, 1985), 76.

110. Devery S. Anderson and Gary James Bergera, eds., *Joseph Smith's Quorum of the Anointed, 1842-1845: A Documentary History* (Salt Lake City: Signature Books, 2005), 240; Cook, *Nauvoo Marriages*, 33, 50-51.

111. In addition to Eliza, Kingsbury married Dorcas Adelia Moore, Mahala Dorcas Eggleston Higley Moore, and Louisa Loenza Alcina Pond.

New York State. In 1838 the Walkers moved again, this time to Missouri, then the next year to Illinois.

Three months after her mother's death in January 1842, Lucy moved into Smith's house. She said she "lived with the prophet's family from that time on up to the date of his martyrdom," although she actually "spent most of the time with Don Carlos's widow," explaining that she was "back and forth between the two families."[112] Sometime in the summer of 1843, she and her oldest sister, Catherine, moved into the Mansion House. It opened for guests on September 15.

When Lucy was asked who else lived with the Smiths in the Nauvoo Mansion, she named "two of Bishop Partridge's daughters"[113] and "the Lawrence girls," adding that Smith "had a Negro cook and a black washerwoman, and he hired a girl to look after the dining room, and we looked after the rest of the house." The girls "did whatever was necessary—some of us did sewing for the family" or prepared the children for "school in the morning"; in fact, dressing the children "was about all that I had to do." She agreed that neither she "nor the Lawrence girls were employed there for any purpose," but "that was our home and Joseph did not look upon us as servants."[114]

She also clarified that Joseph "did not move into the Mansion House until in the fall" of 1843, after he had introduced her to plural marriage. It was long "before that," when they still "lived in the house on the bank of the river" in what was called "the prophet's house," that he had first told her of polygamy.[115] They were married one day after Lucy's seventeenth birthday, on May 1, 1843. Their association went back to January 1842 when Lucy's mother died and Smith offered to take the four oldest of the ten children into his home, then curiously sent their father on a mission to the eastern United States. Lucy and her brother Lorin moved in with the Smiths, and Joseph proposed to the young girl that year. But the fifteen-year-old hesitated. In a detailed, undated statement about her courtship and marriage, Lucy re-

---

112. *Reorganized Church v. Church of Christ,* questions 176-79.

113. Ibid., question 220.

114. Ibid., questions 231-32, 239-40, 242.

115. Ibid., questions 251-54.

called that "in the year 1842, President Joseph Smith sought an interview with me, and said, 'I have a message for you. I have been commanded of God to take another wife, and you are the woman.' My astonishment knew no bounds. This announcement was indeed a thunderbolt to me." When "he asked me if I believed him to be a Prophet of God," she replied, "Most assuredly I do"; then "he fully explained to me the principle of plural or celestial marriage," saying it would "form a chain that could never be broken, worlds without end." When Smith asked her opinion: "What have you to say?" she replied, "Nothing, how could I speak, or what could I say? … No mother to counsel; no father near to tell me what to do."[116]

"The Prophet discerned my sorrow." He consoled her by saying that, "although I can not under existing circumstances acknowledge you as my wife, the time is near when we will go beyond the Rocky Mountains and then you will be acknowledged and honored as my wife."[117] After this gentle persuasion, Smith then proceeded to threaten her, telling her she had a time limit within which she had to respond to what he characterized as a "command of God." "I will give you until tomorrow to decide this matter," he said, and "if you reject this message, the gate will be closed forever against you."

At first she balked. "This aroused every drop of Scotch in my veins," she fumed. "For a few moments I stood fearless before him and looked him in the eye. I felt at this moment that I was called to place myself on the alter a living sacrifice, perhaps to brook the world in disgrace and incur the displeasure and contempt of my youthful companions; all my dreams of happiness blown to the four winds. This was

116. In Lyman O. Littlefield, *Reminiscences of Latter-day Saints* (Logan: Utah Journal Co., 1888), 46-47, from Lucy Walker ("L W") Kimball, Statement, n.d., typescript, LDS Archives.

117. Smith started thinking about going west in 1830 and 1831, expressed in the summary text for D&C 37 about "the future migration of the Church westward" and its relocation to "the Ohio" River, then in D&C 45 about gathering "from the eastern lands" and going "forth into the western countries. On August 6, 1842, Smith prophesied that the church would settle in the Rocky Mountains (Quinn, *Mormon Hierarchy Origins,* 635), and on March 26, 1844, according to the *Times and Seasons,* he recommended that Congress recruit 100,000 armed volunteers for a campaign to Oregon and Texas.

too much."[118] She told Joseph she required a revelation before she would submit. He promised that if she prayed, she would receive her own personal manifestation from God, which she reported she received "near dawn after—a sleepless night"—when a "heavenly influence" and feeling of "supreme happiness … took possession" of her. She ended up marrying Smith on a spring Monday while Emma was away shopping in St. Louis. The ceremony took place at the old Smith homestead rather than in the Mansion House. The older residence had a grand view of the Mississippi River.[119]

There is a Smith family tradition that may offer a glimpse at how emotionally fraught the household was at the time. In May 1945, Nicholas G. Smith recorded that he had heard from his mother-in-law, Tirza Farr Gay, that "Lucy Walker was a hired girl in the home of the prophet and was married to the prophet without Emma knowing it." Lucy said "she felt so guilty and terrible and Emma talked to her about it a[nd] said she hoped she would never make some married woman unhappy by marrying her husband."[120] The day after the wedding, Emma returned from St. Louis and Joseph went to meet her: "About three p.m. the *Maid of Iowa* arrived from St. Louis. I was on the bank of the river, awaiting the arrival of my wife," the diary entry reprinted in the *History of the Church* reads.[121] The following Tuesday, he took his wife and mother and about 100 other guests on an all-day journey aboard the same boat, accompanied by band music.

Fifty years later, Lucy Walker reaffirmed this account of her marriage to Joseph during the Temple Lot hearings. She said he had "taught to me personally" the doctrine of plural marriage and that she married him on "the first day of May 1843," that "Miss Eliza Partridge—was the only witness we had to the ceremony." Clayton performed the wedding.[122] The way Lucy saw it, what she was doing was a

118. Littlefield, *Reminiscences*, 47.
119. Ibid., 48; Smith, *Intimate Chronicle*, 100, 557.
120. Todd Compton to the editor, *Journal of Mormon History* 25 (Fall 1999): x.
121. *History of the Church*, 5:379.
122. *Reorganized Church v. Church of Christ*, questions 21, 25-26.

duty, "giving up of myself as a sacrifice," to help establish celestial marriage on the earth.[123]

When asked to elaborate on what it was the young women in the Mansion House did to occupy their time, Lucy gave another vague answer: "We all did whatever there was for us to do." When asked about the domestic arrangements after a marriage, she said the prophet "did for them whatever was necessary to furnish their home and make them comfortable." She emphasized that "the prophet was a very kind, thoughtful, big hearted man."[124] After they "moved into the mansion there was a great deal to be done, fitting up and getting things in shape." The older Partridge girl was trained as a tailor and was occupied in making clothing.[125] However, none of the girls worked for wages, either inside or outside the home, according to Lucy. "We did not, for that was our home, and there was not one of us that were working there or any other place for regular wages."[126]

She remembered that she was sworn to secrecy; nor was she present at the marriages of the other young women. However, she knew the "Partridge girls were also married to him" and that "moreover Emma knew that they were married to him."[127] Although her sister was living with the Smiths, Catherine was not invited to Lucy's wedding and "knew nothing about it."[128] When they walked to the old Smith homestead for the ceremony,[129] Emma was not present and "did not consent to my marriage." To emphasize this, Lucy repeated that Emma "did not know anything about it at all."[130]

Joseph did introduce Lucy to Heber Kimball, Hyrum Smith, and Brigham Young "as his wife."[131] Although not generally acknowledged, "there was a few [who] knew it."[132] She went by her own name,

123. Ibid., question 29.
124. Ibid., questions 259-63.
125. Ibid., questions 269-70.
126. Ibid., question 271.
127. Ibid., questions 278, 285.
128. Ibid., question 306.
129. Ibid., question 323.
130. Ibid., questions 329-30.
131. Ibid., questions 350-51, 361.
132. Ibid., questions 419-20.

"Lucy Walker," and "the Lawrence girls went by their maiden names also." When asked if she had ever seen a child fathered by Smith, she declined to answer.[133]

After Smith's death, Lucy married Heber C. Kimball in a ceremony performed by Brigham Young on February 8, 1845.[134] Kimball simultaneously stood in for the deceased prophet for the sealing to Lucy for eternity. Both of these ordinances were re-solemnized on January 15, 1846, in the Nauvoo temple. Lucy subsequently accompanied Kimball west and lived with Presendia Buell, Martha Knight, Sarah Ann Whitney, and others of Smith's widows. Lucy had nine children by Kimball. Five survived.[135] Socially engaged, she not only kept in touch with her sister wives in Utah but also traveled to see Agnes Coolbrith in San Francisco. In 1910 in Salt Lake City, Lucy died at the age of eighty-four.

Sarah and Maria Lawrence

wives number 24 and 25
unmarried women
May 1843

On May 11, 1843, only a few days after the Walker marriage and the same day the Partridge sisters remembered being re-married to the prophet with Emma present, Smith wed sixteen-year-old Sarah Lawrence.[136] It may also have been on this same day that he married Sarah's nineteen-year-old sister, Maria. Six years earlier, he had first met the Lawrence sisters when they were eleven and thirteen years of age and he was visiting their recently converted parents in Toronto. Edward and Margaret Lawrence were successful farmers with a family of seven children. Maria was the oldest, born in 1823; Sarah was third, born in 1826.

Two years after the family moved to the states, Edward died, and

133. Ibid., questions 431-32, 463-65.

134. Lucy Walker, Affidavit, Dec. 17, 1902, in Smith, *Blood Atonement,* 68-69; *Reorganized Church v. Church of Christ,* questions 479-88.

135. Ibid., question 547.

136. Marriage possibly on May 23. See note 66.

his widow re-married at the end of 1840. Her new husband, Josiah Butterfield, negotiated with Smith over the disposition of Edward's assets. Smith had arranged in June 1841 to have himself appointed guardian of the children and trustee of the estate.[137] His diary mentions later discussions about the Lawrence estate on April 4 and June 4, 1842. A March 28, 1843, entry in the *History of the Church* captures the dispute with the girls' stepfather: "Josiah Butterfield came to my house and insulted me so outrageously that I kicked him out of the house, across the yard, and into the street."[138]

In Emily Partridge's diary, we read that the Lawrence girls moved into the Smith home in about May 1843 and stayed on when Emily and Eliza left that summer or fall under tense circumstances.[139] Smith's scribe, Willard Richards, and secretary, William Clayton, both recorded the legal wrangling through 1844, which led to Smith's precipitous destruction of the dissenting *Nauvoo Expositor* on June 10, 1844. Financial and marital issues, especially concerning the Lawrence sisters, would inflame public opinion prior to Smith's arrest.[140]

Just a few days before he married Sarah Lawrence and re-married the Partridge sisters, Joseph Smith made note of a celebration. On Saturday morning, May 6, 1843, around 9:30 a.m., he "mounted with my staff, and with the band, and about a dozen ladies, led by Emma, and proceeded to the general parade ground of the Nauvoo Legion, east of my farm on the prairie. ... In the evening attended ... wire dancing [balancing], legerdemain, magic, etc."[141] In the midst of what seemed a conflict with Emma over the re-marriage of the Partridges and courtship of the Lawrences, the prophet was able to take time out for this celebration. This recalls the festivities following his marriage to Beaman in 1841.

---

137. See Gordon A. Madsen, "Joseph Smith as Guardian: The Lawrence Estate Case," *Journal of Mormon History* 34, No. 3 (Summer 2010): 172-211.

138. Dean C. Jessee, ed., *The Papers of Joseph Smith*, 2 vols. (Salt Lake City: Deseret Book, 1992), 2:374, 389; *History of the Church*, 5:316. Butterfield evidently took seriously his responsibility to represent his stepdaughters' interests.

139. Young, "Incidents," 185-86.

140. See Compton, *Sacred Loneliness*, 476.

141. *History of the Church*, 5:384.

Little is known about Smith's relationship to the Lawrence girls after mid-1843, except that his marriage to fiduciary dependents would create outrage while some of the city's elite were already grappling with his July 1843 revelation making polygamy a requirement for faithful priesthood (see chapter 7). With Smith's assassination in 1844, questions arose over what the Smiths owed the Lawrence estate. In the midst of this discussion, Sarah married Heber Kimball, and Maria evidently married Brigham Young while remaining sealed to Smith for the eternities. In 1846 Maria must have changed her mind about being tied to Young, if she in fact had married him or had treated their sealing as an actual marriage, because she became connected for the rest of her short life to Almon Babbitt. Appropriately, Babbitt was the attorney who negotiated the fiduciary settlement for the Lawrences from the Smiths.[142]

As Michael Quinn points out, Young and Kimball usually performed marriages for each other in a coordinated fashion so that each obtained about the same number of wives as the other. Kimball's 1844-45 diary has a lined-through entry on October 12, 1844, that he married Smith's former wife "Sarah L." He was resealed to her in 1846 in the completed temple. Quinn concludes that "it would have been consistent for Maria Lawrence to be sealed 'for time' to Brigham Young on the same occasion he united Sarah and Kimball in a similar proxy marriage in 1844." In addition, Young's daughters, Susa Young Gates and Mabel Young Sanborn, each insisted that their father had married Maria.[143] As a "proxy wife," Maria bore Babbitt a child, although Benjamin Johnson also remembered that she died in childbirth in 1847. Her sister traveled west, separated from Kimball in 1851, and two years later married Joseph Mount. The couple lived together in

---

142. The Nauvoo temple records show that Maria married Almon Babbitt "for time" on January 24, 1846, and that in 1852 she and Joseph Smith, both deceased, were sealed to each other by proxy. Brigham Young served as proxy for Smith.

143. "Brigham Young Genealogy," *Utah Geneal. & Hist. Mag.*, July 1920, 131; Mabel Young Sanborn, *Brigham Young's Wives, Children, and Grandchildren* (Salt Lake: By author, 1940), [4]; Kate B. Carter, *Brigham Young: His Wives and Family* (Salt Lake City: Daughters of Utah Pioneers, 1967), 429-30. Stanley B. Kimball, *Heber C. Kimball: Mormon Patriarch and Pioneer* (Urbana: University of Ill. Press, 1981), 310n17.

California and Hawaii and she eventually resided at 1018 Hyde Street in San Francisco. She died there in 1872 at the age of forty-six.[144]

Helen Mar Kimball

wife number 26
an unmarried woman
May 1843

As Smith's assemblage of plural wives swelled, so did the conflict of interests between building a church community and his continuing affection for young women. In this case his marriage proposal created a conflict for the girl as well. At age fourteen, Helen Mar Kimball would be Smith's youngest wife, married the same month he wed the Lawrence sisters. Joseph's marriage to Helen was complicated by her romantic feelings for nineteen-year-old Horace Whitney, the older brother of her close friend Sarah Ann Whitney. Even so, Smith was able to arrange the marriage through Helen's father, Heber Kimball (see also chapter 4.)

When Joseph was pursuing Helen, the Kimballs lived on Partridge and Munson streets, six blocks from the Smith's home on Water Street. Like Smith and Young, Heber Kimball had moved from Vermont to central New York in the early 1800s and shared similar interests with the other two. All three had farmed and plied such hand trades as carpentry and scrying, being the alleged skill of viewing hidden objects from a distance through supernatural means, by using a crystal or seer stone. Heber was also a potter. Helen, the third daughter of Heber and Vilate Murray Kimball, was born in Mendon, New York, in August 1828, a few months after Smith announced his discovery of buried records in Manchester, New York, not far from the Kimball home.

Helen documented in some detail how her father, then Smith himself, persuaded her to become one of Smith's wives. She left two sets of documents relevant to this account: (1) a private reminiscence,

---

144. Benjamin Johnson, "Historical Mistakes," *Deseret News,* Aug. 6, 1887, 5, cited in Compton, *Sacred Loneliness,* 478-79; see also 477, 484, 744-45.

including a letter to her children, written in the form of an autobiography, and (2) serialized narratives published in the LDS *Woman's Exponent* newspaper from 1880 to 1886, headlined "Early Reminiscences," "Life Incidents," "Scenes in Nauvoo," and "Scenes and Incidents in Nauvoo." The newspaper accounts were edited by Emmeline B. Wells. Helen also published two booklets on plural marriage before her death in Salt Lake City in 1896.[145]

As Helen tells the story, her father asked her one day in 1843 "without any preliminaries" if she "would believe him if he told [her] it was right for married men to take other wives." She responded,

> the first impulse was anger, ... My sensibilities were painfully touched. I felt such a sense of personal injury and displeasure; for to mention such a thing to me I thought altogether unworthy of my father, and as quick as he spoke, I replied to him, short and emphatically, *No, I wouldn't!* ... This was the first time that I ever openly manifested anger towards him ... Then he commenced talking seriously, and reasoned and explained the principle, and why it was again to be established upon the earth, etc.

Helen said that this conversation "had a similar effect" on her emotions as "a small earthquake." However, when she began to "meekly" receive her father's instructions, he took the "opportunity to introduce Sarah Ann [Whitney] to me as Joseph's wife. This astonished me beyond measure."[146]

Helen characterized her father's motivation:

> Having a great desire to be connected with the Prophet, Joseph, he offered me to him; this [arrangement was one which] I afterwards learned from the Prophet's own mouth. My father had but one Ewe Lamb, but willingly laid her upon the alter: How cruel this seemed to the mother [Vilate] whose heartstrings were already stretched until they were ready to snap asunder, for he [Heber] had taken Sarah Noon to wife & she thought she had made sufficient sacrifise but the Lord required more.

145. See Jeni B. Holzapfel and Richard N. Holzapfel, eds., *A Woman's View: Helen Mar Whitney's Reminiscences of Early Church History* (Provo: BYU Religious Studies Center, 1997).

146. Helen Mar Whitney, "Scenes and Incidents in Nauvoo," *Woman's Exponent*, 11 (Aug. 1, 1882): 39; and "Scenes in Nauvoo," *Woman's Exponent* 11 (Mar. 1, 1883): 146.

"I will pass over the temptations which I had during the twenty four hours after my father introduced me to this principle," she confessed.[147] In any case, her father left her to "reflect upon it" and she was initially

> skeptical ... one minute believed, then doubted. I thought of the love and tenderness that he felt for his only daughter, and I knew that he ... loved me too well to teach me anything that is not strictly pure, virtuous and exalting in its tendencies; and no one else could have influenced me at that time or brought me to accept of a doctrine so utterly repugnant and so contrary to all of our former ideas and traditions."[148]

She held this difficult dialogue only with her father, apparently not confiding in her mother.

Granted some time to think it over through the evening, the next morning Helen found Joseph himself at the house. He had walked over to teach her "the principle of Celestial marriage," which he said would provide salvation in the afterlife for herself, her siblings, and her mother and father. It was as though he were asking her to give herself up in exchange for the promise of everlasting life. She obliged because, for her, "this promise was so great that I willingly gave myself to purchase so glorious a reward."[149] One might wonder how someone today would react if a church leader asked for their daughter in bargaining an exchange for eternal life. How might Helen's parents have felt? When finally informed of the transaction, Helen's mother responded succinctly, "If Helen is willing, I have nothing more to say."[150]

On May 28, Apostle Heber C. Kimball solemnly bestowed upon his daughter the right to partake of the "blessings of Abraham, Isaac, and Jacob," or, in other words, plural marriage. He admonished her to "be humble, and listen with care to thy father and mother and all thy

---

147. "Helen Mar Kimball's Retrospection about Her Introduction to the Doctrine and Practices of Plural Marriage in Nauvoo at Age 15," Mar. 30, 1881, Helen Mar Whitney Papers, LDS Archives, published in Holzapfel and Holzapfel, *Woman's View,* 250-54.

148. Whitney, "Scenes and Incidences," 39.

149. Ibid.

150. Ibid.

superiors." Specifically referencing her new husband, the prophet, her father's advice was to "listen with care to his council for he shall be thy head."[151] A glance at the *History of the Church* tells us it was a "cold, rainy" Sunday, May 28, when Joseph Smith "met with Brother Hyrum, Brigham Young, Heber C. Kimball, Willard Richards, ______ Whitney, and James Adams, in the upper room" of Smith's red brick store "to attend to ordinances and counseling."[152]

After Smith's death, Helen would re-marry. Her son Orson knew of his mother's first marriage but believed it took place closer to July. In this, one can see the motivation to place the date near the time of Smith's revelation on celestial marriage, thus justifying Helen's connection to the prophet. Orson would continue this subtle redefinition of the date in a biography of his grandfather: "Soon after the revelation, Helen Mar, the eldest daughter of Heber Chase and Vilate Murray Kimball[,] was given to the Prophet in the holy bonds of celestial marriage."[153] When the Smiths occupied the Mansion House that summer, the newlyweds lived just four blocks apart.

Helen's biographer concludes that she "expected her marriage to Joseph Smith" to be a ceremony "for *eternity* only," not an actual marriage involving physical relations. How surprised she was to discover "that it included [marriage for] *time* also": a physical union at age fourteen with a thirty-seven-year-old man.[154] As she put her ambivalent feelings into verse in her "Reminiscences," Helen had "thought through *this life* my time will be my own," but "the step I now am taking's for eternity alone." She saw her "youthful friends grow shy and cold" as "poisonous darts from sland'rous tongues were hurled." She was "bar'd out from social scenes by this destiny," and faced "sad'nd mem'ries of sweet departed joys." She felt "like a fetter'd bird with

---

151. Heber C. Kimball, Blessing to His Daughter Helen Mar Kimball, May 28, 1843, Helen Mar Whitney Papers.

152. *History of the Church,* 5:412.

153. Orson F. Whitney, *Life of Heber C. Kimball* (Salt Lake City: Kimball Family, 1888), 328.

154. Compton, *Sacred Loneliness,* 500, emphasis added; Linda King Newell and Valeen Tippetts Avery, *Mormon Enigma: Emma Hale Smith* (Garden City, N.Y.: Doubleday, 1984), 147.

wild and longing heart" that "dayly pine[s] for freedom and mur-m[u]r[s] at [its] lot." The poem references the "high celestial law" she knew she would have missed "had this not come through my dear father's mouth."[155]

Not only was Helen saddled by theological imperative to a man two and a half times her age, she longed for the more carefree associations of friends and especially the romantic overtures of her would-be boyfriend. In the end, young love prevailed. After Joseph's death, she married Horace Whitney on February 3, 1846, and raised a family with him. Their marriage was for *time* only, her obligation to her eternal marriage to Joseph Smith still firmly in place. Yet despite the continued allegiance to her first husband and the institution of celestial marriage, she could not shake the feeling of having been victimized by the imposition on her youth, confiding that she "would never have been sealed to Joseph had I known it was anything more than ceremony. I was young and they deceived me, by saying the salvation of our whole family depended on it."[156] When Horace took a plural wife (Lucy Amelia Bloxam) in 1850, then a second, Mary Cravath, in 1856, Helen would become more comfortable with plural marriage and advocate it in her writings.[157]

When the Whitneys journeyed to Utah, they tragically lost two children along the way. Much later, writing from her home near the capital's City Creek Canyon, she recorded her life memories of Joseph Smith and polygamy. Just before her beloved Horace died in 1884, she started a diary in which she continued to record family events and reminisce about the past. She died twelve years later in 1896 at age sixty-eight.

---

155. Helen Mar Kimball Smith Whitney to her children, Mar. 30, 1881, Helen Mar Whitney Papers; qtd. in Stanley B. Kimball, *Heber C. Kimball: Mormon Patriarch and Pioneer* (Urbana: University of Illinois Press, 1981), 109-10.

156. In Catherine Lewis, *Narrative of Some Proceedings of the Mormons* (Lynn, Mass.: N.p., 1848), 19, qtd. in Richard S. Van Wagoner, *Sidney Rigdon: A Portrait of Religious Excess* (Salt Lake City: Signature Books, 1994), 294.

157. See Todd Compton and Charles M. Hatch, eds., *A Widow's Tale: The 1884-1896 Diary of Helen Mar Kimball Whitney* (Logan: Utah State University Press, 2004).

Elvira Holmes

wife number 27
a married woman
June 1843

Smith married an average of one to two wives per month during the first five months of 1843. Continuing that trend, he married two more in June: Elvira Cowles Holmes and Rhoda Richards. Unlike the Partridge and Lawrence sisters, who said they helped with housekeeping at the Smith residence but were not paid for it, Cowles was hired for cleaning and childcare. She was born on November 23, 1813, in Unadilla, New York, 120 miles southeast of Palmyra and 30 miles from Harmony, Pennsylvania. Her father was a Vermont transplant who farmed, taught school, and worked as a mechanic. In early 1830 he and his new wife (Elvira's stepmother) and several children joined the Mormons. Elvira herself waited five years to become a church member in 1835. For two years at least, from 1840 to 1842, she lived in the Smith household. When she got married initially, the first of December 1842, one year prior to her marriage to Smith, she chose another Smith employee and resident of the household, the prophet's bodyguard, Jonathan Holmes. She was twenty-nine and he was thirty-six.

A half year later, she married her husband's boss, her 1869 affidavit from Salt Lake City affirming that "on the first day of June A.D. 1843 at Heber C. Kimball's house, in the City of Nauvoo, County of Hancock[,] State of Illinois, she was married or Sealed for time and all eternity to President Joseph Smith, by Elder Heber C. Kimball, in the presence of Vilate Kimball and Eliza Mariah (Partridge) Smith."[158] This was Smith's twelfth polyandrous marriage. Jonathan must have accepted his wife's marriage to Joseph, since on February 3, 1846, Jonathan acted as a proxy when Elvira was resealed to the deceased Smith. In 1862, Holmes married forty-five-year-old Sarah Floyd as a plural wife.

The Holmeses remained loyal to Smith, while Elvira's father,

158. Elvira A. C. Holmes, Affidavit, Aug. 28, 1869, "Affidavits on Celestial Marriage, 1869-1870."

Austin Cowles, was unconvinced when he heard Joseph's 1843 revelation on polygamy read to the Nauvoo Stake High Council, of which Cowles was a member. That was on August 12, 1843. The next year, Cowles became a counselor in the presidency of the new break-off Latter-day Saint Church in Nauvoo. In June he joined several other dissenters in drafting and publishing the *Nauvoo Expositor.* Simultaneously, thirty-year-old Elvira, a treasurer in the Nauvoo Relief Society, was trying to hush the rumors that were spreading about Smith's polygamous behavior. Elvira and Jonathan later went to Utah and raised five daughters and one adopted boy. She died in Farmington, Utah, in 1871.

Rhoda Richards

wife number 28
an unmarried woman
June 1843

Rhoda Richards was the sister of Apostle Willard Richards. Born on August 8, 1784, in Framingham, Massachusetts, she was the second of eleven children of Joseph and Rhoda Howe Richards. Two of her siblings, Willard and Levi, joined the Mormons in 1836 after visiting Smith in Kirtland. In 1837, Rhoda traveled by rail to New York to investigate the new church, and in mid-year she and her sister Nancy converted; they were baptized on June 2. She was adjusting to the recent loss of her mother, who had died in February that year, and two years later, her father died. Feeling anchorless in the wake of these losses, she decided to move to Nauvoo shortly thereafter, and by May 1, 1843, she was living in Joseph Smiths' red brick store. Her brother, Willard, had just become the first of Smith's inner circle to take a plural wife that year. On Monday, June 12, Rhoda herself, at age fifty-eight, the oldest of Joseph's wives, married her landlord and prophet. On that same day, Willard took a third plural wife. In fact, 1843 was a year of accelerated exchanges of favors among the elite of the city.

Rhoda continued to live at the store, which was also used for Masonic ceremonies, early temple endowments, plural marriage sealings, and priesthood meetings. Moving into the store had been a near alternative to residing in the Smith home itself, where several of the other women Joseph had courted were living. Rhoda affirmed on May 1, 1869, in Salt Lake County that "on the twelfth day of June A.D. 1843 at the city of Nauvoo ... she was married or Sealed to Joseph Smith, President of the church of Jesus Christ of Latter-day Saints, by [her brother] Willard Richards one of the Twelve Apostles of said church."[159] As an aside, Rhoda was a niece of Abigail Howe Young, Brigham Young's mother. Meanwhile, the *History of the Church* for that Monday has Joseph "at the office morning and afternoon" approving resolutions to build an arsenal in the city for the Nauvoo Legion. The following day, Joseph took Emma and the children north to see her sister, Mrs. Wasson, 200 miles away in Dixon, Illinois.[160]

Seven months or so after Smith was killed, Rhoda married her first cousin, Brigham Young, and the ceremony was re-solemnized on January 31, 1846, with Young standing as proxy for Smith. Rhoda and her brothers journeyed to Utah in 1847. Rhoda's marriages exemplified the kinship network at play in Nauvoo whereby Smith married the sister of one of his apostles, a woman who was also the first cousin of another apostle and who was acquired as a responsibility by one of the Twelve when she was widowed. That she was her husband Brigham's cousin was apparently secondary to the grander scheme of interlocking the hierarchy in marriage. It fulfilled Smith's view of the manner in which family relations would be extended into the next world. Rhoda died in Salt Lake City in January 1879 at age ninety-four.

Hannah S. Ells

wife number 29
an unmarried woman
about June 1843

About mid-year, Joseph married three more women. This was after already having acquired twenty-seven plural wives, six of whom Emma

159. Rhoda Richards, Affidavit, May 1, 1869, ibid.
160. *History of the Church*, 5:430-31.

probably knew about. The next three were Hannah Ells and the sisters Mary Ann and Olive Grey Frost, followed shortly thereafter by Desdemona Fullmer.

The first of these, Hannah Ells, was twenty-seven when she moved to Nauvoo in 1840. Born in Newcastle, England, she was one of four foreign wives in Smith's female entourage.[161] It is likely that she traveled with her older brother, Josiah, when he came to America in 1831 and joined the Mormons in New Jersey eight years later. In Nauvoo, she advertised herself in the *Times and Seasons* as a seamstress:

> Miss H. S. Ells begs leave to respectfully inform the Ladies of Nauvoo, and its vicinity, that she intends carrying on the above business, in all its varied branches: and further states, that she has had several years experience in one of the most fashionable French establishments in Philadelphia. Her place of residence is at Dr. Samuel Bennetts where orders will be attended to. Nauvoo, Sept. 30, 1841.[162]

According to John Benbow's 1869 affidavit, Ells married Smith "in the spring or forepart of the summer of 1843." He elaborated, saying she boarded with him for two months that summer and that "President Smith frequently visited his wife Hannah at his (J. B.'s) house." For "several months in 1844, after the Prophet's death," she returned as a boarder.[163] Eliza Snow confirmed that she had been a plural wife of the prophet, as well as the fact that she tragically died "in Nauvoo in Sister Sarah Kimball's house." The hypothesis is that she died of malaria.[164]

In early summer, Missouri officers came once again for Smith, arresting him on a charge of treason on June 23 at the request of Missouri Governor Thomas Reynolds for unsettled past infractions. Illinois Governor Thomas Ford levied the accusation.[165] Sheriff Joseph H. Reynolds of Jackson County, Missouri, accompanied Carthage, Illinois, Constable Harmon T. Wilson to the residence of Emma's niece

---

161. Smith's other foreign-born wives were Maria Lawrence, Sarah Lawrence, and Sarah Scott Mulholland.

162. *Times and Seasons,* Oct. 1, 1841, 566; qtd. in Compton, *Sacred Loneliness,* 535.

163. John Benbow, Affidavit, Aug. 28, 1869, qtd. in Jenson, "Plural Marriage," 222-23.

164. Eliza R. Snow to John Taylor, Dec. 12, 1886, Eliza Snow Letter File, LDS Archives.

165. *History of the Church,* 5:433, 464-65.

in Dixon, where they crept toward the residence with "cocked pistols." As often happened, Smith scrambled to produce a writ issued from Nauvoo against the lawmen, resulting in the lawmen's arrest and Smith's freedom. Back in Nauvoo, Smith voiced his defiance: "I wish you to know and publish that we have all power; and if any man from this time forth says anything to the contrary, cast it into his teeth."[166] As we will see, where another man may have shrunk from courting women under such circumstances, far from having his enthusiasm dampened, Smith seemed to augment his obsession to acquire as many new wives as possible.

Mary Ann and Olive Frost

wives number 30 and 31
married, unmarried
July 1843

The prophet soon married another pair of sisters: Olive Grey Frost and Mary Ann Frost Pratt. Mary Ann was the older of the two, born in January 1809 in Groton, Vermont, the fifth of eleven children of Aaron and Susannah Frost. Her sister Olive was the eighth child in the family, born in July 1816 in Bethel, Maine. They encountered Mormonism from some apostles visiting Maine in 1835, when Mary Ann was already twenty-seven years old and her sister Olive almost twenty. Their parents accepted the apostles' invitation to join their faith. The next year, Mary Ann moved to Kirtland, where in May she married Apostle Parley P. Pratt, who had one child and was recently widowed. His first wife, Thankful Halsey, had died six weeks before. Similarly, Mary Ann had lost a spouse, Nathan Stearns, and had a four-year-old girl named after her mother. In Kirtland, Olive was converted to the faith in 1839, and in the fall of 1840 she accompanied the Pratts to England to serve with them there as a missionary. Not long after relocating to Nauvoo in early April 1843, there is evidence that each of the sisters married Joseph Smith.[167]

166. Ibid., 5:466-67.

167. Mary Ann Pratt, "Frost, (Olive Grey)," in Jenson, "Plural Marriage," 234-35; Cook, *Nauvoo Marriages*, 48n2.

Olive did not leave a personal account of her marriage, but in Mary Ann's biography of Olive published in May 1887, Mary Ann mentioned that by early summer 1843 Olive had accepted the teaching of eternal progression, whereby a man could become a king in heaven and, with his wives by his side, create his own worlds and civilizations and rule over them as a god. Olive, Mary Ann wrote,

> seemed to realize and appreciate the magnitude of the great and important mission allotted to women in the perfect plan of this Gospel dispensation, and she desired to do her part in the good work. She freely accorded to man the title of king, and joyfully accepted the place of queen by his side, for it was at this time that the principle of the plurality of wives was taught to her. She never opposed it, and, as in the case of baptism, soon accepted it to be her creed, in practice as well as in theory. She was married for time and all eternity to Joseph Smith some time previous to his death and martyrdom.[168]

Mary Ann's vagueness about the date of her sister's wedding suggests that it could have occurred about the same time as Mary Ann's own marriage but without her knowledge of it. If they followed the pattern of Smith's courtship of other sisters, the marriage dates would have fallen within a few days or weeks of each other. Though not conclusive, the congruity of the sister marriages would suggest that Olive married Joseph close to the time he presented his celestial marriage revelation to some selected friends in Nauvoo.

If Olive took to polygamy easily, it would not be so for her sister. On July 24, Mary Ann's husband married his first plural wife, Elizabeth Brotherton. She was the sister of the young woman, Martha Brotherton, who had refused Brigham Young in 1842. Although Mary Ann was evidently sealed to Joseph that same day, she could not fully accept Parley's marriages to other women; she held out a decade and then divorced Parley in 1853, the year he courted his tenth wife. Mary Ann was sealed to Parley on June 23, 1843, by Hyrum Smith,[169] but Joseph subsequently canceled the sealing and had her sealed to himself

168. Mary Ann Pratt, "Frost, (Olive Grey)," 234-35.
169. Parley P. Pratt Family Record, copy in author's possession.

on July 24 for time and eternity.[170] Early the next year, Wilford Woodruff reported a meeting of the Quorum of the Anointed in the red brick store, during which Parley "received his 2d Anointing," a unique ceremony for married couples. Joseph drew attention to the anomaly, at least in a technical sense, because Parley "had no wife sealed to him for eternity." He thought Parley needed to go out and find another wife "or els his glory would be Clip[p]ed."[171] Following Joseph's death in 1844, Pratt was sealed to Mary Wood, Hannahette Snively, and Belinda Marden, while Mary Ann was resealed to Smith on February 6, 1846, in the Nauvoo temple, with Pratt acting as the proxy husband. All of this remains shrouded in secrecy. On the Monday Joseph married Mary Ann, the *History of the Church* described only Joseph's morning conversation with Mr. Hoge, Democratic candidate for Congress, about the "governor's sending an armed force to take me" and the settlement of a debt owed Smith by William and Wilson Law.[172]

Mary Ann went west and lived in Utah until her death in 1891. Olive was resealed to Smith five months after his death, on November 7, 1844, with Brigham Young as proxy. Her sealing to Brigham "for time" lasted only one year, because Olive died on October 6, 1845. She was twenty-nine. The ceremony between Olive and Joseph was not repeated vicariously in the Nauvoo temple in 1846 since both spouses were dead.

Nancy Winchester

wife number 32
an unmarried woman
about July 1843

Sometime in 1843, probably by summer or early fall, Smith married

---

170. See Gary James Bergera, "The Earliest Eternal Sealings for Civilly Married Couples Living and Dead," *Dialogue: A Journal of Mormon Thought* 35 (Fall 2002): 56; Bergera, "Identifying Earliest Polygamists," 19-23. See also Cook, *Nauvoo Marriages,* 16-17; Anderson and Bergera, *Joseph Smith's Quorum,* 232; and Lisle G Brown, comp., *Nauvoo Sealings, Adoptions, and Anointings: A Comprehensive Register of Persons Receiving LDS Temple Ordinances, 1841-1846* (Salt Lake City: Smith-Pettit Foundation, 2006), 246.

171. Kenney, *Wilford Woodruff's Journal,* 2:340.

172. *History of the Church,* 5:518.

Nancy Maria Winchester. Born on August 10, 1828, in western Pennsylvania, she was the fourth of six children of Stephen Winchester and Nancy Case. She was four years old when her parents met the Mormon missionaries. Almost immediately her family converted and moved to Ohio, where Nancy was baptized in 1836 at age eight and then apparently married Smith at age fourteen or fifteen.

In May 1842, at the age of thirteen, she was invited to join the Relief Society, which was considered a high honor for such a young woman. Her mother was asked to join a month later.[173] If the marriage between Nancy and Joseph occurred before her birthday in 1843, she would have been fourteen. The precise date remains unknown, but Compton, for instance, concluded that it must have happened about the time Nancy and her mother agreed to help quash rumors about plural marriage through the Relief Society in July 1843.[174] Whatever the exact date, Nancy holds the distinction, with Helen Whitney, of being one of the two youngest brides in Smith's repertoire.

Four months after Smith's death, Nancy married Heber C. Kimball on October 10, 1844, then again in the completed temple on February 3, 1846, Kimball acting as proxy for Nancy's sealing to Joseph Smith. She traveled to Utah with the Kimballs but lived with her parents, the Winchesters. In 1865 she married Amos Arnold in Salt Lake City, by whom she had her only child at age thirty-nine. After several years of poor health, she died at age forty-seven on March 17, 1876.

Desdemona Fullmer

wife number 33
an unmarried woman
July 1843

Desdemona Fullmer, born on October 6, 1809, was the fourth of seven

173. See Maureen Carr Ward, "'This Institution Is a Good One': The Female Relief Society of Nauvoo, 17 March 1842 to 16 March 1844," *Mormon Historical Studies* 3 (2002): 197.

174. Compton, *Sacred Loneliness*, 6, 606, 768. Nancy Maria's mother was Nancy Case Winchester, evidently the "Nancy Winchester" who was welcomed into the Relief Society on April 14, 1842, a month after her daughter. It must be the daughter who mentions that Nancy Case resided with Clarissa Marvel.

children of Peter and Susanah Fullmer, farmers in eastern Pennsylvania. From a prayerful Methodist household that believed in visions and the restoration of "true" Christianity, it was not surprising that at age twenty-five when Desdemona heard her parents read the Book of Mormon aloud, she became convinced that Joseph Smith "was a true prophit." She was baptized in 1836 and then joined the Saints in Kirtland. In her "short histery of my life," she described her conversion.[175]

Later she affirmed that by July 1843, she had become the church president's plural wife, making her the thirty-second plural wife according to the running count we have been keeping. Not unexpectedly, according to the trend that had developed, she was yet another "hired girl" who worked in the Smith home. It is not known when she was hired, but for reasons we can only surmise—possibly relating to Emma—she had to leave the Smith residence and move in with the Claytons in May 1843.

In fact, without specifying exact dates in her autobiography, she identified some tension within the Smith home. During "the rise of poligamy," she wrote, she had a dream warning her that "Amy Smith" (a misspelling that probably indicated how Desdemona pronounced Emma's name) "was a going to poisen me." When she related this to Joseph, he said he thought it was probably true, that Emma "would do it if she could."[176] Desdemona was shunted into the nearby home of Smith's secretary, although this would not prove to be a viable solution. It was not long before she accused Clayton of assaulting her. On January 29, 1844, Clayton recorded that he had "some conversation with Desdemona C. Fullmer. She has treated my family unfeelingly and unkindly in various ways and I requested her to look out for another home. She said she would not until she had counsel from Joseph." The next day she complained to Brigham Young and Heber Kimball that Clayton had threatened to "kick her." Clayton responded that she "lied" and had a "malicious disposition."[177]

175. Desdemona F[ullmer] Smith, Statement, June 7, 1868, Desdemona Wadsworth Fullmer Papers, LDS Archives.

176. Ibid.

177. Smith, *Intimate Chronicle*, 125.

She placed her marriage to Joseph in the context of his revelation on polygamy, specifying the month of July but leaving the day blank, adding that the sealing was performed by Brigham Young "in the presence of Heber C. Kimball."[178] In recalling Smith's February 1843 discussion of "celestial or plural marriage," Clayton confirmed that "Desdemona C. Fullmer and others were [Smith's] lawful wives." Smith himself referenced Desdemona in company with Louisa Beaman, Sylvia Sessions, and Eliza Snow, all of whom were 1841-42 wives. Jenson deduced that Fullmer must have been "among the first,"[179] and it is in fact possible that she married Smith in 1842 or by February 1843 when Clayton mentioned her. Smith ceased marrying anyone in the summer of 1842 in response to John Bennett's verbal attacks, so the marriage to Fullmer may have occurred prior to that time. In all probability, what can be said is that the marriage occurred by July 1843.

Desdemona was resealed to the deceased prophet on January 26, 1846, with Apostle Ezra T. Benson as Smith's proxy.[180] As was customary, Benson simultaneously acquired Fullmer as his dependant, and she joined him and his five other wives in Utah. In 1852 she divorced him. She then re-married a third time, later to separate again. Throughout her later life, she was known simply as Desdemona Fullmer Smith. She died in February 1886.

A revelation

Even as Joseph took as many as four more plural wives in July and as other men in Nauvoo, including some in his own family, engaged in the thinly veiled restoration of an ancient patriarchal order, Smith took the further step of codifying the practice. On July 12 he sat down with Clayton for three hours dictating the now famous revelation on

---

178. Desdemona Fullmer Smith, Affidavit, June 17, 1869, "Affidavits on Celestial Marriage, 1869-1870."

179. Clayton affidavit, Feb. 16, 1874; see also Jenson, "Plural Marriage," 235; compare Jenson, 224-26 and Smith, *Intimate Chronicle*, 557, which omit reference to wife "S. P. Sessions." In affidavit, Clayton names Desdemona C. (Catlin) vs. "W." used by Jenson and Smith.

180. "A Book of Proxey [Sealings]," entry no. 88, Jan. 26, 1846, L. Tom Perry Special Collections.

plural marriage. Clayton said he "wrote it, sentence by sentence, as [Smith] dictated" it.[181]

The basic concept had already unfolded with the conditional passage installed in the 1830 Book of Mormon and the rationale for the 1831 "Lamanite" mission in Ohio. This concept was presented in the early 1840s to Joseph Noble and others and allegedly received Emma's tacit complicity in 1843 in allowing her husband to marry the Partridge and Lawrence sisters. By then, the practice had already become well-rooted in Smith's new city. But his dictation from God in 1843 sealed the doctrine with a stamp of official endorsement. It would not be publicly discussed until 1852 or published as scripture until 1876, but the psychological effect of saying the divine communication had been logged in on a church docket was enormous. Another unintended consequence was that it would place an additional wall of otherness between the Saints and their neighbors. In large part, the revelation would define the boundaries separating this millennialist Christian community from adjacent towns and villages for the rest of the century.

Just as Emily Partridge recognized that her marriage to Smith in March did not fall under the rubric of the July statement, the sanction was too late to validate thirty other marriages. Apologists have hunted for earlier comments they have thought might justify backdating the revelation's reception, if not its actual wording, to at least April 1841. Irrespective of the framework chosen to understand the nearly three dozen women Smith married up to July 1843, the document provided the rationale for the matrix already under construction, and it gave others the necessary validation to help maintain it.

This rationale invoked a variety of responses in its adherents: fear, outrage, pleasure, confidence, and religious fulfillment. What became known as Section 132 of the Doctrine and Covenants would be Smith's last canonized revelation. In this final official expression, he conveyed the idea of a "new and everlasting covenant" that "no one can reject—and enter into my glory" (132:4). Then, as if respond-

181. Smith, *Intimate Chronicle,* 110, 558; *History of the Church,* 5:500-07.

ing to Emma's objections to each of Joseph's wives, the voice of the male deity "command[ed]" Emma, if there had been any question about Joseph's thirty or so wives, to "receive all those that have been given unto my servant Joseph"—more or less confirming the previous alliances and doing little to convince the first lady of the church. The command was followed by a threat: "If she will not abide this commandment she shall be destroyed. … for I am the Lord thy God, and will destroy her if she abide not in my law" (51-54).

Next, to sanction all that had already occurred and had been anticipated for the future, God stated that "if any man espouse a virgin, and desire to espouse another—he is justified. … And if he have ten virgins—he cannot commit adultery for they belong to him" (61-62). Not only for Joseph, but for all worthy Nauvoo men, certain privileges were said to be theirs to enjoy. Once again, recalcitrant wives were threatened with destruction: "If any man have a wife—and teaches her the law—then shall she believe and administer unto him, or she shall be destroyed, sayeth … God, for I will destroy her" (64). The efficacy of this rationale depended, of course, on the ears of the readers, whether they perceived in the message an all-powerful being or merely wishful thinking on the part of his earthly servant. Given the proximity in time and place with other ominous developments and the degree to which followers were immersed in the belief structure, this revelation could be interpreted as both prophetic and individually threatening, especially for women.

Even though Smith and Clayton spent three hours preparing the eloquent language of the "revelation on the eternity of the marriage covenant, including the plurality of wives," Emma was not mollified by this open announcement of her husband's female acquisitions. She lashed out at Clayton on August 21 when she discovered he had delivered Eliza Snow's letters to her husband. She suspected a gold watch in Flora Woodworth's possession was a romantic gift, and "she abused [Joseph] much" over it "when he got home."[182]

The struggle over polygamy was not confined to the leading fam-

182. Smith, *Intimate Chronicle,* 21, 23.

ily; it generated ripples of hostility near and far. In response, Smith began offering ever more elaborate justifications to motivate new participants. He said polygamy represented a higher religious order, that it provided support for the widowed and orphaned and constituted an elite sisterhood, that it would be the means of economic survival. Primarily, he avowed that trust in his leadership of the church showed obedience to God, for which the reward would be a place in heaven. Much of the acceptance of celestial marriage relied on Smith's charisma and the inclination of other men to be drawn to the privileges that Smith convinced them were their birthright.

Melissa Lott

wife number 34
an unmarried woman
September 1843

Two months after dictating the polygamy revelation, Smith married Melissa Lott. Her marriage appears in the Lott family Bible, listing it on September 20, 1843, the same day her parents, Cornelius and Permelia Darrow Lott, were "sealed for eternity" by Joseph's brother Hyrum. When questioned about this during the Temple Lot inquiry, Melissa gave a slightly different date, September 27; but in her 1868 affidavit she still claimed September 20, the date accepted by Andrew Jenson in 1887.[183]

It seems clear that Melissa's father and mother gave her to Smith in exchange for having their own marriage solemnized for eternity. They were thorough going followers who had been loyal to Smith since 1836 when they had moved to Kirtland. Their eldest daughter was born in January 1824 on an eastern Pennsylvania farm, the first of eleven children. Her parents accepted the Mormon message when she was ten. Her father managed Smith's farm in Nauvoo and became a polygamist himself when he was sealed to four other women in 1846, then to two more in 1847, for a total of seven wives.

183. Lott Family Bible, LDS Archives; *Reorganized Church v. Church of Christ,* questions 63-64; Smith, *Blood Atonement,* 72; Jenson, "Plural Marriage," 234.

Melissa moved in with the Smiths in 1842 and spoke of assisting Emma with housework and tending children. In her Temple Lot deposition, she was candid enough about her relationship with Joseph during the fall of 1843 to affirm that she was "a wife in all that word implies." When asked if she ever "room[ed] with" him, she confirmed that she had done so: in "room number one" of the Nauvoo mansion and also at her father's house.[184] She clarified that these were places she had "room[ed] with him as his wife," not beforehand.[185]

She remained several months with the Smiths after the marriage before returning to the farmhouse where her father oversaw the crops and animals and served as one of Smith's bodyguards. In various statements, she offered her views of sex, children, and secrecy in Smith's plural marriages. When her nephew Joseph III visited her in Utah and asked if she were "a wife in very deed," and if so why there had been no children, she answered: "Through no fault of either of us, lack of proper conditions on my part probably," and the limited space of time before he was "martyred nine months after our marriage." She acknowledged that she "did not know of any" children by Smith's other plural marriages.[186]

Melissa confirmed that the marriage was a secret, as were Smith's other polygamous unions. She was not "seen on the streets and in public places with him, as his wife."[187] The marriage took place at her parents' home on the Smith farm. Only hinting at the unannounced event, Joseph's diary reports briefly for that day that he "rode out to his farm." In the *History of the Church,* the entry is amended slightly: "Visited my farm, accompanied by my Brother Hyrum," significant because it was Hyrum who performed the sealing.[188] Most likely, the ceremony was conducted in the morning, since later in the day Smith answered a letter from Illinois Governor Ford and that evening probably visited a phrenologist. We know that six of the apostles had the

184. *Reorganized Church v. Church of Christ,* questions 17, 227-31, 237-38, 255.

185. Ibid., questions 256-59.

186. Melissa Lott, Affidavit, Aug. 4, 1893, in Stanley Ivins Papers, Utah State Historical Society; *Reorganized Church v. Church of Christ,* question 86.

187. Ibid., question 95.

188. Faulring, *American Prophet's Record,* 415; *History of the Church,* 6 (Sep. 20, 1843): 35.

contours of their heads read that evening, and it was an activity Smith usually attended.[189]

Between Smith's marriage to Melissa in September and his November 2 wedding to Fanny Young, he walked "up and down the streets" of Nauvoo "with my scribe" and "gave instructions to try those persons who were preaching, teaching, or practicing the doctrine of plurality of wives; for, according to the law, I hold the keys of this power in the last days; for there is never but one on earth at a time on whom the power and its keys are conferred; *and I have constantly said no man shall have but one wife at a time, unless the Lord directs otherwise.*"[190] While marrying celestial wives himself and offering similar "favors" to some thirty other men, Smith found it useful to reference the conditional restriction on marriage found in the Book of Mormon. By placing himself in the role of determining when and on whom the Lord would bestow this privilege, the prophet could both condemn and allow plural marriage. As he was policing the practice, he was also visiting his wives who were housed with their own families. On Thursday, October 19, he and Clayton traveled to Macedonia to see Almera Johnson. They "arrived there about sundown, and I stayed at brother Benjamin F. Johnson's for the night."[191]

Smith and Clayton returned home on Saturday in time to prepare for Sunday meetings. George A. Smith had just returned home from a mission and heard Hyrum Smith recite from memory "most of the Revelation of Patriarchal Marriage." In this private gathering, "plurality of wives" was portrayed as "an institution which would redeem the female sex from degradation and exalt mankind to celestial glory and increase."[192]

In the second year after Joseph's death, Melissa married John Bernhisel, a forty-six-year-old doctor and close friend of Smith. On that day, February 8, 1846, Bernhisel acted as proxy for Smith so Melissa

---

189. *History of the Church,* 6:36-37.

190. Ibid., 6:46, but not in Joseph Smith's journal. See 1835 D&C 101 (removed from 1876 D&C, but still found in Community of Christ Section 111), recalled in *Times and Seasons,* Oct. 1, 1842, 939.

191. Ibid., 6:59-60.

192. George A. Smith to Joseph Smith III, Oct. 9, 1869.

could be resealed to the prophet. However, Lott soon separated from Bernhisel, and on May 13, 1849, she married Ira J. Willes "with the full understanding it was for time only."[193] Willes was a Mormon Battalion and California gold rush veteran who settled with her in Utah. She died a widow in Lehi, Utah, in 1894.

Sarah Mulholland

wife number 35
a widow
by October 1843

Sarah Scott, born in Armagh, Ireland, in 1816, married Joseph Smith's clerk, James Mulholland, in 1839. Unfortunately, he died the same year he was married, apparently of malaria, like so many others in Nauvoo at the time. Four years later, Sarah is thought to have married Joseph Smith in a union concealed by her October 25, 1843, civil marriage to Alexander Mullinder—a ceremony performed by Apostle John Taylor. On February 3, 1846, Sarah was sealed to Mulholland, Heber Kimball acting as proxy for her deceased first husband. There are two reasons for concluding that Sarah was joined to Joseph for time and eternity. First, in her 1846 sealing ceremony, she was identified as Sarah Smith, indicating a prior marriage to Joseph. Second, in a biography of Heber Kimball, family tradition lists her among "the wives of the prophet" whom Kimball adopted as his own, 1844-46. These included Presendia Huntington, Sarah Lawrence, Martha McBride, Sarah Mulholland, Sylvia Sessions, Lucy Walker, Sarah Ann Whitney, Nancy Winchester, and a less-known woman, Mary Huston (see below).[194] She would have been one of Joseph's wives by the time she married the apparent decoy in October 1843.

Phebe Woodworth

wife number 36
a married woman
October 1843

193. Lott, Affidavit, Aug. 4, 1893.

194. Whitney, *Life of Heber C. Kimball,* 418-19; Brown, comp., *Nauvoo Sealings, Adop-*

On October 29, the mother of Flora Woodworth (see wife 19 above) was initiated into the Holy Order. This event was significant enough for Brigham Young to record it in his 1843 diary, probably because under normal circumstances only plural wives and consenting first wives were admitted to this secret society. Phebe may have joined the inner circle of polygamists at an earlier time, perhaps in March 1843 with Flora in a mother-daughter marriage to Smith. In any case, Phebe's presence among the select order of "the anointed" lends credence to the idea that she had been wedded to Smith, whether in March or October or some time in between.[195]

Mary Huston

wife number 37
an unmarried woman
October 1843

The early Mormon historian Orson Whitney included Mary Huston, born September 11, 1818, in Jackson, Ohio, among the women who had married Joseph Smith and then became attached to Heber Kimball after Smith's death. In fact, in the official sealings record for the Nauvoo temple listing eight widows of the prophet who were given to Kimball, Mary is identified as "Mary Huston Smith," along with "Sarah Scott [Mulholland] Smith" and "Nancy Maria [Winchester] Smith."[196] As an aside, Olive Andrews (see possible wives below) was sealed to Smith for eternity at the same time and then given to Brigham Young as a wife for mortality. If Mary Huston married Joseph Smith during his lifetime, as some historians have assumed, we do not even have an approximate date for it. It is given here as October 1843 to put it toward the end but before the marriage to Fanny Murray, which was said to have been Smith's last.

---

tions, and Anointings, 215; Lyndon W. Cook, comp., *Nauvoo Deaths and Marriages* (Orem, Utah: Grandin Book, 1994), 108; James Wesley Scott, "The Jacob and Sarah Warnock Scott Family 1779-1910," written June 2002, www.scottcorner.org.

195. Brigham Young, Diary, LDS Archives.

196. "Book of Sealings (Living)—Wives to Husbands," Book A, LDS Archives.

Fanny Murray

wife number 38
a widow
November 1843

Fanny Young was married twice prior to her wedding to Smith on November 2. An older sister of Brigham Young, she was born in November 1787, thirteen years before Brigham, the second in a household eventually numbering eleven children. She was nurtured on a farm in Hopkinton, Massachusetts, until 1800 when the Youngs moved to Whitingham, Vermont, where Brigham was born. Four years later the Youngs moved to Mendon, New York, west of Syracuse.

After childless marriages to Robert Carr from 1806 to 1815 and Roswell Murray from 1832 to 1840, Fanny was already fifty-five years old by the time she married Smith. Her second husband was the father of Vilate Murray, who grew up to marry Heber Kimball. In a Sunday sermon thirty years later, on August 31, 1873, in Paris, Idaho, Brigham remembered that his sister had told the prophet she wanted "the privilege of being a ministering angel; that is the labor that I wish to perform. I don't want any companion in that world." Joseph replied to her: "Sister, you talk very foolishly, you do not know what you will want." He then reportedly turned to Brigham and said on impulse, "Here, brother Brigham, you seal this lady to me." Brigham complied, explaining: "I sealed her to him. This was my own sister according to the flesh."[197]

The same day he married his sister to Smith, Young married Augusta Adams and Harriet Cook, his own second and third plural wives. Adams and Cook both affirmed Fanny's marriage to Smith at the same time they married Young. Jenson reported that "Fanny Young, a sister of Pres. Brigham Young, [was] married to Joseph Nov. 2, 1843. Brigham Young officiating."[198] There is no evidence that Fanny ever lived with the Smiths.

---

197. "Discourse by President Brigham Young," *Journal of Discourses,* 26 vols. (London: Latter-day Saint's Book Depot, 1854-86), 16:166-67.

198. Affidavit of Augusta A. Young, July 12, 1869; Harriet Cook, Mar. 4, 1870, "Affidavits on Celestial Marriage, 1869-1870"; Jenson, "Plural Marriage," 234.

After Joseph died, Fanny went to Utah in 1850. From 1856 to 1859, she lived with Brigham's wives in his dormitory-style Lion House. She died in 1859 at age seventy-one. There was significance to the fact that, as Compton points out, she lived to the end of her life under the same roof as Zina Jacobs, Emily Partridge, Eliza Snow, and others of Joseph Smith's widows.[199]

Fanny's marriage to Smith was not re-solemnized in the Nauvoo temple. However, she was included on a list of eleven women LDS Church President Lorenzo Snow believed to have been sealed to Smith during his lifetime. The church president had these women resealed to Smith in 1899 if a record of a prior sealing could not be found.[200]

The pace of Smith's marriages picked up in 1843, indicating that he must have felt greater freedom, or perhaps greater urgency, to couple with select women. Dates are not available for all of the twenty-one women he married before the end of the year; but even though the evidence for some wives is less conclusive than for others, the trend is clear. He may have been motivated by his success in convincing his associates to engage in the same practice. This was the year they overtook him: his colleagues brought thirty-one women home in 1843 to meet their first wives. As the legacy of polygamy was passed to other men, the social structure of the institution evolved. The diaries and letters of these men and women indicate that the original wife was usually told what was going on in each case, and she often helped choose the new wife or wives. Unlike Joseph's domestic arrangements, the plural wives of his followers opted to live together with each other in common households. Accounts of how this took place form the subject of the next three chapters.

Possible marriages

In addition to thirty-eight documented wives of Joseph Smith, there are another six who may be seen as persons of interest. Until

---

199. Compton, *Sacred Loneliness,* 169.

200. Thomas Milton Tinney, *Royal Family of the Prophet Joseph Smith Jr.* (Salt Lake City: Tinney-Green Family Organization, 1973), 41, 63, citing Salt Lake Temple Sealing Records, GS Film 184590, Family History Library; see also *New Mormon Studies CD-ROM* (Salt Lake City: Smith Research Associates, 1998).

further evidence is uncovered, we cannot know with certainty what their status was, even though they look like wives. For instance, Vienna Jacques knew Joseph in Kirtland and was supported financially by the church, based on an 1833 revelation to Joseph Smith (D&C 90:28-29). A later church president, Joseph F. Smith, assumed that Jacques was a plural wife and in 1869 prepared an affidavit for her to sign to acknowledge this. For some reason, she never signed it.

There are indications that Smith may have married five other women: Olive Andrews, Hannah Dibble, Sally Ann Fuller, Aphia Sanburn, and Jane Tibbets. To varying degrees, they were acknowledged or suspected of having been wives and were posthumously sealed to Smith in the Nauvoo temple, following the same procedure as for Smith's known wives when the temple was completed in 1846. In one instance, Brigham Young was proxy for Olive Andrews's sealing to Smith and then received her as his own wife, as was also done for many of Smith's widows.[201]

As noted in chapter 1, Smith demonstrated affection for Fanny Alger from about the time Joseph III was born in 1832. According to subsequent reports, which are suspicious in that they reflect the later understanding of the sealing doctrine, Fanny was assumed to have been sealed to Joseph in about 1833. But Oliver Cowdery called the relationship an "affair," as did other contemporaries. It may be proper to put all of the marriages before July 1843 into that same category—not for the purpose of rendering judgment about them but from a legalistic standpoint because they violated the law of the church at the time, as they arguably did for years to come.

Perhaps no one in Nauvoo—aside from Smith himself—ever knew exactly how many women he married. Bennett's publications in 1842 disclosed what he knew before his departure from the city. By mid-1843, knowledgeable members of the community began making

---

201. Brown, *Nauvoo Sealings,* 281-86. Lyndon W. Cook counts forty-five sealings to Smith during the Nauvoo period (*Nauvoo Marriages,* 12-15). Lawrence Foster notes an additional 300 or more women who were sealed to Smith after Nauvoo, but not because they had been married to him during his lifetime (*Religion and Sexuality: Three American Communal Experiments of the Nineteenth Century* [New York: Oxford University Press, 1981], 156).

their own lists. When the pace of Smith's marriages slowed somewhat in late 1843, Benjamin Johnson was able to list many of Smith's wives: "At this time I knew that the Prophet had as his wives, Louisa Beeman, Eliza R. Snow, Maria and Sarah Lawrence, Sisters Lyon and Dibble, one or two of Bishop Partridge's daughters, and some of C[ornelius]. P. Lott's daughters, together with my own two sisters."[202] Notice that

TABLE 3.1 Joseph Smith's wives

	marriage/sealing	1846 resealing
1. Emma Hale	January 18, 1827	—
2. Louisa Beaman	April 5, 1841	January 14
3. Zina Diantha Huntington (Jacobs)* ~	October 27, 1841	February 2
4. Presendia L. Huntington (Buell)* ~	December 11, 1841	February 4
5. Agnes M. Coolbrith (Smith)	January 6, 1842	—
6. Lucinda Pendleton (Morgan Harris) ~	< January 17, 1842	January 22
7. Mary Elizabeth Rollins (Lightner) ~	February 1842	January 17
8. Sylvia P. Sessions (Lyon)† ~	February 8, 1842	January 26
9. Patty Bartlett (Sessions)† ~	March 9, 1842	—
10. Sarah M. Kingsley (Howe Cleveland) ~	< March 1842	January 15
11. Elizabeth Davis (Brackenbury Durfee) ~	< March 1842	January 22
12. Marinda Nancy Johnson (Hyde) ~	April 1842	—
13. Delcena D. Johnson (Sherman)*	June 1842	—
14. Eliza Roxcy Snow	June 29, 1842	February 3
15. Sarah Rapson (Poulterer) ~	< July 1842	—
16. Sarah Ann Whitney	July 27, 1842	January 12
17. Martha McBride (Knight)	August 5, 1842	January 26
18. Ruth Daggett Vose (Sayers) ~	February 1843	—
19. Flora Ann Woodworth†	March 4, 1843	—
20. Emily Dow Partridge*	March 4, 1843	January 14
21. Eliza Maria Partridge*	March 8, 1843	January 13
22. Almera Woodward Johnson*	< April 25, 1843	—
23. Lucy Walker	May 1, 1843	January 15
24. Sarah Lawrence*	May 11, 1843	January 26
25. Maria Lawrence*	ca. May 11, 1843	January 24
26. Helen Mar Kimball	ca. May 28, 1843	February 4
27. Elvira Annie Cowles (Holmes) ~	June 1, 1843	February 3

202. Johnson, *Life's Review*, 96-97.

TABLE 3.1 *(continued)*

	marriage/sealing	1846 resealing
28. Rhoda Richards	June 12, 1843	January 31
29. Hannah S. Ells	mid-1843	
30. Mary Ann Frost (Stearns, Pratt)* ~	July 24, 1843	February 6
31. Olive Grey Frost*	ca. July 1843	—
32. Nancy Maria Winchester	ca. July 1843	February 3
33. Desdemona Wadsworth Fullmer	< July 1843	January 26
34. Melissa Lott	September 20, 1843	February 8
35. Sarah Scott (Mulholland)	< October 25, 1843	February 3
36. Phebe Watrous (Woodworth)† ~	< October 29, 1843	January 17
37. Mary Huston	ca. October 1843	February 3
38. Fanny Young (Carr Murray)	November 2, 1843	—

* sister-sister marriages
† mother-daughter marriages
~ wives with current husbands

TABLE 3.2 Women of interest

	marriage/sealing	1846 resealing
1. Olive Andrews	<1844	January 15
2. Hannah Dibble	"	—
3. Sally Ann Fuller	"	—
4. Vienna Jacques (Shearer)	"	—
5. Jane Tibbets	"	January 17
6. Aphia Woodman Sanburn (Dow Yale)	"	—

he refers to more than one Lott girl, whereas we know only about Melissa. Earlier that same year, Clayton reported a conversation in which Smith talked about his wives and named a few.[203] Whether we discover that there were more than thirty-eight, Smith's coterie of clandestine marriages is already extensive. Adding six more to the list would bring it to forty-four possible wives, all told (see tables 3.1 and 3.2).

Joseph's last days

From his last dated plural marriage in November 1843 until his death seven months later, on June 27, 1844, Joseph Smith struggled

203. Smith, *Intimate Chronicle*, 557.

with enemies, perceived and real, within and beyond the Nauvoo community. He alerted the Nauvoo police that he was "exposed to far greater danger from traitors among ourselves than from enemies without."[204] Pressure that had been building since Oliver Cowdery's charges in 1838 and John Bennett's publications in 1842 exploded in January 1844 when a member of the LDS First Presidency, William Law, learned of Smith's 1843 revelation and marriage to Maria Lawrence. Law and others filed a lawsuit against Smith and published evidence of his adventuresome marital arrangements in a newspaper they founded in June. Joseph could continue to deny the "rumors," as he called them, but it would no longer be possible for him to marry new wives in the face of such intense local scrutiny. Furthermore, Emma was aware of, and opposed to, plural marriages during this time. Bathsheba Smith, the wife of Joseph's cousin, George A. Smith, paraphrased what Emma said to her female friends: "Your husbands are going to take more wives, and unless you consent to it, you must put your foot down and keep it there."[205] Later that last winter, Emma told the Relief Society "her determination was to do her Duty Effectively … in putting down transgression … [that] it was high time for Mothers to watch over their Daughters & exhort them to keep the path of Virtue."[206]

Through this turbulence, Smith remained either steadfast or headstrong, depending on one's perspective, and not just regarding plural marriage. On November 13, 1843, Smith wrote to New York publisher James Arlington Bennet: "I combat the errors of ages; I meet the violence of mobs; I cope with illegal proceedings from executive authority; I cut the gordian knot of powers, and I solve mathematical problems of universities, with truth … diamond truth; and God is my 'right hand man.'"[207] With such a self-image, it is not surprising that he also aspired to the highest office in the land: the presidency of the United States. In February 1844, Willard Richards nom-

204. *History of the Church,* 6:152.

205. Bathsheba W. Smith, Affidavit, Nov. 19, 1903, LDS Archives.

206. "The Voice of Innocence from Nauvoo," *Nauvoo Neighbor,* Mar. 20, 1844.

207. *History of the Church,* 6:74, 78, letter written for Joseph Smith by W. W. Phelps.

inated him as a candidate in a church-run political party.[208] Smith accepted. Curiously, he also asked the Twelve to "hunt out a good location" in California or Oregon "where we can remove to after the Temple is completed, and where we can build a city in a day, and have a government of our own, get up to the mountains, where the devil cannot dig us out."[209]

On Sunday, April 7, 1844, Smith spoke at the funeral of a Nauvoo constable who had been killed by a falling bucket while working in a well. The deceased had the aristocratic name of King Follett. In his eulogy, Smith took the opportunity to expound on the history and character of God: "God himself was once as we are now, and is an exalted man ... That is the great secret." Further, that "in the beginning, the head of the Gods called a council of the Gods and they came together and concocted a push to create the world and people it." In defending his theology, Smith proclaimed, "I am learned, and know more than all the world put together." He volunteered his views on the immortality of intelligence: "The mind or the intelligence which man possesses is co-equal with God himself."[210]

The confidence to offer such eschatological speculation peaked in the spring of 1844 and was met by growing dissent. Perhaps it was primarily his interest in marrying teenagers or his sealings to married women that ignited the ire of his friends and the displeasure of his "unwavering" first wife. However, the content of his sermons added more fuel to the fire. So did his wedding to nineteen-year-old Maria Lawrence in May 1843, the same month he married her sixteen-year-old sister, Sarah. Some of the inner circle learned that Smith had assumed fiduciary responsibility for the girls' legal and financial well-being. It was more than some of the leadership could accept. His close friend, steam mill operator and high-ranking church leader William Law, expressed the chagrin of many others when he denounced what seemed to be an exploitative relationship. In January

---

208. "For President, Joseph Smith," *Nauvoo Neighbor,* Feb. 28, 1844; notices in the *Illinois Springfield Register* and *Iowa Democrat,* rpt. *History of the Church,* 6:226-27, 268-70.

209. *History of the Church,* 6:222-23.

210. Ibid., 6:302-17.

1844, Law paid a visit to Smith at his office and urged him to give up polygamy (see chapter 4).

George A. Smith recalled that about a month before Joseph Smith was killed, Joseph

> administered a little chastisement to me for not stepping forward as he had indicated in patriarchal marriage. He assured me that the man who had many virtuous wives had great many prizes, though he admitted that the man who had one virtuous wife had one great prize. He testified to me and to my father that the Lord had given him the keys of the sealing ordinance, and that he felt as liberal to others as he did to himself. He remarked that he had given Brigham Young three wives, Heber C. Kimball two, John Taylor three, Orson Hyde two, and many a number of others, and said to me "you should not be behind [in] your privileges."[211]

After Smith's death, the church split according to whether Smith's late doctrines and practices, including polygamy, were of utmost importance. Those who continued in his footsteps expanded their sense of entitlement, as Heber Kimball, Amasa Lyman, Brigham Young, and others divided up Smith's widows among themselves and then added many more women to their respective households.

Children

There is no reason to doubt that Smith's marriages involved sexual relations in most instances, although Sylvia Sessions's testimony to her daughter, Josephine,[212] represents the only concrete claim for a child—and even then the testimony is second-hand. Mary Elizabeth Lightner spoke of "three children" whom she said she "knew he had" by his plural wives. These births would have been disguised because the children would have borne the names of their stepfathers. "They told me. I think two of them are living today but they are not known as his children as they go by other names."[213]

---

211. George A. Smith to Joseph Smith III, Oct. 9, 1869.

212. Josephine F. Fisher to Andrew Jenson, Feb. 24, 1915, LDS Archives.

213. *The Life & Testimony of Mary Lightner* (Salt Lake City: Kraut's Pioneer Press, n.d.); "Mary E. Lightner's Testimony, As Delivered at Brigham Young University)," Apr. 14, 1905, 41-42, compiled by N. B. Lundwall, LDS Archives, at Bancroft Library, University of California, Berkeley; also in Thomas Milton Tinney, *The Royal Family of the Prophet Joseph Smith, Jr.* (Salt Lake City: Tinney-Green Family Organization, 1973).

It was a general rule that children of plural marriages were not acknowledged in the pre-Utah period. Eliza Partridge left home in 1846 with her son, who was fathered by Amasa Lyman. Her sister, Emily, recorded the protocol of secrecy: "While in Nauvoo I had kept my child secreted, and but few knew I had one; but after I started on my journey," she wrote, "it became publicly known, and people would stop at our house [in Winter Quarters, Iowa,] to see a 'spiritual child.'" After one woman told Emily she thought spiritual children were less "smart as other children," Emily remarked that "there was a good deal of that spirit [of resentment] at that time and sometimes it was very oppressive."[214] In an autobiographical account within her diary, she added that "spiritual wives, as we were then termed, were not very numerous in those days and a spiritual baby was a rarity indeed—but few children had been born in the celestial order of marriage."[215] Some children could have been disguised in families where a woman had a civil husband different from the husband she was sealed to.

Perhaps, as Lucy Walker Smith Kimball said, one restraint to fathering plural children was the "hazardous life [Smith] lived[,] in constant fear of being betrayed."[216] While stressful circumstances and a complicated schedule may well have impacted the frequency of marital intimacy, from all outward appearances his conjugal visits were not greatly impeded by social or legal pressure. Smith unquestionably fathered the three sons Emma gave birth to in Nauvoo. The dates of conception are telling. For Don Carlos, it was just months after the family reached Nauvoo. A stillborn son, which was delivered on February 7, 1842, was conceived during the early days of Smith's marriage to Louisa Beaman. And Emma's last child, David Hyrum, was born in November 1844, after Joseph's death, meaning that David was conceived early that year in the midst of enormous turmoil. Until decisive DNA testing of possible Smith descendants—daughters as well as sons—from plural wives can be accomplished, ascertaining

214. Emily Dow Partridge Young, "Written Expressly for My Children, Jan. 7th 1877," in "Diary and Reminiscences."

215. Emily Dow Partridge Young, "Autobiographical Sketch," in ibid., July 24, 1883.

216. Littlefield, *Reminiscences*, 41.

whether Smith fathered children with any of his plural wives remains hypothetical.

Persuasion and refusal

One question that inevitably arises, even a century and a half later, is how Smith persuaded so many teenagers and married women, all of Puritan New England stock, to become his wives. Orson Pratt, known later as "the apostle of polygamy," offered a plausible rationale. After his own objection to Smith's overtures to his wife, Sarah, Pratt explained how important it was to a woman to be married to a "lord," by which he meant a man who was worthy of exaltation in the next world:

> You will clearly perceive from the revelation which God has given that you can never obtain a fullness of glory without being married to a righteous man for time and for all eternity. If you marry a man who receives not the gospel, you lay a foundation for sorrow in this world, besides losing the privilege of enjoying the society of a husband in eternity. You forfeit your right to an endless increase of immortal lives. And even the children which you may be favored with in this life will not be entrusted to your charge in eternity; but you will be left in that world without a husband, without a family, without a kingdom—without any means of enlarging yourselves, being subject to the principalities and powers who are counted worthy of families, and kingdoms, and thrones, and the increase of dominions forever. To them you will be servants and angels.

This is why Presendia Buell, Zina Jacobs, and Mary Elizabeth Lightner risked their marriages to non-Mormons or church members of low ecclesiastical status for a secret marriage with the prophet. This took them to the head of the line at the gates of heaven. Regarding deadbeat husbands, Pratt said it did not matter how great the "morality of such persons may be, nor how kind they may be to you, they are not numbered with the people of God; they are not in the way of salvation; they cannot save themselves nor their families; and after what God has revealed upon this subject, you cannot be justified, for one moment, in keeping their company."[217]

Smith emphasized the same theme as part of his persuasive ap-

217. Orson Pratt, in *The Seer,* Sept. 1853, 140; qtd. in Joseph Fielding Smith, *Conference Report of the Church of Jesus Christ of Latter-day Saints,* Oct. 1946.

proach, offering women a promise of eternal rewards. He accompanied these enticements with warnings of the suffering and damnation they would endure if they refused. Nevertheless, some women did refuse. From their accounts, we learn something about the risks Smith took in courting such a large field of women. There were at least eight failed courtships, including one on behalf of Brigham Young. Some cannot be dated, although most of Smith's solicitations occurred during the active period between the fall of 1842 and the end of 1843. In some instances we have enough details to detect the *modus operandi* Smith employed, as well as the accompanying tensions and risk of exposure. The failures embarrassed him. The women did not feel any compunction about telling what had happened, and their accounts fed the public's indignation toward what they saw as illegitimate marriages. From these failed attempts to woo disinterested women, we also learn when Smith's associates first began courting potential wives.

Some of the women were insulted by the idea of a compound marriage. In 1841, Sarah Pratt firmly rebuffed Smith and remained monogamously committed to her missionary husband.[218] At that point, Smith was the only man (with the exception of John Bennett) who had put the principle into practice, but by mid-1842 he was instructing key associates on how to acquire women. This coincided roughly with Smith's rejection of Bennett's "marriages" and the latter's departure from Nauvoo.

Brigham Young was the first we know about, when his proposal to seventeen-year-old Martha Brotherton in the spring of 1842 failed. Even though he enlisted Smith and Kimball to help him convince her, she stubbornly held her ground. This incident will be discussed in greater detail in chapter 4, but its significance here is in documenting Smith's involvement in persuading Brotherton, followed by his public efforts at damage control.

Nancy Rigdon may have had the highest profile of the women

---

218. "Workings of Mormonism Related by Mrs. Orson Pratt," 1884, LDS Archives; Bennett, *History of the Saints,* 228-31; Breck England, *Life and Thought of Orson Pratt* (Salt Lake City: University of Utah Press, 1985), 77-81; Richard S. Van Wagoner, "Sarah M. Pratt," *Dialogue: A Journal of Mormon Thought* 19 (Summer 1986): 69-99.

who rejected Smith. She was the daughter of one of Smith's counselors in the First Presidency. She gained additional notoriety through Bennett because he emphasized her story in his exposé. With Brotherton and Pratt, Rigdon's refusal created a credibility nightmare for Smith through the spring of 1842.

Among the other women who would repel Smith's romantic overtures are Esther Johnson, Cordelia Morley, Rachel Ivins, and Lydia Moon. The records for their experiences are spotty or vaguely phrased. However, we do know that on April 1, 1843, Smith asked Benjamin Johnson for the hand of two more of his sisters, Almera and Esther. As discussed, Benjamin conveyed Esther's refusal to Smith because she was already engaged.[219]

In 1909, eighty-five-year-old Cordelia C. Morley Cox denied that she had married Smith, despite rumors to the contrary. At the same time, writing her autobiography, she admitted that she had been sealed to him by proxy in January 1846, after his death, and that while he was alive she had rejected his amorous proposal. Her father, Isaac, had invited Smith to stay with his family at Kirtland in 1831. The family joined the church, and when they moved to Adams County, Illinois, about twenty-five miles south of Nauvoo, they founded what became known as Morley Settlement. Cordelia explained that "in the spring of '44, Plural marriage was introduced to me by my pearents" when "Joseph Smith ask[ed] their consent" and "request[ed] me to be his wife. Imagine if you can my feelings," she continued. This was "something I've never thought I ever could be[.] I [k]new nothing of such religion and could not [ac]cept it[,] neither did I."

Having refused him during his lifetime, she nevertheless accepted him after his death. She even enlisted her husband Walter Cox to act as proxy for Smith in sealing her to the prophet in the next world. Explaining this to her children, Cordelia wrote:

> In June 1844 Joseph Smith was martyred. It was a time of mourning for all after Joseph Smith['s] death. I was visited by some of his most intimate friends who [k]new his request & explained to me this religio[us]

219. Johnson, *Life's Review,* 95-96.

> [doctrine,] counseling me to [ac]cept his wishes, for now he was gone & could do no more for himself. I [ac]cepted Joseph Smith['s] desire, [and] in 1846[,] January 27[,] I was married to your Father [Walter Cox] in the Nauvoo Temple. While still kneeling upon the alter[,] my hand clasped in his & now his wife, he gave his consent and I was sealed to Joseph Smith for eternity.[220]

Another woman who resisted Joseph's advances—or perhaps did not, but apparently talked about it all the same—was Eliza Winters. A resident of Harmony, Pennsylvania, at the time the Smiths were living there with Emma's parents, Winters may have been the reason the Smiths left Harmony in a hurry. Martin Harris apparently thought he was defending Joseph Smith by saying it was no crime to seduce a woman. Joseph and Emma's departure from the Susquehanna countryside brought a slow end to the town's agitation over this incident.[221]

Like Cordelia Morley, Rachel Ivins chose to marry Smith posthumously. She was born in New Jersey on March 7, 1821, and met Smith, Erastus Snow, and her husband-to-be, Jedediah M. Grant, when they traveled to New Jersey in 1839-40. She was eighteen or nineteen, and converted in 1841 just prior to her twentieth birthday. In 1842 Rachel moved to Nauvoo with her sister Anna. She soon established close ties to several of the young women who had married Smith. She attended Sarah Ann Whitney's seventeenth birthday party in late March 1842 in "the Masonic room" above Smith's red brick store. In early 1844, Joseph apparently sought an appointment with Rachel. As her granddaughter, Lucy Grant Cannon, later recalled, when "the prophet asked grandmother to meet with him on a certain occasion, she did not keep the appointment because she felt he was going to ask her to enter into the new order of celestial marriage and she did not feel she could do that. This she told me. The Prophet was martyred soon after that time."[222] After Rachel married Jedediah Grant many years later,

220. Cordelia Morley Cox, Autobiographical statement, Mar. 17, 1909, Perry Special Collections.

221. Dan Vogel, *Joseph Smith: The Making of a Prophet* (Salt Lake City: Signature Books, 2004), 178; "Mormonism," *Susquehanna Reg.* 9 (May 1, 1834): 1 in Vogel, ed., *Early Mormon Documents* (Salt Lake City: Signature Books, 1996), 4:296-97, 346.

222. In Truman G. Madsen, *The Heritage of Heber J. Grant* (Salt Lake City: By the author, 1969), 30n17.

they had a son, Heber, who would become the seventh president of the LDS Church (1918-45). Heber heard the same story with a saltier flair to it. His mother told him that on "hearing that [Joseph Smith] was teaching plural marriage and that he undoubtedly was going to propose marriage to her," she told the messenger "she would 'sooner go to hell as a virtuous woman than to heaven as a whore.'"[223]

Following Smith's death, Rachel went back to her hometown of Tom's River, New Jersey. Her biographer, Ronald Walker, found that she had become "bewildered and emotionally scarred" by her experiences in Nauvoo. Her son agreed that "when plural marriage was first taught[,] my mother left the church on account of it." Walker noted that Ivins was "ailing physically as well as spiritually and planning never to mingle with the Saints again."[224] But after about ten years, she decided to travel to Salt Lake City and arrived there in August 1853.

According to Heber Grant, his father, Jedediah, was not allowed to be sealed to Rachel "for eternity, because [Brigham Young] had instructions from the Prophet that if anything happened to him [Smith] before he was married to Rachel Ivins she must be sealed to him for eternity," that she "belonged" to Smith.[225] On November 29, 1855, two years after moving to Salt Lake City, thirty-four-year-old Rachel agreed to a proxy marriage to Smith for eternity and simultaneously to become the seventh wife of Jedediah Grant, "for time only." Grant was Young's counselor in the First Presidency and had been one of the missionaries Rachel had first met in New Jersey.[226] Heber was born just after his father's death in November 1856 and was Rachel's only child. He would eventually preside over efforts to repress the continued practice of plural marriage among "fundamentalist" Mormons.[227]

---

223. Heber J. Grant to Ray O. Wyland, Dec. 12, 1936, LDS Archives.

224. Ronald W. Walker, "Rachel R. Grant: The Continuing Legacy of the Feminine Ideal," *Dialogue: A Journal of Mormon Thought* 15 (Autumn 1982): 109.

225. Heber J. Grant sermon, in *Conference Report of the Church of Jesus Christ of Latter-day Saints,* Oct. 1942.

226. Heber J. Grant, "Remarks at a Birthday Dinner," in Walker, "Rachel R. Grant," 111; Ronald W. Walker, "Grant, Heber J.," *Encyclopedia of Mormonism,* ed. Daniel H. Ludlow (New York: MacMillan, 1992), 2:564-68; see also Quinn, *Mormon Hierarchy Origins,* 549.

227. Walker, "Rachel R. Grant," 111.

According to LDS theology, the posthumous sealing meant that Heber would be Smith's son in the eternities, not the son of his biological father.

Lydia Moon rejected Smith in September 1843 after becoming the object of a tug-of-war between Smith and Clayton, both of whom wanted to marry the seventeen-year-old English immigrant. She was the sister of Ruth and Margaret Moon, both of whom had already married Clayton. Wanting to keep it all in the family, Clayton asked Smith in the fall of 1843 for permission to acquire one more Moon sister. His history with the Moons went back to their common country of origin, where William married Ruth in 1836. The Claytons converted to Mormonism, immigrated to America together, and William married his second wife, Margaret, in Nauvoo in 1843. Five months later his eye fell on the younger sister, and he was disappointed to learn on September 15 that permission to marry her would be denied. As he wrote in his journal: "President Joseph told me he had lately had a new item of law revealed to him in relation to myself. He said the Lord had revealed to him that a man could only take 2 of a family except by express revelation and as I had said I intended to take Lydia he made this known for my benefit." Smith's explanation was that "to have more than two in a family was apt to cause wrangles and troubles." Predictably Smith then asked Clayton if he "would not give L to him." Clayton said he "would so far as I had anything to do in it." When Smith pressed him on this and asked if he would "talk to her," Clayton did so that Sunday. Lydia did not hesitate to give him an answer, and it was "no": "She seems to receive it kindly but says she has promised her mother not to marry while her mother lives and she thinks she won't" marry Smith.[228] After Smith's death, Clayton said that in 1846 Lydia had in principle "agreed to be sealed to me for time and eternity" but that she had become "entangled with my brother James" and "resolved to marry him." She apparently did so in 1847. Belying her polite response to Smith in 1843, her mother had not passed on and would not for another five years.[229]

228. Smith, *Intimate Chronicle*, 120.
229. Ibid., 197.

These first-person accounts by Nancy Rigdon and Sarah Pratt, Clayton's anecdote about his sister-in-law, the negative response from Cordelia Morley relayed through her father, Rachel Ivins's story related by her son, the refusal of Benjamin Johnson's sister Esther, and Martha Brotherton's affidavit on Smith importuning her on behalf of Young all capture the essence of both the danger and delicacy involved in this game of pursuit and evasion, the man trying to reassure the targeted female and the woman adopting strategies of escape ranging from anger to apology.

Emma's dilemma

From the beginning, Emma Hale's parents disapproved of her courtship with the young seer who boarded at their Pennsylvania home in 1825. Against her father's will, Emma eloped with Joseph in 1827. Within just a couple years, her husband was dictating a book which dealt, not only with Native American origins, but also, explicitly, with polygamy. In 1830 he published the work that conditionally sanctioned the practice of plural marriage, and a year later he directed missionaries to marry Native American women. Emma may not have known about this, since no one else seems to know if the directive was carried out or not. But within a year or two, when Joseph became enamored of Fanny Alger, the family's hired girl, it not only became known to Emma but to others as well. This must have been infuriating and embarrassing for Emma. She came to realize that many of the women in their social circles from the 1830s became Joseph's secret wives a decade later. As this dawned on her, it must have made her feel uncertain about his devotion to her, even though there was undeniable love in the marriage and a relationship which, for the most part, seemed to be mutually affectionate and supportive.

Did Emma find herself standing watch over her husband's interactions with the Huntingtons in 1841 or the Partridges in 1841-42 while these girls were living in the Smith household? Lucy Walker affirmed that "Emma knew that they were married to him."[230] When Joseph went into hiding in the summer of 1842, and while Emma was

230. *Reorganized Church v. Church of Christ,* question 285.

calling on the governor for his benefit, she must have wondered about the disproportionate concern for the Whitneys and their daughter. In his warning to Sarah Ann to proceed carefully in order to make sure Emma would not find them in their hiding place, are we to infer that Emma had the habit of appearing unexpectedly and unannounced to surveil his company and demeanor?

Emma seems to have been caught off guard by the marriage to Eliza Snow in June 1842. How else could she have explained the sudden appearance of this woman in their home? Could Emma ignore the ironic discussions in the Relief Society? Was it an issue of respectability for her? Did she face the painful dilemma of tacitly consenting to her husband's plural relationships as long as a façade of gentility was maintained? Assuming that LeRoi Snow's account was accurate, was it Joseph's embrace of Eliza in front of Emma and before their visitor, Charles Rich, rather than the fact of Joseph's marriage to Eliza that triggered Emma's aggression towards Eliza?

What must Emma have thought when the Smiths' former houseguest and church leader John Bennett began to speak of Joseph's wives in the *Sangamo Journal* in 1842? About a month after expelling Eliza Snow, Emma evidently gave her consent for Joseph to marry the Partridge girls, not knowing he had already married them. This suggests further questions. If Emma temporarily accepted these relationships as genuine marriages, did she then accept Joseph's declaration that he was obeying a sanctioned calling? What did it mean in terms of her own faith in his church? What of the marriages to the Lawrence girls later that same spring? Can we assume that Benjamin Johnson, who later championed plural marriage and described it in great detail, would have mentioned it to no one in 1843?

Emma's distaste for Joseph's other wives became clear. Just as Joseph sought comfort from Sarah Ann the day Emma departed from his hideout at the Grangers' farm, the courtships and marriages with other women were interwoven with the births of Emma's children throughout the Nauvoo years. Emma complained about her husband's clandestine relationships and used the Relief Society as a forum for condemning them, but she seemed unable to dissuade Joseph or even the women themselves from pursuing these entanglements. While Emma challenged Joseph when she discovered him with other women, the sheer number of his celestial brides made this kind of hide-and-seek an impossible game for her to win. What Joseph failed to see was that it was equally impossible for him to succeed at this. His insatiable addition of one woman after another to an invisible family endangered the stability of his acknowledged family and increasingly brought peril to himself and the entire community.

After Bennett's announcements in 1842 and Emma's confrontations with Joseph in the spring of 1843, the Smith household was unraveling. By 1843 and 1844, Emma was probably beyond surprise. Some of Smith's closest lieutenants, William Law and others, were deeply troubled. Long before Law published the whole story surrounding the Lawrence girls in the spring of 1844, Maria's situation proved unwieldy. The dispute over Maria precipitated a lawsuit in May, publicity in the *Nauvoo Expositor* in June, then the arrest and incarceration in Carthage prior to Smith's assassination.

"The inauguration of these [plural marriage] principles were a severe trial to your mother," wrote George A. Smith to Joseph Smith III in 1869. "At times she resolved to act upon the same. She gave your father four wives with her own hands; this intelligence I had from your father's mouth."[231] The four wives were the two sets of sisters living in the Nauvoo Mansion, the Partridges and Lawrences. The statement implies that Emma knew about other women. Information from William Clayton, Emily Partridge, and others give us reason to believe Emma knew about Eliza Snow and that she intercepted letters from Flora Ann Woodworth. She was therefore aware of at least six plural wives, as well as of the prolonged dalliance with Fanny Alger.

After all she endured in seventeen and a half years of marriage to Joseph Smith, Emma ultimately took a stand against the principle. She denied its existence to her children. She refused to accompany Brigham Young to the Great Salt Lake Valley. She must have made it

231. George A. Smith to Joseph Smith III, Oct. 9, 1869.

unwaveringly clear in the church's waning years in Nauvoo that any overtures from Young and others to marry her and stand in place of her husband by fathering additional children for Joseph's eternal glory would be unwelcome. So the prophet's first wife, along with his mother, sisters, brother, and children all made their home in the Midwest, separating the immediate Smith family from the growing tradition of plural marriage that would characterize Utah Mormons for years to come.

When Emma had become more fully aware of the underground network of marriages in Nauvoo, beginning in her own home, she reacted forcefully. In July 1843 when her husband presented his revelation sanctioning plural marriage, she threw the written original into the fireplace and destroyed it.[232] The surviving copy was made by

TABLE 3.3 Joseph's courtships and Emma's pregnancies[1]

name	conceptions (est.)	born	died	Joseph's courtships
an unnamed son	Sept. 1827	June 15, 1828	June 15, 1828	Harmony, Pa., Eliza Winters, 1828
twins[2]	Aug. 1830	Apr. 30, 1831	Apr. 30, 1831	Palmyra, N.Y.
Joseph III	Feb. 1832	Nov. 6, 1832	Dec. 10, 1914	Kirtland, Ohio, Fanny Alger, 1832-35
Frederick G.	Sept. 1835	June 20, 1836	Apr. 13, 1862	Kirtland, Ohio, Fanny Alger, 1832-35
Alexander Hale	Sept. 1837	June 2, 1838	Aug. 12, 1909	Ohio, Marinda Nancy Johnson, 1838-41 (marries by 1842)
Don Carlos	Sept. 1839	June 13,1840	Aug. 15, 1841[3]	Nauvoo, Ill. Sept. 1840, plans spring wedding
an unnamed son	May 1841	Feb. 7, 1842	Feb. 7, 1842	Nauvoo, Ill. Apr. 5, 1841, marries Louisa Beaman, courts Zina Huntington, Presendia, & Agnes C.
David Hyrum	Feb. 1844	Nov. 17, 1844	Aug. 29, 1904	Nauvoo, Ill. Feb. 8, 1844, Sylvia Sessions Lyon's disclosed child by Joseph, born Josephine Lyon

[1] Joseph Smith marries Emma Hale in Bainbridge, New York, on Jan. 18, 1827.
[2] The Smith twins die at birth, after which Joseph and Emma adopt the Murdock twins, nine days old and born about the same time as the Smith children. Joseph Murdock dies Mar. 29, 1832; Julia Murdock, married, no children, dies in Nauvoo in 1880.
[3] Joseph's brother, Don Carlos, dies in Nauvoo Aug. 7, 1841, a week before the death of his son, Don Carlos.

232. Smith, *Intimate Chronicle*, 558.

Joseph Kingsbury before Hyrum Smith showed the original to Emma. Kingsbury was the one who fronted for Smith as Sarah Ann Whitney's pretended husband.

In 1846, two years after her husband had been shot to death in Carthage, Emma told Joseph W. Coolidge, administrator of the Smith estate, that "Joseph had abandoned plurality of wives before his death." When Coolidge, himself a polygamist, contradicted her assertion, Emma showed that she would no longer remain mute on this topic and reportedly shot back: "Then he was worthy of the death he died."[233]

Conclusion

Since plural marriage was contrary to the commonly shared standard of American morality, against Illinois law, and offensive even to most of the 10,000 Mormons in Nauvoo, Joseph Smith recognized the need to keep this innovation a closely guarded secret. Smith would be assassinated, in part because of internal resistance to polygamy and opposition to it throughout the Illinois countryside. In his *History of Illinois,* Governor Thomas Ford would list polygamy among the primary reasons Mormons were despised by the older settlers.[234]

Whereas the colleagues Smith selected to follow him into plural marriage maintained secrecy at first, they eventually formed coherent families that were more obvious to onlookers. Nauvoo polygamists typically had two or three wives. The first wife usually set the household schedule and the other wives followed. Children took the surname of their father. After Smith died, the veil over polygamy was further parted as many more families were invited to embrace the principle. By early 1846, when the pioneering Saints crossed the Great Plains to Utah, about 10 percent of the Nauvoo Mormons were living in polygamous families.

---

233. Joseph Coolidge, Diary, Aug. 28, 1870, in Van Wagoner, *Sidney Rigdon,* 306n30.

234. Thomas Ford, *A History of Illinois from Its Commencement as a State in 1818 to 1847* (1854; Chicago: Lakeside Press, 1945), 169, 201, 220-21.

TABLE 3.4 Joseph Smith's inner circle of Nauvoo polygamists

first polygamous marriage			husbands	number of celestial wives by June 27, 1844	Eventually
1.	1842	June 14	Brigham Young	5	55
2.	"		Heber Kimball	2	44
3.	"		Vinson Knight	2	2
4.	"		Reynolds Cahoon	2	3
5.	1843	Jan. 18	Willard Richards	4	11
6.	"	Feb. 5	William Huntington	2	3
7.	"	Feb./Mar.	Orson Hyde	3	9
8.	"	Mar. 9	Lorenzo Young	2	8
9.	"	Mar. 23	Thomas Bateman	2	2
10.	"	Apr. 5	Joseph Noble	3	11
11.	"	Apr. 27	William Clayton	2	10
12.	"	May 17	Benjamin Johnson	2	7
13.	"	July 11	James Adams	2	2
14.	"	July 20	George Miller	2	4
15.	"	July 24	Parley Pratt	2	11
16.	"	July 28	William Felshaw	2	3
17.	"	Aug. 11	Hyrum Smith	5	5
18.	"	Aug. 13	John Smith	3	8
19.	"	fall	William Smith	2	15
20.	"	Nov.	Ebenezer Richardson	2	4
21.	"	Dec. 12	John Taylor	6	18
22.	"	Dec. 19	Isaac Morley	3	10
23.	"	Dec. 28	Edwin Woolley	3	6
24.	"	Dec.	William Sagers	2	10
25.	1844	early	Howard Egan	2	4
26.	"	Mar. 6	Theodore Turley	4	5
27.	"	Apr. 2	Erastus Snow	2	14
28.	"	Apr. 27	Ezra Benson	2	8
29.	"	spring	Joseph Kelting	3	3
30.	"	<June 27	Lyman Wight	4	4
31.	"	<June 27	Joseph Coolidge	2	5
32.	"	<June 27	John Page	2	4
			total wives	**86**	**308**
			average wives per man	**2.7**	**9.6**

FOUR.

Sharing Favors

"All the wives you want"

Sarah Crooks bath[ed] my forehead with rum and gave me some mint drops," wrote twenty-five-year-old William Clayton, proselytizing for his new Mormon faith in Manchester, England, in early 1840. "My feet were very sore to[night]. Sarah washed them and gave me a pint of warm Porter. … We sat together till 2 o'clock [a.m.]" William's wife of three years, Ruth Moon, and their two children were living with her parents not more than fifty miles away. Yet when Sarah contemplated marrying an eligible bachelor, Clayton, apprehensive, confessed: "I don't want Sarah to be married." As she continued to attend to Clayton, he realized he was "much … tempted on her account and felt to pray that the Lord would preserve me from impure affections." Impure thoughts or not, he admitted "I certainly feel my love towards her … increase."[1] On completing his mission and sailing to America with Ruth and the children, Clayton was stunned when Joseph Smith subsequently invited him in February 1843 to take a second wife and suggested that he send for Sarah Crooks.

While continuing to increase his own household domain, Smith was beginning to teach the concept of eternal increase to trusted fol-

1. George D. Smith, ed., *An Intimate Chronicle: The Journals of William Clayton,* 2nd ed. (Salt Lake City: Signature Books and Smith Research Associates, 1995), 32, 41, 52, 29. Clayton was unaware at the time of Smith's plural marriages.

lowers, granting them the "favor" of an additional wife. The proliferation of this practice beyond Smith's own family constitutes an important chapter in the establishment of celestial marriage. In some ways, the protocol remained the same, but in other ways it was transformed. For instance, just as Smith's own weddings went unannounced in the community of restored Latter-day Saints, so too the women his followers brought home to their own families were kept private. However, within the home, the first wife was now informed and became involved in the process. Eventually these discreet transactions involving a select number of families within a small enclave of members would expand to the point that concurrent wives and secrecy would become a contradiction in terms, however much the participants tried to contain the rumors.

Plural marriage had been in the air since the Book of Mormon was published, most especially since Smith began to teach it to such friends as Joseph Bates Noble in 1840-41. These clandestine instructions to one individual at a time grew into a community movement by 1842 as an increasing number of men brought "celestial wives" into their homes. These communal relationships grew slowly at first, more rapidly in 1843, and only momentarily stalled in the wake of Smith's assassination in June 1844. During the remainder of 1844, and into 1845 and 1846, church apostles Brigham Young and Heber Kimball, along with seven other close associates, married twenty-four of Smith's plural widows. In the opening months of 1846, prior to the exodus into the western lands belonging to Mexico, the Saints rushed to complete some 1,500 marriage ceremonies in the just-completed Nauvoo temple. Among these were 300 plural marriages.

The next pages document how polygamy came to 200 Nauvoo families in three stages: first, from 1842 to mid-1844, when Smith urged and even commanded thirty or so hand-picked men to accept the Old Testament custom, saying polygamy was necessary for their exaltation in the next world; second, in the post-assassination period from June 1844 through the end of 1845, when a few of Smith's associates married his widows, then accelerated their own new plural nuptials; and finally, in early 1846, when temple ceremonies upsurged just prior to the westward exodus. Every one of Smith's Twelve Apostles who were present when he began marrying women in 1841 became a polygamist, as did brothers Hyrum and William, and his uncle John. There were a few Nauvoo leaders for whom there is no record of a plural marriage, such as Sidney Rigdon, whose daughter refused Joseph's proposal; John Bennett, whose marriage record may have been deleted after he had a falling out with Smith; and William Law, who opposed polygamy when he discovered it in 1843. These dissenters, like Oliver Cowdery back in the 1830s, were each key Latter-day Saint leaders.

In the accounts recorded by insiders, Smith employed a predictable pattern of persuasion. He would approach someone he had placed into a position of responsibility to suggest that they take a walk together in the woods or to some other solitary place. Smith often chose to stroll at dusk, after a day's work and before a meal, when the sky was ablaze at sunset and a mild breeze blew off the river. Or he would invite a friend on a morning walk through a field and stop to talk when they found a quiet spot under the overhang of a tree or in a shaded grove. William Clayton, Benjamin Johnson, and Lorenzo Snow each confirm a version of the reflective walk with the prophet. By the time each one returned home, his future had been altered. He now had plans to initiate and secrets to keep.

Introducing the Principle

William Clayton

Clayton was born on July 17, 1814, in a rural parish near Penwortham, England, just across the River Ribble from the city of Preston and about twenty-five miles north of Liverpool. The oldest of fourteen children of Thomas Clayton and Ann Critchley, he was tutored by his schoolteacher father and worked in a textile factory as a skilled employee—a bookkeeper—during the Industrial Revolution. He was twenty-three when Mormon missionaries first arrived in England in 1837. Following his wife, Ruth, William was baptized that first year by Heber Kimball. He then served a home mission to nearby Manchester, after which he and his family migrated to Nauvoo in the autumn of 1840. Soon after William met Joseph Smith, he became the prophet's personal secretary, proving to be a meticulous record keeper as he tracked events in England and America in six journals from 1840 to 1853.

"One day in the month of February, 1843," Joseph Smith dropped in for supper at Clayton's home, located at Durphy and Hotchkiss Streets, eight blocks from the Smith homestead in Nauvoo. Before sitting down to a meal, Joseph invited William to step out for a walk. It would have seemed like a normal request since Clayton had worked as a clerk in Smith's office since February and as Smith's personal secretary since October 1842. "During this period the Prophet Joseph frequently visited my house," Clayton wrote in his diary. This allowed Smith to become "well acquainted with my wife Ruth," Clayton added.[2] From the pen of the "private clerk," we have one of the clearest records of how the prophet went about convincing married men to take additional spouses.

By this time, William had been married to Ruth for six years and they were expecting their fourth child. During their private walk, the prophet suggested that Clayton accept the "favor" of the woman to whom he admitted he was still "very much attached," Sarah Crooks of Manchester. Clayton stressed that nothing had happened between them "further than an attachment such as a brother and sister in the Church might rightfully entertain for each other."[3] But in fact, Clayton's journal recorded the emotional intimacy he had shared with her. That recent intimacy with Sarah and Ruth's expectancy made Joseph's timing quite awkward. Here was the married father of three offering another married father of three the "privilege" of a "celestial marriage" to a woman Clayton was in love with while his civil wife, Ruth, was experiencing the discomfort of late pregnancy, minding her three children, and cooking dinner for the two men outside conspiring to amend her marital status. Similarly, Emma was home caring for her

---

2. William Clayton, Affidavit, Feb. 16, 1874, in Andrew Jenson, "Plural Marriage," *Historical Record* 6 (May 1887): 224-26; Smith, *Intimate Chronicle,* 555-56.

3. Smith, *Intimate Chronicle,* 556.

several children with the help of her young house girls Emily and Eliza Partridge, each of whom Joseph would marry a few weeks later.

Smith came to the point and asked Clayton: "Why don't you send for her [Sarah Crooks]?" Clayton demurred. "In the first place," he answered, "I have no authority to send for her, and if I had, I have not the means to pay expenses." Smith pressed the matter, saying he would give him the "authority to send for her, and I will furnish you with means." Smith also had Young convey to Clayton "some instructions on the priesthood," and now Smith was offering to give his secretary "a *favor*" which Clayton had "long desired." Smith left no ambiguity regarding the kind of favor he was willing to grant. He told Clayton, "It is your privilege to have all the wives you want." An ardent believer in the prophet's calling, assured that it was righteous, and knowing that the expenses would be paid, Clayton willingly accepted and sent for Sarah within days. However, instead of waiting for her arrival, he married his legal wife's sister Margaret on April 27. This was before Sarah's ship had even set sail from England.[4]

The young woman from Manchester who had stayed up with Clayton late at night and bathed his head with rum arrived a month after her one-time missionary friend had married his sister-in-law. Three months after Clayton had written to her, she appeared in Nauvoo. It was Wednesday, May 31. Clayton lost no time proposing marriage to her. By Friday, she "appear[ed] willing to comply with her privilege," and on Saturday Clayton took her for a boat ride on the Mississippi River with his sister wives Ruth and Margaret Moon. Ruth had given birth to their son, William Heber, three months earlier on February 28, and Margaret was soon to discover her own pregnancy with Daniel Adelbert, born on February 18 the next year. As ideal as the situation might have appeared to William, his second wife soon quarreled with him, complaining that if he could have three wives, she too might want to marry someone else besides him. At that, "S Crooks

4. Ibid., 94, 99, 107, 556 ("William Clayton's testimony," table 8.2). On March 7, 1843, three weeks after Clayton had already sent for Crooks, Young formally offered Clayton this "*favor*" (emphasis added).

went away abruptly." If her absence from William's journal is any indication, Sarah remained aloof for the next year. When she suddenly reappears, she is married to a William Cook and voicing "enmity to Joseph [Smith]." After Joseph Smith's assassination, her name appeared on a list of those who "brought upon us" that tragedy.[5] However, Kimball spoke "earnestly" to Clayton on September 20, 1844, and promised to help him "accomplish all [his] desires inasmuch as they are right," saying that Clayton "shall yet have S[arah] C[rooks]."[6] Despite the sanguinity of the prediction, Sarah would never become one of Clayton's privileges.

Later, when he had settled in Utah, Clayton would boast about what a good family life he had. "I support a family of near forty persons on a salary of $3,600 per annum," he said, "and we live well, are well clothed and very comfortably situated. … I have six wives whom I support in comfort and happiness and am not afraid of another one. I have [had] three children born to me during the year, and I don't fear a dozen more."[7] Altogether, he married ten women and fathered forty-seven children.

As the prophet's private clerk, Clayton was "thrown constantly into the company of President Smith, having to attend to his public and private business, receiving and recording tithings and donations, attending to land and other matters of business." He related that "during this period [he] necessarily became well acquainted with Emma Smith … and also with the children," as well as with "much of the business being transacted at the residence of the Prophet." On October 7, 1842, Smith appointed Clayton as the Nauvoo temple recorder and told him: "When I have any revelations to write, you are the one to write them."[8] Nine months later, Clayton would record "the revela-

---

5. Ibid., 107-09, 111-12, 129, 135-36. Crooks married Cook on August 16, 1843 (Lyndon W. Cook, comp., *Nauvoo Deaths and Marriages* [Orem, Utah: Grandin Book, 1994], 106).

6. Ibid., 149.

7. William Clayton to Robert Clayton, a nephew, William Clayton Letterbook, Nov. 7, 1869, Bancroft Library, University of California, Berkeley. See also Paul E. Dahl, *William Clayton: Missionary, Pioneer, and Public Servant* (Cedar City, Utah: Dahl, 1959), 226.

8. Jenson, "Plural Marriage," 225.

tion on Celestial marriage given through the Prophet Joseph Smith on the 12th day of July 1843."[9]

With such access to the church president, Clayton not only captured the tone of the invitation to marry when Smith said "you have a right to get all you can,"[10] he bequeathed to us Smith's plan for keeping such obvious marriages secret. After Margaret became pregnant in May or June 1843, Clayton wrote on October 19 about needing to *protect "the truth" by telling untruths*, in this case the strategic charade of publicly rebuking someone while privately embracing them. Clayton wrote about Smith's advice: "Says he[,] just keep her [Margaret] at home and brook it and if they raise trouble about it and bring you before me I will give you an awful scourging and probably cut you off from the church and then I will baptise you and set you ahead as good as ever."[11]

Clayton not only disclosed his own extracurricular romances, he provided the pivotal account of Joseph's struggle with Emma when she agreed to let her husband marry the Partridge sisters and then withdrew her consent as Joseph accumulated other so-called favors (see chapter 2). William wrote of Joseph's May 1843 conversation with "E Partridge," which was the time Joseph held the door shut against Emma, who "called Eliza 4 times and tried to force open the door." Clayton recorded a similar incident in which Emma interrupted a private conversation with Eliza Snow in February that year. Finally, he told in his diary how Emma burned the original copy of Joseph's revelation on plural marriage.[12]

After Nauvoo, Clayton found himself subject to a less accommodating chief executive. Brigham Young was unimpressed by Clayton's performance in defending plural marriage in England in 1853. Instead of persuading the flock of the correctness of the doctrine, Clayton contributed to defections and was personally suspected of "having had unlawful intercourse with women."[13] When he returned to Salt

9. Smith, *Intimate Chronicle,* 110; D&C 132.
10. Smith, *Intimate Chronicle,* 115.
11. Ibid., 122 (emphasis added).
12. Ibid., 100, 105, 557-59.
13. Ibid., xlviii-l.

Lake City, he ran a bookstore, a boarding house, and a mercantile business and participated in local church affairs. He died at age sixty-five and is best remembered today for his pioneer diaries of 1847 and the lyrics he wrote to the hymn, "Come, Come Ye Saints."

Benjamin F. Johnson

Benjamin Franklin Johnson was born on July 28, 1818, in Pomfret, near Chautauqua, in western New York State, an area that would soon be known for its theater, opera, and public lectures.[14] He was the tenth of sixteen children of Ezekiel and Julia Hills Johnson, who heard about Smith's gold plates in the Pomfret village paper in 1829. The Johnsons moved to Ohio in 1832. Three years later, at the age of seventeen, Benjamin joined the Latter-day Saints.

There are three surviving documents in which Johnson recorded his initial and subsequent encounters with Smith regarding plural marriage: an 1870 affidavit; an 1894 manuscript copy of his autobiography, entitled "A Life Review," published in 1947 and more completely in 1992; and a 1903 letter to George F. Gibbs, secretary to the LDS First Presidency. The letter was published in full in 1976.[15] According to Johnson's 1870 affidavit: "President Smith took me by the arm for a walk, leading the way to a secluded spot within the adjacent grove, where to my great surprise, he commenced to offer to me the principle of plural or celestial marriage, but I was more astonished by his asking me for my sister Almeira to be his wife."[16] It will be remembered (see chapter 2) that Benjamin had a vague awareness of polygamy prior to 1843 and that he even surmised that his oldest sister,

14. Founded by Methodist minister Lewis Miller in 1874, Chautauqua was a summer camp offering recreational and educational activities, including training for Sunday school teachers.

15. Benjamin F. Johnson, Affidavit, Mar. 4, 1870, 3-5, in "Affidavits on Celestial Marriage, 1869-1870," a collection of six folders compiled by Joseph F. Smith, Joseph F. Smith Collection, Archives, Church of Jesus Christ of Latter-day Saints, Salt Lake City (also in Jenson, "Plural Marriage," 221-22); Benjamin F. Johnson, "A Life Review," LDS Archives; Benjamin F. Johnson to George F. Gibbs, Apr.-Oct. 1903, LDS Archives; also in Dean R. Zimmerman, ed., *I Knew the Prophets: An Analysis of the Letter of Benjamin F. Johnson to George F. Gibbs* (Bountiful, Utah: Horizon Publishers, 1976).

16. Johnson affidavit, Mar. 4, 1870; also in Andrew F. Ehat and Lyndon W. Cook, eds., *The Words of Joseph Smith* (Provo: Brigham Young University, 1980), 269n9.

Delcena, had married Joseph Smith. But these were still assumptions that did not yet involve him directly. It is also probably significant that his father had left the church by this time and that Benjamin's parents were about to separate over religious issues.

In his manuscript, published fifty years later as *My Life's Review,* Johnson placed the conversation he had with the prophet about plural marriage at "about the first of April, 1843[,] [when] the Prophet with some of the Twelve ... came to Macedonia [Ramus] to hold a meeting ... and as usual he put up at my house."

> Early on Sunday morning he said, "Come Brother Bennie, let us have a walk." I took his arm and he led the way into a by-place in the edge of the woods surrounded by tall brush and trees. Here, as we sat down upon a log he began to tell me that the Lord had revealed to him that plural or patriarchal marriage was according to His law; and that the Lord had not only revealed it to him but had commanded him to obey it; that he was required to take other wives; and that he wanted my Sister Almira for one of them, and wished me to see and talk to her upon the subject.[17]

Sixty years after the event, Benjamin wrote what remains his least edited account of his walk with Joseph:

> It was Sunday morning April 3d or 4th 1843[18] that the Prophet was at my home in Ramus and after breakfast he proposed a Stro[l]l togather and taking his arm our walk led towards a Swail [swale] Surrounded by trees & tall brush and near the forest line not far from my house. Through the Swail Ran a Small Spring [or] brook across which a tree was fallen and was clean of its bark—On this we Sat down and the Prophet proceeded at once to open to me the Subject of plural & Eternal marriage. And he Said That Years ago in Kirtland the Lord had Revealed to him the ancient Order of Plural marriage and the necesity for its practice and did command him then to take another wife."[19]

The prophet went on to ask Benjamin for his sister Almera, provoking his protégé to comment that if Smith did anything to "dishonor and

17. Benjamin F. Johnson, *My Life's Review* (1947; Mesa, Ariz.: 21st Century Printing, 1992), 94-95.

18. In fact, Sunday fell on April 2 in 1843.

19. Johnson to Gibbs, Apr.-Oct. 1903, 28-29.

debauch" his sister, he would have Benjamin to contend with. As Smith casually deflected this threat, his "eye did not move from mine," Johnson reported.

Impressed by the prophet's inner calm but still not fully convinced, Johnson said that "with great hesitation and Stamering I called my Sister to a private audiance and Stood before her Shaking with fear. Just So Soon as I found pow[e]r to *open* my *mouth* it was filled[,] for the Light of the Lord Shone upon my understanding and the Subject that had Seemed So dark, now apeared of all Subjects pertaining to our Gospel the most lucid & plain. and So both my Sister & mySelf ware converted togather." Not long thereafter Almera "stood by the Prophets Side & was Sealed to him as a wife by Brother Clayton."[20] She then stayed in the Smith mansion a few days before returning to Ramus, where Smith occasionally spent the evening with her. Johnson documented these conjugal visits. After briefly mentioning an overnight stay, Benjamin wrote that "some three weeks later the Prophet again Came and at my house ocupied the Same Room & Bed with my Sister that the month previous he had ocupied with the Daughter of the Late Bishop Partridge as his wife."[21]

"Soon after this he was at my house again," Johnson wrote of Smith's frequent visits. Clayton noted a visit to the Johnsons on May 16, 1843, when Smith "gave Brother Johnson some instructions on the priesthood," the code word for a plural wife.[22] At the time, Benjamin was still just twenty-four years old, his wife, Melissa LeBaron, twenty-three, and they had been married only a year and a half. It was at this time that Smith asked Benjamin for his third sister, Esther; but since she was already engaged, or said to be, Johnson suggested that Smith marry the orphan girl, Mary Ann Hale, who was residing at the Johnson residence. The prophet replied, "No, but she is for you. You keep her and take her for your wife and you will be blessed." Shortly thereafter, Smith "sealed me to my First wife for Eternity and gave to me my first Plural wife, Mary Ann Hale ... an

20. Ibid., 31.
21. Ibid., 32.
22. Smith, *Intimate Chronicle*, 101-02.

orphan girl Raised by my Mother" who had since become the responsibility of Benjamin.[23]

Surprised and overwhelmed, Johnson recalled that "this seemed like hurrying up my blessings pretty fast, but the spirit of it came upon me, and from that hour I thought of her [Mary Ann Hale] as a wife that the Lord had given me." In a 1903 letter to Anthon Lund, Johnson confirmed that "on May 17, 1843, [Joseph Smith] sealed me to my first wife and he gave me to be my [plural] wife a young orphan girl then living with us."[24] The orphan girl, Mary Ann, was fifteen years old.

Three months after Smith's springtime stroll with Johnson, he included in his revelation on plural marriage a reference to the biblical parable of the talents. This subtle reference would have been detectable only to those whose ears were attuned to it, but his choice of "ten" as the number of plural wives a man might acquire was significant. If a man had "ten virgins given unto him by this law," the revelation read, "he cannot commit adultery, for they belong to him" (D&C 132:62). Elsewhere Smith elaborated on the hidden meaning, something Johnson thought important enough to mention in his letter to the First Presidency. When Smith explained celestial marriage to his faithful disciple, he said, "I will today preach a Sermon to you that no one but you will understand." This promise was "fulfilled," Johnson said, in that "the Text for his Sermon was Our use of the 'one, Five, & Ten talents.'" There was a coded meaning in this: "As God had now commanded Plural marriage," Johnson wrote, "and as exaltation & dominion of the Saints depended upon the number of the[ir] Righteous posterity—From him who was found but with the one Talent It would be taken & given to him that had Ten."[25] In heaven, the man who had one wife would lose her to the man with ten; this was the meaning Johnson said he was intended to read into the parable.

---

23. Johnson to Gibbs, Apr.-Oct. 1903, 44.

24. Johnson, *Life's Review,* 96, 389; Benjamin Johnson to Anthon Lund, May 12, 1903, LDS Archives. Johnson recalled this as having occurred on May 17, but Clayton recorded that Smith's "instructions" to Johnson "on the priesthood," meaning plural marriage, occurred on May 16.

25. Johnson to Gibbs, Apr.-Oct. 1903, 30; cf. Matt. 25:14-30.

In this way, Smith was able to wrap himself in the authority of the Bible and enhance his prophetic aura while persuading the unconvinced, although in this case only hinting rather than saying explicitly that this was the true meaning of Jesus' parable. For Johnson, the new perspective was compelling. He remembered that the first commandment was to "Multiply" and that it followed, as "the Prophet taught," that "Dominion & pow[e]r in the great Future would be Comensurate with the no. of 'Wives Childin & Friends' that we inheret here and that our great mission to earth was to Organize a Neculi of Heaven to take with us. To the increace of which there would be no end."[26]

When Johnson comprehended the meaning of the sermon, he proceeded on his errand to convince his sister Almera to marry the prophet. A few days later, he accompanied Almera to the home of their sister Delcena, where Joseph, Clayton ("who always acompanied him"), and Hyrum Smith were already assembled. Hyrum sought to allay any fears Benjamin might have: "Now Benjamin you must not be afraid of this new doctrine for it is all Right. ... I know that Joseph was Comanded to take more wives and he waited untill an Angel with a drawn Sword Stood before him and declared that if he longer delayed fulfilling that Command he would Slay him." Johnson declared himself "fully Converted," and with this confession of faith he was sealed to his wife and the "o[r]phan girl Raised by my Mother ... [t]hen living with us ... [w]ho is Still with me and is probably the only wife Still living with the man to whom She was given by the Prophit."[27]

If the private stroll with Benjamin Johnson was part of a general pattern of persuasion, as it seems to have been, the practice of reciprocity is also prevalent. In granting Johnson the privilege of an attractive second wife, Smith took for himself as payment, so to speak, two of Johnson's sisters—Delcena and Almera—in ceremonies that would bind the families together. In a theological explication, perhaps partly inspired by convenience, Smith saw the church hierarchy as an extended family that would continue to live together in an afterlife

26. Ibid., 35.
27. Ibid., 31-32.

community.[28] He performed these reciprocal marriages with the Johnson family just as Clayton had taken additional wives when he performed marriages for Smith and just as Smith and Joseph Noble had married plural wives to each other—Smith to Louisa Beaman in April 1841 and Noble to Sarah Alley two years later.[29] The custom also had a practical side as well, since it added another layer of complicity for those who would have been able to tell tales, thereby further cementing their loyalty to each other.

Johnson "accepted plural marriage as a duty that he owed to his calling as an Elder of the true Church of Christ."[30] By the time he left Nauvoo on February 6, 1846, he had three wives and three children. With Newel K. Whitney, he tried unsuccessfully to convince Emma Smith to follow the Twelve Apostles. His sister Esther, who refused to marry Joseph Smith, became Mrs. David Tulley LeBaron, now twice a sister-in-law to Benjamin's wife, Melissa.[31] Johnson, representative of the mainstream in LDS practice, eventually married seven wives—a few short of the model of ten talents—and became heroic in his family's eyes because of his one-time personal connection to Joseph Smith.

In 1890, Johnson left Utah for Colonia Juárez, Mexico, in the wake of the church's public disavowal of polygamy. The church had silently interpreted the Manifesto as limited to the United States and established the colony about a two-day carriage ride south of El Paso, where selected members could continue to practice plural marriage. The ambivalence about whether Mormons would discontinue polygamy outside the boundaries of the United States lasted until 1904

---

28. D. Michael Quinn, *The Mormon Hierarchy: Origins of Power* (Salt Lake City: Signature Books and Smith Research Associates, 1994), 212; Quinn, *The Mormon Hierarchy: Extensions of Power* (Salt Lake City: Signature Books and Smith Research Associates, 1997), 163-97, citing Herbert R. Larsen, "Familism in Mormon Social Structure," Ph.D. diss., University of Utah, 1954.

29. Jenson, "Plural Marriage," 239.

30. Benjamin F. Johnson, "Open Letter to the President of the United States," Jan. 15, 1886, LDS Archives. An opponent of polygamy, President Grover Cleveland allowed the 1887 Edmunds-Tucker Act to become law, permitting confiscation of church property in response to bigamy violations. However, after the church rescinded polygamy in 1890, Cleveland signed the Utah statehood bill on January 4, 1896.

31. The LeBarons became prominent ex-Mormon fundamentalists who traced their polygamous roots to Benjamin Johnson.

when the church felt compelled to issue a Second Manifesto that forbade plural wives in or out of the country. Johnson argued that "Christ himself was born through a polygamous parentage while nearly all the men of whom and by whom the Holy Bible was written were polygamists." He later returned to Mesa, Arizona, and operated a gardening nursery. He died on November 18, 1905, at the age of eighty-seven.[32]

Lorenzo Snow

Lorenzo Snow, brother of Joseph Smith's thirteenth plural wife, Eliza Snow, was born on April 3, 1814, in Mantua, Ohio. Ten years younger than his sister and the fifth of Oliver and Rosetta Pettibone Snow's seven children, he had grown up on an Ohio farm in a family of Baptists but had the distinction of being able to attend Oberlin College for a half year before joining the LDS Church in June 1836. He then served proselytizing missions in Kentucky, Illinois, Ohio, and England. When he returned from abroad in 1843, Smith admonished him to marry plural wives. Apparently unsettled about this, he waited two years before doing so.

The year before the future church president returned from England, Lorenzo's sister, Eliza, detailed in her biography of him published in 1884 that she had experienced "changes … one of eternal import of which I supposed him to be entirely ignorant. The prophet Joseph had taught me the principle of plural, or Celestial Marriage, and I was married to him for time and eternity. In consequence of the ignorance of most of the saints, as well as people of the world, on this subject, it was not mentioned[,] only privately between the few whose minds were enlightened on the subject." This gave rise to tensions between the two siblings: "Not knowing how my brother would receive it, I did not feel at liberty, and did not wish to assume the responsibility of instructing him in the principle of plural marriage, and either maintained silence, or, to his indirect questioning, gave evasive answers, until I was forced by his cool and distant manner, to feel that he was growing jealous of my sisterly confidence—that I could not con-

32. Johnson, *Life's Review,* 106, 107, 327-28, 339, 341, 351, 377, 381, 387.

fide in his brotherly integrity." When Eliza "could not endure this" any longer, she went to her husband Joseph Smith "and requested him to open the subject to my brother. A favorable opportunity soon presented, and seated together on the lone bank of the Mississippi River, they had a most interesting conversation. The Prophet afterwards told me that he found that my brother's mind had been previously enlightened on the subject in question, and was ready to receive whatever the spirit of revelation from God should impart."[33] Notice again that care was taken in choosing the setting for this conversation: they took a leisurely stroll along the river's bank to find an appropriately secluded area to talk.

According to Eliza, "Joseph unbosomed his heart" to her brother "and described the trying mental ordeal he experienced in overcoming the repugnance of his feelings, the natural result of the force of education and social custom, relative to the introduction of plural marriage." He knew that by violating societal norms, the "whole Christian world stared him in the face" in disapproval but also that a "commandment" had to be "obeyed." According to Eliza, the prophet "hesitated and deferred" until "an angel of God stood by him with a drawn sword, and told him that, unless he moved forward and established plural marriage, his Priesthood would be taken from him and he should be destroyed! This testimony he not only bore to my brother, but also to others—a testimony that cannot be gainsayed."[34]

Lorenzo provided his own version of events:

> In the month of April, 1843 I returned from my European mission. A few days after my arrival at Nauvoo, when at President Joseph Smith's house, he said he wished to have some private talk with me, and requested me to walk out with him. It was toward evening. We walked a little distance and sat down on a large log that lay near the bank of the river. He there and then explained to me the doctrine of plurality of wives; he said that the Lord had revealed it unto him, and commanded him to have women sealed to him as wives; that he foresaw the trouble

---

33. Eliza R. Snow Smith, *Biography and Family Record of Lorenzo Snow* (Salt Lake City: Deseret News, 1884), 68-70; cf. Eliza's 1885 "Sketch of My Life" in chapter 2.

34. Ibid., 69-70.

> that would follow, and sought to turn away from the commandment; that an angel from heaven then appeared before him with a drawn sword, threatening him with destruction unless he went forward and obeyed the commandment.
>
> [The prophet] further said that my sister Eliza R. Snow had been sealed to him as his wife for time and eternity. He told me that the Lord would open the way, and I should have women sealed to me as wives. This conversation was prolonged, I think one hour or more, in which he told me many important things.[35]

Lorenzo added that in his "simplicity," he "besought" Smith to "correct me and set me right if, at any time, he should see me indulging any principle or practice that might tend to lead astray, into forbidden paths; to which he replied, "Brother Lorenzo, the principles of honesty and integrity are founded within you, and you will never be guilty of any serious error or wrong, to lead you from the path of duty. The Lord will open your way to receive and obey the law of Celestial Marriage."[36]

When Lorenzo married his first and second wives, Charlotte Squires and Mary Adeline Goddard, in early April 1845, it was on the same day; he was the only man in Nauvoo who entered into plural marriage straight from bachelorhood. Soon afterward, on April 21, he married his third wife. Eliza related that her brother did "nothing by halves and when he was convinced of [his] duty" he responded by "having two wives sealed to him." Since these relationships could not be divulged, it proved too risky in his case to acknowledge either one of them as his wife.[37] Even so, Eliza considered the time to be propitious because the Nauvoo temple was nearing completion. By the end of the year, these marriages could be properly celebrated and recorded in that sacred edifice. In the first two months of 1846, "thousands of the saints received endowments and sealings," including her

35. Lorenzo Snow, Affidavit, in Joseph Fielding Smith, *Blood Atonement and the Origin of Plural Marriage: A Discussion* (Salt Lake City: Deseret News Press, 1905), 67-68; also in Jenson, "Plural Marriage," 222.

36. Ibid., 70.

37. It would appear that neither wife was married to him civilly. Since only one could be his spouse in the public eye, and since he considered the designation to be arbitrary, he avoided the topic.

brother and his four wives by that time: Charlotte and Mary, Harriet Amelia Squires, and Sarah Ann Prichard.[38]

Two years later he acquired a fifth wife, Eleanor Houtz, whose biographer explained that Lorenzo was twenty-nine years old when "the Prophet, Joseph Smith, had a talk with him and Lorenzo was told it was urgent that he marry right away and do his part in replenishing the earth. As always, he complied as soon as arrangements could be made. He married his first four wives the same [season] in Nauvoo, early in the winter of 1845-1846."[39] In fact, that season he also initiated contact with his fifth wife but found the fourteen-year-old was not ready to be married. As it was delicately framed in Eleanor's history, she was leaving church services with her parents one day when Lorenzo joined them and, "as they walked along, Lorenzo asked Eleanor if she would promise to one day become his wife." She promised that she would. Two years later, on January 19, 1848, the now sixteen-year-old Eleanor became the future church president's fifth wife. She wrote to a friend that day that she had just married and that "soon we shall start for the Salt Lake valley but since the brethern are leaving today I send you this message. I am now a Snow and darlin sis Eliza told me she is proud to be my sister[;] uncle jacob and she said I had digneetee and graceness and I wish [it] to be [so]."[40]

At a family reunion forty years later, Lorenzo spoke publicly about how he had been initiated into the polygamous world: "I was an unmarried man, and to this day would have remained so, had I not received an understanding of the law of celestial marriage—its object

38. Eliza Roxcy Snow (Smith), *Biography and Family Record,* 68-70, 84-85, 484-87.

39. Mildred H. Bray, "Eleanor Houtz Snow, 5th Wife of Pres. L. Snow," typescript, 2-3, LDS Archives. The chronology of the first five marriages is derived from Smith, *Biography and Family Record,* who specified that her brother married Mary Adeline Goddard and Charlotte Squires on the same day and that both of the women were thirty-one years of age (leaving us with the month of April 1845). The third and fourth marriages to Sarah Ann Prichard and Harriet Amelia Squires were recorded by Maude R. Sorenson, "Harriet Amelia Squires Snow," typescript, LDS Archives. The third marriage on April 21, 1845, is corroborated by the Ancestral File, LDS Family History Library, Salt Lake City, see also www.familysearch.org. The date of the fifth marriage is in Bray. D. Michael Quinn has Lorenzo's first three wives married a year earlier in 1844 and the fourth in 1845 (Quinn, *Mormon Hierarchy Extensions,* 701).

40. Bray, "Eleanor Houtz Snow," 2-3.

and necessity in securing eternal glory and exaltation. … Joseph the Prophet, in a private interview at Nauvoo, on the banks of the Mississippi, gave me a full explanation of the principles of celestial marriage, and pointed out to me clearly my duty and privileges in reference to that law." Snow pointed to the risks to his reputation and safety, saying adherence to the "sacred law" was "attended with embarrassments and dangers of no ordinary magnitude. We were surrounded by our enemies, and in our midst were many half-hearted, ignorant Saints, and some of the most wicked apostates, seeking to betray us into the hands of our bitter foes." In Utah he acknowledged his family of forty-two children as the "fruits of my obedience to the law of plural marriage" and promised his descendants that "God will … make you kings and queens in the [afterlife in the] midst of your posterity, to rule in righteousness through the countless ages of eternities."[41]

Snow eventually married nine women, but his sister's 1884 biography acknowledged only the first four, almost certainly wanting to avoid the scandal of a thirty-three-year-old acquiring a sixteen-year-old wife. Having hedged on that detail, she could not very well mention the subsequent brides. Nevertheless, seven of Lorenzo's wives were alive in 1884 and would have been known to Eliza. The women she left out of the family story were Eleanor's sister, Mary Elizabeth Houtz; Phoebe Amelia Woodruff; and Lorenzo's last wife, Minnie Jensen, wed in 1871.

Under political pressure, Lorenzo eventually renounced polygamy. In 1898, when B. H. Roberts was investigated for bigamy and prevented from taking his elected seat in the U.S. House of Representatives, President Snow pushed for an end to the *sub rosa* polygamous transactions which had ironically increased since the church outlawed them in 1890 and especially after Utah had been granted statehood in 1896.[42] While Snow sought to interdict new marriages between 1898 and 1901, Second Counselor Joseph F. Smith, Joseph Smith's neph-

---

41. Smith, *Biography and Family Record,* 68-70, 84-85, 484-87.

42. See Richard S. Van Wagoner, *Mormon Polygamy: A History* (Salt Lake City: Signature Books, 1986), 153-61. Roberts was excluded from the U.S. Congress by a 268-50 vote (Jean Bickmore White, ed., *Church, State, and Politics: The Diaries of John Henry Smith* [Salt Lake City: Signature Books and Smith Research Associates, 1990], 444).

ew, secretly authorized new plural marriages. Again ironically, now-President Joseph F. Smith issued the Second Manifesto in 1904 that applied the 1890 Manifesto to all countries and once and for all closed the door on future polygamy in the church.[43]

For most of his adult life, from 1848 until 1901, Lorenzo Snow lived in Brigham City, Utah, where he ran a cooperative mercantile establishment, although he also traveled on proselytizing missions to Italy, Hawaii, and Malta; toured Palestine; and planned missions in India, Russia, Switzerland, and Turkey. He became church president in 1898 at the age of eighty-four. During his presidency, he helped to reduce the $2.3 million debt burdening the church as a result of the government's escheatment of the church's property under the anti-bigamy Edmunds-Tucker Act of 1887. Snow arranged for the church to issue $1 million in bonds and to sell controlling interest in several businesses.[44] He also advanced foreign missionary work to "warn the nations of the earth and prepare the world for the coming of the Savior."[45] He died in Salt Lake City in October 1901 at the age of eighty-seven and was succeeded as president by Joseph F. Smith.

The lone walks Joseph Smith had with three committed followers reveal how the founder approached and selected men to join his secret enterprise in 1842 and 1843. The records of William Clayton, Benjamin Johnson, and Lorenzo Snow are unequaled in preserving and corroborating the content of those talks and showing a pattern in the way the topic was first discussed in Nauvoo. There were others, too, who were also approached and persuaded in those early years to join the ranks of these brethren in beginning their celestial families.

Expanding Awareness

We do not know how long Joseph Smith had been contemplating

43. Abraham Owen Woodruff, Diary, Aug. 30, Oct. 14, 30, 1900, LDS Archives; Quinn, *Mormon Hierarchy Extensions,* 22-23, 34; Quinn, "LDS Church Authority and New Plural Marriages, 1890-1904," *Dialogue: A Journal of Mormon Thought* 18 (Spring 1985): 83-87.

44. Maureen Ursenbach Beecher and Paul Thomas Smith, "Lorenzo Snow," *Encyclopedia of Mormonism,* ed. Daniel H. Ludlow (New York: Macmillan, 1992), 3:1369-70.

45. B. H. Roberts, *A Comprehensive History of the Church of Jesus Christ of Latter-day Saints* (Salt Lake City: Deseret News Press, 1930), 6:377.

polygamy, but the earliest conversations in which he explicitly addressed the topic were in late 1840 and early 1841, according to the existing records, when his apostles were in England. As the Twelve returned home, he started to hold private conversations with them, as well. Brigham Young's biographer Leonard Arrington thought that "the practice itself was confined to a limited group until after the Mormons moved to the Great Basin."[46] However, as we shall see, this "limited group" included about 200 men and 700 women with children, amounting, all told, to perhaps ten percent of Nauvoo's estimated 1846 population of 12,000.

From reading the recollections of polygamists, historian Juanita Brooks concluded that Joseph Smith had talked about "celestial marriage" for several years, but that "not until 1841" did he "present it to these chosen few as a commandment, a direct order from God, reinforced by an angel with a flaming sword." Again, there were more than a few, and the ones he chose to tell initially were the women he himself married.[47]

Joseph Bates Noble affirmed to a notary in June 1869 that "in the fall of the year A.D. 1840 Joseph Smith taught him the principle of Celestial marriage or a 'plurality of wives,' and that the said Joseph Smith declared that he had received a Revelation from God on the subject" (see chapter 2). One wonders if this discussion might have occurred after the September 14, 1840, death of Smith's father—that is, whether the potential displeasure of his father may have caused him to exercise restraint in the early Nauvoo period. His mother, Lucy Smith, moved in with Joseph and Emma in February 1843, two and a half years after losing her husband and in the second year after her son Don Carlos's death. Then following Joseph's and Hyrum's deaths, she stayed on in the Mansion House. After several years residing with her daughter Lucy and Arthur Milliken, she returned there after Brigham Young had gone west, then in 1851 moved in with Emma and Lewis

---

46. Leonard J. Arrington, *Brigham Young: American Moses* (Urbana: University of Illinois Press, 1986), 102.

47. Juanita Brooks, *John Doyle Lee: Zealot, Pioneer Builder, Scapegoat* (Salt Lake City: Howe Brothers, 1984), 56.

Bidamon for five years, and then briefly to the Smith farm just outside of Nauvoo, where she died on May 14, 1856. If she suspected her son Joseph's romantic interests during his lifetime, she refrained from commenting on the topic, as far as existing evidence allows. Her biographer, Lavina Fielding Anderson, concluded as much, finding "no evidence" that "anyone … ever discussed" polygamy with her "before her death in 1856."[48]

When Smith asked Joseph Noble to "step forward and assist him in carrying out the said principle" of plural marriage, Smith emphasized that he was taking a risk by bringing Noble into his confidence. "I have placed my life in your hands," Smith said, begging his friend not to "betray me to my enemies." This conversation pre-dated by several months the marriage to Noble's sister-in-law, Louisa Beaman, over which Noble would officiate in April 1841.[49]

Juanita Brooks wrote that Young and Kimball learned the new doctrine on May 5, 1842, assuming it was at the same time Smith introduced these men to the Masonic-like endowment ceremonies later associated with temples. Brooks was right that at first the endowment was inextricably connected to polygamy. "Within six weeks, after much hesitation," she wrote of Young and Kimball, "both had taken plural wives." The doctrine was disseminated "slowly at first," but within time "each man initiated" into the Quorum of the Anointed knew he would be "required to take at least one extra wife to fill the law."[50] Young married his first plural wife several months after his conversation with Smith, but the conversation occurred much earlier than Brooks had assumed. Young returned from his British mission in July 1841 and spoke to Smith at some point before Young officiated at Smith's marriage to Agnes Coolbrith in January 1842. Shortly thereafter, prior to April, Young attempted to marry Martha Brotherton.

---

48. Lavina Fielding Anderson, ed., *Lucy's Book: A Critical Edition of Lucy Mack Smith's Family Memoir* (Salt Lake City: Signature Books, 2001), 11-12, 31-34, 125.

49. Joseph B. Noble, Affidavit, June 26, 1869, in "40 Affidavits on Celestial Marriage," 1869.

50. Brooks, *John Doyle Lee,* 56.

Judging from the birth of Kimball's presumed first plural child by Sarah Noon in October 1842, he would have married this wife up to nine months earlier, in about late January. Tradition regards this as a simple "family marriage" that was followed two years later by the formality of a sealing ceremony.[51] If Kimball and Noon married near the time Young sealed Smith to Coolbrith that January, Smith may have urged Young to wed Brotherton around the same time. But as it turned out, when Young married Lucy Ann Decker Seeley five months later on June 14, 1842, this was the first firmly dated polygamous marriage after Smith's initial twelve. His choice of a wife was a twenty-year-old mother of two children who was said to have been separated from her first husband, William Seeley. As tempting as it would be to assign preeminence to this wedding as the first after Smith's, our estimate of the date of the Kimball-Noon wedding puts it a few months before Young's; nor do we have more than approximate dates for Reynolds Cahoon and Vinson Knight, both of whom entered polygamy in 1842—Cahoon marrying Lucina Roberts and Knight marrying Philinda Myrick.

In another claim to be first in line among Smith's adherents, Adeline Belnap said her mother, Martha Knight, Vinson's first wife, was "the first woman to give her consent for her husband to enter Plural Marriage, about May 1842."[52] If Belnap's date was right, it would mean that the Knight wedding occurred before Young's marriage. However, if Vilate gave Heber permission to wed Sarah Noon in January 1842, then Mrs. Kimball was the first wife to give her approval for polygamy. The Knight family's claim would also assume that Emma did not give Joseph permission to marry Louisa, Zina, or Presendia in 1841 or Agnes in January 1842, any one of which would have predated Vilate's involvement in her husband's marriages.

---

51. See *The Wasp,* Apr. 26, 1843, 3. This refers to the death of "Adelmon H. Noon" at six months, implying an October 1842 birth. Cook (*Nauvoo Deaths & Marriages,* 56) has "Adelmone H. Noon," deceased sometime between April 24 and May 8, 1843, according to the Nauvoo sextant's record in the LDS Historical Library, as pointed out to me by Tom Kimball.

52. Della Belnap, "Martha McBride Knight," typescript, LDS Archives, as pointed out to me by Todd Compton.

As Noble reports, Smith discussed polygamy with some others in 1840-41. Not only did Smith prepare Noble to marry him to Beaman, he also talked to John C. Bennett. Another of Smith's counselors in the First Presidency, William Law, later concluded that although "in 1842 I had not heard of such teaching, I believe now that John C. Bennett did know it, for he at the time was more in the secret confidence of Joseph [Smith] than perhaps any other man in the city."[53] Brigham Young's reputed "wife no. 19," Ann Eliza Young, wrote that "one of the first persons to be initiated into the plural-wife doctrine, if not indeed Joseph's confederate in producing it, was Dr. John C. Bennett." She reported that "it is said that the pupil fairly outran the teacher, and his success as special pleader for the system of Celestial Marriage was so decided that he incurred the displeasure of the Prophet, and they quarrelled violently." Ann Eliza thought the reason, although hearsay to her, was that Bennett "taught the doctrine to some ladies whom Smith had intended to convert himself," causing a "rupture." Only after Bennett fell out with Smith in the spring of 1842 were Bennett's relationships with women classified as adulterous, according to this scenario.[54] Either way, the result of the in-house dissonance, which was at least as disruptive as Oliver Cowdery's 1838 accusation that Smith had committed adultery with Fanny Alger, resulting in Cowdery's excommunication, was that Bennett's alliances were expunged from the record. There were vague accusations made about Bennett's character and that he had seduced several women, but, curiously, no details survive. After Bennett left in mid-1842, Young and Kimball would be portrayed in the church's history as the first ones in whom Smith had confided God's most sacred truths, followed soon after by Cahoon and Knight.

After initiating these four associates, along with Noble, who would

---

53. Richard S. Van Wagoner, *Sidney Rigdon: A Portrait of Religious Excess* (Salt Lake City: Signature Books, 1994), 298, citing T. B. H. Stenhouse, *The Rocky Mountain Saints* (New York: D. Appleton and Co., 1873).

54. Ann Eliza Young, *Wife No. 19, or the Story of a Life in Bondage* (Hartford: Dustin, Gilman & Co., 1875), 74. She wrote that some of the events she related depended upon the "experience of those so closely connected with me that they have fallen directly under my observation."

receive his "favor" in 1843, Smith confided in Apostle Willard Richards, who took the leap and expanded his own family in January 1843. Others followed almost immediately, including William D. Huntington on February 5 of that year, Orson Hyde in February-March, Lorenzo Dow Young on March 9, Thomas Bateman on March 23, Joseph Noble on April 5, William Clayton on April 27, and Benjamin Johnson on May 16. They helped spread the practice when Smith resumed his own interest in courting fresh wives after the defensive hiatus in 1842, brought about by adverse publicity and legal threats.

Few in Nauvoo committed their private discussions with Joseph Smith to paper. As Eliza Snow's example tells us, the initiated were at first reluctant, even around close friends and family, to violate their oath of secrecy. However, many were similar to Lorenzo Snow in that they had nurtured suspicions. As rumors circulated, many people were able to discern the truth from cryptic comments Smith repeatedly made about the restoration of ancient practices. Of all the rumors, the most contagious were the ones that originated in failed courtships. Nothing did more to alert the citizens than the story of a young woman who was cornered by a desperate Brigham Young in 1842; her story was followed closely by Nancy Rigdon's anger over Joseph Smith's importunate pleas, telling her that whatever God wanted was right.

The Brotherton debacle

Sometime by early January 1842, Brigham Young prepared to join Smith in polygamy, but his failed attempt to win over Martha Brotherton gives us an unprecedented glimpse at how an older man would go about pressing the merits of plural marriage with a new initiate. Martha was anticipating her eighteenth birthday on May 24, 1842, having been born in 1824 in Manchester, England, the youngest of eight children of Thomas Brotherton and Sarah Hamilton. Struggling in the environment of the declining English textile industry,[55] her

55. Joseph Smith et al., *History of the Church of Jesus Christ of Latter-day Saints,* ed. B. H. Roberts, 2nd ed. rev., 7 vols. (Salt Lake City: Deseret Book, 1963), 4:507-08; William Clayton to William Hardman, Mar. 30, 1842, rpt. *Latter-day Saints' Millennial Star,* Aug. 1842, available online at "Misc. United Kingdom Papers," Dale R. Broadhurst Sites,

family decided to immigrate to America, where they settled with about 200 Saints in Warren, Illinois, in November 1841. Her father's open letter of December 7, 1841, cited the high wages and available work in Nauvoo and confirmed their presence there.[56] Martha is remembered not only for refusing Young's suit but, more importantly, for making a public issue of it. This occurred as early as November 1841, but at least by April 1842, when Hyrum Smith publicly denounced reports of the incident.[57]

After the shock of being solicited by Young, Brotherton left Nauvoo for Warsaw, Illinois, in about July 1842, by way of Missouri, where on July 13 she prepared a statement for John Bennett on "certain propositions made to me at Nauvoo by some of the Mormon leaders." She affirmed her statement before St. Louis County Justice of the Peace Du. Bouffay Fremon. Bennett, in turn, provided Brotherton's affidavit to the *Native American Bulletin* in St. Louis, which published it on July 16. Thereafter newspapers around the country reprinted the "propositions at Nauvoo," which Bennett then included in his *History of the Saints,* published in October. In its first three months, the book went through three printings. Bennett had received permission from Brotherton to do with her statement as he thought best. Its wide circulation brought Nauvoo's underground society into the light of day and formed the most lasting impression the public would have of Mormonism.[58]

According to Brotherton's account, Kimball approached her a few

---

www.sidneyrigdon.com; cf. Richard and Pamela Price, *Joseph Smith Fought Polygamy* (Independence, Mo.: By the authors, 2000).

56. *Latter Day Saints' Millennial Star,* Jan. 1842, 156, quoted in Robert B. Flanders, *Nauvoo: Kingdom on the Mississippi* (Urbana: University of Illinois Press, 1975), 75.

57. *History of the Church,* 4:585.

58. After initial publication in the *Bulletin,* Brotherton's statement was reprinted over the next two weeks in the *Alton Telegraph, Louisville Journal, New York Herald, North-western Gazette and Galena Advertiser* (stating that Miss Brotherton was "called upon to make a public statement of her treatment while among the Mormons"), *Sangamo Journal* (Springfield, Ill.), *Warsaw Signal,* and the *Quincy Whig.* See John C. Bennett, *History of the Saints* (1842; Urbana: University of Illinois Press, 2000), 236-40; Andrew F. Smith, *The Saintly Scoundrel: The Life and Times of Dr. John Cook Bennett* (Urbana: University of Illinois Press, 1997), 122, 127. The location of the original of this affidavit, if it has survived, is not known.

weeks before her eighteenth birthday on May 24, and, as Young's front man, initiated the following conversation:

> "Sister Martha, are you willing to do all that the Prophet requires you to do?" I said I believed I was, thinking of course he would require nothing wrong. "Then," said he, "are you ready to take counsel?" I answered in the affirmative, thinking of the great and glorious blessings that had been pronounced upon my head, if I adhered to the counsel of those placed over me in the Lord.[59]

Her reference to "blessings … pronounced upon my head" may have referred to her "patriarchal blessing," a once-in-a-lifetime prophetic pronouncement church members were then receiving in Nauvoo, as uttered by Hyrum Smith, who rested his hands upon the recipient's head and gazed into the future to tell them what they could expect of their lives. Continuing with a similar theme, Heber told Martha that additional "mysteries of the kingdom" were about to be revealed to her. Then he acquired a foreboding tone and warned, "Martha, you must learn to hold your tongue, and it will be well with you." He said he was going to bring her to "see Joseph, and very likely [she would] have some conversation with him, and he will tell you what you shall do." When they reached Smith's red brick store, Kimball "led me up some stairs to a small room" used for tithing transactions, "the door of which was locked," Martha narrated. "He then left me in the tithing office" with two men: William Clayton, whom she knew from England, and another man she did not know.

"Young came in," she related, "and seated himself before me. … Soon after, Joseph came in," but he and Young went into another room. After a short pause, Kimball came to escort her to the room where Smith and Young had gone.

> I was introduced to the Prophet by Young. Joseph offered me his seat, and, to my astonishment, the moment I was seated, Joseph and Kimball walked out of the room, and left me with Young, who arose, locked the

---

59. *Native American Bulletin,* St. Louis, July 16, 1842, available online at "Readings in Early Mormon History: Newspapers of Missouri," *Dale R. Broadhurst Sites,* www.sidneyrigdon.com; Harold B. Lee Library, Brigham Young University, microfilm holdings; Library of Congress, Newspaper Division [see online].

> door, closed the window, and drew the curtain. He then came and sat before me, and said, "This is our private room, Martha." ... He ... proceeded, "sister Martha, I want to ask you a few questions; will you answer them?" "Yes, sir," said I. "And will you promise not to mention them to anyone?" "If it is your desire, sir," said I, "I will not." "And you will not think any the worse of me for it, will you, Martha?" said he. ... "No, sir," I replied. "Well," said he, "what are your feelings towards me?" I replied, "My feelings are just the same towards you that they ever were, sir." "But to come to the point more closely," said he, "have not you an affection for me, that, were it lawful and right, you could accept of me for your husband and companion?" My feelings at that moment were indescribable. God only knows them. What, thought I, are these men, that I thought almost perfection itself, *deceivers,* and is all my fancied happiness but a dream?

Brotherton collected herself and replied to the question of whether she could accept Young as a husband. "If it was lawful and right perhaps I might," she said; "but you know, sir, it is not."

> "Well, but," said he, "brother Joseph has had a revelation from God that it is lawful and right for a man to have two wives; for, as it was in the days of Abraham, so it shall be in these last days, and whoever is the first that is willing to take up the cross will receive the greatest blessings; and if you will accept of me, I will take you straight to the celestial kingdom; and if you will have me in this world, I will have you in that which is to come, and brother Joseph will marry us here to-day, and you can go home this evening, and your parents will not know anything about it." "Sir," said I, "I should not like to do any thing of the kind without the permission of my parents." "Well, but," said he, "you are of age, are you not?" "No, sir," said I, "I shall not be until the 24th of May." "Well," said he, "that does not make any difference. You will be of age before they know, and you need not fear. If you will take my counsel, it will be well with you, for I know it to be right before God, and if there is any sin in it, I will answer for it. But brother Joseph wishes to have some talk with you on the subject ... he will explain things ... will you hear him?" "I do not mind," said I.

Before Young passed the woman to Smith, he wanted some indication from Brotherton of her frame of mind. "I want you to say something," he said. Brotherton replied sensibly, "I want time to think about it." "Well," said Young, "I will have a kiss, any how." According to Martha, he "then rose, and said he would bring Joseph. He then unlocked the door, and took the key, and locked me up alone. He was absent about ten minutes, and then returned with Joseph." The three of them, according to Brotherton, faced off in the shaded room:

> "Well," said Young, "sister Martha would be willing if she knew it was lawful and right before God." "Well, Martha," said Joseph, "it is lawful and right before God … I know it is. Look here, sis; don't you believe in me?" I did not answer. "Well, Martha," said Joseph, "just go ahead, and do as Brigham wants you to … he is the best man in the world, except me." … "Well," said Young, "we believe Joseph to be a Prophet. I have known him near eight years, and always found him the same.["] "Yes," said Joseph, "and I know that this is lawful and right before God, and if there is any sin in it, I will answer for it before God; and I have the keys of the kingdom, and whatever I bind on earth is bound in heaven, and whatever I loose on earth is loosed in heaven, and if you will accept of Brigham, you shall be blessed … and if you do not like it in a month or two, come to me, and I will make you free again; and if he turns you off, I will take you on." "Sir," said I, rather warmly, "it will be too late to think in a month or two after. I want time to think first." "Well, but," said he, "the old proverb is, 'Nothing ventured, nothing gained;' and it would be the greatest blessing that was ever bestowed upon you." "Yes," said Young, "and you will never have reason to repent it."

Brotherton recorded that Smith became more insistent. "'Well, then,' he said, 'What are you afraid of, sis? Come, let me do the business for you.' 'Sir,' said I, 'do let me have a little time to think about it, and I will promise not to mention it to any one.'" She said she needed to "go home and think and pray about it." The more she resisted, the more Young backed off and placed her request in Smith's hands: "'Well,' said Young, 'I shall leave it with brother Joseph, whether it would be best for you to have time or not.'" Joseph agreed on the repeated condition "never to mention it to any one."

But Martha did inform someone. "The next day being Sunday [probably in March], I sat down, instead of going to meeting, and wrote the conversation, and gave it to my sister [Elizabeth, future plural wife of Parley P. Pratt], who was not a little surprised," Martha wrote. At church that afternoon, she saw Young, who "followed me out, and whispered, 'Have you made up your mind, Martha?' 'Not exactly, sir,' said I; and we parted."

Although Martha only admitted to telling her sister, news of the incident must have circulated before her departure to Warsaw. How shocking it must have been to hear Hyrum Smith, at the church's general conference, April 7, 1842, explicitly repudiate "a report in circulation about Elders Heber C. Kimball, Brigham Young, himself, and others of the twelve, alleging that a sister had been shut in a room for several days, and that they had endeavored to induce her to believe in [men] having two wives."[60] It seems reasonable to suppose that Joseph had asked his brother to offer a defense against Brotherton's story because Hyrum was still opposed to polygamy and probably believed the story to be false. On the other hand, Hyrum must have known, as others did, that his brother had previously advocated plural marriage. Without specific denials from Joseph, he might well have wondered in this case what exactly had happened in the upper room of the store.

Three days after Hyrum's address, Joseph made another effort to minimize reports of the Brotherton incident. He preached in the grove on Sunday morning and "pronounced a curse upon all adulterers, and Fornicators, and unvirtuous persons, and those who have made use of my name to carry on their iniquitous designs."[61] In spite of Smith's pronouncements, Brotherton remained the center of attention in this narrative, and her account seemed to substantiate the rumors that Smith had denied ever since marrying Beaman the previous year. Bennett was on hand in Nauvoo to observe these developments until mid-1842 when he vanished from the city. Soon he would publish the Relief Society's March 1842 investigation of charges against Smith. It is nearly inconceivable to think of, but in the middle of this chaotic environment, Smith importuned Nancy Rigdon that very April. When he went on to send her a letter, Bennett published it as well.[62]

---

60. *History of the Church,* 4:585-86.

61. Ibid., 4:587.

62. A month after his May 11 notice of disfellowshipment, Bennett went to Springfield on June 21 to speak with the *Sangamo Journal.* He returned to Nauvoo for a week, boarding with George Robinson; then on July 1 he left for good, first to Carth-

Brotherton vented her accusations against Smith and the Twelve at a cost. Hyrum defended his brother's integrity, but younger brother and newspaper editor William Smith went straight for Brotherton's virtue. The main objective of *The Wasp,* as William's paper was appropriately called, was to counter stories appearing in the nearby *Warsaw Signal,* edited by Thomas Sharp, a Mormon opponent. While smearing Sharp on August 27, 1842, Smith struck at "John C. Bennett, the pimp and file leader of such mean harlots as Martha H. Brotherton and her predecessors from old Jezebel, whom the dogs [ate]."[63] That same day, Brigham Young swore: "I do hereby testify that the affidavit of Miss Martha Brotherton … is a base falsehood, with regard to any private intercourse or unlawful conduct or conversation with me." A companion affidavit from Nauvoo Stake President William Marks read: "I know of no order in the church which admits a plurality of wives, and do not believe that Joseph Smith ever taught such a doctrine." The church published a broadside to counter Brotherton and devoted it to denials and character slurs. It was circulated by missionaries who carried it in saddlebags to major cities. Mostly it portrayed Brotherton and others who were implicated in polygamy as women of moral laxity. By impugning Brotherton's reputation, the church leaders sought to punish her for her refusal to stay quiet.[64]

The Brotherton affair thus attracted heightened attention through the publicity the church itself devoted to it. The denials continued, even abroad. The August 1842 issue of the *Millennial Star* in England reads as follows:

---

age and St. Louis, then to New York, and ultimately to Polk City, Iowa, where he lived with his wife, Sarah, until 1867. See Smith, *Saintly Scoundrel,* 78-99, 184-85.

63. "Remarks," *The Wasp,* Aug. 27, 1842, "as edited and published every Saturday, by Wm. Smith, at the corner of Water and Bain Streets." The inaugural issue of the paper had appeared on April 16.

64. See *Affidavits and Certificates Disproving the Statements and Affidavits Contained in John C. Bennett's Letters,* Nauvoo, Aug. 31, 1842. In one such statement, Martha's brother-in-law, John McIlwrick (the husband of Mary Brotherton), testified that Martha had "stooped to many actions which would be degrading to persons of common decency, such as lying on the top of a young man when he was in bed, and seeking Aristotle's work from a young seaman's box," a reference to the anonymously published but widely circulated sex manual entitled *Aristotle's Masterpiece.*

> Among the most conspicuous of these apostates, we would notice a young female [Brotherton] who … conceived the plan of gaining friendship and extraordinary notoriety with the world, [so] she accordingly selected President J. Smith, and elder B. Young for her victims, and wrote to England that these men had been trying to seduce her, by making her believe that God had given a revelation that men might have two wives …
>
> But, for the information of those who may be assailed by those foolish tales about the two wives, we would say that no such principle ever existed among the Latter-day Saints, and never will.[65]

Another young woman who rejected plural marriage was Almira Knight, the oldest daughter of one of Smith's wives. It was two years after the Brotherton incident, in the spring of 1844, and almost two years after Joseph had married Vinson Knight's widow, Martha. By this time, Hyrum Smith had been converted to plural marriage and had decided to pursue Martha's sixteen-year-old daughter. While on a visit to Martha's residence, Joseph communicated Hyrum's interest. Through her mother, Almira conveyed her regret. A few months later, on November 10, she married another suitor, Sylvester Stoddard, a tinsmith who had worked for her father. Twenty-six years older than Almira, Stoddard took her to Akron, Ohio, where she was removed from the menace of plural marriage.[66]

After the summer of 1842, celestial marriage would never again function in an entirely *sub rosa* Nauvoo setting. Eyes and ears were attuned to notice who was visiting whom and who was pregnant. Even later, when the temple was completed, church leaders would reprimand those who loitered near the veil in order to see which women belonged to which men. These images filtered out into the general population of the city and from there to neighboring towns. Brotherton eventually returned to England, where she died in 1864. But on August 1, 1870, in Salt Lake City, Brigham Young achieved his romantic pursuit when he had Brotherton sealed to him for eternity. Her

---

65. *Millennial Star,* August 1842, 73-74.

66. Hyrum Belnap, Journal, July 24, 1908, cited in Todd Compton, *In Sacred Loneliness: The Plural Wives of Joseph Smith* (Salt Lake City: Signature Books, 1997), 321, 725.

sister, Elizabeth Brotherton Pratt, plural wife of Apostle Parley Pratt, acted as proxy for the deceased.[67]

Brigham Young

Brigham Young's first wife, Miriam Works, died of tuberculosis in 1832. They had met in Bucksville, New York, along the Erie Canal where Brigham worked at a pail factory. In their eight years of marriage, they had two children. Two years after Miriam's death, Brigham married Mary Ann Angell, a twenty-five-year-old who had heard him preach in Kirtland, Ohio. Throughout his fifty-five plural marriages, she would be "wife number one"[68] and outlive him by five years, dying in 1882 in Salt Lake City.

On July 1, 1841, Brigham arrived home from his mission to England to find a new order of marriage being talked about. His thirty-two-year-old wife, Mary Ann, would give birth to their fifth child, Eunice ("Luna") Caroline Young in August 1842, meaning that the baby was conceived just prior to Brigham's unsuccessful courtship of Martha Brotherton in winter 1841-42. Mary Ann was visibly pregnant with Luna when Brigham began courting Lucy Decker Seeley, whom he married on June 14, two months before Mary Ann delivered their "homecoming daughter." Within a year, Lucy Seeley's mother, Harriet Page Wheeler Decker, after divorcing her husband, Isaac Decker, would marry Brigham's younger brother, Lorenzo Dow Young.[69]

The courtship of Lucy Decker Seeley was in the nature of amplifying a relationship with an old friend—initially not so much with Lucy herself as with her father, Isaac Decker, whom Brigham's father,

---

67. Devery S. Anderson and Gary James Bergera, *The Nauvoo Endowment Companies, 1845-1846: A Documentary History* (Salt Lake City: Signature Books, 2005), 191: "There is too much confusion in these rooms[.] … I have been Amused at the people making [use?] of their eyes to see who takes the sisters through the vail[.] it has nothing to do with the sealing power—they say they cannot receive their endowment without being sealed [and] this [is] to be known hereafter when persons come through the vail"; Lyndon W. Cook, *Nauvoo Marriages, Proxy Sealings* (Provo: Grandin Book, 2004), 7. See also Van Wagoner, *Mormon Polygamy,* 20, 26n7.

68. Stanley P. Hirshson counts seventy wives. See *The Lion of the Lord: A Biography of Brigham Young* (New York: Knopf, 1969), 184-223.

69. Leonard J. Arrington, *Brigham Young: American Moses* (Urbana: University of Illinois Press, 1986), 105, 121, 420.

John Young, had known in New York.[70] After Lucy and William Seeley separated in early 1842, she agreed to let Brigham provide a home for her and her young children. Brigham's interest lay in showing his loyalty to Joseph by following the command to marry a plural wife and pioneering the doctrine of celestial marriage. For Brigham and Lucy, the marriage proved to be mutually advantageous. Lucy did not live with the Youngs but remained in the home she had once shared with her first husband a few blocks away,[71] thus trying to ensure that the Nauvoo community would not know of her second marriage.[72] Even so, she eventually bore Brigham seven children.[73] The first, Brigham Heber, was not born until after a discreet delay of three years. Young did not father any children by his plural wives during Smith's lifetime, as far as is known. His five wives all continued to live in separate residences. Lucy Seeley had two children by her first husband, seven by Brigham, and an Indian girl, Sally, whom she raised as if her own. Sally was captured in a raid and purchased by Charles Decker, Lucy's brother, in about 1847 in exchange for a gun.[74]

---

70. Jeffery O. Johnson, "Determining and Defining 'Wife,'" *Dialogue: A Journal of Mormon Thought* 20 (Fall 1987), 57-70.

71. A family member dates Lucy's separation from William Seeley to about February 1842 (Verna Seely Carter, "When I Die, Let It Be with My Boots On," online at www.rootsweb.com). Devery S. Anderson and Gary James Bergera, eds., *Joseph Smith's Quorum of the Anointed, 1842-1845: A Documentary History* (Salt Lake City: Signature Books, 2005), 221, conclude that they had separated or divorced by 1841.

72. Arrington, *Brigham Young,* 105.

73. Johnson, "Determining and Defining 'Wife,'" 65. Of Young's fifty-five wives, fifteen bore him fifty-five children. Arrington, *Brigham Young,* Appendix C, 420-21, listed only women who bore Young children or for whom Young provided a home and noted them in his will. This excluded, for example, Olive Frost and Maria Lawrence because of early deaths. Arrington conceded that they "might have been on this list if they had lived longer."

74. It should be remembered that "slavery and polygamy were already common practices among the Indians" (Alice M. Bailey, "Last Wife of Chief Kanosh," *Frontier Times,* Mar. 1980, 18) and that captives from a "rival tribe constituted the natural spoils of war. Women were objects of traffic ... bought with ponies, blankets, and other objects, and sometimes branded if they tried to escape."

Mormons saw Native Americans as a cursed people, that "the Lord God did cause a skin of blackness to come upon them" for their waywardness (2 Ne. 5:21). By adopting Sally, Brigham fulfilled prophecy: "The Lord ... put the Saints where they were to help bring about the redemption of the [Indians] and also make them a white and delightsome people" (quoted in the Journal History of the Church of Jesus Christ

After Joseph sealed Brigham to Lucy in 1842, there would be no more weddings for Brigham until November 2, 1843, when he exchanged vows with two at once. On the same day Joseph married Brigham's sister, Fanny, Brigham married Augusta Cobb and Harriett Cook. A half a year later, on May 8, 1844, he followed Smith's example of literally marrying "sister wives" when he added Clarissa Decker to his family, the fifteen-year-old younger sister of Lucy. He had therefore married a total of four women, after his legal wife Mary Ann, prior to Smith's assassination. He would go on to marry thirty-five more in Nauvoo after he assumed church leadership and fifteen more in Winter Quarters and Salt Lake City for a total of fifty-five, the most of anyone in the community. His close friend and fellow apostle Heber Kimball ranked second with forty-four.

We can only speculate as to why Young waited so long to marry his second, third, and fourth wives. Was it because of the trouble stirred up by the Brotherton rejection? Did he give cursory allegiance to the doctrine in only marrying one plural wife and maintaining a separate residence, with no children at first? Did the prophet's own five-month hiatus after August 1842 dampen Young's ardor? Perhaps the conflict with Bennett, as he publicized Young's clumsy attempt to entice Brotherton, as well as Smith's failed courtships with Sarah Pratt and Nancy Rigdon, created a climate that was too adverse for further marriages. Public fury may have temporarily quelled not only the possibility but his desire to be more involved.

None of the other supposed 1842 marriages among Smith's col-

---

of Latter-day Saints, May 12, 1851, LDS Archives). This belief made it easy for the territorial legislature to legalize Indian slavery on March 7, 1852 (Eugene E. Campbell, *Establishing Zion: The Mormon Church in the American West, 1847-1869* [Salt Lake City: Signature Books, 1988], 106-07).

Sally lived with the Young family for about twenty years until, in 1868, Chief Kanosh wanted her for a wife. Young complied with the Indian leader's request and sealed her to him (Journal History, May 11, 1874; Hyrum S. Lewis, "Kanosh and Ute Identity in Territorial Utah," *Utah Historical Quarterly* 71 [Fall 2003]: 332-47). Sally was Kanosh's fourth wife (Bailey, "Last Wife," 17-22, 50-51; Arrington, *Brigham Young,* 210; see also Kate B. Carter, *Our Pioneer Heritage,* 20 vols. [Salt Lake City: Daughters of Utah Pioneers, 1960, 1965], 3:423; 8:97-99; Carter, comp., *Heart Throbs of the West,* 12 vols. [Salt Lake City: Daughters of Utah Pioneers, 1939-51], 8:112-13).

leagues can be dated definitely: neither Reynolds Cahoon to Lucina Johnson, Heber Kimball to Sarah Noon, nor Vinson Knight to Philinda Myrick. All of these may have taken place before Bennett's July 1842 disclosures, without any other plural marriages occurring that year after the Smith/Knight sealing in August.

Although Smith and a few of his associates resumed marrying in early 1843, Young waited until the end of the year. During that period, mid-1842 to late 1843, Young was immersed in missionary activity as well as administrative responsibilities in Nauvoo. In the fall of 1842, he traveled throughout Illinois with Kimball to preach against Bennett. Later that year he developed scarlet fever, but by the spring of 1843 he had been assigned to supervise both domestic and overseas missionaries. In July, he was sent to the eastern states to raise money for the temple and the inn to be called Nauvoo House. Therefore, despite the fog of uncertainty over plural marriage, Young found himself fully employed in the service of the church's efforts in Nauvoo and abroad. He was in the eastern states when Joseph dictated his marriage revelation and would not return to Nauvoo until the end of October, but clearly he had been preparing himself to follow the "many principles … of celestial marriage," even courting his next two wives, Augusta and Harriet. He would later say he had had his own revelation on plural marriage, prior to Smith's revelation and prior to his talk with Smith about polygamy, two years earlier in England. The curious matter of Cobb and Cook is that they planned their marriages to Brigham before he and they were all in Nauvoo and that the marriages took place on the same day, only eleven days after he arrived home.

It seems the courtship of Augusta Cobb, a married woman, occurred in her hometown of Boston while Brigham was on his mission there. She agreed to leave her husband and move to Nauvoo to marry the apostle and took five of her seven children with her. Her soon-to-be sister wife, Harriet Cook, was from a Quaker family located in Oneida County, New York. In 1836 she heard Mormon missionaries preach. She was eleven at the time. In 1842 she was baptized, met Brigham the following year in Boston, and then married him, along with Cobb, in November 1843. She was eighteen, whereas her traveling companion and sister-wife, Augusta, was forty-one.

Smith was increasingly entrusting Young with major responsibilities, both religious and civic. He asked him to "investigate," along with others of the Twelve, possible locations for a westward migration, should it come to that. This was in 1844, simultaneous with Smith's campaign for the U.S. presidency. It is altogether possible that the senior apostle was too busy to court more than the four women he married during Smith's lifetime. However, when he suddenly ascended to the church's top leadership in the latter half of 1844, he married twelve wives, then five more the next year, and eighteen in January and February 1846 before heading west. Perhaps one aspect of his new-found willingness to marry was his conscious assumption of Joseph's position as a role model and his desire to further the founding prophet's legacy. On a more immediate level, the pioneer leader was preparing a self-sustaining family organization before crossing the prairies.

Young is the primary leader, out of all of them, with whom plural marriage is most readily associated. He was the first church leader to acknowledge plural marriage publicly. When he died in 1877, it was a decade before the federal government would force an abandonment of this controversial experiment in marriage.

Brigham's understanding

Young spoke often of plural marriage and usually attributed it to the Old Testament patriarchs. It became part of his overall materialistic theology, derived from Smith's concepts, in which pre-existent and resurrected beings were said to have physical spirit bodies in the likeness of a non-trinitarian godhead. Adam was said to have traveled to earth from another planet and to have planted the human race on earth by sexual propagation with one of his many wives. In line with this, Brigham saw the righteous priesthood brethren as future Adams who would populate future planets.[75]

---

75. Joseph Lee Robinson, Diary, entry dated Oct. 6, 1862, L. Tom Perry Special Collections, Harold B. Lee Library, Brigham Young University, Provo; *Journal of Discourses,* 26 vols. (London: Latter-day Saint's Book Depot, 1854-86), 1:50-51.

Joseph Smith's ideas were thus shaped into a consistent whole by Brigham Young to fit the architecture of a new order. For example, where Smith conceived of multiple worlds occupied by multiple gods, each of which was a perfected human-like being, Young reasoned that the creator of our world must have been "Adam the father of this civilization" and that Adam and God "must be the same person." He ridiculed geologists who "tell us that this earth has been in existence for thousands and millions of years."[76] He considered mankind to be younger than that but at the same time part of an ageless population of ancient gods inhabiting the universe.

Young considered plural wives to be the prerogative of a righteous man. As he explained: "There are multitudes of pure and holy spirits waiting to take tabernacles [human bodies], now what is our duty? … to prepare tabernacles for them; to take a course that will not tend to drive those spirits into the families of the wicked. … It is the duty of every righteous man and woman to prepare tabernacles for all the spirits they can," which could best be accomplished through polygamy. This was "the reason why the doctrine of the plurality of wives was revealed, that the noble spirits which are waiting for tabernacles might be brought forth."[77] Plural marriage was a requirement of every earnest Mormon: "The only men who become gods, even the sons of God, are those who enter into polygamy."[78] Characterizing it as "Joseph Smith's spiritual wife system" and "spiritual wife ism," he had stated already in Nauvoo that "no man can be perfect without the woman, so no woman can be perfect without a man to lead her," and that one man was capable of leading many women.[79]

Young denied that polygamy was a matter of lust. The doctrine of "plurality of wives" was established to "raise up a holy nation," but "not to gratify lustful passion in the least," he said.[80] At times contradicting this apologia, he boasted: "I could prove to this congregation

76. *Journal of Discourses,* 12:271.

77. Ibid., 4:56.

78. Ibid., 11:269.

79. "Speech Delivered by President B. Young, in the City of Joseph," Apr. 6, 1845, in *Times and Seasons,* July 1, 1845, 955; *Journal of Discourses,* 9:38, 307; 11:270; 12:194.

80. *Journal of Discourses,* 9:36.

that I am young; for I could find more girls who would choose me for a husband than can any of the young men," further asserting that "Mormonism keeps men and women young and handsome."[81]

Reflecting on Smith's revelation, Young offered "a few hints" about why men would need to be married to a plurality of wives. "If we could make every man upon the earth get him a wife, live righteously and serve God, we would not be under the necessity, perhaps, of taking more than one wife. But they will not do this; the people of God, therefore, have been commanded to take more wives." He saw polygamy as a counterweight to a man's natural impulses, which he thought were otherwise manifested in promiscuity and solicitation. If a man had enough women to satisfy his needs within the natural order of plural marriage, he would not be led astray. Perhaps contrary to his implied view of the moral superiority of women, he went on to portray females as naturally dependent on men. Differing from the women's rights movement of the day, he spoke as someone whose self image was that of a great leader and progressive thinker—a protector of the weaker sex. "The women are entitled to salvation if they live according to the word that is given to them," he said, "and if their husbands are good men, and they are obedient to them, they are entitled to certain blessings ... that they cannot receive unless they are sealed to men who will be exalted." A woman who "determined not to enter into a plural marriage," by contrast, would lose the right to have a husband in the eternities. However, she would live forever in "single blessedness" as a cosmic sister of mercy, "minister[ing] to the wants of others."

Young and other church leaders may have perceived that women were more easily persuaded than men to join the Mormon faith and that this created a population imbalance which justified plural marriage and prompted the theology of "single blessedness."[82] In 1861 Young again spoke "a few words of doctrine" about those who separated from their husbands and "upgrad[ed]" their marriage by switching to someone who held a "higher" church authority. He then commented on divorce, saying:

81. Ibid., 5:210.
82. Ibid., 16:166-67.

the second way in which a wife can be separated from her husband … I have not revealed, except to a few persons in this Church, and a few have received it from Joseph the prophet as well as myself.

If a woman can find a man holding the keys of the priesthood with higher power and authority than her husband, and he is disposed to take her[,] he can do so, otherwise she has got to remain where she is. …

To recapitulate. First if a man forfeits his covenants with a wife, or wives, becoming unfaithful to his God and his priesthood, that wife or wives are free from him without a bill of divorcement. Second. If a woman claims protection at the hands of a man, possessing more power in the priesthood and the higher keys, if he is disposed to rescue her and has obtained the consent of her husband to make her his wife he can do so without a bill of divorcement.

If after she has left her husband and is sealed to another, [and] she shall again cohabit with him[,] it is illicit intercourse, and extremely sinful.

Young advised the "young sisters" to consider the reward offered a woman who would choose a man of a higher church rank—to "go into the hands of a man, that will lead you into the kingdom of heaven, and exalt you there to become an Eve—a queen of heaven—the wife of a god; and you can remain with that man whom your soul delights, and you take to him your virginity[;] you have obtained a treasure that [a lesser man] could not buy from you, for there is your glory to all eternity."[83] The reference to virginity suggested an initial choice, but he clearly intended to include women who switched husbands to improve their celestial rank. For example, Zina Jacobs left Henry Jacobs to be with Joseph and later with Brigham (see chapter 2).

Five years later, at a general conference in 1866, Young remembered this about Joseph Smith: "He often said to me when speaking upon polygamy, 'I shall die for it: and I would as leave die for it as not. It is the work of God and he has revealed this principle and it is not my business to control or dictate it: to say it shall or shall not be." Young recalled when Hyrum Smith had tried to find out whether the rumors of plural marriage were true. "For a long time," Hyrum had suspected that his brother was involved with other women, and Joseph

83. Brigham Young, "A Few Words of Doctrine," Oct. 8, 1861, LDS Archives.

had "hinted as much." The prophet's brother had "hard things" to say about this. Young continued:

> I recollect in one council where Joseph undertook to teach the brethren and sisters[.] William Law was there[,] and William and Hyrum and a few others were against Joseph. William Law made this expression: "If an angel from heaven was to reveal to me that a man should have more than one wife, and if it were in my power[,] I would kill him." That was pretty hard, but Joseph had to submitt for it. The brethren were not prepared to receive the doctrine. Brother Kimball and others were in that council. Joseph had meetings [on this] in his house time after time and month after month [with the leading brethren], every Sunday evening. Joseph was worn out with it, but as to his denying any such thing, I never knew that he denied the doctrine of polygamy. Some had said that he did, but I do not believe that he ever did.

Young continued with the anecdote about Hyrum, who said, "I am convinced that there is something that has not been told me." Young replied, saying that "Joseph had many wives sealed to him. I told Hyrum the whole story and he bowed to it and wept like a child." Young said he himself had learned "the doctrine of polygamy by revelation" some time ago when he was on his mission "in England before it was revealed to me by Joseph."[84]

On another occasion, Young elaborated:

> Some of my brethren know what my feelings were at the time Joseph revealed the doctrine; I was not desirous of shrinking f[rom] any duty, nor of failing in the least to do as I was commanded, but it was the first time in my life that I had desired the grave, and I could hardly get over it for a long time and when I saw a funeral, I felt to envy the corpse its situation, and to regret that I was not in the coffin, knowing the toil and the labor that my body would have to undergo; and I have had to examine myself, from that day to this, and watch my faith, and carefully meditate, lest I should be found desiring the grave more than I ought to.[85]

It was Young's endorsement and example that sustained his mentor's marital innovation long after Smith had planted it in Nauvoo's

84. Ibid.
85. *Journal of Discourses,* 3:266.

fertile soil. Young gathered polygamy's surviving seedlings and transported them to the west, where they grew into mighty trees of Mormon culture. When the more obvious problems surrounding the practice of plural marriage had been worked out, then, at a safe distance from his critics, Young boldly announced their marital creation to the world.

After Joseph's death

The church was in disarray in mid-1844 after Joseph's martyrdom. Never again would a Mormon leader direct the membership by day-to-day revelation. The apostles were in the role of institutional managers more than innovators. However, in that capacity, Brigham and Heber had stepped in to keep the church intact while Smith spent nearly six months in incarceration in Missouri from November 1838 to April 1839. In doing so, they created an image of themselves in the minds of the Latter-day Saints as suitable substitutes for the president. Young resolved the succession challenges posed by Sidney Rigdon and others in 1844, promising that one of Smith's sons would one day take over the church leadership, and then began consolidating his leadership over the hierarchy. His acclaim rose slowly at first, as he struggled with a haphazard migration across Iowa's rolling prairies to Winter Quarters, but he then was able to tighten control and bring the immigrants safely to their destination in Utah. In part, Smith's organizational labyrinth helped keep the church together, but Young was the real key to its survival. In 1845 Young worked out a scheme that placed church members in companies of "tens" and "fifties" so when the time came he was able to send these companies, comprising 15,000 people, on a march with about five hundred wagons across the Rocky Mountains to the shores of the Great Salt Lake.[86] He kept the wagons moving by establishing way stations that provided the wagon trains with

86. The groups of "tens" and "fifties" are biblical (Ex. 18:10). The first LDS divisions of this kind were in Missouri, where Samson Avard "held meetings to organize his men into companies of tens and fifties ... to rule over this last kingdom of Jesus Christ." He told the men it would soon be their privilege to "take your respective companies and go out on a scout of the borders of the settlements, and take to yourselves spoils of the goods of the ungodly gentiles" (Andrew Jenson, "Caldwell County, Missouri," *Historical Record* 8 [Jan. 1889]: 701).

supplies. When Brigham's pioneers arrived in the Great Basin in 1847, the year after Samuel Brannan reached California by ship in 1846, the church was stretched out across the country from the Mississippi and Missouri Rivers westward to the Pacific Ocean, "eastward across" much of "America and halfway across Europe," as Bernard DeVoto expressed it. DeVoto concluded that "a history of the Mormons in the West would be … a history of a mad prophet's visions turned by an American genius into the seed of life."[87]

Three months after Smith's death, in a response reminiscent of Absalom pitching a tent with his father's wives to show he was now in charge (2 Sam. 16:21-22), Young and Kimball married Smith's widows beginning on September 19, 1844. On one level, Young was pursuing Smith's example of levirate marriage, whereby a man married a brother's widow. But further, as a fraternal bond, the Twelve saw themselves as spiritual brothers who would live together in the hereafter, connected by dynastic marriage. Susa Young Gates recalled that her father, Brigham, approached the widows to tell them that "he and his brethren stood ready to offer themselves to them as husbands" in order to contribute to their comrade's offspring, and that the widows were free to "choose for themselves."[88] Within just a half a year, six of the women married Young, four married Kimball, and one married Amasa M. Lyman. Over the next year and a half, Young, Kimball, and six others—namely Almon Babbitt, John Bernhisel, Ezra Benson, Cornelius Lott, George Albert Smith (Joseph's cousin), and John Smith (Joseph's uncle)—would marry thirteen more of the widows for a total of twenty-four of Smith's thirty-eight wives. Typically these were proxy marriages in which a man substituted himself for Smith for the duration of the couple's lives while re-solemnizing the woman's eternal marriage to Smith. The twenty-four who chose this path were clearly committed to a view of a family hierarchy after death.

---

87. Bernard DeVoto, *The Year of Decision: 1846* (Boston: Houghton Mifflin, 1942), 92-101, 469.

88. Susa Young Gates, "Brigham Young and His Nineteen Wives," Susa Young Gates Papers, 1852-1932, Box 12, Folder 2, Utah State Historical Society, Salt Lake City.

TABLE 4.1 The widows who married LDS leaders

name	re-marriage	new husband	remained sealed to Smith
Louisa Beaman	Sept. 19, 1844	Brigham Young	yes
Zina Jacobs†	Sept. 1844	Brigham Young	yes
Presendia Buell†	ca. Sept. 1845	Heber C. Kimball	yes
Agnes Smith	Jan. 28, 1846	George A. Smith	sealed to 1st spouse
Mary Elizabeth Lightner†	May 22, 1845	Brigham Young	yes
Sylvia Lyon†	Sept. 19, 1844	Heber C. Kimball	yes
Sarah Cleveland†	Jan. 15, 1846	John Smith	yes
Elizabeth Durfee	Jan. 22, 1846	Cornelius Lott	left LDS
Delcena Sherman	Jan. 24, 1846	Almon W. Babbitt	sealed to 1st spouse
Eliza Snow	Oct. 3, 1844	Brigham Young	yes
Sarah Ann Whitney ~	Mar. 17, 1845	Heber C. Kimball	yes
Martha Knight	Oct. 12, 1844	Heber C. Kimball	yes
Emily Partridge	Sept. 1844	Brigham Young	yes
Eliza Partridge	Sept. 28, 1844	Amasa Lyman	yes
Lucy Walker	Feb. 8, 1845	Heber C. Kimball	yes
Sarah Lawrence	Oct. 12, 1844	Heber C. Kimball	yes
Maria Lawrence	ca. Oct. 12, 1844	Brigham Young	yes
"	Jan. 24, 1846	Almon W. Babbitt	—
Rhoda Richards	Jan. 31, 1846	Brigham Young	yes
Olive Frost	Nov. 7, 1844	Brigham Young	yes
Nancy Winchester	Oct. 10, 1844	Heber C. Kimball	yes
Desdemona Fullmer	Jan. 26, 1846	Ezra T. Benson	yes
Melissa Lott	Feb. 8, 1846	John M. Bernhisel	yes
Sarah Mulholland ~	Feb. 3, 1846	Heber C. Kimball	yes
Mary Huston	Feb. 3, 1846	Heber C. Kimball	yes

† polyandrous

~ given a front husband

From late summer 1844 to February 1846, Young married eight of Smith's widows for the duration of their mortal lives, Smith remaining their husband for eternity. When he married Louisa Beaman, Smith's first plural wife, on September 19, 1844, he wrote in his journal in code: "Sta[y]ed at home all day[.] my wife is quite sick[.] I saw sister Louisa B Smith[,] H. C. Kimball & Silv[i]a L[yon] Smith &c &c." As previously noted, the term "saw" followed by a woman's name

TABLE 4.2 The widows who took a different path

name	alternative path	remained sealed to Smith
Emma Smith	married non-Mormon Lewis Bidamon	not resealed
Lucinda Harris†	remained married to George Harris	yes
Patty Sessions†	remained married to David Sessions, then when he died, sealed to Joseph Smith (Joseph F. Smith proxy)	yes
Marinda Hyde†	remained married to Orson Hyde (divorced later)	yes
Sarah Poulterer†	remained married to Tom Poulter/Stephen Poulterer	?
Ruth Sayers	remained married to Edward Sayers	not resealed
Flora Ann Woodworth	married non-Mormon Carlos Gove	not resealed
Almera Johnson	married Reuben Barton	yes
Helen Mar Kimball	married childhood sweetheart Horace Whitney	yes
Elvira Holmes	remained married to Jonathan Holmes	yes
Hannah Ells	remained a widow in Nauvoo	yes
Mary Ann Pratt	remained married to Parley P. Pratt	yes
Phebe Woodworth	remained married to Lucien Woodworth	yes
Fanny Murray	remained widowed with others of Smith's widows at Brigham Young's Lion House	not resealed

† polyandrous marriage to Joseph Smith

was an acronym for "sealed and wedded," as can be shown by comparing entries.[89] The same month he married Beaman, Young also married Emily Partridge and Zina Jacobs. On October 3, he married Eliza Snow; then on about October 12, Maria Lawrence;[90] on November 7, Olive Frost; and on May 22, 1845, Mary Elizabeth Lightner. Mary Elizabeth continued to live with her civil husband, Adam. Young mar-

89. Brigham Young, Journal, Sep. 19, 1844, LDS Archives. As Johnson ("Determining and Defining 'Wife,'" 65) indicates in the case of Beaman and others, Young's and Kimball's journals often coincide in mentioning a Young marriage on the same date.

90. Heber Kimball reported that he sealed Young and Maria Lawrence as husband and wife for time on October 12, 1844 (Heber C. Kimball, Diary, Dec. 12, 1844, LDS Archives, cited by Cook, *Nauvoo Marriages,* 47n5). The 1846 proxy record shows a subsequent sealing to Almon Babbitt for time on January 24, 1846, most likely after a separation from Young (Lisle G Brown, comp., *Nauvoo Sealings, Adoptions, and Anointings: A Comprehensive Register of Persons Receiving LDS Temple Ordinances, 1841-1846* [Salt Lake City: Smith-Pettit Foundation, 2006], 283n270). Dean C. Jessee, like Johnson, excludes Maria Lawrence, concluding she did not marry Young as a plural wife (Jessee, "Brigham Young's Family: The Wilderness Years," *BYU Studies* 19 [1978-79], online at *GospeLink,* http://gospelink.com; Johnson, "Determining and Defining 'Wife,'" 65).

ried Rhoda Richards, Smith's last known wife, on January 31, 1846, in the Nauvoo temple.

Bennett's stories trickled out weeks before his book was published in late 1842 and began to permeate the town and countryside. If Smith wanted to disprove the rumors, issuing a revelation in mid-1843 endorsing polygamy was counterproductive: it only proved them. Incredibly, he saw to it that it was read in meetings through the rest of the year. By the winter and spring of 1844, some of the church leaders who had formerly defended Smith broke ranks, first of all by trying to persuade him to either abandon the practice or exclude dependent women like Maria Lawrence. As community opposition mounted, the number of celestial marriages waned once again. By spring, the lawsuit filed by former officials in the First Presidency and Nauvoo Stake, and publicity in a local newspaper brought marriages to a standstill. When the opposition newspaper appeared and devoted space to polygamy, Smith and the ruling councils had it destroyed.

Although the marriage rate declined in the first half of 1844 to less than half that of the prior year, most of the Nauvoo leadership stood firmly behind polygamy and took a defiant stance with regard to internal and external pressure. So in the second half of 1844, in the wake of Smith's death and when a reconciliation with neighbors and state government seemed unlikely, the marriage rate more than doubled that of the first half of the year (19/49). In 1845 the numbers increased yet again, this time by about 25 percent, and in 1846 there was more than a threefold increase over 1845.

Nauvoo Plural Marriages

1841	1842	1843	1844	1845	1846	total
3	17	52	68	86	295	521

A few of the marriages for which we lack an exact date may have occurred in early 1844 rather than late 1843. The total of 521 wives shown here were married to 196 men. Adding the total number of first wives to plural wives produces a grand total of 717 wives (unadjusted for separation or remarried widows) for an overall ratio of 3.7 wives per husband. We can also see that the number of celestial marriages grew from 91 under Smith to 432 in the later Nauvoo years, for a nearly fivefold increase. Excluding the unusually large families of Smith, Young, and Kimball (these three accounting for thirty-eight wives each, adjusted for Smith's widows), plural families in Nauvoo averaged about three wives. After the migration to Utah, Nauvoo's polygamous men had about five wives.

It may be useful to look more closely at these proportions. In the following list, the families are broken down by (1) Nauvoo, 1841-44; (2) the longer Nauvoo period, 1841-46; and (3) the marital profiles of men who entered polygamy in Nauvoo, extended through the remainder of their lifetimes.

After the westward migration, the 196 families who had practiced polygamy in Nauvoo came to account for a total of 1,134 wives and 3,171 children, an average incidence of 5.8 wives and 16.2 children per family. Excluding the large families of Smith, Young, and Kimball, the average post-migration family had 5.2 wives and 15.8 children per household.[91] Viewed another way, the number of Nauvoo men with four or more wives grew dramatically after they left Illinois. Of 196

TABLE 4.3 Joseph's Nauvoo, 1841-44, families ranked by number of wives

polygamous men	wives per man	total wives
Joseph Smith	38	38
John Taylor	6	6
Hyrum Smith, Brigham Young	5	10
Willard Richards, Theodore Turley, Lyman Wight	4	12
Six other men[a]	3	18
Twenty other men[b]	2	40
Average wives per man (33 men)	3.8	124
Average wives per man (32 men, excl. Smith)	2.7	86

a. Orson Hyde, Joseph Kelting, Isaac Morley, Joseph Noble, John Smith, and Edwin Woolley.

b. James Adams, Thomas Bateman, Ezra Benson, Reynolds Cahoon, William Clayton, Joseph Coolidge, Howard Egan, William Felshaw, William Huntington, Benjamin Johnson, Heber Kimball, Vinson Knight, George Miller, John Page, Parley Pratt, Ebenezer Richardson, William Sagers, William Smith, Erastus Snow, and Lorenzo Young.

91. For the purpose of ranking family size and calculating marriage rates, Joseph Smith's remarried widows are not deducted upon his death.

TABLE 4.4 Nauvoo period, 1841-46, families ranked by number of wives

polygamous men	wives per man	total wives
Brigham Young	40	40
Joseph Smith	38	38
Heber Kimball	37	37
John Taylor	13	13
William Smith	12	12
John Lee	11	11
Samuel Bent	10	10
Willard Richards	9	9
Five other men[a]	8	40
John Bernhisel, Alpheus Cutler, Parley Pratt	7	21
Phineas Young	6	6
Eleven other men[b]	5	55
Twenty-one other men[c]	4	84
Forty-seven other men[d]	3	141
One hundred other men[e]	2	200
Average wives per man (196 men)	3.7	717
Average wives per man (193, excl. Smith, Young, Kimball)	3.1	602

a. Amasa Lyman, Isaac Morley, George Smith, John Smith, and Newel Whitney.

b. John Benbow, William Clayton, Joseph Coolidge, Winslow Farr, Peter Haws, Cornelius Lott, Orson Pratt, Charles Rich, William Sagers, Hyrum Smith, and Lucien Woodworth.

c. James Allred, Almon Babbitt, Rufus Beach, James Brown, John Butler, Dominicus Carter, Lebbeus Coons, Benjamin Covey, Lucian Foster, Aaron Johnson, George Miller, William Miller, John Pack, John Page, Erastus Snow, Lorenzo Snow, Theodore Turley, Lyman Wight, Guy Wilson, Wilford Woodruff, and Joseph Young.

d. John Bair, Ezra Benson, Benjamin Brown, Reynolds Cahoon, Simeon Carter, Isaac Chase, Benjamin Clapp, Raymond Clark, Zebedee Coltrin, Frederick Cox, Charles Dana, George Dykes, Howard Egan, William Felshaw, David Fullmer, Thomas Grover, Edward Hunter, William Huntington, William Huntington Jr., Orson Hyde, Benjamin Johnson, Joel Johnson, Eli Kelsey, Joseph Kelting, Joseph Kingsbury, Reuben Miller, Freeman Nickerson, Joseph Noble, John Parker, William Phelps, Albert Rockwood, Samuel Russell, John Scott, Peregrine Sessions, Abraham Smoot, George Stiles, Hosea Stout, John Tippets, Allen Weeks, Nathan West, Edwin Whiting, Clark Whitney, Stephen Winchester, Daniel Wood, Edwin Woolley, Thomas Woolsey, and Lorenzo Young.

e. J. Adams, J. Allen, I. Allred, W. Anderson, E. Averett, I. Barlow, T. Bateman, O. Bates, J. Bills, W. Blackhurst, C. Bolton, S. Brannan, T. Bullock, H. Burgess, W. Cahoon, T. Callister, C. Canfield, W. Carmichael, A. Carrington, S. Chamberlain, A. Cheney, A. Chesley, A. Coon, C. Crismon, H. Dayton, I. Decker, W. Draper, J. Durfee, W. Edwards, J. Fielding, J. Fleming, E. Fordham, J. Foutz, J. Fullmer, W. Garner, J. Gates, L. Gee, S. Goddard, J. Graham, G. Grant, A. Hadden, C. Hallett, L. Hancock, J. Harmon, E. Harris, I. Hatch, J. Hatfield, H. Herriman, W. Hewitt, W. Hickman, I. Higbee, C. Hunt, J. Hunter, J. Kay, J. Kelly, V. Knight, G. Langley, A. Lathrop, L. Lewis, C. Loveland, J. Loveless, E. Luddington, W. Lyon, S. Markham, D. McArthur, B. McGinnis, J. Meacham, C. Merkley, B. Mitchell, W. Murray, C. Patten, H. Peck, M. Peck, R. Redding, F. Richards, L. Richards, P. Richards, E. Richardson, J. Robinson, O. Rockwell, E. Sanders, L. Scovil, D. Sessions, H. Sherwood, C. Shumway, W. T. Snow, W. Snow, D. Spencer, O. Spencer, L. Stewart, A. Tippets, E. Tuttle, C. Webb, E. Webb, O. Wight, J. Willey, A. Williams, L. Wilson, D. Yearsley, and J. Zundel.

TABLE 4.5 Nauvoo and beyond, families ranked by number of wives

polygamous men	wives per man	total wives
Brigham Young	55	55
Heber Kimball	44	44
Joseph Smith	38	38
John Lee	19	19
John Taylor	18	18
William Smith	15	15
Erastus Snow	14	14
Aaron Johnson, Franklin Richards	12	24
Six other men[a]	11	66
Seven other men[b]	10	70
Five other men[c]	9	45
Eleven other men[d]	8	88
Twelve other men[e]	7	84
Twenty-three other men[f]	6	138
Twenty other men[g]	5	100
Thirty-five other men[h]	4	140
Forty other men[i]	3	120
Twenty-eight other men[j]	2	56
Average wives per man (196 men)	5.8	1,134
Average wives per man (193, excl. Smith, Young, Kimball)	5.2	997

a. James Brown, Joseph Noble, Parley Pratt, Willard Richards, George Smith, and Daniel Wood.

b. Samuel Bent, William Clayton, William Hickman, Isaac Morley, Orson Pratt, William Sagers, and Wilford Woodruff.

c. Dominicus Carter, Orson Hyde, Amasa Lyman, Lorenzo Snow, and Phineas Young

d. Ezra Benson, John Butler, Charles Dana, Hiram Dayton, Stephen Markham, John Pack, Peregrine Sessions, John Smith, Daniel Spencer, Newel Whitney, and Lorenzo Young.

e. James Allred, Ormus Bates, John Bernhisel, Alpheus Cutler, William Draper, George Grant, Isaac Higbee, Benjamin Johnson, Cornelius Lott, William Miller, Phineas Richards, and Lucius Scovil.

f. John Benbow, Curtis Bolton, Frederick Cox, Charles Crismon, George Dykes, Winslow Farr, Jacob Gates, Thomas Grover, Levi Hancock, Jesse Harmon, Eli Kelsey, Chester Loveland, Benjamin Mitchell, William Phelps, Charles Rich, Joseph Robinson, Abraham Smoot, Orson Spencer, Levi Stewart, Chauncey Webb, Edwin Woolley, Thomas Woolsey, and Joseph Young.

g. John Bair, Isaac Chase, Joseph Coolidge, Isaac Decker, Elijah Fordham, James Graham, Peter Haws, Joseph Kingsbury, Elam Luddington, Reuben Miller, Return Redding, Albert Rockwood, John Scott, Charles Shumway, Hyrum Smith, William Snow, Hosea Stout, Theodore Turley, Edwin Whiting, Alexander Williams, and Lucien Woodworth.

h. Joseph Allen, Almon Babbitt, Israel Barlow, Rufus Beach, William Blackhurst, Benjamin Brown, William Cahoon, Thomas Callister, Simeon Carter, Benjamin Clapp, Raymond Clark, Zebedee Coltrin, Abraham Coon, Lebbeus Coons, Benjamin Covey, Howard Egan,

husbands, some 101 ultimately married from four to eight women, which was up from forty-one men in that category in Nauvoo; and twenty-four men later had from nine to nineteen wives, compared to just five such men in Illinois. On the other side of the scale, the men who ended up with just three wives declined from forty-nine to forty, and those who practiced polygamy with two wives dropped from ninety-eight to twenty-eight, making two- and three-wife families a diminishing phenomenon (see table 4.6). Observers sometimes get an exaggerated impression from the well-publicized, upper-echelon polygamists with more than ten wives each, including John D. Lee with his eleven, William Smith with twelve (though briefly), John Taylor with thirteen, and of course the three highest profile polygamists: Joseph Smith, Kimball, and Young with over thirty wives each. At the other extreme, since institutional histories have minimized the incidence and profile of polygamy (see chapter 1), it is easy to imagine that most men who entered polygamy did so in a cursory way. In reality, the typical Utah polygamist whose roots in the principle extended back to Nauvoo had between three and four wives, with a higher incidence of large families.

Looking at percentages, the men who had married just two or three wives before they left for the west in 1846 fell 54 percent, from 147 to 68. The number of men with four wives rose 67 percent, and five-wife families nearly doubled, as did six- to eight-wife families. The results may also be analyzed by comparing the number of polyga-

---

Joseph Fielding, Lucian Foster, Stephen Goddard, Edward Hunter, Joel Johnson, John Kay, Joseph Kelly, John Loveless, Joseph Meacham, George Miller, John Page, Martin Peck, Ebenezer Richardson, Orrin Rockwell, John Tippets, Lyman Wight, Guy Wilson, Lewis Wilson, and Stephen Winchester.

i. Isaac Allred, Samuel Brannan, Thomas Bullock, Harrison Burgess, Reynolds Cahoon, Cyrus Canfield, William Carmichael, Solomon Chamberlain, Aaron Cheney, Jabez Durfee, William Edwards, William Felshaw, Josiah Fleming, Jacob Foutz, David Fullmer, John Fullmer, William Garner, Lysander Gee, Alfred Hadden, Emer Harris, Henry Herriman, Wilkinson Hewitt, William Huntington, William Huntington Jr., Joseph Kelting, Asahel Lathrop, Duncan McArthur, Christopher Merkley, Freeman Nickerson, John Parker, Samuel Russell, David Sessions, Willard Snow, George Stiles, Edward Tuttle, Allen Weeks, Nathan West, Clark Whitney, and Orange Wight.

j. James Adams, William Anderson, Elisha Averett, Thomas Bateman, John Bills, Albert Carrington, Alexander Chesley, Clark Hallett, Isaac Hatch, John Hatfield, Charles Hunt, Jesse Hunter, Vinson Knight, George Langley, Lemuel Lewis, Windsor Lyon, Benjamin McGinnis, William Murray, Charles Patten, Hezekiah Peck, Levi Richards, Ellis Sanders, Henry Sherwood, Alvah Tippets, Edward Webb, Jeremiah Willey, David Yearsley, and John Zundel.

mist men and additional wives and children in three steps: during Joseph Smith's life, after the martyrdom in Nauvoo, and during the Utah period (see table 4.7).

The nucleus of Nauvoo families established the model for polygamy throughout the west. What Joseph Smith began as a secret society involving 150 men and women grew to encompass thousands of families as Brigham Young further restructured the civil society. His radical re-inventing of the assumptions behind families and communities was facilitated by a few key factors: the church's geographical isolation, the country's preoccupation with slavery leading up to the Civil War, and the U.S. government's relative neglect of the region. During the twenty years from the 1840s to the 1860s, the practice of polygamy would grow and flourish in its pristine mountain-desert environment, virtually unchecked by external influence.

After Smith found he was successful in bringing aboard four willing participants in his marriage experiment in 1842, he proselytized energetically among the inner circle of Nauvoo followers over the

TABLE 4.6 Rising incidence of wives

	number of such families		
wives in a family	1841-46	> 1846	
8	5	11	increase
7	3	12	increase
6	1	23	increase
5	11	20	increase
4	21	35	increase
3	47	40	decrease
2	100	28	decrease

TABLE 4.7 Nauvoo plural families

	during Smith's lifetime	Nauvoo after Smith	new wives and children in West	total
husbands	33	163	—	196
wives	124	593	417	1,134
children	710	160	2,301	3,171
total	867	916	2,718	4,501

next year and a half. Twenty-eight newcomers comprised the base of support, as they initiated others into the practice in the later Nauvoo years and especially during the westward migration—a time when Mormons turned their collective gaze to the horizon and imagined a new heaven on earth.

Brigham's wives and children

In addition to Brigham Young's legal wife and four plural marriages during Smith's lifetime, he wed eight of Smith's widows and forty-two additional women between September 10, 1844, and December 8, 1872, fifteen of whom bore him children. As his biographer Jeffery O. Johnson commented, "this does not necessarily mean he did not have conjugal relationships with some of the other" wives, "but the topic of where he spent his nights was apparently not a matter of household discussion."[92] Johnson quoted Young's daughter Susa Young Gates, who recalled that even if she wanted to, she "could tell nothing" of her father's "marital relations, for they were regarded in the family as most sacred."[93] It is probable that some of his marriages did not involve carnal relationships. He told publisher Horace Greeley in 1859 that he had "some aged women sealed" to him, in which instances he no more thought of them as wives, as he put it, "than I would my Grand Mother."[94] Of Young's fifty-five marriages, fifteen ended in separation or divorce.

Three of Smith's widows bore a total of thirteen children to Young, constituting about a fourth of his total progeny. Emily Partridge bore him seven children; Louisa Beaman, five; and Zina Jacobs,

92. The forty-two women were Amy Aldrich, Margaret Alley, Olive Andrews, Phebe Angell, Eliza Babcock, Lucy Bigelow, Mary Jane Bigelow, Martha Bowker, Eliza Burgess, Diana Chase, Mary Cobb, Ann Eliza Dee, Catherine Egan, Elizabeth Fairchild, Harriet Folsom, Emmeline Free, Mary Greene, Abigail Hall, Julia Hampton, Rebecca Holman, Clarissa Homiston, Elizabeth Jones, Mary Kelsey, Hannah King, Sarah Malin, Lydia Mayhew, Mary Peirce, Mary Ann Powers, Ellen Rockwood, Clarissa Ross,Harriet Sagers, Amanda Smith, Susannah Snively, Mary Ann Turley, Naamah Twiss, Nancy Walker, Cynthia Weston, Margaret Whitesides, Emily Whitmarsh, Mary Ellen Woodward, Abigail Works, and Jemima Young.

93. Johnson, "Determining and Defining 'Wife,'" 65; Susa Young Gates, *Unique Story—President Brigham Young* (Salt Lake City: Daughters of Utah Pioneers, 1990), 79.

94. Clerk's Report of Brigham Young's interview with Horace Greeley, July 13, 1859, LDS Archives.

one. One of Young's late wives, Emmeline Free, bore ten children. It would appear to be intuitively obvious that the women who bore him children could be counted among his rumored favorites—the ones he spent the most time with.

In addition, Young's first wife, Miriam Works, had two children before they converted to the LDS Church or heard of polygamy. Miriam died in 1832, five months after their mutual baptisms.

Young's Childbearing Wives

Emmeline Free	10
Emily Partridge Smith	7
Lucy Ann Decker Seeley	7
Mary Ann Angell	6
Clarissa Decker	5
Louisa Beaman Smith	5
Clarissa Chase Ross	4
Lucy Bigelow	3
Margaret Alley	2
Harriet Cook	1
Zina Huntington Jacobs Smith	1
Margaret Peirce Whitesides	1
Martha Bowker	1
Harriet Barney Sagers	1
Mary Van Cott Cobb	1
total for fifteen wives	55

In 1841, Smith's were the only celestial marriages. During the next year, all but four of seventeen plural marriages in Nauvoo were Smith's. From 1843 until Smith's death in mid-1844, his nuptials accounted for less than half of the total, only about thirty-four out of eighty-eight. For the remainder of their time in Nauvoo, his followers eclipsed Smith's volume of wives. This meant that in Nauvoo there was a total of 717 wives for fewer than 200 men.

Relocating polygamy

Antagonism against the Latter-day Saints arose, as it had in Missouri, from bloc-voting influence on local elections and talk of taking over their neighbor's property because God had promised it to them. The legal issues from the Missouri conflict, including the unsolved assassination attempt on Governor Boggs, continued to fester; so did the tendency of Mormon leaders to evade arrest and of Nauvoo police to arrest state officers. When these issues were augmented by alleged eyewitness accounts of incidents involving young girls and acts of adultery, social and political pressure mounted to compel the Mormons to depart, just as had occurred in New York, Pennsylvania, Ohio, and Missouri.

It became clear that the Latter-day Saints would have to move, but where? Young pursued Smith's idea of seeking refuge outside the U.S. on the frontiers of California, Oregon, Texas, Vancouver Island, and the Land of Timpanogos in the midst of the Great Basin. The increase in plural marriages probably indicated early intentions to leave the United States. If so, then the Great Basin, which lacked any permanent Anglo or Spanish settlements, would have been foremost in their minds. Plans were formulated, and the idea of salvaging the community's millennialist hopes filled their imaginations. But to keep his options open, Young continued to negotiate with the U.S. government even while he led his people onto the trail to the Great Salt Lake.[95]

An Ohio lawyer and Western promoter, Lanceford W. Hastings, traveled to the Pacific coast in 1842-43 and wrote the popular *Emigrants' Guide to Oregon and California.* After promoting the book in New York to Mormon publisher Sam Brannan and others, Hastings visited Nauvoo in 1845 and advised Young to lead his following to Upper California, the land between the Wasatch Mountains and the Pacific Ocean. In September 1845, after his visit, the *Nauvoo Neighbor* published extracts from his book announcing that "the Rocky Mountains embosom beautiful valleys, rivers, and parks, with lakes and mineral springs, rivaling … the Alpine regions of Switzerland."[96] On September 9, as Young made plans to send 1,500 men to the Salt Lake

---

95. Hubert Howe Bancroft, *History of Utah, 1540-1886* (San Francisco: The History Company, 1889): 6-15; Klaus J. Hansen, "The Metamorphosis of the Kingdom of God," *Dialogue: A Journal of Mormon Thought* 1 (Autumn 1966): 67-70.

96. *Nauvoo Neighbor*, Sept. 17, 1845.

Valley, he appointed a committee to gather information about westward emigration.[97]

Hastings left Nauvoo and trekked west to Fort Laramie, Wyoming, and from there, based on advice from Jim Bridger, south through Utah and then west on a remarkably snowless trip through the Sierra Nevada Mountains to Sutter's Fort, now Sacramento. Hastings arrived there before Christmas 1845, then returned to the states to advise immigrants about his new direct route to the coast. He had negotiated difficult terrain into the Salt Lake Valley, but he had been traveling light and it was not an impediment. The same would not be true for the Donner-Reed Party in 1846, but until they became snowbound in the mountains it had not been obvious that Hastings had offered uncertain advice. Their favor to the Mormons who followed the next year was that they blazed a trail through previously uncleared stretches of the Wasatch range east of the Salt Lake Valley.[98]

In September 1845, Young announced that the Saints would leave Nauvoo in the spring. In preparation, twenty-four companies of 100 wagons each were outfitted.[99] Robert Baskin, an attorney who

97. *History of the Church,* 7:439.

98. David Lavender, *The Great West* (Boston: Houghton Mifflin, 1965), 250, 253-54, 267-70; Dale L. Morgan, *The Great Salt Lake* (Albuquerque: University of New Mexico Press, 1973), 161-73; Arrington, *Brigham Young,* 124, 172-73; Newel G. Bringhurst, *Brigham Young and the Expanding American Frontier* (Boston: Little Brown, 1986), 75, 95; John D. Unruh Jr., *The Plains Across: The Overland Emigrants and the Trans-Mississippi West, 1840-60* (Urbana: University of Illinois Press, 1982), 288; Richard D. Poll, ed., *Utah's History* (Provo: Brigham Young University Press, 1978), 79-90, 123; see also, Smith, *Intimate Chronicle,* 348-56.

99. A committee on outfitting emigrating families appointed by Brigham Young recommended that "each family consisting of five adults" take "1 good strong wagon, well covered, 3 good yokes of oxen, ... two or more cows, ... one thousand pounds of flour, ... one bushel of beans, one hundred pounds of sugar, ... one good musket or rifle, ... two lbs. tea, 5 lbs. coffee, ... a few goods to trade with the Indians, ... ten to fifty pounds of seed, ... one keg of alcohol," and some farming tools (*History of the Church,* 7:454-55). However, as documented by Richard E. Bennett, these preparations amounted mostly to wishful thinking in 1846 and would not be strictly adhered to until the next year. In 1846, 800 men reported on the Iowa side of the Mississippi River without any provisions at all. Instead of traveling in companies, "wagons often scattered fan-like for miles across the Iowa landscape." Young discovered that Iowa was "a great mud hole" from one side of the state to the other, almost impassable, and the LDS refugees unmanageable (Bennett, *Mormons at the Missouri, 1846-1852* [Norman: University of Oklahoma Press, 1987], 26-45).

investigated Utah's 1857 Mountain Meadows Massacre, suggested that the threat of federal interference if Mormons tried to abandon the Union was fabricated by LDS historian Orson Whitney, whose intent was to demonize the federal response to plural marriage.[100] The first wagons successfully crossed the frozen Mississippi River into Iowa on February 4, 1846. Brigham left his brother Joseph behind to oversee matters in Nauvoo. Wilford Woodruff would return to the city after the wagons had left to officiate in further temple ceremonies, including marriages. Joseph's widow, Emma, remained in Nauvoo until September 1846.

As Nauvoo was gradually depopulated, it became increasingly lawless. Emma rented the Mansion House to a new settler, a Mr. Van Tuyl, and on September 12 traveled with her children 120 miles up the Mississippi to Fulton City, Illinois. But the situation in Nauvoo must have improved because she returned in February 1847 to be courted by Lewis Bidamon, a businessman the Smiths had met in 1844. On December 23, 1847, she and Lewis married and decided to remain in Nauvoo.

In the fall of 1846, Mother Lucy Smith moved in with her daughter and son-in-law, Lucy and Arthur Milliken, in Knoxville, Illinois, eighty-four miles east of Nauvoo. She would return to Nauvoo for periods, as evidenced by her January 1849 letter to her son, William, from the city her other son had built and the Twelve had abandoned.[101] John M. Bernhisel visited Nauvoo in September 1849 and saw her there; but later that fall, the Smith matriarch joined the Millikens again as they moved to nearby Webster, Illinois. After briefly residing in Fountain Green in 1851, Lucy returned to Nauvoo permanently, staying in the Mansion House with the Bidamons and Emma's four sons. When Peregrine Sessions visited in November 1852 from

---

100. Robert N. Baskin, *Reminiscences of Early Utah* (Salt Lake City: Signature Books, 2006), 83-149 (see attached *Reply to Certain Statements by O. F. Whitney,* 1-29); Edwin Brown Firmage and Richard Collin Mangrum, *Zion in the Courts: A Legal History of the Church of Jesus Christ of Latter-day Saints, 1830-1900* (Urbana: University of Illinois Press, 1988), 247.

101. Lucy Mack Smith to William Smith, Jan. 4, 1849, *Melchisedek and Aaronic Herald* 1, no. 2 (Mar. 1849):[1].

Sessions City (Bountiful), Utah, he found Lucy living with Emma. The prophet's mother remained there until she died on May 14, 1856, on the Smith farm just outside of town.

Emma's son Joseph Smith III re-opened the red brick store, but it proved to be unprofitable. In October 1848 an arsonist burned down the three-story temple. Unfazed, the Smiths stayed in town and Joseph III and his brother Frederick went into business managing farmland. Up until the end of Emma's life, writers, reporters, missionaries from Utah, and others came to see her. She died at the Mansion House on April 30, 1879, at seventy-four years of age.

Simultaneous to the westward migration, war broke out with Mexico in May 1846. The famous Mormon Battalion was mustered in Nebraska and marched to California to aid in the campaign and raise money for the Mormon migration. That same year, Sam Brannan sailed with 238 ocean pioneers from New York to Yerba Buena (San Francisco). Once they had settled in the coastal foothills, Brannan tried unsuccessfully to convince Young to move the church to California. Brannan did attract a significant number of the Mormon Battalion soldiers to the area in 1847 when their military service was over. About 100 of them subsequently found work with John Sutter and witnessed the discovery of gold in January 1848. Others made their way east to join their families in Winter Quarters or meet Young's pioneer company investigating the Great Salt Lake Valley. It was Brannan who publicized the gold rush in his newspaper, which was, in fact, the first San Francisco newspaper, the *California Star*. The gold rush provided the Utah settlements a meager income in 1849 as they sold the "Forty-niners" fresh horses, food, and equipment, and repaired their wagons before the hard trek across the salt flats and the Humboldt Sink.[102]

Young was named president of the LDS Church on December 5, 1847, near Winter Quarters, where he had returned after investigating the Salt Lake Valley.[103] Colonization had been delayed through the

102. Arrington, *Brigham Young,* 141; Bringhurst, *Brigham Young,* 82-96.

103. See Gary James Bergera, *Conflict in the Quorum: Orson Pratt, Brigham Young, Joseph Smith* (Salt Lake City: Signature Books, 2002), 53-83.

winter of 1846 by the selection and organization of troops to march on Mexico. In the spring of 1847, a team of 159 pioneers in 72 wagons progressed westward from Winter Quarters, about ten miles a day. The group followed the Oregon trail along the Platte River through Nebraska and by the Sweetwater River in Wyoming, eventually reaching the Great Salt Lake Valley on July 22. Away from Brigham Young's leadership, Brannan's California Saints would resist the polygamous emphasis of the Utah Saints. The original pioneer company in Utah included only three females, but these hardy three happened to be Young's plural wife Clara Decker; her mother, Harriet—the plural wife of Brigham's brother Lorenzo; and Heber Kimball's plural wife Ellen. Most of the men in the company turned back after spending only a month in the valley, to reunite with their families in Winter Quarters. The substantial migration proceeded in 1848.

With some 5,000 settlers in the City of the Great Salt Lake by March 1849, Young decided to form a provisional government for an area comprising present-day Utah; most of Arizona and Nevada; large portions of Colorado, New Mexico, and Wyoming; and parts of Idaho, Oregon, and even a part of the Pacific coast on either side of Baja California. He called this sprawling territory Deseret, which was said to mean "honeybee."[104]

Mormons brought about 100 black slaves with them to Deseret, representing two percent of the total population, from 1847 to 1850. Even more slaves arrived with the so-called "Southern Saints" Young sent to the San Luis Valley in Colorado, north of Santa Fe. Slavery and polygamy formed a witch's brew that isolated Deseret from the rest of the U.S. through its territorial period to the 1890s.[105]

In a further ironic coincidence of slavery and polygamy, Young convinced the territorial legislature to legalize slavery on August 28,

---

104. Dale L. Morgan, *The State of Deseret* (Salt Lake City: Utah Historical Society and Utah State University Press, 1987), 30-33. Notice was given on Feb. 1 of a constitutional convention. On March 10 the constitution was adopted and two days later Brigham Young was elected governor. For *honeybee*, a Book of Mormon term, see Eth. 2:3.

105. Lester Bush, "Mormonism's Negro Doctrine: An Historical Overview," *Dialogue: A Journal of Mormon Thought* 8 (Spring 1973), 23. After thirteen years, slavery was abolished, as it was nationally, when the Confederacy fell in 1865.

1852, the same year he publicly acknowledged plural marriage and defended it as the right of free men. The spokesperson who disclosed the practice of "celestial marriage" was Apostle Orson Pratt, who by then was husband to six wives. He argued that polygamy was sanctioned by the Old Testament and was an alternative to "whoredom, adultery and fornication."[106]

The United States expressed its opinion of this secessionist enclave in the west by sending 2,500 troops in August 1857 to guarantee that a new gubernatorial appointment would be accepted. Characteristically obstinate, Young fended off President Buchanan's emissaries and skillfully negotiated with U.S. General Albert Sidney Johnson to keep federal troops from occupying the city or engaging the Utah militia. Later that year the Mormon attack on a wagon train passing through Mountain Meadows near St. George in southern Utah expressed louder than words the Mormon feelings about outsiders. Young disavowed responsibility for the massacre and avoided execution or jail while his adopted son, John D. Lee, from Lee's perspective the "scapegoat" in the affair, faced a firing squad. Young continued to govern from behind the scenes, presiding over a secret parliament composed of the same Mormon representatives who served in the legislature. When the shadow government approved a measure, it was immediately approved by the legislature; whatever the Council of Fifty disapproved, the legislature rejected.[107]

---

106. *Journal of Discourses,* 3:171.

107. The massacre occurred in 1857, four months after Parley Pratt was killed by his twelfth wife's legal husband near Van Buren, Arkansas. Leading up to this fateful year, the LDS Church had maintained a policy of harassing federal officials, some of whom were killed and others encouraged to flee. In late July, word reached Utah that President Buchanan had dispatched an expeditionary force to the west to guarantee Governor Young's abdication. The Fancher immigrant train had the bad luck of arriving in the middle of this situation when the territory was in a high state of alert and suspicious of outsiders. Despite the hostility they experienced from the Mormon settlers, they opted to take a longer, southerly route through the territory and avoid the fate of the Donner party the year before. However, the Fancher party ended up being killed by a unit of the Utah militia. According to historian Juanita Brooks, between 57 and 96 members of the Fancher train were massacred (*John Doyle Lee: Zealot, Pioneer-Builder, Scapegoat* [Glendale, Calif.: Arthur H. Clark Co., 1961], 372).

See also Brooks's *The Mountain Meadows Massacre* (Stanford, Calif.: Stanford University Press, 1950); Arrington, *Brigham Young,* 257-60, 278-80, 385-86, 479-80. Ar-

After the Civil War, the primary issue affecting Mormon relations with the rest of the United States was celestial marriage. Why Young insisted on defending and expanding this practice is best understood in the context of his unwavering commitment to an independent religious philosophy. This carpenter from the Erie Canal who saw Christian revivalism up close and had no formal education became the unlikely architect of a new society. Despite Young's twelve-year apprenticeship under Smith and his intent to follow his predecessor's footsteps, Young put his own radical stamp on Smith's work. After surviving the panic of 1837 and the failure of the church's "anti-banking society" in Ohio, and after the turmoil in Missouri in 1838, Young was one of the few who remained loyal through defections, all the way through Smith's assassination in 1844. During those years, the triumvirate of Smith, Young, and Kimball had proved a model of organizational rigor and inspirational preaching. On his second mission to England in 1840, Young helped convert several thousand new members to Mormonism. Many of those converts would immigrate to the United States, adding to Young's stature among the rank and file.

Young's recollection of Smith's invitation to marry additional wives was that he had never felt so depressed. No one "could have been more averse to it than I when it was first revealed," he said. "Brother Brigham," Smith said, repeating the same reassurance he gave to each new initiate, "the Lord will reveal it to you."[108] Once converted to the practice, Young never wavered as he began assembling his own latter-day family of wives; especially after he assumed

---

rington recommends C. Kent Dunford, "The Contributions of George A. Smith to the Establishment of the Mormon Society in the Territory of Utah," Ph.D. diss., Brigham Young University, 1970, 178-208, as "a good analysis of the factors that caused the massacre and the extent to which Brigham [Young] and George A. Smith deliberately suppressed the facts of the tragedy to protect the church" (478). For differing interpretations, see Will Bagley, *Blood of the Prophets: Brigham Young and the Massacre at Mountain Meadows* (Norman: University of Oklahoma Press, 2002); Sally Denton, *American Massacre: The Tragedy at Mountain Meadows*, September 1857 (New York: Alfred A. Knopf, 2003), and Ronald W. Walker et al., *Massacre at Mountain Meadows* (New York: University of Oxford Press, 2008).

108. S. Dilworth Young, *Here Is Brigham: Brigham Young, the Years to 1844* (Salt Lake City: Bookcraft, 1964), 299-300; cf. *Journal of Discourses*, 3:266, 18:241.

the primary leadership role, he felt it incumbent on himself to assemble the most number of wives. His fifty-five consorts, although never exceeding thirty-eight at one time (the same as Joseph Smith), made him the most prolific polygamist in the church. LDS Church Historian Leonard Arrington pointed to a hierarchy among Young's wives, beginning with sixteen who bore him children, eleven who did not, and "some thirty women" to whom the church president was sealed for "eternity only" and were not wives in the normal sense of the term.[109]

Heber C. Kimball

"Plurality of Wives!" announced Heber C. Kimball in 1857. "I have a good many wives. How much would you give to know how many? If I were to tell you, you would not believe it ... I have a good many wives and lots of young mustards that are growing, and they are a kind of fruitful seed." When fellow polygamist John Bernhisel posed the rhetorical question, "What did you get these wives for?" Kimball's answer sounded like Brigham Young's: "The Lord told me to get them ... to raise up young 'Mormons' ... not to have women to commit whoredoms with, to gratify the lusts of the flesh, but to raise up children."[110]

Like Young, Kimball joined Smith's church early and stood by the founder through schisms and defections. Kimball wholeheartedly embraced the practice of celestial marriage. These highest-ranking brethren—Smith, Young, and Kimball—married more women than anyone else in the community in keeping with their status. Young married fifty-five women, Kimball forty-four, and Smith thirty-eight. Including the marriages of seventeen of Smith's widows, these three men married 120 women a total of 137 times.

Heber Chase Kimball was born on June 14, 1801, in Sheldon, Vermont, the fourth child of Solomon and Anna Spaulding Kimball.

---

109. Arrington, *Brigham Young*, 121, 170, 420-21. By the time Young completed the Lion House for his plural families, he had, according to Arrington, "eleven connubial wives (those he stayed with on occasion) and thirty-five living children, not counting several caretaker wives [sixteen by recent count]." See also Johnson, "Determining and Defining 'Wife,'" 57-70.

110. *Journal of Discourses*, 5:91.

His parents had seven children in all. When he was ten, again like the Smiths and Youngs, his family moved to New York, specifically to West Bloomfield, Ontario County; and a few years later, Heber moved to Mendon, New York, just twelve miles from Joseph Smith's home in Manchester. In Mendon, Heber found work as a potter. Brigham Young moved into Mendon in 1828 to be near several of his brothers and sisters. Heber recalled that "Brother Brigham and myself used to work hard, side by side, for fifty cents a day." They worked "in the hayfield," raking and binding, "for a bushel of wheat a day, and chop[ped] wood, with snow to our waist[,] for eighteen cents a cord, and t[ook] our pay in corn at seventy-five cents a bushel."[111]

Heber and Brigham probably met before 1830; although they lived in close proximity to the Smiths in central New York state, neither one of them seems to have met Joseph before 1832. That was when Brigham and Heber traveled 325 miles by wagon to Kirtland, the Mormon capital of 1,300 people in Ohio, with the expressed intent of meeting Joseph. Brigham described it: "We went to his father's house, and learned that he was in the woods, chopping [wood]. … He was happy to see us, and bid us welcome."[112] After they met Emma at the Smiths' house, Brigham and Joseph soon spoke in tongues. In 1833, Brigham and Heber trekked together through western New York and Canada, proselytizing; finally moving that fall to Kirtland, they rented a house together and brought their wives, Miriam and Vilate, to live with them.[113]

As an indication of how interwoven the family relationships became, Kimball's biographer, Orson F. Whitney, was Kimball's grandson as well as his nephew. Heber and Joseph were brothers-in-law of his father, Horace, because Joseph married Helen Mar Kimball and Sarah Ann Whitney, and also because Heber married Sarah Ann Whitney the year after Smith's martyrdom in 1844.[114] Whitney relates

111. Ibid., 9:329; see also Arrington, *Brigham Young*, 14-18.

112. Elden J. Watson, *Manuscript History of Brigham Young, 1801-1844* (Salt Lake City: By the author, 1968), 4.

113. Arrington, *Brigham Young*, 34-37.

114. Joseph Smith was also Orson Whitney's uncle and stepfather because he married Orson's mother, Helen Mar, and aunt Sarah Ann.

that Kimball was "not an ardent lover of books, but drew his lessons from life," with "a proneness to melancholy" that blended the "lion like qualities of a leader among men, with the bashfulness and lamb-like simplicity of a child."[115]

Kimball-Whitney Relations

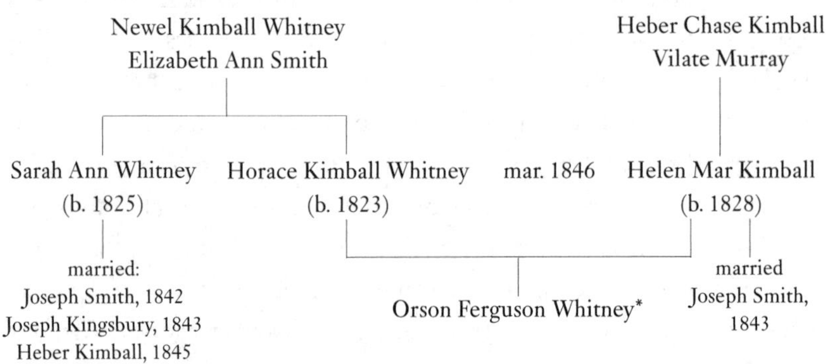

*Orson F. Whitney was Heber C. Kimball's grandson via Helen Mar Kimball and nephew via Sarah Ann Whitney. Joseph Smith was Orson's deceased uncle and "stepfather."

To contemplate Kimball's views on marriage is to recall Joseph Smith's well-known test of Heber's loyalty, in which Joseph demanded his apostle's legal wife, Vilate, for his own. After some anguish, Heber conceded her to Joseph. Initially Heber was reluctant to enter polygamy himself, but the incident surrounding Vilate signaled to him the meaning of restoration of "all things." Later when Joseph asked for Heber's only daughter, Helen Mar, the obedient disciple offered his fourteen-year-old girl without question.[116] This occurred on or about May 28, 1843.

Even Vilate became convinced by "prayer" that "the plural order

115. Orson F. Whitney, *The Life of Heber C. Kimball* (1945; Salt Lake City: Bookcraft, 1977), 4.

116. Helen Mar Whitney, "Scenes and Incidents in Nauvoo," *Woman's Exponent*, 1881-1883; Charles M. Hatch and Todd Compton, eds., *A Widow's Tale: The 1884-1896 Diary of Helen Mar Kimball Whitney* (Logan: Utah State University Press, 2003); Whit-

of marriage was of God."[117] Reportedly, it was more difficult for Heber himself, who "had to be commanded three times to do this thing" and was told by Smith that if he did not he would lose his apostleship and be damned.[118] Vilate was reluctant when it came to putting belief into action, but she made the artful choice of two "old maids" as her recommendation for the women her husband should marry. Smith countermanded Vilate's selection, telling Heber he needed to find a young woman he would want to conceive children with.[119]

In early 1842, Kimball reportedly married Sarah Peak Noon. She was said to have been recently separated from her husband (see above). Like Young, Kimball had delayed marrying and seems to have acted *pro forma*—just enough to meet the minimum requirement. Over two years later, however, Kimball found some enthusiasm and married thirteen more women.[120] No doubt, his hesitation had been similar to Young's, due to the weight of responsibilities involved in running church operations and because of the adverse publicity from Bennett's disclosures.

In 1845 Kimball married six more wives,[121] then sixteen more in the early winter of 1846, and one more in 1847 before the overland trek to Utah.[122] After settling in Utah, he married six more. Of these forty-four women, including Vilate, seventeen of them bore him a total of sixty-six children. Ten of his wives eventually left him.[123] In

---

ney, *Life of Heber C. Kimball*, 333-35; Stanley Kimball, *Heber C. Kimball: Mormon Patriarch and Pioneer* (Urbana: University of Illinois Press, 1981), 93-94.

117. Whitney, *Life of Heber C. Kimball*, 335.

118. Ibid., 336.

119. See Stan Larson, ed., *Prisoner for Polygamy: The Memoirs and Letters of Rudger Clawson at the Utah Territorial Penitentiary, 1884-87* (Urbana: University of Illinois Press, 1993), 12.

120. Lydia Carter, Charlotte Chase, Ann Gheen, Mary Ellen Harris, Martha Smith, Mary Smith, Nancy Smith, Sarah Smith, Sylvia Smith, Frances Swan, Ruth Wellington, Rebecca Williams, and Ellen Ysteinsdatter.

121. Clarissa Cutler, Emily Cutler, Amanda Gheen, Sarah Ann Kingsbury, Lucy Smith, and Presendia Smith.

122. Hulda Barnes, Abigail Buchanan, Sarah Buckwalter, Ruth Cazier, Christeen Golden, Sarah Granger, Sophronia Harmon, Elizabeth Hereford, Margaret McMinn, Theresa Morley, Laura Pitkin, Martha Pitkin, Ruth Reese, Mary Ann Shefflin, Mary Smith, Sarah Smith, and Harriet Ysteinsdatter.

123. Adelia Brown, Eliza Brown, Mary Duell, Dorothy Moon, Hannah Moon, and

1868, near the home where he lived with Lucy Walker, he fell from his wagon and suffered paralysis, speech impairment, and finally death on June 22.[124]

Looking at the way her parents had first embraced polygamy, Helen explained that in early 1842 her mother had suspected something because of Heber's demeanor. Her mother prayed to know what her husband was hiding from her. "He tried to evade her question, saying it was only her imagination, or that he was not feeling well, etc." With some literary license, Helen imagined what her father must have gone through in his mind, saying that

> his anxious and haggard looks betrayed him daily and hourly, and finally his misery became so unbearable that it was impossible to control his feelings. He became sick in body, but his mental wretchedness was too great to allow of his retiring at night, and instead of going to bed he would walk the floor; and the agony of his mind was so terrible that he would wring his hands and weep, beseeching the Lord with his whole soul to be merciful and reveal to his wife the cause of his great sorrow, for he himself could not break his vow of secrecy.[125]

When her mother's "anguish" was so "indescribable" that she was "unable to endure it longer, she retired to her room" to pray,

> and while pleading as one would plead for life, the vision of her mind was opened, ... and before her she saw the principle of Celestial Marriage illustrated in all its beauty and glory, together with the great exaltation and honor it would confer upon her in that immortal and celestial sphere if she would but accept it and stand in her place by her husband's side. She was also shown the woman he had taken to wife, and contemplated with joy the vast and boundless love and union which this order would bring about, as well as the increase of kingdoms, power, and glory extending throughout the eternities, worlds without end.

Mary Smithies. See Kimball, *Heber C. Kimball,* 99; Stanley B. Kimball, ed., *On the Potter's Wheel: The Diaries of Heber C. Kimball* (Salt Lake City: Signature Books and Smith Research Associates, 1987), xxvn1.

124. Whitney, *Life of Heber C. Kimball,* 476-79, citing the *Deseret Evening News,* June 22, 1868.

125. Helen Mar Whitney, "Scenes and Incidents in Nauvoo," *Woman's Exponent* 10 (Oct. 15, 1881): 74.

"Her soul was satisfied[,] ... [her] countenance beaming with joy. ... She related the scene to me and to many others," Helen explained, "and told me she never saw so happy a man as father was" at that moment.[126]

Lorenzo Snow quoted Joseph Smith saying that "no man should ... take a wife unless it was one he could truly love." Smith, according to Snow, was speaking of Vilate Kimball's choice of "two very old maids of quite plain and homely Appearance for her husband." Smith admonished Kimball,

> "Bro K[,] that arrangement is of the devil[.] you go and get you a young wife[,] one you can take to your bosom and love and raise children by. A man should choose his own wife and one he can love and get children by in love. Jesus says you have not chosen me but I have chosen you." Bro S[now] said further[,] one reason why illegitamate children are often so bright and intelligent is because they are begotten in love and unless the children are begotten in love they are not so liable to be so intelligent.[127]

Helen thought the old maids were her father's idea. Faced with having to find more wives, "he thought of the two Sisters Pitkin," Helen wrote, saying "they were both elderly ladies and great friends of my mother's, [whom] he believed would cause her little if any unhappiness. The woman he was commanded to take, however, was an English lady, nearer my mother's age, who came over with her husband and two little girls with a company of Saints in the same ship in which President Brigham Young and my father were returning from their second mission to Europe."[128]

The timing and circumstances of Kimball's first plural marriage are ambiguous. Orson Whitney said Sarah Noon had "left her husband" in England "on account of his drunken and dissolute habits" and that Sarah traveled on the same ship with Heber when he returned from his mission to England. Sarah was already "the mother of

---

126. Ibid.

127. See Larson, *Prisoner for Polygamy,* 12, quoting Lorenzo Snow's conversation with Helon H. Tracy.

128. Helen Mar Whitney, "Scenes and Incidents in Nauvoo," 74; see also Stanley B. Kimball, "Heber C. Kimball and Family: The Nauvoo Years," *BYU Studies* 15 (1975): 461-62.

two little girls."[129] Another Kimball biographer, Stanley B. Kimball, identified Noon as an English convert who was "abandoned in Nauvoo by her husband," William Spencer Noon, when he left her and "returned to England."[130] If that was the case, it suggests that he could have left in 1841-42 because of Heber's courtship of Sarah.

Nauvoo's "first plural child," born to Kimball according to Whitney, was Sarah's son, Adelbert Henry Kimball. If true, the child was not recognized as Kimball's at the time. In contrast to Vilate's son, who was blessed on January 2, 1843, as "Charles Spaulding Kimball," the only mention of Sarah's child in the contemporary record was its April 1843 obituary where the baby's name was reported as "Adelmon H. Noon."[131] There was good reason to avoid public acknowledgment of the offspring, since church leaders were so vigorously denying polygamy at the time. In September 1842, Joseph sent Brigham and Heber, along with a few others, on a two-month mission "to offset the damage done by Bennett," who had just published his eyewitness accounts of plural marriage. Vilate and Sarah were both "about seven months pregnant" in the fall of 1842, so anyone who had cared to investigate could have found evidence if Heber was the father. "With two pregnant wives in Nauvoo, it would have been awkward for him to argue that plural marriage existed only in a spiritual sense," historian Stanley Kimball observed as the rationale for Heber's cover-up.[132]

Even though it is unclear whether the child born in October/November 1842 belonged to William Noon or Heber Kimball, the mother (Sarah Peak Kimball) testified on September 9, 1869, that "President Joseph Smith personally taught her the doctrine of a plurality of wives," after which she was "married or sealed for time and all eternity to Heber C. Kimball by President Joseph Smith in the presence of President Brigham Young."[133] Not recorded as a civil marriage

129. Whitney, *Life of Heber C. Kimball,* 326.

130. Kimball, *Heber C. Kimball,* 95.

131. Whitney, *Life of Heber C. Kimball,* 418.

132. Kimball, "Heber C. Kimball and Family," 467, 468; Arrington, *Brigham Young,* 103; see also *Times and Seasons,* Sept. 15, 1842, 926.

133. Sarah Perry Peak Noon, Affidavit, Sept. 7, 1869, in "40 Affidavits on Celestial Marriage," 1869.

or sealing in 1842, the Kimballs have indicated that this private marriage was later confirmed in a more formal sealing in 1843, as repeated yet again on January 15, 1846, in the Nauvoo temple.[134] Sarah was the first of at least forty-three of Heber's plural wives.

Reynolds Cahoon

Besides Young and Kimball, the two other men who took celestial brides during the first year Joseph introduced the concept were Reynolds Cahoon and Vinson Knight. Cahoon was born April 30, 1790, in Cambridge, New York, east of Saratoga Springs near the Vermont border. He had been married to Thirza Stiles since 1810, but this farmer and veteran of the War of 1812 found himself in Smith's inner circle in the 1830s-40s and encouraged to take additional wives. He had been a church member since fall 1830 in Kirtland, where Smith had appointed him to raise money to support the "inspired translation" of the Bible, then to build the Kirtland temple. Cahoon became a member of the Kirtland bishopric and also worked on construction of the temple.[135] He was chastised by revelation on November 1, 1835, for unspecified "iniquities." In 1842, at age fifty-two, he married Lucina Roberts Johnson, a widow, and later Mary Hilgrath. He was sealed to all three wives in the Nauvoo temple on January 16, 1846.[136]

In addition to being a polygamist, Reynolds was also one of the "princes in the kingdom of God" who had a seat in the secret Council of Fifty. This "kingly form of government" was created by Smith on March 11, 1844. A month later Smith was ordained "a king to reign over the House of Israel forever." The council was to be a shadow government for both the church and civil institutions in Nauvoo; it later helped found colonies in the Southwest and in Central and South America.[137]

Cahoon served as one of the bodyguards when the martyred

---

134. Tom Kimball to author, Feb. 4, 2008.

135. *History of the Church*, 4:205.

136. Reynolds Cahoon, Ancestral File, *Pioneer Women of Faith and Fortitude*, 4 vols. (Salt Lake City: Daughters of Utah Pioneers, 1998), 1:468.

137. Flanders, *Nauvoo Kingdom*, 292-93.

prophet's body was carried back to Nauvoo in June 1844.[138] During the trek west, he was a captain of the sixth company of pioneers. When Cahoon died near Salt Lake City on April 29, 1861, he was the father of ten children.

Vinson Knight

The fourth man to join in celestial marriage was Vinson Knight, born on March 14, 1804, in Norwich, Massachusetts. He had married Martha McBride on July 6, 1826, and with his wife joined the Latter Day Saints in Kirtland in 1834. Along with Oliver Granger, he had served as a church land agent in 1839 when the church purchased 15,000 acres in the "Half Breed lands in the Iowa territory, on the west side of the Mississippi across from Nauvoo." The price was $39,000.[139] He served as a bishop in Nauvoo beginning in 1839 and was designated by revelation in 1841 to be Presiding Bishop of the Church (D&C 124:141). The next year, Joseph Smith invited him to marry Philinda Myrick as a second wife. Her husband, Levi, had died in Missouri in the Haun's Mill massacre four years earlier.[140]

A granddaughter of Vinson and Martha Knight, Della Belnap, wrote about Martha's experiences in Nauvoo. For instance, Martha was present at the organizational meeting for the Female Relief Society in March 1842. Regarding her ancestor's response to polygamy, Belnap wrote:

> It is said that Martha was the first woman to give her consent for her husband to enter Plural Marriage. She knew some thing was worr[y]ing her husband and he couldn't seem to tell her about it. One evening as she was sitting in the grape arbor behind the house Vinson returned home carrying a basket. He explained to her that he had taken some fruit and vegetables to the widow, Mrs. Levi Merrick, whose husband had been killed at Haun's Mill, Mo. He also explained to her that he had been told to enter Plural Marriage. That if he had to, this Sister Merrick would be the one he could help best. He must have been greatly relieved when Martha replied, "Is that all."[141]

138. *History of the Church,* 7:135; see also 2:299.
139. Flanders, *Nauvoo Kingdom,* 36-37.
140. *History of the Church,* 3:325-26.
141. Belnap, "Martha McBride Knight."

There is no date for Knight's marriage to Philinda, nor for Joseph's alleged marriage to Martha after Vinson's death on July 31, 1842. Joseph is thought to have married Martha in early August. Martha Knight was resealed to the deceased Smith on October 12, 1844, at which time she became Heber Kimball's mortal wife, and again on January 26, 1846, when her life-marriage to Kimball was reconfirmed. A half year after Knight's death, Philinda entered into a civil marriage (February 1, 1843) with Daniel Hutchinson Keeler. Then almost exactly three years later, on February 6, 1846, she was sealed to her first husband, Levi Myrick, for eternity with Keeler standing as proxy. Apparently, Knight was not expected to have a companion in the afterlife.[142] Today he is best known for his renovated two-story brick home, still standing on the west side of Main Street between Kimball and Parley Streets in historic Nauvoo.[143]

By the end of 1842, there were thus at least four plural husbands in Nauvoo: Joseph Smith, Brigham Young, Heber Kimball, and Reynolds Cahoon; there would have been six if John Bennett had not been expelled and Vinson Knight had not died. There were already sixteen celestial wives among the four husbands, but only one child thought to have resulted from these unions by this point, the tragically short-lived Adelbert or Adelmon (and this hypothesis comes with a question mark). Smith had nevertheless not only offered the principle to other men, his actions had reached the newspapers and were featured in Bennett's book. Even at the inception of Nauvoo polygamy, the seeds of discord had been sown.

Of the first men to follow Smith into celestial matrimony, Young and Kimball may be the most interesting because of the similar pattern of their marriages in 1844, 1845, and 1846: about thirty-five new wives each for those years (Young: 12, 5, 18; Kimball: 13, 6, 16). This obvious correlation suggests close coordination between Young and Kimball regarding the number of women they married, at least prior

142. Cook, *Nauvoo Marriages,* 47-48.

143. Richard N. Holzapfel and T. Jeffery Cottle, *Old Mormon Nauvoo and Southeastern Iowa: Historic Photographs and Guide* (Santa Ana, Calif.: Fieldbrook Productions, 1991), 121.

to the change in Young's status from president of the Quorum of Twelve Apostles to president of the LDS Church in 1847.

The expanding inner circle

From 1843 through the first half of 1844, Joseph Smith expanded the number of his confidants. John Bennett had broken the story to the newspapers, but publicity had not prevented the inner circle from swelling to thirty-three brethren, excluding Bennett, by the time Joseph and Hyrum Smith were assassinated on June 27, 1844. As we have seen, new plural marriages ceased for a few months after Bennett's intimate accounts in 1842, but the next year and a half saw seventy-one more celestial weddings, twenty-one for Smith and fifty for other men. In fact, celestial marriages more than tripled in 1843. Young married his second and third plural companions on November 2, 1843, the same day Smith married his last plural wife. Kimball would not marry in 1843, but chose to postpone his second plural sealing until the fall of 1844. Cahoon would not marry again, after joining Lucina Johnson in 1842 matrimony, until January 1846. Knight, of course, had died. However, twenty-eight other men complied with the principle: twenty in 1843 and eight in the first half of 1844 (see chapter 5).

Before the Saints left Nauvoo in 1846, this total would swell to 196 men and 719 women. During their lifetimes, these same men would accumulate a total of 1,134 wives for an average of 5.8 wives per family. Excluding the singularly large families of Smith, Young, and Kimball, the remaining 193 men would have 604 wives in Nauvoo, a rate of 3.1 wives per family. During their lifetimes, again excluding the three most-married men, the nearly 200 Nauvoo polygamists would accumulate about 1,000 wives for an average rate of 5.2 wives per family. What Smith cautiously began in secrecy, first for himself, then among two or three dozen church leaders, Young extended to six times as many families. Once out west and acknowledged to the public, these 200 Nauvoo families nearly doubled their number of celestial spouses. Before it was closed down as an option for mainstream LDS members, thousands of polygamists were generated from the culture Smith began in the Midwest and Young amplified in Utah.

TABLE 4.8 Nauvoo plural families by year of inception

Nauvoo husbands	first plural wife	1841	1842	1843	1844[a]	1844[b]	1845	1846	total plural wives: Nauvoo	> Nauvoo	total
1 Smith, Joseph Jr.	Apr 5 1841	3	13	21					37		37
Wives of a man entering polygamy in 1841		*3*	*13*	*21*					*37*		*37*
2 Young, Brigham	Jun 14 1842		1	2	1	12	5	18	39	15	54
3 Kimball, Heber Chase	1842		1			13	6	16	36	7	43
4 Knight, Vinson	< Jul 31 1842		1						1		1
5 Cahoon, Reynolds	1842		1					1	2		2
Wives of men entering polygamy in 1842			*4*	*2*	*1*	*25*	*11*	*35*	*78*	*22*	*100*
6 Richards, Willard	Jan 18 1843			3			2	3	8	2	10
7 Huntington, William Dresser	Feb 5 1843			1				1	2		2
8 Hyde, Orson	Feb/Mar 1843			2					2	6	8
9 Young, Lorenzo Dow	Mar 9 1843			1				1	2	5	7
10 Bateman, Thomas	Mar 23 1843			1					1		1
11 Noble, Joseph Bates	Apr 5 1843			2					2	8	10
12 Clayton, William	Apr 27 1843			1		2	1		4	5	9
13 Johnson, Benjamin Franklin	May 16 1843			1				1	2	4	6
14 Adams, James (Judge)	Jul 11 1843			1					1		1
15 Miller, George	Jul 20 1843			1				2	3		3

a. before June 27
b. after June 27

Nauvoo husbands	first plural wife	1841	1842	1843	1844[a]	1844[b]	1845	1846	total plural wives		
									Nauvoo	> Nauvoo	total
16 Pratt, Parley Parker	Jul 24 1843			1		3	2		6	4	10
17 Felshaw, William	Jul 28 1843			1				1	2		2
18 Smith, Hyrum	Aug 11 1843			4					4		4
19 Smith, John	Aug 13 1843			2				5	7		7
20 Smith, William	< fall 1843			1		3	5	2	11	3	14
21 Richardson, Ebenezer Clawson	Nov 1843			1					1	2	3
22 Taylor, John	Dec 12 1843			1	4		2	5	12	5	17
23 Morley, Isaac	Dec 19 1843			1	1			5	7	2	9
24 Woolley, Edwin Dilworth	Dec 28 1843			2					2	3	5
25 Sagers, William Henry Harrison	ca. Dec 1843			1				3	4	5	9
Wives of men entering polygamy in 1843				*29*	*5*	*8*	*12*	*29*	*83*	*54*	*137*
26 Egan, Howard	early 1844				1			1	2	1	3
27 Turley, Theodore	ca. Mar 6 1844				3				3	1	4
28 Snow, Erastus	Apr 2 1844				1			2	3	10	13
29 Benson, Ezra Taft	Apr 27 1844				1			1	2	5	7
30 Kelting, Joseph Andrew	spring 1844				2				2		2
31 Wight, Lyman	< Jun 27 1844				3				3		3
32 Coolidge, Joseph Wellington	< Jun 27 1844				1			3	4		4
33 Page, John Edward	< Jun 27 1844				1		2		3		3
Wives of men entering polygamy in 1844[a]					*13*	*0*	*2*	*7*	*22*	*17*	*39*

34 Brannan, Samuel	ca. Sep 1844					1			1	1	2
35 Lyman, Amasa Mason	Sep 6 1844					3	1	3	7	1	8
36 Whitney, Newel Kimball	Sep 10 1844					1	4	2	7		7
37 Scovil, Lucius Nelson	Oct 16 1844					1			1	5	6
38 Smith, George Albert	Nov 29 1844					1	4	2	7	3	10
39 Pratt, Orson	Dec 13 1844					2	1	1	4	5	9
40 Grover, Thomas	Dec 17 1844					1		1	2	3	5
41 Johnson, Aaron	Dec 22 1844					1	1	1	3	8	11
42 Bates, Ormus Ephraim	Dec 23 1844					1			1	5	6
43 Butler, John Lowe	Dec 23 1844					1		2	3	4	7
44 Allred, James	Dec 26 1844					1		2	3	3	6
45 Barlow, Israel	fall 1844					1			1	2	3
46 Canfield, Cyrus Culver	1844					1			1	1	2
Wives of men entering polygamy in 1844 [b]						***16***	***11***	***14***	***41***	***41***	***82***
47 Whiting, Edwin	Jan 3 1845						1	1	2	2	4
48 Rich, Charles Coulson	Jan 6 1845						3	1	4	1	5
49 Mitchell, Benjamin Thomas	Jan 7 1845						1		1	4	5
50 Meacham, Joseph	Jan 9 1845						1		1	2	3
51 Brown, James Jr.	Jan 10 1845						1	2	3	7	10
52 Carter, Dominicus	Jan 26 1845						2	1	3	5	8
53 Snow, William	Jan 1845						1		1	3	4
54 Lee, John Doyle	Feb 5 1845						9	1	10	8	18

	Nauvoo husbands	first plural wife	1841	1842	1843	1844[a]	1844[b]	1845	1846	total plural wives		
										Nauvoo	> Nauvoo	total
55	Wight, Orange Lysander	Feb 7 1845						1		1	1	2
56	Scott, John	Mar 2 1845						1	1	2	2	4
57	Kingsbury, Joseph Corrodon	Mar 4 1845						1	1	2	2	4
58	Pack, John	Mar 1845						1	2	3	4	7
59	Stout, Hosea	Apr 20 1845						2		2	2	4
60	Snow, Lorenzo	Apr 1845						2	1	3	5	8
61	Willey, Jeremiah	ca. Apr 1845						1		1		1
62	Cox, Frederick Walter	< Jun 21 1845						1	1	2	3	5
63	Sessions, Peregrine [Perrigrine]	Jun 28 1845						1	1	2	5	7
64	Young, Joseph	Jul 1845						1	2	3	2	5
65	Shumway, Charles	Aug 5 1845						1		1	3	4
66	Nickerson, Freeman	Aug 1845						1	1	2		2
67	Cahoon, William Farrington	Sep 23 1845						1		1	2	3
68	Sessions, David	Oct 3 1845						1		1	1	2
69	Johnson, Joel Hills	Oct 25 1845						2		2	1	3
70	Fullmer, David	Dec 7 1845						1	1	2		2
71	Hunter, Edward	Dec 15 1845						1	1	2	1	3
72	Miller, Reuben	Dec 15 1845						1	1	2	2	4
73	Callister, Thomas	Dec 16 1845						1		1	2	3
74	Goddard, Stephen Hezekiah	Dec 17 1845						1		1	2	3

75 Miller, William	Dec 22 1845						1	2	3	3	6
76 Brown, Benjamin	Dec 23 1845						1	1	2	1	3
77 Coons, Lebbeus Thaddeus	Dec 31 1845						1	2	3		3
78 Spencer, Daniel	Dec 1845						1		1	6	7
79 Rockwell, Orrin Porter	ca. Dec 1845						1		1	2	3
80 Williams, Alexander	ca. 1845						1		1	3	4
81 Fielding, Joseph	ca. 1845						1		1	2	3
82 Smoot, Abraham Owen	ca. 1845						1	1	2	3	5
Wives of men entering polygamy in 1845							*50*	*25*	*75*	*92*	*167*
83 Bills, John	Jan 6 1846							1	1		1
84 Dykes, George Parker	Jan 9 1846							2	2	3	5
85 Haws, Peter	Jan 10 1846							4	4		4
86 Harris, Emer	Jan 11 1846							1	1	1	2
87 Clapp, Benjamin Lynn	Jan 13 1846							2	2	1	3
88 Lewis, Lemuel	Jan 13 1846							1	1		1
89 Stewart, Levi	Jan 13 1846							1	1	4	5
90 Bent, Samuel	Jan 14 1846							9	9		9
91 Cutler, Alpheus	Jan 14 1846							6	6		6
92 Higbee, Isaac	Jan 14 1846							1	1	5	6
93 Allred, Isaac	Jan 15 1846							1	1	1	2
94 Chamberlain, Solomon	Jan 15 1846							1	1	1	2
95 Hatfield, John	Jan 15 1846							1	1		1

Nauvoo husbands	first plural wife	1841	1842	1843	1844[a]	1844[b]	1845	1846	total plural wives		
									Nauvoo	> Nauvoo	total
96 Loveland, Chester	Jan 15 1846							1	1	4	5
97 Spencer, Orson	Jan 15 1846							1	1	4	5
98 West, Nathan Ayres	Jan 15 1846							2	2		2
99 Herriman, Henry	Jan 16 1846							1	1	1	2
100 Luddington, Elam	Jan 17 1846							1	1	3	4
101 Young, Phineas Howe	Jan 18 1846							5	5	3	8
102 Averett, Elisha	Jan 19 1846							1	1		1
103 Carter, Simeon	Jan 19 1846							2	2	1	3
104 Woodworth, Lucien	Jan 19 1846							4	4		4
105 Stiles, George Philander	< Jan 19 1846							2	2		2
106 Bernhisel, John Milton	Jan 20 1846							6	6		6
107 Kelsey, Eli Brazee	Jan 20 1846							2	2	3	5
108 Langley, George Washington	Jan 20 1846							1	1		1
109 Peck, Martin Horton	Jan 20 1846							1	1	2	3
110 Russell, Samuel Jr.	Jan 20 1846							2	2		2
111 Crismon, Charles	ca. Jan 20 1846							1	1	4	5
112 Beach, Rufus	Jan 21 1846							3	3		3
113 Chase, Isaac	Jan 21 1846							2	2	2	4
114 Cheney, Aaron	Jan 21 1846							1	1	1	2
115 Covey, Benjamin	Jan 21 1846							3	3		3

116 Durfee, Jabez	Jan 21 1846							1	1	1	2
117 Fullmer, John Solomon	Jan 21 1846							1	1	1	2
118 Gates, Jacob	Jan 21 1846							1	1	4	5
119 Lathrop, Asahel Albert	Jan 21 1846							1	1	1	2
120 Rockwood, Albert Perry	Jan 21 1846							2	2	2	4
121 Sherwood, Henry Garlic	Jan 21 1846							1	1		1
122 Webb, Chauncey Griswold	Jan 21 1846							1	1	4	5
123 Farr, Winslow Sr.	Jan 22 1846							4	4	1	5
124 Lott, Cornelius Peter	Jan 22 1846							4	4	2	6
125 Bullock, Thomas	Jan 23 1846							1	1	1	2
126 Dana, Charles Root	Jan 23 1846							2	2	5	7
127 Grant, George Davis	Jan 23 1846							1	1	5	6
128 Babbitt, Almon Whiting	Jan 24 1846							3	3		3
129 Foster, Lucian Rose	Jan 24 1846							3	3		3
130 Hallett, Clark Thatcher	Jan 24 1846							1	1		1
131 Huntington, William Jr.	Jan 24 1846							2	2		2
132 Patten, Charles Wetherby	Jan 24 1846							1	1		1
133 Redding, Return Jackson	Jan 24 1846							1	1	2	3
134 Merkley, Christopher	Jan 24 1846							1	1	1	2
135 Benbow, John	Jan 26 1846							4	4	1	5
136 Bair, John	Jan 27 1846							2	2	2	4
137 Blackhurst, William	Jan 27 1846							1	1	2	3
138 Dayton, Hiram	Jan 27 1846							1	1	6	7

Nauvoo husbands	first plural wife	1841	1842	1843	1844[a]	1844[b]	1845	1846	total plural wives		
									Nauvoo	> Nauvoo	total
139 Richards, Levi	Jan 27 1846							1	1		1
140 Wood, Daniel	Jan 27 1846							2	2	8	10
141 Carmichael, William	Jan 28 1846							1	1	1	2
142 Draper, William	Jan 28 1846							1	1	5	6
143 Tippets, John Harvey	Jan 28 1846							2	2	1	3
144 Woolsey, Thomas	Jan 28 1846							2	2	3	5
145 Decker, Isaac Perry	Jan 29 1846							1	1	3	4
146 McArthur, Duncan	Jan 29 1846							1	1	1	2
147 Tuttle, Edward	Jan 29 1846							1	1	1	2
148 Webb, Edward Milo	< Jan 29 1846							1	1		1
149 Hickman, William Adams	Jan 30 1846							1	1	8	9
150 Markham, Stephen	Jan 30 1846							1	1	6	7
151 Whitney, Clark Lyman	Jan 30 1846							2	2		2
152 Edwards, William	Jan 31 1846							1	1	1	2
153 Foutz, Jacob	Jan 31 1846							1	1	1	2
154 Richards, Franklin Dewey	Jan 31 1846							1	1	10	11
155 Robinson, Joseph Lee	Jan 31 1846							1	1	4	5
156 Zundel, John	Jan 31 1846							1	1		1
157 Hunter, Jesse Divined	Feb 2 1846							1	1		1
158 Loveless, John	Feb 2 1846							1	1	2	3

159 Phelps, William Wines	Feb 2 1846							2	2	3	5
160 Sanders, Ellis Mendenhall	Feb 2 1846							1	1		1
161 Anderson, William	Feb 3 1846							1	1		1
162 Fordham, Elijah	Feb 3 1846							1	1	3	4
163 Garner, William	Feb 3 1846							1	1	1	2
164 Graham, James	Feb 3 1846							1	1	3	4
165 Murray, William Ellis	Feb 3 1846							1	1		1
166 Parker, John Davis	Feb 3 1846							2	2		2
167 Wilson, Lewis Dunbar	Feb 3 1846							1	1	2	3
168 Allen, Joseph Stewart	Feb 4 1846							1	1	2	3
169 Peck, Hezekiah	Feb 4 1846							1	1		1
170 Bolton, Curtis Edwin	Feb 6 1846							1	1	4	5
171 Burgess, Harrison	Feb 6 1846							1	1	1	2
172 Clark, Raymond	Feb 6 1846							2	2	1	3
173 Coltrin, Zebedee	Feb 6 1846							2	2	1	3
174 Harmon, Jesse Pierce	Feb 6 1846							1	1	4	5
175 Hewitt, Wilkinson	Feb 6 1846							1	1	1	2
176 Winchester, Stephen	Feb 6 1846							2	2	1	3
177 Fleming, Josiah Wolcott	Feb 7 1846							1	1	1	2
178 Hunt, Charles Jefferson	Feb 7 1846							1	1		1
179 Weeks, Allen	Feb 7 1846							2	2		2
180 Yearsley, David Dutton	Feb 7 1846							1	1		1
181 Kelly, Joseph	Feb 7 1846							1	1	1	2

Nauvoo husbands	first plural wife	1841	1842	1843	1844[a]	1844[b]	1845	1846	total plural wives: Nauvoo	> Nauvoo	total
182 Richards, Phineas Howe	Feb 8 1846							1	1	5	6
183 Gee, Lysander	Feb 12 1846							1	1	1	2
184 Lyon, Windsor Palmer	ca. Feb 1846							1	1		1
185 Woodruff, Wilford	Apr 15 1846							3	3	6	9
186 Snow, Willard Trowbridge	May 14 1846							1	1	1	2
187 Hatch, Isaac Burrus	spring 1846							1	1		1
188 Wilson, Guy Carlton	< 1846							3	3		3
189 Tippets, Alvah Lewis	ca. 1846							1	1		1
190 Carrington, Albert	ca. 1846							1	1		1
191 Kay, John Moburn	ca. 1846							1	1	2	3
192 McGinnis, Benjamin	ca. 1846							1	1		1
193 Hadden, Alfred Sidney	ca. 1846							1	1	1	2
194 Chesley, Alexander Philip	1846							1	1		1
195 Coon, Abraham	1846							1	1	2	3
196 Hancock, Levi Ward	1846							1	1	4	5
Wives of men entering polygamy in 1846								*185*	*185*	*191*	*376*

TABLE 4.9 Total wives in plural families by year of inception

	1841	1842	1843	1844[a]	1844[b]	1845	1846	Nauvoo	> Nauvoo	total
Wives of 1 man entering polygamy in 1841	3	13	21					37		37
Wives of 4 men entering polygamy in 1842		4	2	1	25	11	35	78	22	100
Wives of 20 men entering polygamy in 1843			29	5	8	12	29	83	54	137
Wives of 8 men entering polygamy in 1844[a]				13	0	2	7	22	17	39
Wives of 13 men entering polygamy in 1844[b]					16	11	14	41	41	82
Wives of 36 men entering polygamy in 1845						50	25	75	92	167
Wives of 114 men entering polygamy in 1846							185	185	191	376
Total plural wives by year	*3*	*17*	*52*	*19*	*49*	*86*	*295*	*521*	*417*	*938*
Plus first wives										*196*
Total wives										*1,134*

a. before June 27
b. after June 27

TABLE 4.10 Wives per family

	plural wives	total wives	average wives per man
	Smith, Young, and Kimball		
Nauvoo:	112	115	38.3
lifetime:	134	137	45.7
minus 17 Smith widows*:	117	120	40.0
	193 other husbands		
Nauvoo:	409	602	3.1
lifetime:	804	997	5.2
minus 7 Smith widows*:	797	990	5.1
	All 196 husbands		
Nauvoo:	521	717	3.7
lifetime:	938	1,134	5.8
minus 24 Smith widows*:	914	1,110	5.7

*Remarried widows are subtracted to reduce double counting of the same wives.

FIVE.

A Surge in Plural Families

"I have six wives . . . and am not afraid of another"

In 1843 twenty more men joined Joseph Smith's fraternity of polygamists. Recovering from the hiatus of late 1842, a time of arrests and antagonistic publicity, Smith further institutionalized plural marriage, characterizing it as a Christian obligation. He applied Jesus' parable of ten talents to ten virgins betrothed to one worthy man, and in other ways he linked his marriage system to the Bible. His eighteenth wife was Mrs. Ruth Sayers, the gardener's wife, whom he married in February 1843. This was one month after his record keeper, William Clayton, became one of the first twenty participating husbands. By the end of the year, a total of twenty-five men had accumulated seventy-two wives, a trend that was becoming increasingly difficult to keep from the public view.

Willard Richards

Born in Massachusetts in 1804, Willard Richards was an educated, reliable scribe to Smith. On January 18, 1843, he led a surge of new participants by marrying his first plural wife, Sarah Longstroth, a sixteen-year-old from England. Sarah had come to America in early 1842 with three sisters. Willard, a cousin of Brigham Young, had traveled as a missionary to England in 1837 with the Twelve Apostles. Three years later at a conference in Preston, England, Richards replaced Apostle Thomas B. Marsh, who had been excommunicated a year earlier. After four years in England, Willard and his British wife, Jennetta, sailed for Massachusetts in mid-1841, where he left his wife and baby with his family and continued on to Nauvoo. He was quickly put to use as a member of the city council, city recorder, and clerk for the municipal court. In 1844 he escaped death at the Carthage Jail when the Smiths were killed. Under Brigham Young, Richards served as a clerk and Church Historian.[1]

A year after Jennetta's arrival in America, Willard had gone west to Nauvoo and she was still living in Richmond, Massachusetts, near Boston. In the spring of 1842, she wrote to Joseph Smith with a "request" that Smith notes, perhaps concerning her husband's absence—her letter is not available. Smith replied to Jennetta with the news that her husband would soon return to gather his family. He then seeks to prepare her for the advent of more women in her household—there would be ten. As he broached the topic, Smith positioned himself as a confidante, an ally she could help to persuade her husband to enter into polygamy. In a seemingly friendly communication, Joseph appealed to Jennetta on June 23, 1842: "Agreabley to your request … I now imbrace a moment to adress a few words to you. … I want you[,] beloved Sister, to be a Gen[e]ral in this matter, in helping him along, which I know you will[.] he will be able to teach you many things which you never have heard." Smith continued this intimate tone, writing that he had "formed a very strong Brotherly friendship and attachment for you in the bonds of the Gospel. Although I never saw you I shall be exceedingly glad to see you face to face."[2] Just days after

1. Andrew Jenson, *Latter-day Saint Biographical Encyclopedia,* 4 vols. (Salt Lake City: Andrew Jenson History Co., 1901-36), 1:53-56; Joseph Smith et al., *History of the Church of Jesus Christ of Latter-day Saints,* ed. B. H. Roberts, 2nd ed. rev., 7 vols. (Salt Lake City: Deseret Book, 1963), 4:382; "History of Willard Richards," *Latter-day Saints Millennial Star,* Feb. 24-Mar. 18, 1865.

2. Joseph Smith to Jennetta Richards, June 23, 1842, in *History of the Church,* 5:40-41; Dean C. Jessee, ed., *The Personal Writings of Joseph Smith,* rev. ed. (Salt Lake City: Deseret Book, 2002), 551.

Joseph's letter to Jennetta, Willard returned to his wife and family in Massachusetts.

It took six months for Willard and Jennetta to persuade each other that plural marriage was from God. By that time they embraced the practice with enthusiasm, Willard marrying Sarah and Nanny Longstroth, the first two of three sisters, on January 18, 1843; in three years a third sister, Alice Longstroth would become his fifth plural wife. Another Longstroth girl, Ann, came to America and agreed to marry John Kimball Whitney, a son of Newel and Elizabeth. After his first two plural wives in 1843, Willard married another that year—Susannah, the same day Joseph married Rhoda Richards, Willard's sister, then five more in Nauvoo after the prophet's death, and two more after leaving Nauvoo, for a total of ten plural wives—with Jennetta eleven wives in all—and eventually fourteen children.

Willard's fifty-eight-year-old sister Rhoda was the oldest woman Joseph married. In 1846 the widow married her cousin Brigham Young as she was simultaneously resealed to Smith, Young acting as proxy. Willard died in 1854. Attentive to Willard's widows, Brigham asked them to marry Willard's nephew Franklin. Four of them, Mary, Nanny, Rhoda, and Susannah, agreed.[3] By 1846, Franklin D. Richards already had begun amassing a family of wives and eventually married twelve. Willard's brothers Levi and Phineas had two and seven wives respectively.

The next two men to marry in 1843 were a brother-in-law of the prophet by plural marriage, William Huntington, and Smith's friend and neighbor Orson Hyde, who was also one of the Twelve Apostles. Huntington, the brother of Joseph's 1841 wives, Zina and Presendia, became a polygamist in February, followed shortly thereafter by Hyde, whose legal wife, Marinda, Joseph had already taken as his own.

William Huntington and Orson Hyde

After his scribe, Smith invited a brother-in-law and a neighbor-apostle. When Joseph Smith married Zina Diantha Jacobs and Pre-

3. Minerva E. Richards Knowlton, "Nanny Langstroth," in *Richards Family History,* ed. Joseph Grant Stevenson (Provo: Stevenson's Genealogical Center, 1991), 286.

sendia Buell in late 1841, their brother William D. Huntington, age twenty-three, had embarked upon a coffin-making enterprise in Nauvoo with his brother-in-law Henry Jacobs, Zina's legal husband. Their parents, William and Zina Dorcas Huntington, converted to Mormonism in the 1830s when they were well into their forties and had six children. Attentive to the spiritual revival of the period, they had become swept up in the religious enthusiasm which had carried over to their view of the Smith family's callings. When Joseph Smith Sr. and his brother John Smith told them in 1836 to sell their prosperous ranch and produce farm near Watertown, New York, and relocate to Kirtland, Ohio, they did so. Their two oldest children, Dimick and Presendia, had their own families by then and traveled separately. William D., the oldest remaining son, and his three younger siblings traveled with their parents.[4]

In Kirtland, Joseph Smith had recently acquired the famous Egyptian mummies. When the Huntingtons had settled into their house, Smith found it convenient to occasionally hide the mummies with them. Joseph Sr. and his sons Hyrum, Samuel, and Don Carlos also hid in their house to "escape from the persecutions" that developed in Kirtland.[5] In 1839, Mother Zina Huntington died of malaria, and the next year, Father William Huntington married the widowed Partridge matron, Lydia, whose own five children included Emily and Eliza. When the newlywed parents moved in together, William brought his sons Oliver and John with him to the Partridge home in 1840, although with so many people in a small space, Oliver soon moved out. Joseph and Emma Smith then took two of the Huntington siblings, Zina D. and John, into their Nauvoo home just as they would Emily and Eliza Partridge that year.

Within a year or so, William D. discovered that Joseph Smith had courted and married three boarders: William's sister Zina and two stepsisters, Emily and Eliza Partridge, as well as William's older sister,

---

4. Martha Sonntag Bradley and Mary Brown Firmage Woodward, *Four Zinas: A Story of Mothers and Daughters on the Mormon Frontier* (Salt Lake City: Signature Books and Smith Research Associates, 2000), 51-53, 105-11.

5. Jenson, *Biographical Encyclopedia,* 1:369.

Presendia, who lived with her legal husband, Henry Jacobs. After William D.'s mother died, he stayed for a while with the Rigdons and then, in the summer of 1839, with the Smiths. On September 24, now twenty-four years old, young William married Caroline Clark. A few years later, he acquired two celestial wives himself: Caroline's sister, Harriet Clark, on February 5, 1843, and Ann Maginn in 1846. His father waited, but in the end brought home two new women himself to meet Lydia in 1846. A captain of ten in Amasa Lyman's evacuation company, Father William contracted a fever along the way across Iowa and died in August 1846.

Orson Hyde reported seeing a "wonderful lustful spirit" on his visit to the polygamous Cochranite community in Saco, Maine, in 1832 (see chapter 9). In 1834 he acquired his own lustful spirit in Marinda Johnson, the sister of two future apostles, Luke and Lyman Johnson, who would be his colleagues in the Quorum of the Twelve after 1835. In April 1842, while Hyde was on a three-year mission to Palestine to the end of 1842, Marinda secretly entered into a celestial union with Joseph Smith. There is no contemporary record of Orson's reaction, but Brigham Young's "nineteenth wife," Ann Eliza Webb, later asserted that "Hyde was in a furious passion." Nevertheless, moving beyond monogamy, he accepted Smith's "favors" in 1843 and married two more women, then another six in Utah for a total of eight plural wives. Hyde was ready to join in by early 1843 when Smith invited him to wed Martha Browett; he accepted and married her on February 5, less than two months after his return from the Holy Land. In April that same year, Orson married Mary Ann Price (Thomas Bullock recorded it as July 20).[6] The four of them found some equilibrium in their complex marriage until they settled in Utah and six more wives joined the family. Marinda would later report matter-of-factly of her husband's entrance into polygamy: "Having accomplished a three-years mission, he returned, and shortly after, in accor-

6. Mary Ann Price Hyde, Autobiography, Bancroft Library. For the context of proposals involving husbands and wives of existing marriages, see Todd Compton, *In Sacred Loneliness: The Plural Wives of Joseph Smith* (Salt Lake City: Signature Books, 1997), 241.

dance with the revelation on celestial marriage, and with my full consent, married two more wives."[7]

When Joseph Smith first "endeavored to teach" the subject of plural marriage to Mary Ann Price, Hyde's third wife, at first she "resisted it with every argument [she] could command," saying the "tradition … was most repulsive to my feelings and rendered me very unhappy, as I could not reconcile it with the purity of the Gospel of Christ." When Hyde asked if she "would consent to enter his family," she replied, "I could not think of it for a moment." Then she thought otherwise, realizing that "Mr. Orson Hyde was a conscientious, upright and noble man," and so she "became his third wife." She reported that she learned to love the first Mrs. Hyde, who "in the Spring of 1843 received me into her house as her husband's wife." She was "sealed to [Orson] by Joseph, the prophet, in [Marinda's] presence." Mary Ann reports that her husband "married three young wives," and they too got along well for they all "lived together until the offspring became so numerous we were compelled to have separate homes." Toward the end of her life, Mary Ann reflected that after receiving the principle of plural marriage, she had "never doubted this being the work of God," that it was "destined to usher in the millennium, when peace shall reign on the earth."[8]

Orson and Marinda's thirty-six-year marriage survived both her sealing to Joseph Smith and Orson's acquisition of eight wives to rival her claim to him. During Joseph's lifetime, Marinda was considered to be Orson's wife, although she was not sealed to him. Toward the end of her marriage, on May 1, 1869, she affirmed that in May 1843 she had been "married or Sealed to Joseph Smith, President of the Church of Jesus Christ of Latter Day Saints, by Brigham Young, President of the Quorum of the Twelve Apostles," at approximately the time of Orson's first two plural marriages.[9] If there was a sealing at

---

7. Compton, *Sacred Loneliness,* 242, citing Edward Tullidge, *The Women of Mormondom* (New York: Tullidge & Crandall, 1877).

8. Hyde, Autobiography, 2-5.

9. Marinda Nancy Johnson Hyde, Affidavit, May 1, 1869, in "40 Affidavits on Celestial Marriage," 1869.

that time, as she averred, it may have re-commemorated an earlier 1842 ceremony, unless Joseph considered the earlier relationship an informal levirate-like caring for the wife of a brother in the gospel during his long absence. After Smith's death the following year, Orson and Marinda were then sealed to each other on January 11, 1846, the same day Orson was sealed to wives two and three, Martha and Mary Ann. The following day Orson and Marinda were sealed to their twin daughters.[10]

While the otherwise loquacious Orson Hyde and otherwise strong-willed first wife, Marinda, left no written record of their reactions to polygamy or the convoluted means by which they were introduced to it, the discrepancies in their 1840s-50s sealings and their 1870 divorce speak volumes. Orson married wife number four, Charlotte Quindlin, in 1852. Five years later he married two more wives, Ann Vickers and Helen Winters, after which, on July 31, 1857, Marinda chose to be resealed to Joseph rather than to Orson, who nevertheless acted as Joseph's proxy. Her decision at age forty-two to be reconnected to Smith coincided, curiously enough, with her conception of one last child with Orson. Zina Virginia Hyde, their tenth, was born in April 1858. In the next few years, Orson married Julia Reinart, Elizabeth Gallier, and Sophia Lyon. In 1870, well after her husband had married his tenth wife, Marinda obtained a divorce, though she did not leave him entirely without someone to care for him. Orson retained a family of eight wives and thirty-one children.[11]

Lorenzo Young, Thomas Bateman, and Joseph Bates Noble

In late winter 1842-43 and early spring, Smith brought in three more participants: two friends and the man who had married him two years ago to his own first plural wife. Lorenzo Dow Young greeted the com-

10. Smith revealed after-life worlds, attained by children being sealed to their parents to form permanent family networks throughout the eternities. See Lisle G Brown, comp., *Nauvoo Sealings, Adoptions, and Anointings: A Comprehensive Register of Persons Receiving LDS Temple Ordinances, 1841-1846* (Salt Lake City: Smith-Pettit Foundation, 2006), x-xi.

11. Howard H. Barron, *Orson Hyde* (Salt Lake City: Horizon, 1977), 214, 223-24.

ing spring by wedding Harriet Decker, his first plural wife. Their celestial marriage occurred on an unseasonably warm March 9. Four years later, Harriet would be among the three pioneer women on the trail to Utah. Like Emily Dow Partridge, Lorenzo Dow Young was named for the Methodist preacher from Connecticut, Lorenzo Dow (1777-1834), who, in his eccentric style was said to have been a forerunner of the evangelist Charles Finney. Lorenzo was older than his brother, Brigham, but followed Brigham's lead in marriages. He wed another plural wife in 1846 and five more in Utah, forming a family of eight wives and twenty-five children.[12]

Plural marriages were beginning to proliferate. As each took place, it became easier and presumably more socially acceptable for men to accept Joseph's call to be married and procreate new Saints. On March 23, 1843, Thomas Bateman was united with his first celestial wife, Elizabeth Ravenscroft. Two weeks later, on April 5, Joseph Bates Noble, Joseph Smith's "brother-in-law" through polygamy, married twenty-three-year-old Sarah B. Alley. Not long thereafter, on June 28, Noble married fifteen-year-old Mary Ann Washburn.[13] Noble's first wife, Mary Beaman (sister of Smith's wife Louisa Beaman), bore him nine children; Alley gave him one child; and Washburn gave birth to five children, for fifteen in all by three Nauvoo wives. Including post-Nauvoo wives, Noble would marry a total of eleven women and father thirty-one children. Young, Bateman, and Noble were all close friends of Smith and willingly obeyed his directives that spring when the momentum was shifting away from the chill of John Bennett's disclosures, in favor of plurality.[14]

---

12. There was a change in the weather on Wednesday, March 8. It had been cold but turned "pleasant and calm. Much floating ice in the river." By Friday it was cold again (Scott H. Faulring, ed., *An American Prophet's Record: The Diaries and Journals of Joseph Smith,* 2nd ed. [Salt Lake City: Signature Books and Smith Research Associates, 1989], 328-29); Jenson, *Biographical Encyclopedia,* 3:743; Marguerite L. Sinclair to Frank M. Young, June 21, 1947, Lorenzo Dow Young Papers, A 1108-3, Utah State Historical Society, Salt Lake City; Lorenzo Dow Young Family Record, MS 1538, LDS Archives; "Diary of Lorenzo Dow Young, 1846-1852," *Utah Historical Quarterly* 14 (1946), 25-132.

13. See chapter 2 for Noble's role in marrying Joseph Smith to Louisa Beaman.

14. Jenson, *Biographical Encyclopedia,* 2:591, 4:691; Ancestral File, LDS Family History Library, Salt Lake City, also www.familysearch.org; Devery S. Anderson & Gary

Three previously mentioned husbands

Smith's efforts at persuasion, detailed in the previous chapter, would continue to bear fruit. He approached his secretary William Clayton in February 1843, and Clayton married a plural wife in April. Three months later Clayton would take dictation from Smith for the revelation on plural marriage. Another Smith intimate, Benjamin Johnson, was advised of his responsibilities in the beginning of April. Johnson took a wife on May 16. Smith also approached Lorenzo Snow, brother of Smith's thirteenth plural wife, Eliza Snow, in April. For reasons that are not clear, Lorenzo demurred and did not follow through until April 1845, ten months after Smith's death. Despite this, the pattern of accelerated involvement in celestial marriage is manifest.

James Adams, George Miller, Parley P. Pratt, and William Felshaw

The summer of 1843 began with four more men who would eventually marry sixteen more wives. James Adams, a close friend of the Smith family who performed marriages for Joseph, chose Roxena Rachel Repsher. Like the Smiths, Adams was a Mason—Deputy Grand Master of the Second Grand Lodge of Illinois—and had helped establish Nauvoo's lodge. Since 1821, he had made his home in the state's capital of Springfield, converted to Mormonism in the mid-1830s, and was elected Sangamon County Judge in 1841. Tragically, he died on August 11, 1843, exactly a month after his plural marriage of July 11.[15]

James Bergera, *Joseph Smith's Quorum of the Anointed, 1842-1845: A Documentary History* (Salt Lake City: Signature Books, 2005), 230; Joseph Bates Noble, Autobiography, 1810-1834, typescript, MSS 968, L. Tom Perry Special Collections, Harold B. Lee Library, Brigham Young University, Provo, Utah (see also online at "Diaries, Journals, and Histories of Some Early Mormons," *Book of Abraham Project,* www.boap.org); Andrew Jenson, "Plural Marriage," *The Historical Record,* 6 (May 1887): 237-38; Hazel Noble Boyack, *A Nobleman in Israel: A Biographical Sketch of Joseph Bates Noble* (Cheyenne: Pioneer Print Co., 1962), 1-3, 11, 16-17, 21, 28, 29-34. At the time of this writing, David L. Clark's *Joseph Bates Noble: Polygamy and the Temple Lot Case* was still forthcoming from University of Utah Press.

15. Mervin B. Hogan, "James Adams and the Founding of the Grand Lodge of Illinois," LDS Archives; Kent Walgren to Gary Bergera, Oct. 13, 2001, copy in author's possession.

The next summer marriage took place between George Miller and Julia Chapman on July 20 while Smith and Apostle Lyman Wight were on an expedition to Wisconsin Territory seeking lumber for Nauvoo. A Virginia farmer prior to bringing his wife, Mary Catherine, to Illinois, Miller offered Joseph and Emma Smith shelter during their flight from Missouri in the early 1830s. He and his wife joined the nine-year-old church in 1839. In Nauvoo, George was made a bishop and a brigadier general in the Nauvoo Legion, a member of the city council, a prince in the Council of Fifty, and grand master of the Nauvoo Masonic Lodge. At Smith's request on March 2, 1841, Miller prepared a statement, published in 1842, saying he had "made inquiries" into John Bennett's pre-Nauvoo life and discovered that Bennett's "wife [had] left him under satisfactory evidence of his adulterous connections." Two years later, on August 15, 1844, Brigham Young performed a second anointing ceremony for George and Catherine.[16] Referred to as having their "calling and election made sure," this ordinance was said to guarantee their position in heaven.[17] In 1846, before leaving Nauvoo, Miller married two more wives. A year later he quarreled with Brigham Young and ended up leaving the Utah church in favor of Wight's LDS faction in Texas, then James Strang's in Michigan. Miller died in Illinois in 1856 at age sixty-one.[18]

---

16. D. Michael Quinn, *The Mormon Hierarchy: Origins of Power* (Salt Lake City: Signature Books and Smith Research Associates, 1994), 632, 647-48.

17. This ordinance involved being anointed "kings and queens, priests and priestesses" to God. The Doctrine and Covenants refers to the ordinance in uniquely Mormon terms, guaranteeing that the recipients would be numbered among the first resurrection, promising "thrones" and "kingdoms," and concluding that the anointed would "pass by the angels, and the gods" to become gods themselves. "Then shall they be gods, … then shall they be above all, because all things are subject unto them" (D&C 132:19-26). The ordinance was administered for the first time on September 28, 1843, to Joseph and Emma Smith, as Joseph's journal reads: "Baurak Ale [code name for Joseph] was … anointed & ord[ained] to the highest and holiest order of the priesthood (& companion)" (Faulring, *American Prophet's Record,* 416; David John Buerger, "'The Fulness of the Priesthood': The Second Anointing in Latter-day Saint Theology and Practice," *Dialogue: A Journal of Mormon Thought* 16 [Spring 1983]: 21-22).

18. Lavina Fielding Anderson, *Lucy's Book: A Critical Edition of Lucy Mack Smith's Family Memoir* (Salt Lake City: Signature Books, 2001), 844-45; Dean C. Jessee, ed., *The Papers of Joseph Smith: Autobiographical and Historical Writings,* 2 vols. (Salt Lake City: Deseret Book, 1989), 2:561.

Four days after Miller's marriage and twelve days after the July 1843 polygamy revelation, Apostle Parley Parker Pratt secretly married Elizabeth Brotherton on July 24. His legal wife, Mary Ann Frost, seemed unaware of her husband's new wife. Pratt justified this deception by explaining that his deceased wife, Thankful, had appeared to him in a dream to give him permission. He went on to marry five additional women in Nauvoo and four out west, for a total of twelve wives (one legal, ten plural, one deceased), who bore him thirty-two children, one of them Thankful's. His last wife, Eleanor McComb McLean, whom he met in San Francisco, was sealed to him without divorcing her legal husband, who fatally shot Parley near Van Buren, Arkansas, the proximate cause of the Mountain Meadows Massacre.[19]

A biographer of Pratt reports that according to Pratt family legend, Parley was at first shocked by Smith's request that he practice polygamy, which he considered to be akin to "free love." Smith insisted that the apostles had a duty to set an example. He told Pratt to pray for a revelation. He did, and this was when Thankful appeared to tell him "that by taking other wives he would be adding to his own glory in the next world and thus would make her a queen over the other wives who would become her handmaids."

On June 29, 1843, Vilate Kimball wrote to her husband, Heber, about the mood swings Mary Ann was experiencing in coming to terms with Parley's intent to marry additional women:

> I have had a viset from brother Parley and his wife. ... It appears that J[ose]p[h] has taught him some principles and told him his privilege and even appointed one for him. I Dare not tell you who it is [as] you would be astonished and I guess some tried. She has be[e]n to me for counsel. I told her I did not wish to advise in such matters. Sister Pratt has be[e]n rageing against these things. She told me her self that the devel had be[e]n in her until within a few days past. She said the Lord has shown her it was all right. She wants Parley to go ahead, says she will do all in her power to help him. They are so ingagued I fear they will run to[o] fast. ... I rather they would go to those that had authority to teach.[20]

---

19. Scott F. and Maurine J. Proctor, *Autobiography of Parley P. Pratt,* rev. (1874; Salt Lake City: Deseret Book, 2000), 586-99.

20. Vilate Kimball to Heber C. Kimball, June 29, 1843, LDS Archives.

Pratt's biographer notes that as the apostle grew older, he chose increasingly younger wives. Elizabeth Brotherton was twenty-seven years old when they married in 1843. In 1844 and early 1845, he married four women who were twenty-two and twenty-three years of age, then in 1847 he married seventeen-year-old Ann Walker.[21] Mary Ann had reconciled herself to these theological philanderings but reportedly had not understood that they would involve conjugal relations resulting in offspring. In January 1846, Belinda bore Parley's polygamist child, Nephi,[22] which caused a scandal as Mary Ann then refused to have anything to do with her husband.[23] Instead of leaving Nauvoo with the apostles in late 1846, Mary Ann and her children stayed behind with Emma Smith; after visiting her family in Bethel, Maine, she went west. By 1853, in Salt Lake City, she divorced Parley. Yet in 1869, she affirmed the practice of celestial marriage and signed her name as Mary Ann Pratt.[24] On October 22, 1852, Parley wrote from Salt Lake City to "Mrs. Mary Ann Pratt," noting that back in 1846 he had sent a wagon to bring her and the children to Council Bluffs, Iowa, but that she had sent back the wagon without explanation.[25]

Another 1843 polygamist was William Felshaw, who had been converted in Boston in 1832 by Joseph's brother Samuel and Orson Hyde. Felshaw worked as a carpenter for the Kirtland temple and then migrated with the Saints to Missouri and Illinois. In the summer of 1843 in Nauvoo, he accepted the "principle" and asked Charlotte Walters to join him and Mary Harriet Gilbert, his first wife, in marriage. Eighteen-year-old Charlotte accepted, marrying the forty-

---

21. Reva Stanley, *A Biography of Parley P. Pratt: The Archer of Paradise* (Caldwell, Idaho: Caxton Printers, 1937), 182. The four were Sarah Huston, Belinda Marden, Martha Monks, and Phoebe Sopher.

22. In 1897, Nephi's son, Nephi James Pratt, married Myrtle Pettit, daughter of Orson Hyde Pettit, whose family was converted in Hempstead, New York, in the 1830s by Parley Pratt and Orson Hyde—one example of missionary families wedding convert families.

23. Stanley, *Biography of Parley Pratt,* 189-90.

24. Mary Ann Pratt, Affidavit, Sept. 3, 1869, in "[Affidavits] Book No. 2," 1869-1870, a collection of six folders compiled by Joseph F. Smith, Joseph F. Smith Collection, LDS Archives. Mary Ann died in Pleasant Grove, Utah, in 1891.

25. The letter is reproduced in Stanley, *Biography of Parley P. Pratt,* 190-91.

three-year-old William on July 28. She subsequently bore him four children, adding to the thirteen by his first wife, Mary.[26]

The Immediate Smith Family

Joseph's brothers Hyrum and William and Uncle John Smith (brother of Joseph Smith Sr.) were the next in line to join the polygamous circle. John's son, George A. Smith, would follow the example of his father in 1844.

Hyrum was almost six years older than Joseph. In 1830 he was one of eight witnesses to the Book of Mormon. In 1841 he was named Presiding Patriarch and Assistant Church President. Although he is known to have initially opposed polygamy, he finally gave in and married his first wife's sister, Mercy Fielding Thompson, on August 11, 1843, followed by Catharine Phillips and, evidently, Lydia Dibble Granger that same month, then Louisa Sanger on September 17—a total of four plural wives in just over a month.[27]

Hyrum had denounced the pervasive rumors regarding his brother's involvement with women as late as May 14, 1843, yet it appears that he may have performed some sealings before this date—at which time Joseph had already married twenty-four supernumerary wives and convinced eleven other men to go and do likewise. But before indulging in the practice himself, Hyrum had proclaimed that "many wifes & concubines" was an "abomination in the Sight of God" and that "if an angel should come and preach such doctrine[,] [someone] would be sure to see his cloven foot and cloud of blackness over his head."[28] A week later, Joseph's secretary, Willard Richards, warned that "a plot" was "being laid" by "bro H and others," with the intent to "entrap the brethren" with women.[29] The previous year, Hyrum had

---

26. *Deseret News Weekly*, Nov. 27, 1867, 336; Jessee, *Papers of Joseph Smith*, 2:544, citing Frank Ellwood Essholm's 1913 *Pioneers and Prominent Men of Utah*.

27. Mercy Thompson gave the date as August 11, but Joseph Smith's diary has "Hyrum, Brigham, William, and Sis[ter] Thompson <were married>" on May 29, 1843, as noted by Brown, *Nauvoo Sealings*, 279n199.

28. Levi Richards Journal, 1840-1853, typescript, May 14, 1843, LDS Archives.

29. George D. Smith, ed., *An Intimate Chronicle: The Journals of William Clayton*, 2nd ed. (Salt Lake City: Signature Books and Smith Research Associates, 1995), 105; see

publicly defended the prophet and his ever-reliable senior apostle, Brigham Young, against accusations of improper proposals to Martha Brotherton, Sarah Pratt, and Nancy Rigdon.[30]

Hyrum's May exhortation against the "abomination" he detected in the church came only two months before the revelation on plural marriage. Surprisingly, Hyrum experienced an abrupt change of heart by August and would be the one to announce his brother's revelation to the Nauvoo High Council. To persuade his skeptical older brother, Joseph had told Hyrum that if he embraced the doctrine, he could have his deceased wife, Jerusha Barden, sealed to him in the next world. In addition, he could have his current wife, Mary Fielding, sealed to him as an eternal companion. And furthermore, if he wished, he could have his wife's sister Mercy sealed to him, as well. Hyrum appeared to be tempted. To influence his deliberations, Brigham confided to Hyrum that his brother Joseph had "many wives."[31] To Joseph, the acquiescence of his oldest living sibling was a signal milestone that came just after Emma's presence in some of Joseph's marriages. These were no doubt inducements for Hyrum to announce two months later, in August, that God had given his official sanction to plural marriage.

Two of Hyrum's four plural wives were widows. His wife's sister, one of the Fielding women, had been married to Robert Thompson, who like her was from England. In 1840 Robert was employed by the church in Liverpool as a clerk, then in 1841 as associate editor of the *Times and Seasons.* Another of Hyrum's plural wives, Lydia Dibble, was the widow of Oliver Granger, a church land agent and a brother of Carlos Granger, the non-Mormon resident of Nauvoo who offered Joseph sanctuary when he was in hiding the previous year.

Brother Don Carlos Smith, like Hyrum, had opposed polygamy.

---

also Richard S. Van Wagoner's narrative in *Mormon Polygamy: A History* (Salt Lake City: Signature Books, 1986), 54-55.

30. *History of the Church,* 4:585, 586.

31. Brigham Young Address, Oct. 8, 1866, unpublished typescript, LDS Archives. See also Thomas Bullock, Conference Report, Apr. 8, 1844, 30-33 (LDS Archives) in "Notecard Resource Library, 157. Plural Marriage," online at www.mormonmiscellaneous.com/; description in Newel and Avery, *Mormon Enigma,* 141-42, 332nn47-48.

When he died in 1841, Joseph married his widow, Agnes Coolbrith Smith. Widowed again in 1844, Agnes married Joseph's cousin George A. Smith until, after wedding three members of the Smith family, she decided to go her own way and find a husband elsewhere, thereafter separating her family from the LDS community.

Hyrum's children and descendants followed Brigham Young and remained influential in the Utah church. Joseph and Emma's children, along with their mother and grandmother, were predominant among Saints who remained in the Midwest, eventually forming the leadership of the Reorganized Church of Jesus Christ of Latter Day Saints (now Community of Christ). The children vigorously denied that their father had ever taught or practiced polygamy, and Joseph Smith III went so far as to travel to Salt Lake City in an effort to convince his Utah cousins of his point of view. In turn, the prophet's nephew, Joseph F. Smith, and others in Utah argued the case for polygamy. A prominent example of this dialogue of opposites is found in *Blood Atonement and the Origin of Plural Marriage,* published in 1905 by Joseph F. Smith's son and namesake, Joseph Fielding Smith.

Another Smith sibling, Apostle William, assumed that the church presidency would be his after his two brothers were killed and the other remaining brother, Samuel, died in July 1844.[32] When the members rejected William's bid for the position, he affiliated for a time with some smaller factions and then retired to the eastern part of the country, where he remained apart from the major strains of Mormonism. William was born in 1811 and was five years younger than Joseph.[33] In 1842 he was elected to the Illinois legislature. In May 1845 he was or-

32. Dean Jessee attributes Orson Hyde as describing Samuel Harrison Smith (1808-44) as "a man of slow speech" yet "of good faith" (*Papers of Joseph Smith I*, 594-95); he was the third person to join his brother's church, and soon offered to sell his brother's translation of "a history of the origins of the Indians," the Book of Mormon (Jenson, *Biographical Encyclopedia*, 1:279).

33. Smith evidently adopted the middle initial "B" during the Civil War to distinguish himself from other William Smiths. See Paul M. Edwards, "William B. Smith: The Persistent Pretender," *Dialogue: A Journal of Mormon Thought* 18 (Summer 1985): 128-39. Quinn adds that William adopted an alias, "William Francis Smith," on Feb. 21, 1889, for marriages two weeks before his legal wife died (*Mormon Hierarchy Origins,* 595.)

dained Church Patriarch to take the place of the martyred Hyrum, though before long he was rejected by Young and the Twelve for having a temperament and lifestyle that seemed at odds with the office. William's first wife was Caroline Amanda Grant; they married on February 14, 1833. Ten years later William married his first plural wife, Mary Ann Covington Sheffield, evidently by the fall of 1843. A year later he married two sisters, Sarah and Hannah Libby, and another woman, Susan Clark. In 1845 he married perhaps as many as ten more women, followed by four additional wives over the next twelve years to 1858 and, as a conclusion to this marital odyssey, a final wife, Rosella Goyette Surprise, in 1889, just four years before William's death.[34]

In 1844, Brigham Young assumed administrative control of the church but left open the possibility that Joseph Smith III would one day assume the reigns of leadership. Young Joseph was eleven years old at the time. Young was dismissive of Sidney Rigdon's argument that, just as he had been Smith's spokesperson during his life, he should continue in that role as the most able orator in the First Presidency. Rigdon said he would do so "until Joseph Smith himself shall descend as a mighty angel."[35] Another contender for the throne was James J. Strang, who was outwardly the most like Joseph Smith in that he produced written revelations and found and translated ancient buried works. He led many of Smith's followers to Wisconsin and an island in Lake Michigan. Members of this group, after Strang's assassi-

---

34. See Quinn, *Mormon Hierarchy Origins,* 594-97; Kyle R. Walker, "William Smith's Quest for Ecclesiastical Station: A Schismatic Odyssey, 1848-93," in *Scattering of the Saints: Schism within Mormonism,* eds. Newel G. Bringhurst and John C. Hamer (Independence: John Whitmer Books, 2007), 92-114; Lyndon W. Cook, *Revelations of the Prophet Joseph Smith: A Historical and Biographical Commentary of the Doctrine and Covenants* (Provo: Seventy's Bookstore, 1981), 276-77; *Reorganized Church of Jesus Christ of Latter Day Saints v. Church of Christ of Independence, Missouri, et al.* 60 F. 937 (W.D. Mo. 1894), 313, 499-502. The 1845 wives included Mary Jones, Priscilla Mogridge, Henriette Rice (Aug. 8), Mary Jane Rollins (June 22), and Elizabeth Weston. Next came Rhoda Alkire and Abeanade Archer in 1846, Roxie Ann Grant in 1847, and Eliza Elsie Sanborn in 1857. Roxie Ann was probably the younger sister of his deceased wife, Caroline Amanda Grant (1814-45).

35. Smith, *Intimate Chronicle,* 141; Richard S. Van Wagoner, *Sidney Rigdon: A Portrait of Religious Excess* (Salt Lake City: Signature Books, 1994), 337-38, 348n63, citing Andrew F. Ehat, "Joseph Smith's Introduction of Temple Ordinances and the 1844 Mormon Succession Question." M.A. thesis, Brigham Young University, 1982, 187-98.

nation, would form the nucleus of the church later headed by Joseph Smith III.

Young wrote in his journal after asserting himself during the August 1844 conference: "This day is long to be remembered by me, it is the first time I have met with the Church at Nauvoo since Bro Joseph and Hyrum was kild—and the occasion on which the Church ca[l]le[d] was somewhat painful to me, … now Joseph is gone and it see[med] as though manny wanted to draw off a party and be leaders, but this cannot be, the church must be one or they are not the Lords."[36]

Despite these conflicts, the various groups found common ground in a commitment to the patrilineal right of Joseph III. While everyone was waiting for the young Joseph to show an interest in taking a leadership role, two issues became significant: (1) Emma Smith's dislike of Brigham Young and (2) Emma's disdain of plural marriage. Embarrassed over her husband's retinue of mourning widows, Emma maintained a solid wall of denial that the church founder had ever had anything to do with these women. Joseph III adopted his mother's distaste for what he considered to be an assault on his father's honor.

Young oversaw the evacuation of Nauvoo, but Emma remained in the city for over ten years, only leaving for a brief five-month period, September 1846 to February 1847, when the town became so lawless that she felt impelled to take her family 120 miles north to Fulton City, Illinois. There they joined former Nauvoo stake president William Marks, Lorin Walker, and other Nauvoo dissenters. During this time, Joseph III was being raised in a Protestant church rather than as a Mormon. When Emma re-married in 1847, it was on her deceased husband's birthday. Her new husband, Lewis Bidamon, taught Joseph III the dry goods business and other enterprises. The family attended the Methodist Church in Nauvoo.

As Joseph III was growing up, the Midwestern Mormons were growing older. William Smith supported James Strang for a time. Other prominent Mormons who trekked to Wisconsin and Michigan in support of Strang were George J. Adams, John C. Bennett, Jason W.

---

36. Roger D. Launius, *Joseph Smith III: Pragmatic Prophet* (Urbana: University of Illinois Press, 1988), 33, citing Brigham Young Journal, Aug. 8, LDS Archives.

Briggs, Zenas H. Gurley, Lorenzo Dow Hickey, William E. Marks, George Miller, and John E. Page. Lucy Mack Smith remained in Illinois but supported Strang, as did some other members of the Smith family, but not Emma. Strang sought Joseph III's participation. When word leaked out that Strang, like Joseph Smith, practiced polygamy on the underground, the Smith family was no longer interested. Two influential members of Strang's faction, Briggs and Gurley, left Strang to throw their support to William Smith in 1850. Once again, it became known that the aspirant to Joseph Smith's legacy was following in the prophet's marital footsteps.[37] Finally the branches of disillusioned believers from northern Illinois and southern Wisconsin "disclaimed in an 1852 conference in Beloit, Wisconsin, the 'pretentions' of Brigham Young, James Strang, William Smith, and others and resolved that the successor of Joseph Smith, Jr., 'must of necessity be the seed of Joseph Smith, Jun.'" Their declaration preceded the public proclamation of polygamy in Utah by two months, although the practice was apparent by that time to anyone familiar with the situation in Utah, as was the contempt for polygamy expressed by the deceased prophet's family.[38] The Reorganized Church actively sought out twenty-four-year-old Joseph Smith III in 1856 to issue him a "calling" to succeed his father. He decided to accept the calling, and they ordained him as their first president on April 6, 1860.

His assumption of the new church's leadership drew a fair amount of press, both positive and skeptical that he, son of the man responsible for all the controversy, would organize a non-polygamous alternative to the Utah church. But with time, Joseph III came to be respected in his community as a justice of the peace and a competent religious leader. The *Carthage Republican* thought he was doing more to "purify the Church, ... reforming its ... evil practices, than all the troops which the government could send to Salt Lake."[39] A *New York Times* editorial spoke of the disgust of Midwest Mormons for "the proceed-

37. Vickie Cleverley Speek, *"God Has Made Us a Kingdom": James Strang and the Midwest Mormons* (Salt Lake City: Signature Books, 2006); Launius, *Joseph Smith III*, 84.

38. Launius, *Joseph Smith III*, 88.

39. Ibid., 122-24.

ings of the Saints in Utah" and applauded any "steps to get rid of the tyranny of Brigham Young."[40] Although Joseph III agreed to lead the reorganization, he was at first preoccupied with making a living as a farmer and real estate developer and with politics, in his support of Abraham Lincoln and the Republican Party. In August 1860 when Hancock County residents expressed outrage that Mormons were once again gaining a foothold in their state, curiously enough Thomas C. Sharp, who had been a vocal opponent of Mormonism in the 1840s, defended the right of Joseph III and his people to practice their religion. Nevertheless, to avoid conflict, Joseph decided to move the mother church to Plano, Illinois, and then to Independence, Missouri.

Although the Reorganized Church continued to eschew polygamy, in 1983 its historians acknowledged the overwhelming evidence for its presence in Joseph Smith's life. After so many years of persuasion, denials, and struggle, it is ironic that the two churches have come to the same ideological ground in recognizing its practice in the church's formative years yet rejecting its current suitability. However, the RLDS Church (Community of Christ) has allowed for cultural norms in Africa and India which accept plural families among its members there, although, ironically, the LDS Church has not.[41]

The Extended Smith Family

The sons of Joseph Smith Sr. were not the only Smiths to practice polygamy. Joseph Sr.'s brother John, one of ten siblings, married Clarissa Lyman in 1815, then married his first plural wife, Mary Aikens Smith, in the summer of 1843. Mary was the widow of Joseph's brother, Silas (1779-1839). Polygamy must have suited the elder Smith because later that same year, after turning sixty-two, he married Julia Ellis Hills Johnson. She was the mother of Benjamin Johnson and had recently separated from her husband, Ezekiel, over Mormonism. Because of her own plural marriage, one can assume she approved of her daughters, Almera and Delcena, marrying Joseph Smith Jr. To sum-

40. *New York Times*, Apr. 11, 1860.

41. Richard P. Howard, "The Changing RLDS Response to Mormon Polygamy: A Preliminary Analysis," *John Whitmer Historical Journal* 3 (1983): 14-29.

marize the Smith family's involvement in celestial marriage, the prophet's Uncle John was persuaded to marry the mother of two of Joseph Jr.'s own plural wives. The Smith family was connected to the Johnsons through multi-generational intermarriage, only underscoring D. Michael Quinn's thesis of a kinship hierarchy conceived of by Joseph Smith as extending into a successive world.[42]

Uncle John is also important as the father of George A. Smith (1817-75), who in November 1844 married his first of ten plural wives and in 1854 would be appointed the official LDS Church Historian. He helped edit Joseph Jr.'s journals into the multi-volume *History of the Church.* George A. was the progenitor of several George Smiths

Four Generations of the Smith Family[43]

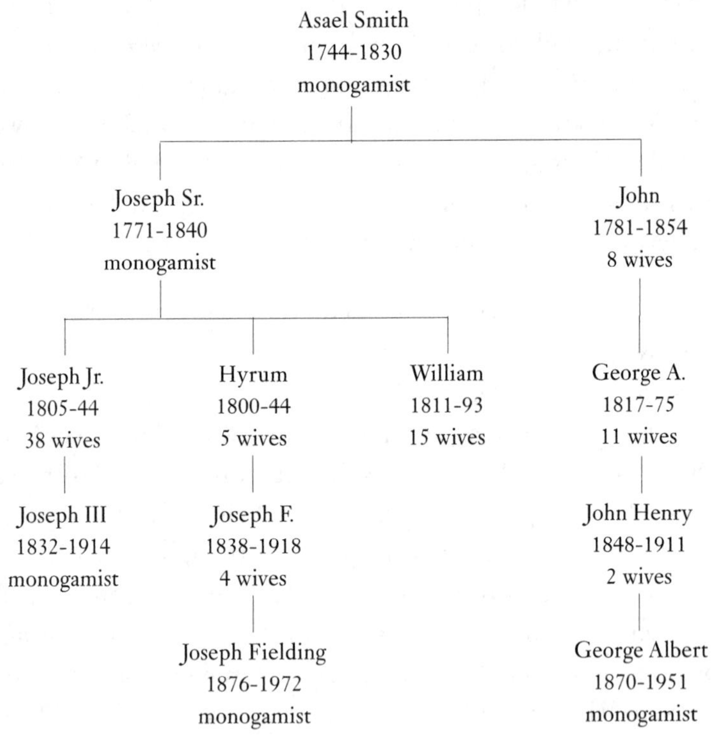

42. D. Michael Quinn, *The Mormon Hierarchy: Extensions of Power* (Salt Lake City: Signature Books, 1997), 163-97.

43. The siblings of Joseph Smith Jr. and Sr. are found on pp. 16 and 139n225.

(the author of the present work excluded), including George Albert Smith, the first monogamous LDS church president, 1945 to 1951.

Ebenezer Richardson, John Taylor, Isaac Morley, Edwin Woolley, and William Henry Harrison Sagers

In late autumn 1843, five men took their first plural wives. Ebenezer Richardson (1815-74), later president of the South African mission (1857), in November married a second wife, Polly Ann Childs. He would eventually have four wives and thirty-five children. In December, Apostle John Taylor brought home the first of those who would amount to seventeen additional wives. Isaac Morley, a father of ten, took a plural wife in 1843, another in 1844, and five more in 1846, for a total of seven in Nauvoo. Edwin Woolley married two of six plural wives in Nauvoo, while Harrison Sagers took the first of nine supernumerary women to wife.

John Taylor (1808-87), a cabinet-maker from England, moved to Toronto in 1832. The next year he married a recent immigrant from the Isle of Man, Leonora Cannon. Both were Methodists and John served as a traveling minister. But after listening to the two Pratt apostles and Freeman Nickerson in 1836, they converted to Mormonism and never looked back. John was ordained an apostle in the LDS Church in December 1838; in July 1841, he returned from a two-year mission to England. At some point over the next two years, perhaps around the time Joseph Smith began circulating his revelation on plural marriage in 1843, Taylor was instructed in the celestial law. He entered into polygamy with Elizabeth Kaighan in December 1843, and the next year, while Smith was still alive, married Jane Ballantyne, Mary Cook, and Ann Vowles. After Smith's death, he went on to marry eight more women in Nauvoo and five more in the west. He had thirteen wives by the time he left Nauvoo in 1846. Some of these women, such as Mary Ann Oakley in April 1845, married him under the utmost secrecy. From Winter Quarters, Taylor, Orson Hyde, and Parley Pratt were called on a second mission to England. Back home the following year, Taylor resumed marrying, adding Sophia Whitaker to his family at Council Bluffs, Iowa, in April 1847. Eight months later he married

Sophia's older sister Harriet as his fifteenth spouse—three wives away from his total of eighteen before his death. As church president (1880-87), Taylor was a strong advocate of plural marriage—the last president, in fact, to defend the practice without ever wavering. Over the course of his life, seven of his eighteen wives bore him thirty-five children. After a final address to the church in 1884, he went into exile to avoid prosecution for bigamy and died in hiding in 1887.[44]

On December 19, 1843, Isaac Morley (1786-1865) married Abigail Snow Leavitt, the first of nine plural wives. She was a sister of Lorenzo and Eliza Snow and was separated, but not divorced, from her legal husband Enoch Virgil Leavitt. Morley's daughter Cordelia refused an invitation from Joseph Smith to marry him in 1843/44 but in 1846 chose to be sealed to the deceased prophet for eternity rather than being sealed to her legal husband, Frederick Cox. A member of Smith's inner circle and supporter of plural marriage, Morley's ten wives would nevertheless bear him only thirteen children, ten of them by his civil wife, Lucy Gunn.[45]

Edwin D. Woolley (1807-81) was a farmer and merchant from Chester County, Pennsylvania, who became Brigham Young's business manager and a member of the Utah territorial legislature. In Nauvoo, he owned and operated a general store, where he was at work

---

44. Dean C. Jessee, ed., "The John Taylor Nauvoo Journal, January 1845-September 1845," *BYU Studies* 23 (Summer 1983): 1-64, 78-95, 102-05. B. H. Roberts, *The Life of John Taylor* (Salt Lake City: Bookcraft, 1963), 98-101, 465-68, 473-95, reports seven wives but has Taylor and Pratt directing the westward migration from Nauvoo in June 1847 (477). Andrew Jenson has Taylor leaving Nauvoo in 1846 for Winter Quarters, then undertaking a round trip to England before the 1847 pioneer trek to the Salt Lake Valley (*Biographical Encyclopedia,* 1:17). See also Quinn, *Mormon Hierarchy Origins,* 597-99. After Taylor's death in 1887, the next church president, Wilford Woodruff (1887-98), yielded to U.S. government pressure and threats to assume control of church property and on September 24, 1890, issued a "manifesto" calling for an end to the practice. Strong advocates within the LDS community would cite an earlier revelation to John Taylor purportedly commanding him to continue the practice and one to Woodruff in 1889 confirming the same (Jedediah S. Rogers, ed., *In the President's Office: The Diaries of L. John Nuttall, 1879-1892* [Salt Lake City: Signature Books and the Smith-Pettit Foundation, 2007], 393-96). Woodruff had waited until most Mormons had left Nauvoo to wed his first plural wives.

45. Cordelia Morley Cox Autobiography, MS 6105, LDS Archives; Maureen Ursenbach Beecher, ed., *The Personal Writings of Eliza Roxcy Snow* (Logan: Utah State University Press, 2000), 89-90, 245, 273.

and within earshot of Hyrum Smith one day in October 1843 when Hyrum mentioned his younger brother's revelation on marriage. In the next few months, Woolley's rapid transformation from stolid Quaker to a thrice-married man was outlined by a son who credited the family patriarch with being "among the first who adopted the principle of plural marriage as taught by the Prophet Joseph Smith ... in the autumn of 1843." Edwin's first plural wife was Louisa Chapin Rising. The ceremony was performed by Joseph Smith. In what by now will be recognized as a common storyline, Woolley had met Louisa when he was on a mission to Connecticut. He converted her and, even though she was not divorced from her legal husband, she agreed to marry her missionary. "Afterwards," on December 28, Edwin "received a second plural wife," Ellen Wilding, "by the same authority," meaning that of Joseph Smith, "so that before leaving Nauvoo at the time of the exodus in 1846," Woolley "had three living wives."[46]

Edwin and his wife of twelve years, Mary Wickersham, were friends of Joseph and Emma and often rode horseback with them for pleasure. The day in October when Hyrum came to the store, Edwin closed the door and pulled the blinds and, along with a female boarder named Jermain, gathered around a table to listen. As Hyrum explained the state of things, Jermain "went to the southwest window, raised the curtain, looked out, then turned around and, refusing the new marriage principle, said, 'Brother Hyrum, don't read any more, I am full up to here' drawing her hand across her throat."[47] In contrast, Edwin quickly accepted the idea, even if his wife took longer to warm up to it. Their daughter Rachel wrote that for days her mother "would not leave her room." Walking in on her one day, she found her mother "crying as though her heart would break."[48] Rachel remembered one night coming down from her room to witness what were likely plural

46. Edwin Gordon Woolley, Autobiography, 1845-98, typescript, 2-3, LDS Archives; Rebecca Bartholomew, *Audacious Women: Early British Mormon Immigrants* (Salt Lake City: Signature Books, 1995), 121-22. See also Leonard Arrington, ed., *From Quaker to Latter-day Saint: Bishop Edwin D. Woolley* (Salt Lake City: Deseret Book, 1976).

47. Arrington, *From Quaker to Latter-day Saint,* 111.

48. In Kate B. Carter, comp., *Heart Throbs of the West,* 12 vols. (Salt Lake City: Daughters of Utah Pioneers, 1939-51), 11:157.

marriage ceremonies taking place: "I came down stairs and opened the door at the foot of the steps, but was immediately discovered and unceremoniously sent back to bed again, but in the few seconds I stood there, I saw several persons standing in the center of the floor as though receiving some rites or ceremonies, but of what nature, I cannot say."[49] Her father eventually married three more plural wives; altogether his six wives bore him twenty-six children.

In November 1843, Harrison Sagers (1814-96) was accused of "trying to seduce" Phebe Madison. Then he married her. If this had been young love, it may not have appeared to be out of the ordinary; but there was nothing ordinary about this affair between a twenty-eight-year-old and his wife's twenty-three-year-old sister.[50] The charge against Sagers was made public by none other than Joseph Smith, who reported it to the High Council meeting above Smith's red brick store. Smith announced that Harrison had been "trying to seduce a young girl, living at his house[,] by the name of Phebe Madison … [and] using my name in a blasphemous manner, by saying that I tolerated such things in which thing he is guilty of lying &c. &c." The council acquitted Sagers on the questionable logic of having been "taught false doctrine which was corrected by President Joseph Smith."[51] Five months later Lucinda Madison appeared before the First Presidency and Twelve to accuse her husband of adultery, threatening to take the matter to the civil courts if she found no satisfaction from the church:

> Inasmuch as you have declared officially that you will deal with all per-

---

49. Ibid., 11:157; Arrington, *From Quaker to Latter Day Saint,* 113.

50. Ellis Sagers Swanson, *The Sagers Clan: William Henry Harrison Sagers and His Descendants* (Tucson, Ariz.: n.p., 1980), 35, 61, 65-66. Joseph Smith denied he had taught Harrison polygamy, but Harrison's wife Lucinda said he had been guilty of "spiritual wives" since Dec. 1843. A Phebe "Matteson" married Henry Pearmain on Nov. 19, 1843, but whether this was our "Phoebe Madison" is unclear. See Lyndon W. Cook, comp., *Nauvoo Deaths and Marriages* (Orem, Utah: Grandin Book, 1994), 96. Lucinda's Ancestral File, LDS Family History Library, also www.familysearch.org shows a Dec. 22, 1834, marriage and 1846 sealing. There is no comparable record for Phoebe.

51. Minutes of the High Council of the Church of Jesus Christ of Nauvoo, Illinois, Nov. 21, 1843, Book No. 3, p. 21, LDS Archives, from a typescript prepared by Lyndon W. Cook, 1978; Scott G. Kenney, ed., *Wilford Woodruff's Journal,* 9 vols. (Midvale, Utah: Signature Books, 1983), 2:328.

> sons who teach or have taught the abominable doctrine of Spiritual wives. This is to notify you that Harrison Sagars is guilty of ~~that~~ said sin, which thing can be proven by credible witnesses[,] and if he is not chastised for it by the church the law of the land will be enforced against him. H. Sagars left his family in December last[.] since such time he has not provided for them in any way what ever. The cause of the innocent demand[s] action immediately and you are the ones to take the matter in hand.[52]

The First Presidency referred the matter back to the High Council, which on April 13, 1844, "decided that as the first part of the charge had been brought before the Council before … and [Sagers was] tried on it; … the Council had no wright to deal with him on that item, and that the Second part was not sustained and therefore he should remain in the Church."[53] Thus, it appears that Sagers was concurrently married to both Lucinda and Phoebe with Joseph Smith's approval and the tacit endorsement of the High Council. In 1869, Nathan Tanner affirmed that "in the Spring of 1844 at Montrose, Lee County, Iowa, he heard President Joseph Smith, while in conversation with … Harrison Sagers, [blank] Daniels and others, teach the doctrine of celestial marriage or plurality of wives."[54] Harrison's fifth wife, Harriet Barney, left him, and their sealing was cancelled on August 23, 1855,[55] so she could become Brigham Young's forty-ninth wife on March 14, 1856.

The year 1843 closed with twenty new plural families in the Mormon capital. In addition to twenty-nine willing women who agreed to marry twenty new polygamous men, Brigham Young married another two women and Joseph married twenty-one more, including Brigham's sister Fanny.

Howard Egan, Theodore Turley, Erastus Snow, Ezra Taft Benson, Joseph Kelting, Lyman Wight, Joseph Coolidge, and John E. Page

In early 1844, Howard Egan led a group of eight more entrants into

52. Nauvoo High Council minutes, Apr. 11, 1844.

53. Ibid., Apr. 10, 1844.

54. Nathan Tanner, Affidavit, Aug. 28, 1869, "40 Affidavits on Celestial Marriage," 1869.

55. Swanson, *Sagers Clan,* 91.

the select society. This was also the year that several prominent church leaders became reformers, led by Smith's second counselor, William Law. These latter-day reformers directed their criticisms against secret combinations among the elite in Nauvoo whereby the inner circle was meeting behind closed doors and engaging in *sub-rosa* political discussions, performing arcane rituals, and solemnizing plural marriages. However, even as the protective facade began to be peeled back, the marrying continued. These final eight men joined Joseph's Quorum of the Anointed before his death in June 1844.

Howard Egan took as the first of three plural wives the widow Catherine Clawson in early 1844. Two years later he married Nancy Redding, and Zephaniah Clawson three years after that. Along with his first love, Tamson Parshley, he had four wives and nine children. A colorful figure who was born in Ireland and orphaned in Canada, he had been a sailor and rope maker in Massachusetts before he and Tamson converted to Mormonism in 1842 through the efforts of Apostle Erastus Snow. The Egans moved to Nauvoo, and in 1847 he served as a captain of ten wagons in the pioneer company that explored the Salt Lake Valley. He later went on to the California gold fields, then explored and rode the mail route from Salt Lake City to Carson City and Sacramento. He died at age sixty-two in 1878 while guarding Brigham Young's grave in Salt Lake City.[56]

Theodore Turley (1801-71) was another of the eight men initiated into Smith's polygamy fraternity in 1844. He converted to the Mormon faith in 1837 in Canada, where he was a Methodist preacher. Having immigrated there from England with his wife, Frances Kimberly, in 1825, when they settled among the Latter-day Saints he became— in a particularly odd turn for a minister—a bodyguard for Joseph Smith

56. William M. Egan, ed., *Pioneering the West, 1846-1878: Major Howard Egan's Diary* (Richmond, Utah: H. R. Egan Estate, 1917); see also Jaromy D. Jessop, "Pioneer Played Key Role in Story of Old West," *Tooele Transcript Bulletin,* Nov. 11, 2005. When Egan was away in California in 1851, his first wife, Tamson, became pregnant by a neighbor, James Monroe. Egan killed Monroe and then reported his act to the police. A jury acquitted him (Kenneth L. Cannon, "Mountain Common Law: The Extralegal Punishment of Seducers in Early Utah," *Utah's Lawless Fringe: Stories of True Crime,* ed. Stanford J. Layton (Salt Lake City: Signature Books, 3-6).

and a gun maker. On March 6, 1844, he married two sisters, Mary and Eliza Clift, then the next month married a third sister from the same family, Sarah Ellen Clift. Mary's background reveals something of the social dynamics of polygamy as it intersected with the age-old problem of the unwed mother. Family tradition has it that Theodore and Mary were sealed to each other in 1842 because of Mary's pregnancy and birth of a son, Jason, in October of that year. However, the minutes of the Nauvoo Stake High Council tell a different story. On September 3, 1842, Gustavus Hills was charged with "illicit intercourse with a certain woman by the name of Mary Clift by which she is with child[,] and for ... teaching the said Mary Clift that the heads of the Church practised such conduct & that the time would come when men would have more wives than one &c." [57] The council disfellowshipped Hills the next day, and on September 15 the Nauvoo Municipal Court ruled that Hills was the legal father of the unborn child and therefore needed to pay Mary $200 quarterly "in provisions or clothing suited to the condition of the said child," plus $20 annually for the infant's first three years, presumably allowing time for the mother's recovery. [58]

The courts based their rulings partly on an affidavit from Mary, dated August 29, that "she was pregnant with a child" and that "Gustavus Hills was the father of such child." She had also stated that Hills had tried to convince her to "remove to Columbus (Adams County, Ohio) until after her confinement and he would assist her with support as far as his means would permit."[59] On September 4, Mary swore in another affidavit that Hills had told her "he was intimate with another woman in town besides his wife & that the authorities of the church countenanced and practiced illicit connexion with women & said there was no harm in such things provided they kept it secret."[60] As was more common than one would like to think, the baby lived only one year and died on October 26, 1843. It was not long thereafter

57. Nauvoo High Council minutes, Sept. 3, 1842.

58. In Newel K. Whitney Papers, Perry Special Collections.

59. Journal History of the Church of Jesus Christ of Latter-day Saints, Aug. 29, 1842, LDS Archives.

60. In Danel Bachman, "A Study of the Mormon Practice of Plural Marriage before the Death of Joseph Smith," M.A. thesis, Purdue University, 1975, 227.

that Turley became Mary's husband, most likely through his interest in her sister, Eliza, and perhaps through the encouragement of the prevailing wisdom in Nauvoo, that if a man was going to marry someone who was not his initial wife, he might as well marry her sister.[61] In 1850 he married a fourth wife, Ruth Giles.

In April of 1844, Erastus Snow (1818-88) married Minerva White as the first of his thirteen plural wives, and Ezra Taft Benson (1811-69) married the younger sister of his legal wife, the first of seven marital adjuncts to Pamela Andrus Benson. Erastus was a cousin of Eliza and Lorenzo Snow. After converting in 1833, Erastus served missions to Massachusetts, New Jersey, Pennsylvania, and Vermont. He married Artimesia Beaman in 1838, the sister of Joseph Smith's 1841 wife, Louisa Beaman. In April 1844 Snow campaigned in Vermont for Smith's U.S. presidential candidacy. He was a member of the Council of Fifty, an 1847 pioneer, an apostle from 1849, and he helped found the town of St. George in southern Utah in 1861. He died in Salt Lake City in 1888, leaving behind thirty-six children.

The other April 1844 polygamist, Ezra Taft Benson, was the first son of John and Chloe Taft Benson, farmers from Mendon, Massachusetts. Ezra was baptized a Mormon in 1840 in Quincy, Illinois, where he had encountered Orson Hyde and John Page on their arrival from Missouri. In 1846, Benson was called to be an apostle, and the next year he participated in the pioneer company that found its way to the Great Basin. Eventually, he settled in Logan, Utah. His service to the church included missions to the eastern United States, Europe, and the Sandwich Islands (Hawaii). Before being elected to the Utah Territorial House of Representatives, he became an officer in the secretive Provisional State of Deseret. Following in his political foot-

61. Quinn, *Mormon Hierarchy Origins*, 632, notes that on Feb. 6, 1841, Smith told the Nauvoo High Council not to excommunicate Turley for "sleeping with two females" and only require that he confess "he had acted unwisely, unjustly, imprudently, and unbecoming." See also Nancy R. Turley and Lawrence E. Turley, *The Theodore Turley Family Book* (Mesa, Ariz.: By the authors, 1978), 56. Mary and Eliza were resealed to Theodore on Feb. 3, 1846, or Feb. 2, according to Ella Mae Turley, "Theodore Turley Biography and Autobiography," MS 7661, LDS Archives. The Ancestral File (www.familysearch.org) shows Theodore marrying Mary Clift in Jan. 1842, and the Nauvoo High Council records a child, Jason Turley "born Oct. 20, 1842, died Oct. 26, 1843."

steps, his great-grandson, Ezra Taft Benson (1899-1994), a correspondent of FBI Director J. Edgar Hoover, was appointed U.S. Secretary of Agriculture by President Dwight D. Eisenhower in 1952, then succeeded Spencer W. Kimball as church president in 1985.[62]

Four other men qualified for the first time as polygamists in the spring of 1844. Joseph Andrew Kelting was born in 1811 at Philadelphia and died in or after 1903 in southern California. For several years Kelting was a deputy sheriff of Hancock County and a lawyer for LDS Bishop George Miller. In 1894 Kelting testified:

> For some time previous to the death of Joseph Smith, the Mormon prophet, I lived at Nauvoo, Hancock County, Illinois. ... I heard rumors to the effect that Joseph Smith was practicing polygamy; the matter frequently being repeated especially by Wm and Wilson Law and the Higbees. Calling at the house of the prophet one day, early in the spring of 1844, on some business or other not now remembered, the prophet invited me into a room up stairs in his house, called the Mansion. After we entered the room he locked the door and then asked me if I had heard the rumors connecting him with polygamy. I told him I had. He then began a defense of the doctrine by referring to the Old Testament. I told him I did not want to hear that as I could read it for my self. He claimed to be a prophet[,] I believed him to be a prophet—and I wanted to know what he had to say about it. He expressed some doubts as to how I might receive it, and wanted to know what stand I would take if I should not believe what he had to say about it. I then pledged him my word that whether I believed his revelation or not, I would not betray him. He then informed me that he had received a revelation from God, which taught the correctness of the doctrine of a plurality of wives, and command[ed] him to obey it. He acknowledged to having married several wives. I told him that was alright. He said he would like a further pledge from me that I would not betray him. I asked him if he wanted me to accept the principle by marrying a plural wife. He answered yes. A short time after this I married two wives in that order of marriage.[63]

---

62. Jenson, *Biographical Encyclopedia*, 99-102; John H. Evans & Minnie E. Anderson, *Ezra T. Benson: Pioneer, Statesman, Saint* (Salt Lake City: Deseret News Press, 1947), 63-65, 355-57, 364-65; Donald B. Alder & Elsie L. Alder, *The Benson Family: The Ancestry and Descendants of Ezra T. Benson* (Salt Lake City: Ezra T. Benson Genealogical Society, 1979), 38, 54.

63. Joseph Andrew Kelting, Affidavit, Mar. 1, 1894, in "Affidavits [on Celestial Marriage], 1869-1915."

The two wives Kelting referred to were Minerva Orrilla Woods and Lucy Matilda Johnson, both from upstate New York. Kelting had married his first wife, Elizabeth Ann Martin, in 1832. In 1903 he issued a second affidavit, this time from his home near San Bernardino, California, again describing his conversation with Joseph Smith about plural marriage.[64]

Lyman Wight (1796-1858), a farmer from Fairfield, New York, near the Adirondack Mountains, married Harriet Benton in 1823. Evidently, he married three more wives by the time of Joseph Smith's death in June 1844. He was already a father many times over, a veteran of the War of 1812, and a Campbellite Baptist when he converted to Smith's church in 1830. He was present at the Kirtland temple dedication in 1836. In Nauvoo he was the principal fundraiser and procurer of lumber for the Nauvoo temple and Nauvoo House, the lumber having to be floated and hauled from the church pineries in Wisconsin. In May 1844 he went on the stump for Smith's presidential campaign. As a member of the Quorum of the Twelve, in 1845 he led an expedition to Texas looking for a new home for the Latter-day Saints. Three years later he was excommunicated over a dispute with Brigham Young and died in 1858 having just abandoned his congregation of about 160 individuals near San Antonio.[65]

Another of the 1844 polygamists was Joseph W. Coolidge (1814-71), a carpenter, miller, and lumber dealer from Bangor, Maine. In 1834 he married Elizabeth Buchanan, who would become the mother of eleven children. In 1838 they joined the Latter-day Saints in Missouri. At some time before Joseph's Smith's death, Coolidge married his wife's sister, Mary Ann, and then three more wives in 1846. He was the administrator of Joseph Smith's estate after the prophet's death. Eventually he worked in San Francisco as a lumber dealer.[66]

---

64. Ibid.

65. Jer[e]my Benton Wight, *The Wild Ram of the Mountain: The Story of Lyman Wight* (Bedford, Wyo.: Star Valley Llama, 1996), 211, 214-22, 236-41, 441-44, 500-01; B. H. Roberts, *Successions in the Presidency of the Church of Jesus Christ of Latter-day Saints,* 2nd ed. (Salt Lake City: George Q. Cannon & Sons, 1900), 122-24.

66. Jessee, *Papers of Joseph Smith,* 2:536; Linda King Newell and Valeen Tippetts Avery, *Mormon Enigma: Emma Hale Smith* (Garden City, N.Y.: Doubleday, 1984), 208.

John E. Page (1799-1867) from Oneida County, New York, converted in 1833 in Ohio, where he was living at the time. After dissenters abandoned the prophet in 1838 and left vacancies in the Council of the Twelve, this devout follower was ordained an apostle and sent east in 1841 to preside over the church in Pittsburg. After the deaths of two wives in succession, he married Mary Judd, the mother of eight children, in 1839, and by mid-June 1844 had evidently married his first plural wife, Nancy Bliss, followed by Rachel and Lois Judd, sisters of his legal wife, Mary. In 1846 he became disillusioned with Brigham Young and threw his support instead to James Strang, which resulted in his excommunication from the LDS apostolic tradition on June 26 of that year. He later supported Granville Hedricks's effort to acquire the temple property at Independence, Missouri, for the Church of Christ Temple Lot. Page died in Dekalb City, Illinois.[67]

Looking back over the three years of Joseph Smith's activity as a polygamist in Nauvoo, between April 1841 and June 1844, a few conclusions are apparent. We know that during this time he launched at least 33 families into plural marriages. The 33 known husbands married 124 plural wives, or an average of nearly four wives per family out of a total population of 11,000 in Nauvoo. It should be noted that the westward expanding population was fluid and not all factors potentially affecting these numbers are precisely accounted for, such as individuals moving in and out of the community, excommunications, and marriages to women who were already married—not to mention marriage to widows already in the count, divorce and re-marriage, and death. Even so, this snapshot of 157 male and female polygamists on June 27, 1844, is accurate enough to provide a sense of the demographics of the city.

In his own study of the earliest Mormon polygamists, Gary James Bergera summarized:

---

67. Joseph Fielding Smith, *Blood Atonement and the Origin of Plural Marriage: A Discussion* (Salt Lake City: Deseret News Press, 1905), 49-50; Quinn, *Mormon Hierarchy Origins,* 567-68; Minutes, LDS Council of Twelve, May 5, 1954, Alma Sonne Collection, Msf 678 #2, Bx 3, Fd 5, LDS Archives; John E. Page to Brigham Young, July 13, 1845, Brigham Young Collection, d1234, box 41, fd 2, LDS Archives.

> The "average," or representative, early Mormon polygamist husband was twenty-four years old when he married civilly and thirty-nine years old when he first married plurally. He had been ordained to the office of high priest in the Melchizedek Priesthood and, prior to Joseph Smith's death, was either a member of the Quorum of the Anointed or Council of Fifty, or had received his second anointing. The "average" wife was twenty-one years old at the time of her civil marriage or twenty-eight years old at the time of her plural marriage. If a plural wife, she had never previously married and was not a member of Nauvoo's Relief Society (unless she was married plurally to Joseph Smith). A civilly married couple's first child was born thirteen months after their marriage, while a plurally married couple's first child was born two years after their marriage, which would put this birth after the death of Joseph Smith.[68]

Over the next two years, to June 1846, there would be overlapping periods of sorrow, fear of assault, political and religious zeal, and appeals to the governor and other state authorities. But against this backdrop of starts and stops in other areas, there would be no sustained alteration in the momentum behind polygamy. Brigham Young, Heber Kimball, and seven others of the hierarchy brought twenty-four of Smith's widows into their households, some of these as early as September 1844 and others as late as February 1846. Through the fall of 1844, there were forty-nine new celestial marriages, eighty-six in 1845, and 276 in the early months of 1846 while waves of travelers left Nauvoo and crossed the Mississippi.[69] The 163 new polygamous men brought the total number of families living the marriage principle to 196. These were the vanguard who would shape the practice as they passed the tradition on to others of the faith and to the next generation in the valleys of the Intermountain West.

---

68. Gary James Bergera, "Identifying the Earliest Mormon Polygamists, 1841-44," *Dialogue: A Journal of Mormon Thought* 38 (Fall 2005): 51.

69. Brigham Young's diary, often written in code, suggests other marriages. On October 8, 1844, Young's diary reads: "ME [marriage for eternity] Br. [Heber C.] Kimball and myself stop[p]ed at sister Knoons [Sarah Peak Noon]. saw [sealed and wed] sisters Sarah All[e]y and Clary [Clarissa] Blake [(Morriston)][,] [Kimball performing the ceremony]." Alley, a wife of Joseph Bates Noble, may have married Young along with Clarissa Blake, a known wife. Alley was not resealed to Noble in 1846. Margaret Alley (not a sister) married Young in 1846.

SIX.

How Plural Marriage Worked

"It was whispered . . . the authorities were getting more wives"

Several themes naturally emerge out of a consideration of the thirty-three Nauvoo plural families and their growth to two hundred by the time of the 1846 exodus:

- *Discovery and persuasion.* When and how did the people in Nauvoo become aware of polygamy? Joseph Smith introduced plural marriage to one individual at a time, yet by 1846, over 1,000 people had adopted the practice. It was at first necessary to convince a critical base in order to launch this community of celestial wives.

- *Acceptance and rejection.* Smith applied considerable pressure on both women and men to conform to this new doctrine. He respected, to a greater or lesser degree, a woman's decision not to become a plural wife. The men he invited to accept their "privileges" generally acquiesced, sometimes after a delay.

- *Life in polygamous households.* The first wives often helped to choose subsequent spouses, an important contribution in forming a cohesive family. Family connections between "sister wives" (women married to the same man) were important, as were kinship relationships between biological sisters and mother-daughter wives. The arrangement of domestic authority to allocate work and other day-to-day affairs became important considerations. Plural families felt close to one another, but also expressed jealousy and tension.

- *Secrecy and security.* Some plural wives were sent to board with other families. Some of Smith's wives were housed by his bodyguards. Family networks cooperated to protect the secret of their lives.

The social climate in Nauvoo during Joseph Smith's years and after his death is relevant in tracing polygamous families. Extant portions of the historical record derive mostly from narratives written down in the late 1860s by people who confided in the deceased prophet's nephew, Joseph F. Smith, and through often involuntary depositions in the 1892 Temple Lot Case. Efforts to suppress the story of Nauvoo until the 1852 announcement restricted the breadth and depth of the records that were kept, as did the 1890 rescission of the practice. Thereafter, the image of Mormonism was modified through under-representation and denial, which extended into the twenty-first century as the church struggled with its efforts to phase out a practice the prophet had mandated as essential to salvation. Polygamy was no longer a source of religious or community pride, but an embarrassment. The effects of this suppression of evidence and LDS-sponsored historical revisionism will be the focus of chapter 7. Chapter 8 will explore the historiography of reconstructing forgotten Nauvoo events in the face of the redacted official accounts.

Over the five years of Nauvoo polygamy, many people kept first-person records which corroborate their marital relationships in subtle ways. These accounts constitute the core of an eyewitness record of how plural marriage developed in the community. Contemporary diaries and letters indicate who was where at the time and their related preoccupations. Occasional coded references to liaisons and marriages amplify official sealing records from the Nauvoo temple to confirm the veracity of the later apologetics.

Assistant LDS Church Historian Andrew Jenson invited Mary Elizabeth Lightner to join Smith's other plural wives in 1887 in composing a personal account for Jenson's periodical, the *Historical Record.* Plural wife and suffragist Emmeline B. Wells encouraged Lightner, explaining that "Br. Jensen … wants to get interesting biographical sketches and incidents of all those who were sealed to the prophet Joseph Smith." She referred to the other wives as "Aunt Eliza," "Aunt Presendia," and "Aunt Zina."[1] In a follow-up letter, Wells reminded Lightner to include vital statistics, especially ("positively") regarding her "marriage ceremony to Joseph, on what day, and by whom performed, and who were the witnesses if any." Taking charge, Wells added that "perhaps you had better direct it to me though it will all be submitted to someone in authority before being published." She ended with love from Eliza Snow, Helen Mar Kimball, and Lucy Walker Kimball and with this question: "Do you know the particulars about Sister Marinda Hyde's being sealed to Joseph & on what day or in what year, or who officiated in the ceremony?"[2] Wells may have thought the proximity of their marriages to the ceremony involving Marinda, apparently about three months after Mary Elizabeth, would have meant that she would know about it. Such a matter-of-fact exchange illuminates the transition from utmost secrecy to a time of open discussion, when events had become so commonplace that these plural ceremonies were treated as mundane genealogical information.

Discovery and Persuasion

Although a few close friends were aware of Joseph Smith's ideas about plural marriage in the 1830s, most only learned the rationale and its defense by 1846, when a plethora of new and resolemnized wedding ceremonies were celebrated in the closing weeks of the long awaited Nauvoo temple, just prior to their departure for the West. However, Smith's own family, his parents and children, somehow remained unexposed to polygamy as a doctrine. Smith neglected to include his parents in these rites, although his mother was inducted into the anointed

1. Emmeline B. Wells to Mary Elizabeth Rollins Lightner, Feb. 10, 1887, LDS Archives.

2. Wells to Lightner, Mar. 12, 1889, LDS Archives.

quorum in 1843. He apparently did not want a second mother. Joseph waited until seven months after his father's death to introduce polygamy as a formal institution involving a sealing ceremony.

Early in the five years of practice from spring 1841 to winter 1846, most of Nauvoo apparently knew nothing of this. Joseph's mother may have referred to polygamy when she wrote after his death that someone had "told a tremendous tale which [William] Law believed."[3] It would be hard to imagine that she was entirely unfamiliar with, for instance, John Bennett's accusations in 1842 or the general substance of the *Nauvoo Expositor*'s exposé in 1844. Lucy died a decade later in 1856, sixteen years after her husband's death (the year her son explained polygamy to Joseph Noble and recruited him to perform the first celestial marriage), and four years after Orson Pratt announced plural marriage as a doctrine in Utah (which was a world away from the immediate Smith family in the Midwest). There were members of the extended Smith family in the leadership of the Utah church, with whom the Midwestern Smiths sometimes communicated. Uncle John Smith had become a polygamist in Nauvoo when he was in his mid-sixties. At the other end of the Smith family arc, John's great-grandson George Albert Smith would be the first monogamist LDS Church president when he ascended to the office a century later, in 1945.

Franklin D. Richards was twenty-two years old and his wife, Jane, twenty-one, when Hyrum Smith divulged the secret of polygamy to him in 1844. Frank and Jane had been married less than two years. She later said she was under the impression that few in the church knew anything about polygamy at the time, also that she and her husband lacked a full understanding of it themselves until the winter of 1845-46 when most church members were informed of it. That was also

---

3. Robert P. Cooper, "Martha Jane Knowlton Coray and the History of Joseph Smith by His Mother," 1965, an eighteen-page typescript, photocopy in possession of Lavina Fielding Anderson; Lavina Fielding Anderson, ed., *Lucy's Book: A Critical Edition of Lucy Mack Smith's Family Memoir* (Salt Lake City: Signature Books, 2001), 12, 31-34, 125, concludes that Lucy "omits" mention of the practice of polygamy because she "knew women who were her son's plural wives and names nine of them or their relatives in her history."

when Frank crossed the threshold from belief to action and took the first of eleven plural wives.[4]

From a privilege to a requirement

In 1842, as the reality shifted from one man with unspoken numbers of wives to a community of polygamists, the practice evolved from a privilege to a required doctrine. Initially, the practice challenged the traditional beliefs of church members about marriage and family. The prophet and his brother Hyrum at first found it difficult to convince men to follow their lead. Even Hyrum for a while dragged his feet, opposing and denying the practice before taking four wives in quick succession in 1843. Like Hyrum, others entered into these covenants but struggled to rationalize the new sexual morality and what they considered an imposition on their own religious sensibilities. But as Joseph applied intense pressure to act, and they risked being marginalized or even banished from the community as heretics, those chosen to accept their celestial privileges eventually consented.

Some people discovered the state of marital confusion in Nauvoo simply because they were Latter-day Saints and lived there. Sarah Leavitt had been a Freewill Baptist who accepted the possibility of universal salvation before she converted to the LDS Church. She had never spoken directly to Joseph Smith herself but said she "had seen him and heard him preach" and felt that he was "a prophet of God." She wrote:

> It was whispered in my ear by a friend that the authorities were getting more wives than one. I have thought for many years that the connections between a man and wife were as sacred as the heavens and ought to be treated as such, and I thought that the Anointed of the Lord would not get more wives unless they were commanded to do so. But still I wanted a knowledge of the truth for myself. I asked my husband if he did not think we could get a revelation for ourselves on that subject. He said he did not know. … [That evening] my mind was carried away from the

4. "Reminiscences of Mrs. F[ranklin] D. Richards [Jane Snyder Richards]," San Francisco, 1880, Bancroft Library, University of California, Berkeley; Carol Cornwall Madsen, *In Their Own Words: Women and the Story of Nauvoo* (Salt Lake City: Deseret Book, 1994), 176.

> earth and I had a view of the order of the celestial kingdom. ... I have seen so much wrong connected with this ordinance that had I not had it revealed to me from Him that cannot lie[,] I should have ... doubted the truth of it, but there has never a doubt crossed my mind concerning the truth of it since the Lord made it known to me by a heavenly vision.[5]

Prevalence presaged discovery

Orange Wight, son of Lyman Wight, said he learned about polygamy from his neighbors and members of his ward. As described in chapter 3, the young man faced a dilemma when he inadvertently sought out the company of Flora Ann Woodworth, only to learn that she had been married to Joseph Smith. Wight elaborated:

> At first the Doctrine was taught in private. The first I knew about it was in John Hig[be]e[']s family[.] He lived close to us and being well acquainted with him and family I discoverd he had two wives. The next I noticed [was] when in company with the young folks the girls were calling one another spirituals [spiritual wives]. ... Now altho only in my 20th year ... I concluded to look about and try to pick up one or more of the young Ladies before they were all gone, so I commenced keeping company with Flora Woodworth, Daughter of Lucian Woodworth.

After being informed by Flora's mother that her daughter was taken, Orange decided to look for another companion.

> I was no[w] called on a mishion to go up the river 5 or 6 hundred miles to make lumber for the Nauvoo house and Temple. ... I knew of a Girl that I thought I could induce to go. She was over in Ioway across the river. I went over in a skiff. Found the Girl and she agreed to go at once, she was a Daughter of Gideon Carter that was killed in the crooked river battle in Missoury[.] She had neither Father nor Mother. So I thot maby I had the right one this time.
>
> Then we all borded a steamboat and started for Black river Wisconsin. Long before we reach our destination, I got acquainted with the Hadfield fam[i]ly. There were two young Girls. I had them away where I thought I could induce them to take up with me. Now it remaines to see how I succeeded. I at once commenced keeping company with Miss Sa-

5. "Autobiography of Sarah S. Leavitt, from Her History," ed. Juanita Leavitt Pulsipher, June 1919, 23, Utah State Historical Society Library, Salt Lake City.

rah Hadfield and at the same time paid close attention to Miss Matilda Carter.

Now it would be uninteresting to you to [have] related [to you] all the ups and downs I had in my courtship, so I will mearly say I succeeded in marrying both of them. The sister [of] Miss Matilda Carter I maried some years afterward.

In all this time I did not hear [P]ress. Brigham Young['s] name mentioned in connection of Plurel marrage. The Doctrine was taught me by other Apostels Bishops and members of the church. Bishop George Miller, [W]m Claton and David Claton, Bishop Isac Higbee, John Higbee, and others, also by Joseph Smith the Prophet by prec[e]dent and Revelation.[6]

After confirming the doctrine from people he knew, Wight went looking and found wives for himself "before they were all gone."

Family encouragement

One of Heber Kimball's wives, Mary Ellen Able Kimball, believed she was among the first to know about polygamy when she was confided in sometime in 1842:

In the course of conversation br. George [A. Smith] says a [female] friend of his at Cincinnati had apostacized because she thought some of the people had more wives than one. How foolish I replied. There is nothing in the book of Mormon or Doctrine and Covenants to uphold such a doctrine. He smiled and said nothing. I was surprised at this. And after arriving at Nauvoo [I] told sis. Clawson of it. Well she said I think there is something in it. I thought not because I knew ... this people were slandered in a most reediculous manner ... but replied I[,] why do you think so. Well she asked, what did the Lord say to David? ... Thinking it would be a day of barbarism in earnest [if polygamy were practiced,] I knew of none except Arabs or Turks who practiced such a life ... [and] learned that br Hyrum Smith saw this subject in the same light as I did until he had a revelation on the subject. Finally I fe[l]l in company with br. Hyrum[,] who in a few words made the subject plainer to my understanding. Yet I thought others could live it much better than I could. ... I remember saying I do not believe there is a man in this church who would give his daughter in plural marriage. I firmly believed this, but in a few weeks I learned that El[der] H[eber] C. Kimball gave his daughter

6. Orange Lysander Wight, untitled reminiscence, 1903, LDS Archives.

> and she was an only daughter too. ... After learning this lesson I fell to look upon plural marriage as differently as day is from night. ... I was sealed to Br. H. C. Kimball at the house of Br. Erastus Snow ... in the fall of 1844. ... I do remember those who knelt at the altar at the same time; and [Heber's first wife,] sister Vilate Kimball[,] placed each of our hands in that of her husband's.[7]

Plural marriage had a strong effect on children when they learned that their father would marry—or had already married—other women. Parents were understandably slow to inform their children about these changes in their father's intimacies. Thirteen-year-old Helen Mar Kimball was not aware her father had married Sarah Noon, even after Sarah gave birth to a child: "I had no knowledge then of the plural order, and therefore remained ignorant of our relationship to each other until after his [the child's] death, as he only lived a few months. It's true I had noticed the great interest taken by my parents in behalf of Sister Noon, but ... I thought nothing strange of this."[8] When Heber explained his compound marriage to her in the summer of 1843, prior to her own marriage to Joseph Smith—she was fourteen by then—various "fears and temptations ... flashed through my mind," Helen wrote. She continued: "The next day the Prophet called at our house, and I sat with my father and mother and heard him teach the principle and explain it more fully, and I believed it."[9]

Artemisia Beaman was Erastus Snow's first wife and would bear him eleven children. In April 1844, Erastus married Minerva White. Artemisia later expressed her endorsement of this step her husband took:

> Sisters, I am a sincere believer in plural marriage. In 1844 my husband first asked my consent to take to himself other wives. I freely gave it, believing such an order of marriage to be a pure and holy principle, revealed from the heavens to our beloved Prophet, Seer, and Revelator. Knowing it to be a principle practiced anciently by those, who now sit at the right hand of our Father in Heaven, and knowing also my husband to

7. Mary Ellen Able Kimball, "Sketch of Pioneer History," 1895, LDS Archives.

8. Helen Mar Whitney, "Scenes and Incidents in Nauvoo," *Woman's Exponent* 11 (July 15, 1882): 26.

9. Ibid., Aug. 1, 1882, 39.

> be a virtuous man, and entering into that order out of pure motives in obedience to the will and commandments of Heaven, I say I freely gave my consent. I have lived in the order of Celestial marriage thirty-five years. I have no wise—I have no desire—to have it changed or abolished.[10]

From the perspective of the woman who became the proverbial third wheel in the family, Minerva White found it more difficult to be the plural wife than Artemisia did to accept her into the marriage. Snow's biographer found it difficult to acknowledge the next two wives in the family, the sisters Achsah and Louisa Wing, and opted not to mention them, skipping over to the next woman, Elizabeth Rebecca Ashby, and calling her the third wife. Despite a New England Puritan heritage, Elizabeth married Snow at the age of sixteen on December 19, 1847.[11]

Amasa Lyman moved to Nauvoo in 1841 and worked for a while in Theodore Turley's gun repair shop, then served missions in Illinois, Indiana, New York, Tennessee, and Wisconsin. He was preparing to go to Boston in the spring of 1844 when Joseph Smith spoke with him about plural marriage. As Lyman reported it, "a few days after the [April] conference, I had an interview with the Prophet, in which he taught me some principles on celestial marriage. On the day of my parting with him, he said as he warmly grasped my hand for the last time, 'Brother Amasa, go and practice on the principles I have taught you, and God bless you.'"[12]

Lyman's biographer reported that "meetings with the Prophet" were "always occasions of delight and always too infrequent," paraphrasing the subject of the biography. Lyman "stood nearer than any other man to Joseph" Smith and was "eligible to all the inner confidences." He was also the only counselor in the First Presidency to remain faithful to Smith after William Law and Sidney Rigdon became disaffected. Lyman understood that the "plurality of wives" was

10. Andrew Karl Larson, *Erastus Snow: The Life of a Missionary and Pioneer for the Early Mormon Church* (Salt Lake City: University of Utah Press, 1971), 747.

11. Ibid., 87, 745-51.

12. Andrew Jenson, "The Twelve Apostles: Amasa M. Lyman," *Historical Record* 6 (Jan. 1887): 130-31.

a matter that "as yet was to be kept carefully from the ears of the world." In Lyman's last conversation with the prophet, Smith used "impressive words" to emphasize "the import and obligation of this ancient law," saying that "to obey that law" was "one of the essentials to salvation."

Joseph's ultimatums

At first, Lyman found polygamy to be "strange, startling, astonishing" and "rather too much to grasp in a moment." He also perceived a "tone" of "power and authority" in Smith's voice. More and more often, Joseph would threaten colleagues with eternal damnation if they did not accept the promised rewards of plural marriage. If Lyman rejected this principle, Joseph told him, "he would be damned." Lyman anticipated "difficulty and danger, the shame, disgrace and loss of friends it might involve" and the possible "hopeless tangles of dissatisfaction, discouragement, separation, bitter estrangement, and irreparable heart-break" should he falter on this point. When he returned from the East, he dutifully married eight women and by old age would father thirty-seven children.[13]

Sometimes Joseph phrased the matter in terms of being free to go beyond the normal "bounds." Brigham Young said, "The spiritual wife doctrine came upon me while abroad, in such a manner that I never forget." He said that when he returned home,

> Joseph said to me—"I command you to go and get another wife." I felt as if the grave was better for me than anything, but I was filled with the Holy Ghost [and] … could jump up and holler. My blood was as clear as a West India rum, and my flesh was clear. I said to Joseph, "Suppose I should apostacize, after taking another wife, would not my family be worse off?" Joseph answered—"There are certain bounds set to men, and if a man is faithful and pure to these bounds, God will take him out of the world; if he sees him falter, he will take him to himself. You are past these bounds, Brigham, and you have this consolation." But I never had any fears of not being saved. Then I said to Joseph, I was ready to go ahead.

13. Albert R. Lyman, *Amasa Mason Lyman: Trailblazer and Pioneer from the Atlantic to the Pacific* (Delta, Utah: Melvin A. Lyman, 1957), 114-15.

The next statement from Young was a telling concession that the normal rules governing social interaction had not applied to Smith as he had set about instigating polygamy. "He passed certain bounds," Young explained, "before certain revelations were given."[14]

In an address in 1883 to the Mormon settlements around Bear Lake, Idaho, future church president John Taylor, who was then a senior apostle, described the ultimatum that had accompanied the command to practice polygamy:

> Joseph Smith told the Twelve that if this law was not practiced, if they would not enter into this covenant, then the Kingdom of God could not go one step further. Now, we did not feel like preventing the Kingdom of God from going forward. We professed to be the Apostles of the Lord, and did not feel like putting ourselves in a position to retard the progress of the Kingdom of God. The revelation ... says that "All those who have this law revealed unto them must obey the same." ... It was the Prophet of God who revealed that to us in Nauvoo, and I bear witness of this solemn fact before God, that He did reveal this sacred principle to me and others of the Twelve, and in this revelation it was stated that it is the will and law of God that "all those who have this law revealed unto them must obey the same."

Taylor said he "had always entertained strict ideas of virtue, and I felt as a married man that ... [polygamy was] an appalling thing to do. The idea of my going and asking a young lady to be married to me, when I had already a wife! ... I have always looked upon such a thing as infamous, and upon such a man as a villain." His reaction was understandable: "We [the Twelve] seemed to put off, as far as we could, what might be termed the evil day." But for Taylor, the strength of Smith's persuasive argument eventually prevailed: "Some time after these things were made known to us, I was riding out of Nauvoo on horseback, and met Joseph Smith coming in, he, too, being on horseback ... I bowed to Brother Joseph, and having done the same to me, he said; 'Stop;' and he looked at me very intently. 'Look here,' said he, 'those things that have been spoken of must be fulfilled, and

14. Brigham Young Manuscript History, Feb. 16, 1849, LDS Archives; William S. Harwell, ed., *Manuscript History of Brigham Young, 1847-1850* (Salt Lake City: Collier's Publishing Co., 1997), 158.

if they are not entered into right away, the keys will be [re]turned.'" Taylor replied: "Brother Joseph, I will try and carry these things out."[15] Taylor's biographer noted that within two years the apostle had married Jane B. Ballantyne, Elizabeth Kaighan, and Mary Ann Oakley and that in Utah, Taylor married Harriet Whitaker, Sophia Whitaker, and Margaret Young.[16] In fact, he would marry another eleven women as well.

Elizabeth Ann and Newel K. Whitney

Elizabeth Ann Whitney was close to Emma Smith as her counselor in the Relief Society presidency. Together they expressed public opposition to the "rumors of plural marriage" even as Elizabeth was arranging conjugal visits between her daughter, Sarah Ann, and Emma's husband in 1842, as documented in chapter 2. In her reminiscences, Elizabeth described how Joseph Smith invited her husband, a trusted Mason, to accept the revelation.

> It was during the time we lived at the Brick Store that Joseph received the revelation pertaining to Celestial Marriage ... He had been strictly charged by the angel who committed these precious things into his keeping that he should only reveal them to such persons as were pure, full of integrity to the truth, and worthy to be entrusted with divine messages; that to spread them abroad would only be like casting pearls before swine, and that the most profound secrecy must be maintained, until the Lord saw fit to make it known publicly through His servants. Joseph had the most explicit confidence in my husband's uprightness and integrity of character; he knew him capable of keeping a secret, and was not afraid to confide in him, as he had been a Free Mason for many years. He therefore confided to him, and a few others, the principles set forth in that revelation, and also gave him the privilege to read it and to make a copy of it, knowing it would be perfectly safe with him. It was this veritable copy, which was preserved, in the providence of God, that has since been published to the world; for Emma (Joseph's wife) afterwards becoming indignant, burned the original, thinking she had destroyed the only written copy upon the subject in existence.

---

15. *Journal of Discourses,* 26 vols. (London: Latter-day Saint's Book Depot, 1854-86), 24:230-31.

16. B. H. Roberts, *The Life of John Taylor* (Salt Lake City: Bookcraft, 1963), 101.

While Elizabeth and Emma were combating rumors of polygamy, Elizabeth's husband, Newel, was guarding a copy of the revelation justifying the doctrine.[17] Elizabeth said, "Our faith [was] made so perfect that we were willing to give our eldest daughter, then only seventeen years of age, to Joseph, in the holy order of plural marriage." She commented that their daughter "had been raised in the strictest manner as regarded propriety, virtue and chastity; she was as pure in thought, in feeling and in impulse as it was possible for a young girl to be, yet, laying aside all our traditions and former notions in regard to marriage, we gave her with our mutual consent." In fact, Elizabeth was proud of the fact that her daughter would be "the first woman ever given in plural marriage" with the consent of her parents. The only reason for problems, in Elizabeth's view, was because some of the early practitioners failed to keep the practice confidential: "Of course, these things had to be kept an inviolate secret; and as some were false to their vows and pledges, persecution arose, and caused grievous sorrow to those who had obeyed, in all purity and sincerity, the requirements of the celestial order of marriage."

Elizabeth acknowledged the difficulty with which some weaker individuals received the new marriage practice: "They themselves did not comprehend what the ultimate course of action would be, but were waiting further developments from heaven … It was not strange that many could not receive it; others doubted, and only a few remained firm and immovable." She and her husband clearly considered themselves stalwarts, and yet Newel himself was reticent to answer the call to espouse another woman: "Although my husband believed and was firm in teaching this Celestial order of Marriage, he was slow in practice. Joseph repeatedly told him to take a wife, or wives, but he wished to be so extremely cautious … that in Joseph's day he never took a wife. When he did so, he did it to fulfill a duty to the principles of divine revelation as he understood his duty." When

---

17. William Clayton, Affidavit, Feb. 16, 1874, in "Affidavits [on Celestial Marriage], 1869-1915," a collection consisting of six folders compiled by Joseph F. Smith, LDS Archives. George D. Smith, ed., *An Intimate Chronicle: The Journals of William Clayton* (Salt Lake City: Signature Books and Smith Research Associates, 1991), 557-59.

Newel married another woman, he found it was not as bad in practice as it had seemed in theory; he warmed up to the idea and soon had "several" wives to his credit. "With one or two exceptions," Elizabeth observed, "they came into the same house with me, and my children; therefore, I believe I am safe in saying that I am intimately acquainted with the practical part of polygamy."[18]

Delay among Nauvoo leaders

In his voluminous journals, Wilford Woodruff wrote of the difficulty in persuading Latter-day Saints to take up the cause in 1844. He recorded Joseph's words before a large assembly of Saints at the site of the future temple: "The Saints will be divided & broken up & scattered before we get our salvation secure …. [A]ny person who is exhalted to the highest mansion has to abide a celestial law & the whole law, to[o]. But there has been a great difficulty in getting anything into the heads of this generation." Joseph wondered "how many will be able to abide a Celestial law."[19]

Although high in the LDS hierarchy and eventually serving as church president, Woodruff was among those who did not take additional wives in Joseph Smith's lifetime. Perhaps contributing to his initial hesitancy was his extensive involvement away from home in missionary activities. When the rest of the Saints were beginning their haphazard winter trek across Iowa in February 1846, Woodruff was returning from a mission to England and then remained in Nauvoo for a time, marrying Mary Ann Jackson in the temple there on April 15, 1846, then Mary Barton on August 2. Eventually he acquired nine plural wives and fathered thirty-five children. In his diaries, he obsessively recorded his mileage on his various missions, giving a total of 61,692 miles he had traveled across North America and Europe by 1846 during which time he had planted 51 churches, wrote 1,040 let-

18. Madsen, *In Their Own Words*, 200-03, citing Elizabeth Ann Whitney's reminiscence, "A Leaf from an Autobiography," *Woman's Exponent* 7 (Dec. 15, 1878): 105.

19. Scott G. Kenney, ed., *Wilford Woodruff's Journal, 1833-1898*, 9 vols. (Midvale, Utah: Signature Books, 1983-85), 2:341-43; see also Joseph Smith et al., *History of the Church of Jesus Christ of Latter-day Saints*, ed. B. H. Roberts, 2nd ed. rev., 7 vols. (Salt Lake City: Deseret Book, 1963), 6:183-85.

ters, and confirmed 813 new members into the church, according to his meticulous calculations.[20]

Persuasion by revelation

On August 12, 1843, as Hyrum Smith read his brother's month-old dictated revelation to a dozen or more individuals at a Nauvoo Stake High Council meeting, reactions were mixed. Reports of the event contain references to dissent in the leadership for the first time since Oliver Cowdery's private objection in 1838 to the prophet's conduct with Fanny Alger or the year-ago protest of President John Bennett when he defected over what he called "gross sexual improprieties, ethical degradation, financial misbehavior, theft, and murder."[21] Four supporters of plural marriage, James Allred, David Fullmer, Thomas Grover, and Aaron Johnson, as well as a critic, Leonard Soby, reported on the meeting in letters and affidavits.

Fullmer recalled in an affidavit that "Dunbar Wilson made enquiry in relation to the subject of plurality of wives as there were rumors afloat respecting it, and he was 'satisfied there was something in those rumors, and he wanted to know what it was.'" In response, Hyrum went to obtain "a copy of the revelation on celestial marriage given to Joseph Smith July 12, 1843, and read the same to the High Council." Fullmer recalled that besides himself, Smith, and Wilson, there were at least twelve others at the meeting: James Allred, Samuel Bent, Austin A. Cowles, Thomas Grover, George W. Harris, William Huntington, Levi Jackman, Aaron Johnson, William Marks, Phinias Richards, Leonard Soby, and Dunbar Wilson. He singled out Cowles, Marks, and Soby as the ones who were most disturbed by this perceived infraction of the ten commandments. The three detractors, Fullmer said, "were the only persons present who did not receive the Revelation and Testimony of Hyrum Smith."[22] Fullmer verified that

20. Thomas G. Alexander, *Things in Heaven and Earth: The Life and Times of Wilford Woodruff, a Mormon Prophet* (Salt Lake City: Signature Books, 1991), 124-25; Kenney, *Wilford Woodruff's Journal*, 3:111-12.

21. John C. Bennett, *The History of the Saints: Or an Exposé of Joe Smith and Mormonism* (1842; Urbana: University of Illinois Press, 2000), vii. Bennett's charges are summarized in Andrew F. Smith's introduction to the 2000 edition.

22. David Fullmer, Affidavit, June 15, 1869, Salt Lake County, in "40 Affidavits on

the revelation published in the *Deseret News* September 14, 1852, was an accurate copy.[23]

Thomas Grover affirmed Fullmer's memory and "further sayeth that Hyrum Smith reasoned upon said Revelation for about an hour, clearly explaining the same, and enjoined it upon said [High] Council, to receive and acknowledge the same, or they would be damned." Grover confirmed that Cowles, Marks, and Soby "refused" to do so, that they began at that moment to "dwindle" in faith until eventually they made a clean break with the church.[24]

James Allred recalled that the meeting was "held in Hyrum Smith's Brick office." He said Hyrum "read the revelation on celestial marriage to said High Council, and enjoined it upon them to manifest their willingness to receive or reject the same, at the same time bearing his testimony of its truth." Cowles, Marks, and Soby had "voted against the Revelation and the Testimony of Hyrum."[25]

Leonard Soby emphasized the significance of the meeting in showing that the revelation on marriage "did not originate with Brigham Young" after Smith's death, "as some persons had falsely stated, but was received by the Prophet Joseph Smith."[26] Soby was living near the Delaware River north of Philadelphia in Beverly, New Jersey, when he recorded his reminiscence. He believed himself to be "about the only person now [1886] living who was present at the High Council meeting at which the revelation on celestial marriage was read." He reiterated that he "was there and did hear the revelation read." His motivation for saying so was that Zenos Gurley, a follower of Joseph Smith III, had questioned whether there had been a plural marriage revelation at all.[27]

Celestial Marriage," 1869.

23. David Fullmer et al., Affidavit, Oct. 10, 1869, Salt Lake City, in "[Affidavits] Book No. 2," 1869-1870.

24. Thomas Grover, Affidavit, July 6, 1869, Salt Lake City, in "40 Affidavits on Celestial Marriage," 1869.

25. James Allred, Affidavit, Oct. 2, 1869, Utah County, in "40 Affidavits on Celestial Marriage," 1869.

26. Leonard Soby, Affidavit, Mar. 23, 1886, Salt Lake City, in "Affidavits [on Celestial Marriage], 1869-1915."

27. Jenson, "Plural Marriage," 227-28, citing the *Ogden Herald,* Jan. 1886.

Hyrum explained the revelation to some other prominent citizens before and after the High Council meeting. Howard Coray said it was

> on the 22nd day of July, A.D., 1843, [when] Hyrum Smith, the martyred patriarch, came in a carriage to my house in Nauvoo; he invited me and my wife to take a ride with him [in his carriage] … in the direction of Carthage [Illinois]. Having gone a short distance, he observed to us that his brother Joseph Smith the Prophet, had received a revelation on marriage, that was not for the public yet, which he would rehearse to us, as he had taken pains to commit it to memory.[28]

Charles Rich was starting on a mission to Michigan in May 1844 when he too was taught "the principle of polygamy or celestial marriage" by Hyrum Smith. Hyrum told Rich that he should consider it "his privilege to take other wives" when he returned from his mission.[29]

Not long afterward, two members of the High Council, Cowles (father of Smith's plural wife, Elvira Cowles) and Soby, withdrew from the church and revealed the content of the revelation to the public. It created a wave of confusion and discontent as these formerly esteemed leaders accused Smith and others of marital infidelity. Citizens in the surrounding area needed little prompting to join their own voices to the chorus of protesters.[30] It was during this period, before and after the Smith brothers' martyrdom, that many first realized that plural marriage was, in fact, a reality among the LDS hierarchy. Sarah Leavitt is a representative example of how church members confronted the issue and struggled with it but soon decided they would continue to support the leadership. Bathsheba W. Smith, the first wife of Apostle George A. Smith, went through these emotional currents until she "firmly" concluded that she should "participate with him [George A.] in all his blessings, glory and honor." She compared herself to "Sarah of old" because she "had given to my hus-

---

28. Howard Coray, Affidavit, June 12, 1882, Salt Lake County, in "Affidavits [on Celestial Marriage], 1869-1915."

29. Charles C. Rich, Affidavit, July 12, 1869, Salt Lake County, in "40 Affidavits on Celestial Marriage," 1869.

30. Juanita Brooks, *John Doyle Lee: Zealot, Pioneer Builder, Scapegoat* (Salt Lake City: Howe Brothers, 1984), 56-57.

band five wives," whom she defended as "good, virtuous, honorable young women."[31]

Teaching others

In 1843 Smith initiated new participants in polygamy with caution, usually in a secluded area, carefully chosen, and often in a natural setting. Over the next year these extra marriages became more visible as Joseph would even call attention to his own wives. By 1844, Smith had become even more nonchalant in introducing the topic to loyal adherents. Amos Fielding affirmed by affidavit that "in December A.D. 1843, on his arrival at Nauvoo from a mission to England, he was informed that Joseph Smith had obtained a Revelation on Celestial Marriage, and on or about the 9th of March 1844, while in conversation with the Prophet at the Mansion, a young lady passed through the room where they were sitting, when President Smith remarked 'that is one of my wives.'"[32]

In another affidavit, John Benbow affirmed that in summer 1843 at his home just outside of Nauvoo, Joseph came to speak to him and his wife together and brought Hyrum with him. After telling John and Jane about the "doctrine of Celestial Marriage or plurality of wives," Joseph arranged to use the Benbow home for intimate visits with one of his wives, Hannah Ells, who lived with the Benbows.[33]

Acquiescence among bodyguards

Four of Smith's approximately forty bodyguards had their own unique experiences with these strange innovations of their client. Aware at an early date of the numerous intimacies of the lifestyle, they had a model on which to structure their own families. John D. Lee, one of the most famous of the bodyguards, exhibited enough self-awareness to know it was not until he had acquired "a large home" and sufficient "standing in the church" that he would be considered

31. Ibid., 64-65.

32. Amos Fielding, Affidavit, Salt Lake County, in "40 Affidavits on Celestial Marriage," 1869.

33. John Benbow, Affidavit, Aug. 28, 1869, County of Salt Lake, in "40 Affidavits on Celestial Marriage," 1869; also quoted in Jenson, "Plural Marriage," 222-23.

"one of the elect who might practice celestial marriage."[34] His narrative is important for its discussion of an alternative means to link leading families by what they called "adoption," meaning that an adult was "adopted" into the family of another adult for a family pedigree that they thought replicated the interconnectedness that the elite would enjoy in heaven. Lee wrote on February 5, 1845, "Nancy Bean was adopted into my family." On April 19, "Louisa Free was also admitted —taking upon her my name. On the same day Caroline Williams was registered on my list—and on the 3rd day of May 1845 Abigail Woolsey, and Rachel her daughter was likewise acknowledged."[35]

In Lee's deathbed "confessions," he explained that he had pursued plural marriage as aggressively as adoption, with the intent of adding to his celestial possessions:

> My second wife, Nancy Bean, was the daughter of a wealthy farmer who lived near Quincy, Illinois. She saw me on a mission and heard me preach at her father's house. She came to Nauvoo and stayed at my house three months, and grew in favor and was sealed to me in the Winter of 1845. My third and fourth wives were sealed to me soon afterward in my own house ... Amasa Lyman officiated at the ceremony. At the same time Sarah C. Williams, the girl that I had baptized in Tennessee, when but a child ... stood up and claimed a place in my family ... In the Spring of 1845 Rachel Andora was sealed to me ... She was a sister to my first wife. Her mother, Abigail Sheffer, was sealed to me for an eternal state.[36]

With his relatively large number of wives, nineteen in all, Lee broadcast his standing to the community.[37] Like marrying into royalty, Lee's wives significantly came from the most prominent families: two Vances, three Williamses, four Woolseys, and two Youngs among them. That was the shape of Lee's kingdom which he projected into the next world, where he believed family standing would count for something.

Another bodyguard, Hosea Stout, received encouragement di-

---

34. Brooks, *John Doyle Lee,* 65.

35. Ibid., 65-66.

36. John Doyle Lee, *Mormonism Unveiled: Or the Life and Confessions of the Late Mormon Bishop, John D. Lee, Written by Himself* (St. Louis: Bryan, Brand & Co., 1877), 166-67.

37. Brooks, *John Doyle Lee,* 378-84.

rectly from Joseph Smith to take a plural wife, which Stout did on April 20, 1845, choosing Lucretia Fisher. A descendant, Wayne Stout, calculated that Lucretia was born May 23, 1830, meaning "she was only 15 [14] years old at that time," twenty years younger than Hosea Stout. The descendant found it astonishing that Stout could keep peace in his family with his first wife, the twenty-three-year-old Louisa Taylor, while marrying a teenager. And the marrying went on:

> Forty days later (June [May] 30) he accomplished a feat more incredible than the first. He married a third wife. This time it was nineteen-year-old Marinda Bennett, ... born August 26, 1826, at Bedford, Tennessee. It is indeed very remarkable that he could induce this charming lady in the very prime of life to be the third wife to a man 16 years her senior! The case illustrates the great influence which the teachings of Joseph Smith have on the people at that time.[38]

A third bodyguard, the noted gunslinger Orrin Porter Rockwell,[39] gave literal meaning to "taking a wife," according to the *Warsaw Signal* of December 10, 1845. The newspaper editorialized:

> O. P. ROCKWELL — This delectable specimen of humanity, who was once the peculiar pet of Joe Smith and has since been regarded as the main champion of Zion in the holy city, ... has taken to himself a wife—not his own wife, for be it remember[ed] that he cast off the woman that law regarded as his wife long since; but he has appropriated to himself the wife of Amos Davis [a Nauvoo legion captain]. ... So fashionable is it for the Heads of the church to appropriate the wives of other men to their own purposes, that it is regarded as no crime for one man to steal the companion of his neighbor and live with her in open unconcealed adultery. What a beautiful moral code is Mormonism![40]

A fourth bodyguard, George A. Smith, had experiences with plural marriage that were documented by biographer Merlo Pusey. "In the spring of 1841, or earlier," Pusey narrated, Joseph Smith "began

38. Wayne Stout, *Hosea Stout: Utah's Pioneer Statesman* (Salt Lake City: By the author, 1953), 48.

39. Journal History of the Church of Jesus Christ of Latter-day Saints, Oct. 9, 1845, LDS Archives; *History of the Church*, 7:481; see also Harold Schindler, *Orrin Porter Rockwell: Man of God, Son of Thunder* (Salt Lake City: University of Utah Press, 1966).

40. *Warsaw [Illinois] Signal*, Dec. 10, 1845.

marrying plural wives in deep secrecy, the facts being known only to the bride, her parents, the officiating church leader, and sometimes his first wife Emma."[41] Some of the hierarchy, including George A., were "deeply shocked." It was George A.'s opinion that if polygamy had been preached in the 1830s, "perhaps we should all have apostatized at once."[42] To focus on the actual practice might have seemed unsavory, whereas presented as a theological concept, celestial marriage seemed to have a "profound appeal."

George A.'s wife, Bathsheba, said the prophet "counseled the sisters not to trouble themselves in consequence of it, that all would be right, and the result would be for their glory and exaltation." She went on to state that she was "proud of my husband" and that their love for each other was not diminished by George's love for these other women; instead, "he would not love them less because he loved me more," she concluded. As compensation, she felt "joy in having a testimony that what I had done was acceptable to my Father in Heaven."[43]

It was probably not insignificant that George A. was the missionary who converted Bathsheba in her small town in what is now West Virginia. She was fifteen years old, and George A. and a companion, Marcellus F. Cowdery (cousin to Oliver), had crossed the Ohio River in mid-August 1837 for a debate. While there, they met her parents, Mark and Susanah Bigler, who farmed a 300-acre plantation. Four years later, in July 1841, Bathsheba married her missionary and agreed to "keep his cabin." She wrote that she and "Mr. Smith believed firmly" in Joseph Smith Jr. as the "prophet of the Most High." She also acknowledged that she "became thoroughly convinced as well as my husband that the doctrine 'plurality of wives' as taught … in our hearing" by Joseph Smith "was a revelation from God." It was because she had "a fixed determination to attain Celestial Glory" that she "felt to embrace [this] very principle." It was "for my husband's exaltation that he should obey the rev[elation] on P[lural] M[arriage] in order to at-

---

41. Merlo J. Pusey, *Builders of the Kingdom: George A. Smith, John Henry Smith, George Albert Smith* (Provo: Brigham Young University Press, 1981), 48.

42. Ibid. "Destroying angel" Bill Hickman had one wife when he guarded Joseph.

43. Bathsheba W. Smith, Autobiography, 13, LDS Archives.

tain kingdoms, thrones, principalities and powers." She "firmly believ[ed]" that she would "participate with him in all his blessings, glory and honor." In pursuit of this conviction, she decided to help him find suitable wives. Bathsheba was still a young woman of twenty-two years at the time. George A. was twenty-seven.[44]

Bathsheba reported that it was after her husband returned from a mission to Boston in the fall of 1843 that they were "sealed under the holy order of Celestial Marriage" which she said was "revealed July 12, 1843." She may well have been unaware of any previous plural marriages. She and her husband considered themselves close to the prophet and were often with him in the room over his red brick store, which is also where the temple endowment ceremony was first introduced. She heard Joseph give his counsel to the women that they should do as they were instructed and it would be "for their glory and exaltation."[45] Some of the plural wives, and some of the celestial husbands, repeated nearly by rote this same reasoning in their personal accounts. Among Joseph Smith's wives, Sarah Cleveland, Marinda Hyde, Mary Lightner, and Sylvia Lyon uttered similar words.[46] "Many—but not all—of the men and especially women entering into Joseph Smith's order of plural marriage," wrote historian Gary James Bergera,

> did so primarily as a show of loyalty, obedience, and sacrifice to Smith, coupled with Smith's assurance that blessings unimaginable awaited them. For Smith, plural marriage represented the pinnacle of his theology of exaltation: the husband as king and priest, surrounded by queens and priestesses eternally procreating spirit children … [for] additional glory, power, and exaltation—the entire process of exaltation cycling forever worlds without end.[47]

Practical expectations

Charles Rich (1809-83), was a rugged Mormon frontiersman, born in Kentucky with some of the adventure of a Daniel Boone. He

44. Ibid. See also Pusey, *Builders of Kingdom*, 24-25.

45. Smith, Autobiography.

46. Linda Newell, "Women's Reaction to Early Mormon Polygamy, 1841-45," LDS Archives.

47. Gary James Bergera, "Identifying the Earliest Mormon Polygamists, 1841-44," *Dialogue: A Journal of Mormon Thought* 38 (Fall 2005): 4.

colonized San Bernardino and then the even more remote area of Bear Lake Valley in Idaho. A Southerner, he was traditional in his personal morals; he found the quest for eternal life to be all-consuming. Before he was taught the new doctrine of marriage, he had believed that monogamy was a necessary part of personal integrity. He understood why women might reject polygamy. But now he was being asked to accept that a man might live in intimacy with several women, without blame. If that were not enough, the prophet was telling him that unless he embraced plural marriage he would incur God's displeasure. It was only Rich's confidence in the prophet, believing him to be God's spokesman, that enabled him to convert his thinking and marry five plural wives. He came to believe that each male priesthood holder could more effectively look after his "kingdom" within the structure of plural marriage. Each man was "a God in embryo," according to the 1840s teachings, with a potential to create worlds of their own and populate them with endless families, so it made sense that plural marriage would facilitate this process. Lest he be tempted by the flesh, Rich let his legal wife, Sarah Pea, decide whom they would invite into their family circle and how often. The Riches were convinced that love, or the absence of it, did not matter. They lived in plural marriage because it was the "revealed" word of God and was "right," that it would facilitate Charles's progress toward becoming a future god who would rule his own world. Sarah instructed Charles's first four plural wives in the principle, and upon receiving the consent of the young women's parents, church authorities performed the four ceremonies.[48]

Rich's youngest plural wife, Harriet Sargent, was only fourteen years old when they married. His biographer indicated that she was "a beautiful young woman, fully matured," and "much sought after, both by married and by single men." A married Mormon man could stay active in courting young women, especially if he was one of the church leaders. When Rich asked her what she thought of plural mar-

48. John Henry Evans, *Charles Coulson Rich: Pioneer Builder of the West* (New York: MacMillan, 1936), 91-96. See also Leonard J. Arrington, *Charles C. Rich: Mormon General and Western Frontiersman* (Provo: Brigham Young University Press, 1974).

riage, she told him she believed it to be "right" or "it would not have been revealed to the Prophet." He asked her if she would be interested in a polygamous marriage with one or another interested "brethren" among the church authorities, which she denied. Later he asked if she would, more specifically, consider becoming his wife. "But you don't love me, Brother Rich, do you?" she asked. He responded frankly, "You don't love me either, do you?" Rich quickly added that he "admired and respected" her, as did his first wife, Sarah. After discussing the matter and assuring her that celestial marriage was a "true principle, necessary to the highest glory in the next world," she accepted his proposal.[49] His experience, even in persuading a fourteen-year-old to be his plural wife, exemplified one of the reasons Mormon polygamy was potentially workable, both in theory and practice: it relied upon the theological underpinning of plural gods and an infinite number of worlds.

Natural tensions between women in a plural marriage were mitigated by bringing the first wife in on the decision to select additional wives. In her autobiography, Sarah Rich wrote that "many may think it very strange that I would consent for my dear husband, whom I loved as I did my own life and lived with him for years, to take more wives; this I could not have done if I had not believed it to be right in the sight of god, and believed it to be the one principle of His Gospel, once again restored to the earth, that those holding the Priesthood of Heaven might, by obeying this Order attain to a higher glory in the eternal world."[50]

Another of Rich's wives, Mary Phelps Rich, wrote that "on January 6, 1845, after considerable deliberation, I embraced the principle of plural marriage. I was married to Charles C. Rich, with the full con-

---

49. Ibid., 96-97. Rich later asserted: "It is just as natural for a girl to marry an old man, as it is to marry a young one, provided both parties have their agency and choice; and the girls would do better in many instances, to marry good and tried men, if they were old, than to marry young, and thoughtless, boys, who would get drunk [at] every opportunity" (John R. Patrick, "The School of the Prophets: Its Development and Influence in Utah Territory," M.A. thesis, Brigham Young University, June 1970, 118).

50. Sarah DeArmon Pea Rich, Autobiography, LDS Archives.

sent of his first wife, I being his third wife. We then lived in the hope of soon moving to the Rocky Mountains, where we would be free to live our religion and be acknowledged as wives."[51] For Mary, a large cohesive family provided the security she needed for the long walk into the unknown to escape persecution. Wife number five, Emeline Grover Rich, underscored that this had little to do with love for many women. Her son asked her if she had ever loved his father, and she answered: "We learned to love him."[52] As with fourteen-year-old Harriet, Emeline, also fourteen, had not considered affection a prerequisite to marry polygamously.

Joseph Lee Robinson said "the little he knew about" plural marriage "had come directly from the prophet" and that after the deaths of Joseph and Hyrum the Lord had granted him a vision of the "remarkable, sacred, and interesting doctrine." He was taught that a large number of intelligent spirits had been "kept back in reserve" in a pre-earth existence to be born in the latter days. A chair maker, Robinson was working in a wood shop when this vision fell upon him and demonstrated that "polygamy is an institution from heaven ... for the purpose of raising up seed unto the Lord."[53] He believed he would be among those who would populate infinite worlds.

Hyrum Smith's first plural wife, Mercy Rachel Fielding, sister of his legal wife, Mary Fielding, said she was persuaded against her initially negative disposition to go ahead and marry her brother-in-law:

> On the 11 of August 1843 I was called by direct revelation from Heaven through Brother Joseph[,] Prophet[,] to enter into a state of Plural Marriage with Hyrum Smith[,] Patriarch. This subject when first communicated to me tried me to the very core of my former traditions and every natural feeling of my Heart rose in opposition to this Principle but I was convinced that it was appointed by him who is too wise to err and too good to be unkind. Soon after Marriage I became an inmate with my sister in the House of Hyrum Smith where I remained until his Death sharing with my sister the care of his numerous family [and where] I had

51. Mary Phelps Rich, "Autobiographical Sketch," cited in Evans, *Charles Coulson Rich,* 110.

52. Evans, *Charles Coulson Rich,* 111.

53. Joseph Lee Robinson, Journal, 10-11, Utah State Historical Society Library.

> [been] from the time I moved to his House acting as scribe Recording Patriarchal Blessings.[54]

Margaret Peirce Whitesides wrote in her journal that she became Brigham Young's nineteenth living wife "on January 22, 1846," formalizing their earlier sealing of January 1845. She reflected: "I have no regrets that I went into that Sacred Order. We did what we thought was right; we were conscientious; we broke no law of the land. Those of us who entered that Order soon will have passed to the great beyond where we will be judged by the Father, who knows our hearts."[55] At age twenty-one, she had made a conscious decision to enter polygamy in preparation for the next world. But in later life, one can detect a hint of doubt in her statement—perhaps regret that she missed the natural excitement of a youthful romance—even though her commitment to the principle of plural marriage was unwavering. She lived to be eighty-three, dying in January 1907.

Lucy Walker explained how she felt about polygamy: "Instead of a feeling of jealousy, it was a source of comfort to us. We were as sisters to each other." She said that by being Joseph Smith's plural wife she had "acted in accordance with the will of God ... not for the gratification of the flesh." To say they had "accepted this principle for any lustful desires" would have been "preposterous" and "utterly impossible." This was "a principle that would benefit the human family," she insisted, one which would "emancipate them from the degradation into which they, through their wicked customs, had fallen." Castigation of the morals of monogamist society is a recurring theme in the stories of polygamists that reflects both the official propaganda and expresses the depth of insult Mormons felt over their portrayal as a people of low moral integrity.

So polygamy was said to be a remedy for social ills, and beyond that, Lucy perceived a personal benefit to it. "A tie had been formed that will bring me into the highest and most glorious destiny," she believed. That is, plural marriage would bring her into the Celestial

---

54. Untitled autobiographical sketch by Mercy Rachel Fielding Smith Thompson, Dec. 20, 1880, LDS Archives.

55. Margaret Peirce Young, Journal, 1903, MS 5716, LDS Archives.

Kingdom.[56] Lucy went on to explain the day-to-day reality of being one of many women married to the same man:

> Since 1845, I have been the wife of President Heber C. Kimball, by whom I have had nine children, five sons and four daughters, who have lived in the same house with other members of his family; have loved them as dearly as my own sisters, until it became necessary, as our children began to grow up around us, to have separate homes. Every mother had her own mode of government, and as children grow in years, it is more pleasant to have them under the immediate dictation of their own mother. I can truthfully state, however, that there is less room for jealousy where wives live under the same roof. They become interested in each others welfare; they love each other's children[;] beside[s], in my experience, I find the children themselves love each other as dearly as the children of one mother.

Even so, living together naturally required more than the usual amount of patience: "It is a grand school. You learn self control, self denial, it brings out the nobler traits of our fallen natures, and teaches us to study and subdue self, while we become acquainted with the peculiar characteristics of each other."[57]

Acceptance and Rejection

In 1880, Ebenezer Robinson wanted to clear the air on what he considered a "subject which is not pleasant to dwell upon[,] but it is not wise for us as individuals or as a people to ignore the truths of the past, but to look the history of the past squarely in the face." To the question of when and where polygamy was introduced, he wrote that "the doctrine of 'spiritual wives' was taught privately in the church in Nauvoo, in 1841." Plural marriage emerged out of spiritual wivery ("This I always considered polygamy"). Hyrum Smith "instructed me in Nov. or Dec. 1843, to make a selection of some young woman," Robinson continued. Hyrum said "he would seal her to me, and I should take her home."[58] Despite this ecclesiastical advice, Robinson

56. Statement of Mrs. L. W. Kimball (typescript), Bancroft Library, University of California; see also microfilm of holograph, LDS Archives and in Lyman Omer Littlefield, *Reminiscences of Latter-day Saints* (Logan, Utah: Utah Journal Co., 1888), 48-49.

57. Ibid., 7, 8.

58. Ebenezer Robinson to Jason W. Briggs, Jan. 28, 1880, LDS Archives.

remained married to one woman. His brother, Joseph Lee Robinson, on the other hand, endorsed the theology and married six wives.

Jane Richards said that when Joseph Smith received the revelation, he "talked of it in confidence with my husband, who mentioned it to me, though I spoke of it to no one." She thought it "a strange thing" and was "uncertain" at first as to "the result" within a family and society generally if people embraced it.[59] It seemed logical enough in theory, but the thought of actually bringing another woman into her marriage was nearly unconscionable. It was not until she saw Joseph Smith in a vision (previously mentioned) that she was satisfied enough to venture into it.

Then the day came when theory turned to reality. She related the circumstances to her biographer, who wrote that "about eight months after her marriage, Elder Richards told her he felt he should like to have another wife."

> It was crushing at first, but she said that … if it was necessary to her salvation that she should let another [wife] share her pleasures, she would do so even if it was necessary for her to do the other thing. He wanted to know what that was and [said that] if she thought she could not be happy in such a relation he would not enter into it. She said if she found they could not live without quarrelling she should leave him.

This must have been sufficient enough of an ultimatum for Franklin to postpone diversifying their marital union for several years to mollify his wife's feelings. Finally he announced that the time had come. "In three or four days," he declared he would bring home a wife. When he mentioned who, "it was a surprise to her that he should select as he did; she knew the young woman very well." But she did her best to make the situation comfortable for the new bride, knowing it would be as difficult for her as it was for Jane. Elizabeth, as it turned out, "was amiable" and "all lived happily together" until the young woman died of tuberculosis on the journey toward Utah.[60]

---

59. "Reminiscences of Mrs. Richards"; Madsen, *In Their Own Words,* 176.

60. Matilda G. Bancroft, "The Inner Facts of Social Life in Utah," an interview with Jane Snyder Richards, San Francisco, 1880, Bancroft Library.

A reason to resist

Having agreed, at twenty-two years old, to share her husband with sixteen-year-old Elizabeth McFate, Jane admitted that she did not know what she would do if children came. She thought she would "feel like wringing the neck of any other child than hers that should call him papa."[61] This undercurrent of resentment may be why Franklin Richards admitted reluctantly that plural marriage was "a bitter pill" but that "the Lord required it, and we had to look for the explanation and reason afterward."[62] After taking one "bitter pill," Frank and Jane decided to wait more than three years before taking another, although the decision to find an added wife was no doubt influenced by the tragedy of Elizabeth's death.

Emancipation

One of the most intriguing episodes in the plural marriage saga was that of Emmeline B. Wells. As a woman's advocate and future associate of Susan B. Anthony in the suffrage movement, Wells seemed an unlikely convert to polygamy. Yet she not only married three times, in two of these nuptials she took her place in line along with several other wives. Emmeline's feelings for the particular husbands involved and her own religious commitments might explain how this proponent of women's rights became persuaded to join these polygamous families.

At the age of fifteen, the daughter of David and Deiadama Woodward, she married sixteen-year-old James Harvey Harris, the son of a presiding Mormon elder near Worcester, Massachusetts. In 1844, only a year into their marriage, the young couple moved to Nauvoo where James quickly became disaffected and left the LDS Church, as did his parents. The Harrises all moved to New Orleans; James died shortly afterward. Emmeline stayed in Nauvoo and taught school to support herself. Among her students were the children of Newel and Elizabeth Ann Whitney. One day the Whitneys drew Emmeline aside to instruct her in plural marriage. Newel's concern was not limited to ped-

61. Ibid.
62. Ibid.

agogy, however; he felt affection for the teenager and was considering her for a wife. On February 24, 1845, the sixteen-year-old Emmeline married fifty-year-old Newel Whitney. Newel had recently wed two other women, and with Emmeline, his total number of wives came to eight. Newel's weddings were ahead of the large wave of plural marriages solemnized prior to the westward migrations from Nauvoo. When the time came to leave in February 1846, Emmeline traveled with the Whitney family. Upon reaching Winter Quarters, Nebraska, she again taught school.

In Salt Lake City, Emmeline gave birth to Isabel and Melvina Whitney. When Newel died in 1850, Emmeline was now twice widowed and still only twenty-two. In desperation, she turned to her husband's close friend, Daniel H. Wells, and indirectly proposed to him by letter. This prominent figure—an attorney, superintendent of public works, and second counselor to Brigham Young—still had a modest number of wives, six in all. Emmeline described herself as "a true friend" and appealed to Wells to "consider the lonely state" she found herself in, saying she hoped to be "united with a being noble as thyself." She asked if he would "return to her a description of his feelings for her."[63] She became his seventh wife in 1852. His first six wives lived in what was known as the "big house" on South Temple Street. Emmeline and her five daughters, three of them by Wells, lived a few blocks away in a smaller home.

Emmeline became active with the national suffrage movement twenty years later in the 1870s. In a curious twist of circumstance, the national group led by Susan Anthony ended up supporting Mormon polygamy. From 1867 on, the U.S. Congress had considered granting women in Utah Territory the vote as a way to empower them to abolish polygamy. It was during these political negotiations that the Utah territorial legislature passed its own suffrage proposal in 1870 and Mormon feminists like Wells surprised Congress by coming out in full support of plural marriage. In response, Congress attempted to

---

63. Carol Cornwall Madsen, "Emmeline B. Wells: Romantic Rebel," in *Supporting Saints: Life Stories of Nineteenth-Century Mormons* (Provo: Religious Studies Center, Brigham Young University, 1985), 309.

disenfranchise Mormon women. This political maneuvering put one faction of the national women's movement on the side of Mormons and the other against them. According to Carol Cornwall Madsen, Wells's theological perspective was that plural marriage would be the means to "exalt woman until she is redeemed from the effects of the Fall, and from that curse pronounced upon her in the beginning." This was, again, the concept of exaltation, whereby men and women would be forever bound together in pursuit of godhood.[64]

In actuality, Emmeline saw plural marriage as a means for personal emancipation. Her attitude was, no doubt, derived from her early experiences as a fifteen-year-old bride to a husband she barely knew. She wanted to be "released from the hands of a cruel guardian who pretended so much respect for me that he did not wish me to associate with my own mother and sister because they were … Mormons."[65] For Emmeline, plural marriage was a vehicle for escaping her husband. She wanted a husband with so many wives, he could not smother her personal avocations; a disinterested husband was, "in truth," the "lover" she sought.[66] In her diary of February 1845, she expressed antipathy for her absent spouse, James Harris: "Here was I brought to this great city by one to whom I was expected to look for protection and left dependent on the mercy and friendship of strangers."[67] This abandonment made the concept of a stable afterlife even more attractive, wherein the "curse" on women due to Eve's disobedience would be removed. Emmeline actively promoted the equality of women in the workplace and in civic and social endeavors—in every situation but the church hierarchy. In doing so, she constituted a strange bedfellow for national feminists.

Nauvoo citizens accepted plural marriage

The primary expressed reasons for practicing polygamy were be-

---

64. Carol Cornwall Madsen, "Emmeline B. Wells: 'Am I Not a Woman and a Sister?'" *BYU Studies* 22 (Spring 1982): 176-77, quoting George Q. Cannon in *Journal of Discourses,* 13:207.

65. Emmeline B. Wells, Diary, Feb. 20, 1845, L. Tom Perry Special Collections, Harold B. Lee Library, Brigham Young University, Provo, Utah.

66. Ibid.

67. Ibid.

lief in the "revealed word" of God and a demonstration of loyalty to Joseph Smith. By this logic, if it had not been "right," the prophet would not have revealed it. Smith exercised remarkable influence over his followers. He assured them that plural marriage was necessary for celestial-afterlife glory and that there was an urgent need to "raise up seed unto the lord" in this life, promising them a world of spiritual splendor. This caught their imagination and drove them to feats of endurance and devotion.

As Lucy Walker described it, she was Joseph Smith's wife according to the "will of God." Plural marriage was a principle that would "emancipate" the human family from "degradation." It enabled participants to school their thoughts. She said she offered herself up as a "sacrifice" for the sake of this brave new world.[68] Furthermore, Joseph told Lucy "the day would come" when she would be known as Mrs. Smith.[69]

Life in Polygamous Households

The leadership of a first wife

Polygamy changed the way families functioned. The lead wife was usually considered chief among the women. She allocated jobs, scheduled affection, and called for votes on whether or not to endorse the husband's desire for a new wife. Among prominent examples, George A. Smith explained, "my wife, under the law of Abraham and Sarah, gave me five wives." He named them: Nancy Clement, Hannah Maria Libby, Sarah Ann Libby, Lucy Smith, and Zilpha Stark.[70] Perhaps spoken with rhetorical exaggeration, yet Bathsheba was at least involved in making accommodations for the new wives and probably witnessed the marriages.

Heber Kimball wrote communal letters to his wives from abroad, according to their groupings in various houses. In 1855 he wrote to

---

68. *Reorganized Church of Jesus Christ of Latter Day Saints v. Church of Christ of Independence, Missouri, et al.* 60 F. 937 (W.D. Mo. 1894), deposition testimony (question 450), electronic copy prepared by Richard D. Ouellette.

69. Ibid., question 466. For the "biological basis of social behavior," see "Sociobiology," *Encyclopedia Britannica 2008,* online at www.britannica.com.

70. Andrew Jenson, "George Albert Smith," *Historical Record* 5 (Dec. 1886): 101.

Ann, Amanda, Lucy, and Sarah Ann with some instructions: "[To] [a]ll my wives[:] [T]each our children… I have no time to teach children. I teach you and you teach them and my head teaches me. This is your Calling and lurn to hear me and Listen to my voice as you would like to have your Children Listen to you."[71]

Accepting new wives

Margaret Thompson Smoot, wife of Abraham O. Smoot, affirmed that she knew plural marriage had come through Joseph Smith by "revelation from God"; that Joseph "had other wives, th[a]n Emma his first wife"; and that "the doctrine" of plural marriage was "true, pure and chaste, and ennobling to man and woman." When her husband married other women, she was "perfectly willing, and gave my fullest and freest consent, believing and receiving it as a part of my religion, from which I have never faltered or swerved, and I bear testimony that my husband and his wives are virtuous, chaste and honorable to their marriage vows, and their children are legitimate, and heirs to the priesthood of the God."[72]

John Fullmer's first wife, Mary Ann, asked their housekeeper, Olive Amanda Smith, if she would be her husband's second wife. Olive "decided she would never find a more noble com[p]anion, and she accepted them both," marrying him on January 21, 1846.[73] John's younger brother, David, married Rhoda Ann Marvin in 1831. Then in January 1846, as Rhoda Ann remembered, she "fulfilled the law of Sarah," a term that occurs frequently in women's narratives in discussing polygamy. Rhoda Ann "gave to my husband … Margaret Philips and Sarah Sophronia [Oyster]banks. I felt happy and greatly blessed in fulfilling the law."[74] Frederick Cox's biographer suggested

71. Heber C. Kimball to wives Ann, Amanda, Lucy, and Sarah Ann Kimball, Dec. 31, 1855, LDS Archives.

72. "A brief sketch of the Life & History of Margaret Thompson Smoot," LDS Archives.

73. Olive Amanda Smith Markham, biographical sketch, LDS Archives.

74. "A Brief Sketch of the Life of Rhoda Ann Marvin Fullmer," Nov. 29, 1885, Fullmer Family Notebook, 73, LDS Archives. If the women had been asked where they had heard about the "law of Sarah," they would have answered that it was in the revelation on plural marriage, at least after it became D&C 132 in 1876 (see vv. 64-65). However, the revelation makes only passing reference to this "law of Sarah" and even

that because the first wife assisted in selecting the others, this "probably contributed substantially toward the love and harmony that existed in the Cox family during later decades."[75]

Challenge to a husband's leadership

Love and harmony were not the terms many men chose to describe their domestic circumstances under the law of Sarah. Joseph Fielding said that plural marriage was his "greatest trial" and that there was "more trouble on the Subject of Plurality of Wives than anything else. … [S]ome of the best of our Sisters are tiranised over by some of the meanest."[76]

Writing to his daughter in 1887, Erastus Snow emphasized that "the first wife should not usurp the functions of her husband in the control and government of his wives and their children." In an interesting departure from what one might expect, he followed up by saying that "each wife should retain … separate and independent control of her own affairs and household." Speaking of the first wife's role in raising the stakes of a polygamous tent, Snow added: "there is, however, recognized in the revelations of God a right of the first wife called the 'law of Sarai' to [require that the first wife] be consulted by her husband and to give approval to his taking a second [wife] into the family[,] and the same right also extends to the second where a third is to be taken in order that all may be done by common consent in order to maintain mutual confidence and fellowship and love in the whole family circle."[77]

A woman's decision: The Richards family

Eight days after Franklin Richards was sealed to his first wife,

---

then puts it in a negative light, stating that if a woman refuses to consent to polygamy, she is a "transgressor" and her husband is therefore free to take whomever he chooses as a wife. The emphasis on the woman's right to ascent or be damned was exaggerated even further in commentaries (see Orson Pratt's 1854 essay in the *New York Messenger,* later reprinted in the *Seer,* quoted in Richard S. Van Wagoner, "Sarah M. Pratt: The Shaping of an Apostate," *Dialogue: A Journal of Mormon Thought* 19 [Summer 1986]: 83-84).

75. John Clifton Moffitt and Frederick Walter Cox, "Frontiersman of the American West," 4, LDS Archives.

76. Joseph Fielding, Journal, 1832-59, 178, LDS Archives.

77. Erastus Snow to Eliza [Snow], Salt Lake City, Aug. 7, 1887, LDS Archives.

Jane, he married Elizabeth McFate. Frank explained that Elizabeth's father, James McFate, "presented me his daughter Elizabeth" at the altar, then "Jane gave her to me" in a ceremony performed by Brigham Young.[78] Jane assessed that her co-wife was "young, (about 17 and pretty) and amiable." Jane was, in fact, appreciative of the fact that Elizabeth was "very considerate—and kind to me; never in our associating together was there an unkind word between us." Jane elaborated:

> I was in delicate health and from the time she first entered my house, three or four days after her marriage, she seemed only concerned to relieve me of trouble and labor. She was ready to take hold and do anything, always asking me for direction. We lived in our two story brick house, she occupying the upper portion. To those in the church who knew of the doctrine, I always spoke of her as Mrs. Elizabeth Richards, but even [then] it was not publicly talked about. I knew of other families, at this time, living in polygamy, but as yet it was a new thing.[79]

Jane suggests that she did not fully appreciate how far and wide polygamy had spread by 1846 in Nauvoo, involving some two hundred polygamous families, or about 10 per cent of Nauvoo's population, as already discussed in chapter 4.[80]

Even though males were given social preference in the community and could choose as many wives as they wished if they remained in good standing, Jane fantasized about choosing her own husband upon remarrying after her first spouse died. While "the man can be sealed to as many wives as he pleases," she found a loophole for a widow, who would also be "at liberty to make that choice." She could choose her second husband as her eternal mate "if she feels that her second husband is her preference," she reasoned. Jane seems to reflect a woman's desire to compensate for the injustice of men having greater liberty in choosing spouses.

Jane and Franklin were committed to their unique bond even

78. Franklin L. West, *Life of Franklin D. Richards* (Salt Lake City: Deseret News Press, 1924), 58.

79. "Reminiscences of Mrs. Richards," 18-19.

80. Estimating 200 husbands plus 700 wives and about 200 children yields about 1,100 people in polygamous families, or ten percent of an 1845 population of 11,000, which was approximately the same in 1846.

within polygamy. "Previous to Mr. Richards taking a plural wife," her interviewer explained, "she had made him promise that any matter that concerned any one of them individually should be always talked over with him in private." So far, he had "lived up" to that promise. He "told her that he would not marry" additional women "if he did not think she would love his wives as much as he himself."

When asked if the other wives in the family had objected to Frank's subsequent choices for brides, Frank answered that the family had encountered no such difficulties. Jane had heard of instances where the man had resorted to strategy, first talking to the wife who was "likely to prove refractory" before consulting any others or even waiting until a wife's "confinement" (pregnancy) or the delivery of a child when she would be too busy to care. In the Richards family, Franklin spent so little time at home, the issue of which wife he may have favored was of secondary concern. Jane reported that "in the first 15 years of her married life he was away on missions 10 years." She said that if she were to "divide [her] time with other wives, when [he was] away 9 weeks in 10," she could "dispense with the money," alluding to how household expenses were divided according to how many people were in each house, apparently a little extra being allotted to feed Frank when he was with one of his wives.

Sometimes the first wife was in a position to mentor a young woman and play the role of a matchmaker. A young girl came to Jane for a job and Jane found her a place in another house. In a few months, according to plan, the young woman "married the master of the house; and the two wives had two daughters with but 12 days' difference in their ages."[81]

Family interconnections

Joseph Smith sought to connect his loved ones to other families through cross-family marriages to form a close, interrelated hierarchy. Those who came after him saw the value in this practice. Women found a sense of elite belonging when Smith invited them to join the secret religious order he had started among the high-ranking priest-

81. Bancroft, "Inner Facts," 1-18.

hood men. This Quorum of the Anointed was the repository of the secrets of plural marriage. All of the members initiated into this secret society knew of, and accepted, polygamy. Most were practicing polygamists. When plural families included biological sisters, mutual understanding and trust were expected.

Widows and orphans were offered family support by polygamous men. In 1835, Henry Sherwood married Jane McManagle as his second wife. Jane had been married previously to Nathaniel Stoddard and Arza Judd, both of whom had died. She brought with her three stepdaughters, Arza's children by another wife: Lois, Mary, and Rachel. All three sisters married the polygamist John Page.[82] Like their mother, they had been considered unattractive marriage candidates except for the polygamous system, which had a way of finding a place for everyone, including a twice-widowed woman and three orphans. This more-or-less guarantee was something Brigham Young argued was an advantage of plural marriage.

Sixty Nauvoo men, about one-third of all male polygamists, married sisters over the course of their lives. The popularity of the practice is masked by some men marrying more than one pair each, taking seventy-six sets of sisters in all. The sisters were distributed as five pairs for Heber Kimball; four pairs each for Joseph Smith and Brigham Young; three sets for John Lee; and for Clayton, Higbee, G. A. Smith, and Taylor, two sets per husband. Through mid-1844 the

---

82. Joseph Fielding Smith, *Blood Atonement and the Origin of Plural Marriage: A Discussion* (Salt Lake City: Deseret News Press, 1905), 49-50; Justin E. Page letters to P. A. Watts, Mar. 16, 1936, and Wilford Poulson, Mar. 20, June 11, Sept. 12, 1936, Wilford Poulson Papers, Perry Special Collections; D. Michael Quinn, *The Mormon Hierarchy: Origins of Power* (Salt Lake City: Signature Books and Smith Research Associates, 1994), 567-68; Arza Judd, Jane McManagle, Henry G. Sherwood Ancestral File, www.familysearch.org. A note at the bottom of John E. Page to Brigham Young, 1845, Box 41, fd 2, Brigham Young Collection, LDS Archives, suggests that Page was excommunicated "for adultery[.] J E P whored it with a Miss Bliss from Boston." In a circular way, the note is quoting another annotation at the bottom of Joseph Smith III to Joseph F. Smith, June 30, 1883, Joseph F. Smith Collection. However, Page's first wife, Mary Eaton, was interviewed in 1904 and confirmed that "John E. Page [did] have [other] wives than [herself] … he wanted them[,] and I gave them to him … in the days of the Prophet Joseph Smith" (Council of the Twelve, minutes, May 5, 1954, Alma Sonne Collection, Msf, 678, #2, bx 3, fd 5, LDS Archives).

Nauvoo men acquired a total of thirteen sets of sisters. Through the rest of the Nauvoo period, they acquired another thirty-one sets. The rest joined their families after the migration to Utah. These biological sister-wives were considered to be, far from incestuous, a theological extrapolation on the levirate tradition of the Old Testament, whereby a man was obligated to marry his brother's widow.[83]

After William Clayton married his legal wife's sister as his first plural wife, in 1843 he asked Smith for permission to marry a third sister. Smith offered an impromptu reply that taking more than two sisters of a family was forbidden. Such a limitation was absent in the instances of Theodore Turley and John Page, previously cited, although normally several sisters would marry different husbands. The three daughters of Alva and Sally Beaman were examples. Mary Adeline married Joseph Noble in 1834 as his first wife and her two sisters married Joseph Smith and Erastus Snow, respectively.

Perhaps to care for older women, many polygamists married their wives' mothers prior to the trek west. This produced unique family histories: "On the 19th day of January, 1846, David [Fullmer] was sealed to Sarah Sophronia [Oyster]banks and her mother, Margaret Philips. The sealing to Margaret Phillips was later revoked and cancelled."[84] John L. Butler married a third wife, Sarah Lancaster, on February 3, 1846. Three days later he married her mother. However, he found that she "was too old and feeble to go on such a journey as it was to Salt Lake," so he sent her "back to Indiana."[85]

Female subordination

In their domestic relations, plural husbands tended to occupy a role as king of the household. For Heber Kimball, the subordination of women was a popular topic, a matter of order and decorum. As his ninth wife, Mary Ellen Able, explained, when Heber brought a new woman into the family he liked to stage a ritual whereby his wives

83. For the law of the levirate, see James R. Baker, *Women's Rights in Old Testament Times* (Salt Lake City: Signature Books, 1992), 51, 142-43, 147, 151-53.

84. E. Nilson Raymond, comp., "The Fullmer Family," typescript, 7-8, LDS Archives.

85. John L. Butler, Autobiography, 48, LDS Archives.

symbolically gave their consent to the marriage by forming a line and symbolically passing her up to him. This was to "stop the[ir] mouths," Heber said in his characteristically brash way, reminding them that he would "keep what he ha[d] received in peace." Like a man's relationship to God, the woman's responsibility, he said, was to anticipate what the man wanted, to allow her desires to be "swallowed up in his will" and "impregnated with his will and spirit" in order to "become one in spirit."[86]

Israel Barlow echoed:

> In all the Kingdoms of the world you will find that there will be only one King. All will be governed as one great family; and every man will preside over his own family. … You and your children will rise up and administer to your children and children's children, and you will rule over your posterity, and they may increase into tens, hundreds, thousands, and millions. Yet all will finally join with Adam, who will be King of all under Christ. … This is the order of the Kingdom of Heaven, that men shall rise up as Kings and Priests of God. We must have posterity to rule over.[87]

Examples of Nauvoo families

Lorenzo Snow described his life in Nauvoo with four plural wives in accounts collected by his sister Eliza. He said his "humble family mansion was a one-story edifice, about 15 by 30, constructed of logs, with a dirt roof and brown floor, displaying at one end a chimney of modest height, made of turf cut from the bosom of Mother Earth." For light during dinner they "selected the largest and fairest turnips—

86. Mary Ellen Able Kimball, 1818-1902, MS 42182, LDS Archives. Heber preached that "the man was created, and God gave him dominion over the whole earth, but saw that he never could multiply, and replenish the earth, without a woman. And he made one and gave her to him. He did not make the man for the woman; but the woman for the man, and it is just as unlawful for you to rise up and rebel against your husband, as it would be for man to rebel against God. When the man came to the vail, God gave the key word to the man, and the man gave it to the woman. But if a man dont use a woman well and take good care of her, God will take her away from him, and give her to another" (Devery S. Anderson and Gary James Bergera, eds., *The Nauvoo Endowment Companies, 1845-1846: A Documentary History* [Salt Lake City: Signature Books, 2005], 120).

87. Ora H. Barlow, *The Israel Barlow Story and Mormon Mores* (Salt Lake City: By the Author, 1968), 212.

scooped out the interior, and fixed short candles in them, placing them at intervals around the walls, suspending others to the ceiling above, which was formed of earth and cane." During the evening they "served up a dish of succotash" and entertained themselves with "short speeches, full of life and sentiment, spiced with enthusiasm, appropriate songs, recitations, toasts, conundrums, exhortations, etc."

By the time they left for Pisgah, Iowa, Snow's family was "composed of the following individuals: Mary Adeline [Goddard] (my eldest wife) … Charlotte [Squires], Sarah Ann [Prichard], [and] Harriet Amelia [Squires] … [A]ll of the wom[e]n above-mentioned were sealed to me as my wives in the Temple at Nauvoo, where we all received our second annointings,"[88] a ceremony that guaranteed a place in the Celestial Kingdom, similar to the Protestant doctrine of predestination.

Erastus Snow, Lorenzo's cousin, and his wife Artemisia arrived in Nauvoo in April 1839 just a few months after their marriage. They were separated for long periods of time while Erastus was away on preaching assignments. In 1843 they built a home "with means Artemisia had acquired from her father's estate. It was while they were in this home that Artemisia gave her consent to Erastus' marriage to Minerva White, her close friend." Snow's biographer asserted that Artemisia was dedicated to "this difficult principle" and was "the soul of cooperation in wishing Erastus to inherit the blessings of eternal glory through a large posterity."[89] In 1878 this advocate of polygamy spoke before a large gathering of women at St. George, Utah. The speech was printed in the *Woman's Exponent.* She said:

> I have reared a large family in the marriage system. I have been the mother of 11 children. My husband has been the father of 35, [with] 26 now living, all equally honorable inasmuch as they might pursue an upright, righteous course through life. Of that number, there are 16 sons.

---

88. Eliza R. Snow Smith, *Biography and Family Record of Lorenzo Snow* (Salt Lake City: Deseret News, 1884), 92-3. D. Michael Quinn, *The Mormon Hierarchy: Extensions of Power* (Salt Lake City: Signature Books, 1997), 701, has Charlotte, Mary, and Harriet married in 1844 and Hannah Goddard, sister of Mary Adeline, married and separated in 1845, then remarried in 1849.

89. Larson, *Erastus Snow,* 746.

> Not one of them has ever committed any crime that has brought a stain upon the character or a dishonor upon the heads of their parents. Not one of them is given to tickling [the palette with spirits] or drunkenness, not one smokes or chews tobacco, and as fast as they arrive at mature age, [they] earn their living by the sweat of the brow, or by the labor of their own hands. Why should they not be honorable? Their father is an honorable man. He is honored with that priesthood that emanates from the Gods.
>
> We have children born in the new and everlasting covenant of marriage, who are walking in the footsteps of their father and mothers. And, I trust, will honor it.
>
> My sister, Louise Beaman, next older than myself, was the first woman given in plural marriage. She lived and died a good, faithful Latter-day Saint, true to the principles she embraced and is now rejoicing with her husband, our beloved Prophet, in the eternal worlds. If I can walk in her footsteps, imitate her example, attain that glory and exaltation that I believe she has, I will be satisfied.
>
> It looks very odd to me nowadays to see a man living alone with one wife, especially a middle-aged man. It does very well for new beginners, just starting out on the journey of life to begin with one, and then add to. But to see a man in the decline of life, I say it looks odd. It looks selfish, contracted, drawn up into a nutshell.[90]

Artemisia was outspoken and strong-willed, while Erastus's second wife, Minerva, was noteworthy for her domestic neatness and formality. When speaking to others, "she always referred to her husband as 'Mr. Snow.'" Particular about her dress, she "kept her curly hair plastered close to her head because she did not like the curls."[91] She and Artemisia were close friends, the two of them living together with their husband.

After Erastus joined the 1847 pioneers in the Great Salt Lake Valley, he returned for his family and married sixteen-year-old Elizabeth Ashby, whom he had met six years earlier. She apparently thought he was the "handsomest man she had ever seen." Erastus would have thirty children by these three women and six more children by another nine wives. With such an expansion in the marriage, it would be

90. Ibid., 747-48.
91. Ibid., 350.

difficult to maintain the cohesion his family had known in Nauvoo. In Salt Lake City, Elizabeth lived in a tent and wagon box until a home could be constructed for her. Her husband built what he called his "big house" on the corner of First North and Main Streets, but this was not just for his wives; it doubled as a hotel. Here Elizabeth was renowned for entertaining "salesmen, cattlemen, and mining men, who were pleased with her cheerful disposition and the good food and comfortable, clean rooms which she furnished."[92]

Helen Callister was the second wife of Thomas Callister, the father of thirty-two children and about 500 grandchildren. She staunchly defended her marriage:

> To raise my voice in public has never been a source of much embarrassment to my sensitive nature ... [D]uty and justice demand that my voice should now be heard[,] and would that my words of faith in the defence of my religion might re-echo and find an accordance in the heart of every true-hearted woman through the length and breadth of our country. I know the principle of Plural Marriage to be a truth. I have lived in polygamy for the last thirty-three years and was among the first to enter that sacred principle. I have shared hunger, poverty, and toil with my husband's first wife whom I love as a dear sister: together we trod the trackless wilds to reach these then sterile valleys; together we battle[d] the hardships of the "first year," ... I have see[n] my husband stagger for want of food. I have heard my babies cry for bread and had nothing to give them ... [but] through those trying scenes[,] ties closer than those of sister-hood bound us together and the principle of plural marriage was firmly planted in our souls.[93]

As another example of the friendship shared by wives, Vilate and Sarah Kimball were each about seven months pregnant with Heber's children in October of 1842 when Vilate wrote to him. He was on his mission in southern Illinois defending the reputation of Joseph Smith against allegations of polygamy. She expressed her love for Heber's second wife, "our friend S," writing that "as ever, we are one." Her sister-wife, Sarah, added this postscript:

---

92. Ibid., 749-52.

93. Helen Mar Clark Callister, Statement, LDS Archives; see also "Important Incidents in the Life of Thomas Callister," 13, LDS Archives.

> Your kind letter was joyfully received. I [have] never read it [a letter from you,] but I received some comfort and feel strengthened, and I thank you for it. You may depend upon my moving as soon as the house is ready. I feel anxious as I perceive my infirmities [pregnancy] increasing daily. Your request with regard to Sister Kimball I will attend to. Nothing gives me more pleasure than to add to the happiness of my friends; I only wish that I had more ability to do so. I am very glad we are likely to see you so soon, and pray that nothing may occur to disappoint us. When you request Vilate to meet you, perhaps you forget that I shall then stand in jeopardy every hour, and would not have her absent for worlds. My mind is fixed and I am rather particular, but still, for your comfort, I will submit. "I am as ever."[94]

Disputes among wives

Not all plural relationships were warm and caring. Tension between husbands and wives over subsequent, younger wives permeated the writings of several of Nauvoo's plural families. Twenty-two-year-old David Sessions, born in Vermont, married his seventeen-year-old sweetheart, Patty Bartlett, on June 28, 1812, in Oxford County, Maine, not far from her birthplace in rural Bethel. Over thirty years later, David and Patty, both in their fifties, welcomed younger women into their household. In October 1845, David married thirty-year-old Rosilla Cowen, who was twenty years younger than Patty. The first wife poured out her thoughts and feelings to her diary. Her relationship with Rosilla was strained even from the start and deteriorated further over time. Ten months into the compound marriage, writing from Winter Quarters on the first Sunday in August 1846, Patty told her diary that "Mr. Sessions took Rosilla and asked me to go to the river[,] then took her and waided across the river [and] left me on this side[.] [He] was gone 2 or 3 hours … I went back to the wagons[.]"[95]

On Monday, September 7, Patty wrote, "Mr Sessions is more kind to me"; but she was upset the next day because he had "talked with Rosilla and she filed his ears full and when he came to my bed I was also quite ch[il]led[,] he was gone so long[,] and I was so cold [and]

94. Whitney, "Scenes and Incidents," *Woman's Exponent* 11 (June 1, 1882): 2.

95. Donna Toland Smart, ed., *Mormon Midwife: The 1846-1888 Diaries of Patty Bartlett Sessions* (Logan: Utah State University Press, 1997), 60.

had been crying." She wrote that he had begun to "talk hard to me before he got into bed and thretens me very hard of leaving me[.] Oh may the Lord open his eyes and show him where he is deceived by listening to her false tales," she wrote.[96] Patty tried to talk with Rosilla, but the younger woman was "very abusive," Patty wrote. On Sunday, October 25, "Mr. Sessions and I had a talk with Rosilla[. S]he was very willful and obstinate," so "he told her to come into the tent and if she did right she should be used well." At this, Patty expressed exasperation: "I told her it was a big cud for me to swallow to let her come in after she had abused me so shamefuly." Patty made sure that David "knew she had abused me worse than I had her."[97]

Patty hinted at another issue common to some plural families, insisting that if Rosilla became part of the family, Patty "should be boss over the work." Patty considered Rosilla to be insubordinate, saying she had "twisted and flung at" her sister wife.[98] The subject of work resurfaced a few days later. Patty said she

> got but 2 hours sleep last night and I have cut the meet of the bones of the beaf and salted it[.] I have to work all the time and[,] not withstanding all he has said to her about helping me[,] she … gave me the lie many times and talked very saucy to me and when I could bear it no longer I told her to hold her toungue and if she gave me the lie again I would thro[w] the tongs at her[. S]he then talked very saucy to me[,] [so] I told her there was the tent door and she might walk out if she could not cary a better toungue in her head."[99]

Rosilla continued to resist domestic chores. The next day "she came into the tent but will not work[.] I cook[,] she eats." Nevertheless, David seemed to spend more time with Rosilla than with Patty: "He has lain with her three nights[;] she has told him many falsehoods and is trying to have him take her to Nauvoo and then to Maine and leave me for good." Patty stopped speaking to Rosilla, but the second wife claimed the first had quarreled with her all day. Patty reported that

96. Ibid., 61.
97. Ibid., 64.
98. Ibid.
99. Ibid., 65.

Rosilla had not done one thing to help her, then "said [she would] if I would ask her[.] I then asked her to clean the dishes[.] I waited 3 hours she then went over the river and never touched them." When Rosilla returned, according to Patty, she was again "very saucy to me [and] said she would eat but she would not work for me."[100]

Given the circumstances, the women decided the best resolution was for Rosilla to stay permanently on the opposite side of the river. On Friday, November 20, Patty recorded that "Mr. Sessions went over the river to see Rosilla" and "staid all night." A week later "Rosilla came back here[,] sais she is going back to the Missis[s]ip[p]i river [and] she left word for Mr. Sessions to come over and see her," a message Patty was not eager to convey. On Sunday "he went over at night and staid with her." Then, Patty wrote on Monday, November 30, that David "did not speak to me when he came home." Patty concluded her contemporary observation of her sister wife on December 3, writing that Rosilla had "started for Nauvoo," after which Patty, a midwife, delivered three children within a week, baked mince pies, and recorded an intrusion of "Mohakgh" Indians.[101] In early 1850, Patty wrote in her diary that "Rosilla Cowin was sealed" to David Sessions four years previously on Oct 3, 1845, that Rosilla "left him" three years previously on December 23, 1846, and that they had "not seen her since."[102] Two years later, Patty's son Perrigrine heard that Rosilla had married a man named "Baley."[103] And so Patty leaves us wondering how unique her experiences might have been but suspecting that in some ways her story was probably more representative than unusual.[104]

Secrecy and Security

Considering the explosive nature of what was unfolding, Joseph Smith, according to one of his plural wives, "lived in constant fear of being be-

---

100. Ibid., 65.

101. Ibid., 67-68.

102. Smart, *Mormon Midwife*, 142. Smart notes that later in 1850, Perrigrine would see Rosilla.

103. Ibid., 67n127. Perrigrine Sessions, Diary, Nov. 3, 1852, LDS Archives.

104. For example, recall Emily Partridge's view of Joseph's first wife, Emma, as "our bitter enemy" (Emily Dow Partridge Young, "Diary and Reminiscences, 1874-

trayed."[105] Jane Richards explained that when Smith married more women a few months before his death, he was compelled to do so without even the normal amount of what she called "publicity" because of the high level of "mob spirit," where people were "already quite excited."[106] According to Mary Horne, the topic could "scarcely be mentioned" at first because "the brethren and sisters were so averse to it."[107] Joseph Lee Robinson put it bluntly: "There are some on this stand that would cut my throat or take my hearts blood," he said, if he told them what God had revealed to him.[108] This level of paranoia, which permeated the church at the time, indicates an appreciation of how heretical their secret beliefs and practices were. This is why, as Nancy Tracy recalled, Smith taught the "Celestial Order of Marriage" only to those who "could bear it."[109]

Front husbands and concealed marriages

The same motif recurs in many stories about early polygamy. When the pregnancy of William Clayton's first plural wife threatened public exposure, Smith told Clayton he might have to publicly excommunicate him.[110] Sarah Ann Whitney engaged in a sham marriage to Joseph Kingsbury to conceal her connection to Smith. As previously quoted, he wrote in his autobiography that he "agreed to stand by Sarah Ann Whitney as though I was supposed to be her husband [in] a pretended marriage" (see chapter 3).[111]

When Smith died, Kingsbury and Whitney continued to live in the same household even though there was no longer a reason to keep

---

1899," 6, Perry Special Collections; cf. Jenson, "Plural Marriage," 240; Emily Partridge Young, "Autobiography," *Woman's Exponent,* Dec. 1884-Aug. 1885; *Reorganized Church v. Church of Christ,* question 365).

105. Littlefield, *Reminiscences,* 50.

106. "Reminiscences of Mrs. Richards," 18.

107. Mary Isabella Hales Horne, "Migration and Settlement of the Latter Day Saints," 1884, typescript, Utah State Historical Society, from 42-page holograph, Bancroft Library.

108. Robinson Journal, 24, Utah State Historical Society Library.

109. "A Sketch of the Life of Nancy Naomi Tracy," 20, Utah State Historical Society.

110. Smith, *Intimate Chronicle,* 122.

111. "History of Joseph Kingsbury, Written by His Own Hand, 1846, 1849, 1850," Utah State Historical Society, photocopy, original holograph and typescript at Marriott Library.

up appearances. On January 26, 1845, they walked together to Parley P. Pratt's store to receive their endowments. Kingsbury was being groomed to begin choosing his own plural wives. As he wrote in his journal, he "was Recd into the Corum of the Priesthood" and "Recd. instructions Verry Benefitial." Initiation into this secret society entailed entrance into a "quorum" of men and women who periodically met together to engage in the endowment rituals. As Kingsbury put it, they "met … at times & offerd up Prayer."[112] On March 4, Kingsbury married Dorcas Moore. A few days later, on March 17, Sarah Ann was sealed to Heber Kimball for mortality, while her sealing to Smith for eternity was re-confirmed. In all of this, her marriage to Kingsbury was ignored. There was no divorce—no sense of a need to grant the sham marriage any further legitimacy. However, Sarah Ann continued living with Kingsbury. When she became pregnant with Kimball's child, it naturally appeared to be Kingsbury's. Simultaneously, Kingsbury's "plural" marriage to Moore was kept secret. Webs of appearances grew further tangled.

In January the next year, Kingsbury married Louisa Loenza Alcina Pond. On the same day, he was sealed to his deceased wife, Caroline Whitney, and Dorcas Moore, her proxy. Two days later, on January 28, he received the "ordinances of the fulness of the priesthood" or "second anointings for himself and his three eternal wives, meaning that they were now guaranteed resurrection to the celestial kingdom," as explained by biographer Lyndon Cook. In a stark change in surroundings from the furtive former marriages in secluded rooms and gardens, Kingsbury now knelt, kinglike, on "the scarlet, damask cushions of the alter in the upper northeast room of the [Nauvoo] temple" and was "ordained a priest and anointed a king unto God," his two living wives Dorcas and Louisa "anointed priestesses and queens unto their husband."[113]

A year after the refugees from Nauvoo founded their temporary

112. Lyndon W. Cook, *Joseph C. Kingsbury: A Biography* (Provo, Utah: Grandin Books, 1985), 89; for an overview of how the endowment was introduced, see Devery S. Anderson and Gary James Bergera, eds., *Joseph Smith's Quorum of the Anointed, 1842-1845: A Documentary History* (Salt Lake City: Signature Books, 2005).

113. Cook, *Joseph C. Kingsbury*, 93-94.

settlement near present-day Omaha, Nebraska, which they called Winter Quarters, Patty Sessions wrote in her diary in mid-1847: "I cal[l]ed to Sarah Ann['s] this evening with E R Snow[.] [S]isters Whitney and Kimbal came in … [T]hings were given to us that we were not to tell of but to ponder them in our hearts and profitt thereby … E [Louisa] Beamon[,] E Pa[r]tri[d]ge[,] [and] Zina Jacobs came here [and] laid their han[ds] on my head [and] blesed me, and so did E Snow[,] thank the Lord."[114] The bond formed by their formerly unspoken marriages to the same husband, Joseph Smith, had drawn these women close together.

Sharing a code of silence

In the winter of 1845-46, polygamy moved briefly out of the shadows as the ostensibly secret marriages were shared with the general church membership. John D. Lee confirmed that "in the Winter of 1845 meetings were held all over the city of Nauvoo" to teach "celestial marriage." He told of men scrambling to add wives to their families, then discovering incompatibilities and wanting to renegotiate relationships. In a few instances, men made exchanges between themselves, trading one woman for another. All of this was done under the continuing censorship of public discussion outside of the few, strictly guarded church gatherings. It was a confusing time. People "had to be kept still" lest they reveal anything to an outsider, and this meant that "a young man [still] did not know when he was talking to a single woman."[115] Making the same point from a woman's perspective, Eliza Partridge wrote that "a woman living in polygamy dared not let it be known."[116] Jane Richards corroborated the fact that the winter of 1845-46 was when "polygamy was now made known to us for the first time." Her take was different than John Lee's, in that Mrs. Richards

114. Smart, *Mormon Midwife,* 84; see also Linda King Newell, "Gifts of the Spirit: Women's Share," in *Sisters in Spirit: Mormon Women in Historical and Cultural Perspective,* eds. Maureen Ursenbach Beecher and Lavina Fielding Anderson (Urbana: University of Illinois Press, 1987), 111-15.

115. John Lee added that "many a night" he had stood guard for Brigham Young "while he spent an hour or two with his young brides" (*Mormonism Unveiled,* 165-72.)

116. Eliza Maria Partridge Lyman, Autobiography and Diary, 1846-1885, LDS Archives.

thought, "while the majority of the church were made acquainted with the doctrine, it was only practically entered into by a few."[117]

Leonora Cannon Taylor advised Mrs. Richards to be vigilant in keeping her marriage troubles to herself. Jane was "not [doing] very well" in polygamy, but Leonora encouraged her, saying: "You have too much pride and grit to let any of your domestic trials be known to the world." Richards would pass on this "code of silence" to a younger woman, telling her with some satisfaction that "as long as she had lived in polygamy she had never spoken to any one of her troubles or allowed that she had any trials."[118]

John D. Lee felt no such qualms about divulging emotional complications or in revealing the underlying political corruption he detected in the system:

> Now the first wife of D. H. Wells [Louisa Free] … and her sister Emmeline were both under promise to be sealed to me. One day Brigham Young saw Emmeline and fell in love with her. He asked me to resign my claims in his favor, which I did, though it caused a great struggle in my mind to do so, for I loved her dearly. … The two girls did not want to separate from each other; however, they both met at my house at an appointed time and Emmeline was sealed to Brigham and Louisa was sealed to me. … By Louisa I had one son born who died … She lived with me about one year after her babe was born. She then told me that her parents were never satisfied to have one daughter sealed to the man highest in authority and the other below her. Their constant teasing caused us to separate, not as enemies, however. Our friendship was never broken. Her change made her more miserable than ever. After we got into Salt Lake Valley, she offered to come back to me, but Brigham would not consent to her so doing. Her sister became a favorite with Brigham, and remained so until he met Miss Folsom, who captivated him to a degree that he neglected Emmeline, and she died broken-hearted.[119]

Celestial indoctrination

Hosea Stout recorded in his diary how Lee himself had helped to indoctrinate others in plural marriage. On April 19, 1845, Stout was

117. "Reminiscences of Mrs. Richards," 19.
118. Bancroft, "Inner Facts," 17-18.
119. Lee, *Mormonism Unveiled,* 166-67.

"sent for by Brother Lee who wanted to see me," upon which Stout witnessed Lee's double marriage to Louisa Free and Sarah Caroline Williams. Stout wrote that the following day "myself and wife Lucretia Fisher went to Br John D. Lee's to a Social meeting ... Prest A Lyman, Br Lee & wife & others were present." Stout did not divulge that on this date, at Lee's house, Stout married Lucretia, as he felt bold enough to list in his family Bible. Two months later on June 30, Stout went to the home of Charles Shumway, where a large crowd had gathered. "We [drank] what wine we wanted," Stout wrote. This time, he neglected to mention that this was the occasion of his second plural marriage uniting with Marinda Bennett. His biographer detected in this reticence "evidence of how secret it was." Neither Stout nor Lee felt able to articulate Lee's double marriage on April 19 or Stout's marriages in April and June.[120] Only the genealogical sheets of Stout's Bible were considered safe enough to preserve a record of these solemnities.[121]

Lee explained that even though "the ordinance of celestial marriage was extensively practiced," only a relatively "few men" in comparison to the general population "had dispensations granted to them" to transcend the normal constraints on sexuality. He firmly believed that plural marriage was "the stepping-stone to celestial exaltation." He said that "without plural marriage, a man could not attain to the fullness of the holy priesthood and be made equal to our Saviour. Without it he could only attain to the position of the angels, who are servants and messengers who attain to the Godhead." Lee felt that the inducement to become one of the council of gods in heaven "caused every true believer to exert himself to attain that exalted position, both men and women." He reported that the women would often initiate plural relationships in order to attain royal credentials for an aristocratic afterlife: "In many cases the women would do the 'sparking,' through the assistance of the first wife."[122]

---

120. Brooks, *John Doyle Lee,* 66-67, dates this narration to May 19-20, 1845, whereas the Stout Family Bible cites April 19-20. See Juanita Brooks, ed., *On the Mormon Frontier: The Diary of Hosea Stout, 1844-1861,* 2 vols. (Salt Lake City: University of Utah Press and Utah State Historical Society, 1964), 1:21, 22, 35n60, 50.

121. Ibid., 35n64, 50n12.

122. Ibid., 166.

John D. Lee recorded that marriage in Nauvoo was discounted to the point that two men in one of his examples got together and "mutually agreed to exchange wives," thinking nothing of it. Lee gave as an example Lorenzo Young and a Mr. Decker, who "both seemed happy in the exchange."[123] Lee suggested that plural marriage required the permission of the president of the church; but eventually local leaders assumed this responsibility, as cited in the example of Orange Wight. Either way, this represented a significant departure from Smith's pleading with his male friends to take more wives when, in the late Nauvoo period, each man was left to determine for himself how many times he would marry. After amassing many wives over two decades, Lee stopped. "After 1861 I never asked Brigham Young for another wife," he wrote. By his nineteenth wife, he had had enough. Even from a financial standpoint, fathering sixty-four children formed a formidable natural barrier to engaging more wives.[124]

Polygamy after Joseph Smith's Death

The demographic impact of Nauvoo polygamy on the culture of the west, including the five-fold expansion after Joseph Smith's death, cannot easily be minimized by ignoring the extent of commitment that grew out of the Nauvoo period over the next forty years. The impact of reaching this critical mass can be seen today among the fundamentalist Mormons, who continue to remind us of the church's historical image.

While the journals and personal writings tell a complex human story, the raw numbers themselves add some precision to the overall picture. In 1844 the number of plural marriages rapidly increased. In the autumn, Brigham Young took twelve wives; Heber Kimball, thirteen; Parley Pratt, three; William Clayton, two; and George A. Smith, one. William Smith married three wives sometime during that year. Of the sixty-eight plural marriages in 1844, forty-nine (about two-thirds) took place after Joseph Smith's death. Only eleven of these were women who had previously been married to the prophet.

---

123. Ibid., 165.
124. Ibid., 288-89.

Plural marriages accelerated even more in 1845, when (1) it became clear the church would leave the United States and members would be beyond the reach of the law and (2) the Nauvoo temple opened its doors on December 10. When Young urged the highest-ranking members to set a good example, the inner circle of thirty-three polygamous men now broadened to nearly two hundred.

Added to eighty-six marriages in 1845, the early months of 1846 witnessed 275 more plural couplings, an amazing number considering that most were performed in January and February. During this wedding marathon, Heber C. Kimball acquired nineteen wives; Brigham Young, eighteen; Samuel Bent, nine; John Bernhisel and Alpheus Cutler, six each; John Taylor, Willard Richards, and John Smith, five each; and Winslow Farr, Peter Haws, Cornelius Lott, and George A. Smith, four each. Seven other men married three wives each, thirty-eight men took two wives each, and some eighty-seven added one more wife to their families. By the end of the Nauvoo period, 196 men had married 717 women. Over 80 percent of the city's plural marriages had occurred after Smith's death. As a necessary qualifier, the wives of Smith, Kimball, and Young constituted over one-fifth of the total number of plural wives: 115 of 521. Heber referenced the disproportionate number of wives he married when Vilate died. At her funeral, he pointed to the coffin and said: "There lies a woman who has given me forty-four wives."[125]

In the realms of American social history, Joseph Smith's experience with plural marriage was distinctive. His thirty-eight wives lived apart in separate households or in his house under the auspices of being hired help. His followers in Nauvoo, by comparison, married fewer wives per husband and formed more coherent families. Of the thirty-three male polygamists in Nauvoo during Smith's life, the majority, a full twenty of them, had only two wives each. Four had only three wives per man. Willard Richards, Theodore Turley, and Lyman Wight had four wives each; Brigham Young had five. As the number of

125. Orson F. Whitney, *The Life of Heber C. Kimball, an Apostle: The Father and Founder of the British Mission* (Salt Lake City: Kimball Family, 1888), 436n. Whitney affirms that Kimball was the husband of forty-five wives and father of sixty-five children.

polygamous families increased in 1846, so did the number of wives per family, growing to an average of 3.7 wives per husband for a given polygamous family. The tendency continued in Utah. Thomas Callister was near the average in that he remained a twenty-four-year-old bachelor in Nauvoo until 1845, when he married two women. He married two more in Utah and became "the husband of four wives and had," as he phrased it in his autobiography, "a posterity of 32 children and about 500 grandchildren of various degrees of relationship."[126]

Conclusion

In April 1830 when the church was founded, Joseph Smith was twenty-four. (Oliver Cowdery, one of his three witnesses, was twenty-three.) Of his eight witnesses, there were three in their twenties and three had turned thirty that year. In 1830 the men who would be called to the original Quorum of Twelve Apostles were still an average of twenty-four years old, the same age as Smith.[127] The founders of Mormonism were young men.

Joseph Smith initiated a social system that appealed to deeply held human concerns. People want to be counted among the elite, the initiated few, the chosen of God or, as Joseph promised, to be given the unheard of opportunity to become as gods themselves. Some women yearn to marry powerful men; some men seek the comforts of several women. At the same time, the social-religious mechanism which made men and women special as plural families destined for a celestial kingdom was repugnant to some, violating the deepest moral values of many Latter-day Saints who, for a while, were left in the dark along with their Illinois neighbors. It was inevitable that "rumors" of polyg-

126. "Important Incidents," 13.

127. Peter Whitmer was 25 and Martin Harris 46. Of the eight witnesses, Samuel Smith, John Whitmer, and Peter Whitmer Jr. were 22, 28, and 21 respectively. Hiram Page, Hyrum Smith, and Jacob Whitmer were coincidentally all 30 years of age. Joseph Smith Sr. was 59. For the Quorum of the Twelve, Joseph Smith chose young men who were about his same age, but four were still teenagers the year the church was founded. Although the quorum was not organized until 1835, for the sake of comparison their ages on April 6, 1830, were: John F. Boynton, 18; Orson Hyde, 25; Luke S. Johnson, 22; Lyman E. Johnson, 18; Heber C. Kimball, 28; Thomas B. Marsh, 30; William E. McLellin, 24; David W. Patten, 30; Orson Pratt, 18; Parley P. Pratt, 22; William Smith, 19; and Brigham Young, 28.

amy among the Saints would spread within a year of Smith's first formal induction ceremony. He could hold off non-Mormons at the perimeter, but when his own people in Nauvoo rebelled—John Bennett in 1842, William Law in 1843-44—he was in trouble at home. Joseph had already fled three states under pressure that arose, in part, from suspicious relationships with young women. Perhaps he could have anticipated the violence coming to his kingdom on the Mississippi from his Illinois neighbors; but a homegrown assault was too much to endure. As town mayor in 1844, he had the city council order the destruction of the printing press and the suppression of the only edition of the *Nauvoo Expositor* the dissenters at home would print. His own colleagues took Joseph Smith to court and published his marital relationships in the newspaper, thereby revealing all that he had publicly denied. Suppression of a newspaper without due process brought a swift response from the Illinois authorities. On June 25 they arrested the prophet for violating freedom of the press: he had destroyed the newspaper without allowing the publishers to defend themselves.

When the Saints moved west beginning in 1846 and 1847, the United States expanded westward as well. In 1848 the United States and Mexico signed the treaty of Guadalupe Hidalgo, augmented in 1854 through the Gadsden Purchase and confirmed by the treaty of Mesilla. When the winds settled, the Mormons were once more on United States soil, no longer part of the Mexican territory called Upper California. Mexican land that had once included present-day Utah was redefined as American territory.[128] In January 1848 Brigham Young went back from the Great Salt Lake to Winter Quarters (Nebraska) to be sustained for the first time as president of the LDS Church. From there he organized the substantial "emigration of

128. The land acquired through the Gadsden Purchase in southern New Mexico was where the Mormon Battalion, led by U.S. Captain Philip St. George Cooke, had found a passable road for wagons in 1846-47. Their trail would become the westbound route of the Santa Fe Railroad. The Territory of Utah was created in 1850 when California became a state and Utah was carved out of its western edge. The maps from the previous decade had referred to the area as the Great Sandy Plain of Upper California, then part of "New Mexico" (Bernard DeVoto, *The Year of Decision, 1846* [Boston: Little, Brown and Company, 1943], 491; maps of the American West from 1841, 1842, 1845, and 1846, online at *David Rumsey Map Collection,* www.davidrumsey.com).

1848." Four years later, as Salt Lake City was still emerging from the desert floor, polygamy was publicly announced as official church doctrine.

The announcement came from the pulpit of the "old tabernacle," which was a simple adobe building with a barn-like roof, not yet a year old and much more modest than its famous successor with the oblong metal roof. In summer, meetings on Temple Square, which did not yet boast of a temple, were still held in the thatched-roof bowery.[129] Five years after the announcement of polygamy, U.S. troops were sent to the territory. In those days, it still took a month or more to send a letter to the east coast, so the war unfolded slowly, only gradually permeating the land. Over the next two decades, through the Civil War, the church played a cat and mouse game with the United States. Having fought a war to end slavery, the federal government went after the second "relic of barbarism." Polygamy went back into hiding.

Having come full circle—denial, secrecy, discovery, open advocacy, secrecy, and denial again—the next step for the Latter-day Saints was to forget they had ever countenanced polygamy. Rather than explore this curious, and perhaps most fascinating aspect of its esoteric past, the church mounted an effort to dispel plural marriage from memory. However, as Latter-day Saints began discovering a renewed interest in their past, they reconstructed the lives of their ancestors, and this "lost" chapter of the church's pilgrimage from east coast to west began to make more sense. That the church had sought to disclaim this colorful aspect of its past became motivation to locate primary documents—diaries and affidavits—in dusty attic spaces and from the shelves of church archives which were tended by wary gatekeepers.

Joseph's "celestial marriage" became a term referring to all temple marriages rather than to sacred plural wifery, which had been the key to afterlife kingdoms on distant planets where husbands would raise multiple families. Contemporary church officials would come to disclaim polygamy as "not a part of us," or only as an aspect of be-

129. Nelson B. Wadsworth, *Set in Stone, Fixed in Glass: The Mormons, the West, and Their Photographers* (Salt Lake City: Signature Books, 1992), 19, 20, 64.

grudging permission that had been given to frontiersmen to assist their journey across the plains. No longer a critical part of celestial exaltation, this keystone of Joseph's restoration of the ancient church would be dismissed in the twentieth century as unacceptable, a violation of the "Christian" code of behavior.

This is the diminished legacy of Joseph's amplified life which is not found in official church histories but is now available to be restored to the expurgated *History of the Church.* Historians now can place in more complete perspective Smith's determined willingness to share the *favors and privileges* of celestial marriages with his Nauvoo inner circle. This once secret practice, denied publicly but recorded privately in diaries and journals, forms a lost, indeed, a suppressed, history that is present in the original documents.

SEVEN.

A Silenced Past

"No Man Shall Have But One Wife"

The earliest Mormon record-keepers faced a dilemma in writing about Nauvoo: since Joseph Smith had repeatedly denied that he or others had engaged in "illegal" bigamous marriages, the clandestine practice of marrying plural wives could hardly be cited as a precipitating reason for the prophet's assassination and the expulsion of his "restored" church from borders of the United States. Peeling back the layers of rationalization, this is the picture that confronts us. The tradition of secrecy itself defined and delineated this tragedy. Despite the marital rumors, many of the rank-and-file convinced themselves that what was unfolding right in front of them must have been an illusion, not reality. Others interpreted the odd glance, the subtle nod, or the oblique, coded reference to mean something they recognized, but could not express.

As increasing numbers of men accepted their own privileges of having celestial wives, word of this practice spread in correspondingly greater arcs across Hancock County, beyond the Mississippi River, and throughout neighboring states. Those in the immediate towns and villages looked on with mounting astonishment. Their alarm was registered in the *Alton-Quincy Whig*, the *Sangamo Journal*, and the *Warsaw Signal*, and was carried even to New York. Onlookers were inclined to believe John Bennett, and the related testimonials from other dissenters in Latter-day Saint leadership councils only confirmed what Nauvoo's neighbors had already accepted as true.

Some twenty years later, LDS roles were reversed as a prominent member of the Quorum of the Twelve collected and publicized polygamy testimonials for the sake of the skeptical midwestern family of Joseph Smith. But after forty years of openly encouraging plural marriage, roles would revert back to officially foreswearing the outlawed practice. As the LDS Church assisted federal and state authorities to identify and prosecute fundamentalist Mormons; the Utah church, in ironic unity with its Missouri counterpart, would even come to deny that polygamy had been central to Smith's theology. Schismatic colonies that held to the Nauvoo prophet's restoration of "all things" emerged throughout the Rocky Mountains from British Columbia to Mexico, but especially in the bedroom communities filling the Salt Lake Valley.[1]

As accounts of concurrent marriages began to fade from the public record at the turn of the twentieth century, the term "celestial marriage" was counterintuitively redefined to mean its opposite, first-time, monogamous marriage. Already in the 1880s, "celestial" had been used in reference to temple marriages, which were said to be eternal, and not specific to polygamous marriage. This practical adjustment made it difficult for U.S. marshals to determine which marriages were plural. Today, "celestial" marriages are strictly monogamous except when a widower remarries, in which case he is promised two wives in the hereafter. Women, however, can be sealed eternally to only one husband.[2] Historian B. Carmon Hardy noted that the

1. Fundamentalist Latter-day Saints are centered in Hildale, Utah, on the Arizona border. The Allred group, headquartered in the Salt Lake Valley, was associated with the FLDS until 1952; the Kingston family and other fundamentalist Mormons are also separate. See Brooke Adams and Peg McEntee, "FLDS Church May Be Building First Temple at Its Texas Enclave," *Salt Lake Tribune*, Dec. 4, 2004, B2; Anne Wilde, "Fundamentalist Mormonism: Its History, Diversity, and Stereotypes, 1886-Present," in Newell G. Bringhurst and John C. Hamer, eds., *Scattering of the Saints: Schism within Mormonism* (Independence, Mo.: John Whitmer Books, 2007), 258-89.

2. Some men have been counseled against seeking a temple divorce after separating from a wife. They have been told the woman will form part of the spacious family kingdom the man will rule over in the next life ("Celestial Polygamy," public forum letter, *Salt Lake Tribune*, May 10, 2008).

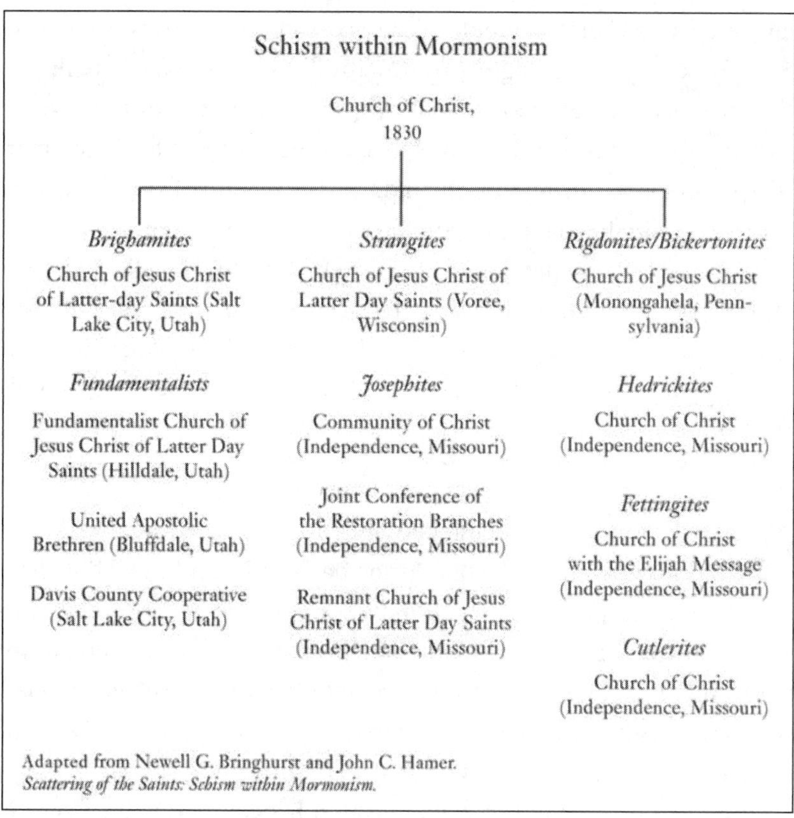

wording in the headnote for Doctrine and Covenants 132 had already been rewritten in the 1890s to reflect the change in theology and practice.[3] During the U.S. Senate's Reed Smoot hearings a decade later, church authorities enforced the change in usage so that no one could misunderstand that celestial marriage might include polygamy. It would remain for historians a half century later to rediscover the marital commotion in Nauvoo as interest reignited in this period of LDS ecclesiastical history.[4]

Given the initial secrecy and later revisionist history, how is it that

3. B. Carmon Hardy, *Solemn Covenant: The Mormon Polygamous Passage* (Urbana: University of Illinois Press, 1992), 297; LaMar Petersen, *Problems in Mormon Text: A Brief Study of Changes in Important Latter-day Saint Publications* (Salt Lake City: By the author, 1957), 18.

4. See Harvard S. Heath, ed., *In the World: The Diaries of Reed Smoot* (Salt Lake City: Signature Books and Smith Research Associates, 1997).

anyone can be certain about those once-forgotten events? In a sense, the process of forgetting evolved naturally from the eerie reality of secret marriage ceremonies held in the redecorated upper level of Smith's Red Brick Store in Nauvoo. Evidence of these forgotten marriages appeared during a brief window of availability from about 1850 to 1890 before becoming unpopular and again forgotten as polygamy was outlawed and abandoned after the manifestos of 1890 and 1904. Yet in the latter half of the twentieth century, the inception of these end-of-world marriage practices beside the Mississippi River was once again rediscovered as Latter-day Saints reawakened to their bold and colorful Nauvoo past.[5]

Keeping Secrets

When nineteen-year-old Orange Wight noticed the attractive sixteen-year-old Flora Woodworth one spring day in 1843, how could he have known she was already married, and was even a secret wife of the Mormon prophet? He had returned home from a year-long mission to the eastern United States and was not yet familiar with the changed social landscape in Nauvoo. He was surprised to discover that many of the young women he wanted to befriend were someone else's secret wives. Did he feel disoriented or even question his commitment? After devoting part of his youth to a church mission, was he disappointed that no one told him what was transpiring at the center of the church he was serving?[6]

John D. Lee arrived back from a Tennessee mission in the autumn of that same year. As if he were in a masquerade, he also found it difficult to distinguish a maiden from a married woman.[7] Sarah Leavitt

5. A recent rediscovery, forty years after Brigham Young University acquired the Reed Smoot diaries in 1960 (see note 4), the autobiographical writings of Zina Diantha Huntington, plural wife to Joseph Smith, then Brigham Young, were recently deposited in the Brigham Young University Library (Zina D. H. Young Family Papers and Photographs, 1876-1898, L. Tom Perry Special Collections, Harold B. Lee Library); see Martha Sonntag Bradley and Mary Brown Firmage Woodward, *Four Zinas: A Story of Mothers and Daughters on the Mormon Frontier* (Salt Lake City: Signature Books and Smith Research Associates, 2000).

6. Orange Lysander Wight, "Recollections," 1903, typescript, L. Tom Perry Special Collections; original in LDS Archives, Salt Lake City.

7. As previously quoted, he summed up the situation by saying "a young man did

found celestial marriage practiced by "more and more" of the "brethren." She recalled the ubiquitous whisperings about that time, hearing that men were taking more wives (see chapter 6).

Just as young men like Wight and Lee were once unaware of the social changes in Nauvoo but quickly adapted, so too, other Mormons had to make sense of Joseph Smith's mockery of the claim that he had "seven wives" when, as he said, he had looked for them and could "only find one."[8] To conclude otherwise was said to be a characteristic of disbelievers, or even "anti-Mormons." The faithful were expected to dismiss the abundant rumors. Smith's scribes carefully excluded anything from the records they kept that might allude to the denied practice. Smith's diaries, which inadvertently contained only carefully masked hints, were used to write the seven-volume *History of the Church of Jesus Christ of Latter-day Saints,* published in book form from 1902 to 1912. Although the history was previously serialized, beginning with installments in the Nauvoo *Times and Seasons* from 1842 to 1846, the installments only brought the record forward to 1834, thereafter continuing in the *Millennial Star* in England and then the Salt Lake City *Deseret News* which, by1858, completed the story to the end of Joseph Smith's life. Smith's scribe, Willard Richards, was responsible for writing the history for the period up to March 1843, and George A. Smith completed it to the end of Smith's life in 1844, then brought the historical narratives to 1846 when the Saints left Nauvoo. B. H. Roberts finally edited the whole series for final publication in seven volumes.[9] Like Smith's diaries, the official history ignored Nauvoo's increasingly public secret and was never revised.

If no one was talking, how did we learn so much about this

---

not know when he was talking to a single woman" (John D. Lee, *Mormonism Unveiled: Or the Life and Confessions of the Late Mormon Bishop, John D. Lee* [St. Louis: Bryan, Brand & Co., 1877], 167).

8. Joseph Smith et al., *History of the Church of Jesus Christ of Latter-day Saints,* ed. B. H. Roberts, 2nd ed. rev., 7 vols. (Salt Lake City: Deseret Book, 1963), 6:411.

9. Dean C. Jessee, *The Papers of Joseph Smith,* 2 vols. (Salt Lake City: Deseret Book, 1989-1992), 2: xxxi-xlix, 1-3; Leonard J. Arrington, "The Writing of Latter-day Saint History: Problems, Accomplishments, and Admonitions," *Dialogue: A Journal of Mormon Thought* 14 (Autumn 1981): 121-22.

curious episode in American history? Years after the events in question, eyewitnesses began to step forward and offer personal testimony as well as recorded events in their personal diaries from the time of early courtships and marriages, augmented by later impressions in autobiographies. Moreover, the 1846 temple sealings, which re-commemorated previously conducted plural marriages, were carefully noted in Nauvoo temple records. Then in 1852, the official church records became increasingly detailed and more open in the wake of the public disclosure in Salt Lake City of Mormon marriage practices. This once-hidden custom flowered into visibility and was then vigorously pressed on anyone who denied that such marriages characteristically defined Nauvoo. Emma Smith told her children it was Brigham's invention, not Joseph's, but the ground beneath her story eroded under waves of documentary evidence proclaimed from the Mountain West. In response to her denials, the deceased founder's nephew, Joseph F. Smith, collected notarized personal accounts in 1869 from wives and witnesses to prove to his doubting cousins that his uncle Joseph, the prophet, had in fact initiated plural marriage in Nauvoo as part of his "restoration of all things," which importantly included the biblical marriage practices. Then, in 1887, LDS Assistant Church Historian Andrew Jenson published a number of these, along with others he himself collected, in his Salt Lake City periodical, the *Historical Record*.[10]

From the temple books and statements gathered by church officials, as many as 938 polygamous marriages were documented, including 521 in Nauvoo and 417 more by the same men after they had moved west and acquired a cumulative total of almost six wives each (see chapter 4, appendix B). In 1892, just two years after the church agreed to abandon plural marriage, involuntary accounts of polygamy were elicited in the Temple Lot court case over the land Joseph Smith had designated for a temple in Independence, Missouri.[11]

---

10. Jenson stated in his publication that it was "devoted exclusively to historical, biographical, chronological and statistical matters, at $1.25 per annum, 154 North Second West, Salt Lake City."

11. Andrew Jenson, "Jackson County, Missouri: The Temple Lot," *Historical Record* 7 (Dec. 1888): 647.

Joseph Noble recalled having heard about polygamy in 1840, the year before he was asked to perform Smith's marriage to Louisa Beaman. The vow of secrecy, complete with ritualized threats of disclosure, were reminiscent of ancient times—the secrecy surrounding Mithraic rites of bread and wine conducted behind closed doors. Trying to move undetected about a city to stage secret rituals was difficult. The furtive nature of these unexplained happenings only aroused suspicion and rumors. On the edge of the Mississippi, Louisa's hat-and-coat disguise might have initially deflected attention but planted an unforgettable picture in the memory of those who later heard of it.

Joseph disguised the practice by indirection. Clayton was told he might be expelled from the church, then quietly rebaptized, just as the Female Relief Society investigated moral infractions while many of the town's leading women had become intimate with the prophet, an ironic setting akin to the tale of "the bear at the hunter's ball."[12] Hyrum Smith told Ebenezer Robinson in 1843 that if he were to marry a "young woman" and "she should have an offspring," they would "give out word that she had a husband, an Elder, who had gone on a foreign mission." When asked in unambiguous words forty years later whether there was "a place appointed in Iowa, 12 or 18 miles from Nauvoo to send female victims to hid[e] polygamous births," Robinson replied, "We were told that there was a place, a few miles out[,] ... where females were sent for that purpose."[13] In spite of this managed discretion, a rising tide of gossip spilled through Nauvoo and abroad in the land. In response, other churchmen initiated events that would lurch inexorably out of control.

John Bennett's July 1842 disclosures correctly identified Louisa Beaman, Presendia Buell, Elizabeth Durfee, Sylvia Sessions, and Agnes Smith as a few of the concealed wives of the prophet.[14] When he wrote eight letters to the *Sangamo Journal* (in Springfield), he ex-

12. George D. Smith, ed., *An Intimate Chronicle: The Journals of William Clayton* (Salt Lake City: Signature Books and Smith Research Associates, 1991), 122.

13. Ebenezer Robinson to Jason W. Briggs, Jan. 28, 1880, LDS Archives.

14. John C. Bennett, *The History of the Saints: Or an Exposé of Joe Smith and Mormonism* (1842; Urbana: University of Illinois Press, 2000), 256.

panded the existing areas of concern regarding the ever-problematic Mormons. The Whigs of Sangamon County were already irritated over the choreographed bloc voting for Democrats where the Mormons lived. Illinois was solidly Democratic except for the Whig stronghold in Springfield. It was in the state capital that Lincoln, over the next decade, would build a new Republican base of power.[15] For the minority party at that time, Bennett's disclosures came as a windfall. After these highly charged revelations about Nauvoo appeared in print, the well-regarded Bennett assembled these scraps of suspicion in his new book, *History of the Saints*, which was released in the fall. Smith was so concerned, he apparently ceased marrying from about August 1842 to February 1843, denied the charges, and vigorously counter-attacked. But however much he tried, resorting to calling Bennett a heretic and the women in question, harlots, Smith could not entirely neutralize the negative impression Bennett had created. Not only in Springfield, but also in Nauvoo, the increasingly aware citizens sensed that where there was smoke, there might be fire—that there was something amiss in Smith's response—and began to ask questions.

On March 15, 1843, the church periodical, *Times and Seasons*, published an editorial that sought to dissociate Nauvoo from American utopian communities that were known to share property and wives. The newspaper's editor, John Taylor, who was not yet a polygamist, is presumed to be the author. He wrote: "We [Latter-day Saints] are charged with advocating a plurality of wives, and common property. Now this is as false as the many other ridiculous charges which are brought against us. No sect has a greater reverence for the laws of matrimony, or the rights of private property."[16] Taylor's was among the most civil of participants in the generally heated exchanges between Mormons and outsiders. Bennett and Smith were still locked in

---

15. John C. Bennett, "The Mormon War," *Sangamo Journal,* June 17, 1842. Lincoln arrived in Springfield in 1837 and practiced law until his debates with state senator Stephen A. Douglas catapulted him to political notice in 1858. See Doris Kearns Goodwin, *Team of Rivals: The Political Genius of Abraham Lincoln* (New York: Simon and Schuster, 2005), 7-8, 27, 106.

16. "What Do the Mormons Believe," *Times and Seasons,* Mar. 15, 1843, reprinted from the *Boston Bee.*

a contest of wills, each trying to outdo the other in the defamation of character.

When on July 12, 1843, the prophet dictated his revelation to convince Emma and others about the restoration of Old Testament polygamy, it may have seemed like the beginning of a new era, but for him it would be the final chapter in a saga that could not continue. This occurred just four months after the public denial in print. Hyrum, previously an opponent of plural marriage, became an advocate to help his brother resolve his domestic trouble and convince others to join the inner circle of celestial marriage. In an August 12 meeting of the Nauvoo Stake High Council held at Hyrum Smith's office, Lewis Dunbar Wilson, then monogamous, "made inquiry in relation to the subject of plurality of wives, as there were rumors about respecting it." This portentous High Council meeting was held on a day when neither Joseph nor Emma was anywhere to be seen in the city. Emma had been out of town in St. Louis and would return that day, while Joseph was sequestered at home in a sick bed.[17] In the prophet's absence, Hyrum took the query, briefly adjourned the meeting, and walked home to get a copy of the revelation issued exactly a month before. After reading the document to the High Council, he admonished those who believed the words of the revelation to "go forth and obey the same" and "be saved." Those who rejected it would be "damned." Or so it was remembered by high councilman Thomas Grover, a one-time Erie Canal boat captain, when he wrote of these events to Amos Musser in January 1885.[18]

Even after offering the revelation to an unscreened audience, the Smiths and others of high office in the church continued to deny the existence of the marriage doctrine to the larger community. On October 5, 1843, the prophet denounced it as sin and falsehood. And in his personal journal of that date, his scribe Willard Richards, who was Smith's first initiate into polygamy that year, recorded the prophet's

17. The date was Aug. 12, 1843; see *History of the Church,* 5:528.

18. Jenson, "Plural Marriage: Thomas Grover's Testimony," *Historical Record* 6 (May 1887): 226-27; see also Richard S. Van Wagoner, *Mormon Polygamy: A History* (Salt Lake City: Signature Books, 1986), 63-64, citing Charles A. Shook, *The True Origin of Mormon Polygamy* (Cincinnati: Standard Publishing, 1914).

contrary assertion that "no man shall have but one wife."[19] Even though this was for public consumption, and the apostles and high councilors would have been told something different with regard to "trying" supposed offenders, the statement did not find its way into the *Times and Seasons*. However, as late as February 1, 1844, Joseph and Hyrum Smith did co-author a letter for the *Times and Seasons* planning to "cut off from the church, for his iniquity," a Michigan member who was "preaching Polygamy, and other false and corrupt doctrines."[20]

It was a different story at home, where Joseph continued to lobby his wife in favor of his marriages to other women. Just days after Hyrum presented the revelation to the high council—a month after Emma first repudiated it—she again "resisted the P[riesthood]," presumably a reference to her rejection of plural marriage.[21] Two days later, Joseph instructed Samuel James, a cousin of Sidney Rigdon, in "the order of the Holy Priesthood," meaning polygamy. This was the time that the prophet announced to Clayton, "You have a right to get all you can."[22]

Nevertheless, Smith realized the possible damage to his reputation and went on the offensive to protect his moral character. Beginning in a meeting the previous year, July 22, 1842, he had publicly asked Orson Pratt, who was struggling with Smith's recent overtures to his wife, Sarah: "Have you personally a knowledge of any immoral act in me toward the female sex, or in any other way?" Pratt had answered categorically: "Personally, toward the female sex, I have not." Then Heber Kimball, William Law, and Hyrum Smith defended the prophet

---

19. In Scott H. Faulring, ed., *An American Prophet's Record: The Diaries and Journals of Joseph Smith* (Salt Lake City: Signature Books and Smith Research Associates, 1987), 417.

20. "Notice," *Times and Seasons*, Feb. 1, 1844, 423. On October 1, 1843, the *Times and Seasons* carried excerpts from Joseph Smith's December 1830 manuscript history (later published as *History of the Church*, 1:133). From 1842-1846, the *Times and Seasons* serialized Smith's history for the years 1805-1834; nothing yet of Smith's personal writings from the 1840s (see Arrington, "The Writing of Latter-day Saint History," 122). The opposition to polygamy was apparently serious enough in February 1844 that Joseph and Hyrum considered it necessary or expedient to write a letter denying it.

21. See Smith, *Intimate Chronicle*, 117.

22. Ibid., 115, 117.

by bearing "testimony of the iniquity of those [Bennett] who had calumniated Pres. J. Smith's character." But Pratt, Sidney Rigdon, and George Robinson refused to certify the prophet's "high moral character."[23] On August 25 of that year, Smith had admonished his twelve apostles and others to "support the character of the prophet, the Lord's anointed." He criticized "O. Pratt and others of the same class [who had] caused trouble by telling stories to people who would betray me, and they must believe those stories because his Wife told him so!" The prophet said that as for Pratt, Rigdon, and Robinson, he could "kick them off [his] heels" anytime he wanted to.[24] His supporters agreed to "disabuse the public mind in relation to the false statements of Dr. J. C. Bennett," so that in late August the church was able to assemble the somewhat fanciful "Affidavits and Certificates, Disproving the Statements and Affidavits Contained In John C. Bennett's Letters."[25]

Early the next year, on February 21, 1843, Smith approached the Female Relief Society concerning the frequent rumor that the society was a front organization to conceal Smith's wives—or that it was where young women were groomed to be "wives of Joe Smith."[26] The next week the *Times and Seasons* once again denied that Smith had ever "advocate[ed] a plurality of wives.[27] Even as the prophet challenged the rumor, he was fueling it. A few days after his speech, he married Emily and Eliza Partridge (see chapter 3.) Over the next few months, he would marry seven more women, then formally record the revelation at mid-year. News of this momentum ineluctably spread throughout Nauvoo and environs. Ironically, the one who would lead the charge against Smith when he learned there was an increasing number of undisclosed marriages among the leadership was William Law, one of the three who had so ardently defended Smith against Bennett.

Law came out in opposition to Smith when he discovered Smith's marriage to the Lawrence sisters, for whom he had also arranged to have himself appointed executor and guardian. In the spring of 1843,

23. *Times and Seasons*, Aug. 1, 1842, 869-78.
24. Faulring, *American Prophet's Record*, 253-54.
25. Manuscript History of the Church, Aug. 29, 1842, LDS Archives.
26. *History of the Church*, 5:286.
27. *Times and Seasons*, Mar. 15, 1843, 143.

the girls had moved into the Smith household and became Joseph's wives in May of that year.[28] William Law had been named a bondsman to guarantee Smith's fiduciary responsibility for the Lawrences; he asserted that Emma had endorsed the girls' marriages to her husband for access to the girls' inheritance of "about $8000 in English gold."[29] Perhaps it was Smith's conflict of interest that enraged Law. Maybe it was their age, Sarah at sixteen and Maria at nineteen, still teenagers. Law may have soon realized the sheer volume of wives Smith had married. As soon as Law discovered Joseph's marriage to Maria, for which he was unrepentant, Law first pleaded with him to end his love bonds with these young women, then broke off his relationship with the Mormon leader and never looked back. Joseph's marriage to Maria was cited in his arrest and in the attempts to interdict Smith's relentless accumulation of more wives in his household.

William Law (1809-92), a merchant and miller from northern Ireland, had migrated to America and then Canada, where he joined the LDS Church. In 1837 he met Smith and moved to Nauvoo in 1839 with his brother, Wilson (1807-77), where they began accumulating real estate in and around the town. Law provided Smith with financial support, and Smith in turn chose Law to be a counselor in the First Presidency (1841-44). Law appraised Smith as "an honest upright man" but acknowledged that his spiritual mentor had some unspecified "follies."[30] In May 1842, Law joined Smith's Anointed Quorum

28. Their inheritance amounted to about $4,000, which converted to twenty-first-century currency would be more than $100,000, a staggering sum for seven orphans—as fatherless children were considered by Illinois law. See Robert B. Flanders, *Nauvoo: Kingdom on the Mississippi* (Urbana: University of Illinois Press, 1965), 177; Todd Compton, *In Sacred Loneliness: The Plural Wives of Joseph Smith* (Salt Lake City: Signature Books, 1997), 742-43, drawing on Gordon Madsen, "Joseph Smith as Guardian: The Lawrence Estate." Emma's welcome of the Lawrence sisters was suggested by Emily Dow Partridge, "Incidents in the Life of a Mormon Girl," 185-86, LDS Archives. See also chapter 2.

29. Lyndon W. Cook, *William Law: Biographical Essay, Nauvoo Diary, Correspondence, Interview* (Orem, Utah: Grandin Book, 1994), 119, reproducing Law's interview with Wilhelm Wyl, Mar. 30, 1887 (see *Salt Lake Daily Tribune,* July 31, 1887). The $8,000 may represent the size of the bond, by law twice the $4,000 inheritance (Compton, *Sacred Loneliness,* 743).

30. William Law to Isaac Russell, Nov. 29, 1840, LDS Archives; Cook, *William Law,* 11.

and participated in the endowment lodge meetings until January 1844. He may have been aware of the onset of polygamy in the church, but kept his silence. A good soldier in support of his leader, Law assured Nauvoo in 1842 that "spiritual wifery" was not condoned by Smith or the church.[31]

In early 1843, the Law brothers came into a related dispute with Smith over his conduct as trustee-in-trust for the church. In that capacity, Smith had appropriated church members' charitable donations for real estate speculation, buying low and reselling high to those immigrants who could afford to pay. Sometime later that year, William evidently began hearing disturbing aspects of plural marriage, such as Smith's keeping company with other men's wives. The rumors circulating among church leaders were confirmed by the revelation on plural marriage, presented to the High Council in August. Law was not present that evening, but in 1887 he recalled that he visited Hyrum Smith in the late summer or early fall of 1843 to ask about the revelation. Law found the wording and structure of the revelation, which made plural marriage incumbent on all worthy men, unquestionably repugnant: "All those who have this law revealed unto them must obey the same ... or be damned; for no one can reject this covenant and be permitted to enter into ... glory" (D&C 132:2-4). Law said of the revelation that

> Hyrum gave it to me in his office, told me to take it home and read it and then be careful with it and bring it back again. I took it home and read it and showed it to my wife. She and I were just turned upside down by it, we did not know what to do. I said to my wife, that I would take it over to Joseph and ask him about it. I did not believe that he would acknowledge it, and I said so to my wife. But she was not of my opinion. She felt perfectly sure that he would father it. When I came to Joseph and showed him the paper, he said: "Yes, that is a genuine revelation." I said to the prophet: "But in the Book of Doctrine and Covenants there is a revelation just contrary of this [the 1835 article on marriage]."[32] "Oh," said

---

31. *Times and Seasons*, Aug. 1, 1842, 872-73.

32. The section referred to was D&C 101:4. It read, "Inasmuch as this Church of Christ has been reproached with the crime of fornication, and polygamy: we declare

> Joseph, "that was given when the church was in its infancy, then it was all right to feed the people on milk, but now it is necessary to give them strong meat."[33]

Law gave a similar account in an 1885 affidavit, saying that Joseph told him plural marriage was "a great privilege granted to the *High Priesthood*."[34] The one-wife rule, Law affirmed, echoing Smith's argument, was given to "babes [who] … had to be fed on *milk*, but now they were strong and must have *meat*."[35] For Law, the revelation "gave the finishing touches to my doubts and showed me that [Smith] was a rascal." He took the revelation back to his wife and "told her that Joseph had acknowledged it." When he asked her, "What shall we do?" she advised him to keep still and sell their property quietly for what he could get, presumably in order to leave Nauvoo and the church. William then returned the document to Hyrum.[36]

Law hesitated for months. He initially tried to persuade Smith to quit Maria; on January 8, 1844, he asked Joseph to withdraw the doctrine. William wrote, "It was of the Devil and that he should put it down."[37] As a member of the First Presidency, Law appealed to the president for the sake of collegiality, but to no avail. That winter and spring, two other prominent members of the church, Nauvoo Stake President William Marks and Nauvoo Legion officer Robert D. Foster, a surgeon, decided to stand with Law in opposition to what they saw as church-sponsored philandering.

Smith was aware of Law's disaffection. Evidence of Smith's apprehensions about Law was deleted from the *History of the Church* as part of the sanitization of incriminating references to polygamy. However, a document that was bowdlerized in the official history remains clear

---

that we believe, that one man should have one wife." This was deleted from the 1876 D&C.

33. Cook, *William Law,* 119, 127-29.

34. See Shook, *True Origin,* 126.

35. William Law, Affidavit, July 17, 1885, reprinted in Cook, *William Law,* 98-99, emphasis in original.

36. Cook, *William Law,* 128.

37. Ibid., 18n, 46-47, reproducing William Law's diary, which contains a record of events in Nauvoo in 1844, Jan. 8, 1844.

in the original, the minutes of a Nauvoo City Council session on January 3, 1844:

> Mayor [Joseph Smith] said he was not afraid of any thing but [that there was] a doe head [dough-head: fool] in our midst! [Law] … [W]e referred to spiritual wives … [Eli] Norton said Bro. Law knew about the spiritual wife system. … Mayor [Joseph Smith] spoke on Spiritual wife System and explained. The man who promises to keep a secret and does not keep it he is a liar and not to be trusted.[38]

Dissent

William Law's efforts to dissuade Smith from acquiring more young women like Maria and Sarah Lawrence ran into stiff opposition, both personal and political. Law learned on January 2, 1844, from "remarks made by J. Smith before the city council and police," that Law was "suspected of being a Brutus, and consequently, narrowly watched." Even as Smith was declaring to Law that they were "very good friends," the prophet's counselor heard another rumor, that "Warren Smith one of the Police men said he believed I was the Brutus and that Wm Marks was another, and that we had better keep out of his way or he would pop us over," slang for killing someone. Law reported this to Smith on January 8, but the latter "became very angry" that anyone would think Smith "would encourage such a thing, and said that he had a good mind to put them (police) on us any how, we were such fools." Law was indignant "to find the mayor of the City, threaten two innocent men, with forty armed poliece, because they complained to him of threats … against their lives."[39]

After Law had pressed his case against Smith, he was dropped from the Quorum of the Anointed and from the First Presidency. Law responded: "I confess I feel annoyed very much by such unprecedented treatment, for it is illegal, inasmuch as I was appointed by revelation first [and sustained] twice after by unanimous voice of the general Conference."[40] On April 18, Law was excommunicated, along

---

38. Nauvoo City Council, Minutes, Jan. 3, 1844, in Cook, *William Law,* 38n7; cf. *History of the Church,* 6:162-65.

39. Cook, *William Law,* 38-42, for diary, Jan. 2-4, 1844.

40. Ibid., 46-47, for Jan. 8, 1844.

with his wife, Jane, and brother Wilson.[41] On May 10, 1844, they joined a few others in issuing a prospectus for an opposition newspaper, *The Expositor,* which was to appear every Friday at a cost of two dollars per annum by subscription, five cents per issue. Law led a list of seven publishers identified in the prospectus.

Two weeks later, William Law, William Marks, and Robert Foster took formal action against Smith. The problems the church president had confronted in the past over female relationships were nothing compared to the disapprobation the Maria Lawrence affair was about to bring to him. On Thursday, May 23, Law filed a complaint in the Hancock County Circuit Court in Carthage alleging that Smith had lived with Maria Lawrence "in an open state of adultery" from October 12, 1843, to May 23, 1844, while serving as her guardian and co-executor of her father's estate. The initial date cited in the complaint corresponds with the date on which Smith confirmed to Law his involvement with young girls. While the lawsuit was pending, there was only silence from Smith, who felt it unnecessary to respond to charges of vice and a conflict of interest. He simply complained about being charged "with polygamy, or something else" and characterized the evidence as hearsay, saying it was based "on the testimony of William Law, that I had told him so!"[42]

That Sunday, Smith addressed the charge from the pulpit. Taking as his text a passage from the eleventh chapter of Second Corinthians, he likened himself to the apostle Paul, asserting that he himself had "suffered more than Paul did." He taunted his opponents, saying if they "want a beardless boy to whip all the world, I will get on the top of a mountain and crow like a rooster: I shall always beat them … I will come out on the top at last. I have more to boast of than ever any man had. I am the only man that has ever been able to keep a whole church together since the days of Adam. A large majority of the whole have stood by me. Neither Paul, John, Peter, nor Jesus ever did it. I boast that no man ever did such a work as I."

41. *History of the Church,* 6:341.

42. Ibid., 6:405. Smith had been acting as guardian and executor for the Lawrence sisters from about 1841 but had himself appointed legal guardian on June 4, 1844.

Ignoring specific legal charges, he asserted that his "enemies cannot prove anything." His temerity was laced with contempt:

> I had not been married scarcely five minutes, and made one proclamation of the gospel, before it was reported that I had seven wives …
>
> This new holy prophet [William Law] has gone to Carthage and swore that I had told him that I was guilty of adultery. This spiritual wife-ism! Why, a man dares not speak or wink, for fear of being accused of this.
>
> A man asked me whether the commandment was given that a man may have seven wives; and now the new prophet has charged me with adultery. I never had any fuss with these men until that Female Relief Society brought out the paper [*The Voice of Innocence from Nauvoo*] against adulterers and adulteresses. …
>
> What a thing it is for a man to be accused of committing adultery, and having seven wives, when I can only find one.[43]

As he issued his most resounding denial yet, Smith only aggravated the difficulties for his wives and other men with whom he had shared the "privileges." When he then took the further step of ordering the destruction of the *Expositor*, Smith committed a fatal strategic error that subjected him to more intense scrutiny and more serious legal action. The situation was rapidly escalating out of control.

The dissidents published their charges in the first and only edition of the *Nauvoo Expositor* on June 7. In it, Law editorialized that the paper would be sent out "to the world, rich with facts" and with "expositions" that would "make the guilty tremble and rage. 1,000 sheets were struck and 500 mailed forthwith."[44] In the preamble, the editors affirmed that they "all verily believe[d] [in] … the religion of the Latter Day Saints," that "its precepts are invigorating, and in every sense of the word, tend to dignify and ennoble man's conceptions of God and his

---

43. A synopsis of Smith's May 26, 1844, Sunday address was reported by his scribe Thomas Bullock and included in *History of the Church,* 6:408-11. Smith's journal only mentioned that he "preached at the stand about Jackson and the mobocrats." By Jackson, he meant the self-styled undercover agent Joseph H. Jackson. Afterward, Smith "rode out in the p.m." and met with his "lawyers," Babbit and Richardson. See also *A Narrative of the Adventures and Experience of Joseph H. Jackson* (Warsaw, Ill.: Signal Office, 1844), available online at *Joseph Smith's History Vault,* www.olivercowdery.com. The Relief Society's *Voice of Innocence* was circulated on Mar. 9, 1844.

44. Cook, *William Law,* 55, for diary, June 7, 1844.

atributes." However, "many items of doctrine, as now taught, some of which, however, are taught secretly, and denied openly," were of a nature that they could not be believed in. Reflecting their pleadings with Smith over the last several months, they reported that they had called upon him "to repent" and "stood ready to seize him by the hand of friendship." "Many of us," they wrote, "have sought a reformation in the church, without a public exposition of the enormities of crimes practiced by its leaders ... but our petitions were treated with contempt." Smith "would not make acknowledgment."

Among other issues the editors wanted to draw attention to, they reported that "it is a notorious fact, that many females in foreign climes ... have been induced, by the sound of the gospel, to forsake friends, and embark upon a voyage across waters that lie stretched over the greater portion of the globe." And "what is taught them on their arrival at this place?" They are told that "God has great mysteries in store for those who love the Lord, and cling to brother Joseph. They are also notified that Brother Joseph will see them soon, and reveal the mysteries of heaven." After a short time, they are "requested to meet brother Joseph, or some of the Twelve, at some insolated ... room" where a sign hangs on the door, "Positively NO Admittance."

Upon meeting Smith, the women are "sworn in one of the most solemn manners, to never divulge what is revealed to them, with a penalty of death attached." They are told that "God Almighty has revealed it to him, that she should be his (Joseph's) Spiritual Wife." This is justified as "right anciently" and approved again, even though "we must keep those pleasures and blessings from the world." The woman is no doubt "thunderstruck," but "the Prophet damns her if she rejects." Such were the conditions in Nauvoo, where the "wretchedness of females in this place," the editors wrote, was beyond adequate description. The newspaper stated its intent to ferret out misdeeds and denounce false doctrines such as "a plurality of gods" and the "plurality of wives." It meant to put a stop to Smith's autocracy; his sale of property at "exhorbitant prices," some at a "tenfold advance"; and his "secret societies" which employed "penal oaths."

Their primary concern, however, was the "plurality of wives." After listing fifteen resolutions for reform, Law included his own affirmation, notarized on May 4, 1844, that in 1843 "Hyrum Smith did … read to me a certain written document" that, William's wife, Jane, certified, "sustained in strong terms the doctrine of more wives than one at a time, in this world, and in the next." Jane Law testified that she saw the revelation and that it "authorized some [men] to have [up] to the number of ten [wives], and set forth that those women who would not allow their husbands to have more wives than one should be under condemnation before God."[45]

The publishers closed with a note that they had engaged the services of Sylvester Emmons as editor, then signed their names at the end of this first number: William Law, Wilson Law, Charles Ivins, Francis M. Higbee, Chauncey L. Higbee, Robert D. Foster, and Charles A. Foster. Most of them were converts to Smith's church and all were successful businessmen and community leaders. To introduce them briefly: Charles Ivins (1799-1875) had a business across the Mississippi from Nauvoo in Keokuk, Iowa, where he was a town official. He had converted to Mormonism in New Jersey in 1841 and moved to Nauvoo. A pious man, when Law created his Reformed Church in April 1844, Ivins was appointed bishop. The two Higbee brothers, Francis (b. 1820) and Chauncey (1821-84), were sons of a prominent Missouri high councilman and church recorder, Elias Higbee. Chauncey became a state senator in Pike County, Illinois, and later a circuit and appellate judge. He was dismissed from the church in May 1842. His brother, Francis, was appointed a colonel with the Nauvoo Legion. A friend of Nancy Rigdon, Francis had become concerned in 1842 over Smith's advances toward her. He left the church in June 1843; in 1844 he became an apostle in the Reformed Church. Robert Foster, born in Northampton, England, was a physician and brigadier general in the Nauvoo Legion, as well as a Hancock County magistrate. His younger brother, Charles, was born in 1822 in Watertown, New York, and lived in Nauvoo at the time he joined Law's Reformed Church in 1844.[46]

45. William and Jane Law, *Nauvoo Expositor,* June 7, 1844.

46. See Cook, *William Law,* 45n12, 51, 55, 93, 108.

The editor, Sylvester Emmons, came from New Jersey (b. 1808). In Philadelphia, Emmons had studied law. Since May 1843, he had been a member of the bar in Illinois, which was no doubt useful for a newspaper editor. He was not a Mormon, but he was chosen a member of the Nauvoo City Council and had helped the city craft ordinances. Even after being named editor of the *Expositor,* he was addressed favorably by John Taylor, who also served on the city council.

Emmons, aged thirty-six at the time, included his own introduction to the first issue of the *Expositor,* advocating "free toleration in religious sentiments" and decrying despotism "engendered by an assumption of power in the name of religion." He announced that he would help facilitate "radical reform" in Nauvoo because of the "departure from moral rectitude" and creeping "abuse of power" in the city, which had grown to "intolerable" proportions. Perhaps referring to *The Wasp,* in which Joseph's brother, William, had denigrated Martha Brotherton (August 27, 1842) and other innocents, Emmons expressed his regret that the press should be "the medium through which the private character of any individual should be assailed." He similarly regretted the use of "illegal force" in the city, although he must not have foreseen its use against his newspaper. Later in 1844, when he moved north, halfway to Springfield, he operated the *Beardstown Gazette.* In February 1850 he received a letter of introduction from Abraham Lincoln. He won election as mayor of Beardstown and served in the office for sixteen years. He was also the town's postmaster, as well as a county clerk and justice of the peace. Emmons was married and had four children.[47]

Throughout the first number of the *Expositor,* several references were made to the "two indictments" against Smith, or "adultery" and "perjury," the latter resulting from a complaint filed by Robert Foster and Joseph Jackson. A county grand jury had heard testimony regard-

---

47. Proceedings of the Nauvoo City Council, June 8, 1844, published in the *Deseret News,* Sept. 23, 1857; William Alexander Linn, *The Story of the Mormons: From the Date of Their Origin to the Year 1901* (New York: Macmillan, 1923), 291; William Henry Perrin, ed., *History of Cass County, Illinois* (Chicago: O. L. Baskin & Co., 1882); cf. *Church History in the Fullness of Times: Religion 341-43,* 2nd ed. (Salt Lake City: Intellectual Reserve, 2003), online at *LDS Seminaries and Institutes of Religion,* www.ldsces.org.

ing the perjury charge in May but had decided to postpone making a decision until its October term, when it hoped to hear from material witnesses.[48]

In another affidavit, submitted by Austin Cowles for the *Expositor* and notarized on March 4, Cowles set forth his reason for leaving the church, rehearsing for readers what occurred on the evening Hyrum Smith introduced the revelation on marriage to the Nauvoo High Council. Cowles objected to two doctrines contained in the revelation: "the sealing up of persons to eternal life, against all sins," called the "second anointing," and "the doctrine of plurality of wives or marrying virgins." The "evidence that the aforesaid heresies were taught and practiced in the Church," he said, "determined me to leave the office of first counselor to the [stake] President of the Church at Nauvoo, inasmuch as I dared not teach nor administer such laws." He had resigned from the High Council in September 1843.[49]

To say that the *Expositor* caused a sensation would be an understatement. In 1905, John W. Rigdon, son of Sidney Rigdon, of the Nauvoo First Presidency, remembered that "in the afternoon … Henry Phelps, a son of W. W. Phelps, came down Main Street selling this paper, the *Nauvoo Expositor,* and everyone who could raise five cents bought a copy."[50] Three days after publication, Robert Foster, Charles Ivins, and William and Wilson Law went to Carthage upon "invitation by twenty five of the most respectable citizens" of the city to lecture on "Nauvoo legislation and usurpation &c." They advised "being patient and allowing the law to have its course" and to "avoid anything like an outbreak" since that "would only tend to create a false sympathy for those that opposed us."[51] While they were away for

48. *History of the Church,* 6:403, 405, 412-13; Edwin Brown Firmage and Richard Collin Mangrum, *Zion in the Courts: A Legal History of the Church of Jesus Christ of Latter-day Saints, 1830-1900* (Urbana: University of Illinois Press, 1988), 106.

49. Nauvoo High Council minutes, Sept. 23, 1843, LDS Archives; Austin Cowles Affidavit, May 4, 1844, in *Nauvoo Expositor,* June 7, 1844; see also Roger D. Launius, *Joseph Smith III: Pragmatic Prophet* (Urbana: University of Illinois Press, 1988), 195.

50. John W. Rigdon, Affidavit, July 28, 1905, in Joseph Fielding Smith, *Blood Atonement and the Origin of Plural Marriage* (Salt Lake City: Deseret News Press, 1905), 84.

51. Cook, *William Law,* 55, for diary, June 10, 1844.

their lecture that Monday, the mayor met with the Nauvoo City Council from 10:00 a.m. to 1:20 p.m. After an hour break, they resumed meeting until 6:30 p.m. At the end of the day, the council passed a libel ordinance that would allow action against the *Expositor*, then, based on the ordinance just passed, they declared the *Expositor* a "libelous and slanderous" nuisance and requested the mayor to "abate the said nuisance." Smith ordered the city marshal to destroy the press "without delay." He also ordered Major-General Jonathan Dunham of the Nauvoo Legion to assist if necessary. At 8:00 p.m., Marshal John P. Green returned to report that he had "removed the press, type, printed paper, and fixtures into the street, and destroyed them." That evening, Smith addressed hundreds of citizens who had returned with the marshal and blessed them "in the name of the Lord."[52]

Law recorded in his diary for June 10 that "to my utter astonishment tonight upon returning from Carthage to Nauvoo, I found our press had actually [been] demolished by the Marshall J. P. Green, by order of the Mayor (Jos. Smith) and the City Council." Furthermore, the publishers had been threatened with punitive action. "The Marshal said his instructions were to burn the houses of the proprietors if they offered any resistance."[53] The next day, Law learned of a threat against his life. He was also told he would be fined $500 and risk a six-month prison sentence if he spoke "disrespectfully of the City Charter." Law suspected "this plan was resorted to that they might ... rob us of our property, and get us into prisons to take away our lives."[54] On June 12, the second day after the press was destroyed, William, his wife, Jane, and three children (she would give birth to a fourth two days later) left Nauvoo, along with four other families. They took a steamboat headed for Burlington, Iowa.

That same day, Smith was arrested in Nauvoo on a complaint by Francis Higbee that the mayor and seventeen others had "commit[ted] a riot" when they "broke into the office of the *Nauvoo Expositor*" and "destroyed the printing press." The Nauvoo court immediately

52. *History of the Church*, 6:432-33.
53. Cook, *William Law*, 55-56, for diary, June 10, 1844.
54. Ibid., 56-57, for Jan. 2-4, 1844.

released Smith.[55] The next day, people gathered in Warsaw, Illinois, to discuss the situation and draft an appeal to Governor Thomas Ford. Hearing of this the next day, Smith addressed his own letter to Ford questioning the sincerity of the dissenters' moral objections and their standing in the community as reasonable and serious-minded adults. There can be no doubt about the standing of the individuals who published the *Nauvoo Expositor.* Based on any criteria, they were, as LDS historian Dean Jessee has written, "prominent in Church and civic affairs in Nauvoo." Jessee concluded that "as news spread of the … seemingly flagrant case [in] which Joseph Smith and the members of the city council avoided legal consequences, indignant county residents held meetings and adopted resolutions, and the Hancock County countryside took on the appearance of an armed camp as determined men prepared to take the law into their own hands."[56] What Jessee does not express is that armed men who were ready to take the law into their own hands appeared on both sides of the conflict.

The way Smith dismissed the civic and religious contributions of the dissenters could not have been stated in starker contrast to the historians' characterizations. Smith asserted that the "proprietors" of the *Expositor* were

> a set of unprincipled, lawless, debouchees, Counterfeiters, Bogus Makers, Gamblers, [and] peace disturbers, and that the grand object of said proprietors was to destroy our constitutional rights and chartered privileges; to overthrow all good and wholesome regulations in society; to strengthen themselves against the municipality, to fortify themselves against the church of which I am a member, and destroy all our religious rights and privileges by libels, slanders, falsehoods, perjury &[c.,] and sticking at no corruption to accomplish their hellish purposes. [A]nd that said paper of itself was libelous of the deepest dye, and very injurious as a vehicle of defamation,—tending to corrupt the morals, and disturb the peace, tranquility and happiness of the whole community, and especially that of Nauvoo.[57]

---

55. *History of the Church,* 6:453, 456-58.

56. Dean C. Jessee, comp., *The Personal Writings of Joseph Smith* (Salt Lake City: Deseret Book, 1992), 602.

57. Joseph Smith to Thomas Ford, June 14, 1844, in *History of the Church,* 6:466-67.

Smith's grandiloquence failed to persuade the governor, who could not have overlooked his rhetorical embellishments. Three days later, on June 17, Smith was re-arrested, although once again released by the Nauvoo authorities.

On the same day, Smith wrote to his sixty-two-year-old uncle, John Smith, urging him to take up arms if he saw any agitation over his nephew's stand against the state. John lived twenty miles southeast in Macedonia (Ramus), the residence of two of Joseph's plural wives, Almera and Delcena Johnson. In answer to his uncle's letter regarding vigilante gatherings, Joseph wrote: "And we want this to be your motto in common with us, … 'that we will never ground our arms until we give them up by death.' … never give up your arms, but die first."[58]

The following day, Smith placed the city under martial law and assembled the Nauvoo Legion. Appearing before this vast municipal army, he drew his sword and called on "all men" to deliver "this people." He shouted to the soldiers: "Will you all stand by me to the death, and sustain at the peril of your lives, the laws of our country, and the liberties and privileges which our fathers have transmitted unto us, sealed with their sacred blood?" As "thousands" replied with a resounding yes, Major General Smith "call[ed] upon all men, from Maine to the Rocky Mountains, and from Mexico to British America … to come to the deliverance of this people from the hand of oppression."[59] In this last speech to the legion, he exclaimed: "I call God and angels to witness that I have unsheathed my sword with a firm and unalterable determination that this people shall have their legal rights, and be protected from mob violence, or my blood shall be spilt upon the ground like water, and my body consigned to the silent tomb."[60] Then he added even more fuel to the fire by mounting his steed and parading the legion through the streets of Nauvoo, an act for which he would be charged with treason—marshaling a military force while resisting arrest.[61]

---

58. *History of the Church,* 6:485-86.
59. Ibid., 6:498-500.
60. Ibid., 6:499.
61. Ibid., 6:504-05, 561-62.

Events moved swiftly now. Governor Ford wrote from nearby Carthage to inform Smith on June 22 that his "conduct was a very gross outrage upon the laws and the liberties of the people." The *Expositor* "may have been full of libels, but this did not authorize you to destroy it." Expressing his "regard for the liberty of the press and the rights of a free people in a Republican government," even when abused by newspapers, Ford wrote: "I would shed the last drop of my blood to protect those presses from any illegal violence."[62]

Having been an Illinois circuit court judge and a member of the state supreme court before he ran for governor in 1842, Ford was more than adequately qualified to interpret the law. "You have violated the Constitution in at least four particulars," he explained. The first of these was over the principle that "printing presses shall be free." A libelous press could be charged in court, but it had the "right to give truth in evidence." In this instance, the *Expositor* was given "no notice." Furthermore, the Constitution protects against "unreasonable searches and seizures" and grants "due process" of a trial.

Ford observed that Smith's action would not be tolerated in any other "state, county, city, [or] town" in the United States or even in Europe. It was "just such another act in 1830 [that] hurled the king of France from his throne." The governor admonished Smith that "no civilized country can tolerate such conduct, much less can it be tolerated in this free country of the United States."[63] He admonished the mayor to "submit" to arrest and to "interpose no obstacles … either by writ of *habeas corpus* or otherwise."[64]

---

62. Ibid., 6:533-37.

63. After Napoleon abdicated in 1814, France restored its royalty. However, the French did not expect Charles X to behave like his executed brother and sister-in-law, Louis XVI and Marie Antoinette, and deposed him in the July Revolution of 1830 for stifling the press, as he attempted to restore the absolute monarchy.

64. Dallin H. Oaks asserted that the "abatement of newspapers publishing scandalous or provocative material" was not considered a violation of freedom of the press at the time ("The Suppression of the *Nauvoo Expositor*," *Utah Law Review* 9 [Winter 1965]: 902, quoted in Firmage and Mangrum, *Zion in the Courts*, 112-13, 390n13), drawing no distinction between the destruction of a newspaper without a trial and a libel charge being tried in the courts. The Illinois Senate Committee on the Judiciary agreed with Governor Ford that the destruction of the *Expositor* was a "flagrant" violation.

Smith replied the same day that he "dare not" leave Nauvoo. "Writs, we are assured, are issued against us in various parts of the country," he wrote. "For what? To drag us from place to place, from court to court, across the creeks and prairies, till some *bloodthirsty* villain could find his opportunity to shoot us. We dare not come, though your Excellency promises protection ... Sir, we dare not come, for our lives would be in danger, and we are guilty of no crime."[65] Aside from the legal issues, it is clear that Smith was aware of the danger he faced. He addressed a second letter to Ford later the same day, calling accounts in the *Expositor* and elsewhere about his multiple marriages "false" and "libelous." He denounced "the vast excitement which has been got up by false report and libelous publications," commenting that the alternative press "was established for the express purpose of destroying the city."[66]

Denouement

Ford had traveled from Springfield to Carthage on Friday, June 21, in order to monitor the Nauvoo situation more closely. Over the weekend Smith came to realize that he had no other choice but to turn himself in. He and other church leaders, including his scribe, Willard Richards, arrived in Carthage late Monday evening, June 24, and checked into Hamilton's Hotel. The next morning, fifteen days after the destruction of the press, they surrendered at the Hancock County courthouse and were taken into custody on the charge of "riot." Later that morning Joseph and Hyrum Smith were also charged with the capital crime of "treason" for suspending civil rights and calling up the Nauvoo Legion, which with 5,000 troops was credited as the largest military unit in the United States.[67] In a hearing that same day be-

65. *History of the Church,* 6:540.

66. Ibid., 6:525-27.

67. Robert B. Flanders, *Kingdom on the Mississippi Revisited: Nauvoo in Mormon History* (Urbana: University of Illinois Press, 1996), 57, 113n41, citing Hamilton Gardner, "The Nauvoo Legion, 1840-1845: A Unique Military Organization" and *St. Louis Reporter;* Philip M. Flammer, "Nauvoo Legion," *Encyclopedia of Mormonism,* ed. Daniel H. Ludlow (New York: Macmillan, 1992), 3:998; Andrew F. Smith, *The Saintly Scoundrel: The Life and Times of Dr. John Cook Bennett* (Urbana: University of Illinois Press, 1997), 94.

fore a municipal judge, bail of $500 was set and paid for each of the fifteen defendants charged with riot; but a circuit judge was needed to set bail for the capital crime.[68] The Smiths were imprisoned until a scheduled Saturday appearance of Francis Higbee to offer testimony. On Wednesday, Smith told Ford he was willing to satisfy all legal claims if the governor could show how the Nauvoo City Council had transcended its bounds in acting against the *Expositor*. He also argued that the Nauvoo Legion had been mustered for ceremonial purposes, as a show of force for the protection of the city, and not to threaten or invade the state.[69] On Thursday, June 27, Joseph wrote to Emma that he knew he was not guilty of treason.[70] That same day, while Ford went to Nauvoo in search of evidence, Joseph and Hyrum were shot to death in the Carthage jail.

After Smith's arrest, Law had written in his diary that Smith had surrendered to the governor and a large army and had appeared before justice of the peace Robert F. Smith. After posting bail, Joseph Smith was "arrested on the charge of Treason, and sent to jail, to be tried tomorrow."[71] A continuance was granted in order to secure witnesses; the Laws and Fosters were summoned to appear and testify regarding the charge of treason. Law reported his response to these events: "In the morning by daylight we heard the news of the death of the Smiths. We could hardly believe it possible … [T]he judgment of an offended god had fallen upon them." He expressed the depth of his bitterness over what he had seen transpire in Nauvoo, writing that one of "Smith's weakest points" had been "his jealousy of other men."

> He could not bear to hear other men spoken well of. If there was any praise it must be of him; all adoration & worship must be for him. He would destroy his best friend rather than see him become popular in the eyes of the Church or the people at large. His vanity knew no bounds. He was unscrupulous; no man's life was safe if he was disposed to hate him. He sat the laws of God and men at defiance. He was naturally base,

---

68. *History of the Church,* 6:561-631; Firmage and Mangrum, *Zion in the Courts,* 116.

69. *History of the Church,* 6:577-79.

70. Joseph Smith to Emma Smith, June 27, 1844, Community of Christ Library-Archives, Independence, Missouri.

71. Cook, *William Law,* 59, for diary, June 25, 1844.

> brutish and corrupt and cruel. He was one of the false prophets spoken of by Christ who would come in sheep's clothing but inwardly be a rave[n]ing wolf. His works proved it. One great aim seemed to be to demoralize the world, to give it over to Satan, his master; but God stopped him in his mad career & gave him to his destroyers. He claimed to be a god, whereas he was only a servant of the Devil, and as such met his fate. His wife was about as corrupt as he was.[72]

Not quite a month later, on July 20, 1844, William wrote to Isaac Hill, an 1833 Pennsylvania convert who had made bricks for him in Nauvoo. William expressed shock, yet perhaps a sense of poetic justice, in the "judgment" he found in "the wicked slay[ing] the wicked."

> My family & myself are all well and have enjoyed good health and peace since we left Nauvoo, although the Events which have transpired since, were very shocking to my feelings[;] yet as they [Joseph and Hyrum] brought it on themselves, and I used my influence to prevent any [outrage] even from the Commencement of the Excitement, believing that the Civil law had power to expose in[i]quity and punish the wicked[,] I say consequently I look on Calmly and while the wicked slay the wicked, I believe I can see the hand of a blasphemed God Stretched out in judgment[.] [T]he cries of innocence & virtue, have ascended up before the throne of God & he has taken sudden judgment.[73]

Smith's destruction of the *Expositor* appeared to be a clear act of personally motivated violence that made his arrest inevitable. As he avoided answering the state's charges for this action, the more people suspected that he had acted without cause. The denouement in Carthage occurred just a month after Law had traveled there in May to charge Smith with polygamy and fiduciary neglect of his teenage responsibility, Maria Lawrence. Reviewing his own actions forty years later, Law concluded that Joseph was not the only one who had taken advantage of a defenseless girl. Emma, he believed, was equally complicit. "Emma complained about Joseph's living with the L[awrence] girls, but not very violently," he wrote. "It is my conviction that she was his *full accomplice*." With Hyrum Smith's death, William Law, the other

72. Ibid., 60-61, for diary, June 27-28, 1844.
73. William Law to Isaac Hill, July 20, 1844, in Cook, *William Law*, 88-89.

bondsman for the Lawrences, felt acutely the responsibility he bore, ultimately reimbursing Joseph's $3,000 worth of expenses charged to the estate—the amount Joseph had claimed as the value of room and board. After Law settled the account, he noted that "Emma didn't pay a cent."[74] He might have pointed out that Joseph had used celestial marriage as a means to access another fortune, that of Sarah Cleveland, who shared her Quincy, Illinois, home with the Smiths. In 1842, at age fifty-three, she married the prophet, became one of Emma's Relief Society counselors, and then gave financial support to various Mormon projects (see chapter 2).

Later that fateful summer, on August 15, 1844, William Clayton portrayed Emma as "cross" and "angry." She thought Clayton was a "liar" for insinuating that she had "ever committed a crime." She accused Clayton of "neglect[ing] her and the [family] business," which involved plans for an inn called the Nauvoo House, and charged that Clayton spent his time in the "secret counsel of the Twelve." It was such "secret things which had cost Joseph and Hyrum their lives," she anguished. In a "threatening manner," she prophesied that it would be their ruin. Clayton said she "raged" and used "severe threats" and "intended to make [secret things—polygamy] cost us our lives."[75]

Others mentioned Emma's preoccupation with pecuniary matters. Clayton commented that "she don't want to give up the" $200 he had used from the Smith estate to pay a debt. Never had he met such "tyranny … from any person … as I have borne from that woman." Suspecting her of having removed important papers from Joseph's desk, Clayton concluded that her "treachery" was probably "unbounded."[76] In a similar vein, Helen Mar Kimball reminisced about the dancing parties at the Smith home in 1843 and said Emma "had become the ruling spirit, and money had become her God."[77] Emma's biographers, Newell and Avery, commented on Emma's concern over

74. Cook, *William Law,* 120 (emphasis in original).

75. Smith, *Intimate Chronicle,* 143-44.

76. Ibid., 145-46.

77. Linda King Newell and Valeen Tippetts Avery, *Mormon Enigma: Emma Hale Smith* (Garden City, N.Y.: Doubleday, 1984), 166, citing Helen Mar Whitney, *Woman's Exponent* 11 (Nov. 15, 1882): 90.

a gold watch her husband had given Flora Woodworth, wherein the value of the gift seemed an issue.[78]

The same biographers raised the question of a rumored "spiritual swop" of spouses. Joseph was interested in Jane Law and Emma then expressed interest in Jane's husband, William, out of retaliation, so the story went.[79] Newell and Avery introduce the possibility only to dismiss it. Their quotation from Law is nevertheless curious. William said Joseph had "offered to furnish his wife, Emma, with a substitute ... by way of *compensation* for his neglect of her."[80] Nevertheless, the Smiths and Laws had been close, as William had financed Joseph's endeavors for several years. Whatever was behind the talk of Emma or William as a sacrificial offering for sake of harmony at home could not have gone over well with the Laws.

Another irony of the story appeared as Smith wrote to the church in 1839 to inveigh against the very type of polygamous society he had inaugurated. "I would further suggest the impropriety," he wrote, "of the organization of bands or companies, by covenant or oaths, by penalties or secrecies" because "pure friendship always becomes weakened the very moment you undertake to make it stronger by penal oaths and secrecy."[81] Contrary to this statement of principle, the entire understructure of Nauvoo society, as Smith repeatedly emphasized to the Relief Society, was based on providing information only on a need-to-know basis.

When polygamy was discovered, Elizabeth Ann Whitney responded to opposition within the Mormon community, which she considered to be persecution of Joseph Smith. In 1879 she reflected that he "had no peace, his life was sought continually by his enemies." She considered disclosures to be "wicked misrepresentations," which "increased rapidly" in 1844. She identified dissenters John Bennett, Robert Foster, and William and Wilson Law as turncoats who were attempting to overthrow our cause.[82] In a sense, Sidney Rigdon shared

78. Newell and Avery, *Mormon Enigma,* 159.

79. Ibid., 176.

80. Ibid.

81. In *History of the Church,* 3:303.

82. Carol Cornwall Madsen, *In Their Own Words: Women and the Story of Nauvoo*

her perspective in an October 1844 letter to James Greig, in which he suggested that the system of plural marriage was "introduced by the Smiths some time before their death"; Rigdon concluded that polygamy was "the thing which put them into the power of their enemies, and was the immediate cause of their death[s]."[83]

In 1844 an unbridgeable gulf separated two views of polygamy, as either God's will for his true believers or Smith's path to destruction. Benjamin Johnson tied the dissent and apostasy to its beginning in Kirtland when Smith was involved with Fanny Alger: "And I Can now See that as at Nauvoo ... So at Kirtland[,] That the Suspician or Knowledge of the Prophet's Plural Relation was one of the Causes of Apostasy & disruption ... altho at the time there was very little said publickly upon the Subject."[84] No doubt, within as well as outside the theocratic township, Smith's numerous courtships incited much of the trouble the Saints endured.

Governor Ford's statement of grievances, which he mailed to Brigham Young on April 8, 1845, captured the feelings of the common citizens of Illinois. Ford explained that he was in favor of Young taking the Mormons out of Illinois: "Your religion is new and it surprises the people. ... The impression on the public mind everywhere is that your leading men are imposters and rogues and that the others are dupes and fools ... this impression in the minds of the great mass is sufficient to warrant them in considering and treating you as enemies and outcasts." Recalling that "General Joseph Smith last summer ... contemplated a removal west," Ford recommended that "if you can get off by yourselves you may enjoy peace." He advised Young to "take possession of and conquer a portion of the vacant country, and establish an independent government of your own subject only to the laws of nations." He added, confidentially, that "if you once cross the line

---

(Salt Lake City: Deseret, 1994), 203-04, citing Elizabeth Ann Whitney, "A Leaf from an Autobiography," *Woman's Exponent* 7 (Jan 1, 1879): 115; 7 (Feb. 15, 1879): 191.

83. Richard S. Van Wagoner, *Sidney Rigdon: A Portrait of Religious Excess* (Salt Lake City: Signature Books, 1994), 371, citing the *Messenger and Advocate* of Pittsburgh, Oct. 1844.

84. Benjamin Johnson to George F. Gibbs, 1903, available in Dean R. Zimmerman, *I Knew the Prophets* (Bountiful: Horizon Publishers, 1976), 33.

of the United States territories, you would be in no danger of being interfered with" by state or federal officials.[85] One might ask whether Ford's prompting was what nudged Young to make plans for a mass migration out of Illinois or if the governor just confirmed what Young had already determined to do. Young was under constant pressure to leave Illinois. Inside or outside the boundaries of the United States, the question would still be raised about the primary cause of Joseph Smith's death—the marriage doctrine—which could not yet be answered because the church had yet to acknowledge its polygamy. Emma's denials only cemented the obscurity of why she had lost her husband, and Nauvoo had lost its prophet.

Suppression

Instead of evaluating a difficult past in order not to repeat it, the church leadership tried to separate its troubles from their apparent causes. They ascribed the death of Joseph and Hyrum Smith to subterranean forces and malevolent conspiracies of assailants who attacked them, interrupting fulfillment of their foreordained work. Portrayed in this dichotomy, darkness had overtaken the forces of truth. The turmoil over plural marriage was minimized, as was the political opposition to bloc voting, the church's millennialist predictions, and its perceived threat to the social order in neighboring communities. Ford's letter captured some of the antagonism directed toward the Saints of the expected latter days, who denied their marriages even as these plentiful couplings were becoming more and more detectable.

Revision of the death narrative as early as August 1844 marked the beginning of a second wave of the church's revision of its history. It began with the Smith family's rejection of any tangible cause for Joseph's death involving, for instance, financial dealings, destruction of the local newspaper, or polygamy.[86] On the opposite side of the spectrum, Nauvoo Stake President William Marks disclosed that Joseph had told him in his waning days that the "doctrine of polygamy or Spiritual Wife System … will prove our destruction and overthrow … it is

85. In *History of the Church,* 7:396-98.

86. Launius, *Joseph Smith III,* 37.

wrong; it is a cursê to mankind, and we shall have to leave the United States soon, unless it can be put down."[87] Emma would have assumed that with Joseph's death, polygamy would end, and the insult to her reputation would subside. But Brigham married several of Joseph's widows, making it clear that her chagrin would continue. George A. Smith went to see Emma's oldest son, Joseph III, on two occasions, in 1849 and 1856. The apostles assumed the youngster would one day become the church's leader. In 1856, Wilford Woodruff called on Brigham Young and heard the president's son report on a recent trip to Nauvoo. Brigham H. Young said Emma had convinced her children "that it was President Young who had caused the death of Joseph and Hyrum Smith."[88] It made sense that, if "secret things" were the cause of all the trouble, Emma would associate Young's continuation of these esoteric rites and practices as an indication of at least partial culpability.[89] In 1882, three years after Emma died, Woodruff told a congregation in the tabernacle that "Emma … maintained to her dying moments that her husband had nothing to do with the patriarchal order of marriage, but that it was Brigham Young [who] got that up."[90]

From the time of Smith's assassination to the dedication of the Nauvoo temple in early 1846, many, if not most, of Nauvoo's twelve-thousand citizens became aware of plural marriage. Some five-thousand endowments and marriage sealing ceremonies, many solemnizing already polygamous unions, were performed over a two-month period in January and February 1846. Young found it "amusing" to watch the brethren loitering in the temple "to see who takes the sisters through the vail," indicating a possible plural wife.[91] As widely as the unofficial word may have spread among most Nauvoo citizens, the

---

87. William Marks, *Zion's Harbinger and Baneemy's Organ,* St. Louis, Missouri, July 7, 1853.

88. Scott G. Kenney, ed., *Wilford Woodruff's Journal,* 9 vols. (Midvale, Utah: Signature Books, 1983), 4:485-86.

89. Smith, *Intimate Chronicle,* 144.

90. *Journal of Discourses,* 26 vols. (London: Latter-day Saint's Book Depot, 1854-86), 23:131.

91. In Devery S. Anderson and Gary James Bergera, eds., *The Nauvoo Endowment Companies, 1845-1846: A Documentary History* (Salt Lake City: Signature Books, 2005), 191.

practice was still not acknowledged to outsiders. Letters between Ford and the Nauvoo leaders dealt euphemistically with the marriage issue. Ford observed to former bishop George Miller that "these people ... [have] been in difficulty with all the people they ever lived amongst," listing the states of Ohio, Missouri, and Illinois.[92] Why was this? Even pioneer families in Utah looked back on the Nauvoo period with a degree of confusion, unable to state with precision "some cause or other" for their expulsion. Nevertheless, if one had asked what people knew about plural marriage from 1846 on, almost all Mormons who had been in Nauvoo would have known about it, even while they continued to deny it to "gentiles." European Mormons were a different matter. They would have scarcely believed the rumors.

In the late 1840s, securely garrisoned in the Rocky Mountains, 1,200 miles west of the Mississippi River, the Saints could do what they pleased with impunity—or so they thought. Gradually, however, reports began trickling back east from gold rush travelers who conveyed their impressions to the eastern press. In early 1852, Young's counselor Jedediah M. Grant complained that polygamy had been a "bone in the throat" and it was time to expel it—meaning to acknowledge it publicly.[93] The previous year, Young had ventured to speak on the topic in an address before the General Assembly of Deseret on February 4, 1851. His words were not intended for the general public, although it was a more or less public address. Deseret was the provisional government prior to the creation of the Territory of Utah in September 1850. It was about to be replaced by a new legislative body, at which time Deseret would go underground and continue to rule the region as a shadow government. Just the day before his speech to the Assembly of Deseret, Young was ceremoniously installed as territorial governor. There were no federal officials on hand. None had yet arrived in the territory. Young felt secure enough to speak to his fel-

92. *History of the Church,* 7:396-98, 505-08.

93. Jedediah M. Grant to Brigham Young, March 20, 1852, cited by David J. Whittaker, "The Bone in the Throat: Orson Pratt and the Public Announcement of Plural Marriage," *Western Historical Quarterly* 18 (July 1987): 293-314; see also the *New York Herald,* Jan. 10, 1842.

low Saints—the most trusted among them—and also perhaps to send up a trial balloon before ending their self-imposed quarantine altogether. In the speech, Young twice mentioned the desire of Latter-day Saints to "have more wives than one." He took the opportunity to chastise "Gentile Christian Nations" who "make it almost Death for a man to have two wives but they will have as many whores as they please." He risked being prosecuted, should his words reach the U.S. Congress, by boldly announcing: "I have more wives than one," adding that "I am not ashamed to have it known."[94]

The next year, Young asked Apostle Pratt to announce the doctrine from the tabernacle pulpit, simultaneously sending a polygamy mission to England to inform the largest number of converts outside of the United States. William Clayton wrote of the difficult reception the announcement received in England. Baptismal rates declined 88 percent and over fifteen-thousand members were purged from the church rolls from 1853 to 1859. Clayton told Young that this "unfortunate mission of 1852-3" was the "most unpleasant and bitterest period of my life." His discussion of plural marriage was at once turned into a charge of having had "unlawful intercourse with women."[95]

Observers have tried to assess how significant the announcement of 1852 was in terms of hostility engendered against Mormons. Lawrence Foster found it unlikely, in his opinion, that polygamy could have been the major cause of persecution until 1852, although it was "a major disruptive factor *within* the Mormon movement." John Hallwas and Roger Launius acknowledged a larger role for polygamy but placed it in the context of a "struggle between two cultures—that is, groups with differing social visions." It was Smith's theocracy, they wrote, as he "extended his religious ideology into temporal affairs … suppress[ing] their civil rights through institutionalized violence,"

94. In Dale L. Morgan, *The State of Deseret* (Logan: Utah State University Press, 1987), 61; Kenney, *Wilford Woodruff's Journal,* 4:11-12. See also Eugene E. Campbell, *Establishing Zion: The Mormon Church in the American West, 1847-1869* (Salt Lake City: Signature Books, 1988), 208-10.

95. In Smith, *Intimate Chronicle,* xlix-l; Richard L. Jensen and Malcolm R. Thorp, eds., *Mormons in Early Victorian Britain* (Salt Lake City: University of Utah Press, 1989), 179-93.

that made it impossible for Mormons and non-Mormons to live in peace. In this view, polygamy was already a part of the problem extending back to the Nauvoo period. "The Mormon conflict [in Illinois] was not a matter of religious persecution," they concluded. "Non-Mormons did not much care for the oddities of Mormon belief—and some reacted with emotions ranging from curiosity to horror—but they did not try to suppress faith in the Book of Mormon or the prophet's revelations or prevent the Saints from worshiping as they pleased." The neighbors did care about temporal issues—what the Mormons did, in other words, as opposed to what they believed.[96]

As with the church members' own reactions to polygamy, the nation was dumbfounded to witness its growth. Polygamy was linked with slavery on the 1856 Republican platform and characterized as one of the "twin relics of barbarism." Thus, while church leaders continued on their way, relatively undisturbed in the Mountain West, political opposition had coalesced at the national level. Federal action was delayed because of the bitter, long-festering struggle over slavery through the Civil War. The only action Utahns saw during this period was the continuing quarrel with midwestern Latter Day Saints over doctrine. In 1869, four years after Lee surrendered at Appomattox and the year the railroad arrived in Utah Territory, Hyrum Smith's son, Joseph F., began collecting his seventy-five affidavits on Nauvoo celestial marriage. He had determined to affirm incontrovertibly, once and for all, what the actual facts of the matter were. In 1874, William Clayton wrote an affidavit of his own, in which he named several of Joseph Smith's wives, augmenting what he had already hinted at in his journals.

It is difficult today to appreciate the significance of the article on "Plural Marriage" published in May 1887 in Andrew Jenson's *Historical Record.* Jenson included twelve of the affidavits Joseph F. Smith had

---

96. Lawrence Foster, *Women, Family, and Utopia: Communal Experiments of the Shakers, the Oneida Community, and the Mormons* (Syracuse, N.Y.: Syracuse University Press, 1991), 125, emphasis added; John E. Hallwas and Roger D. Launius, *Cultures in Conflict: A Documentary History of the Mormon War in Illinois* (Logan: Utah State University Press, 1995), 1-8. Hallwas and Launius emphasize that "the most explosive issue within Nauvoo was polygamy" and that it "scandalized non-Mormon[s]" (115).

collected and others he himself gathered. Despite this victory for historiography, however, Jenson's article appeared on the down-side slope of the historical peak in polygamy, three years before the Manifesto of President Woodruff that announced the end of the practice. In fact, Woodruff complained to Jenson: "We do not think it a wise step to give these names to the world at the present time in the manner in which you have done ... Advantage may be taken of their publication and in some instances, to the injury, perhaps, of families or relatives of those whose names are mentioned."[97]

Following statehood, as sensitivities relaxed somewhat, seventeen of Joseph F. Smith's affidavits were published by his son, Joseph Fielding Smith, in his book of the less than subtle title, *Blood Atonement and the Origin of Plural Marriage.*[98] Together, only twenty-four affidavits were published by Jenson and Smith, comprising about a third of those collected by Joseph F. Smith.

When the 1892 Temple Lot depositions were taken, polygamy was suffering a heavy political toll. Some of the responses sound distinctly involuntary. The practice had been forced underground, and soon the historical records and even talk of what had occurred in Nauvoo would follow the same path. Some primary sources were simply neglected and remained, for want of interest, unexamined in libraries and archives. Writing to fellow apostle Orson Pratt, Joseph F. Smith recalled when a "few years ago [he had] tried to get affidavits regarding Joseph Smith and 'celestial marriage'" and was "astonished at the scarcity of evidence ... almost total absence of direct evidence upon the subject as connected with the prophet Joseph himself."[99]

Fourteen years after LDS Church President Wilford Woodruff's 1890 Manifesto ostensibly ended polygamy, in April 1904 President

97. Van Wagoner, *Mormon Polygamy,* 135, citing Wilford Woodruff to Andrew Jenson, Aug. 6, 1887; cf. Kenney, *Wilford Woodruff's Journal,* 8:451, where the entry for Aug. 7, 1887, refers to correspondence with "A Jenson."

98. Smith, *Blood Atonement,* 67-94.

99. Joseph F. Smith to Orson Pratt, July 19, 1875, Joseph F. Smith Letterbooks, Ms d 1325, LDS Archives, from notes by Scott G. Kenney. Smith went on to say to Pratt that "if you personally know that he was (the author), I would like to have or see your testimony as a witness on the subject."

Joseph F. Smith issued a so-called "Second Manifesto," declaring Mormon polygamy would no longer be countenanced anywhere in the world. From 1890 to 1904, although the practice continued *sub rosa,* as D. Michael Quinn has documented, the LDS First Presidency published twenty-four denunciations and denials that any new plural marriages were being performed.[100] In 1904, Joseph F. Smith stated:

> Inasmuch as there are numerous reports in circulation that plural marriages have been entered into contrary to the official declaration of President Woodruff, of September 24, 1890, commonly called the Manifesto … I, Joseph F. Smith, President of the Church of Jesus Christ of Latter-day Saints, hereby affirm and declare that no such marriages have been solemnized with the sanction, consent or knowledge of the Church of Jesus Christ of Latter-day Saints.[101]

During that same year, church attorney Franklin S. Richards asked the First Presidency to discipline renegade apostles Matthias F. Cowley and John W. Taylor for continuing to perform plural marriages and to require Senator Reed Smoot to resign his political office in order to stop the Senate investigation into plural marriage. However, Taylor and Cowley were sustained as apostles at the October 1904 general conference and Smoot managed to keep his Senate seat. In 1909, two years after Senate hearings, the Senator noted in his diary that "the question of new polygamy cases is being discussed and I told Pres Smith the only way to stop them was to handle the parties that do the marrying." To end the adverse publicity, President Smith arranged for Cowley to be disfellowshipped and for Taylor to be excommunicated.[102]

---

100. D. Michael Quinn, "LDS Church Authority and New Plural Marriages, 1890-1904," *Dialogue: A Journal of Mormon Thought* 18 (Spring 1985): 9.

101. Ibid., 10.

102. Harvard S. Heath, ed., *In the World: The Diaries of Reed Smoot* (Salt Lake City: Signature Books and Smith Research Associates, 1997), 23; Quinn, "LDS Church Authority," 101. Smoot had been elected to the Senate in 1902, but a Senate committee investigated him for over two years, charging that he belonged to a "self perpetuating fifteen member ruling body that controlled Utah's elections and economy … [which was] secretly continuing to preach and permit plural marriages." The committee took 4,000 pages of testimony, and although the committee recommended Smoot's expulsion, the full Senate allowed him to retain his seat. See Richard S. Van Wagoner and

However, polygamy was a hardy plant that refused to be uprooted. B. Carmon Hardy has identified 220 Mormon men who engaged in 262 post-1890 plural marriages.[103] Joseph F. Smith attached to his 1904 statement a directive to bishops and stake presidents to excommunicate new polygamists and withdraw support of the renegade polygamists in the so-called Mexican colonies of Colonia Dublán and Colonia Juárez. Most Mormons were struggling to be accepted as normal Americans and wanted to forget about their ancestors' marriages. Apostle Francis M. Lyman concluded in 1910 that the new Manifesto implied that the church should stop performing marriages in the temple.[104] A revived series of excommunications lowered the rate of new polygamy in 1911. The next year, the Mexican Revolution compelled Mormons to descend from the high country of Chihuahua northward into Arizona and other parts of the western United States. Plural marriage was no longer being talked about as an essential belief, but more often as an embarrassing historical anomaly. Supporting this reduced profile, a third wave of censorship made it difficult to glean much hard evidence about what seemed to be an increasingly exotic past, a darkened window through which observers had to gaze in trying to imagine Nauvoo in the 1840s.

Mormon historians became increasingly enamored with the church's interconnectedness with the great western myths of pioneering life: cowboys, miners, railroads, and Indians. Church-employed historians did not want to portray a people maintaining an outpost on the fringe of American society. Mormons accepted as sufficient the explanation that Joseph Smith's death was due to an angry mob, without caring to know specifically what those Illinois neighbors had been angry about. It was the broader society of Illinois that was now seen as backward, barbaric, and primitive in the face of a civilizing force of Latter-day Saints.[105]

Steven C. Walker, *A Book of Mormons* (Salt Lake City: Signature Books, 1982), 314-19; Michael Harold Paulos, ed., *The Mormon Church on Trial: Transcripts of the Reed Smoot Hearings* (Salt Lake City: Signature Books, 2008).

103. Hardy, *Solemn Covenant,* 389 ff.

104. Ibid., 298, 307n87.

105. See B. H. Roberts, *A Comprehensive History of the Church of Jesus Christ of Latter-*

One LDS educator in 1967 wrote about the "causes" of conflict in Nauvoo and mentioned Smith's death as a watershed moment, a dividing mark that separated the eras, without mentioning plural marriage.[106] The sexual habits of the Latter-day Saints had been buried so deeply in the past, it was no longer necessary even to deny them. Polygamy had become a taboo subject for the church.[107] Access to documents that reflected Mormon plural marriage was restricted at LDS Church archives. This kind of negative thinking, so the protocol went, was a curiosity that distracted from the missionary effort. In fact, in the mid-twentieth century, an LDS authority who seemed to have been assigned the task as part of his apostolic duties utilized surveillance to ferret out polygamists, excommunicate them, and refer them to the police in order to obscure this embarrassing reminder of former days.[108] Then came the flood of family diaries, letters, and testimonials by people who felt a desire to make sense of their marginalized ancestors—no one knowing that their seemingly anomalous branch on the family tree was actually normative for Latter-day Saints. With these sources as tools, historians were able to begin the task of fleshing out this complex tale.

---

day Saints, 6 vols. (Salt Lake City: Church of Jesus Christ of Latter-day Saints, 1930); Orson F. Whitney, *Life of Heber C. Kimball, an Apostle* (Salt Lake City: Juvenile Instructor Office, 1888); Joseph Fielding Smith, *Essentials of Church History* (Salt Lake City: Deseret News Press, 1922); William E. Berrett, *The Restored Church* (Salt Lake City: Deseret Book, 1940); Leonard J. Arrington and Davis Bitton, *The Mormon Experience* (New York: Alfred A. Knopf, 1979).

106. Kenneth W. Godfrey, "Causes of Non-Mormon Conflict in Hancock County, Illinois, 1839-1846," Ph.D. diss., 1967, chap. 7; Wallace Stegner, *Mormon Country* (Lincoln: University of Nebraska Press, 1981).

107. See Martha S. Bradley, "Changed Faces: The Official LDS Position on Polygamy, 1890-1990," *Sunstone* 14 (Feb. 1990): 26-33.

108. Ibid., 31.

EIGHT.

In Search of Lost History

A Record of Unpublicized Marriages

Nauvoo's missing wives began to reappear in 1852. Although Orson Pratt's public announcement of celestial marriage in Salt Lake City did not exactly rewrite Nauvoo's obscure history, by starting to speak openly, the long suppressed stories of seven-hundred plural wives came to the surface. Now proud and bold, the Salt Lake leaders even encouraged Nauvoo's migrant families to tell their stories. Diaries, journals, letters, and affidavits would confirm the rumors that had flooded Nauvoo and Illinois farm towns just a few years back. The days of denial were past. The Saints were their own masters. Now was a time of pride, time to tell it all.

The process of discovery continued through 1869, when Apostle Joseph F. Smith began to collect affidavits of undocumented marriages, and into 1892 when participants and witnesses testified in the Federal Court Temple Lot case, then in 1904-07 when a U.S. Senate subcommittee probed the political dimensions of polygamy in a series of hearings to consider the election of Utah's Senator Smoot. When polygamy was outlawed at the end of the nineteenth century, the story went underground, not to resurface again until more than a half century later when researchers began assembling evidence from a variety of sources. The documents they found can be summarized in five categories: personal writings, public records, sworn affidavits, court depositions, and Senate testimony. Since the renaissance in Mormon studies in the 1970s, there have been path-breaking studies that assembled new evidence of polygamy, along with interpretive essays, documentary collections, and narrative histories,[1] all presented to a receptive audience.

Personal writings

Letters, diaries, and autobiographies provided detailed eyewitness descriptions of how plural marriage unfolded in Nauvoo. Among the most useful sources, including both contemporary and retrospective impressions, are accounts by Martha Brotherton, Oa Jacobs Cannon, William Clayton, Benjamin Johnson, Helen Mar Kimball, Joseph Kingsbury, Mary Elizabeth Rollins Lightner, Joseph Bates Noble, Eliza Partridge, Emily Partridge, Patty Sessions, Bathsheba Smith, Eliza Snow, Lorenzo Snow, Orange White, Brigham Young, and Zina Huntington Jacobs Young. Writing from the perspective of a teenaged live-in baby tender, Emily Partridge was shocked when her married employer proposed and asked her to burn the letter he would write. For context, Joseph Smith's own diaries, while silent on his courtships and marriages, offer confirmation of his whereabouts and observations about people and events. His diaries formed the basis of six of the seven volumes in the official *History of the Church.*

Eyewitness narratives give a sense of the Nauvoo ambience and provide many of the intimate descriptions we are aware of. By contrast, Joseph Smith left euphemistic clues, but neglected to say up front just what occurred at the days and times of his uncelebrated marriages. His diary offers the disarmingly mundane information that he "rode out to the farm," or "met with my counselor," without mentioning that a plural marriage occurred at the farm or that the counselor was the one who performed it. While Lucy Walker's father managed the Smith family farm, Joseph's visits there included courtship, marriage, and conjugal stopovers, according to Lucy's Temple Lot testimony taken in Salt Lake City. The interplay between moments

1. See Davis Bitton, "Ten Years in Camelot: A Personal Memoir," *Dialogue: A Journal of Mormon Thought* 16 (Autumn 1983): 9-33.

with Emma, occasional visits to other wives, shifting from place to place to avoid arrest, planning a city, and running a church, reveals a talent for remaining calm amid the storm. In a life with such involvements, it is hard to see when he found time for reflection and contemplation to prepare for writing, speaking, and theologizing, not to mention pronouncing "revelations" to guide his thousands of followers.

While the space Smith devoted in his diary to his marriages is significant for its understatement, in 1843 one of his scribes appended a retrospective April 1842 record of Smith's marriage to Marinda Johnson, the only specific mention of a plural marriage in the prophet's personal journals. The *History of the Church* deleted even that one citation.

Equally graphic are the surviving letters which mention town events or convey impressions from former citizens. A year following the inception of Nauvoo celestial marriage, Smith's remarkable 1842 letter to Sarah Ann Whitney and her parents, urging them to visit him in hiding but to take precautions in case Emma is present, comprises an heirloom of history. Smith's letter to Nancy Rigdon, in which he argues that "whatever is asked … is right" sounds as if it were drawn from a medieval romance. The entire corpus of Smith's correspondence, including affectionate notes to Emma, helps frame the timing and feeling of the dual life he led. George A. Smith's 1869 letter to Joseph Smith III, in which George cited the founder's admonition not to fall behind in his "privileges" (to wed additional women), is equally telling. Clayton echoed Smith's invitation to accept these "favors," and his "right" to "get" all he could.

Public records

Complementing these diaries and letters, newspapers and periodicals such as the *Times and Seasons, Sangamo Journal, Nauvoo Expositor, Historical Record,* and *Deseret News* document events like Zina Huntington's marriage to Henry Jacobs months before her connubial bond with Joseph Smith (*Times and Seasons*) and John Bennett's public disclosure of Joseph's persuasive appeals (*Sangamo Journal*). Organizational minutes of the Nauvoo Stake High Council and the Nauvoo Female Relief Society show how the town leader dealt with internal marital disputes while keeping these complex relationships private.

The Nauvoo temple records were not publicly available until the 1970s. When researchers were allowed to scrutinize them, they found that the notations about marriages for "time and eternity" (this life and the next), and some for "time" only, largely confirmed what had been claimed by other sources.[2] The Nauvoo temple ledger titled "Sealing Book A" listed the ceremonies as they occurred in 1846, often resealings of prior undisclosed weddings. In 2004 they were reproduced in the same chronological format by Lyndon W. Cook in his *Nauvoo Marriages, Proxy Sealings: 1843-1846,* then in 2005 by Devery S. Anderson and Gary James Bergera in their volume, *The Nauvoo Endowment Companies, 1845-1846.* The following year, the same information was arranged alphabetically, with annotation, by Lisle G Brown in his work, *Nauvoo Sealings, Adoptions, and Anointings.* Information from the diaries and reminiscences can now be cross-checked against the Nauvoo temple records. In this volume, readers may consult a condensed summary of this information in Appendix B, where the demographic data (births, deaths, marriages, sealings) for nearly 200 men and over 500 plural wives in Nauvoo are presented.

Affidavits

In 1869, Apostle Joseph F. Smith collected affidavits from wives and eyewitnesses to his uncle Joseph Smith's marriages and other LDS sealings from as far back as twenty-eight years earlier. When the RLDS Church established a mission in Utah in 1863 and the Mormon founder's children refused to believe the assertions of their Rocky Mountain cousins that Joseph Smith had been a polygamist, Joseph F. began looking for supporting documents. Initially he was confronted by a dearth of evidence for the well-disguised Nauvoo events. In an 1875 letter to his colleague Apostle Orson Pratt, Joseph F. complained

2. Historian D. Michael Quinn noted in 1988 that "although [church] authorities give Latter-day Saints a solemn obligation to verify all [temple] ordinance data (including polygamous sealings for their ancestors), the [LDS] Historical Department withholds that information not only from rank-and-file Mormons but also from the Genealogical Department and Temple Department" ("Remarkable Book about Memorable Polygamy," a review of *Mormon Polygamous Families: Life in the Principle* by Jessie L. Embry, *Sunstone,* Nov. 1988, 47-48).

that his first cousin Joseph III had spun an imaginative tale about why Utahns had falsely attributed polygamy to his father—basically in order to cover their own sins. Joseph III, president of the RLDS Church, accused Brigham Young of having "steadied the ark" at the deaths of Joseph and Hyrum Smith in a well intentioned but seriously misguided act of treason—then led the church astray with his invention of polygamy. "The idea," Joseph F. wrote to Pratt,

> has been advanced in a pamphlet written by Young Joseph … [and] it is held [to] with tenacity by this apostate clique … [A] few years ago [I] tried to get affidavits regarding Joseph Smith and "celestial marriage"… I was astonished at the scarcity of evidence. I might say almost total absence of direct evidence upon the subject as connected with the prophet Joseph himself … If you personally know that he was (the author [of plural marriage]), I would like to have or see your testimony as a witness on the subject.[3]

None of the affidavits Joseph F. Smith gathered were published until 1879, four years later and the year Emma Smith died. Six months after Emma's April 30 death, the RLDS Church published an edited conversation with her wherein she stated that her husband had "never taught nor practiced polygamy."[4] The same month the interview was printed, Emma's nephew Joseph F. Smith sent a rebuttal to the *Deseret News.* His letter of October 17 promised "sworn statements and affidavits of a few reliable persons," which he said would "present a much better appearance of voracity than the dialogue between Joseph Smith [III] and his mother." He noted that Emma's lips were

3. Joseph F. Smith to Orson Pratt, Sr., July 19, 1875, Joseph F. Smith Letterbooks, Joseph F. Smith Collection, LDS Archives, from notes by Scott G. Kenney, with permission. That Brigham Young had stepped in to steady the ark and then corrupted the church was being proposed by Isaac Sheen as early as 1849 in the *Aaronic Herald,* a precursor of the RLDS *Saints' Herald* ("The Man of Sin," *Aaronic Herald,* Feb. 1, 1849, online at "Miscellaneous Southern Newspapers," *Uncle Dale's Readings in Early Mormon History,* www.sidneyrigdon.com). Orson Pratt evidently declined to prepare an affidavit in response to Joseph F. Smith's request (see also Orson Pratt, *The Essential Orson Pratt* [Salt Lake City: Signature Books, 1991]).

4. Joseph Smith III, ed., "Last Testimony of Sister Emma," *Saints' Advocate,* Oct. 1879, 49-52.

conveniently "sealed in death," so she could not vouch for the accuracy of the published dialogue.[5]

Ultimately, in this first salvo against Smith family denials, Joseph F. Smith offered as evidence seven eyewitness affidavits. The witnesses included a wedding officiator, two of Joseph Smith's wives, two men whose sisters had married Smith, and two witnesses to conjugal visits. The witnesses were Joseph Noble, who conducted the ceremony when Smith married his first plural wife; wives Emily and Eliza Partridge; brothers-in-law Benjamin Johnson and Lorenzo Snow; and observers John Benbow and Lovina Walker. With permission implied by the publication of these initial accounts, others would gradually begin to add their voices to these seven. A week later in the October 22, 1879, *Deseret News,* another of Smith's widows, Eliza R. Snow, added her memories to the public record. Four years later, Emily Partridge began publishing excerpts from her autobiography, which appeared in the *Woman's Exponent* beginning with the August 1, 1883, issue for the period when she was courted by and married Joseph Smith while living in his home. Three years later the *Deseret News* published an article by Joseph F. Smith about his uncle's teachings to some of the "leading members" in 1842 and the dictation of the revelation in 1843. William Clayton's 1874 affidavit listing some of Smith's plural wives was included in the same issue of the newspaper.[6]

Andrew Jenson published twelve of the affidavits that Joseph F. Smith had collected, including eight that had appeared in the 1879 *Deseret News,* and also gathered thirteen new statements in the 1887 edition of the *Historical Record.* Five years into the new century, Joseph Fielding Smith (son of Joseph F. Smith), published seventeen affidavits, of which five were duplicated from Jenson's *Historical Record,* as "expressions of eye and ear witnesses."[7] Although Joseph Fielding Smith characterized his father's collection as comprising "one hundred or more" statements, today we only know of seventy-five.

5. Andrew Jenson, "Plural Marriage," *Historical Record* 6 (May 1887): 220, quoting Joseph F. Smith.

6. *Deseret News,* May 20, 1886.

7. Joseph Fielding Smith, *Blood Atonement and the Origin of Plural Marriage* (Salt Lake City: Deseret News Press, 1905), 67-88.

Reports of Nauvoo Polygamy

1869 Joseph F. Smith begins a collection of 75 affidavits, now found in the Affidavits on Celestial Marriage collections consisting of six folders in LDS Archives. The documents are allocated among (1) "40 Affidavits on Celestial Marriage," May 1-Oct. 13, 1869; (2) "Book No. 2," with twenty-one affidavits, 1869-1870; and (3) "Affidavits, 1869-1915," with twenty-seven affidavits, thirteen of them duplicating others in "Book No. 2."

1879 Emma Smith is quoted posthumously in the *Saints' Advocate,* saying that "Joseph never taught nor practiced polygamy."

Joseph F. Smith publishes eight affidavits in the *Deseret News.*

Eliza Snow's rebuttal of Emma Smith appears in the *Deseret News.*

1883 Emily Partridge Young's account is published in the *Woman's Exponent.*

1886 The *Deseret News* publishes Joseph F. Smith's account of his uncle's teachings and revelation on plural marriage and William Clayton's 1874 affidavit.

1887 Andrew Jenson publishes twelve affidavits in the *Historical Record* (the eight from *Deseret News* plus four new ones). He also includes thirteen statements.

1905 Joseph Fielding Smith publishes twelve new affidavits in *Blood Atonement and the Origin of Plural Marriage* (plus five already found in the *Historical Record*) to produce a total of twenty-four published affidavits. He also includes three unnotarized statements.

When Joseph F. Smith began collecting these affidavits in 1869, he started with his uncle's widows: Elvira Cowles, Mary Ann Frost, Desdemona Fullmer, Presendia and Zina Huntington, Marinda Johnson, Melissa Lott, Sylvia Lyon, Martha McBride, Eliza and Emily Partridge, Rhoda Richards, Ruth Sayers, Eliza Snow, Lucy Walker, and

Sarah Ann Whitney, as well as with Hyrum's widow Mercy Thompson. Andrew Jenson published and explained the provenance of four of those statements in 1887. Sixteen years later Joseph Fielding Smith published the affidavits of six of Joseph's wives, five of which were newly put into print.[8]

TABLE 8.1 Published affidavits of Joseph's widows

	A. Jenson* 1887	J. F. Smith** 1905	
Almera Johnson		*BA*	
Melissa Lott		*BA*	
Martha McBride		*BA*	
Eliza Partridge	*HR-DN*		
Emily Partridge	*HR-DN*		
Rhoda Richards		*BA*	
Eliza Snow	*HR*		
Lucy Walker Kimball	*HR*	*BA*	
Sarah Ann Whitney		*BA*	
	4	6	
		-1	
	4	5	4 + 5 = 9 published widows' affidavits
			+7 unpublished
			16 total widows' affidavits

*Jenson's 1887 article, "Plural Marriage," in the *Historical Record* (*HR*); Jenson quotes affidavits from Joseph Fielding Smith, October 17, 1879, *Deseret News* (*HR-DN*).

** Joseph Fielding Smith's 1905 *Blood Atonement and the Doctrine of Plural Marriage* (*BA*).

The main archival collection of "40 Affidavits on Celestial Marriage" became a primary source of evidence for Nauvoo polygamy during a later time when people were discouraged from investigating the topic. The initial forty affidavits, which are recorded in a notebook that could be designated as book number 1, are complemented by both "Book No. 2" and a third "book." These three books form a combined collection of seventy-five affidavits.

The first collection begins on May 1, 1869, with the statements of

8. Jenson, "Plural Marriage," 219-40; Smith, *Blood Atonement*, 67-76. As noted in chapter 3, neither Sylvia Lyon's nor Vienna "Jaques's" affidavits are signed. Vienna is considered a possible wife.

Joseph's second and third plural wives, Zina and Presendia Huntington. It concludes on October 13, 1869, with a sworn statement from Roxena Adams, plural wife of a Smith family friend, James Adams. Book number 1 includes Joseph Noble's account of performing Smith's first plural marriage. The folders comprise an original affidavit book and a duplicate (noted "Du"). The forty affidavits of book number 1 and the twenty-one affidavits of Book No. 2 are entirely distinct; there is no overlap.

Book No. 2 contains twenty-one affidavits from 1869 and 1870, along with the duplicate copy of a 1903 statement by Bathsheba Smith commenting on Emma Smith's denials of polygamy. The original documents are housed separately in LDS Archives. Book No. 2 also contains Elizabeth Ann Whitney's and Sarah Ann Whitney's affirmations that Joseph Smith wrote a letter on August 18, 1842, inviting them to visit him in hiding so he could complete "the transaction" in "saf[e]ty."

The third collection, "Affidavits, 1869-1915," contains twenty-seven affirmed statements, thirteen of which replicate affidavits from the Book No. 2 series. For instance, the third collection repeats the statements of Orson Hyde, Eliza Partridge (four affidavits), Mary Ann Pratt, and Lorenzo Snow—as well as the 1903 document from Bathsheba Smith, adding a second affidavit by Bathsheba from a day earlier. It concludes with Josephine Rosetta Fisher's 1915 assertion that she was a child of Joseph Smith. This [Book 3] collection includes two accounts by John Rigdon, Sidney Rigdon's son, one affirming that Joseph Smith propositioned his sister, Nancy—the second account being a shortened version that was edited for the *Deseret News* (see table 8.2).

LDS historian Andrew Jenson, in his 1887 article on "Plural Marriage," explained:

> As a number of apostates and other opponents of the truth are continually attempting to deny certain facts connected with the introduction of plural marriage among the Latter-day Saints by Joseph Smith, the Prophet, it has been deemed proper, in connection with our other historical labors, to compile and republish in the *Record* the following state-

> ments, testimonies, affidavits, etc., from truthful and reliable parties, who have been eye and ear witnesses to the circumstances and incidents of which they speak; and also to add new proofs and testimonies to those already made public.

As intimated by Jenson, it was the argument between the Utah and Missouri churches that originally inspired the movement in Utah to collect documentation of what had occurred almost three decades earlier, in Nauvoo.

After Joseph Smith III assumed the RLDS Church leadership in Amboy, Illinois, on April 6, 1860, he would turn his attention to two things: (1) clearing his father's name of what he regarded as a malicious insult involving polygamy and (2) converting the Utah Saints back to the original church he believed they had abandoned when they went west. Smith was tolerant of the Utah Saints but not of their leader, Brigham Young, whom he regarded as an evil doer comparable to a southern slave holder. Joseph III felt the Reorganization had the potential to call together the scattered elements of the Restoration. In the midst of the Civil War, the young Smith sent a delegation to Utah. Edmund C. Briggs, one of the RLDS Twelve, met with Brigham Young on August 11, 1863, but the LDS president forbade his guest from preaching anywhere in the territory and told Briggs he could not guarantee his safety. However, the RLDS apostle did preach in the territory and began to convert a sizeable number of Saints. One of those converts was George P. Dykes, a polygamist, who switched churches that November. By the next year, the mission had acquired three hundred converts and expanded to California. In an 1877 letter, Joseph III wavered over the question of "whether or not Joseph Smith did practice it [polygamy],"[9] but continued to condemn it. As the deceased prophet's son matured, the RLDS mission survived through the 1880s. The church president himself made four trips to Utah in 1876, 1885, 1887-88, and 1889.[10]

The first affidavit Joseph F. Smith cited in his 1879 letter to the

---

9. In Roger D. Launius, *Joseph Smith III: Pragmatic Prophet* (Urbana: University of Illinois, 1988), 201.

10. Ibid., 229.

Deseret News was the extraordinary account of fifty-nine-year-old Joseph Bates Noble, registered by notary public James Jack on June 6, 1869. Noble was in a position to know about Nauvoo polygamy because he had been chosen to marry Joseph Smith to his first plural wife, the sister of Noble's own wife, Mary Adeline Beaman.[11] Next came the statement of fifty-one-year-old Benjamin Johnson, given on March 4, 1870. Johnson had intimate knowledge of Smith's relationship with his two sisters, Almera and Delcena. The next affidavit was that of Lorenzo Snow, brother of Smith's wife, Eliza Snow.

Joseph F. went on to explain that John Benbow, an English immigrant and farmer who had given financial support to the prophet, stated on the same date as Lorenzo Snow in 1869 that "in the spring or forepart of the summer of 1843, at [Benbow's] house, four miles from Nauvoo, … President Joseph Smith taught him [Benbow] and his wife, Jane Benbow, the doctrine of celestial marriage, or plurality of wives, Hyrum Smith being present." In this same affidavit, Benbow noted that "Hannah Ells Smith, a wife of the Prophet, boarded at his house two months during the summer of the same year" and that "President Smith frequently visited his wife Hannah at his (J. B's.) house."

Following these four initial affidavits came statements by two of Smith's wives, Emily and Eliza Partridge, as well as excerpts from Emily's autobiography, which would be serialized in the 1883 *Woman's Exponent.* Both sisters, now forty-five and forty-nine years old respectively, affirmed on May 1 and July 1, 1869, that they were "married or sealed" to Joseph Smith "in the presence of Emma (Hale) Smith, (now Emma Bidamon)." Then came the June 16, 1869, statement of Hyrum Smith's daughter, Lovina Walker, in which she affirmed that "while I was living with Aunt Emma Smith, in Fulton … Illinois, in the year 1846, she told me that she, Emma Smith, was present and witnessed the marrying or sealing of Eliza Partridge, Emily Partridge, Maria Lawrence and Sarah Lawrence to her husband, Joseph Smith, and that she gave her consent thereto."

---

11. See Joseph B. Noble, Affidavit, June 26, 1869, in "40 Affidavits on Celestial Marriage," 1869, LDS Archives; also in Jenson, "Plural Marriage."

In the *Woman's Exponent,* Emily would add:

> The first intimation I had from Brother Joseph that there was a pure and holy order of plural marriage, was in the spring of 1842, but I was not married until 1843. I was married to him on the 11th of May, 1843, by Elder James Adams. Emma was present. She gave her free and full consent. She had always, up to this time, been very kind to me and my sister Eliza, who was also married to the Prophet Joseph with Emma's consent. Emma, about this time, gave her husband two other wives—Maria and Sarah Lawrence.

When Joseph F. Smith put pen to paper again to document Nauvoo polygamy in a letter that appeared in the *Deseret News* on May 20, 1886, he made the extraordinary claim that polygamy had been "first revealed to Joseph Smith in 1831." And at that early date, ten years before Joseph's first Nauvoo marriage, he had only told "a very few of his intimate associates" about it: Oliver Cowdery and Lyman Johnson, both of whom left the church in 1838, and Orson Pratt, who was disciplined in 1842 but reinstated in 1843. However, the prophet had waited until 1842 to instruct some "leading members" in the doctrine—"those whom he could trust"—and they practiced it as an "unwritten law." Even that restriction changed in 1843 when, according to Joseph F., "a portion of the revelation was written." By claiming that only "a portion" of the full revelation was written down, Joseph F. was able to insinuate that there were more instructions, explications, and promises yet to be divulged.[12] In this way, he was able to portray polygamy as part of a grand plan that was being revealed gradually, thereby explaining away the inconvenient detail that it had been practiced before the revelation was recorded.

As if speaking to Joseph Smith's widow and son, Utah nephew and cousin Joseph F. Smith then emphasized that no one other than the church founder himself had served as God's spokesman to announce the doctrine to the earth; that the founder "did practice" it himself. Conceding that the Nauvoo *Times and Seasons* had published "seeming denials" of polygamy attributed to the prophet and others, Joseph F.

---

12. In Jenson, "Plural Marriage," 219-20.

claimed that when carefully scrutinized, these were actually "proofs of the *true coin,* the counterfeit of which they denounced."[13]

To the affidavits of these eight key witnesses quoted by Joseph F. Smith, Andrew Jenson added seventeen other commentaries, including four formal affidavits. For instance, he quoted Eliza Snow's statement of *"fact"* (emphasis in original), published in the *Deseret News* in October 1879, that Emma "of her own free will and choice, gave her husband four wives," two of whom Emma taught "the doctrine of plural marriage and urged them to accept it." Eliza signed her letter to the newspaper, "Eliza R. Snow. A wife of Joseph Smith, the Prophet."

Jenson included the testimonies of William Clayton (1874), Howard Coray (1882), David Fullmer (1869), Thomas Grover (1885), Lucy Walker Kimball (undated), Sarah M. Kimball (undated), Joseph C. Kingsbury (1886), Lyman O. Littlefield (*Millennial Star,* 1883), Orson Pratt (1878: "Lyman Johnson ... told me himself that Joseph had made known to him as early as 1831, that plural marriage was a correct principle"), Erastus Snow (undated), Leonard Soby (1886), Allen J. Stout (1885), Mercy R. Thompson (1883, 1886), and Samuel A. Woolley (undated). To these he added "additional testimony" from, for instance, Arthur Stayner of the Farmington Ward bishopric, who read Grover's affidavit at an LDS stake conference in Centerville, Utah, in 1883. Thomas Grover had attested to the fact that, as a former member of the Nauvoo Stake High Council, he was present at the 1843 meeting when Hyrum Smith read to all there "the revelation on celestial marriage." There were also statements by Joseph B. Noble (again), LDS President John Taylor, and LDS Apostle George Q. Cannon.

Jenson then listed twenty-seven women he had identified as Joseph Smith's plural wives, based on their own declarations, and provided sketches of their marital experiences. Following this, in a "miscellaneous" section, he offered information about Louisa Beaman, provided by Joseph Noble, who also described his own plural marriages and recollections of Joseph Smith and other Nauvoo history; Olive Frost, provided by her sister, Mary Ann Frost Pratt; Emily Partridge

13. Ibid.

Young, from her autobiography; and Desdemona Fullmer, Almera Johnson, Lucy Walker Kimball, and Eliza Partridge Lyman.

Two descriptions of the prophet's liaisons, published before Joseph F. Smith's letters, were notably absent from Jenson's 1887 *Historical Record.* In the *Salt Lake Tribune* of October 6, 1875, one of the original Twelve Apostles of the LDS Church, William E. McLellin, had described conversations with Emma Smith about her husband's involvement with Fanny Alger in Kirtland. McLellin had also written to Joseph Smith III about this in 1872,[14] but no doubt because McLellin had left the church, Joseph F. Smith chose not to include his testimony among those of the other eyewitnesses, even though Joseph F. thought plural marriage had its beginnings in Kirtland (see also chapter 1). Jenson, no doubt, followed the church president's lead in this judgment.

Another valuable source comes from a former bodyguard of both Joseph Smith and Brigham Young. In his 1877 deathbed confessions, John D. Lee described how plural marriage had been presented to church members as "the stepping stone to celestial salvation." Sealed to his second wife, Nancy Bean, in the winter of 1845, Lee documented marriages to her and eighteen other plural wives. He recalled that in Nauvoo these unions were not made public, then observed that Brigham Young was careful to have only his first wife at home with him, explaining: "Many a night have I gone with [Young], arm in arm, and guarded him while he spent an hour or two with his young brides, then guarded him home."[15] Lee's conviction and execution for the 1857 Mountain Meadows Massacre may explain his absence from Jenson's *Historical Record.*

Court depositions

More testimony about Joseph Smith's plural wives came out in 1892 during the enigmatic and untimely Temple Lot case, two years after Wilford Woodruff promised to end polygamy. The LDS Church

---

14. Stan Larson and Samuel J. Passey, eds., *The William E. McLellin Papers, 1854-1880* (Salt Lake City: Signature Books, 2007), 483-95.

15. John D. Lee, *Mormonism Unveiled; Or the Life and Confessions of the Late Mormon Bishop, John D. Lee* (New York: Bryan, Brand & Company, 1877), 166, 167ff.

was not a defendant in the lawsuit, at least not formally, but was the object of scrutiny. As plaintiff, the RLDS Church sued Granville Hedrick's Church of Christ for claiming of a piece of property once owned by Joseph Smith's Church of Christ denomination in Independence, Missouri. Polygamy became a surrogate issue in determining whether the RLDS Church represented the Mormon community that had purchased the land in 1831. If Hedrick's church could demonstrate that Joseph Smith, himself, had acquired dozens of plural wives, then presumably it could successfully challenge the monogamous RLDS Church's claim to this Missouri land. The site held religious significance for all three denominations because Smith had said it was where Christ would return to earth at the outbreak of the millennium.

Originally the prophet hoped to build a temple on a sixty-three-acre plot of land at the summit of a hill in Independence. Sidney Rigdon dedicated the site for a temple on August 3, 1831,[16] and Bishop Edward Partridge purchased the land on December 19 for $130. After the Mormons were expelled from Independence in 1833, they built a temple in Kirtland, Ohio, instead. Then in 1837 and 1838, divided by financial turmoil and theological schism, the Mormons left Ohio for Missouri. A year later, in the winter of 1838-39, they were forced out of Missouri and moved to Illinois. In 1848, Lydia Partridge, the widow of Edward Partridge, and her three daughters then living in Iowa sold the property to James Pool of Jackson County, Missouri. That next year, Pool's land was sold, and from 1869 to 1877 Granville Hedrick acquired eight lots for $1,175. This two and a half acres became the so-called "Temple Lot." The Hedrickites built a small meeting house on the northeast corner of the lot ten years later and began holding regular meetings. After the Temple Lot suit, the RLDS managed to acquire other parts of the sixty-three-acre tract, but joint discussions with the Hedrickites,[17] which had begun in 1885, proved fruitless.

---

16. The *History of the Church* names Joseph Smith.

17. Jenson, "The Temple Lot," *Historical Record* 7 (Dec. 1888): 647-48. R. Jean Addams, "The Church of Christ (Temple Lot): Its Emergence, Struggles and Early Schisms," *Scattering of the Saints: Schism within Mormonism,* eds. Newell G. Bringhurst and John C. Hamer (Independence, Mo.: John Whitmer Books, 2007), 206-23.

The LDS Church in Utah became involved on October 14, 1890, one week after President Woodruff's Manifesto was approved by a general church conference, and offered a $20,000 bank loan to the Hedrickites, accepting "the Temple Block as security." Frustrated by failed attempts to merge, purchase, or obtain it through the 1887 "Notice to Vacate," Joseph III decided to proceed with formal legal action and filed suit in the U.S. Circuit Court for Western Missouri in Kansas City, claiming the RLDS were the legal inheritors of Joseph Smith's church, and he asserted that the Partridge family had not owned the property and was not in a position to sell it.[18]

Eventually the argument over the rightful successor to Joseph Smith's church hinged on whether Smith had initiated plural marriage, something he had never publicly acknowledged. If the Hedrickite lawyers, supported by Utah Mormons, could establish Smith's role in introducing polygamy, they would win. But if no evidence linked Smith to plural wives, the much-married Utah Mormons would have a weaker claim than the monogamous RLDS.

The RLDS asserted that Brigham Young, not Joseph Smith, had instigated polygamy. The Church of Christ (Hedrickite) produced LDS witnesses to testify to the contrary. One historian's summary of the evidence concluded that "fully three-fourths of all the testimony" had dealt with the question of succession.[19] However, with so many individuals who claimed an authentic line of authority, the issue turned again on whether or not Joseph Smith had endorsed polygamy.

Temple Lot depositions brought out previously unimaginable details. When people keep diaries or write memoirs, they usually have in mind presenting themselves and their friends in a favorable light, whereas adverse questioning brings out events that otherwise might be suppressed in personal narratives. When Joseph Noble attempted to avoid searching questions about his mentor and friend by claiming

---

18. Ibid., 647-48; Scott G. Kenney, ed., *Wilford Woodruff's Journal, 1833-1898,* 9 vols. (Midvale, Utah: Signature Books, 1983-85), 9:118. The State of Missouri deeded land to settlers such as Jones H. Fluorney in 1827, and in this instance Fluorney sold it to Partridge four years later.

19. Launius, *Joseph Smith III*, 317n51.

for himself illness and forgetfulness, persistent questions eventually led him to divulge what constitutes a trove of memories about how the prophet lodged in Noble's home during what Noble called "the wedding night."[20] After prodding, Noble waxed loquacious, relating fond memories of the events he described. Once into the story, he even recalled advising Smith to get into bed with his new wife and "blow the candles out" (see chapter 2).

Other witnesses painted similarly colorful pictures of Nauvoo polygamy. As the women explained themselves, they seemed to have relished the assurance given to them by the proposing prophet that they would live in a blessed afterlife. The depositions most relevant to plural marriage came from Lucy Walker Kimball, Melissa Lott, Bathsheba W. Smith, Mercy Rachel Thompson, Mary Ann West, and Emily Partridge Young. These women spoke in stark contrast to the complainant's witnesses, ironically led by William Smith, himself a polygamist, who testified that plural marriage had not been practiced in Nauvoo. William thus took sides against the LDS Church, whose apostles had rejected his filial bid for leadership. The wives' testimonies, especially, constituted a strong final confirmation, placed in the public record, of the religious society of a forgotten era.[21]

Senate testimony

To say there were some surprise moments in the U.S. Senate Committee on Privileges and Elections hearings in 1904-06 would be an understatement. The Senate challenged Reed Smoot's qualifications for "election." In those days, the state legislatures appointed Senatorial delegations, so Smoot had been chosen by a small group of state representatives rather than the general population—he actually re-

---

20. *Reorganized Church of Jesus Christ of Latter Day Saints v. Church of Christ of Independence, Missouri, et al.* 60 F. 937 (W.D. Mo. 1894), deposition testimony (questions 627-708), electronic copy prepared by Richard D. Ouellette.

21. Ibid. The Circuit Court awarded the Temple Lot to RLDS complainants in 1894 based on the 1839 deed, decreeing that the RLDS Church was the rightful "successor" to Joseph Smith. However, in 1895 the U.S. Court of Appeals in St. Louis concluded that the RLDS had waited too long to prosecute, so the Temple Lot remained with the Hedrickite Church. However, the appellate court did not challenge the lower court's ruling that Joseph III was the rightful heir to his father's congregations.

ceived only ten of eighteen votes in the Utah Senate and thirty-six of forty-four votes in the House to qualify for the appointment.[22] Complicating Smoot's bid for the U.S. Senate, he also happened to be a member of the second-highest ranking administrative body in the LDS Church, the Quorum of Twelve Apostles. In fact, behind the scenes, church president Joseph F. Smith had smoothed the path for his appointment.

The Senate was concerned that Mormons exhibited more fealty to their church president than to the law of the land. Reports had reached the Senate that in their temple, LDS people swore blood oaths against the United States and secretly continued to perform additional plural marriages, even after giving Congress assurances to the contrary.[23]

Utahn Henry Lawrence, a younger brother of Joseph Smith's wives Maria and Sarah Lawrence, considered himself unlucky to have been subpoenaed to testify.[24] Asked if in the temple Mormons took an "oath of vengeance" against the nation for the deaths of Joseph and Hyrum Smith, Lawrence replied that he did "not want to say anything about it"; but when pressed, he responded: "During my administration the word 'nation' was not used." Perplexed, the committee inquired what he meant by his "administration": "Do you mean you administered the oath?" Lawrence replied: "No, sir—yes, sir. I mean I officiated there with the rest of them." The committee wanted to know how many times he administered the oath: "Did you administer it hundreds of times?" Lawrence replied, "I will say, yes."[25] Although this witness had married plural wives in 1862 and 1868, the committee neglected to ask him about the Nauvoo origins of the practice.

---

22. Michael Harold Paulos, ed., *The Mormon Church on Trial: Transcripts of the Reed Smoot Hearings* (Salt Lake City: Signature Books, 2008), 4n. 77-80, 374n. Smoot was re-appointed by the state legislature in 1908 and then went on to win three general elections, serving to 1933.

23. Ibid., xiv-xvi.

24. John S. McCormick and John R. Sillito, "Henry W. Lawrence: A Life in Dissent," in *Differing Visions: Dissenters in Mormon History,* eds. Roger D. Launius and Linda Thatcher (Urbana: University of Illinois Press, 1994), 221, 223-25, 238n. Henry was nine years old when he left Nauvoo for the West. He later left the LDS Church over issues of freedom of thought, especially in the political and financial arenas.

25. Paulos, *Mormon Church,* 657-60.

Another dramatic moment occurred when George Reynolds, secretary to the late church president Wilford Woodruff, was asked if he had understood the Manifesto to include a prohibition against cohabitating with existing plural wives. He first answered in the negative, then said yes. To a follow-up question about whether he had "take[n] the trouble to read the declaration [him]self at the time" the Manifesto was published, Reynolds responded that he had, in fact, "assisted to write it." Clarifying this further, he explained that church president Wilford Woodruff had given his office staff "the substance" of the Manifesto and then Reynolds and others had "put it in shape for publication." Woodruff's presumed intention to dissolve existing plural relationships had apparently come to Reynolds "gradually" after the fact.[26]

In light of the LDS Church's repeated guarantees that polygamy would cease, the biggest surprise at the hearings was from Joseph F. Smith, then president of the church, who admitted that he had fathered eleven children by five wives since the Manifesto. He went on to confirm that the church founder had married Eliza Snow, Eliza Partridge, and others. A future church apostle, James E. Talmage, took the stand to offer apologetic explanations for the early denials of polygamy by Joseph Smith and others. Questions were asked about the revelation on plural marriage, specifically how a document that required Mormons to "obey it or be damned" could be set aside by the Manifesto. Children of Nauvoo polygamists testified about what they knew of their parents' marriages. A polygamist himself, church leader Francis Lyman said of his father, Amasa, "I can hardly remember when my father was not a polygamist ... so that[,] as my earliest recollections[,] I remember my father's wives and families as I remember ... my own mother."[27]

Twentieth-century studies

Although the *History of the Church* neglected to address the "restoration of all things" in regard to polygamy, and even though Joseph

26. Ibid., 311-14, 318-21.

27. Ibid., 52-57, 54-55n, 141-42, 158-59, 342, 486-91, 500-504, 506-8, 526, 543.

Smith's own diary was crafted with careful omissions, amateur historian Stanley Snow Ivins found sufficient evidence of the practice when in the 1930s he began a survey of the available documents. Ivins initiated the first serious attempt to uncover the outlines of Nauvoo polygamy since 1905 when Joseph F. Smith had assembled the reliable sources. Ivins deposited his records with the Utah State Historical Society.

Apologizing to RLDS Church President Israel Smith, Ivins wrote, "I have been making an intensive study of this subject for more than 20 years, and I long ago realized that if the facts about it were to be told, the chance of offending someone must be taken."[28] He compiled a list of eighty-four possible plural wives of Joseph Smith, some of whom would turn out to be posthumous brides and others inadequately documented.[29] Through his two decades of work, Ivins published only one article on polygamy.[30] His contributions are most evident in the help he gave historian Juanita Brooks with her study of the Mountain Meadows Massacre and, along with Dale Morgan, in his correspondence with Fawn Brodie on Joseph Smith and Brigham Young. At Ivins's death in 1967, Brooks commented that "every student of early Mormon history in any of its phases will be benefitted by the work done by Stanley S. Ivins."[31]

Fawn Brodie published a list of forty-eight wives of Joseph Smith in the appendix to her 1945 biography of Smith, *No Man Knows My History.* Although not without errors, her scholarship was impressive. Brodie brought a broad perspective since she was both an insider and outsider—a niece of LDS Church President David O. McKay, but not a practicing Mormon herself; an academic who would become a lecturer at UCLA, yet aware of the currents in Mormon thought and a frequent correspondent with Juanita Brooks, Stanley Ivins, and Dale

---

28. Stanley Ivins to Israel Smith, Sept. 17, 1956, Stanley Snow Ivins Papers, Utah State Historical Society.

29. See Ivins Papers, Utah State Historical Society.

30. Stanley S. Ivins, "Notes on Mormon Polygamy," *Western Humanities Review* 10 (Summer 1956); 229-39, repr. *Utah Historical Quarterly* 35 (Fall 1967): 309-21.

31. Quoted in "Scope and Content," *The Stanley Snow Ivins Papers, 1850-1968,* online at http://history.utah.gov.

Morgan. These four researchers launched analytic Mormon history in the twentieth century.

Fawn Brodie raised important questions about the marital life of the founder of Mormonism. Where Joseph Smith had striven to conceal information about his domestic affairs, Brodie's biography contained solid information that cast a spotlight on this facet of Latter-day Saint culture.

Almost two decades later, Jerald and Sandra Tanner, founders of the Salt Lake City-based Modern Microfilm Company (later Utah Lighthouse Ministry), gathered copies of documents relating to Mormon polygamy and included them in their exposé of the LDS Church, *Mormonism: Shadow or Reality,* first published in 1963, the most recent edition in 2008.

Ten years after the first *Shadow*, genealogist Thomas Milton Tinney included some of the sealing records from the Nauvoo temple in *The Royal Family of the Prophet Joseph Smith, Jr.*, followed in 1975 by a master's thesis at Purdue University by Danel Bachman. Bachman's "A Study of the Mormon Practice of Plural Marriage before the Death of Joseph Smith" was a comprehensive work that listed 133 affidavits and interviews on plural marriage in Nauvoo. Many of these documents had been previously unavailable to researchers. In 1981, Lawrence Foster completed an insightful study of Mormons, the Oneida Community, and Shakers in his impressive *Religion and Sexuality.* In his follow-up, *Women, Family and Utopia,* Foster listed fourteen women he thought had been married to Smith.[32] In 1986, Richard S. Van Wagoner completed a short but sweeping survey of plural marriage from the beginning to the present, *Mormon Polygamy: A History.* Then in 1992, B. Carmon Hardy published *Solemn Covenant: The Mormon Polygamous Passage,* documenting the post-1890 Manifesto period. In 1994, D. Michael Quinn contributed a two-volume study of the *Mormon Hierarchy* with vast documentation of polygamy. That same year, I

32. Lawrence Foster, *Religion and Sexuality: Three American Communal Experiments* (New York: Oxford University Press, 1981), 151-58; Foster, *Women, Family, and Utopia: Communal Experiments of the Shakers, the Oneida Community, and the Mormons* (Syracuse, N.Y.: Syracuse University Press, 1991), 135-61.

wrote an article summarizing preliminary findings about Nauvoo marriages, a precursor to the present work.[33] In 1997, Todd Compton compiled his exhaustive analysis of thirty-three of Smith's plural wives, *In Sacred Loneliness.* Lyndon W. Cook published *Nauvoo Marriages, Proxy Sealings: 1843-1846* in 2004, a compilation of sealing records that updated and corrected Tinney's 1973 publication. In 2005, Devery S. Anderson and Gary James Bergera completed *The Nauvoo Endowment Companies, 1845-1846: A Documentary History,* with an extensive listing of all Nauvoo temple ceremonies, including plural marriages. Finally, in 2006, Lisle G Brown released his alphabetized and annotated *Nauvoo Sealings, Adoptions, and Anointings,* which is a facilitator for genealogists. The present discussion benefits in many ways from the entire preceding outpouring of scholarly documentation and analysis.

Conclusion

Awareness of celestial marriage has waxed and waned from 1841, when only a small proportion of Nauvoo's few thousand citizens knew of the practice, to 1846 when up to 10 percent of the population, swollen to about 14,000, was now counted among polygamist families and many more were undoubtedly aware. Public dissent on the part of some of Joseph Smith's closest confidants—Oliver Cowdery in 1838, John Bennett in 1842, and William Law in 1844—brought attention to his extra-family relationships. We can assume that from 1852 to 1890 almost everyone knew about the "principle." Lowell Bennion's forthcoming study on the incidence of plural marriages in western communities is expected to document the Utah period to the date of the Manifesto,[34] when awareness of Mormon polygamy once again began eroding, only to be rediscovered when once-restricted archival collections were re-opened and re-examined in the twentieth century. By then, even the term "celestial wives" had come to mean something en-

33. D. Michael Quinn, *The Mormon Hierarchy: Origins of Power* (Salt Lake City: Signature Books, 1994); Quinn, *The Mormon Hierarchy: Extensions of Power* (Salt Lake City: Signature Books, 1997); George D. Smith, "Nauvoo Roots of Mormon Polygamy," *Dialogue: A Journal of Mormon Thought* 27 (Spring 1994): 1-72.

34. See Bennion's preliminary report, "The Incidence of Mormon Polygamy in 1880: 'Dixie' versus Davis Stake," *Journal of Mormon History* 11 (1984): 27-42.

tirely different than the polygamous "favors" bestowed by Smith for the purpose of populating celestial kingdoms in the hereafter.

Joseph Smith's thirty-eight or more wives and their children may be further understood when molecular biologists apply DNA findings to family trees of the Mormon community and as more family records are coordinated with genealogical collections. Future submissions from families with Nauvoo ancestors may enhance available collections of letters, diaries, autobiographies, and papers held by historical archives.

In spite of the conscious effort since 1890 by church leaders to remove any association with polygamy from Latter-day Saint perspectives, including the use of surveillance and excommunications from the 1950s,[35] documentary records and eyewitness commentary have reincorporated numerous clandestine marriages into visible Mormon history. Although the polygamous family associations of Joseph Smith, and now even Brigham Young, are not acknowledged in LDS gatherings, there is no reason to doubt the church founders' departure from a traditional monogamous family.

The next chapter considers antecedents to the nineteenth-century Mormon effort to "restore" plural marriage as found in the Old Testament. As a comparable Christian community sprang up in Europe 300 years earlier, their attempt to establish a polygamous society was also met with the assassination of its leaders. Like the Mormons, these antecedent "saints" were expelled from their "city," where they had looked to the imminent return of Jesus in the last days. While not suggesting a causal relationship between the two end-times societies, such comparable historical examples suggest the plausibility of restorationist communities concluding that polygamy would be a necessary and proper part of that restoration.

---

35. Martha S. Bradley, "Changed Faces: The Official LDS Position on Polygamy, 1890-1990," *Sunstone*, Feb. 1990, 26-33; see also Vern Anderson, Associated Press, "Mormon Church Manual Paints Polygamist [Brigham] Young as Monogamist," Apr. 4, 1998.

TABLE 8.2 Affidavits by date and provenance

			Affidavits on Celestial Marriage (LDS Archives)			LDS Publications		
	Date	Affiant	Book 1, 1869, fds. 5-6	Book 2, 1869-1870, fds. 5-6	Book 3, 1869-1915, fds. 1-4	*Historical Record*	*Blood Atonement*	*Deseret News*
1	May 1,1869	Zina D. H. Young	p. 5					
2	"	Presenda L. H. Kimball	p. 7					
3	"	Ruth Vose Sayers	p. 9					
4	"	Emily D. P. Young	p. 11					
5	"	Emily D. P. Young	p. 13			x		x
6	"	Marinda Nancy Johnson Hyde	p. 15					
7	"	Rhoda Richards	p. 17				x	
8	"	Dimick B. Huntington	p. 19					
9	"	Fanny Maria Huntington	p. 21					
10	May 20, 1869	Malissa Lott Willes	p. 23				x	
11	June 7, 1869	Eliza R. Snow Smith	p. 25					
12	June 15, 1869	David Fullmer	pp. 27-28			x	x	
13	June 16, 1869	Lovina Walker[a]	p. 30			x	x	x
14	June 17, 1869	Desdemona Fullmer Smith	p. 32					
15	June 19, 1869	Mercy R. Thompson	p. 34					
16	"	Sarah Ann Kimball	p. 36				x	
17	June 26, 1869	Joseph B. Noble	p. 1			x	x	x
18	"	Joseph B. Noble	p. 38			x		x

a. Certified rather than notarized.

19	July 1, 1869	Eliza Maria (Partridge) Lyman		p. 30	fd. 3, p. 11			
20	"	Eliza Maria (Partridge) Lyman		p. 32	fd. 3, p. 3			
21	"	Eliza Maria (P.) Lyman		p. 33	fd. 3, p. 7	x		x
22	"	Eliza Maria (P.) Lyman		p. 34	fd. 3, p. 15			
23	July 6,1869	Thomas Grover	p. 42					
24	"	Thomas Grover	p. 44					
25	July 8, 1869	Martha McBride Kimball		p. 36	fd. 2, p. 25		x	
26	July 10, 1869	Mary Ann Young	p. 46					
27	"	Lucy Ann D. Young	p. 48					
28	July 12, 1869	Augusta (Adams) Young	p. 50					
29	"	Augusta (Adams) Young	p. 52					
30	"	Charles C. Rich	p. 54					
?	July 20, 1869	Vienna Jaques[b]			fd. 4, p. 56			
31	July 22, 1869	John Pack	p. 58					
32	1869	Cylvia Lyon[c]	p. 62					
33	Aug. 2, 1869	Elizabeth B. Pratt	p. 64					
34	Aug. 3, 1869	Christopher Merkley		pp. 21-23	fd. 3, p. 19			
35	Aug. 6, 1869	Mary Ellen Kimball	p. 66					
36	Aug. 9, 1869	Lucy W. Kimball[d]	p. 68					
37	"	Wm. Clayton[e]	pp. 69-70					

b. Unsigned.
c. Unsigned.
d. Compare Kimball's statement of Dec. 17, 1902 (Affidavit 68).
e. This journal extract was certified by Joseph F. Smith.

			Affidavits on Celestial Marriage (LDS Archives)			LDS Publications		
	Date	Affiant	Book 1, 1869, fds. 5-6	Book 2, 1869-1870, fds. 5-6	Book 3, 1869-1915, fds. 1-4	*Historical Record*	*Blood Atonement*	*Deseret News*
38	Aug. 13, 1869	Elizabeth & Sarah A. Whitney[f]		pp. 25-28				
39	Aug. 24, 1869	Amos Fielding	p. 72					
40	Aug. 28, 1869	John Benbow	p. 76			×		×
41	"	Nathan Tanner	p. 78					
42	"	Elvira A. C. Holmes	p. 80					
43	"	Lorenzo Snow		pp. 19-20	fd. 4, p. 38	×	×	×
44	Aug. 30, 1869	Elizabeth Ann Whitney[g]	p. 74				×	
45	Sep. 3, 1869	Mary Ann Pratt		p. 38	fd. 3, p. 23			
46	"	Mary Ann Pratt		p. 40	fd. 3, p. 27			
47	Sep. 5, 1869	Adeline B. A. Benson		p. 42	fd. 1, p. 7			
48	Sep. 6, 1869	Pamelia A. Benson		p. 44	fd. 1, p. 11			
49	Sep. 7, 1869	Sarah Perry Peak Kimball	p. 82					
50	Sep. 15, 1869	Orson Hyde		pp. 45-46	fd. 2, p. 7		×	
51	Oct. 2, 1869	James Allred	p. 84					
52	"	Aaron Johnson	p. 86					
53	Oct. 10, 1869	David Fullmer, Thomas Grover, Aaron Johnson, and James Allred		pp. 47-48				
54	Oct. 13, 1869	Roxsena R. Adams	p. 88					
55	Mar. 4, 1870	Benjamin F. Johnson		pp. 3-9		×		×

f. Compare Elizabeth Whitney's statement of Aug. 30, 1869 (Affidavit 44).
g. Compare Elizabeth's and Sarah A. Whitney's statement of Aug. 13, 1869.

56	"	Harriet Cook Young		p. 12			
57	"	Harriet Cook Young		p. 14			
58	"	Clara Decker Young		p. 16			
59	Mar. 7, 1870	Joseph Kingsbury[h]		p. 18			
60	Apr. 23, 1870	Jacob Peart Sen.		p. 50			
61	Feb. 16, 1874	William Clayton			fd. 1, p. 28A	×	
62	Feb. 27, 1874	Gideon Carter			fd. 1, p. 15		
63	Jun. 12, 1882	Howard Coray			fd. 1, p. 38	×	×
64	Aug. 1, 1883	Almira W. Johnson Smith Barton			fd. 1, p. 3		×
65	Mar. 23, 1886	Leonard Soby[i]			fd. 4, p. 42		×
66	May 22, 1886	Joseph C. Kingsbury[j]			fd. 2, p. 29	×	
67	Mar. 1, 1894	Joseph A. Kelting[k]			fd. 2, p. 11		
68	Dec. 17, 1902	Lucy Walker Smith Kimball[l]			fd. 2, p. 21		×
69	Jan. 28, 1903	Catherine Phillips Smith			fd. 4, p. 10		×
70	Sep. 11, 1903	Joseph A. Kelting[m]			fd. 2, p. 17		
71	Nov. 18, 1903	Bathsheba W. Smith[n]			fd. 4, p. 8		
72	Nov. 19, 1903	Bathsheba W. Smith[o]		pp. 51-54[p]	fd. 4, p. 6		×

h. Compare Kingsbury's statement of May 22, 1886 (Affidavit 66).
i. Soby was present at an Aug. 12, 1843, high council meeting during which the revelation of plural marriage was taught.
j. Compare Kingsbury's statement of Mar. 7, 1870 (Affidavit 59).
k. Compare Kelting's statement of Sept. 11, 1903 (Affidavit 70).
l. Compare Kimball's statement of Aug. 9, 1869 (Affidavit 36).
m. Compare Kelting's statetment of Mar. 1, 1894 (Affidavit 67).
n. Not notarized.
o. Expanded from the Nov. 18, 1903, version.
p. Found only in the duplicate copy of Book 2.

	Date	Affiant	Affidavits on Celestial Marriage (LDS Archives)			LDS Publications		
			Book 1, 1869, fds. 5-6	Book 2, 1869-1870, fds. 5-6	Book 3, 1869-1915, fds. 1-4	*Historical Record*	*Blood Atonement*	*Deseret News*
73	Jul. 28, 1905	John W. Rigdon			fd. 3, pp. 35 & 89		×	
74	"	John W. Rigdon			fd. 3, p. 83			
75	Feb. 24, 1915	Josephine Rosetta Fisher			fd. 1, p. 11			
			40	21	27 -13* 14	12	17 -5** 12	(8 incl. in HR & BA)
			75 total affidavits			24 published affidavits		

*duplicated from Book 2

**duplicated from *Historical Record*

NINE.

Antecedents and Legacy

Marriage Allowed by the Law of Moses is Not Forbidden

In 1534 CE, in Münster, Germany, the prophet king sat in a grand hall with sixteen wives. One of the women at a long dinner table found a wooden marker at her chair indicating that she would be that night's queen, with whom the king, John Bockelson, would share his bed. Formerly a tailor in Holland, Jan Beukelszoon van Leiden led the Anabaptists of Münster, located thirty-five miles east of the Dutch border, in one of the most radical movements of the Protestant Reformation.[1] Pious ancestors of the Amish, the Anabaptists were preparing for the imminent end of the world. Like the Latter-day Saints, who would form their own millennialist community some 300 years later in America, they were intent on restoring biblical truths, including polygamy.

The Münsterites were not the only Protestant group to practice communal marriage in the 1530s. Another branch of Anabaptists, the so-called Hessian "dreamers," also shared wives. These sects flourished for reasons similar to those advanced by Joseph Smith: a perceived urgency in preparing for the last days, loyalty to their prophetic leader, a "modern" cure for the social ills surrounding promiscuity, and

---

1. Bockelson's Dutch name, Jan Beukelszoon van Leiden, implied that Jan was the son of Beukel from Leiden. The German version of his name was Johann Bockelson von Leiden. The English further rendered his name into a convenient shorthand, as John Bockelson.

the creation of a home for orphans and widows. Although there is no direct evidence that Smith, or indeed anyone in the Mormon hierarchy, focused much attention on the Münster Anabaptists, some Nauvoo leaders knew about them—despite the fact that the Mennonites had downplayed this embarrassingly violent and non-traditional era in their history. During the Great Awakening in America, people were generally attentive to religious movements from the time of Jesus to the eighteenth century. They were especially cognizant of the ways Christians in years past had prepared for the expected end-times. Christians from the Roman era to the present had continually looked for the return of Jesus. This persistent waiting often included extraordinary measures ranging from celibacy to polygamy, advanced as spiritual obligations that took precedence over secular laws and mores.

Pre-Reformation Antecedents

Not only did polygamy emerge as a trajectory of the Protestant Reformation, it continued a long practice in world history involving *polygyny* (plural wives) and in rarer instances *polyandry* (plural husbands), which across the spectrum of world cultures has been more often normative than aberrant. Polygamy has typically been found in a small part of most cultures. A recent study of early human sexuality concluded that, while modern man is often culturally obliged to one spouse, he (and she) may not be biologically predisposed to monogamy. For instance, primates which are dimorphic, meaning that the males are larger in stature than females, tend to be polygynous. Gorillas are one example. Over time, the males pass on their genes in favor of larger, stronger gorillas in general, including females, and while the dimorphism decreases, some polygyny continues. Polygyny may have existed among the hominid ancestors of human beings with the polygynous impulse becoming less pronounced over time. Even if the trend is away from polygamy, it is still represented in many societies.[2]

For instance, polygamous customs are found today in Africa, Aus-

2. Lynn Margulis and Dorion Sagan, *Mystery Dance: On the Evolution of Human Sexuality* (New York: Summit Books, 1991); John Noble Wilford, "New Clues to History of Male and Female," *New York Times,* Aug. 26, 1997, B-7.

tralia, China, India, Indonesia, the Middle East, and Nepal; they were prevalent in the early Americas among the Eskimos and among the early Germanic tribes in Europe. Polygyny was also practiced in pre-Islamic Arabic cultures.[3] Only in 656 CE did the Qur'an restrict Muslim husbands to a maximum of four wives.[4] There have been men with more than one wife in about 80 percent of 853 cultures on record, living either according to a cultural expectation or an acceptable alternative. In a sampling of 1,267 contemporary communities representing 186 of the "world's known and well-described cultures" today, 82.5 percent contain some polygamous relationships. Among these scattered communities, 46.4 percent practice polygyny as the norm. In 35.8 percent, polygyny is practiced "occasionally" in independent nuclear families according to changing circumstances involving wealth and status. Only 0.3 percent of these communities are said to be polyandrous. Researchers have found it useful to consider two additional dichotomies where polygamy is prevalent: "sororal polygyny," where co-wives are typically sisters or cousins (15%), versus "non-sororal" (85%); and communities where co-wives live together (38.4%), versus co-wives living in separate dwellings (61.6%).[5]

Men of prominence in ancient Mesopotamia had multiple wives

---

3. See James A. Brundage, *Law, Sex, and Christian Society in Medieval Europe* (Chicago: University of Chicago Press, 1987), 28-36, 52, 128, 225, 256, 299, 304, 478-79, 577, 615; Vern L. Bullough and James A. Brundage, *Sexual Practices and the Medieval Church* (Buffalo, N.Y.: Prometheus Books, 1982), 118-28.

4. According to the Qur'an: "And if (you wish to marry them [orphans] and) you fear that you will not be able to do justice to the orphan girls, then (marry them not, rather) marry of women (other than these) as may be agreeable to you, (you may marry) two or three or four (provided you do justice to them), but if you fear that you will not be able to deal (with all of them) equitably then (confine yourselves only to) one, or (you may marry) that whom your right hands possess (your female captives of war). That is the best way to avoid doing injustice" (Amatul Rahman 'Omar and 'Abdul Mannân 'Omar, trans., *The Holy Qur'an: Arabic Text—English Translation* (Hockessin, Del.: Noor Foundation, 2000), Sura (chapter) 4, verse 3; the translators placed implied text, necessary to the English translation, within parentheses.

5. George P. Murdock and Douglas R. White, "Standard Cross-Cultural Sample," *Ethnology* 8 (Oct. 1969): 329-69; Murdock, *Ethnographic Atlas* (Pittsburgh: University of Pittsburgh Press, 1967); Murdock, *Atlas of World Cultures* (Pittsburgh: Pittsburgh Press, 1980); White, "Ethnographic Atlas Codebook," *World Cultures* 10 (1998): 86-136; see also Delta Willis, *The Hominid Gang* (New York: Viking, 1989), 259.

and concubines. The mythic lives of such figures as Abraham, David, and Solomon included a hierarchy in which the leader was granted the most wives. Under the emerging influence of Christianity, however, when the teachings of Jesus became the primary religion in the Roman Empire, bigamy became regarded as a legal offense. But it was still a man's world. The Justinian Code defined marriage in the sixth century in terms of female subjugation: a husband could have concubines, in addition to a wife, but a wife was severely punished if she strayed beyond her marriage.[6] The Apostle Paul's emphasis on celibacy might have influenced the culture away from polygamy. Although in the New Testament, Jesus is silent on conjugal relationships, Paul's letters were written with the view that Christians should eschew earthly matters such as marriage and procreation, since the world was about to expire.[7] The asceticism of early Christianity, according to historian James A. Brundage, discouraged sex in marriage.[8]

As time went by, the Church Fathers relaxed their views on marital relationships. As one example, St. Augustine (354-430 CE) justified polygamy by noting that men were not forbidden from having more than one slave—why then should he be permitted only one wife?[9] But after Constantine integrated the Christian church into the Roman government in 326 CE, he forbade married men to take concubines. The Church Fathers came to oppose polygamy, not only because of

---

6. On February 13, 528 CE, Emperor Justinian appointed a commission to revise eleven centuries of Roman law. The twelve books of the *Codex Justinianus* were enlarged to fifty books in four divisions: the Code, Digest, Institutes, and Novels, comprising the *Corpus juris civilis* of Roman law. (See Brundage, *Law, Sex, and Christian Society,* 113, 118-19; for concubinage, see Cod. 5.27.8; 6.57.5.2; 7.15.3; Nov. 18.5(536); 89.2-6; for adultery, see Nov. 117.15; 134.10). Through the Nauvoo period in America, polygamy was a criminal act under the Illinois 1833 anti-bigamy laws, which remained unchanged during the statute revision of 1845. Each count of bigamy referred to an illegal secondary marriage, so a person with three spouses might be charged with two counts of bigamy. Polygamy, thus defined, was punishable by fines of $1,000 and a two-year imprisonment for previously married persons, $500 and one-year imprisonment for previously single persons (*Revised Laws of Illinois 1833 and Revised Statutes of the State of Illinois 1845,* Secs. 121, 122, University of Chicago Law Library).

7. Brundage, *Law, Sex, and Christian Society,* 2, 5, 57-61, 74.

8. Ibid., 60.

9. Eugene Hillman, *Polygamy Reconsidered: African Plural Marriage and the Christian Churches* (Maryknoll, New York: Orbis Books, 1975), 181.

the church's heritage of self denial, but because they wanted to distinguish Christian practice from Old Testament customs. As Christians sought to dissociate themselves from Judaism, they reasoned that Yahweh had approved polygamy for only a short period of time so the elect of their day could "increase and multiply." By the eleventh century, monogamy would become the norm for Jews as well.[10]

The situation changed in the sixteenth century when the question of marriage was submitted to new scrutiny in determining whether it was scripturally based. It was an issue that was influenced by the Protestant Reformation, the invention of the printing press, and a beleaguered papacy. By the time the Münster prophet John Bockelson claimed the right of a different wife each night, polygamy had already surfaced among kings and reformers as a mostly theological but sometimes practical matter.

Protestant Polygamy

The changes in Europe during the Reformation were both incremental and sweeping, fueled by conquests, inventions, integration of new concepts and technologies, and the disintegration of older societies. When the Ottoman Turks conquered Constantinople in 1453, Byzantine scholars fled to Europe with Greek manuscripts, bringing with them an awakening which encouraged the study of biblical literature in its original language. Moveable type, invented in the mid-1450s, allowed greater popular access to the written word in broadsheets, pamphlets, and picture books.[11] Both events advanced literacy among the populace. Reading and biblical interpretation would no longer be the exclusive province of priest, monk, or scholar. This democratization of access to the Bible stirred debate and challenge. As the Dutch humanist Erasmus (1466-1536) translated and annotated what Aristotle and Augustine had actually said, a new dialectic arose.

---

10. Brundage, 65-66, 77, 87, 98-99.

11. In the twelfth century, Spanish Moors introduced the Chinese invention of paper to the west. Printers smeared engraved wooden blocks with ink until the era of Gutenberg when removable letters were placed in hollow metal forms, leading to large-scale printing and greater diffusion of ideas. See John Carter and Percy H. Muir, eds., *Printing and the Mind of Man: A Descriptive Catalogue* (London: Cassell and Co., 1967).

No doubt the boldest proclamation was that of Martin Luther in nailing his grievances to the door of the Wittenberg cathedral in 1517. His ninety-five theses upheld the authority of the Bible over that of Pope Leo X, igniting a religious, social, and political revolution. His influential translation of biblical texts into German, published in 1534, made the Bible available to common people and, incidentally, helped standardize the German language.

Across the channel, Henry VIII contributed to the decentralization of religious control, declaring England's ecclesiastical independence when Pope Clement VII (1523-34) refused to annul Henry's marriage to his first wife, Catherine of Aragon. As we recall, Catherine bore Henry no living male heirs to perpetuate the royal house of Tudor; and since Henry desired the younger, winsome, and presumably more progenitive Anne Boleyn, the king took matters into his own hands. In 1531 he sought and received advice from Protestant reformers about a second wife and eventually broke with the Roman Catholic Church, although for a while he still considered himself Catholic; he then established the Church of England, closed monasteries and nunneries, and gave much of the church property to the English nobility. Henry's actions had far-ranging social and political consequences.

Social reform in continental Europe and England extended into matters that had traditionally been the exclusive province of the church. Political and ecclesiastical reform spawned the rise of capitalism, particularly in the textile industry, in the exploitation of iron and coal deposits located on what had been church properties, and in agricultural changes which eventually gave rise to a class of dispossessed farm workers. Propertied radicals advocated social reform over revolution, but there was no question that the Industrial Revolution had been unleashed.[12] As the Protestant Reformation rent the monolithic

12. See Christopher Hill, *Puritanism and Revolution: Studies in Interpretation of the English Revolution of the Seventeenth Century* (London: Secker and Warburg, 1965), 32-39, 99-102. Henry deprived the Catholic church of its "tenths" (tithing) and the "first fruits" of farming and industry, as well as the income derived from judicial appeals to Rome.

social order that had once looked to Rome, the Counter-Reformation, initiated in 1540 by Pope Paul III, sought to revitalize the Catholic Church with its own modifications. Evangelizing missions were sent to North and South America and to the Far East.

Canon law, natural law, and plural wives

As customs adapted to the changing social climate, marital practices became more flexible. New leaders wondered if marriage was a matter of nature rather than a spiritual event to be regulated by the church. Even though many Protestant reformers no longer took the Catholic position that marriage was a sacrament involving divinity, they continued the long-standing Catholic ban on divorce.[13] Remarriage was still considered adulterous, despite the six wives of King Henry VIII, two of whom were briefly concurrent. But to those who were plumbing the Bible for answers to social questions, the example of the multiple wives of Jacob, David, and Solomon presented polygamy as a potential alternative (see Deut. 24:1-4; Mark 10:2-12).

The number of women who might cohabit with a man, whether as concubines (extra-legal partners) or plural wives, and the legitimacy of their children had long concerned heads of state. Concubines had played a significant role in families but were granted lower social status than a wife. Like the Germanic "morganatic" marriages (the term deriving from a gift given in the morning after consummation), concubines lacked property rights and legitimacy for their children. If the man was unmarried and took a concubine to wife, the inheritance rights sometimes accrued to the children. In reality, polygyny was sometimes tolerated, albeit contrary to law.

The style of concubinage practiced in Rome resembled monogamy in that it often involved one female at a time. Property rights represented the primary difference. Germanic invasions into the Roman Empire during the fourth and fifth centuries extended polygyny among the noble classes, at least before their conversion to Christian-

13. Luther considered marriage to be "an estate of the earthly kingdom ... subject to the prince, not the pope" (John Witte Jr., *From Sacrament to Contract: Marriage, Religion, and Law in the Western Tradition* [Louisville, Ky.: Westminster John Knox Press, 1997], 70).

ity; but the church eventually prevailed and by the twelfth century the jurist Gratian completed a textbook of canon law which defined fornication as either "simple" (sexual relations between two unmarried persons) or "double" (one of the two was married).[14]

Thirteenth-century canonists argued against polygyny under the assumption that a man could not satisfy more than one woman and so could not expect to meet his "conjugal" debt.[15] Since property rights followed the presumption of conjugal debt, in time a concubine, often the mistress of a powerful man, was allowed to spell out what property rights she shared with her beloved, as well as the status of her children.[16]

As late as the early seventeenth century, Pope Alexander III sought to remedy the declining economic position of women where their husbands had sometimes deserted them for mistresses. The pope was also concerned about the welfare of the mistresses and concluded that if a man had exchanged "marital consent" with a mistress prior to a legal marriage, the concubine should be regarded by the courts as the legitimate spouse.[17] He held that children born to a concubine prior to marriage were legitimized by the subsequent marriage.

Whereas the canonists recognized a widow's free choice to remarry ("constructive bigamy"), a man's marriage to two spouses at the same time ("simultaneous bigamy") was considered unlawful.[18] Long-term cohabitation without marital intent (common law marriage) was legitimate if neither had another spouse. They ruled out "plural concubinage."[19] Because canon law concerned itself with women who were vulnerable to exploitation, it ruled out the polygamous relationships that would be subsequently advocated by natural law proponents in fifteenth- and sixteenth-century Europe. The rights of women were argued in both canon law and natural law theaters, but

14. Brundage, *Law, Sex, and Christian Society*, 229, 304-05.

15. Ibid., 359n.

16. For example, King James I of Aragon and Countess Aurembaix of Urgel, Oct. 23, 1228, in ibid., 370.

17. Ibid., 341n.

18. Ibid., 407.

19. Ibid., 444n.

conclusions diverged regarding plural relationships. In the thirteenth century, Thomas Aquinas declared concubinage contrary to natural law. By the early fourteenth century, strict penalties were applied to concubinage, although it was still common in certain regions such as Carcassonne, France; Worcestershire, England; and in parts of Italy and Spain.[20]

Radical reform

Renewed interest in plural marriage sprang out of the Reformation as people read and interpreted the Bible for themselves. The New Testament does not explicitly prohibit polygamy, neither in the words attributed to Jesus nor among such influential Church Fathers as Jerome (347-420) and Augustine (354-430). The mainstream Protestant leaders such as Martin Luther, Huldrych Zwingli, and John Calvin did not embrace or recommend a return to Old Testament practices. But neither could they adequately answer the question posed by such powerful men as Henry VIII or Philip of Hesse when they requested an exemption from customary practice.

A Protestant dispensation for Henry VIII

England's heirless King Henry had a problem for which polygamy seemed to provide a simple resolution. His appeal for a marriage annulment was rebuffed by the pope in 1527, so Henry took his case to a succession of other Catholic and Protestant leaders, hoping for a better outcome. His Spanish wife, Catherine of Aragon, had borne him a daughter in 1516, but no male heirs. Henry claimed his marriage was invalid because, in a denial of the levirate, he must have wrongfully married his brother's widow. When Catherine was fifteen, she had wed Henry's older brother, Arthur, who was fourteen at the time. After just four and a half months, Arthur died. Henry argued that according to Leviticus 20:21, his marriage to Catherine must have violated the passage that reads: "And if a man shall take his brother's wife, it is an unclean thing." In response to Henry's claim, Catherine asserted that this brief, youthful marriage had remained unconsummated and that she was therefore Henry's legal spouse; she

20. Ibid., 444-45.

countered with the Deuteronomic (25:5-7) admonition that "the duty of an husband's brother" toward a childless widow was to "go in unto her, and take her to him to wife."

Important subtexts to these arguments lay not only in Henry's want of a male heir but in his documented interest in Anne Boleyn, a member of the queen's household who, in her mid-twenties, was fifteen years younger than the queen. In 1526, a year before he sought to divorce Catherine, Henry began to write love letters to Anne. The letters, which are extant at the Vatican Library in Rome, suggest at minimum a playful relationship. Catherine, at forty years of age, was in poor health. The king, at thirty-four, proposed that Catherine, now "middle aged" and ill, should enter a nunnery. The queen steadfastly rejected this proposal.

Another subtext in Henry's appeal to biblical authority was an assault on the authority of the pope and his ability to issue dispensations contrary to a presumed higher law. In the political realm, Catherine's nephew, Charles V, was elected emperor of the Holy Roman Empire in 1519. The same month that the pope's emissary, Cardinal Woolsey, began to review the validity of the king's marriage, in May 1527, the emperor's troops sacked Rome and held Pope Clement VII captive for seven months for having supported France against the emperor's forces in Italy. The pope's capture by the queen's nephew would seem to have biased his view in favor of his captor's aunt, and against King Henry.

The king might have expected that at least the English bishops would oblige him and condemn his marriage to Catherine in order to free him to marry Anne, but they found his marriage to the queen to be valid. Granting Henry a sliver of hope, Rome sent word in December 1527 that if the king could demonstrate that his brother had consummated his marriage with the young Spanish princess, the pope would grant a dispensation allowing Henry to marry Anne. On May 31, 1529, a tribunal began hearing testimony. Catherine asserted that when she married her second husband, Henry, "I was a true maid, without touch of man." Diametrically opposed to her testimony was that of Sir Anthony Willoughby, a former steward of the king's household, who reported that when the couple married in 1501, Prince Arthur emerged from the bed chamber the following morning and exclaimed, "Willoughby, bring me a cup of ale, for I have been this night in the midst of Spain."[21] In the face of this conflicting evidence, the pope's tribunal delayed issuing a ruling.

In the meantime, the pope decided he would hear the case himself. Henry had previously insisted that the tribunal be held in England. The parliament responded to the pope's perceived meddling by giving the king a new title: Supreme Head of the Church and Clergy of England. King Henry himself rebuffed the pope by saying, "I care not a fig for all his excommunications." As tensions rose, the standoff ended in July 1531 when Henry simply decided to leave Windsor Castle, where he and Catherine had made their home, never to return again. The next month, German Protestant leaders favorably answered Henry's request for private permission to marry a second wife.

The first response from the German Protestants came from the reformer Philip Melanchthon, undoubtedly representing Luther and other colleagues. His memorandum of August 1531, entitled "On bigamy for the King of England," agreed that there was "public utility" in seeing a "new marriage for the sake of an heir." Not the least bit squeamish, Melanchthon resolved: "Although I would not like to concede polygamy to the common people, "in this case … I decide thus: it would be safest for the king if he marries a second wife, not divorcing the first, because it is certain that polygamy is not prohibited by divine law, nor is the practice entirely uncommon." He pointed out that "Abraham, David and other holy men have had many wives, whence it is clear that polygamy is not against divine law."[22] Just as Joseph Smith would stake his case on an appeal to the Old Testament, so did the sixteenth-century theologians when it suited them.

Melanchthon cited Emperor Valentinian I (364-75 CE), who proclaimed a law allowing "two wives at once" and then married

---

21. Antonia Fraser, *The Wives of Henry VIII* (New York: Knopf, 1992), 161-63; see Henry Ansgar Kelly, *The Matrimonial Trials of Henry VIII* (Eugene, Ore.: Wipf and Stock, 2004), 75-131; cf. Shakespeare, *Henry VIII,* 2.4.

22. Leo Miller, *John Milton among the Polygamophiles* (New York: Loewenthal Press, 1974), 17-19.

Justina, not having divorced his first wife, Severa. Considering the political realities of the day, "it may be advantageous," Melanchthon opined, if Henry considered "seek[ing] a papal dispensation that would permit polygamy to the king."[23] From here on, matters would not proceed quite so smoothly. Instead of waiting for the pope's imprimatur, Henry remarried in January 1533, then divorced his first wife in May 1533, prompting the pope to order him to quit his second wife. The following year, on March 23, 1534, the pope decreed that Queen Catherine's marriage to Henry had always been valid. Pope Clement VII died six months later.[24]

Luther himself had addressed Henry VIII's problems in a letter to a third party, Robert Barnes, a Lutheran adherent in England, on September 3, 1531. Echoing Melanchthon's memorandum of the prior month, Luther agreed that although the New Testament frowned on divorce, the Old Testament "permits the king to marry a second queen, by the example of the patriarchs, who had many wives even before the Law."[25] This royal privilege, which Luther and Melanchthon did not want publicized, predated Henry's marriage to Anne, but it is not known whether this biblical example or Melanchthon's letter primarily influenced the king's decision. At the time of her wedding, Anne was pregnant with Henry's daughter, Elizabeth. This child, born on September 7, would become Queen Elizabeth I and rule England for over four decades. In 1535, Pope Paul III excommunicated Henry. Henry's next wife, Jane Seymour, bore him the son and heir he had long desired, King Edward VI, crowned in 1547, and succeeded by Catherine's daughter, Mary Tudor, in 1553.

Henry VIII would eventually marry six wives, although only the first two marriages would overlap. Not only did he feel free to engage in these new relationships, he felt equally confident about disposing

---

23. Ibid., 6, 102-03, 205n. Miller cites the 28-volume compilation of Karl Gottlieb Brettschneider and Heinrich Ernst Bindseil, *Philippi Melanthonis Opera quae Supersunt Omnia,* published from 1834 to 1860.

24. Fraser, *Wives of Henry VIII,* 195, 207.

25. Miller, *Milton among Polygamophiles,* 21. Miller cites the 67-volume series, *Dr. Martin Luthers sämmtliche Werke,* published from 1826 to 1932, and translates the document.

of less-than-satisfactory wives (two were executed) at will. He was not a polygamist, but the commentary he elicited from the reformers, in concert with similar advice given to a German aristocrat, Philip of Hesse, conveys a recurring line of reasoning that endorsed selective polygamy.

Philip of Hesse

Another early challenger to monogamous restraints, Count Philip the Magnanimous, Landgrave of Hesse (1504-67), ruled over and organized political alliances in one of the first Lutheran states of Germany. The Hessian land baron was loosely subject to Charles V, Holy Roman Emperor from 1519, and resided in Marburg, southwest of Wittenberg and southeast of Münster—in other words, near where Luther began the Protestant movement in 1517 and near the city where the Dutch and German Anabaptists would form their unique millennialist society within a similar time frame.

Philip had married Christina of Saxony in about 1523 but never felt he had "found a fit mate" in her, eventually concluding that a second wife would be desirable.[26] Although she would bear him six or seven children, Christina was evidently unappealing to her husband in some way. After three years of marriage, he asked Luther if he could follow the Old Testament example. Luther answered on November 28, 1526: "It is my faithful warning and advice that Christians especially should not have more than one wife, not only because it is a scandal." Luther assumed that the "old patriarchs had many wives" out of necessity and had "inherited the wives of their friends under Moses' law," a seeming extension of the levirate to deceased friends. "It is not enough for a Christian to appeal to the conduct of the patriarchs," Luther continued, but then opened the door a crack by saying that one "must also have a divine word for himself." If Philip were in "highest need," Luther explained, "as for example, if the wife ha[d] leprosy," then it would be a different matter. Otherwise, Luther advised Philip to avoid such thoughts.[27]

---

26. Miller, *Milton among Polygamophiles*, 13.

27. Ibid, 13-15. Miller cites the ongoing 123-volume series, *Dr. Martin Luthers Werke: Kritische Gesamtausgabe*, published from 1883 to the present, translating letter 1,056.

In 1539, a decade after his rebuff, Philip again raised the question of a second wife. Seventeen-year-old Margaretha von der Saal, he wrote, "was so very much bent on marriage." Now Luther and other Protestant leaders responded with a public "no" but a private "yes." Philip had heard about the permission granted to Henry VIII and recognized that it bore the mark of Luther's influence. Perhaps Henry had similarly heard of Philip's overtures in 1526. Whether one influenced the other or vice versa, their estrangement from Rome and deference to the Protestants established a commonality between them. For his part, Philip would later quote back to Luther the very advice he and Melanchthon had given to Henry VIII. Through Martin Bucer, with whom Philip "discussed his desires," Luther and Melanchthon joined their voices of assent to polygamous marriage as long as it was done discreetly.[28] In approving this course of action, Luther was proposing a worldly interpretation of marriage in which a ruler could grant exceptions because the authority was vested in him. The Protestant leaders relinquished the sacramental character of marriage and upheld the argument that state law is man-made and therefore malleable.

The confessional advice (*Beichtrat*) that Luther, Melanchthon, and others issued on December 10, 1539, from Wittenberg giving Philip of Hesse a secret exemption from church law regarding marriage is significant enough to excerpt at length. As directed by his spiritual advisors, Philip obtained his wife Christina's written consent. The polygamous wedding was performed on March 4, 1540.[29] The document authorizing this marriage, addressed to "the illustrious high-born prince and Lord Philip, landgrave of Hesse," included the following instructions and explanations:

> As Your Princely Grace has indicated to us through Dr. Bucer [the] certain long-time burden of your conscience[,] ... this is our thought....
>
> Now we cannot advise that any should make a public introduction,

28. Ibid., 21-22.

29. Paul Mikat, *Die Polygamiefrage in der frühen Neuzeit* (Opladen: Westdeutscher Verlag, 1988), 15-16, translation courtesy of Henry L. Miner. Mikat cites *Luthers Werke,* 8:638-43; see also Miller, *Milton among Polygamophiles,* 22.

that is, a law, that it is allowable to marry more than one wife ... Your Princely Grace could perceive that such [public] would take this for a common law, from which great scandal and trouble would result ... [for] all [those who are] married. ...

God has instituted marriage as a society between two persons alone, and not more, so nature does not become destroyed. So we have the passage, These two shall become one flesh, and thus it was at first. But Lamech introduced the example of having more than one wife, which is spoken of concerning him in the Scriptures as bringing in something against the first rule. Accordingly it became a custom with the unbelieving, until Abraham and his descendants took more wives; and so it came to be allowed in the law of Moses, Deut. 2[1], If a man have two wives. For God allowed something to [those who are] weak [in] nature.

But inasmuch as at the beginning and conformably to the creation, a man was not to have more than one wife, so such a law is praiseworthy and [is] therefore to be received in the Church; and no other law is to be made against it. For Christ repeats this passage, They too shall be one flesh, Matt. 19, and reminds us of how it was before the time of human weakness.

But that in a certain case a dispensation might be given, as for instance in the case of a captive in a strange land, who has become free and brings his wife with him, or in the case of some chronic disorder such as was thought of for a time with lepers—that in such cases, with the advice of their pastor, a man might take a wife again, not to bring in a law but as counsel for his necessity, this we do not condemn. *Because it is one thing to bring in a law and another to use a dispensation, this we humbly beg you to observe.*

First, caution is to be used in every way that this affair is not brought into the world publicly as a law which others might follow. Second, though it is no law but a dispensation, yet Your Princely Grace must think of the scandal, namely that the enemies of the Gospel will cry out that we are like the Anabaptists who take many wives. They will also say that the Evangelicals seek freedom to have as many wives as they wish, just like the Turks. Third, what a prince does becomes noised abroad much more than what happens in the case of a private person. Fourth, when private persons hear of such an example they will permit the same things to themselves, so one sees how easily such a thing spreads. Fifth, Your Princely Grace has [to reckon with] a wild nobility, of whom many[,] as in all lands on account of the great enjoyment they have from the Cathedral foundations [and who] are passionately opposed to the

> Gospel[,] [will take advantage of the situation]. So we know that from these great young lords very unfriendly speeches will be heard … Sixth, by God's grace Your Princely Grace has a praiseworthy name even with foreign kings and potentates, and is feared by them, of which reputation this would make a lessening.
>
> Because then, so much scandal would be sowed, we humbly pray Your Princely Grace to think diligently and well over this matter. …
>
> Therefore, Your Grace must take into consideration all these things, the scandal, the other cares and work, the weakness of the body, and also the truth that God has already given to Your Grace[,] [as well as the] fine heirs and girls with this wife; and have her for good, as many others in their married state [who] have to exercise patience, to ward off scandal….
>
> As now Your Princely Grace has finally concluded to have another wife, so we think that such is to be held secret, as is said above of a dispensation …
>
> So [by this means] there would follow no special talk or scandal, for it is common for princes to have concubines. And as not everyone would know what the occasion was, reasonable people (who did know) would remind themselves and have more pleasure in such modest behaviour than in adultery and other wild unchaste living.
>
> Also not all talk is to be noticed if a conscience is right. So far we hold this for right that what was permitted concerning marriage in the law of Moses is not forbidden by the Gospel.[30]…

When Philip's dual marriage became public knowledge in about 1541, the reformers' fears were realized, in that it embarrassed both the political establishment and theologians. An anonymous dialogue satirized Luther's secret permission to marry and dispatched the pointed reference: "You Lutherans want to carry on like the Turks and the Münsterites."[31]

Historian Paul Mikat observes that although Luther and the re-

30. John Alfred Faulkner, "Luther and the Bigamous Marriage of Philip of Hesse," *American Journal of Theology* 17 (April 1913): 206-31, emphasis added.

31. Johann Lenning, a defender of Philip's bigamous marriage, wrote on the subject in 1541 under the pseudonym Huldrich Neobolus, whose writing influenced Bernardino Ochino, a former friar who was open-minded on polygamy and referred to Neobolus in Dialogue XXI of his 1563 *Dialogi XXX*. See George Huntston Williams, *The Radical Reformation* (Philadelphia: Westminster Press, 1962), 785-86 (for quote, see Williams's 3rd ed., 786); Miller, *Milton among Polygamophiles*, 23.

formers extended privileges for concurrent wives to Henry and Philip, they sustained the Lutheran requirement that marriage be generally limited to monogamy. The "incomparable importance" Luther "bestowed [on] the polygamy problem" was beyond anything previously found in the "theological and legal marital literature."[32] In fact, it took the discussion of plural marriage as a permissible reflection of Old Testament practices out of the radical camp and established a mainstream precedent for it. Luther's status gave the issue a certain *gravitas* which it would have otherwise lacked.

Anabaptists and social protest

Initially the great sixteenth-century reformers wanted to work within the legal structure of the Roman Church. Even after separating from Rome, the reformers were too conservative for some radical sects. Men such as Melchior Hofmann (1495-1543) and Bernhard Rothmann (ca. 1495-1535) grew impatient with what they saw as the overly cautious leadership of Martin Luther. When the French theologian John Calvin (1509-64) became a Protestant in 1533 and advanced the Reformation in Geneva, he also seemed too cautious. The radicals wanted to go beyond reformation to what they called a restoration of the original liturgy and practice of the earliest Christian churches. They complained that Luther "tore down the house, but built no new one in its place." The spread of the Bible among common people produced literal-minded assumptions about the past.[33] Apart and separate from Luther's qualified permission to practice polygamy in special cases, various groups openly challenged the tradition of marriage. Their re-interpretation of Christian life made its way into German historian Johann Lorenz von Mosheim's 1755 book, *Institutes*

---

32. Mikat, *Polygamiefrage*, 25, citing Werner Elert's *Morphologie des Luthertums*, 1931.

33. Franklin Hamlin Littell, *The Anabaptist View of the Church: An Introduction to Sectarian Protestantism* (Chicago: American Society of Church History, 1952), 19, 24. Some scholars translate the German word *Wiederherstellung* as "restitution," but *Langenscheidt's New College German Dictionary* (Berlin: Langenscheidt KG, 1995) has "restoration" as the preferred meaning. This is the contemporary usage by the LDS Church, as in "die Wiederherstellung," *Kirche Jesu Christi der Heiligen der letzten Tage*, www.kirche-jesu-christi.org. In fact, the Anabaptists used two terms, "Restitution" and "Wedderstellinge," dialect for "restitution" and "restoration" (see note 61).

of Ecclesiastical History, Ancient and Modern, a copy of which Joseph Smith owned. Historian D. Michael Quinn observed that with Mosheim, "Joseph Smith could have had [at least] a textbook knowledge of the Anabaptists."[34] John Fox's *Book of Martyrs* and the writings and hymns of other sixteenth-century radicals were also in wide circulation during the rise of Mormonism.[35]

The Anabaptists' object was to reconstruct apostolic Christianity. One church reformer who inspired them was the Dutch scholar Desiderius Erasmus (1466-1536), a resident of Basel, Switzerland. He wished to return to the assumed simplicity of Jesus' time. The first radical Baptist schismatics assembled in Switzerland in 1525, about eight years after Luther inscribed his ninety-five theses; among other doctrines, they rejected the validity of infant baptism practiced by Catholics and various Protestant sects. This meant that adult converts who had been baptized as infants would need to be re-baptized. As a result of this heresy, they acquired the nickname *ana-baptist* from the Greek *ana baptizo* (German *Wiedertäufer*), meaning to re-baptize.

There were philosophical predecessors to the Anabaptists in Germany and elsewhere, but the first formally organized sect developed among disagreements with the Swiss reformer Huldrych Zwingli (1484-1531), who had made a cautious break with Rome similar to what Luther had undertaken in Germany. By contrast, the Anabaptists seemed to want nothing less than the complete destruction of the church as it had existed in Zurich and neighboring cantons. In 1531,

34. At least by January 1844, Joseph Smith had a copy. The book was first published in Latin as *Institutiones Historiae Ecclesiasticae Antiquae et Recentioris*, and when it appeared in English in 1765, the translator had anglicized the author's name to John Lawrence Mosheim. For more on Smith's familiarity with Mosheim, see D. Michael Quinn, "Socio-Religious Radicalism of the Mormon Church: A Parallel to the Anabaptists," in *New Views of Mormon History: A Collection of Essays in Honor of Leonard J. Arrington*, eds. Davis Bitton and Maureen Ursenbach Beecher (Salt Lake City: University of Utah Press, 1987), 378, 386n; also Kenneth W. Godfrey, "A Note on the Nauvoo Library and Literary Institute," *BYU Studies* 14 (Spring 1974): 388.

35. The Mennonites had their own expanded version of Fox's work, *The Martyrs' Mirror*, published in English in 1837 in Pennsylvania. Nauvoo Mormons were also aware of the Waldensians, radical reformers of the French Alps (Michael W. Homer, "The Waldensian Valleys: Seeking 'Primitive Christianity' in Italy," *Journal of Mormon History* 31 [Summer 2005]: 136n, 159-60).

two years before Calvin's rise in Geneva, Zwingli died in battle against a Catholic army intent on defeating Protestantism. The smaller and more radical branch of Swiss Protestantism, the so-called Swiss Brethren (*Brüder in Cristo,* literally "Brothers in Christ"), believed in modern-day prophecy and spirit possession, revivalism, dancing, speaking in tongues, and following the "inner word." Their idealism, and their related contempt for the status quo, can be explained in part by the fact that they were relatively young people at the time, coming on the heels of the ill-fated Peasants' War of 1524-25 in which radicals had fought for legal rights for farmers and feudal townspeople. The Swiss Brethren formed its first congregation outside of Zurich in 1525. Another important movement, which had been in existence half a century, was the similarly sounding Dutch organization, Brethren of the Common Life (*Broeders des gemeenen levens*), which promoted scripture reading, meditation, and imitation of the apostles' lives.[36] These Swiss and Dutch brotherhoods presaged a throng of Anabaptist believers who gathered in Münster, Germany.

Influenced by these currents of religious discontent, a one-time furrier from Austria, Melchior Hofmann, became inspired by the work of Erasmus and others and felt called to carry the simple gospel message into northwest Germany and the Netherlands. The year 1530 found him in Strassburg, along the Rhine trade route (now Strasbourg, across the border from Germany). While there, Hofmann converted to Anabaptism.[37] More than others in the movement, Hofmann began articulating an eschatological version of the theology, predicting that Christ would return during his lifetime.[38] Drawing

---

36. "Brethren of the Common Life," *Encyclopaedia Britannica,* 2008, online at www.britannica.com. Bernhard Rothmann received humanist training at the sect's Deventer school (Carl Adolf Cornelius, *Historische Arbeiten vornehmlich zur Reformationsgeschichte* [Leipzig: Duncker und Humboldt, 1899], 1-33; D. Reichling, *Johannes Murmellius: Sein Leben und seine Werke* [Nieuwkoop, 1963]).

37. James M. Stayer, *Anabaptists and the Sword,* 2nd ed. (Lawrence, Kans.: Coronado Press, 1976); also in the *Mennonite Quarterly Review* 44 (Oct. 1970): 371-75; Littell, *Anabaptist View,* 20-33; Stephen F. Nelson and Jean Rott, "Strasbourg: The Anabaptist City in the Sixteenth Century," *Mennonite Quarterly Review* 58 (July 1984): 3:230-39; Williams, *Radical Reformation,* 362-86.

38. Williams, *Radical Reformation,* 3rd ed., 621-23.

upon Jewish apocalyptic themes, he imagined a religion originally established by Adam and Eve. Hofmann would then move from the cosmic to the mundane and speak of the "historical Adam attending the first church." He believed this Adamic church had the same doctrines and rituals as were preserved in early Christianity.[39] Three hundred years later, Joseph Smith and his successor Brigham Young expressed equal fascination with Adam and Eve. "When our father Adam came into the Garden of Eden," Young proclaimed from the pulpit in Salt Lake City, "he came into it with a *celestial body,* and brought Eve, *one of his wives,* with him."[40]

Hofmann and his "Melchiorite" followers literally believed there would be a "holy city" (Rev. 21:2) at Christ's Second Coming which would be spared while the rest of the world was destroyed by fire. They speculated about which city would be favored by this honor. When Hofmann announced that it was Amsterdam, Anabaptists began flocking there. However, when Charles V became emperor of the Holy Roman Empire in 1530, he turned up the heat on heresy in the low countries in what has been called the Dutch Inquisition. Rather than exercising prudence, the Anabaptists, convinced that they were right and would prevail against the anti-Christ, denounced the Catholic teaching that the Eucharist was the literal body and blood of Christ and marched through Amsterdam waving swords, threatening to seize the city from Satan. Some of the radicals walked naked through the city to announce the "naked truth" of the imminent millennium. Many were apprehended. When eight of Hofmann's disciples were beheaded in the Hague on December 5, 1531, this became for Menno Simons and Obbe Philips "a turning point in the[ir] spiritual evolution." After the Münster debacle, described below, Simons

---

39. Littell, *Anabaptist View,* 50-51.

40. Henry W. Naisbitt remembered that "Joseph Smith the prophet taught that Adam had two wives" ("Communities Are Made Up of Family Organizations ... Eternity of Marriage Necessarily Leads to Plural Marriage," a sermon delivered in the Tabernacle, Mar. 8, 1885, in *Journal of Discourses,* 26 vols. [London: Latter-day Saint's Book Depot, 1854-86], 26:115; Brigham Young, "Self-Government, ... Adam, Our Father and Our God," a sermon delivered Apr. 9, 1852, in *Journal of Discourses,* 1:50, emphasis in the original.

and Philips directed the scattered flock toward a less radical and non-violent Mennonitism.[41] Hofmann left Amsterdam and was arrested in Strassburg in 1533, where he would die in prison ten years later. Despite his personal fate, he inspired yet more radicals to congregate in Münster in 1534 to fulfill his dream of a New Jerusalem.

Anabaptism had developed into a widespread underground movement by 1534. It included, as Luther might have said, a "priesthood of all believers"—sailors, fishermen, cooks, small business owners, and common laborers who had suffered hard times. The Netherlands became the center of activity, complementing the re-baptizers in Switzerland and elsewhere, including Bohemia and Moravia (now the Czech Republic, Slovakia, and part of Austria). Germany itself was a country in turmoil, where a Catholic bishop, the Hapsburg emperor, and a governing council of district representatives competed for political dominance. Apocalyptical doctrines about Christ's second coming provided the rationale for popular revolt. Economic stagnation in the Netherlands, a trade blockade, and bread shortages pitted peasants against dukes. Trade guilds rose up in the 1520s to be followed by millennialist agitators in the 1530s. Located in Germany near the border with Holland, Münster lay at the heart of the Anabaptist ferment.

Münster's Anabaptists

Disillusioned by events in Amsterdam and moved by the texts of Daniel and Revelations, the more radical Anabaptists looked elsewhere for a place where they could practice their faith and await the end of the world.[42] They were punished for their beliefs and practices by church

41. Williams, *Radical Reformation,* 540-47. Charles V received the low countries by inheritance as Duke of Burgundy in 1506. He initiated the Inquisition in 1522, then continued his agenda of rooting out heresy with added vigor as emperor.

42. The Book of Daniel was written in about 167 BCE by Jewish Maccabees revolting against Seleucid (Syrian-Greek) persecution. The Book of Revelation, written about 90 CE, borrowed imagery from Daniel to address the scattered Christians of Asia Minor with vivid images, including the four horsemen of the apocalypse and the "mark of the beast," perhaps referring to Roman oppressors. See Jaroslav J. Pelikan, *The Christian Tradition: A History of the Development of Doctrine* (Chicago: University of Chicago Press, 1973), 1:123-27. See also Public Broadcasting Service, *Apocalypse! The Evolution of Apocalyptic Belief and How It Shaped the Western World,* a production of *Frontline,* 2000, at www.pbs.org.

and civil authorities wherever they were, whether in Catholic or Protestant regions. British historian Diarmaid MacCulloch estimated that the "excitement about the Last Days" was so "common in the 1520s and 1530s" that the Anabaptist converts numbered in the thousands.[43] One of the larger groups of self-proclaimed "saints of the last days,"[44] these Anabaptists found Münster to be ideal. It was a gateway for both travel and news because of its stature as a commercial center and university town.[45] Impressed by the degree of tolerance that allowed such topics as adult baptism to be discussed openly, the radicals came to be convinced that Münster was destined to become the apocalyptic holy city.

At the center of these events was Bernhard Rothmann, who was educated at the Cathedral School in Münster and became a theologian and pastor of the church of St. Moritz outside of the city. In 1529 he toured the great centers of the Reformation, including Marburg, Strassburg, and Wittenberg. When he returned in 1531, he was censured by more conservative reformers for his stridency and then removed from his cathedral post.[46] Undaunted, he presented Lutheran articles of protest against the Catholic Church in 1532, the year the city council formally authorized a "reformation" in the city. Rothmann received protection from admirers, especially among the trade guilds, who were likewise looking for reform. However, when Rothmann began to preach against infant baptism, he became too heretical

43. Diarmaid MacCulloch, *Reformation: A History* (New York: Viking, 2004), 183.

44. See Williams, *Radical Reformation*, 578-79. A two-part series on the Anabaptists, *King of the Last Days* (*Der König der letzten Tage*) aired on German television in 1993; see commentary by Thomas Seifert, *Die Täufer zu Münster* (Münster: Agenda Verlag, 1993).

Both Anabaptists in Germany (1534-35) and Mormons in America (1830-90) read warnings of the last days in the Bible. In the King James Bible, the "last days" are referred to in Genesis 49:1, Isaiah 2:2, and John 6:39; "latter days" in Deuteronomy 4:30 and Job 19:25; and "latter times" in 1 Timothy 4:1. The term "saints" is used in Deuteronomy 33:2, 1 Samuel 2:9, Psalms 50:5, Daniel 7:18, Matthew 27:52, Romans 1:7, and 1 Corinthians 1:2; 14:33. "Saints of the last days," or "latter day saints," are concepts that each group of believers would have derived from the Bible.

45. Williams, *Radical Reformation*, 556-57; Gary K. Waite, "From Apocalyptic Crusaders to Anabaptist Terrorists: Anabaptist Radicalism after Münster, 1535-1544," *Archiv für Reformationsgeschichte* 80 (1989): 173-93, 180n.

46. Cornelius Krahn, *Dutch Anabaptism: Origin, Spread, Life, and Thought, 1450-1600* (1968; Scottdale, Penn.: Herald Press, 1981), 123.

even for fellow Protestant sympathizers. Later that year, when armed citizens captured some of the Catholic clergy while the city council looked the other way, the new bishop, Franz von Waldeck, conscripted troops to besiege the city. Over the next two years, a Dutch Anabaptist prophet would assume power in Münster, expelling Catholics and Lutherans alike. Strict obedience to the prophet and polygamy were among the new expectations of the populace, enforced within the city as it held off the surrounding armies and waited for Jesus to return to the earth to rescue them.

Philip of Hesse arrived from Marburg on February 14, 1533, to try to mediate peace between the competing religious interests in the city. But by then, Rothmann's radical movement had nearly overwhelmed its opponents. In the March 3 election, the city replaced four incumbent councilmen with Anabaptists. The electorate retained twelve councilmen who had recently converted to Anabaptism, giving Rothmann and his followers a total of sixteen of twenty-four council seats.[47] The previous year, the city council had already given Rothman a new clerical position as pastor of St. Lambert's, adjacent to the cathedral, to the bishop's great dismay. Rothman was also beginning to entertain traumatized Melchiorites from Holland. Among those was the future king, John Bockelson, who visited briefly and then returned to Holland.

Münster's Catholics and conservative Protestant parties began a formal debate ("disputation") over their theological differences in early August 1533. Surprisingly, they found themselves united on many topics. Mostly, they were both opposed to Rothmann. They lobbied the city council to take note of their positions and agree that Rothmann was beyond the line of reasonableness. The discussion came to involve Martin Bucer of Strassburg, who would later become a divinity professor at Cambridge University in England. He and other mainstream reformers realized that the heresy they thought they had defeated in Strassburg had begun to spread throughout Europe.[48] The

47. Ernst Laubach, "Die Täuferherrschaft in Münster," *Geschichte in Wissenschaft und Unterricht* 45 (1994): 503.

48. Krahn, *Dutch Anabaptism,* 123, 124, 135.

Wittenberg scholars—Melanchthon, Johannes Bugenhagen (a close friend of Luther), and Nikolaus von Amsdorf—tried to convince Rothmann of his error, to no avail. Theologians sent by Philip of Hesse from Marburg on November 15, 1533, were less severe than Luther and Melanchthon, who said they favored execution of the Anabaptist agitators.[49] Feeling cornered, the city council ordered Rothmann exiled.

Rothmann defied the city's edict and, with popular support, preached in all but two of Münster's churches over the next few months. He welcomed two emissaries from Holland in January 1534 and allowed himself to be baptized by them. They then began baptizing other converts. Bishop von Waldeck issued an edict to imprison anyone who performed an adult baptism.[50] However, with the optimistic report that John Bockelson had taken back to the Netherlands, hundreds of immigrants were already streaming into the area—some from Strassburg.[51] If the bishop had known of the internal dissent that existed within the Anabaptist ranks at the time, he might have been able to exploit their differences. For instance, Hofmann had declared that the world would end in December 1533, at which time—but not beforehand—they could start baptizing each other. Simultaneously, one of Hofmann's leading disciples in Holland, Jan Mathijs, grew impatient and initiated the "believer's sacrament." The people of Münster were less directly influenced by Hofmann than others in the Anabaptist fold and seem not to have troubled over Hofmann's unfulfilled prophecy. They received his emissaries and responded well to their call for defiance against the bishop. By the end of January, the Dutch evangelists had baptized some 1,400 converts in Münster.[52]

In the Netherlands, Mathijs had been busy establishing an eccle-

49. See entries for Bucer, Bugenhagen, Luther, Melanchthon, and Rothmann at the *Global Anabaptist Mennonite Encyclopedia Online* (www.gameo.org); also Williams, *Radical Reformation,* 560.

50. Krahn, *Dutch Anabaptism,* 123, 124, 135.

51. Claus-Peter Clasen, "Anabaptist Sects in the Sixteenth Century: A Research Report," *Mennonite Quarterly Review* 46 (July 1972): 256-79; Krahn, *Dutch Anabaptism,* 115.

52. Laubach, "Täuferherrschaft in Münster," 504.

siastical structure to support the Anabaptist theology. At the top of the organization were apostles; although not stopping at twelve, Mathijs commissioned twenty-seven of them by 1534.[53] One of the anointed was Bockelson. He too returned to Münster on January 31 and was pleased to find a thriving congregation there. The adherents were mostly women. As Münster historian Karl-Heinz Kirchhoff discovered when he analyzed the demographics of the conflict, there were more women than men among the believers to begin with, and toward the end of the siege in 1535, after casualties and departures, Münster would have about five women for every man.[54]

There were enough men among the congregation to flex some political muscle. The Anabaptists used their numerical superiority to seize full political control of the city in February 1534; they designated Münster the "New Jerusalem" and called upon the elect to move there. In the words of German historian Ralf Klötzer, "It was here the saints were to gather[,] ... [to] live through God's judgment, and with the returning Christ possess the kingdom of peace in the last days."[55] When Mathijs himself arrived in February, he was the de facto leader because of his stature among the re-baptized. A Rothmann supporter by the name of Bernard Knipperdolling was appointed *Bürgermeister,* or mayor, on February 23. It was an office that the city council filled, and its members were already under Mathijs's influence. Next, Mathijs announced his intention to expel from the city the "godless" who had refused to join the "covenant" of re-baptism. As startling as this was to his followers, they consented to his authority and watched as their Catholic and Lutheran neighbors fled the city. Simultaneously, Bishop Waldeck tightened his grip, encircling Mün-

53. Portentously, this was the eve of the Feast of Epiphany commemorating the arrival of the three magi or, in the Greek Orthodox tradition, the baptism of Christ.

54. Karl-Heinz Kirchhoff, "Was There a Peaceful Anabaptist Congregation in Münster in 1534?" trans. Elizabeth H. Bender, *Mennonite Quarterly Review* 44 (Oct. 1970): 357-70, a translation of Kirchhoff's groundbreaking 1964 essay ("Gab es eine friedliche Täufergemeinde in Münster?" *Jahrbuch des Vereins für westfälische Kirchengeschichte* 55/56 [1962/1963], 7-21), that began the "new look" into Anabaptist history in western Germany.

55. Ralf Klötzer, *Täuferherrschaft von Münster: Stadtreformation und Welterneuerung* (Münster: Aschendorff Verlag, 1992), 153.

ster with ever more troops and printing broadsides and leaflets to propagandize Germany in his favor.[56]

The bishop hired about 8,000 mercenaries who brought forty cannons with them—this compared to the city's population of about 9,500, of whom only about 900 were armed men. Since so many of the men had fled, and some had died in fighting, there were already about three women to each man at this early stage of the siege.[57] As the standoff continued, the Anabaptists had few options to resolve the situation. On February 28, Bishop Waldeck's soldiers completed their blockade of all roads leading to Münster. Little more than a month later, on the Easter Sunday Mathijs had said would prove their salvation, Mathijs was killed as he led an armed raid against the surrounding army. That evening, Bockelson stepped into the martyred prophet's shoes and announced that he would be the one to continue his predecessor's work, setting for this encircled community the ambitious goal of converting the world.[58] On that same day, an Anabaptist blacksmith, Jacob von Ossenburg, "confessed" under torture by surrounding armies that Bockelson had said he was the reincarnation of Enoch, that Melchior Hofmann was Elijah, and that Christ had promised to stage his second coming before Easter: "The world will be cruelly punished so that not even one tenth of the population will survive. ... Only in Münster will there be peace and security, since it will be the city of the Lord and the New Jerusalem."[59]

---

56. Ernst Laubach, "Das Täuferreich zu Münster," *Westfälische Zeitschrift* 141 (1991): 123-24.

57. Before the Anabaptist phenomenon, Münster was a member of the Hansa League of northern trade cities and had a population estimated at 10,000. Kirchhoff noted that between 1534 and 1535, the population declined to 7,000-8,000, of whom 1,500-2,000 were men, about 5,000 women, and about 1,200 children (*Die Wiedertäufer in Münster,* a catalog for the opening exhibit of the Münster City Museum, October 1, 1982, 2nd enlarged ed. [Münster: Aschendorff Verlag, 1986]; Seifert, *Täufer zu Münster;* Krahn, *Dutch Anabaptism,* 144).

58. Laubach, "Täuferherrschaft in Münster," 508.

59. Krahn, *Dutch Anabaptism,* 137, 276n: Johann Heinrich Joseph Niesert, *Beiträge zu einem Münsterischen Urkundenbuche aus vaterländischen Archiven* (Münster: Coppenrath, 1823), 1:123, 154 ff.; Karl-Heinz Kirchhoff, "Die Täufer im Münsterland: Verbreitung und Verfolgung des Täufertums im Stift Münster, 1533-1550," *Westfälische Zeitschrift,* 113 (1963): 21ff.; see also Klötzer, *Stadtreformation und Welterneuerung,* 9-11.

As Bockelson "purified" Münster of infidels, he urged Anabaptists everywhere to come to the city. "I do not simply tell you about it, but command you in the name of the Lord to obey without delay." A tract addressed to "All Believing Covenanters in Christ" throughout the world urged people to leave their property except for some "money, linen, and enough food for the trip" because there was enough in the way of "supplies for the saints" in the city. Historian Cornelius Krahn painted the picture: "From North Holland they came by the hundreds. From South Holland ... they came to the harbors of the Zuiderzee [Lake Ijssel] to cross it by boat ... From other parts of the country they came by foot or with horse, cart, men, women, and children moving in the direction of Münster." Some sources speak of 14,000 to 16,000 pilgrims responding to Bockelson's summons. Many were intercepted on their way and incarcerated or slaughtered by outraged Christians.[60]

Bernhard Rothmann became Bockelson's primary spokesperson. In the space of nine months, from October 1534 to June 1535, Rothmann produced four tracts defending the course of events in Münster, arguing that human history is a repeating cycle of apostasy and restoration and that Münster represented the final stage in that cycle. Just as Mormons would speak of historic "dispensations" leading to the gathering of Israel in the last days, Rothmann wrote of the Saints of Münster and their New Zion, how they had "restore[d] again the kingdom to Israel" (Acts 1:6). Rothmann used two terms for what was transpiring: a *restitution* and a *restoration,* implying that things would return to the way they had been or that there would be a re-implementation of the previous *statute,* which is the etymological root of *restitution.* The term was theologically dependent on Acts 3:21, which alluded to everything returning to how it once was ("the times of restitution of all things"), a passage Mormons would also employ in their reinstatement of Old Testament plural marriage. In October 1534, Rothmann published his most famous pamphlet, *A Restitution or Restoration of Proper and Healthy Christian Teachings about Faith and Life,* defending polygamy.

60. Krahn, *Dutch Anabaptism,* 146.

In December, in the second of his four major works, *Van der Wrake* (*On Vindication*), Rothmann portrayed the developments in Münster as the intended result of history, writing that "the reformation in Germany, through the revolution in Münster, has reached perfection as a pattern to be emulated." While mainstream Protestant reformers sought a return to classical, or what they saw as "magisterial," Christianity, restorationists like Rothmann harkened back to the formative years of the church for their redefinition of Christianity, extending back even before the advent of Jesus.

Rothmann's followers believed in a kind of eternal Christianity that manifested itself over time as sequential chapters of the same book, a process Mormons would also formalize in their view of a Christianized Old Testament. The Münsterites saw world history as a series of three dispensations: (1) from the Creation to the Flood, (2) from Noah to the sixteenth century, and (3) from 1534 to a future millennial kingdom, for which Münster was the "cosmically ordained preparation." Rothmann traced Adam's fall and redemption, the fall of Israel and return to Canaan, the establishment of Christ's church and later apostasy in the second century, and the final restoration "begun by Erasmus and Luther and climaxing in John Bockelson." "Behold," Rothmann continued, "how through Erasmus, Luther, and Zwingli the [new] beginning was made, but only in Melchior [Hofmann], John Mathijs and here in our brother, John of Leiden, has the truth been gloriously established."[61] In Hofmann's restorationism, Paradise, Old Israel, and the apostolic church were all part of a preparation for the universal rule of Christ, a view shared in some form among various restorationist sects.

---

61. Bernhard Rothmann, *Eyne Restitution edder Eine wedderstellinge rechter unde gesunder Christlicher leer gelovens unde levens* (Münster, 1534), in Robert Stupperich, ed., *Schriften von evangelischer Seite gegen die Täufer,* vol. 3 in the *Schriften der münsterischen Täufer und ihrer Gegner* series (Münster: Aschendorff, 1983), 172-83; Andreas Knaake, ed., *Flugschriften aus der Reformationszeit* (Halle: Niemeyer, 1888): 7:16-17, cited in John Cairncross, *After Polygamy Was Made a Sin: The Social History of Christian Polygamy* (London: Routledge and K. Paul, 1974), 224; and Williams, *Radical Reformation,* 3rd ed., 576. For the Mormon view of the Old Testament, see Melodie Moench Charles, "The Mormon Christianizing of the Old Testament," *Sunstone,* Nov.-Dec. 1980, 35-39.

Polygamy in Münster

The Münster prophets considered polygamy and New Testament communal life to be important aspects of their restitution, with all its striking similarities to nineteenth-century Mormonism.[62] It is noteworthy that neither LDS people nor Mennonites today boast of this part of their ancestral past. Like the Mormons in Nauvoo, no undertaking in Münster burdened the Anabaptist reputation as much as polygyny after it was initiated in July 1534. Their neighbors referred dismissively to the practice as the *Vielweiberei,* which loosely means "the many wivery."[63] It took Bockelson only three months from the prophet's martyrdom until he decided to demonstrate his authority as Mathijs's successor by marrying the prophet's widow. It may well have been true, and at least the later dramatic presentations hint at this, that the enchanting widow, Divara, happened to be a woman of beauty. Bockelson already had a wife and two children in Leiden; but after marrying this woman he called his "queen," he proceeded to marry the mayor's daughter, Clara Knipperdolling, thus solidifying political alliances just as Joseph Smith would later do.[64] Bockelson did not appear to construct his own doctrinal justification for accumulating wives beyond that which his spokesperson, Rothmann, devised; it took Rothmann only three months to develop a theological justification for multiple marriages and put it into print in his famous *Restitution.*

Bockelson did claim to have received a communication from God compelling him to marry Divara. She was familiar with the genre of

62. See Krahn's *Dutch Anabaptism;* William E. Juhnke, "Anabaptism and Mormonism: A Study in Comparative History," *Mennonite Life* 40 (Dec. 1985): 22-25; Juhnke, "Anabaptism and Mormonism: A Study in Comparative History," *John Whitmer Historical Journal* 2 (1982): 38-46; David Brion Davis, "The New England Origins of Mormonism," *New England Quarterly* 26 (June 1953): 148-65; Quinn, "Socio-Religious Radicalism," 363-86; Andrew Bolton, "Learning from Anabaptism: A Major Peace Tradition," *Restoration Studies,* 5 vols. (Independence, Mo.: Herald Publishing House, 1993), 5:13-24; and Frederick S. Buchanan, "Mormons Meet the Mennonites: A View from 1884," *Mennonite Quarterly Review* 62 (Apr. 1988): 159-66.

63. Laubach, "Täuferherrschaft in Münster," 500, translation courtesy of Henry L. Miner.

64. Klötzer, *Stadtreformation und Welterneuerung,* 116.

revelation, since her deceased husband had been the prophet of the end-times. Now Bockelson learned through the same medium that he was apparently greater than her previous husband—the "redeemer," implying a second manifestation of Christ. In a study of charismatic succession, Margrit Eichler has traced the Anabaptist leadership in Amsterdam from Hofmann to Mathijs, then to Bockelson after the move to Münster. With each successive claim to power, the leadership became bolder in its published credentials. Hofmann considered himself to be Elijah's avatar, the first witness to Jesus' return; Mathijs had viewed himself as the prophet of the last days; then in a more assertive step in the summer of 1534, Bockelson became Jesus Christ himself. The fact that Bockelson had heretofore claimed something more akin to inspiration than outright visions, which would have been a greater stamp of charisma, "was compensated for by deification. This culminated in [his] recognition as the Messiah."[65] Bockelson was responsible for initiating the shift in the scriptural basis of Anabaptist theology from the New Testament to the Hebrew Bible and for defining their denomination as "new Israelites."[66] In claiming the prophetic mantle, he pushed many more of the men out of Münster. Whether or not the end of days was upon them, for the Anabaptists of Münster the final chapter had begun.

Bockelson dissolved the city council in April 1534. God's spokesman on earth had little need for a deliberative body of that kind.[67] With the Parousia not yet a reality by July, Bockelson appointed twelve elders—analogous to the twelve tribes of Israel and Christ's twelve apostles—and designated himself as the divinely appointed king, son of David, who would rule the world until God the Father reclaimed his scepter of authority.[68] Bockelson's claims suggested that

---

65. Margrit Eichler, "Charismatic Prophets and Charismatic Saviors," *Mennonite Quarterly Review* 55 (Jan. 1981): 53, 59, citing Otthein Rammstedt's *Sekte und soziale Bewegung: Sociologische Analyse der Täufer in Münster,* 1966. Eichler suggests that Bockelson had more charisma than Rammstedt allows.

66. *Wiedertäufer in Münster* (catalog).

67. Krahn, *Dutch Anabaptism,* 137, 276n; Niesert, *Beiträge,* 1:123, 154ff.; Kirchhoff, "Täufer im Münsterland," 21ff.; see also Klötzer, *Stadtreformation und Welterneuerung,* 1-19.

68. Hermann von Kerssenbroick, in Klemens Löffler, *Die Wiedertäufer zu Münster,*

the Second Coming, presumptively his, had already occurred. He told the elders that plural marriage was a patriarchal right, an apologetic that anticipated what Mormons would later call "patriarchal marriage."[69] On August 31, another self-proclaimed Anabaptist prophet, Johann Dusentschuer, announced a vision in fulfillment of Jeremiah 23 and Ezekiel 37, proclaiming Bockelson "King of the New Zion." Similar millennialist themes were voiced by early Mormons.[70]

In September, triumphant in holding the bishop's troops at bay, Bockelson staged a coronation ceremony at which he was crowned "king of righteousness over all" and was handed a sword by the twelve elders as one of them anointed him, announcing: "Upon the command of the Father, I anoint thee to be King of the people of God in the New Temple; and in the presence of all the people, I proclaim thee to be ruler of the new Zion." Thereafter, Bockelson made ritual appearances in the marketplace three times a week. One observer wrote:

> Some of the women and girls stayed on after he had preached, danced about and cried in a loud voice, Father, Father, Father, give! give! give! Then they leapt up, raised their hands to the sky and clapped. Their hair[,] undone, hung round their neck or down their back. They stared at the sun and imagined that God the Father was sitting up there in his glory. Then they danced like maenads in pairs through the streets and gazed at the sun till they were exhausted, white and deadly pale.[71]

As king, Bockelson would accumulate fourteen more wives, all of them recognized as "queens." In addition to Divara van Harlem, or Gertrud von Utrecht, as she was also known, and Clara Knipper-

---

1534-35: Berichte, Aussagen, und Aktenstücke von Augenzeugen und Zeitgenossen (Jena: Eugen Diederichs, 1923), 79; also in Eichler, "Charismatic Prophets," 54.

69. Klötzer, *Stadtreformation und Welterneuerung,* 97-102. I have not found any indication that Münsterites claimed, as the Mormons later did, that Jesus was a polygamist (*Journal of Discourses,* 2:81-83, 11:327-28, 25:90).

70. Krahn, *Dutch Anabaptism,* 144-45, 277. Krahn cites three sources: (1) Kerssenbroch's *Anabaptistici Furoris Narratio* (Münster, 1899), 2:650 ff.; (2) Löffler, *Berichte, Aussagen,* 124 ff.; (3) and Krahn's "Münster" in the *Mennonite Encyclopedia* (Hillsboro, Kans.: Mennonite Brethren Publishing House, 1955-59), 4:779. For the Mormon view, see Grant Underwood, *The Millenarian World of Early Mormonism* (Urbana: University of Illinois Press, 1993), 24-31.

71. Löffler, *Berichte, Aussagen,* 75; translation in Cairncross, *After Polygamy Was Made Sin,* 10; Kirchhoff, "Peaceful Anabaptist Congregation."

dolling, who was previously married to someone named Hangesbeck, who had died, Bockelson married Elizabeth Wantscherer—a brief marriage because Bockelson beheaded her in May 1535. He also married Anna Kippenbrock, if that was her name. She may well have been the daughter of a previous mayor, Kibbenbrock. Another of Bockelson's consorts was Anna Knipperdolling, the mayor's wife; the mayor had died in July. The foreign wives returned to their homeland after the breakup of the Münster idyll in 1535.[72] Perhaps giving a more complete accounting of the king's wives, a pamphlet published in the wake of Münster's collapse gave their names in two columns, following the name of his first plural wife who must have been considered superior to the others. In all, sixteen women were mentioned, as follows.[73]

Dissere von Harlum

Maria Hecker	Katherina Miling
Anna Laurentz	Engelle Kerckerinck
Anna Uberweg	Elizabeth Wantscherer
Elisabeth Treger	Anna Knipperdolling
Clara Knipperdolling	Katherina Uberweg
Anna Kippenbrock	Christina Röde
Margareta Morsonne	Margaret Grolle
Elisabeth von dem Bussche	

After initiating polygamy in the new zion, Bockelson ordered all eligible men to take additional wives. Fourteen-year-old males and twelve-year-old females were deemed to be of a marriageable age. Bockelson publicized twelve "articles" to govern marriage and attributed them to a revelation from God. One of the articles required that a woman should recognize her husband as her lord, another that a man could take as many wives as he desired. This experiment with

72. Karl-Heinz Kirchhoff to the author, April 20, 2008.

73. *Wiedertäufer in Münster* (catalog), 196-97; Max Geisberg, comp., *Die Wiedertäufer in Münster: Bildwiedergaben ausgewälter Urkunden und Akten zur Geschichte Westfalens,* 12 Bd. (Velen, Westfallen: Archivbildstelle, 1930), with a photographic reproduction (vol. 4) of *Neue Zeitung, wie die Stadt Münster erobert [wurde],* 1535.

polygamy lasted eleven months, until the city's fall in late June 1535. In the aftermath of the conquest, Bockelson was interrogated and then executed along with the other Anabaptist leaders. A month before the final struggle, according to Krahn, the total population of Münster was estimated to be 9,500. Of these, there were 900 men and 5,500 women—over six women to each man—and the rest children.[74]

During this period, according to Klötzer, the subordination of women was defended in sermons. Women were told their relationship to men was like the community's relationship "to Christ, the heavenly husband." The joining of male and female also had a mystical dimension, oddly enough a "sacramentally conceived concept of marriage which the patriarchate of Münster took responsibility for, and through which the liberty for the man to take several wives would be able to be realized."[75] The Anabaptists had come full circle in rejecting the sacramental model for Catholic marriage and replacing it with their own, while mainstream Protestants insisted that marriage was a secular institution, yet still regulated it as if it were a church ordinance.

Unmarried women were required to accept a marriage proposal unless, for some extraordinary reason, they were unable to. This compulsion prompted single women to stay out of sight and sparked a frenzy among the men, who each wanted to be the first to ask available girls.[76] Some of the men employed existing wives to make contact with potential wives, just as Sarah had done for Abraham in biblical times and as some Mormon women would do for their husbands in the mid-1800s. The man with the most wives was considered the winner of this unacknowledged competition.

For three days in July 1534, as Bockelson shared intimacies with Divara, Rothmann preached in the marketplace about how God had appointed plural marriage for the New Israel. Rothman himself would accumulate nine wives, which he could now see was necessary in or-

74. Krahn, *Dutch Anabaptism,* 159, Karl-Heinz Kirchhoff, "Die Belagerung und Eroberung Münsters, 1534/35," *Westfälische Zeitschrift* 112 (1962); Kerssenbroch, *Anabaptistici,* 2:141-44, 700, 736, 833-856.

75. Klötzer, *Stadtreformation und Welterneuerung,* 156-57.

76. Williams, *Radical Reformation,* 3rd ed., 566-80, 755-98.

der to fulfill the command to "be fruitful and multiply and fill the earth" (Gen. 1:28). It also facilitated the promise to Abraham that he would have innumerable descendants (Gen. 22:17, Ps. 46:4, 87:3; Rev. 7:1-8, 14:1). Rothmann now envisioned a progeny that would be numbered among the 144,000 who would receive Christ at his coming.[77] These are familiar themes for millennial societies.

The expressive theologian further advised that if "a man is so richly blessed that he is able to fructify more than one woman," he should do so. A man should not let a woman lead him about "like a bear on a rope." Playing to feelings of uncertainty over where society might be moving in the wake of the Reformation, Rothmann complained that the weaker sex had been "everywhere ... getting the upper hand" and needed to submit to its masters, just as men do to Christ and Christ to God.[78] In much the same vein, Brigham Young would announce in Nauvoo that a "woman will never get back [to God], unless she follows the man back ... The man must love his God and the woman must love her Husband," in that order. LDS Apostle George A. Smith said outright that "the woman ought to be in subjection to the man." Heber Kimball instructed Mormons that God "did not make man for the woman, but the woman for the man" and said God "made one [a female] and gave her to him."[79] Both the Münster Anabaptists and the Mormons stressed the importance of male dominance in their respective patriarchal societies.

The parallels between these two disparate communities, separated by centuries, are eerily close. As the Münster prophet accumulated more authority, he seemed even less grounded in the temporal sphere. One dissenter, Henry Mollenhecke, gathered some citizens to surprise and imprison Bockelson on July 29, 1534, intending to overturn the marital confusion in the city. Freed by townspeople who

77. Ibid., 517, 568, 570. The passage, "multiply and fill the earth," is used to make a case for polygamy in Mormon theology (cf. 2 Ne. 20:22, a virtual reproduction of Isa. 10:22, which itself follows Gen. 1:28).

78. Rothmann, *Restitution edder Eine wedderstellinge,* 75, 81, 85; Williams, *Radical Reformation,* 3rd ed., 577-78; Krahn, *Dutch Anabaptism,* 144.

79. In George D. Smith, ed., *An Intimate Chronicle: The Journals of William Clayton* (Salt Lake City: Signature Books and Smith Research Associates, 1991), 227, 239.

were loyal to him, Bockelson put Mollenhecke and forty-eight other insurgents to death. After the "Mollenhecke uprising," polygyny became even more strictly enforced. Wives disobedient to their husbands were threatened with the same fate as the insurgents. In the autumn of 1534, Bockelson jailed and executed additional members of the community, including a few of the so-called "stiff-necked" women.[80] Reminiscent of Brigham Young's policies, by late fall 1534, after the men had endured unresolvable strife among their multiple wives, over one hundred women were allowed to divorce the men they had been forced to marry.[81]

Stayer's article on *Vielweiberei* concludes that polygyny caused such indignation toward the Münster Baptist movement on the part of Europeans that it "has not been silenced" to "the present day." In his "Restitution" of October 1534, Rothmann rejected as slander the charge that the people of Münster were living in illegal marriage. He then confirmed that they had restored the ancient practice of polygamy, which he justified as fulfilling the "biblical laws of purity and procreation." Heinrich Gresbeck, an Anabaptist who wrote an exposé after fleeing the besieged city, reported that men had been required to take all "virgins, servant girls, widows, and all that are marriageable, whether of the nobility, the bourgeoisie, believers or worldly." On January 2, 1535, Bockelson forbade adultery (Article 7) and followed up with an allowance that when a man was absent three days and three nights, his wife was free to take another man (Article 13). Previous marriages were thus suspended if the husband was not in the city, which was true for many of Münster's women because couples had decided it was safe for the woman to stay behind to keep a claim on the house while the man fled. A wrinkle in the law was in regard to girls who were not yet of marriageable age.[82] Those besieging

80. Klötzer, *Stadtreformation und Welterneuerung,* 99-101.

81. Williams, *Radical Reformation,* 3rd ed., 570; Klötzer, *Stadtreformation und Welterneuerung,* 97-102; Laubach, "Täuferherrschaft in Münster," 517.

82. James M. Stayer, "Vielweiberei als 'innerweltliche Askese': Neue Eheauffassungen in der Reformationszeit," *Mennonitische Geschichtsblätter* 37 (1980), translated for the author by Henry L. Miner; Darren T. Williamson, "'For the Honor of God and to Fulfill His Will': The Role of Polygamy in Anabaptist Münster," *Restoration Quar-*

Münster heard of pre-teens who had been forced to marry. Heinrich Dorpius spoke of "little girls of ten, twelve or fourteen years of age"; Kerssenbroeck spoke of eleven- to thirteen-year-old girls. Young girls were among those who were allowed to apply for divorce in the fall of 1534.[83]

Bockelson's apocalyptic pitch, tainted by what seemed to be sexual license, appeared outrageous to traditionalists. As a measure of the Protestant response to the Anabaptists, when the king sent out twenty-eight apostles to proselytize in various German cities in October 1534, all but one were executed.[84] Luther considered "the rabble in Münster," as he called them, a regrettable second front on the war against superstition and excess.[85] Yet the Anabaptists were also, to the Lutheran mind, an indication of the demonic powers that the Bible warned would precede the apocalypse, a "gross example of devil's play in Münster," as Luther said. "What spirit," he asked, "would try to harm faith by going off and taking more wives or husbands? ... But to be so shameless as to claw at the crown and [take] as many women as one's desire and impertinence allow" was too much.[86] What nefarious spirit would inspire such behavior? The Wittenberger held such contempt for the Anabaptists that he could not resist indulging in sarcasm and expletives when discussing them. They would be punished without mercy for such an insult against God, he promised, although he then tempered his view to explain that the

---

terly 42 (2000): 27-38, online at www.acu.edu/sponsored/restoration_quarterly/archives. An interesting, distinctly medieval, way of distributing tracts from Münster was to attach them to arrows and shoot them over the city walls into the troops' quarters. According to Williams, they were "thrown from the walls or fired in canisters into the enemy camp." Their favorite proselyting tract was a 1533 pamphlet, *Bekentones des globens und lebens der gemein Christe zu Monster,* meaning *Confessions of the Faith and Life of the Community of Christ at Münster* (*Radical Reformation,* 560, 568).

83. Karl-Heinz Kirchhoff, "Das Phänomen des Täuferreichs zu Münster, 1534/35," in *Der Raum Westfalen,* Hrsg. Franz Petri u.a., 6 Bd. (Münster: Aschendorff, 1989), 1:393.

84. Krahn, *Dutch Anabaptism,* 138; Williams, *Radical Reformation,* 574.

85. Jaroslav Pelikan and Helmut T. Lehman, eds., *Luther's Works,* 55 vols. (St. Louis: Concordia Publishing and Fortress Press, 1955-86), 24:92; available on CD-ROM from Augsburg Fortress, 1999.

86. Martin Luther, Vorrede, *Neue Zeitung von den Widertäufern zu Münster,* 1535, in Stupperich, *Schriften von evangelischer Seite,* 51-55.

heretics would be punished by God, that human beings need not interfere with cosmic justice.

> No matter how you judge the Anabaptists, they are doing wrong, blaspheming and dishonouring God's discipline. It is, nevertheless, not correct—and I am dreadfully disappointed to see this—that one murders, burns and gruesomely kills such wretched people. One should let everyone believe what he wants to believe. If his faith is incorrect, he will be punished enough by the eternal flames in hell.[87]

If Luther was an idealist, Bishop von Waldeck was not. His forces broke through the city's walls on the evening of June 24, 1535, entering through a gate that was weakly defended, as two collaborators (including Gresbeck) had tipped them off, and massacred a good portion of the inhabitants. The leaders were all executed except, perhaps, for Rothmann, who was missing. The city of Münster has since remained predominantly Catholic to the present day, even though it is entirely surrounded by Protestant lands.[88]

When Münster fell, the Anabaptist movement splintered into several factions: nonviolent groups led by David Joris, Obbe Phillips, and Menno Simons and smaller radical groups such as the roving bands of mercenaries led by John of Batenburg. After a period of disorganization, Strassburg became the new focal point of Anabaptist conferences from 1554 to 1607. Hofmann had proclaimed Strassburg the city that would become the "New Jerusalem." It remained important, but it was also the site where Anabaptists were repeatedly tried and sentenced as late as 1590.[89] It did not matter if one belonged to one of the new moderate Anabaptist groups throughout Germany, Italy, Lithuania, the Netherlands, Poland, or even England, or if one's

---

87. Ibid.

88. Cairncross, *After Polygamy Was Made Sin,* 2-30; Pelikan and Lehman, *Luther's Works,* 5:239, 41:242; E. Belfort Bax, *The Rise and Fall of the Anabaptists* (1903; New York: A. M. Kelley, 1970), online at *Marxists Internet Library,* www.marxist.org. Bax is cited here for his excellent narrative of the city's demise, although his interest is mainly in the communal experiment in Münster.

89. Nelson and Rott, "Strasbourg"; John S. Oyer, "The Strasbourg Conferences of the Anabaptists, 1554-1607"; Jean Séguy, "The French Anabaptists: Four and One-Half Centuries of History," *Mennonite Quarterly Review* 58 (July 1984).

allegiance was to one of the surviving militant cadres, primarily in Germany—all were suspected of being revolutionaries. Reformers called all Anabaptists Münsterites, which was intended as a slur, and some Catholics pointed to the Münster incident as the predictable end result of Protestantism generally.[90] However, Menno Simons, the pacifist after whom the Mennonites were named, and Obbe Phillips, another non-violent Anabaptist, adhered to adult baptism without the chiliastic teachings of the imminent end of the world, and without polygamy.

When Münster was approaching its nadir in 1535, Menno Simons, then a Catholic priest, wrote a tract against Bockelson. The next year, this northern Dutch priest converted to the Anabaptists and was rebaptized by Obbe Philips. He then went underground to avoid persecution. In the following years, Simons re-emerged to gather the "poor straying sheep," as he called them, who had been deceived by "the ungodly doctrines of Münster."[91] In 1545, as he assumed leadership of the pacific Melchiorites and consolidated much of Anabaptism in the Netherlands and lower Germany, his first name came to be applied to almost the entire movement.[92] Like Lutherans, though more literal in applying biblical strictures, the Mennonites sought to avoid the path the Münsterites had trod by subordinating "revelation or heavenly inspiration" to the "expressed written work of the Lord." Menno was not a "seer or prophet," nor was he specifically an Elias, Enoch, or "third David."[93] Following his death in 1561, the movement, now apolitical and pacifist, spread back into Switzerland where much of the early theologizing had begun. It was from this reaction to Münster that Mennonitism as we know it today, typified by pacifism and plain living, had its roots. It was transplanted to America in 1683 when the first Mennonite and Quaker families arrived in Pennsylvania and in 1749 when the Amish bishop, Jacob Hertzler of Switzerland, immigrated to

---

90. Cornelius Krahn, Nanne van der Zijpp, and James M. Stayer, "Münster Anabaptists," *Global Anabaptist Mennonite Encyclopedia Online* (www.gameo.org).

91. Williams, *Radical Reformation,* 589-95.

92. Ibid., 723-28, 1229.

93. Littell, *Anabaptist View,* 46.

the New World, as well. Neither Mennonites nor the Amish, conservative in their marital relationships, practice polygamy.[94]

Other Protestant Experiments

Other German experiments with marriage appeared almost simultaneously with the Münster debacle. In about 1531, the Dreamers (*Träumer*), a gathering of peasants from the outskirts of Nüremberg, Germany, instituted "spiritual marriage," a term which anticipated the later use of "spiritual wifery."[95] Two representative families, the Maiers and the Kerns, were among those who practiced "reciprocal spouse exchange amongst a small circle of believers, many of whom were related." Historian Lyndal Roper noted that "two fathers held their children in common just as they held their goods in common." So too, the wives. Although the men oversaw a strictly patriarchal society, the women apparently suggested couplings with the men after they heard a voice instructing them in that direction. Else Kern, a "former maid," became "mistress of Hans Schmidt's house" even though Hans' previous wife still resided there. Typically a man was guided by dreams to approach other women; but Roper noted an instance of a woman traveling from another town and "candidly inform[ing] Marx Maier that he was to be her spouse." The Dreamers described their sexual unions as submitting to the will of God rather than as self-initiated acts.[96]

The backdrop for the Dreamers was the establishment of Anabaptism in Thuringia in 1527 under John Römer, who had stood by Thomas Müntzer during the Peasants' Revolt of 1524-25. Römer and Müntzer were influenced by John Hut, a visionary who foresaw Christ's return in 1528. Their convictions were secured through the doctrine of the "inner world," a feeling of spiritual guidance that was not open

---

94. The name "Amish" derives from Jakob Ammann (b. 1661) of Bern, Switzerland. The Quakers were an English branch of Anabaptism and were communitarian, pacifistic, non-sacramental, and spiritualist (Williams, *Radical Reformation,* 3rd ed., 649n, 1209-11).

95. Lyndal Roper, "Sexual Utopianism in the German Reformation," *Journal of Ecclesiastical History* 42 (July 1991): 398-400.

96. Ibid., 401-02.

to examination.[97] They said that their behavior was summoned the same way other Christians responded to the Holy Ghost. These radicals could not be persuaded otherwise by reason or by the likelihood of persecution and death. Hut escaped prison to Austria, and the Hutterites (followers of Jacob Hutter, a different family than Hut) continued to preach Hut's ideas, including in 1547 the right of a woman to divorce an unbelieving spouse.

From greater self-reliance for women to the right of a man to have more wives, the theology often followed a determination to behave in a given way. The Dreamers were not the only ones in Europe who based their actions on the wide-open theology of spiritual promptings, as Mormons would also later do. In the German state of Hesse, another branch of Dreamers was known as the *Blutfreunde* ("friends of blood," meaning of the blood of Christ). They sought to attain what they considered to be an ecstatic essence of Christ through "fleshy mingling," the only true sacrament, according to their theology. In tantric fashion, they viewed the body as a bridge to the divine.[98] Their leader, Louis of Tungeda, did away with baptism altogether in about 1550 in favor of sexual unions. Historian George Williams wondered if the intercourse might have been achieved during a group ritual, implying some kind of collective marriage.[99] The confession of Jorg Schuchart is ambiguous on this point. He defended their couplings as the way to salvation, as long as one's partner was "pure"—a devout believer, in other words.[100] The Dreamers were not, strictly speaking, polygamists, but their reinterpretation of Christian marriage and reliance on feelings as a guide to spirituality represent variations on important themes—both similar to later Mormon thinking, which would promote inner promptings or "having the spirit." Another similarity

97. Williams, *Radical Reformation,* 266-69.

98. Robert Rodgers, "An Introduction to Anabaptism," *Evangelical Quarterly* 54 (Jan.-Feb. 1982): 39.

99. Williams, *Radical Reformation,* 667, 781-82, citing Paul Wappler, *Die Stellung Kursachsens und des Landgrafen Philipp von Hessen zur Täuferbewegung,* 1910; Gary N. Waite, "Post-Münster Melchiorite Debate on Marriage: David Joris response to Johannes Eisenburg, 1537," *Mennonite Quarterly Review* 63 (1989) 367-99.

100. Roper, "Sexual Utopianism," 403-05; Paul Wappler, *Die Täuferbewegung in Thüringen von 1526-1584* (Jena: Verein für Reformationsgeschichte, 1913), 481.

can be found in the idea of eternal marriage in the Anabaptist theology at Eisenach in western Thuringia.[101]

Whether at the fringe or at the heart of the movement, Anabaptists could not reconcile the Catholic view of marriage with their understanding of salvation involving an individual standing alone before God. In the eyes of Protestant reformers such as Wolfgang Capito and Martin Bucer of Strassburg, the Anabaptists had succumbed to unbridled sensuality. In fact, the Dreamers and Quakers and related sects represented just a few of the "bewildering variety" of Anabaptist currents in the sixteenth century. Historian Claus-Peter Clasen has identified no fewer than twenty major groups in Austria, south and central Germany, Moravia, and Switzerland between 1525 and 1618.[102] How many of these sympathized to some degree with polygamy is difficult to determine.

Until recently, Mennonites (like Mormons) selectively preserved and emphasized what they considered to be the positive aspects of their heritage and downplayed contradictory examples. Then a generation of young Mennonites began researching and publishing their findings in the peer-reviewed *Mennonite Quarterly Review,* presenting a fuller picture. Simultaneously, the first comprehensive survey of Anabaptism in the English language, George H. Williams's *The Radical Reformation,* appeared in 1962, amplified by Karl-Heinz Kirchhoff's "new look" at Münster in 1964, translated into English by 1973. Other European attempts to re-evaluate Anabaptist history followed. It was no longer possible for Mennonites to claim a clear, unbroken theological lineage back to a small group of religiously conservative pacifists in Zurich in 1525. The history was more complex. For Europeans, where the popular understanding of Anabaptism had been largely negative, their early religious non-conformists could no longer be dismissed as simple-minded, deluded fanatics who had been misled by exploitive autocrats.[103] In the "Reformation," Münster's evolution had

101. Clasen, "Anabaptist Sects," 270.

102. Ibid., 256-57.

103. Rodgers, "Introduction to the Anabaptists," 36-45, citing H. L. Ellison, foreword to Leonard Verduin, *The Reformers and Their Stepchildren* (Grand Rapids: Eerdmans, 1964).

been ascribed to the devil; during the Enlightenment, it had been chalked up to mass hysteria. In modern times, Catholics had spoken of the "excesses of the Reformation" and Protestants had referred to the "evils of cults."[104]

In preparation for the 1983 anniversary of the fall of Münster, current historian Ernst Laubach gave a lecture in which he reviewed how historical sources have been misused over time, either for propagandistic reasons or because researchers uncritically had accepted what essentially amounts to hearsay evidence. He called for a change —for historians to give priority to what the Anabaptists said about themselves. With similar objectives, Cornelius Krahn, Nanne van der Zijpp, and James M. Stayer compiled a bibliographic essay in 1957 on "Münster in the Press" and "Münster in Fiction," updated in 1987 and adapted by the online *Global Anabaptist Mennonite Encyclopedia.* At the related "Anabaptist Mennonite Ethereal Library," readers can find some of the relevant historical documents. In that bibliographic essay, the authors single out the scholarship of Karl-Heinz Kirchhoff regarding Anabaptists in Münster, indicating that despite the introduction of communal property, the religious leaders were "well to-do" citizens of "the old order." For our purposes, the authors' finding, based on their survey of the literature, is significant in that after Münster fell in 1535, "the majority of Melchiorite Anabaptists turned away from polygamy."[105]

Traditionally the Münster story was told from the viewpoint of the sixteenth-century enemies of the Anabaptists.[106] It was not until source-critical historiography in the nineteenth and twentieth centuries that we began to see a more balanced examination of the events. In prior popular-media presentations, John Bockelson has been portrayed as lustful, brutal, and cowardly, such as in Giacomo Meyerbeer's romantic opera, *Le Prophète* (*The Prophet*), produced in Paris in 1849 and Münster in 1853. Swiss playwright Friedrich Dürrenmatt's *Es steht Geschrieben* (*It Is Written)* produced in Zurich in 1947 and re-

104. Laubach, "Täuferreich," 125, 127-29, 135, 145.
105. Krahn et al., "Münster Anabaptists."
106. Laubach, "Täuferherrschaft in Münster," 501.

written twenty years later as a social parody, *Die Wiedertäufer* (*The Anabaptists*), cast Bockelson as a failed actor whose people could not see through his make-believe.[107] In 1935 the Nazis celebrated the four-hundred-year anniversary of Münster's collapse as the fall of medieval Bolshevism. Two years later a Prussian, Friedrich Reck-Malleczewen, portrayed John Bockelson as a dictator with parallels to Hitler, for which Reck-Malleczewen was executed at Dachau in 1945.[108]

A popular 1981 French novel, *Le Roi des Derniers Jours* (*The King of the Last Days*), inspired a 1993 German television documentary film of the same name (*Der König der letzten Tage*), in which a fictional couple was placed in the middle of the action in Münster. Borrowing from Dürrenmatt, the script writers assumed that Bockelson was an international charlatan.[109] German writers have liked to show the events in Westphalia's capital in the context of the problems of "modernity" or, like Reck-Malleczewen, as a prototype for National Socialism.[110] Others have concluded that the Anabaptist leaders were poor "deluded souls," not self-conscious frauds, but nevertheless, products of an age of magic and superstition.[111]

Robert Stupperich's critical edition of Bernhard Rothmann's writings became a new starting point for writing about Münster.[112] The important narrative by one-time Anabaptist Heinrich Gresbeck was discovered in the archives of St. Paul's Church in Münster in the 1840s by Karl Adolph Cornelius, a Catholic graduate student working on his dissertation. Cornelius was the first to realize the value of considering what the Anabaptists themselves said had happened; he edited Gresbeck's report and drew heavily on the writings of Rothmann for context. While it was true that Gresbeck was a disillusioned Anabaptist, he did not carry the bias of, for instance, Hermann von

---

107. Laubach, "Täuferreich," 140.

108. Ibid., 140-45.

109. Laubach, "Täuferherrschaft in Münster," 500.

110. Mary E. Bender, "The Sixteenth-Century Anabaptists as a Theme in Twentieth-Century German Literature," Ph.D. diss. abstract, Indiana University, 1959, in *Mennonite Quarterly Review* 42 (July 1968): 226-27.

111. Laubach, "Täuferreich," 131-32, 142, 148-49.

112. Robert Stupperich, ed., *Die Schriften Bernhard Rothmanns,* vol. 1 in *Die Schriften der Münsterischen Täufer und ihrer Gegner* series (Münster: Aschendorff Verlag, 1971).

Kerssenbrock, who began researching and writing about the Anabaptist takeover in the 1550s while serving as rector of the cathedral school in Münster. His evidence came mostly from the testimony of Anabaptists as they were tortured and interrogated a day or two prior to their executions.[113]

Another scholar in the tradition of Cornelius and Kirchhoff, who has looked at the Anabaptists more sympathetically, is Ralf Klötzer. Utilizing contemporary letters and fragments of official files, as well as Rothmann's tracts, he has introspectively mined the world view of the Anabaptists.[114] A simultaneous development in Europe has been to discontinue referring to the radical reformers as *Wiedertäufer* (Anabaptists) in favor of the more neutral term *Täufer* (Baptists).

Debate in Europe and America

For three centuries following the Reformation, polygamy has been a subject of intermittent discussion in Europe, although mostly as an abstract idea.[115] The dominant culture had long considered polygamy in Africa and the Middle East to be heathen, even while revering the Old Testament as part of its own religious tradition. Christian sacred literature spanned the spectrum of sexual norms, from the Apostle Paul's celibacy to Solomon's harem of 700 wives and 300 concubines.[116] When Landgrave Philip received an exemption from the monogamy standard in 1539, it did not reverse the reality that polygamy was illegal everywhere in the Hapsburg-led Holy Roman Empire. In 1563 the Catholic Council of Trent denounced polygamy, stating: "If anyone says that it is not unlawful for Christians to have several wives at the same time, and that it is not forbidden by any

113. Laubach, "Täuferreich," 136-37.

114. Rothmann's *Bekentones des globens und lebens der gemein Christe zu Monster* (*Confessions of the Faith and Life of the Community of Christ at Münster*), completed in June 1534, rejected slanderous rumors about the community, "that in Münster marriage was being abused; that it had complete control of the totality of a woman, and didn't even accept the boundaries of familial relationships in the sexual order of things."

115. See Cairncross, *After Polygamy Was Made Sin,* 36-51.

116. Ursula Vogel, "Political Philosophers and the Trouble with Polygamy: Patriarchal Reasoning in Modern Natural Law," *History of Political Thought* 12 (Summer 1991): 229-51.

divine law ... let him be anathema." Such language was the equivalent to a death warrant.[117] Even as the church and empire outlawed polygamy, philosophers and theologians continued to discuss it. Following in the wake of St. Augustine (354-430), German natural-law jurist Samuel von Pufendorf (1632-94) and French historical philosopher Baron Montesquieu (1689-1755) found that polygamy provided a provocative context for discussing truth, knowledge, and reason. Such discussions demonstrated the efficacy of social philosophy compared to medieval theology.

Polygamy's subplot: female subordination

By the eighteenth century, Denis Diderot in France and von Pufendorf in Germany both concluded that the procreative impulse and the need to legitimize offspring were the chief reasons why some societies had developed polygamy. Human customs had developed from the authority of instinct.[118] Going a step further, Dutch legal scholar Hugo Grotius (1583-1645) concluded that natural law justified polygamy.[119] British philosopher David Hume wrote in his 1741 *Essays Moral, Political, and Literary* that marriage was "an engagement entered into by mutual consent" and that "it is mere superstition to imagine that marriage can be entirely uniform and will admit only of one mode or form."[120] He gave the example of sailors on board the *Tonquin,* an American-made merchant ship, who had contracted monogamous marriages with temporary spouses while in port. He also cited Athenian men who were allowed to marry two wives "in order to repair the waste" of war and pestilence. There were also ancient Britons who had had families in common.[121] In comparing the advantages

117. Hillman, *Polygamy Reconsidered,* 218.

118. Vogel, "Political Philosophers," 229-51. Vogel here cites Denis Diderot's *Encyclopédie ou Dictionnaire Raisonné des Sciences,* 1751-80; Samuel von Pufendorf, *Acht Bücher von Natur und Völkerrecht,* 1711; and Stephan Buchholz, "Erunt Tres aut Quattuor in Carne Una: Aspekte der neuzeitlichen Polygamiediskussion" in *Zur Geschichte des Familien und Erbrechts,* 1987.

119. Hugo Grotius, *De Jure Belli ac Pacis, 1625,* 1.2.6; 2.5.5, 9; trans. A. C. Campbell, *On the Law of War and Peace,* London, 1814.

120. David Hume, *Essays: Moral, Political, and Literary* (1741; London: Grant Richards, 1903), 185-95.

121. Ibid., 187.

and disadvantages of monogamy, divorce, and polygamy, Hume summarized the secular patriarchal view:

> The advocates of polygamy may recommend it as the only effectual remedy for the disorders of love, and the only expedient for freeing men from that slavery to the females which the natural violence of our passions has imposed upon us. By this means alone can we regain our right of sovereignty; and, sating our appetite, reestablish the authority of reason in our minds, and, of consequence, our own authority in our families.[122]

Hume's criticism of polygamy was that it implied male domination of women, a barbarism which deprived couples of genuine love. He was an advocate of divorce as a natural, necessary escape mechanism: "If the public interest will not allow us to enjoy in polygamy that variety which is so agreeable in love: at least, deprive us not of that liberty which is so essentially requisite."[123]

During the English Revolution of the 1630s-40s, when common people attempted to propose their own solutions to the problems of their time, there was a general questioning of the foundations of society. This was the era of Diggers, Ranters, Revelers, and other groups composed mostly of lower-class British people who wanted to overturn the tyranny of the nobility. They considered the clergy to be the enablers of the rich. During this same general period, views of propertied marriage gradually shifted to the Puritan ideal of marriage by choice, accompanied by fidelity, especially for women. Issues of morality, economics, social control, and the status of women were all open to question, as were divorce, polygamy, and free love.[124]

Some writers considered what they called a "surplus of carnal desire" over what was necessary for propagation and concluded that it would be a violation of natural law to act on it. This was especially true when this was detected in women. Referring to the Anabaptist punishment for female promiscuity, German scholar Ursula Vogel has called

122. Ibid., 187-88.

123. Ibid., 192.

124. Christopher Hill, *World Turned Upside Down: Radical Ideas during the English Revolution* (New York: Viking, 1972), 247.

this female subordination "the subplot in the story of polygamy."[125] The customary view of adultery, based on canon law, was that the unfaithful wife had violated her marriage. The husband did not necessarily "violate" his marriage, only if he had been involved with another married woman. In that case, it was the betrayed husband, not the betrayed wife, who was thought to be the injured party. It is easy to see that on this basis, another woman in a marriage would not require much of a stretch of the imagination.[126] Another wrinkle in the philosophical reasoning involved the irony that women sometimes supported the institution that treated them as second-class citizens. When Christian Thomasius (1655-1728) took all the various details into consideration, he concluded that polyandry was as justifiable as polygyny. If a woman married several men, he reasoned, it would not frustrate the biological impulses toward procreation and social tranquility.[127]

Well before natural-law philosophers took the discussion of marriage outside the bounds of religious imperatives, Bernard Ochino (1487-1564), an anti-Trinitarian Italian friar in exile in England, wrote *Thirty Dialogues* and published it in Basel, Switzerland. It was soon banned in Zurich. In one of the most objectionable dialogues, the antagonist gave a rationale for divorce; in another, someone defended multiple wives. The latter argument was reprinted in England in 1657 as *A Dialogue of Polygamy.*[128]

Ochino was succeeded ideologically a century later by Johann Leyser of Leipzig (1631-84), who argued that polygamy was not only permitted by God, it was a commandment.[129] He preached this

125. Vogel, "Political Philosophers," 237.

126. Mikat, *Polygamiefrage,* 32. A passage of the Doctrine and Covenants (49:16) supports monogamy, in contradiction to Section 132, by borrowing the biblical imagery of "one flesh." The natural law philosophers would have found this an unconvincing argument.

127. Vogel, "Political Philosophers," 247n, citing Christian Thomasius, *De Crimine Bigamiae,* Halle, 1685.

128. Miller, *Milton among Polygamophiles,* 24-27; E. Geoffrey Parrinder, *The Bible and Polygamy: A Study of Hebrew and Christian Teachings* (London: Society for Promoting Christian Knowledge, 1950), 13-28, 60-65.

129. Stephan Buchholz, *Political Implications and Perspectives* (Frankfurt: Mohnhaupt and Klostermann, 1987), 77; Williams, *Radical Reformation,* 3rd ed., 965. Johannes

throughout Europe and in 1673 published a pamphlet that spoke of the "sins that spring from monogamy," especially how "it drives women to arrogance and domination over men." Not only would abortion, adultery, and whoremongering be abolished with polygamy, "nowhere does the Bible say that one man should be limited to one woman." If a man "cannot be satisfied with one wife, let him take another," Ochino wrote. "If he has an old, sterile Sarah, let him take a young Hagar. If he has got into a tangle with Leah and Rachel, let him marry both in order to keep his word with one and save the other's honour. If he sees a beauty among the Philistines or on his travels, let him carry her home."[130]

Leyser wrote at a time when the male population of Germany had been devastated by the Thirty Years' War (1618-48). In Nüremberg in 1650, a regional council of Catholic Franconia (now Bavaria), with approval of the archbishops of Bamberg and Wurzberg, authorized men to take two wives over the next ten years to remedy the problem. Over the next few years, while Leyser was speaking and writing, the Dutch philosopher Spinoza and German jurist von Pufendorf each took up this advocacy of polygamy.[131] Cairncross thinks that Spinoza, with numerous friends in the Dutch Anabaptist community, may have "looked with favour on the practices of his Jewish forebears."[132] Lorenz Beger, a German in Amsterdam, supported Leyser in 1670, reiterating that the want of men in the population made polygamy reasonable.[133] Even Napoleon Bonaparte in 1816 expressed his support of polygamy to increase the population.[134]

Social Reformers in America

Utopianism has often implied communal living and some kind of al-

---

Leyser, *Polygamia Triumphatrix,* Frankfurt, 1676; Cairncross, *After Polygamy Was Made Sin,* 74-93; Buchholz, *Recht, Religion und Ehe* (Frankfurt: Klostermann, 1988), 389n.

130. Leyser, *Discursus de Polygamia,* 1673; *Das königliche Mark aller Länder,* 1676; quoted in Cairncross, *After Polygamy Was Made Sin,* 77, 78.

131. Cairncross, *After Polygamy Was Made Sin,* 74-93.

132. Ibid., 85.

133. Ibid., 86.

134. Ibid., 122, citing Emmanuel de Las Cases, *Le Mémorial de Sainte Hélène,* Paris, 1951.

ternative marriage arrangement. Reformers have generally appealed to both religious precedent and natural law to defend their innovations. For instance, Martin Madan was a Methodist-leaning minister in London in the late eighteenth century, best known as co-author of the Christmas carol, "Hark! The Herald Angels Sing." In 1780 he argued in a three-volume work, *Thelyphthora,* that "God himself" "allowed" polygamy and that if it were instituted, it would restore men to their rightful patriarchal role.[135] He reasoned that since the Bible forbids divorce and remarriage,[136] polygamy was the best solution for the social ills surrounding promiscuity: "If a man (having a wife) entices a virgin, and lies with her, this last shall surely be his wife, as much as the first."[137] Madan's writing provoked emotional denunciations;[138] but as late as 1869, American writer E. N. Jencks came upon Madan's work in a Boston public library and included its arguments in his study of the *History and Philosophy of Marriage.* Demonstrating how far removed from the focus of nineteenth-century letters the Mormons appeared to be, Jencks was apparently unaware that such a relatively large Christian denomination was practicing polygamy on American soil.[139]

Münster Anabaptists and Mormons

We have considered two millennialist societies 300 years apart, each claiming to be the saints of the latter days. In 1632 the Mennonites endorsed a Confession of Faith that outlined their views of God and man; the "restoration"; "washing of the saints' feet"; the believer's baptism; "matrimony of two free, believing persons," both of them required to be Mennonites; pacifism; swearing oaths (forbidden); separation of church and state; "shunning" those who had been excommunicated; and other points of doctrine. By 1683 Anabaptists of various

---

135. B. Carmon Hardy, *Solemn Covenant: The Mormon Polygamous Passage* (Urbana: University of Illinois Press, 1992), 2, quoting *Thelyphthora; or, A Treatise on Female Ruin, in Its Causes, Affects, Consequences, Prevention, and Remedy; Considered on the Basis of the Divine Law; under the Following Heads, viz Marriage, Whoredom, and Fornication, Adultery, Polygamy, Divorce, with Many Other Incidental Matters,* London, 1781.

136. Deut. 24:1; Mark 10:10-12; Madan, *Thelyphthora.*

137. Madan, *Thelyphthora.*

138. Miller, *Milton among Polygamophiles,* 146-49, 331-33.

139. E. N. Jencks, *The History and Philosophy of Marriage* (Boston: James Campbell, 1869), microfilm, New York Public Library, ZAN T 3340: R336, no. 2900, 78 ff, 224.

denominations began arriving in the American colonies. William Penn invited the Mennonites and Quakers to settle in Germantown north of Philadelphia. They were joined briefly in 1708 by the Swiss Brethren, who then moved farther west to found their own settlements. By about 1800, the Amish arrived. They had split from the Swiss Brethren in 1693 in favor of Jakob Ammann's stricter church discipline. They are best known today for their resistance to modernity, as typified by horsedrawn buggies and "plain" clothing. Another Anabaptist denomination, the Hutterites, immigrated to the United States in 1874.

Of all the separatist groups, the German Baptist Brethren, also known as Pietists, provided the largest number of Anabaptist immigrants to Pennsylvania in the eighteenth century. Influenced by Mennonite writings, they had organized themselves and began baptizing each other in Germany in 1708. Of interest to Mormon history, one of their leaders, Alexander Mack, had the same surname as Joseph Smith's mother, Lucy Mack Smith.[140] Even before the American republic was formed, Anabaptists exerted moral influence by providing humanitarian aid even to the British "enemy" during the Revolutionary War.[141]

Recently UCLA professor Val D. Rust studied the "radical origins" of early Mormon converts and discovered, first of all, that many of them had Anabaptist ancestors in colonial Connecticut, Massachusetts, Maine, New Hampshire, and Rhode Island. The Anabaptist congregation founded by Roger Williams in Providence, Rhode Island, as one example, included the forebears of Reynolds Cahoon, Isaac Morley, and the brothers Orson and Parley Pratt. Descendants of Connecticut's Anabaptist settlers included Louisa Beaman Smith, Vinson Knight, and Vilate Murray Kimball.[142]

---

140. See entries for "Alexander Mack," "Amish," "Anabaptist," "Brethren," and "Mennonite" in the *Encyclopedia Britannica,* online at www.britannica.com; William R. Estep, *The Anabaptist Story* (Grand Rapids: Eerdmans, 1974), excerpts online at www.anabaptists.org; "Mennonites," *BELIEVE Religion Information Source,* http://mb-soft.com.

141. "Amish, Mennonites, and Brethren Timeline," online at *Christian History & Biography,* www.christianitytoday.com.

142. Val D. Rust, *Radical Origins: Early Mormon Converts and Their Colonial Ancestors* (Urbana: University of Illinois Press, 2004), 95-107, 228n7, 230n46.

The distinctive nature of the German-speaking Separatists in Pennsylvania was familiar to Emma Hale's family, who lived just south of the Susquehanna River, and probably also to the Smith men as they worked there in the 1820s. Long after John Bockelson's abbreviated charismatic reign over Münster in 1534-35, it is possible that Joseph Smith may have heard of this "latter-day" millennialist by oral tradition. The Quakers, a sister denomination of the Anabaptists, were hunted and persecuted for promoting their esoteric, mystical leaning which the Puritans found so threatening. The Mennonites disagreed with the Quakers; but more importantly, they did not want to elicit the same kind of attention, giving them all the more reason to keep certain aspects of their controversial past as private as possible. While seventeenth-century millennialism in New England was exciting a countryside labeled the "Burned-Over District" in central New York, which in itself contained an echo of the same apocalyptic zeal that was manifested in Münster in 1534-35, Mennonites chose to be observers rather than participants this time around. However, try as they might, they were unable to avoid harassment, even for being aloof. Mormon writer Milton Backman has commented that the 1818 book, *Anabaptism Disapproved,* "summarized the controversy concerning baptism which divided Protestants" in Joseph Smith's day.[143] Backman believed Smith must have been familiar with at least some of the issues that had burned in the hearts of sixteenth-century millennialists.

Two concrete examples of a general awareness of Münster Anabaptism are, first, a line from John C. Bennett's book comparing Mormons to Reformation-era Anabaptists. Bennett said the German millennialists "gave themselves out for '*Latter Day Saints,*'" a "chosen" people commanded to "assemble at the New Zion," the "city of Münster."[144] Secondly, there was a letter in the *Times and Seasons* in 1843 by a "brother in the new covenant," John Greenhous. He re-

143. Milton V. Backman Jr., *Joseph Smith's First Vision* (Salt Lake City: Bookcraft, 1971), 94; see also Timothy Merritt, *Anabaptism Disapproved, and the Validity and Sufficiency of Infant Baptism Asserted: In Two Letters from a Minister to His Friend* (New York: Methodist Episcopal Church, 1818).

144. John Bennett, *History of the Saints* (1842; Urbana: University of Illinois Press, 2000), 304-5.

ferred to the "horrible successes" of the "Ana-baptists" under the lead of "Mathias, a baker, and Boccold [Bockelson], a tailor." Greenhous knew they had had "all things [in] common," including "a plurality of wives." Reportedly, "Boccold" had proclaimed that "the kingdom of Zion was at hand. He had fourteen wives at one time" and was put to death in "Munster," Greenhous explained.[145]

John Milton's polygamy treatise

When Joseph Smith met Emma Hale in Pennsylvania in 1825, an important treatise on polygamy was being published. The English poet John Milton had written a defense of bigamy in the mid-1600s, apparently inspired by personal considerations. His wife, Mary, had left him in 1642, and he had tried to convince his close friend, a "Miss Davis," and civil authorities that bigamy was a righteous state of marriage. Divorce was not yet conceivable. The poet cited Paul's comments in the Bible about not being "under bondage" to a prior spouse who had "depart[ed]" (1 Cor. 7:15). "A person deserted, which is something lesse than divorc't, may lawfully marry again," Milton reasoned. Paul had said so! Miss Davis was not so sure. When Milton's wife returned, he presumably lost interest in the topic.[146]

However, Milton's argument that if polygamy were wrong, it would make Abraham and the patriarchs fornicators and their offspring bastards remained valid (Deut. 23:2). Deemed too sensitive to publish when he wrote it, his *De Doctrina Christiana* (*Treatise on Christian Doctrine*) was forgotten until an employee of the government archive at Whitehall happened upon it in 1823 and then published it two years later.[147] In 1826, social critic William Ellery Channing praised it

145. John Greenhous to the editor, *Times and Seasons,* Apr. 15, 1843, 165-66.

146. Geoffrey Cumberlege, ed., *Complete Prose Works of John Milton,* vol. 6, gen. ed. Don M. Wolfe (New Haven: Yale University Press, 1980), 762-63, originally published ca. 1658; Miller, *Milton among Polygamophiles,* 8. See also Lowell W. Coolidge, ed., *Complete Prose Works of John Milton,* vol. 2, gen. ed. Don M. Wolfe (New Haven: Yale University Press, 1980), 137-48, 217-356, including introductory chapter by Ernest Sirluck, "The Divorce Tracts and Aeropagitica," and Milton's "Doctrines of Discipline of Divorce," originally published ca. 1643.

147. Following its discovery in 1823 by Robert Lemon Sr., Deputy Director of His Majesty's State Papers, Milton's *De Doctrina Christiana* was translated and published by Charles Sumner as *A Treatise on Christian Doctrine* (Cambridge, Eng.: Cambridge Uni-

in a periodical printed in London and Boston, the *Christian Examiner and Theological Review*, as did Thomas Macaulay in the *Edinburgh Review*. It had come from the same renowned seventeenth-century author whose *Paradise Lost* had heavily influenced the Garden of Eden account preached in Europe and America, so on that basis it drew wide interest. Milton's belated publication advocating polygamy was reviewed in more than fifty British and American periodicals.[148] One year later, Joseph Smith began dictating the Book of Mormon manuscript, which would introduce plural marriage to the nineteenth-century Latter-day Saints.

American polygamy before Joseph Smith

The records of early New England communities indicate that polygamy was sometimes a topic of discussion. One free-spirited author, John Miner, argued the doctrine in 1780 at the Norfolk, Connecticut, village church, claiming there were others in the church who concurred with his opinion. He was excommunicated.[149] Early Mormons were aware of utopian communities and millenarian expectations. The breakaway Baptist church of Alexander Campbell (1788-1866) expected an imminent millennium. It was Campbell's denomination that provided large numbers of early converts to Mormonism in Ohio in 1830-31. Campbellite leader Sidney Rigdon became vitally important to Smith's church. Christian utopian societies included the Perfectionists in Oneida, New York (1848-81); the Harmonists in New Harmony, Pennsylvania, from 1790; French utopians after Charles Fourier (1772-1837) in Utopia, Ohio, and elsewhere; Ann Lee's Shaking Quakers ("Shakers"); and the Pietists who emerged from Lutheranism in the late seventeenth century and inspired the Methodist and Brethren movements, as well as the Inspirationists in the Amana Colonies.[150]

---

versity Press, 1825; Boston: Cummings, Hilliard and Co., 1825); see Cumberlege, *Complete Prose Works*, 6:126-850.

148. See Don M. Wolfe, ed., *Complete Prose Works of John Milton*, vol. 1 (New Haven: Yale University Press, 1980), 3-10; James G. Nelson, *The Sublime Puritan: Milton and the Victorians* (Madison: University of Wisconsin Press, 1963), 176n.

149. Miller, *Milton among Polygamophiles*, 150, citing *Dr. Miner's Defense, Being a Concise Relation of the Church's Charge against Him, for Professing the Doctrine of Polygamy, or the Lawfulness of Having a Plurality of Wives* (Hartford: Hudson and Goodwin, 1781).

150. See Lawrence Foster, *Religion and Sexuality: Three American Communal Experi-*

Among these idealists, Jacob Cochran promoted what he called "spiritual matrimony" in communities he established in Maine and New Hampshire beginning about 1817. Sexual relations were "sanctioned by a ceremony" Cochran introduced, by which "any man or woman, already married or unmarried, might enter into [a union,] choosing at pleasure a spiritual wife or spiritual husband." A former Campbellite pastor in Ohio, Orson Hyde, visited one of Cochran's communities in Maine as an LDS missionary in 1832. In his journal, he commented on their "wonderful lustful spirit, [manifest] because they believe in a 'plurality of wives' which they call spiritual wives, knowing them not after the flesh but after the spirit, but by the appearance they know one another after the flesh."[151] Hyde, who would later have nine wives of his own, might have been sensitized by Joseph Smith's 1831 suggestion of plural marriage to Native Americans and therefore judged the Cochranites less harshly than otherwise.[152] Elsewhere in the new country, John Humphrey Noyes and his New York Perfectionists practiced another form of group marriage for a half century from the 1830s on. Settling in Oneida, New York, in 1848 and convinced that the millennium had begun, more than 500 followers shared land, clothes, sex partners, and child rearing.

The Americans no doubt borrowed the term "spiritual matrimony" from their European predecessors. In New England, Perfectionist Simon Lovett referred to his "spiritual wife" in 1835 when he was involved with a married woman, indicating that the term had become a euphemism for an extramarital union.[153] Long before Lovett, an eccentric Swedish theologian from the eighteenth century, Eman-

ments (New York: Oxford University Press, 1981), 21-177; Cairncross, *After Polygamy Was Made Sin,* 173, 178. Separatists from the Lutheran state churches of the early 1700s, and with origins in the German Pietist communities, the Amana came first to the Seneca Indian Reservation near Buffalo, New York, then to Amana, Iowa, in 1855. It was there that the Amana brand of industrial freezers emerged in the 1930s ("Amana Church History," online at *Amana Church Society,* www.amanachurch.org).

151. Richard S. Van Wagoner, *Mormon Polygamy: A History* (Salt Lake City: Signature Books, 1986), 8, quoting Orson Hyde's Journal, Oct. 11, 1832.

152. Anonymous, "The Cochran Fanatacism in York County [Maine]," Aug. 3, 1867, in *Maine Historical Quarterly* 20 (Summer 1980): 30; see also Orson Hyde's description of the Cochranites in Van Wagoner, *Mormon Polygamy,* 8.

153. Cairncross, *After Polygamy Was Made Sin,* 173.

uel Swedenborg, wrote of soul mates in heaven, a romantic idea that lay behind the concept of spiritual wives. As Swedenborg imagined it, "in heaven as on earth[,] there are males and females" united "eternally" by love, and "these celestial spouses … have the utmost pleasures of conjugal love[,] and [which are] much more delicious than mortals have because the senses of the spiritual body are incomparably more perfect."[154] Cairncross speculated that Joseph Smith may have "transformed these ideas" into his own "conception of celestial marriage, designated for those in the highest of three afterlife kingdoms."[155] Outsiders spoke dismissively of the Mormons' "spiritual wives," but the Mormons themselves sometimes used the term. Plural wife Emily Partridge mentioned that it was how "they called it in those days" and said that, in addition to "spiritual wives," there were "spiritual babies" in Nauvoo, although rare.[156] In a 1903 reminiscence, Orange Wight called plural wives in Nauvoo "spirituals."[157] In an 1845 sermon, Brigham Young referred to "Joseph Smith's spiritual wife system."[158] So Mormons were aware of the term and used it occasionally despite its generally pejorative connotation.

Sensitive to public opinion, Emma Smith denied that her husband had ever even claimed to have had a revelation on polygamy. In the 1879 interview conducted by her son, she stated that "no such thing as polygamy, or spiritual wifery, was taught, publicly or privately, before my husband's death, that I have now, or ever had any knowledge of." She did acknowledge that "at one time my husband came to me and asked me if I had heard certain rumors about spiritual marriage, or

---

154. Ibid. Swedenborg was celibate. Perhaps he had not found his soul mate, an idea he promoted by writing that "two souls which grew up together before life are bound to find each other again on earth" (174).

155. Ibid. Joseph divided three afterlife kingdoms into "telestial," reminiscent of the eighteenth-century term, "teleology," for the study of design in nature; "terrestrial," meaning earth-like; and "celestial," the highest, meaning heaven-like (D&C 76:64-119).

156. Emily Partridge Young, "Diary and Reminiscences, 1874-1899," entry for July 24, 1883, L. Tom Perry Special Collections, Harold B. Lee Library, Brigham Young University, Provo, Utah; also Smith, *Intimate Chronicle,* 122.

157. Orange Lysander Wight, Untitled Reminiscence, 1903, LDS Archives.

158. "Speech Delivered by President B. Young, in the City of Joseph," Apr. 6, 1845, *Times and Seasons,* July 1, 1845, 955.

anything of the kind; and assured me that if I had, that they were without foundation; that there was no such doctrine, and never should be with his knowledge, or consent. I know that he had no other wife or wives than myself, in any sense, either spiritual or otherwise." Her biographers gave her the benefit of the doubt and allowed for the possibility that she might have been cleverly "sidestepping her son's questions." By interpreting a spiritual wife to mean one not married and a plural wife to be one that was legally married, she was able to deny that any wives had been sealed to her husband by a higher ordinance than civil marriage.[159]

Fifteen miles from the Mormon temple in Ohio, a Cleveland newspaper printed a letter in 1837 signed "Enquirer" that argued for polygamy as a remedy for the "distress" of "so many old maids." If a man first obtained "the consent of his wife, or wives," the writer asked, "what evil would arise" from allowing him "as many more wives as he may judge proper?" It would be "more desirable to be the second or even third wife of a generous man, than to remain an old maid, neglected and laughed at … and it would eminently lessen prostitution in one sex and ranging [about] in the other." Furthermore, it would "not be more expensive for a man to have two wives, than to have one wife, and hire a seamstress," the reference to a fashion assistant being, of course, a humorous acknowledgment of a mistress.[160]

In the same year as the letter from "Enquirer," the LDS Quorum of Seventy threatened to deny fellowship to anyone "guilty of polygamy." Solomon Freeman was tried for assuming he could "liv[e] with another woman" on the frontier when he had a wife in Massachusetts.[161] The

---

159. Linda King Newel and Valeen Tippetts Avery, *Mormon Enigma: Emma Hale Smith* (Garden City, N.Y.: Doubleday, 1984), 301-02, quoting "The Memoirs of President Joseph Smith [III], 1832-1914," *Saints' Herald,* Apr. 2, 1935, 432; Joseph Smith III, "The Last Testimony of Sister Emma," *Saints' Herald,* Oct. 1, 1879, 289-90; also in the *Saints' Advocate,* Oct. 1879, 49-52.

160. "Enquirer" to the editor, *Cleveland Liberalist,* Feb. 4, 1837, 164. In a similar tone, Benjamin Franklin advised a young man to find an older mistress who would be attentive to his needs and prevent him from "ruining his Health and Fortune among mercenary Prostitutes" (Larzer Ziff, ed., *The Portable Benjamin Franklin* [New York: Penguin Books, 2005], 475-76).

161. "Resolution," *LDS Messenger and Advocate,* May 1837, 511; Elders Quorum Re-

incident blurred the line between polygamy and adultery. In most cases during this period, the latter resulted in a reprimand and nothing more if the transgressor repented. The Seventies seem to have become concerned about how it would look to outsiders if a brother felt justified in maintaining two households.

Mormon Polygamy's Legacy

After Mormons publicly announced themselves as committed polygamists in 1852, Europeans continued to debate the related philosophical issues. The German philosopher Arthur Schopenhauer (1788-1860), who considered *woman* to be "nature's knockout blow," endorsed the Mormons, since nature's aim was to increase the species.[162]

No doubt LDS men were attracted to females as much as Schopenhauer; but what they talked about incessantly was the need to prepare for the millennium with proper sacraments, including marriage. Joseph Smith had offered a time frame for Jesus' return, deciding that "fifty-six years should wind up the scene and the Saviour should come to his people." He made this assessment in February 1835.[163] But what "wound up" was the polygamy scene, not the millennium predicted a half century earlier, as Mormons officially ceased practicing, according to the 1890 "manifesto." During that half-century of polygamy, the Latter-day Saints installed a remarkable new social system while awaiting the world's end. Prior to legislation that was hostile to plural marriage, criminal prosecution, and a revelation to stop marrying multiple wives, the number of practitioners had expanded exponentially. Demographic historian Lowell Bennion noted that by the end of Brigham Young's life and before the federal raids on polygamists, about 33 percent of the Mormons in the St. George

---

cord, Nov. 23, 1837, Archives, Community of Christ, Independence, Missouri; also in Fawn M. Brodie, *No Man Knows My History: The Life of Joseph Smith,* 2nd ed. (New York: Alfred A. Knopf, 1971), 185.

162. Cairncross, *After Polygamy Was Made Sin,* 91-92, citing Arthur Schopenhauer, *Parerega und Paralipomena,* Wiesbaden, 1947; Cairncross also refers to Bertrand Russell's 1945 *History of Western Philosophy.*

163. A. Karl Larson and Katharine Miles Larson, eds., *Diary of Charles Lowell Walker* (Logan: Utah State University Press, 1980), 2:522.

Stake and 67 percent in Orderville, Utah, lived in polygamous households.[164] Similarly, Stanley S. Ivins found that a sample of 1,651 families in Utah produced an average of fifteen children per family. A sampling of 1,784 known polygamous men showed that 66 percent had only one extra wife, 21 percent had three wives, nearly 7 percent had four, and 6 percent five or more wives. Applying these ratios to an 1890 census that detected 2,451 plural families, we can estimate that about 45,000 people were involved in polygamy at its zenith.[165] Continuing research into this subject should produce more definitive statistics.

This new form of marriage unalterably divided the Latter-day Saints. One of the first signs of rapprochement occurred in 1983 when RLDS Church Historian Richard P. Howard presented a research paper reassessing the Missouri church's rejection of the evidence for polygamy. Prior to this time, the RLDS people had not accepted the evidence that Smith could have been the originator and chief proponent of plural marriage.[166] RLDS leaders had focused on the last weeks before his death when Smith had reportedly confessed to several people that his revelation on marriage had been a mistake. "We are a ruined people," he had surmised. "This doctrine of polygamy, or spiritual wife system, that has been taught and practiced among us, will prove our destruction and overthrow. I have been deceived ... it is wrong; it is a curse to mankind, and we shall have to leave the United States soon, unless it can be put down."[167]

After the first wave of Mormon pioneers reached the Great Basin, it did not take long for outsiders to notice their atypical domestic ar-

---

164. Lowell Bennion, "The Incidence of Mormon Polygamy in 1880: 'Dixie' versus Davis Stake," *Journal of Mormon History* 11 (1984): 27-42.

165. See Stanley Snow Ivins, "Notes on Mormon Polygamy," *Utah Historical Quarterly* 35 (Fall 1967): 311, 313-14, 318. The total estimated polygamists is the sum of 2,451 husbands, 6,200 wives ([2,451 x .66 x 2] + [2,451 x .21 x 3] + [2,451 x .07 x 4] + [2,451 x .06 x 5]), and 36,765 children (2,451 x 15).

166. Richard P. Howard, "The Changing RLDS Response to Mormon Polygamy: A Preliminary Analysis," *John Whitmer Historical Journal* 3 (1983): 14-29.

167. Recalled by William Marks in a July 1853 letter to *Zion's Harbinger and Beneemy's Organ,* a publication of Charles Thompson, leader of a schismatic LDS group in St. Louis, Missouri.

rangements. In 1850, John W. Gunnison, a U.S. Army officer in charge of a government survey expedition to Utah, found that the "large number of wives" per husband was "perfectly manifest to anyone residing among them and indeed the subject begins to be more openly discussed informally."[168] It was the following year, on February 4, that Brigham Young told the Deseret legislature he was not ashamed to say he had more than one wife.[169]

Then on August 29, 1852, Apostle Orson Pratt, addressing the semi-annual church conference "upon the principle … [of] a plurality of wives," warned his listeners that this would be "new ground to the inhabitants of the United States" but " well known … to the congregation before me," the church having a decade earlier "embraced the doctrine of a plurality of wives, as a part of their religious faith." Ten years earlier, in 1842, Pratt had feuded over Smith's proposal to Sarah, Orson's wife, and now he was the one in the national spotlight defending and justifying the practice. The purpose of polygamy was not to "gratify the carnal lusts" of man, he said, but was related to the doctrine of the pre-existence of souls—a teaching he admitted differed widely "from the views of the Christian world." At that time, Mormons spoke of Christians as a world from which they stood apart and remained distinct.

He spoke of previously created spirits which were waiting to inhabit earthly "tabernacles," a process facilitated by polygamy. Pratt referred to the "Book of Abraham, translated from the Egyptian papyrus by the Prophet Joseph Smith," which spoke of "the intelligences that were organized before the world was." The admonition in Genesis "to multiply and replenish the earth" implied "germs of intelligence" that were "destined, in their times and seasons, to become not only sons of God, but Gods themselves." He pictured "an endless increase, even of one family," which would "require an endless increase of worlds." Since there was "no end to the increase of [Abraham's]

168. Eugene E. Campbell, *Establishing Zion: The Mormon Church in the American West, 1847-1869* (Salt Lake City: Signature Books, 1988), 164.

169. Scott G. Kenney, ed., *Wilford Woodruff's Journal, 1833-1898,* 9 vols. (Midvale, Utah: Signature Books, 1983), 4:12.

posterity," on course to become "as numerous as the sand upon the sea-shore," there must be "an infinity of worlds for their residence," he argued. It would have been "rather a slow process," he thought, "if Abraham had been confined to one wife, like some of those narrow, contracted nations of modern Christianity." He concluded that "some of the nations of Europe and America" had not honored God's promise to Abraham and had limited their ability to contribute to the patriarch's innumerable offspring. God wanted large families with many children, best produced by polygamy, Pratt orated. He speculated that "only about one-fifth of the population of the globe … believe in the one-wife system; the other four-fifths believe in the doctrine of a plurality of wives."

In addition to the argument of religious tradition and the necessity to produce bodies for spirit children waiting to come to earth, Pratt gave social reasons for polygamy. It addressed the problem of promiscuity, he said, characterizing it as something that had been "licensed" by "Gentile Christendom." Among other conclusive aspects of this comment, Pratt indicated how insular the LDS people had become. As part of the "we" versus "them" tone of the address, Pratt's usage of the term "gentile" was uniquely LDS and meant "non-Mormon," terminology that elsewhere would have been unintelligible. "There is another reason why this plurality should exist among the Latter-day Saints," he said, and that was because of the temptations of the flesh which had "doomed" other people "to destruction." He said the question of plural marriage was about more than how many children to conceive, but also concerned where and when they would be born—the choice spirits being "appointed to come and take their bodies here," in the Utah Territory among the Saints, that the children might be "raised up among the righteous"—one more indication that Pratt was preaching to a congregation of believers. He went on, saying:

> The Lord had not kept [the spirits] in store for five or six thousand years past, and kept them waiting for their bodies all this time to send them among the Hottentots, the African negroes, the idolatrous Hindoos, or any other of the fallen nations that dwell upon the face of this earth. They are not kept in reserve in order to come forth to receive such a de-

> graded parentage upon the earth; ... [T]hose who were chosen before they were born ... long to come [to earth], and they will come among the Saints of the living God.

Was it "reasonable, and consistent that the Lord should say unto His faithful and chosen servants, ... take unto yourselves more wives, like unto the Patriarchs, Abraham, Isaac, and Jacob of old," and deny it to people of a later generation? No, Pratt concluded. It was perfectly consistent that God had introduced a "new revelation" about the matter to the "Prophet, Seer, and Revelator, Joseph Smith, on the 12th day of July, 1843; only about eleven months before he was martyred for the testimony of Jesus."[170]

Following this address, Brigham Young stood to confirm to the assembled church that Joseph Smith's revelation "contain[ed] a doctrine [that] a portion of the world is opposed to" but was nevertheless from God. "I can deliver a prophecy upon it," Young said. "It will sail over, and ride triumphantly above the prejudice and priest-craft of the day. It will be fostered and believed in by the more intelligent portions of the world, as one of the best doctrines ever proclaimed to any people." In this address and repeatedly thereafter, Young would justify polygamy on the basis of Old Testament precedent and modern revelation. However, he and other Mormon defenders would occasionally, mostly in informal settings such as in letters or private discussions, append intermediate justifications for plural marriage such as social utility or economic practicality, following Pratt's lead in those areas.[171]

Having announced the practice to the world, the Utah church simultaneously launched an active outreach to Americans and Europeans to explain it to them. Pratt wrote articles on the subject for his new magazine, *The Seer,* created for the purpose of promoting polygamy and published in Washington, D.C. In the January 1853 issue, Pratt reiterated that polygamy was "four times more popular among the inhabitants of the earth, than the one wife system." He noted that the U.S. Constitution and federal laws "do not interfere with marriage relations, but leave the nation free to believe in and practice the doc-

170. *Journal of Discourses,* 1:53-66.
171. Ibid., 1:66-71.

trine of a 'plurality of wives,'" allowing "the several States and Territories to enact such laws as they see proper in regard to the Marriages." He acknowledged that the "European nations who have been for centuries restricted by law to the one-wife theory" would consider "the plurality system" a "shocking innovation," yet reasonable people would see that it had been sanctioned in the Old Testament.[172] The "first great commandment" was to "be fruitful, and multiply, and replenish the earth" (Gen. 1:28), so polygamy was desirable in fulfilling that aim. Whenever discussing the topic, Pratt was quick to draw a distinction between the virtue of polygamy and the vice of adultery, even the thought of which was impermissible, quoting Jesus: "Whosoever looketh on a woman to lust after her" had already committed adultery in his heart.[173]

European Mormons lived in another kind of isolation, far distant from the mother church, and were unprepared for the news from Salt Lake City. They were astonished and repelled. To be more precise, they had begun to hear rumors about polygamy earlier in the year, and mission president Samuel W. Richards had written in April 1852:

> Much opposition has existed in this country [England] for a few months past and much still continues. The report of the [clergy] in relation to polygamy etc. in the [Salt Lake] Valley has been one great cause of it. Many are turned out of employment for embracing the work and … attempts are made to poison elders, etc. … Women in this country are shamefully abused with [strong] language if they will not le[a]ve this church. They are told that polygamy is practiced by it and every other filthy thing the wicked can imagine.[174]

In order to preach the good news of plural marriage in 1853, Mormon elders found themselves in an awkward position, defending what they had been denying for years. William Clayton found that on his return to England, people had heard that church leaders would "tak[e]

---

172. Orson Pratt, "Celestial Marriage: A Revelation on the Patriarchal Order of Matrimony or Plurality of Wives, Given to Joseph Smith, the Seer, in Nauvoo, July 12, 1843," *The Seer*, Jan. 1853, 1, 7-16.

173. Ibid., 25, 57, 28.

174. Samuel W. Richards to Mary Richards, Apr. 25, 1852, LDS Archives.

a man's wife from him and giv[e] her to another, without her consent; and tak[e] young women and giv[e] them to men contrary to their feelings &c."[175] The leaders in Salt Lake seemed to misjudge, if not misunderstand, British sensibilities. They failed to comprehend how unsavory it appeared for a man of high priesthood rank to claim the wife of someone of lower status if a missionary's wife was loaned to someone else during the husband's absence.[176] Both Joseph Smith and Brigham Young had set such examples.[177]

Ultimately the polygamy mission to Britain was unsuccessful. After the doctrine was announced in the Liverpool-published *Latter-day Saints' Millennial Star* on January 1, 1853, British membership declined 60 percent from a high of 33,000 in 1851 to about 13,000 by the end of the decade. Although immigration to Utah accounted for a part of the decrease, baptismal rates plummeted by 88 percent during the 1850s.[178] Yet in Utah, a "reformation" was initiated in 1856 by President Young's counselor Jedediah M. Grant, intent on shoring up support for polygamy and other uniquely Mormon doctrines. In a letter which is reminiscent of reports from Münster and Nauvoo, Apostle Wilford Woodruff wrote on April 1, 1857, to fellow Apostle George A. Smith, "All are trying to get wives, until there is hardly a girl fourteen years old in Utah, but what is married, or just going to be."[179]

After the Civil War, Congress campaigned to end the remaining "relic of barbarism" in America, as they referred to polygamy. President Lincoln had already signed the Morrill Anti-Bigamy Act into law on July 8, 1862, to "punish and prevent the practice of polygamy in the Territories of the United States and to disapprove and annul

---

175. Smith, *Intimate Chronicle*, 493.

176. S. George Ellsworth, ed., *The Journals of Addison Pratt* (Salt Lake City: University of Utah Press, 1990), 515; Smith, *Intimate Chronicle*, 227n.

177. Van Wagoner, *Mormon Polygamy*, 37-46; Brodie, *No Man Knows*, 34, 442-44; Newell and Avery, *Mormon Enigma*, 100-01.

178. Richard D. Poll, "The British Mission During the Utah War, 1857-58," in *Mormons in Early Victorian Britain*, eds. Richard L. Jensen and Malcolm R. Thorpe (Salt Lake City: University of Utah Press, 1989), 226; Jensen, "Church Councils and Governance," in ibid., 179-93.

179. Wilford Woodruff to George A. Smith, Apr. 1, 1857, Journal History of the Church of Jesus Christ of Latter-day Saints, a scrapbook of daily events, LDS Archives.

certain acts of the territorial legislature of Utah." But Lincoln was preoccupied and had neither the resources nor the inclination to prosecute polygamists in the west. Asked by Mormon journalist T. B. H. Stenhouse how vigorously he intended to pursue the matter, Lincoln reportedly answered:

> When I was a boy on the farm in Illinois, there was a great deal of timber on the farms which we had to clear away. Occasionally we would come to a log which had fallen down. It was too hard to split, too wet to burn, and too heavy to move, so we plowed around it. That's what I intend to do with the Mormons. You go back and tell Brigham Young that if he will let me alone, I will let him alone.[180]

While the president was distracted by the Civil War, Mormons went their own way, actually cheering on the destruction of armies and cities in the East, which they called retribution for the country's mistreatment of the Mormons. Many LDS leaders believed the war was a prelude to the millennium. The American government would be brought low and "hang by a thread," so the prophecy went. On January 19, 1863, Brigham Young told the Utah Territorial Legislature that, though it was "called the State Legislature," the time would come when "we shall be called the kingdom of God." The national government, he said, "is going to pieces and it will be like water that is spilled upon the ground that cannot be gathered. … The time will come when we will give laws to the nations of the earth. … We should get all things ready, and when the time comes, we should let the water on the wheel and start the machine in motion."[181] During the war years, LDS leaders freely predicted the collapse of the American nation. Brigham Young wrote to Utah territory Congressman William H. Hooper: "It seems that many are looking with some hope, apparently not yet realizing that the corruption of the nation has sealed its doom, which will be consummated sooner or later."[182] Similarly, Young's successor as

180. T. B. H. Stenhouse to Brigham Young, June 7, 1863, LDS Archives; see also Gustive O. Larson, *The Americanization of Utah for Statehood* (San Marino, Calif.: Huntington Library, 1971), 60; *Journal of Discourses,* 10:306; Preston Nibley, *Brigham Young: The Man and His Work* (Salt Lake City: Deseret Book, 1937), 369.

181. Kenney, *Wilford Woodruff's Journal,* 6:93.

182. Larson, *Americanization of Utah,* 28.

church president, John Taylor, expected that the nation would be "shaken to its center and ... will continue to fall and to crumble until it is no more."[183]

As such predictions failed to materialize, federal opposition to polygamy intensified from 1862 to 1890. While Congressman Morrill's 1862 act defined bigamy as marrying a woman when one had not divorced a previous spouse, it proved unenforceable since Mormon wives were not legally married. The act also annulled the church's articles of incorporation. The 1874 Poland Act empowered U.S. attorneys and marshals to bring cases to federal territorial courts rather than allowing Mormon-influenced probate courts to regulate marriage. In 1875, Brigham Young's secretary George Reynolds was convicted of bigamy, then effectively a second time in 1876, and his case was appealed to the U.S. Supreme Court. In *Reynolds v. United States,* the court ruled in 1879 that although people were free in their religious *beliefs*, the country had every right to regulate the *practice of those beliefs.* In the eleven years following the *Reynolds* decision, the Supreme Court ruled on eighteen polygamy cases. The issue also elicited comments from leading politicians. U.S. President James Garfield said the Mormon Church "offends the moral sense of manhood," and President Chester Arthur characterized polygamy as such an "odious crime" it was "revolting to the moral and religious sense of Christendom." In 1882 the Edmunds Act made cohabitation a crime, upheld in the 1885 Supreme Court case involving Angus M. Cannon, brother of one of the church presidency, George Q. Cannon. Two years later the Edmunds-Tucker Act called for more aggressive prosecution of polygamy and made adultery a federal crime, also repealing woman's suffrage for Utah Territory. As Congress once again dissolved the LDS Church corporation, it directed the territorial attorney to seize all church holdings. This was upheld by the U.S. Supreme Court in 1890 in *The Late Corporation of the Church of Jesus Christ v. United States.*[184]

---

183. *Journal of Discourses,* 11:26.

184. Ken Driggs, "The Prosecutions Begin: Defining Cohabitation in 1885," *Dialogue: A Journal of Mormon Thought* 21 (Spring 1988): 109-25.

Plural wives and women's rights

American women crusading to liberate plural wives from the oppression of polygamy were surprised to find that LDS women actively supported the practice. Artemisia Beaman Snow was the outspoken wife of Apostle Erastus Snow. She gently chided her well-intentioned female liberators for interfering where they were not needed or wanted. Addressing the St. George Relief Society, composed of Mormon women in Southern Utah, she lectured:

> We have been driven from a should-be land of freedom and liberty. We have wended our way over a trackless dessert, foot sore and bleeding, to these valleys of the mountains, thinking here the weary could find rest. Thinking here we could live in peace, enjoy our rights and freedom, and worship God according to the dictates of our own conscience. But in this we have been disappointed. Our persecutors[,] not being satisfied with driving us from county to county, from state to state, and at last from the United States, have followed us here. And from time to time have gotten up their crusades against us to annoy and perplex, and last of all our Christian sisters have taken it in hand, to deliver us from that awful yoke of bondage and oppression with which we are bound, and raise us from the low state of degradation into which we have fallen. My Christian sisters, this is a mistaken idea of yours! We are not the kind of women you take us to be. There are just as pure, virtuous, noble spirited women in Utah, as you will find any where on the footstool of God. You need not be to the trouble. We can deliver ourselves if we choose. We can live in the plural marriage system or out of it. There is no compulsion whatever. Wait till we solicit your aid. We have not asked your services. We do not need them. We do not want them. They are voluntary. It is what I call offered service, and it is a stink in our nostrils!

Snow protested that if these well-intentioned women did not "like our religion" or the "principles which we practice," then "hie ye away to your own cities and homes from whence ye came, and there get up your petitions to Mrs. [Rutherford B.] Hayes to use her influence for Congress to legislate for the morality of your own cities and towns."[185]

As in Nauvoo, some polygamous wives in Utah found that plural marriage was a way to keep men at arm's length while they pursued

185. In Larson, *Americanization of Utah,* 748.

their own interests, seeing their husbands once a week or less. In this way, it proved to be a good arrangement for women who wanted to pursue a career. Assisted by her sister-wives, Martha Hughes Cannon studied medicine in the east and became a physician. She also successfully ran for office in the Utah legislature. She spoke approvingly of the system, saying that if a woman's "husband has four wives, she has three weeks of freedom every month."[186] Ironically, Mormons favored inclusion of women in the political franchise, while many suffragists opposed giving Mormons the vote. This contradiction was most pronounced among non-Mormons in Utah. One of the territory's chief opponents of suffrage was Phoebe W. Couzins, a single, non-Mormon, female attorney. She argued in 1872 that women should not get involved in politics and should stay at home to raise their children. By contrast, LDS leaders called for female suffrage while telling women they were duty bound to obey their husbands.[187]

When polygamy was outlawed as a condition for statehood, plural families fled south of the Rio Grande and established expatriate Mormon towns, the remnants of which are still found there. Some "fundamentalist" Mormons have continued to practice polygamy throughout the American west and Canada, apparently numbering some 37,000 inhabitants.[188] According to news reports, the same customs involving marriages to young teenage women and to blood relatives, for instance, are still practiced. Rightly or wrongly, these customs have spawned similar stereotypes of lecherous prophets and submissive girls that plagued the early LDS Church.[189] Even in the current LDS

186. Van Wagoner, *Mormon Polygamy,* 102, quoting an interview in the *San Francisco Examiner,* Nov. 8, 1896.

187. Martha Sonntag Bradley, *Pedestals & Podiums: Utah Women, Religious Authority, and Equal Rights* (Salt Lake City: Signature Books, 2005), 459; Marvin S. Hill, "Counter-Revolution: The Mormon Reaction to the Coming of American Democracy," *Sunstone,* June 1989, 28, quoting Apostle Jedediah Grant's reminder to women that they had covenanted to "abide the law of th[eir] husband" and noting that Brigham Young "considered women to be inferior beings who derived guilt from original sin. Men must rule them. For a sister, Young explained, 'it is a law that a man shall rule over me; his word is my law, and I must obey him.'"

188. Newell G. Bringhurst and John Hamer, eds., *Scattering of the Saints: Schism within Mormonism* (Independence, Mo.: John Whitmer Books, 2007), 258-89.

189. In June 2002, fifteen-year-old Elizabeth Smart was kidnaped from her Salt

Church, which excommunicates polygamists, belief in plural marriage drives a policy which allows men to be married in temple sealing ceremonies to a second woman if a first wife dies but denies similar options to widows wanting to be sealed to another husband.[190]

As Mormon polygamy peaked in the 1880s, other social changes were afoot in the old world. Karl Marx died, and his philosophical partner, Friedrich Engels, advocated freer relationships between men and women. "It is a curious fact," Engels wrote, "that with every great revolutionary movement the question of 'free love' comes into the foreground." For some, it represented "revolutionary progress, as a shaking off of old traditional fetters, no longer necessary; with others [it was] a welcome doctrine, comfortably covering all sorts of free and easy practices between man and woman."[191]

Continuing aftershocks

What do LDS people today think about their polygamous history, enshrouded as it is with secrecy and ambiguity? The church does not officially acknowledge that polygamy existed until the Utah period under Brigham Young, and then it has gone to great lengths to obscure even Young's family arrangements. Tours of his Salt Lake City home, the Beehive House, notably omit mention of Young's numerous wives. An LDS Church manual on the second LDS Church president care-

---

Lake City home by a man reportedly impelled by revelation to "take" her for a second wife. She was recovered a year later. On September 25, 2007, FLDS polygamous leader Warren Steed Jeffs, of Hildale, Utah, and Colorado City, Arizona, which straddle the state line, was convicted in southern Utah for marrying a fourteen-year-old girl to her nineteen-year-old cousin six years earlier. He awaits trial on additional felony counts in Arizona and Texas for sexual conduct with a minor and incest (see Brooke Adams, "Jeffs to Face Judge in Arizona Today," "Texas Grand Jury Indicts Jeffs," *Salt Lake Tribune,* Feb. 27, July 22, 2008; John Dougherty, "Polygamist Is Indicted in Assault of a Child," *New York Times,* July 23, 2008; Kirk Johnson and John Dougherty, "Raid on Sect in Texas Rattles Polygamist Faithful Elsewhere," *New York Times,* May 8, 2008).

190. Dana Miller, "Celestial Polygamy," May 9, 2008, Public Forum letter to the *Salt Lake Tribune.*

191. Hill, *World Turned Upside Down,* 247, citing Engels's manuscript, "The Book of Revelation," written in 1883 and published in an anthology in the twentieth century by Moscow's Progress Publishers. Engels "rejected the institution of marriage" but lived with his long-time partner, Mary Burns, "as husband and wife"; when she died, he went to live with Mary's sister, Lizzy, "on similar terms," eventually marrying her ("Friedrich Engels," *Encyclopaedia Britannica,* online at www.britannica.com).

fully edited his statements and expurgated elements of his life story to make him appear to have been a monogamist.[192] The church does not acknowledge the internal dissent over polygamy which led to Joseph Smith's arrest and assassination. Not just a few Latter-day Saints still dismiss reports about Nauvoo polygamy as anti-Mormon propaganda, based on unfounded rumors, and hold fast to Joseph Smith's answer to William Law's court charge when Smith shrugged off talk of "seven wives" when he could "only find one."[193] The community of Nauvoo polygamists has been effectively forgotten. Despite the official attitude of the LDS Church, some Latter-day Saints take pride in their polygamous past, as one finds a nineteenth-century outlaw or European royalty in the family tree. For others, the association with polygamy runs deeper than that. Dana Miller of Idaho Falls was told by his church leaders that "men will have more than one wife in the celestial kingdom. It's doctrinal." When he divorced his first wife and remarried another woman, his priesthood leaders told him not to cancel his temple sealing to his first wife because she would need "the blessings of a husband" in the celestial kingdom just as much as his second wife.[194]

Plural families have been common in small proportions among many cultures, in pockets of non-conformists in monogamous societies. Communal marriage has been discussed, practiced, venerated, and outlawed in Middle Eastern, European, and American religious com-

192. See Vern Anderson, "Mormon Church Manual Paints Polygamist [Brigham] Young as Monogamist," Associated Press Release, Apr. 4, 1998; Klaus Hansen, "The World and the Prophet," review of *Nauvoo: Kingdom on the Mississippi* by Robert Bruce Flanders, *Dialogue: A Journal of Mormon Thought* 1 (Summer 1966): 107. Hansen wrote that "Preston Nibley, it will be remembered, wrote an entire book on Brigham Young without mentioning the dread word [polygamy] once." Nibley was Assistant Church Historian under Joseph Fielding Smith; his book, *Brigham Young: The Man and His Work,* was published by the Deseret News Press in 1936. For a more recent example of this anxiety of plural marriage, see "Cut and Recut: New Emma Smith Film Skirts Polygamy," *Sunstone,* July 2008, 76-77.

193. During a recent discussion about polygamy on a community radio station in Salt Lake City, a caller stated his opinion that "Joseph Smith had one wife, and her name was Emma," a view not infrequently voiced (Lorna Vogt, host, with Mary Batchelor, Doe Daughtery, Richard Dutcher, and Anne Wilde, RadioActive, KRCL 90.9, Salt Lake City, Mar. 15, 2006).

194. Miller, "Celestial Polygamy."

munities. What seemed to be a counter-theme to a modern norm may, in fact, reflect the variations in lifestyle of our earliest human ancestors. Both the Münster Anabaptist and Mormon communities, sharing common beliefs while separated by 300 years, drew upon Old Testament models as they attempted to restore an early biblical world. For a while these two "latter-day" communities spoke of similar goals in equally prepossessing terms, but neither was able to overcome internal dissent or external revulsion. The Münsterites were exterminated by Christians, and their memory was shunned by the broader Anabaptist world. The Mormons were able to isolate themselves for a time and resist pressure to conform to the norms of the surrounding culture but were eventually forced to abjure. Today Latter-day Saints look away from what are defined as less desirable episodes in church and family history; at least they keep their family narratives politely ambivalent regarding the topic.

Conclusion

Looking back from the twenty-first century to the sixteenth-century millennialists and then forward to their counterparts in nineteenth-century Illinois, the social innovations in these two groups appear to be palpably comparable. The German community, begun by Dutch Anabaptists and lasting only one year—in the context of privileges granted to English and German leaders by Protestant theologians—stimulated discussions about marriage in Europe and America for centuries thereafter. Mormon celestial marriage lasted five years in Nauvoo, followed by a forty-five-year segue into the Rocky Mountain environment. Ostensibly renounced in 1890, the practice never came to a complete end. Contrary to the Münster example, Mormon polygamy continues today, at least among committed descendants of pioneer families from Illinois.

Speaking in Salt Lake City's open-air Bowery in August 1866, President Young used polygamy to distinguish the Latter-day Saints from "the Christian world," as he called it.[195] It had been a year since Appomattox and a decade since the Republican Party platform had

195. "Beneficial Effects of Polygamy," *Journal of Discourses,* 11:266-72.

railed against the "twin relics of barbarism—slavery and polygamy." Young observed that only one of the "twin relics" had been abolished. Anticipating a federal assault on the other "relic," he warned that it would not be Brigham Young they would "fight" but rather "the Lord Almighty," and that the Lord was "going to do just as he pleases." Wondering whether "we shall ever be admitted as a State into the Union without denying the principle of polygamy," Young said he would be content if the territory were never admitted.[196]

Separating his Saints from what he mockingly called the "refined Christian society" of the day, he accused Christians of abusing women, whom he claimed were often defiled and cast off "dishonored," according to the norms of the prevailing culture. Those who "set up such a howl against the doctrine of polygamy," he said, were the "very class of men" who victimized women. Deriding what he detected as feigned morality from critics, he continued:

> If a woman wants to live with me as a wife, all right; but the law says you must not marry her, and own her as your wife openly ... [S]he can come home to me, not as my wife, you know; she can sweep my house, make my bed, help me to make the butter and cheese, and share in all my pleasures and wealth, but the ceremony of marriage must not be performed. This is what is practiced in the outside world from the President "on down." They have their mistresses, and thereby violate every principle of virtue, chastity and righteousness.[197]

In the "large cities of the east" where Young had gone as a missionary, men had "hire[d] and support[ed] girls ... the same as you would hire a horse." "You go out a few days for a ride," Young said, then return your horse and "pay down your money, and you are freed from all further responsibility." Young alluded to his right as president of the church to receive revelation if God decided to bless him with one, saying that "if it is wrong for a man to have more than one wife at a time, the Lord will reveal it by and by."[198]

Polygamy remains very much on the minds of Mormons today,

196. Ibid., 269.
197. Ibid., 270.
198. Ibid., 268.

whether in the LDS Church, the Community of Christ, the Restoration Branches, or fundamentalist organizations. Each group looks back to Nauvoo through a different lens. The "Texas Polygamy Raids" of 2008, as various headlines summarized the events, recall the umbrage that was taken and the criminal complaints filed when Joseph Smith married the teenaged Maria and Sarah Lawrence, for whose father's estate Smith was the executor. These issues ignited intense social and political indignation which eventually drove mainstream Latter-day Saints away from plural marriage.

As fundamentalist Latter-day Saints continue to embrace the principle of plural marriage, the thirteen-million-strong mainstream LDS Church tries to suppress the memory of a half century of polygamy. Yet, at the same time, Smith's 1843 proclamation, dictated to William Clayton,[199] officially sanctioning celestial marriage of a man to plural wives—and still considered scripture—makes the practice difficult to forget.

199. Appendix A.

Photographs

Emma Hale Smith, the long-suffering first wife of Joseph Smith, attended a few of her husband's plural marriages but may have been uncertain about exactly what these ceremonies implied. Her own marriage to the prophet was in secret and against her parents' wishes.

Joseph Smith as Lieutenant-General of the Nauvoo Legion. Painting by John Hafen, one of the LDS Church's "art missionaries" who studied at the Academie Julian in Paris in the 1890s.

In 1841, under a literal cloak of secrecy wearing a man's coat and hat, Louisa Beaman became Joseph Smith's first documented plural wife. After Smith's death, she married Brigham Young and had five children, including two sets of twins, all of whom died as infants. At age thirty-five, she succumbed to breast cancer. *Used by permission, Utah State University, all rights reserved*

Agnes Coolbrith met Joseph Smith in Boston in 1832 and later married his brother, Don Carlos Smith. Five months after Don Carlos died of malaria in 1841, Agnes became one of Joseph's plural wives. Her daughter, Josephine Donna Smith, became a famous California poet under the pen name Ina Coolbrith. As a measure of her success, "Ina" was named an honorary member of the all-male Bohemian Club in San Francisco. *Courtesy Community of Christ Archives, Independence, Missouri*

Joseph B. Noble conducted the marriage ceremony between Louisa Beaman and Joseph Smith in 1841. Afterward, he loaned them his house for the evening, advising them to "blow out the lights and get into bed, and you will be safer there."

As mobs burned and ransacked the press that was printing Joseph Smith's revelation in Independence, Missouri, in 1833, fifteen-year-old Mary Elizabeth Rollins risked personal harm by gathering up the freshly printed sheets that had been thrown out the print shop window. In 1905 Rollins spoke to an assembly of Brigham Young University faculty and students to explain the details of her marriage to Joseph Smith. *Used by permission, Utah State Historical Society, all rights reserved*

Benjamin F. Johnson had two sisters who married Joseph Smith. A third sister took in a boarder, Fanny Alger, at a time when Fanny was reported to be involved with Joseph Smith. Benjamin's parents separated over the church's innovations in Illinois, but Benjamin took three wives in Nauvoo and four more in Utah where he became an icon to later fundamentalist Mormons.

Eliza R. Snow was twenty-seven years old when she met Joseph Smith. She had been part of Sidney Rigdon's Campbellite Baptist Church prior to converting to Mormonism. She was Smith's fourteenth wife.

As governor of Missouri, Lilburn W. Boggs echoed LDS rhetoric by declaring that "the Mormons … must be exterminated," "treated as enemies," and "driven from the State if necessary" to protect "the public peace." Joseph Smith's counselor Sidney Rigdon had previously said the same about non-Mormons.

John C. Bennett, assistant president of the LDS Church, quarreled with Joseph Smith in Nauvoo and then wrote an exposé of polygamy, published in October 1842 as the *History of the Saints*.

Parley P. Pratt and wife Elizabeth Brotherton. Pratt was an apocalyptic apostle who spoke of "lightnings from the east" and "the voice of thunderings" and "tempests." His sister-in-law, Martha Brotherton, became famous for rejecting Brigham Young's marriage proposal.

Eliza Maria Partridge, along with her younger sister, Emily, boarded with the Smith family, where they were employed as servants. Joseph told the girls about celestial marriage and then secretly married them. When Emma later gave consent to the marriages, unaware that ceremonies had already been performed, Joseph staged another ceremony for Emma's benefit. However, Emma soon changed her mind and forced the girls from her home. Eliza later married Apostle Amasa Lyman.
Courtesy International Society, Daughters of Utah Pioneers

Brigham Young is well known as the pioneer leader and colonizer of the American West. His rise to prominence began as one of Joseph Smith's closest confidants in the Midwest, where he was also one of the first polygamists. In addition to an already prodigious household, he took eleven of Joseph Smith's widows under his roof as additional wives.

Emily Dow Partridge and sister Eliza worked as maids for Joseph and Emma Smith for three years. After marrying Joseph, Emma harassed them to the point that they no longer felt comfortable or safe. In Emily's later autobiographical sketches and court testimony, she offered rich insight into the character of polygamy. *Used by permission, Utah State Historical Society, all rights reserved*

Lucy Ann Decker was Brigham Young's first plural wife. Her marriage to him in June 1842 was the first firmly dated polygamous marriage for anyone other than Joseph Smith.

Heber C. Kimball was one of the most prolific LDS polygamists. Unruffled by Joseph Smith's involvement with Fanny Alger, Kimball assumed that where there was intimacy, there must have been a marriage.

When Lucy Walker's mother died in 1842, Joseph Smith invited her and three siblings to board in the Smith home, then proposed marriage to her. Fifteen years old, Lucy demurred, and Joseph agreed to wait until she was older. Accordingly, waiting until her seventeenth birthday, Joseph repeated his proposal, citing a revelation demanding their union and giving her one day to reply. She consented, and they were married on May Day 1843. She later married Heber Kimball.
Courtesy International Society, Daughters of Utah Pioneers

Helen Mar Kimball was the oldest daughter of Heber and Vilate Kimball. When she was fourteen, her father convinced her to become Joseph Smith's youngest wife. With evident bitterness she later wrote: "My father had but one ewe lamb, but willingly laid her upon the altar." Her serialized reminiscence in the *Woman's Exponent* from 1860 to 1886 is an important polygamy narrative. *Used by permission, Utah State Historical Society, all rights reserved*

Hyrum Smith comforted the uninitiated by telling them the prophet resisted God's command to take more wives until an angel threatened him "with a drawn sword." Hyrum had been his brother's most formidable polygamy opponent until he read the 1843 revelation. Once converted to the doctrine, he became one of its strongest advocates and personally took four plural wives. *Used by permission, Utah State Historical Society, all rights reserved*

Orson Pratt was suspended from the Quorum of Twelve Apostles after quarreling with Joseph Smith about an incident involving Smith and Orson's wife, Sarah. In later years, Brigham Young used this brief suspension to prevent Pratt from ascending to the church presidency. In 1852, standing in the Old Tabernacle in Salt Lake City, Pratt was the first to publicly defend Mormon polygamy.

Joseph F. Smith with his family. In 1901 he became sixth president of the LDS Church. In the 1860s, as an apostle, he collected seventy-five affidavits from early participants in plural marriage, mostly wives of Joseph Smith. Although he secretly authorized some post-Manifesto plural marriages, Joseph F. eventually issued a Second Manifesto curtailing them.

Lorenzo Snow was among the earliest initiates into plural marriage and the fifth president of the LDS Church. His sister Eliza was Joseph Smith's thirteenth plural wife.

John Taylor performed the 1843 artificial marriage of Sarah Mulholland to Alexander Mullinder to conceal Sarah's marriage to Joseph Smith. In 1880, Taylor became president of the LDS Church; he married a total of eighteen women.

Jan van Leiden (John Bockelson in English) was the Anabaptist king of Münster, Germany. As part of his millennialist agenda for the "saints of the last days," he promoted the Old Testament practice of polygamy. Of sixteen plural wives, his first was the widow of the prophet Jan Mathijs. *Copper engraving by Heinrich Aldegrever, 1536. Photograph by Tomasz Samek. Courtesy Stadtmuseum Münster. All rights reserved*

Appendix A
The 1843 Revelation (excerpts)

Joseph Smith's "celestial marriage" revelation, which explicates and defends a "plurality of wives," was recorded on July 12, 1843, in Nauvoo, Illinois. However, it was not made available to the general public until September 14, 1852, a month after polygamy was announced to the world from the podium of the Old Tabernacle in Salt Lake City. The *Deseret News* distributed the text of the revelation as part of an extra edition, as if it were breaking news, and about a quarter century later in 1876 the revelation was published by the LDS Church as Section 132 of the Doctrine and Covenants. It is not in the RLDS Doctrine and Covenants. The following is drawn from pages 26-28 of the *Deseret News Extra.*

Verily thus saith the Lord, unto his servant Joseph, that inasmuch as you have enquired of my hand, to know and understand wherein I the Lord justified my servants, Abraham, Isaac, and Jacob; as also Moses, David, and Solomon, my servants, as touching the principle and doctrine of their having many wives, and concubines: Behold! and lo, I am the Lord thy God, and will answer thee as touching this matter: Therefore, prepare thy heart to receive and obey the instructions which I am about to give unto you; for all those, who have this law revealed unto them, must obey the same; for behold! I revealed unto you a new and everlasting covenant, and if ye abide not that covenant, then are ye damned; for no one can reject this covenant, and be permitted to enter into my glory; ...

And again, verily I say unto you, if a man marry a wife by my word, which is my law, and by the new and everlasting covenant, and it is sealed unto them by the Holy Spirit of promise, by him who is anointed, unto whom I have appointed this power, and the keys of this priesthood, and it shall be said unto them, ye shall come forth in the first resurrection; … Then shall they be Gods, because the[y] have no end, therefore shall they be from everlasting to everlasting, because they continue; then shall they be above all, because all things are subject unto them. Then shall they be Gods, because they have all power, and the angels are subject unto them. …

Abraham received promises concerning his seed, and of the fruit of his loins—from whose loins ye are, viz, my servant Joseph—which were to continue, so long as they were in the world; and as touching Abraham and his seed, out of the world, they should continue; both in the world and out of the world should they continue as innumerable as the stars; or, if ye were to count the sand upon the sea-shore, ye could not number them. This promise is yours, also, because ye are of Abraham, and by this law are the continuation of the works of my Father, wherein he glorifieth himself. Go ye, therefore, and do the works of Abraham—enter ye into my law, and ye shall be saved. But if ye enter not into my law, ye cannot receive the promises of my Father which he made unto Abraham.

God commanded Abraham, and Sarah gave Hagar to Abraham, to wife. And why did she do it? Because this was the law, and from Hagar sprang many people. This, therefore, was fulfilling, among other things, the promises. …

Abraham received concubines, and they bare him children, and it was accounted unto him for righteousness, because they were given unto him, and he abode in my law: as Isaac also, and Jacob did none other things than that which they were commanded: and because they did none other things than that which they were commanded, they have entered into their exaltation, according to the promises, and sit upon thrones; and are not angels, but are Gods. David also received many wives and concubines, as also Solomon, and Moses my servant, as also many others of my servants, from the beginning of creation until this time; and in nothing did they sin, save in those things which they received not of me.

David's wives and concubines were given unto him, of me, by the hand of Nathan, my servant, and others of the prophets who had the keys of this power; …

I am the Lord thy God, and I gave unto thee my servant Joseph, an appointment, and restore al[l] things; ask what ye will, and it shall be given unto you, according to my word; and as ye have asked concerning adultery—verily, verily I say unto you, if a man receiveth a wife in the new and everlasting covenant, and if she be with another man, and I have not appointed unto her by the holy anointing, she hath committed adultery, and shall be destroyed. If she be not in the new and everlasting covenant, and she be with another man, she has committed adultery; and if her husband be with another woman, and he was under a vow, he hath broken his vow, and hath committed adultery; and if she hath not committed adultery, but is innocent, and hath not broken her vow, and she knoweth it, and I reveal it unto you, my servant Joseph, then shall you have power, by the power of my Holy Priesthood, to take her, and give her unto him that hath not committed adultery, but hath been faithful; for he shall be made ruler over many; for I have conferred upon you the keys and power of the priesthood, wherein I restore all things, and make known unto you, all things, in due time.

And verily, verily I say unto you, that whatsoever you seal on earth, shall be sealed in heaven; and whatsoever you bind on earth, in my name, and by my word, saith the Lord, it shall be eternally in the heavens, …

Verily I say unto you, a commandment I give unto mine handmaid, Emma Smith, your wife, whom I have given unto you, that she stay herself, and partake not of that which I commanded you to offer unto her, for I did it, saith the Lord, to prove you all, as I did Abraham, and that I might require an offering at your hand, by covenant and sacrifice: and let mine handmaid, Emma Smith, receive all those that have been given unto my servant Joseph, and who are virtuous and pure before me, and those who are not pure, and have said they were pure, shall be destroyed, saith the Lord God; for I am the Lord thy God, and ye shall obey my voice; and I give unto my servant Joseph, that he shall be made ruler over many things, for he hath been faithful over a few things; and from henceforth I will strengthen him.

And I command mine handmaid, Emma Smith, to abide and cleave unto my servant Joseph and to none else. But if she will not abide this commandment, she shall be destroyed, saith the Lord, for I am the Lord thy God, and will destroy her, if she abide not in my law; but if she will not abide this commandment, then shall my servant Joseph do all things for her even as he hath said, and I will bless him and multiply him, and give unto him an hundred fold in this world, of fathers and mothers, brothers and sisters, houses and lands, wives and children, and crowns of eternal lives in the eternal worlds. And again, verily I say, let mine handmaid forgive my servant Joseph his trespasses, and then shall she be forgiven her trespasses, wherein she hath trespassed against me; and I the Lord thy God will bless her, and multiply her, and make her heart to rejoice. …

And again, as pertaining to the law of the Priesthood—if any man espouse a virgin, and desire to espouse another, and the first give her consent; and if he espouse the second, and they are virgins, and have vowed to no other man, then is he justified; he cannot commit adultery, for they are given unto him; for he cannot commit adultery with that, that belongeth unto him, and to none else; and if he have ten virgins given unto him by this law, he cannot commit adultery, for they belong to him, and they are given unto him—therefore is he justified.—But if one, or either of the ten virgins, after she is espoused, shall be with another man, she has committed adultery, and shall be destroyed, for they are given unto him to multiply and replenish the earth, according to my commandment, and to fulfil the promise which was given by my Father before the foundation of the world, and for their exaltation in the eternal worlds …

And again, verily, verily I say unto you, if any man have a wife who holds the keys of this power, and he teaches unto her the law of my Priesthood, as pertaining to these things; then shall she believe, and administer unto him, or she shall be destroyed, saith the Lord your God, for I will destroy her; … Therefore, it shall be lawful in me, if she receive not this law, for him to receive all things, whatsoever I the Lord his God will give unto him, because she did not believe and administer unto him, according to my word; and she then becomes the transgressor, and he is exempt from the law of Sarah, who administered unto Abraham according to the law, when I commanded Abraham to take Hagar to wife. And now, as pertaining to this law—verily, verily I say unto you, I will reveal more unto you hereafter; therefore, let this suffice for the present. Behold, I am Alpha and Omega—AMEN.

Appendix B
Nauvoo Polygamous Families

The following chart lists 196 male polygamists in Nauvoo and their 717 wives, which would expand to 1,134 after the westward migration. This information is derived from diaries and journals, census and Church records, and various biographical writings. When differences arise in dates of birth, death, or marriage, or in the spelling of a name, weight is given to documents that have proven to be reliable or to the consensus of available documents. The primary sources upon which this chart is based, and their availability at different periods of time, are discussed in chapter 8.

Two symbols appear on the chart. An asterisk (*) indicates that an individual was part of the inner circle of about thirty Nauvoo men, members of the so-called Quorum of the Anointed. A dagger (†) shows that a wife was married "for time only," as long as she and her husband "each shall live," rather than "for time and eternity," which means for this life and the next. The doctrine of celestial marriage conceived of other worlds in vast planetary systems hosting infinite afterlife civilizations. Whereas a husband might have some wives "for eternity" and others "for time only," possibly because these women were sealed to someone else "for eternity," a wife in the Latter-day Saint community could only be married to one man at once, whether "for time" or "for eternity," unless a "temple divorce" allowed her to be sealed to someone else. When Joseph Smith's colleagues married his widows, the women were regarded as their spouses "for time" only even though the stand-ins for Joseph Smith might have fathered children with these wives. These children were thought to belong to their eternal sealing partner in the next world, not to their natural fathers. A prominent example would be Heber J. Grant, whose mother avoided Joseph's pursuits in Nauvoo (see chapter 3) but by Joseph's demand was sealed to him after Joseph's death, making Grant a son of Smith in the afterlife.

Nauvoo Polygamous Families

	husbands & wives	birth	death	marriage	sealing	marriage age: husb	marriage age: wife	in JS life: wives	in JS life: children	> JS death: wives	> JS death: children	> Nauvoo: wives	> Nauvoo: children	total: wives	total: children
1	**Adams, James (Judge)***[1]	**Jan 24 1783**	**Aug 11 1843**					**2**	**5**	**0**	**0**	**0**	**0**	**2**	**5**
	Harriet Denton[2]	Jan 31 1787	Aug 21 1844	1809	May 28 1843	26	22								5
	Roxena Rachel Repsher[3]	Mar 20 1805		Jul 11 1843	Jul 11 1843	60	38								0
2	**Allen, Joseph Stewart**	**Jun 25 1806**	**Apr 25 1889**					**1**	**4**	**1**	**1**	**2**	**15**	**4**	**20**
	Lucy Diantha Morley[4]	Oct 4 1815	Oct 19 1908	Sep 2 1835	Feb 4 1846	29	19								12
	Nancy Jane Putnam	Feb 20 1825	Jan 30 1853	Feb 4 1846	Feb 4 1846	39	20								0
	Karen Marie Hansen	Nov 5 1835	Aug 7 1885	Jan 28 1854	Jan 28 1854	47	18								8
	Ingeborg K. Jespersen (Hanson Pehl)[5]	Jan 10 1802	Jun 3 1869	Sep 11 1857	Sep 11 1857	51	55								0
3	**Allred, Isaac**	**Jun 28 1813**	**May 12 1859**					**1**	**6**	**1**	**3**	**1**	**9**	**3**	**18**
	Julia Ann Taylor[6]	Feb 9 1815	May 16 1898	Oct 11 1832	Jan 15 1846	19	17								10
	Mary Henderson	Feb 18 1823	Dec 27 1910	Jan 15 1846	Jan 15 1846	32	22								6
	Emma Dewey	Apr 28 1826	Apr 21 1909	Oct 7 1856	Oct 7 1856	43	30								2
4	**Allred, James**	**Jan 22 1784**	**Jan 10 1876**					**1**	**12**	**3**	**0**	**3**	**0**	**7**	**12**
	Elizabeth Warren[7]	May 6 1786	Apr 23 1879	Nov 14 1803	Jan 14 1846	19	17								12
	Elizabeth Davis	ca. 1782		Dec 26 1844		60	62								na
	Sarah Ann (Sally) Warren (Allred)†[8]	Nov 25 1794	May 28 1858	Jan 28 1846	Jan 28 1846	62	51								0
	Elizabeth Patrick (Taylor)†	Dec 9 1795	Oct 25 1880	Feb 3 1846	Feb 3 1846	62	50								0
	Kisner Olsen	Feb 7 1844		Mar 14 1857	Mar 14 1857	73	13								na
	Annie Marsina Christensen			Mar 14 1857	Mar 14 1857	73									na

	Annie Maria Hansen	Nov 9 1840		Mar 14 1857	Mar 14 1857	73	16								
5	**Anderson, William**	**Mar 29 1809**	**Sep 12 1846**					**1**	**3**	**1**	**1**	**0**	**0**	**2**	**4**
	Emeline Tellone Stewart	Sep 25 1812	Sep 26 1871	Sep 6 1831	Jan 30 1846	22	18								4
	Druzilla Sargent	Feb 1 1826		Feb 3 1846	Feb 3 1846	36	20								0
6	**Averett, Elisha**[9]	**Dec 12 1810**	**Oct 22 1890**					**0**	**0**	**2**	**0**	**0**	**14**	**2**	**14**
	Dorcas Willis (Witt)[10]	Feb 1 1810	Feb 6 1843	Jan 15 1838	Jan 19 1846	27	27								3na
	Cherizade Grimes[11]	Jun 27 1812	Jan 1 1896	Jan 16 1846	Jan 16 1846	35	33								0
	Sarah Jane Witt[12]	Feb 1 1831	Dec 31 1875	Jan 19 1846	Jan 19 1846	35	14								14
7	**Babbitt, Almon Whiting**[13]	**Oct 1 1813**	**Oct 24 1856**					**1**	**3**	**3**	**0**	**0**	**3**	**4**	**6**
	Julia Ann Johnson[14]	Nov 9 1808	Oct 23 1857	Nov 23 1833	Jan 24 1846	20	25								6
	Delcena D. Johnson (Sherman Smith)†[15]	Nov 19 1806	Oct 21 1854	Jan 24 1846	Jan 24 1846	32	39								0
	Mary Ann Tulley	Nov 26 1810		Jan 24 1846	Jan 24 1846	32	35								0
	Maria Lawrence (Smith)[16]	Dec 18 1823	1847	Jan 24 1846	Jan 24 1846	32	22								0
8	**Bair, John**	**Nov 26 1810**	**Oct 11 1884**					**1**	**1**	**2**	**1**	**2**	**23**	**5**	**25**
	Lydia Regester[17]	Nov 17 1804		Aug 29 1829	Jul 15 1989	18	24								7na
	Lucinda Owen (Tyler)[18]	Jan 10 1819	Jul 4 1893	Oct 19 1843	Jan 24 1846	32	24								7
	Belinda Owen	Apr 21 1822	Jan 20 1847	Jan 27 1846	Jan 27 1846	35	23								2
	Jerusha Ann Richardson (Card)†	May 15 1818	Mar 16 1861	Jan 27 1846	Jan 27 1846	35	27								7
	Lucy Ann Maria Cole	Sep 15 1830	Mar 3 1924	Jul 1 1852	Jul 1 1852	41	21								9
	Mary Jane Bigler	Oct 15 1827	Sep 26 1868	Apr 8 1856	Apr 8 1856	45	28								0
9	**Barlow, Israel**	**Sep 13 1806**	**Nov 1 1883**					**1**	**2**	**1**	**2**	**2**	**11**	**4**	**15**
	Elizabeth Haven[19]	Dec 28 1811	Dec 25 1892	Feb 23 1840	Jan 17 1846	33	28								7

husbands & wives	birth	death	marriage	sealing	marriage age husb	marriage age wife	in JS life wives	in JS life children	> JS death wives	> JS death children	> Nauvoo wives	> Nauvoo children	total wives	total children
Elizabeth Barton[20]	Sep 10 1803	Oct 21 1874	fall 1844	Jan 28 1846	38	41								0
Lucy Heap	Sep 24 1836	Jul 4 1901	Dec 2 1855	Dec 2 1855	49	19								8
Cordelia Maria Dalrymple	Oct 4 1822	Mar 29 1905	May 27 1865	May 27 1865	58	42								0
10 Bateman, Thomas*	**Sep 17 1808**	**Nov 29 1852**					**2**	**8**	**0**	**1**	**0**	**3**	**2**	**12**
Mary Street[21]	May 12 1810	Mar 4 1891	Aug 12 1829	Jan 29 1846	20	19								12
Elizabeth Ravenscroft[22]	ca. 1819		Mar 23 1843		34	23								0
11 Bates, Ormus Ephraim	**Mar 25 1815**	**Aug 4 1873**					**1**	**4**	**1**	**2**	**5**	**40**	**7**	**46**
Phoebe Mariah Matteson[23]	Jan 31 1817	Mar 6 1888	Aug 20 1835	Nov 14 1847	20	18								9
Morilla Spink	Dec 31 1823	Feb 17 1906	Dec 23 1844	Oct 15 1859	29	20								11
Matilda Reeves	Apr 11 1827	1882	Nov 15 1847	Nov 15 1847	32	20								7
Ellen B. Mecham	Jul 4 1836	Aug 1 1872	Jan 25 1853	Jan 25 1853	37	16								4
Margrette Alice Busenbark	Dec 29 1836	Mar 23 1915	Jun 23 1853	Jun 23 1853	38	16								6
Sarah Alameda Weir	Dec 18 1841	Aug 31 1876	Oct 10 1862	Nov 16 1862	47	20								4
Sarah Hymas	Dec 6 1841	Nov 27 1929	Nov 10 1862	Nov 16 1862	47	20								5
12 Beach, Rufus	**May 8 1795**	**1850**					**1**	**0**	**3**	**0**	**0**	**2**	**4**	**2**
Laura Ann Gibbs[24]	Apr 5 1814	Jul 26 1893	Sep 16 1833	Jul 22 1977	38	19								1
Mary Catherine Aber[25]	Dec 24 1825		< Jan 21 1846	Jan 21 1846	50	20								0
Eliza Jane Fosdick[26]	Apr 16 1825		Jan 21 1846	Jan 21 1846	50	20								0
Harriet Cordelia Williams	Nov 10 1829	Nov 7 1907	1846	Mar 4 1939	50	16								1
13 Benbow, John	**Apr 1 1800**	**May 12 1874**					**1**	**0**	**4**	**0**	**1**	**1**	**6**	**1**

	Jane Holmes	Jan 12 1792	Nov 27 1846	Oct 16 1826	Jan 26 1846	26	34								0
	Agnes Taylor	Oct 2 1821	Dec 12 1911	Jan 26 1846	Jan 26 1846	45	24								0
	Elizabeth Holmes[27]	ca. 1800		ca. 1846		46	46								0
	Charlotte Spencer[27]	ca. 1800		ca. 1846		46	46								0
	Mary Dart[27]	ca. 1800		ca. 1846		46	46								0
	Rosetta Wright (King Peacock)	Sep 1 1819	Mar 17 1894	Sep 3 1851	Sep 18 1857	51	32								1
14	**Benson, Ezra Taft***	**Feb 22 1811**	**Sep 3 1869**					**2**	**5**	**1**	**1**	**5**	**28**	**8**	**34**
	Pamelia Andrus[28]	Oct 21 1809	Sep 14 1877	Jan 1 1832	Nov 19 1843	20	22								8
	Adeline Brooks Andrus[29]	Mar 18 1813	Apr 20 1898	Apr 27 1844	Apr 27 1844	33	31								3
	Desdemona Wadsworth Fullmer (Smith)†[30]	Oct 6 1809	Feb 9 1886	Jan 26 1846	Jan 26 1846	34	36								0
	Eliza Ann Perry	Mar 30 1829	Apr 30 1913	Mar 4 1847	Mar 4 1847	36	17								7
	Lucinda Barton (West)†	Oct 22 1826		Mar 4 1847	Mar 4 1847	36	20								0
	Olive Mary Knight	Jan 24 1830	Mar 27 1905	Jul 12 1851	Jul 12 1851	40	21								7
	Elizabeth Gollaher	Dec 30 1831	May 4 1903	Jun 4 1853	Apr 10 1856	42	21								7
	Mary Larsen	Dec 19 1844	Feb 21 1926	Sep 15 1866	Sep 15 1866	55	21								2
15	**Bent, Samuel**	**July 19 1778**	**Aug 16 1846**					**1**	**0**	**9**	**0**	**0**	**0**	**10**	**0**
	Mary Kilburn[31]	Mar 4 1785	Jul 5 1836	May 3 1805	Jan 14 1846	26	20								4na
	Lettis Hawkins (Palmer)†[32]	Jun 27 1785		Sep 1837	Jan 14 1846	59	52								0
	Phebe Palmer	Oct 29 1788	1858	Jan 14 1846	Jan 14 1846	67	57								0
	Cynthia Noble[33]	Jun 19 1806	Jun 17 1873	Jan 14 1846	Jan 14 1846	67	39								0
	Marial Thompson (Crosby)	May 7 1808	May 19 1893	Jan 14 1846	Jan 14 1846	67	37								0
	Asenath Slafter (Janes)	Aug 18 1796	Oct 5 1867	Jan 28 1846	Jan 28 1846	67	49								0

	husbands & wives	birth	death	marriage	sealing	marriage age husb	marriage age wife	in JS life wives	in JS life children	> JS death wives	> JS death children	> Nauvoo wives	> Nauvoo children	total wives	total children
	Anna Hartshorne[34]	Apr 9 1787	Jun 13 1846	Jan 28 1846	Jan 28 1846	67	58								0
	Elizabeth "Betsy" Burgess (Matthews)	Aug 4 1789		Jan 28 1846	Jan 28 1846	67	56								0
	Vina Clearwater (Hollister)†[35]	Dec 19 1799	July 18 1872	Jan 28 1846	Jan 28 1846	67	46								0
	Polly Miller (Smith)†[36]	Oct 18 1795		Jan 30 1846	Jan 30 1846	67	50								0
	Naomi Harris (Duel Kellogg)[37]	May 5 1800	Mar 29 1884	<Feb 6 1846		67	45								0
16	**Bernhisel, John Milton**	**Jun 23 1799**	**Sep 28 1881**					**0**	**0**	**7**	**0**	**0**	**9**	**7**	**9**
	Julia Ann Haight (Van Orden)[38]	Oct 6 1805	Jan 23 1865	1845	Jan 20 1846	46	39								1
	Dolly Ransom (Mecham)	Aug 26 1801	ca. 1853	<Jan 20 1846	Jan 20 1846	46	45								0
	Catherine Paine	Jun 1795		Jan 20 1846	Jan 20 1846	46	50								0
	Fanny Spafford	Feb 5 1802		Jan 20 1846	Jan 20 1846	46	43								0
	Elizabeth Barker[39]	Feb 8 1830		Feb 3 1846	Feb 3 1846	46	15								8
	Catherine Burgess (Barker)[40]	Aug 12 1809	Nov 7 1884	<Feb 3 1846	Feb 3 1846	46	37								0
	Melissa Lott (Smith)[41]	Jan 9 1824	Jul 13 1898	Feb 8 1846	Feb 8 1846	46	22								0
17	**Bills, John**	**Sep 19 1819**	**Feb 19 1850**					**1**	**3**	**1**	**1**	**0**	**3**	**2**	**7**
	Elizabeth Scott[42]	Jan 1 1817	1854	Jan 7 1834	Jan 16 1846	14	17								5
	Elizabeth Hall[43]	Nov 20 1820	Mar 17 1897	Jan 6 1846	Jan 6 1848	26	25								2
18	**Blackhurst, William**	**Jun 22 1807**	**Sep 9 1864**					**1**	**2**	**1**	**1**	**2**	**4**	**4**	**7**
	Margaret Stephenson	May 5 1804	Jun 5 1847	1836	Jan 27 1846	29	32								3
	Catharine Bimford (Stephenson)†[44]	Jan 16 1771	Apr 14 1847	Jan 27 1846	Jan 27 1846	38	75								0
	Jane Hamilton	Jul 20 1805	Jan 4 1874	by 1850	by 1850	43	45								0

	Isabella Mecham	Apr 6 1837		Sep 25 1857	Sep 25 1857	50	20								4
19	**Bolton, Curtis Edwin**	**Jul 16 1812**	**12 6 1890**					**1**	**1**	**1**	**1**	**4**	**9**	**6**	**11**
	Eleanor Post	Jan 26 1808	Jul 23 1837	Jun 15 1836	Aug 4 1869	23	28								1na
	Rebecca Baks Bunker (Merritt)[45]	Mar 19 1810	Feb 7 1891	Sep 12 1839	Feb 6 1846	27	29								6
	Ellen Coil Merritt	Feb 27 1829	Sep 1877	Feb 6 1846	Feb 6 1846	33	16								4
	Sarah Brettell	Sep 1824	Mar 23 1882	Aug 2 1869	Aug 2 1869	57	44								1
	Agnes Post			Aug 4 1869		57									0
	Jane Juliet Post			Aug 4 1869		57									0
	Mary Elizabeth Powell			Aug 4 1869		57									0
20	**Brannan, Samuel**	**Mar 2 1819**	**May 5 1889**					**1**	**0**	**1**	**1**	**1**	**3**	**3**	**4**
	Harriet Hatch	May 30 1821	1842	1841		22	20								1na
	Ann Eliza "Lisa" Corwin[46]	Apr 1 1823	Dec 7 1916	by Jun 1844		25	21								4
	Sarah E. Wallace[47]	Jul 12 1825	Mar 17 1845	ca. Sep 1844		25	19								0
	Carmelita Carmen de Llaguno	> 1817	1874	Mar 25 1882		63									0
21	**Brown, Benjamin**	**Sep 30 1794**	**5 22 1878**					**1**	**5**	**2**	**1**	**1**	**0**	**4**	**6**
	Sarah Mumford	Apr 20 1795	Jan 1 1879	Sep 22 1819	Jan 19 1846	24	24								5
	Mary Ann Barker	Feb 18 1825	Sep 8 1846	Dec 23 1845	Jan 19 1846	51	20								1
	Polly Thompson	Jan 29 1822		Feb 6 1846	Feb 6 1846	51	24								0
	Abigail "Abba" Cadwalder	Jan 31 1797	Aug 22 1872	Oct 18 1857		63	60								0
22	**Brown, James Jr.**	**Sep 29 1801**	**Sep 30 1863**					**1**	**1**	**3**	**1**	**7**	**13**	**11**	**15**
	Martha Durfee Stephens	Oct 12 1806	Sep 28 1840	Mar 2 1823	Jan 10 1846	21	16								9na
	Susan Foutz[48]	Feb 14 1823	Aug 18 1842	Jan 25 1841	Jan 10 1846	39	17								na

husbands & wives	birth	death	marriage	sealing	marriage age: husb	marriage age: wife	in JS life: wives	in JS life: children	> JS death: wives	> JS death: children	> Nauvoo: wives	> Nauvoo: children	total: wives	total: children
Esther Jones (Raper)[49]	Jan 7 1814	> 1880	Nov 20 1842	Jan 10 1846	41	28								4
Sarah Steadwell (Wood)[50]	Mar 31 1814	Mar 18 1893	Jan 10 1845	Jan 10 1846	43	30								1
Abigail Smith (Abbott)[†51]	Sep 11 1806	Jul 23 1889	Feb 8 1846	Feb 8 1846	44	39								0
Mary McRee (Black)[†52]	Oct 17 1819	Nov 1 1907	Jul 16 1846		44	26								5
Phebe Abigail Abbott	May 18 1831	Apr 10 1914	Oct 17 1850	Oct 17 1850	49	19								3
Cecelia Henrietta Cornu Robellaz[†]	May 17 1825	Sep 14 1882	Dec 26 1854	Dec 26 1854	53	29								2
Mary Wollerton	ca. 1805		Feb 7 1855	Feb 7 1855	53	50								0
Darthula Catherine Shupe	Dec 27 1834	Mar 3 1911	Feb 17 1856	Feb 17 1856	54	21								0
Lavinia Mitchell	Jul 22 1837	Mar 16 1905	Sep 7 1856	Sep 7 1856	54	19								0
Harriett Wood (Yancey)	Dec 21 1834	Dec 22 1873	Sep 17 1859	Sep 17 1859	57	24								0
Maria Mitchell	Apr 14 1843	Feb 19 1923	Oct 7 1859	Oct 7 1859	58	16								0
23 Bullock, Thomas	**Dec 23 1816**	**Feb 10 1885**					**1**	**3**	**1**	**1**	**1**	**19**	**3**	**23**
Henrietta Rushton[53]	Feb 13 1817	Oct 19 1897	Jun 25 1838	Jan 23 1846	21	21								9
Lucy Caroline Clayton[54]	Mar 21 1820	Apr 16 1879	Jan 23 1846	Jan 23 1846	29	25								6
Betsy Prudence Howard	Jul 22 1835	Jun 12 1893	Dec 9 1852	May 30 1856	35	17								8
24 Burgess, Harrison	**Sep 3 1814**	**Feb 10 1883**					**1**	**0**	**1**	**0**	**1**	**11**	**3**	**11**
Sophia Minerva Foster	Apr 12 1810	Sep 1 1889	Jul 1 1835	Jan 21 1846	20	25								0
Amanda Melvina Hammond	May 6 1827	Aug 8 1882	Feb 6 1846	Feb 6 1846	31	18								11
Rachel Crampton	ca. 1818		Aug 8 1860		45	41								0
25 Butler, John Lowe	**Apr 8 1808**	**Apr 10 1860**					**1**	**8**	**3**	**0**	**4**	**7**	**8**	**15**

	Name	Birth	Death	Married	Sealed										
	Caroline Farozine Skeen[55]	Apr 15 1812	Aug 4 1875	Feb 3 1831	Sep 23 1843	22	18								12
	Charity Skeen	Mar 15 1808	Jul 7 1854	Dec 23 1844	Dec 23 1844	36	36								0
	Sarah Lancaster	Mar 23 1806		Feb 3 1846	Feb 3 1846	37	39								0
	Sarah Bryant (Lancaster)	Jun 28 1771		Feb 6 1846	Feb 6 1846	37	74								0
	Lovisa Hamilton	Sep 25 1837	Jul 9 1924	Mar 9 1857	Mar 9 1857	48	19								1
	Ester Ogden	Aug 6 1839	Jan 2 1923	Mar 9 1857	Mar 9 1857	48	17								0
	Ann Hughes	Feb 19 1795		Mar 9 1857	Mar 9 1857	48	62								0
	Henrietta S. Blyth	Jun 6 1831	Aug 10 1924	Sep 8 1857	Sep 8 1857	49	26								2
26	**Cahoon, Reynolds***[*]	**Apr 30 1790**	**Apr 29 1861**					**2**	**8**	**1**	**1**	**0**	**1**	**3**	**10**
	Thirza Stiles[56]	Oct 18 1789	Nov 20 1866	Dec 11 1810	Jan 16 1846	20	21								7
	Lucina Roberts (Johnson)[57]	Mar 5 1806	1861	1842	Jan 16 1846	52	36								3
	Mary Hilgrath[58]	Oct 21 1794		Jan 16 1846	Jan 16 1846	55	51								0
27	**Cahoon, William Farrington**[59]	**Nov 7 1813**	**Apr 6 1893**					**1**	**6**	**1**	**0**	**2**	**10**	**4**	**16**
	Nancy Miranda Gibbs[†60]	Jul 27 1817	Oct 6 1867	Jan 17 1836	Jan 29 1846	22	18								12
	Mary Wilson Dugdale (Casson)[†61]	Dec 1 1814	Mar 24 1882	Sep 23 1845	Sep 23 1845	31	30								4
	Elvina Marshall Jones	Aug 5 1824	1915	Jun 12 1871	Jun 12 1871	57	46								0
	Oleana Olsen	ca. 1820	ca. 1910	Feb 28 1878		64	58								0
28	**Callister, Thomas**[62]	**Jul 8 1821**	**Dec 1 1880**					**0**	**0**	**2**	**0**	**2**	**32**	**4**	**32**
	Caroline Clara Smith	Jun 6 1820	Jan 8 1895	Aug 31 1845	Oct 10 1863	24	25								8
	Helen Mar Clark	Jul 17 1829	Dec 4 1917	Dec 16 1845	Dec 16 1845	24	16								12
	Mary Lavina Phelps	Sep 27 1845	Mar 9 1828	Dec 19 1863	Dec 19 1863	42	18								11
	Caroline Eliza Lyman	Aug 1 1851	Mar 20 1879	Feb 14 1878	Feb 14 1878	56	26								1

husbands & wives	birth	death	marriage	sealing	marriage age: husb	marriage age: wife	in JS life: wives	in JS life: children	> JS death: wives	> JS death: children	> Nauvoo: wives	> Nauvoo: children	total: wives	total: children
29 Canfield, Cyrus Culver	**Dec 20 1817**	**Dec 1889**					**1**	**0**	**1**	**1**	**1**	**4**	**3**	**5**
Louisa Jones[63]	Oct 17 1812	Nov 25 1872	Oct 9 1841	Jan 31 1846	23	28								0
Clarissa Jones	Jul 6 1815	Nov 27 1892	1844	Jan 31 1846	26	29								5
Laura Albina Allen (Shaw)	Sep 19 1829	Jun 2 1871	Jun 15 1851		33	21								0
30 Carmichael, William	**Aug 15 1804**	**Apr 21 1868**					**0**		**2**		**1**		**3**	**0**
Mary Ann Wilson	Oct 29 1808	Oct 26 1866	Jan 17 1846	Jan 17 1846	41	37								
Mary Clark (Wilson)†[64]	Sep 8 1788	Aug 19 1852	Jan 28 1846	Jan 28 1846	41	57								
Emma Wright	May 27 1849		Feb 9 1867	Feb 9 1867	62	17								
31 Carrington, Albert	**Jan 8 1813**	**Sep 19 1889**					**1**	**4**	**1**	**1**	**0**	**10**	**2**	**15**
Rhoda Maria Woods[65]	Mar 22 1824	Aug 1 1886	Dec 6 1838	Jan 31 1846	25	14								15
Mary Ann Rock[66]	Mar 4 1822	Jun 1 1895	ca. 1846	Jan 31 1846	33	24								0
32 Carter, Dominicus	**Jun 21 1806**	**Feb 2 1884**					**1**	**1**	**3**	**1**	**5**	**34**	**9**	**36**
Lydia Smith[67]	Jan 17 1809	Oct 23 1838	May 11 1828	Jan 13 1846	21	19								na
Sylvia Ameretta Meacham[68]	Jul 28 1820	May 24 1894	Mar 28 1839		32	18								1
Mary Durfee[69]	Mar 21 1830	Dec 6 1885	Jan 26 1845	Jan 26 1845	38	14								13
Sophronia Babcock[69]	Jul 14 1822	Aug 26 1847	Nov 15 1845	Nov 15 1845	39	23								1
Eliza Babcock[70]	Oct 8 1828	1874	Jan 10 1846		39	17								0
Polly Miner	May 5 1832	Mar 15 1896	Oct 9 1851	Oct 9 1851	45	19								10
Elizabeth Brown	Jun 18 1833	Sep 9 1914	Jun 20 1852	Jun 20 1852	45	19								8
Caroline Maria Hubbard[71]	Mar 22 1833	Oct 2 1907	Oct 20 1854	Oct 20 1854	48	21								2

Frances Nash	Oct 4 1837	May 16 1908	Jan 6 1857	Jan 6 1857	50	19							1
Charlotte Duke	Sep 30 1856	Apr 4 1921	Dec 10 1873		67	17							0
33 Carter, Simeon	**Jun 7 1794**	**Feb 3 1869**					**1**	**2**	**2**	**0**	**1**	**3**	**4**	**5**
Lydia Kenyon	Dec 11 1801	Dec 10 1866	Dec 2 1818	Dec 15 1845	24	16							2
Hannah Dunham	Jan 23 1800		Jan 19 1846	Jan 19 1846	51	45							0
Matilda Phebe Cochran	Jan 26 1828	Apr 8 1896	Jan 20 1846	Jan 20 1846	51	17							0
Louisa Gibbons	Jan 27 1820	Oct 22 1902	Nov 4 1849	Nov 26 1849	55	29							3
34 Chamberlain, Solomon	**Jul 30 1788**	**Mar 26 1862**					**1**	**3**	**1**	**0**	**1**	**1**	**3**	**4**
Hopestill Haskins	Apr 7 1787	Jan 12 1847	Oct 23 1809		21	22							3
Emiline Shepherd	Oct 6 1805		Jan 15 1846	Jan 15 1846	57	40							0
Terressa Morse (Bridges)[72]	Oct 20 1813	Mar 20 1862	1847		59	33							1
35 Chase, Isaac	**Dec 12 1791**	**May 26 1861**					**1**	**6**	**2**	**0**	**2**	**0**	**5**	**6**
Phoebe Ogden (Ross)	Dec 7 1794	Jul 10 1872	Aug 18 1818	Jan 21 1846	26	23							6
Rosanna Whipple	Jun 14 1793		Jan 21 1846	Jan 21 1846	54	52							0
Rebecca Pierce	Nov 13 1791	Jul 31 1851	Jan 27 1846	Jan 27 1846	54	54							0
Elizabeth Calvert	Feb 3 1825	Mar 20 1885	Jul 7 1850	Jul 7 1850	58	25							0
Charlotte Walters (Felshaw)	Nov 28 1824	Sep 12 1884	Apr 15 1855	Apr 15 1855	63	30							0
36 Cheney, Aaron	**Jul 14 1787**	**Sep 18 1862**					**1**	**8**	**1**	**0**	**1**	**0**	**3**	**8**
Mehitable Wells	Jan 31 1787	Nov 30 1869	Aug 14 1807	Jan 16 1846	20	20							8
Sarah Griffith	Sep 12 1790		Jan 21 1846	Jan 21 1846	58	55							0
Louisa Pizel	ca. 1791												0
37 Chesley, Alexander Philip	**Oct 22 1814**	**Aug 9 1884**					**1**	**1**	**1**	**1**	**0**	**9**	**2**	**11**

	husbands & wives	birth	death	marriage	sealing	marriage age husb	marriage age wife	in JS life wives	in JS life children	> JS death wives	> JS death children	> Nauvoo wives	> Nauvoo children	total wives	total children
	Mary Eliza Haws[73]	Oct 30 1822	Nov 21 1870	1843	Apr 3 1848	28	20								6
	Emily Haws[74]	Jul 23 1826	Aug 11 1902	1846	Apr 3 1848	31	19								5
38	**Clapp, Benjamin Lynn**	**Aug 19 1814**	**Oct 31 1865**					**1**	**5**	**2**	**0**	**1**	**7**	**4**	**12**
	Mary Rachel Shultz[75]	Apr 2 1815	Nov 13 1874	ca. 1830	Jan 13 1846	16	15								10
	Elvira Randall	Feb 26 1825	Sep 25 1876	Jan 13 1846	Jan 13 1846	31	20								0
	Ann Bingham Thomas	Apr 1 1813	Nov 24 1887	Jan 26 1846	Jan 26 1846	31	32								0
	Ane Kjerstine Mortensen	Sep 14 1837	Apr 12 1898	Oct 12 1856	Oct 12 1856	42	19								2
39	**Clark, Raymond**	**Feb 20 1798**	**Sep 22 1853**					**1**	**6**	**2**	**1**	**1**	**4**	**4**	**11**
	Louisa Gill	Jan 25 1810	Feb 19 1847	Sep 16 1827	Feb 2 1846	29	17								7
	Mary Carpenter	Dec 26 1819		Feb 6 1846	Feb 6 1846	47	26								0
	Elizabeth Andrews	Mar 13 1822		Feb 6 1846	Feb 6 1846	47	23								0
	Hannah Miller	Jan 2 1811	Feb 11 1887	May 2 1847		49	36								4
40	**Clayton, William***	**Jul 17 1814**	**Dec 4 1879**					**2**	**5**	**3**	**2**	**5**	**40**	**10**	**47**
	Ruth Moon[76]	Jun 13 1817	Jan 15 1894	Oct 9 1836	Jul 22 1843	22	19								10
	Margaret Moon[77]	Jan 14 1820	Aug 25 1870	Apr 27 1843	Apr 27 1843	28	23								6
	Alice Hardman[78]	Apr 5 1816	Nov 11 1894	Sep 13 1844	Sep 13 1844	30	28								4
	Jane Hardman[79]	May 23 1805	Jan 2 1868	Nov 20 1844	Nov 20 1844	30	39								0
	Diantha Farr	Oct 12 1828	Sep 11 1850	Jan 9 1845	Jan 9 1845	30	16								3
	Augusta Braddock	Nov 24 1833	Mar 13 1924	Oct 5 1850	Oct 5 1850	36	16								8
	Sarah Ann Walters	Nov 16 1838	Mar 1 1915	Nov 30 1856	Nov 30 1856	42	18								11

	Maria Louisa Lyman[80]	May 8 1849	Jul 5 1877	Oct 3 1866	Oct 3 1866	52	17								1
	Elizabeth Mort Ainsworth	1824	Sep 10 1877	Dec 19 1869	Dec 19 1869	55	45								0
	Anna Elizabeth Higgs	Dec 28 1853	Jan 24 1947	Dec 30 1870	Dec 30 1870	56	17								4
41	**Coltrin, Zebedee**	**Sep 7 1804**	**Jul 20 1887**					**1**	**1**	**2**	**1**	**1**	**8**	**4**	**10**
	Julia Ann Jennings	Jun 1 1813	Oct 24 1841	ca. 1828	Jan 20 1846	24	15								na
	Mary Mott	Nov 27 1820	Mar 3 1886	Feb 5 1841	Jan 20 1846	36	20								10
	Sarah Oyler (Mackley)[†81]	Dec 8 1801	Jan 8 1886	Feb 6 1846	Feb 6 1846	41	44								0
	Hannah Husted (Marsh)[†82]	Feb 28 1797	1862	Feb 6 1846	Feb 6 1846	41	48								0
	Lavina Elizabeth Fullmer[83]	Mar 5 1838	Jul 21 1907	Feb 25 1857	Feb 25 1857	52	18								0
42	**Coolidge, Joseph Wellington***	**May 31 1814**	**Jan 13 1871**					**2**	**5**	**3**	**2**	**0**	**6**	**5**	**13**
	Elizabeth Buchanan[84]	Jul 1 1815	Jun 23 1913	Dec 17 1834	Jan 21 1846	20	19								11
	Mary Ann Buchanan[85]	Aug 1 1829		<Jun 27 1844	Jan 21 1846	30	14								0
	Elizabeth Jane Tuttle	Sep 6 1823	May 4 1890	Jan 21 1846	Jan 21 1846	31	22								2
	Rebecca Atwood	Oct 25 1825	Nov 24 1906	Jan 26 1846	Jan 26 1846	31	20								0
	Rosilla Milla Carter[86]	Feb 22 1825		Feb 6 1846	Feb 6 1846	31	20								0
43	**Coon, Abraham**	**Apr 3 1810**	**Mar 28 1885**					**1**	**8**	**1**	**1**	**2**	**7**	**4**	**16**
	Elizabeth Yarbrough[87]	Dec 23 1808	Jan 15 1894	1829	May 11 1848	19	20								10
	Frances Yarbrough	Mar 3 1825	Apr 1847	1846	May 11 1848	36	21								1
	Mary Elizabeth Wilson	Feb 19 1827	Jul 2 1856	ca. 1847	May 11 1848	37	20								5
	Sarah Wright (Curtis)[88]	Feb 7 1812	Feb 6 1882	Feb 7 1858		47	46								0
44	**Coons, Lebbeus Thaddeus**	**May 13 1811**	**Jul 7 1872**					**1**		**3**		**0**		**4**	**0**
	Mary Ann Williamson	Aug 11 1812	Nov 24 1867	Jan 24 1832	Jan 24 1846	20	19								

	husbands & wives	birth	death	marriage	sealing	marriage age: husb	marriage age: wife	in JS life: wives	in JS life: children	> JS death: wives	> JS death: children	> Nauvoo: wives	> Nauvoo: children	total: wives	total: children
	Esther Harvey	ca. 1811		Dec 31 1845	Jul 13 1867	34	34								
	Sarah King (Hillman)†	Aug 24 1793	May 25 1870	Jan 24 1846	Jan 24 1846	34	52								
	Elizabeth Maria Defoe	Mar 31 1809		Jan 24 1846	Jan 24 1846	34	36								
45	**Covey, Benjamin**	**Mar 9 1792**	**Mar 13 1868**					**1**	**4**	**3**	**0**	**0**	**0**	**4**	**4**
	Almira Mack (Scobey)[89]	Apr 23 1806	Mar 13 1886	Oct 23 1836	Jan 21 1846	44	30								4
	Diana Cole	May 27 1819	Dec 9 1847	Jan 21 1846	Jan 21 1846	53	26								0
	Phoebe Cowles	Jul 6 1796	Apr 6 1850	Jan 21 1846	Jan 21 1846	53	49								0
	Elizabeth Skinner[90]	Jan 1 1805		Jan 21 1846	Jan 21 1846	53	41								0
46	**Cox, Frederick Walter**	**Jan 20 1812**	**Jun 5 1879**					**1**	**4**	**2**	**2**	**3**	**33**	**6**	**39**
	Emeline Sally Whiting[91]	Jul 23 1817	Mar 4 1896	Jul 22 1835	Jan 27 1846	23	17								12
	Cordelia Calista Morley†[92]	Nov 28 1823	Jun 10 1915	<Jun 21 1845	Jan 27 1846	33	22								8
	Jemimah Losee	Sep 30 1823	Mar 8 1901	Jan 27 1846	Jan 27 1846	34	22								9
	Lydia Margery Losee	Jul 24 1837	Dec 27 1921	Oct 11 1854	Oct 11 1854	42	17								3
	Mary Ann D. Richardson	Feb 28 1818		Oct 11 1854	Jan 8 1858	42	36								2
	Emma Smith Peterson	Jul 27 1850	Nov 22 1900	Oct 11 1869	Oct 11 1869	57	19								5
47	**Crismon, Charles**[93]	**Dec 25 1807**	**Mar 23 1893**					**1**	**6**	**1**	**0**	**4**	**28**	**6**	**34**
	Mary "Polly" Hill[94]	Oct 1 1814	May 15 1892	May 6 1830	Jan 20 1846	22	15								11
	Elizabeth Hill	Nov 14 1818	Dec 27 1882	<Jan 20 1846	Jan 20 1846	38	27								0
	Louisa Christine Bischoff	Mar 30 1843	May 3 1911	May 10 1862	May 10 1862	54	19								12
	Ellen Wilcox	Oct 24 1840	Feb 23 1921	May 10 1862	May 10 1862	54	21								10

	Christina Amelia Hassel	Jun 27 1852	Apr 16 1903	Oct 12 1867		59	15							1
	Mary Grey	ca. 1811												0
48	**Cutler, Alpheus**	**Feb 29 1784**	**Aug 10 1864**					**1**	**11**	**6**	**0**	**0**	**0**	**7**	**11**
	Lois Lathrop[95]	Sep 24 1788	Mar 23 1878	Nov 17 1808	Nov 15 1843	24	20							11
	Luana Beebe	Oct 13 1814		Jan 14 1846	Jan 14 1846	61	31							0
	Margaret Carr	Oct 16 1771		Feb 3 1846	Feb 3 1846	61	74							0
	Abigail Carr	Oct 4 1780		Feb 3 1846	Feb 3 1846	61	65							0
	Sally Cox	Feb 26 1794		Feb 3 1846	Feb 3 1846	61	51							0
	Disey Caroline McCall	Oct 26 1802		Feb 3 1846	Feb 3 1846	61	43							0
	Henrietta Clarinda Miller	Nov 16 1822		Feb 3 1846	Feb 3 1846	61	23							0
49	**Dana, Charles Root**	**Nov 8 1802**	**Aug 7 1868**					**1**	**7**	**2**	**0**	**5**	**17**	**8**	**24**
	Margaret Kennedy	Apr 1 1807	Jun 15 1850	1827	Jan 23 1846	25	20							7
	Susan Luce (Thomas)[†96]	Jan 1 1808	May 9 1886	Jan 23 1846	Jan 23 1846	43	38							0
	Emily Waterman	Dec 15 1826		Jan 23 1846	Jan 23 1846	43	19							0
	Harriet Elizabeth Gibson	Apr 4 1831	1858	Dec 1 1850	Jan 20 1852	48	19							2
	Jane Dorothy Culley	Jan 2 1831	Sep 2 1899	Sep 14 1857	Sep 14 1857	54	26							5
	Mary Ann Cato	Aug 19 1833	Jul 9 1922	Sep 14 1857	Sep 14 1857	54	24							7
	Ann Barlow	Nov 16 1837	Mar 25 1895	Sep 14 1857	Sep 14 1857	54	19							0
	Elizabeth Culley	Oct 11 1835	Jul 26 1905	Sep 14 1857	Sep 14 1857	54	21							3
50	**Dayton, Hiram**	**Nov 1 1798**	**Dec 10 1881**					**1**	**11**	**1**	**0**	**6**	**9**	**8**	**20**
	Permelia Bundy[97]	Jul 28 1799	Jan 10 1881	Nov 1 1820	Jan 13 1846	22	21							11
	Sophia Lance (Thorton)	Feb 1 1826	Dec 22 1861	Jan 27 1846	Jan 27 1846	47	19							7

	husbands & wives	birth	death	marriage	sealing	marriage age husb	marriage age wife	in JS life wives	in JS life children	> JS death wives	> JS death children	> Nauvoo wives	> Nauvoo children	total wives	total children
	Nancy Lance	Nov 2 1818	Apr 28 1879	Feb 24 1848	Feb 24 1848	49	29								2
	Mary Lance	Dec 9 1819		Feb 24 1848		49	28								
	Lucy Ann Millard	1802		May 26 1857	May 26 1857	58	55								0
	Nancy Allen	1802		Jul 6 1870		71	68								0
	Mindwell Bundy	1798		Jul 6 1870		71	72								0
	Louise Jones	1802		Jul 6 1870		71	68								0
51	**Decker, Isaac**	**Dec 29 1799**	**Jun 13 1873**					**0**	**0**	**2**	**0**	**3**	**12**	**5**	**12**
	Harriet Page Wheeler[98]	Sep 7 1803	Dec 23 1871	< Dec 31 1820	Jan 26 1846	21	17								6na
	Maria Louisa Roberts	Nov 11 1824	Sep 16 1903	Jan 29 1846	Jan 29 1846	46	21								0
	Fanny Eliza Green	Jan 17 1821	Mar 7 1901	Jan 29 1846	Jan 29 1846	46	25								0
	Hannah Herbert	Dec 11 1840	Dec 13 1865	Feb 15 1857	Feb 15 1857	57	16								5
	Anna Lucas	Mar 22 1835	May 17 1886	May 31 1857	May 31 1857	57	22								7
	Delight Day	Mar 6 1804	Oct 24 1883												0
52	**Draper, William**	**Apr 24 1807**	**May 28 1886**					**1**	**8**	**1**	**1**	**5**	**46**	**7**	**55**
	Elizabeth Staker[99]	Feb 25 1806	Apr 9 1888	Jun 11 1827	Jan 28 1846	20	21								11
	Martha Raymer (Weaver)[†100]	Jul 8 1804	Oct 28 1849	Jan 28 1846	Jan 28 1846	38	41								1
	Mary Ann Manhardt	Aug 15 1827	Jul 30 1909	Apr 27 1848	Apr 27 1848	41	20								14
	Marial Thompson (Crosby Bent)	May 7 1808	May 19 1893	May 6 1848	May 6 1848	41	39								1
	Mary Howarth	Feb 14 1831	Mar 9 1902	Dec 18 1853	Dec 18 1853	46	22								10
	Fannie Newton	Mar 1 1834	Mar 18 1907	Dec 18 1853	Dec 18 1853	46	19								7

	Ruth Hannah Newton	Apr 1 1837	Apr 14 1896	Apr 17 1854	Apr 17 1854	46	17								11
53	**Durfee, Jabez**	**Dec 26 1791**	**Apr 1867**					**1**	**0**	**1**	**0**	**1**	**0**	**3**	**0**
	Electa Cranston	1790	ca. Feb 1834	1811	Jan 21 1846	19	21								8na
	Elizabeth Davis (Goldsmith Brackenbury)[101]	Mar 11 1791	Dec 16 1876	Mar 3 1834		42	42								0
	Magdalena "Laura" Pickle (Durfee)[†102]	Jun 3 1788	May 17 1850	Jan 21 1846	Jan 21 1846	54	57								0
	Sarah[103]	ca. 1800													
54	**Dykes, George Parker**	**Dec 24 1814**	**Feb 25 1888**					**1**	**2**	**2**	**1**	**3**	**3**	**6**	**6**
	Dorcas Keeling	Nov 30 1811	Dec 17 1881	Nov 1 1835	Jan 9 1846	20	23								3
	Cynthia Soles	Feb 6 1800	Jan 11 1847	Jan 9 1846	Jan 9 1846	31	45								0
	Alciva Durfee	Mar 24 1831		Jan 9 1846	Jan 9 1846	31	14								0
	Louisa Jane Stevenson	Jan 4 1808	Jan 10 1863	Oct 25 1853		38	45								3
	Cornelia A. Hill	1839	1888	Oct 31 1872		57	33								0
	Mary Rice[104]														0
55	**Edwards, William**	**May 16 1810**	**Jun 3 1883**					**1**	**0**	**1**	**0**	**1**	**4**	**3**	**4**
	Eliza M. Allred[105]	Aug 31 1826	Aug 16 1875	Jan 1 1844		33	17								0
	Elizabeth Gilbert	Oct 2 1802		Jan 31 1846	May 5 1848	35	43								0
	Ruth Lucas	Jan 7 1835	Jan 31 1903	Dec 9 1854	Dec 9 1854	44	19								4
56	**Egan, Howard***	**Jun 15 1815**	**Mar 15 1878**					**2**	**1**	**1**	**0**	**1**	**8**	**4**	**9**
	Tamson Parshley[106]	Jul 27 1824	Mar 31 1905	Dec 1 1838	Jan 23 1846	23	14								6
	Catherine Reese (Clawson)[107]	Jan 27 1804	Nov 7 1860	early 1844	1844	28	40								
	Nancy A. Redding	Oct 6 1825	Apr 3 1892	Jan 23 1846	Jan 23 1846	30	20								2
	Mary Ann Tuttle	Jun 5 1830	Dec 10 1910	1849	Nov 9 1860	34	19								1

husbands & wives	birth	death	marriage	sealing	marriage age: husb	marriage age: wife	in JS life: wives	in JS life: children	> JS death: wives	> JS death: children	> Nauvoo: wives	> Nauvoo: children	total: wives	total: children
57 Farr, Winslow Sr.	**Jan 12 1794**	**Aug 25 1867**					**1**	**6**	**4**	**0**	**1**	**0**	**6**	**6**
Olive Hovey Freeman[108]	Jun 23 1799	Mar 10 1893	Dec 5 1816	Jan 9 1845	22	17								6
Almira Randall	Nov 28 1814		Jan 22 1846	Jan 22 1846	52	31								0
Adelia Maria Clemens (Gribble)	Oct 14 1820	Sep 5 1904	Jan 22 1846	Jan 22 1846	52	25								0
Amanda Bower Colburn	Dec 29 1826	Feb 8 1850	Feb 7 1846	Feb 7 1846	52	19								0
Roxana Porter (Freeman)†[108]	Sep 18 1796	> 1860	Feb 22 1846	Feb 22 1846	52	49								0
Achsach Cole	Dec 20 1818	Jan 26 1883	Feb 3 1856	Feb 3 1856	62	37								0
58 Felshaw, William*	**Feb 3 1800**	**Sep 24 1867**					**2**	**9**	**1**	**2**	**0**	**6**	**3**	**17**
Mary Harriet Gilbert[109]	Jun 23 1808	Aug 26 1871	Feb 1 1827	Jan 16 1846	26	18								13
Charlotte Walters	Nov 28 1824	Sep 12 1884	Jul 28 1843	Feb 7 1846	43	18								4
Elizabeth Cheney	Jun 7 1814		Jan 29 1846	Jan 29 1846	45	31								0
59 Fielding, Joseph	**Mar 26 1797**	**Dec 19 1863**					**1**	**3**	**1**	**2**	**2**	**5**	**4**	**10**
Hannah Greenwood[110]	Sep 4 1808	Sep 9 1877	Jun 11 1838	Jan 23 1846	41	29								7
Mary Ann Peake (Greenhalch)[111]	Oct 29 1802	Jan 12 1885	ca. 1845	Jan 23 1846	48	43								3
Mary Duff	Jan 16 1782													0
Mary Farras														0
60 Fleming, Josiah Wolcott	**Apr 25 1808**	**Jan 6 1873**					**1**	**2**	**1**	**0**	**1**	**0**	**3**	**2**
Nancy Ann Bigler (Whiteman)[112]	Aug 6 1810	Jul 3 1886	Jun 3 1828	Feb 7 1846	20	17								2
Nancy Simpson Henderson[113]	Jan 13 1827	Dec 18 1863	Feb 7 1846	Feb 7 1846	37	19								0
Mary Bunnell	Jun 18 1842		Feb 26 1857	Feb 26 1857	48	14								0

61	**Fordham, Elijah**	**May 12 1798**	**Sep 9 1879**					**1**	**3**	**1**	**0**	**3**	**5**	**5**	**8**
	Jane Ann Fisher	Apr 13 1802	Jul 17 1828	Nov 23 1822	Jan 16 1846	24	20								2na
	Bothia Fisher	Apr 12 1805	Mar 11 1834	Apr 12 1830	Jan 16 1846	31	25								na
	Anna Bibbins Chaffee[114]	May 24 1811	Dec 8 1881	Oct 3 1838	Jan 16 1846	40	27								6
	Clarissa Brooks	Aug 15 1799		Feb 3 1846	Feb 3 1846	47	46								0
	Elizabeth Hughes	Mar 31 1839	1839	Mar 21 1856	Mar 21 1856	57	16								1
	Jane McCausland	Mar 12 1828	Mar 5 1905	Apr 1 1856	Apr 1 1856	57	28								1
	Amelia Brown (Spencer)[115]	May 15 1804	May 18 1877	Apr 1 1856	Apr 1 1856	57	51								0
62	**Foster, Lucian Rose**[116]	**Nov 19 1806**	**Mar 18 1876**					**0**	**1**	**4**		**0**		**4**	**1**
	Harriet Eliza Burr	Nov 22 1814		by 1846	Jan 24 1846	39	32								1
	Mary Ann Graham	Apr 25 1819		Jan 24 1846	Jan 24 1846	39	26								
	Ann Maria Still	Aug 31 1825		Jan 24 1846	Jan 24 1846	39	20								
	Maria Fosdick	Apr 7 1827		Feb 6 1846	Feb 6 1846	39	18								
63	**Foutz, Jacob**	**Nov 20 1800**	**Feb 14 1848**					**1**	**10**	**1**	**1**	**1**	**1**	**3**	**12**
	Margaret Mann[117]	Dec 14 1802	Aug 5 1896	Jul 22 1822	Jan 28 1846	21	19								12
	Lucinda Loretta Loss	Feb 17 1823		Jan 31 1846	Jan 31 1846	45	22								0
	Mattie Secrest				Oct 24 1888										0
64	**Fullmer, David**	**Jul 7 1803**	**Oct 21 1879**					**1**	**5**	**2**	**1**	**0**	**14**	**3**	**20**
	Rhoda Ann Marvin[118]	Feb 12 1813	Aug 17 1892	Sep 18 1831	Fall 1843	28	18								11
	Sarah Sophronia Oysterbanks	Sep 22 1822	Jan 1 1906	Dec 7 1845	Jan 19 1846	42	23								9
	Margaret Phillips[119]	May 26 1800	1890	Jan 19 1846	Jan 19 1846	42	45								0
65	**Fullmer, John Solomon**	**Jul 21 1807**	**Oct 8 1883**					**1**	**4**	**1**	**1**	**1**	**26**	**3**	**31**

husbands & wives	birth	death	marriage	sealing	marriage age husb	marriage age wife	in JS life wives	in JS life children	> JS death wives	> JS death children	> Nauvoo wives	> Nauvoo children	total wives	total children
Mary Ann Price[120]	Sep 16 1815	Nov 29 1897	May 24 1837	Jan 15 1846	29	21								8
Olive Amanda Smith (Cook)	Sep 15 1825	Mar 17 1885	Jan 21 1846	Jan 21 1846	38	20								10
Sarah Ann Stevenson	Jul 31 1835	Sep 7 1901	Sep 3 1856	Oct 12 1856	49	21								13
66 Garner, William	**Jan 22 1817**	**Mar 29 1892**					**1**	**4**	**1**	**2**	**1**	**7**	**3**	**13**
Sarah Workman[121]	Jan 27 1818	May 11 1904	Sep 4 1838	Feb 3 1846	21	20								12
Elizabeth Ann Dunn	Sep 20 1828		Feb 3 1846	Feb 3 1846	29	17								1
Bethzina Burns	Nov 4 1842		Mar 16 1857		40	14								0
67 Gates, Jacob	**Mar 9 1811**	**Apr 14 1892**					**1**	**0**	**1**	**0**	**4**	**13**	**6**	**13**
Mary Minerva Snow	Jul 30 1813	Feb 9 1891	Mar 16 1833	Jan 21 1846	22	19								0
Elizabeth Caroline Hutchings	Jul 7 1826	Sep 15 1846	Jan 21 1846	Jan 21 1846	34	19								0
Emma Forsberry	Jul 27 1830	Oct 12 1907	Oct 23 1853	Sep 17 1859	42	23								6
Lydia Clementine Wise	Apr 1 1840		Jul 13 1856	Jul 13 1856	45	16								0
Sarah Meredith	Jul 13 1842		Nov 1 1861	Nov 1 1861	50	19								0
Mary Ware	Feb 19 1844	Jan 7 1909	Oct 25 1862	Oct 25 1862	51	18								7
68 Gee, Lysander	**Sep 1 1818**	**Jun 27 1894**					**1**	**1**	**1**	**0**	**1**	**21**	**3**	**22**
Amanda Melvina Sagers[122]	May 5 1821	Oct 22 1848	Sep 5 1838	Feb 4 1846	20	17								2
Theresa Bowley[123]	Oct 7 1828	May 9 1902	Feb 12 1846	Jul 18 1850	27	17								11
Maryetta Rowe[124]	Oct 3 1831	12 20 1866	Jul 18 1850	Jul 18 1850	31	18								9
69 Goddard, Stephen Hezekiah	**Aug 23 1810**	**Sep 10 1898**					**1**	**0**	**1**	**0**	**2**	**0**	**4**	**0**
Isabella Bisbee[125]	May 26 1812	ca. 1839	Nov 14 1833	Jan 19 1846	23	21								na

	Zerviah Norwood Roby	Feb 20 1803	> 1851	Sep 11 1839	Jan 19 1846	29	36								0
	Alamantha Goddard	May 31 1831	Apr 24 1847	Dec 17 1845	Feb 6 1846	35	14								0
	Lucinda Vaughan				Apr 21 1857										
	Mary Ann Sears Lewis		Mar 10 1873		Nov 27 1871										
70	**Graham, James**	**Oct 11 1804**	**Dec 9 1857**					**1**	**9**	**1**	**2**	**3**	**2**	**5**	**13**
	Mary Ann Butler[126]	Apr 18 1804	Sep 19 1846	ca. 1824	Feb 3 1846	20	20								11
	Orilla Crandall	Jan 29 1803		Feb 3 1846	Feb 3 1846	41	43								0
	Sarah Thompson	Sep 10 1810		Feb 28 1848	Feb 28 1848	43	37								0
	Christiana Gregory (Read)	Mar 19 1795	Mar 25 1874	ca. 1849	Sep 9 1849	44	54								0
	Hannah Tucker Reed	May 10 1821	Dec 11 1904	Sep 9 1849	Sep 9 1849	44	28								2
71	**Grant, George Davis**	**Sep 10 1812**	**Sep 29 1876**					**1**	**3**	**1**	**2**	**5**	**10**	**7**	**15**
	Elizabeth Wilson	Apr 26 1816		Jan 22 1834	Jan 23 1846	21	17								7
	Margaret Leonisa Redding	Feb 17 1823		Jan 23 1846	Jan 23 1846	33	22								0
	Elizabeth Dubois (Lamb)	Aug 25 1823	Jul 22 1911	Feb 2 1851	Feb 2 1851	38	27								5
	Magdalene Baxter	Apr 22 1833	Jan 30 1927	Jan 18 1857	Jan 18 1857	44	23								1
	Susan Fairchild Noble	Jul 25 1832	Mar 9 1914	Jan 1 1858		45	25								1
	Rosetta Robison	Apr 26 1833	May 18 1873	Feb 16 1858		45	24								0
	Sarah Ann Thurston	May 26 1835	Mar 3 1909	Feb 16 1858	Apr 25 1868	45	22								1
72	**Grover, Thomas**	**Jul 22 1807**	**Feb 20 1886**					**1**	**2**	**2**	**3**	**3**	**38**	**6**	**43**
	Caroline Whiting	Jun 25 1809	Oct 17 1840	1828	Aug 1843	20	18								na
	Caroline Eliza Nickerson (Hubbard)[127]	Jun 25 1808	Jul 28 1889	Feb 20 1841	Aug 1843	33	32								4
	Hannah Tupper	Mar 23 1823	Dec 15 1893	Dec 17 1844	Dec 17 1844	37	21								14

husbands & wives	birth	death	marriage	sealing	marriage age husb	marriage age wife	in JS life wives	in JS life children	> JS death wives	> JS death children	> Nauvoo wives	> Nauvoo children	total wives	total children
Laduska Salome Tupper	May 22 1828	Mar 27 1902	Jan 20 1846	Jan 20 1846	38	17								7
Emma Walker	Mar 15 1837	Dec 5 1920	Oct 29 1856	Oct 29 1856	49	19								9
Amaretto Acton	Apr 19 1838		Dec 28 1856	Dec 28 1856	49	18								
Elizabeth Walker	Oct 17 1839	Mar 1 1918	Jan 24 1857	Jan 24 1857	49	17								9
73 Hadden, Alfred Sidney	**Jan 13 1813**	**Apr 27 1895**					**1**	**4**	**1**	**0**	**1**	**21**	**3**	**25**
Julia Ann Hall	Aug 9 1813	May 1847	Oct 10 1831	Sep 16 1961	18	18								4
Mary Caroline Carter[128]	Mar 6 1827	Oct 19 1869	ca. 1846	Mar 28 1847	33	18								11
Sarah Ann Carter[129]	Jun 5 1829	Jun 18 1916	Mar 28 1847	Mar 28 1847	34	17								10
74 Hallett, Clark Thatcher	**May 5 1810**	**1852**					**1**		**1**		**0**		**2**	**0**
Phebe Bray	Apr 25 1808	1852	Sep 18 1830	Jan 20 1846	20	22								
Anna Rassory Gould	Feb 10 1818	1852	Jan 24 1846	Jan 24 1846	35	27								
75 Hancock, Levi Ward	**Apr 7 1803**	**Jun 10 1882**					**1**	**6**	**1**	**1**	**4**	**12**	**6**	**19**
Clarissa Reed	Dec 18 1814	Jan 17 1860	Mar 29 1833	Jan 16 1846	29	18								9
Fanny Myrick[130]	Aug 11 1831	May 9 1911	1846		43	14								0
Emily Melissa Richey	Mar 12 1830	Apr 26 1857	Feb 24 1849	Feb 24 1849	45	18								4
Elizabeth Woodville Hovey	May 11 1835	May 24 1879	Feb 19 1856	Feb 19 1856	52	20								0
Anne Tew	Jul 18 1835	1884	Jul 19 1857	Jul 19 1857	54	22								6
Maren Morgansen (Anderson Pedersen)	Sep 8 1819	1880	Aug 9 1868	Aug 9 1868	65	48								0
76 Harmon, Jesse Pierce	**Aug 11 1795**	**Dec 24 1877**					**1**	**4**	**1**	**0**	**4**	**0**	**6**	**4**
Anna Barnes	Mar 6 1798	Jan 16 1847	Apr 29 1819	Jan 24 1846	23	21								4

Margaret Allen	Jan 11 1798		Feb 6 1846	Feb 6 1846	50	48								0
Nancy Calkins	ca. 1840	ca. 1875	Oct 19 1861	Oct 19 1861	66	20								0
Lucy Calkins				Dec 26 1870										0
Lovina Hazl				Dec 26 1870										0
Laura Ann Shaw				Dec 26 1870										0
77 Harris, Emer	**May 29 1781**	**Nov 28 1869**					**1**	**4**	**1**	**1**	**1**	**0**	**3**	**5**
Roxana Peas	Dec 5 1781	Feb 9 1814	Jul 22 1802	Dec 19 1961	21	20								6na
Deborah Lott	Nov 1799	Mar 18 1825	Jan 16 1819	Aug 28 1867	37	19								5na
Parna Chappel	Nov 12 1792	Jun 4 1857	Mar 29 1826	Jan 30 1846	44	33								4
Polly Chamberlain[131]	Feb 6 1812	Jun 9 1849	Jan 11 1846	Jan 11 1846	64	33								1
Martha Allen (Richards)	Mar 15 1803	May 4 1860	Sep 10 1855	Sep 10 1855	74	52								0
78 Hatch, Isaac Burrus	**Feb 14 1823**	**Mar 25 1853**					**0**	**0**	**2**	**0**	**0**	**5**	**2**	**5**
Mary Jane Garlick[132]	Aug 12 1822	Jul 8 1900	Sep 10 1845	1858	22	23								3
Hannah Garlick	Jun 1 1818	Jun 5 1892	Spring 1846		23	27								2
79 Hatfield, John	**Nov 29 1818**						**1**	**0**	**1**	**0**	**0**	**0**	**2**	**0**
Lucy Clark[133]	Jul 14 1821		Dec 31 1840	Jan 15 1846	22	19								0
Lucinda Curtis[134]	Mar 24 1829	Mar 21 1915	Jan 15 1846	Jan 15 1846	27	16								0
80 Haws, Peter	**Feb 17 1796**	**1862**					**1**	**0**	**4**	**0**	**0**	**6**	**5**	**6**
Charlotte Harrington	Apr 8 1798		Jul 1824	Jan 10 1846	28	26								6
Betsy Harrington	Jul 15 1790		Jan 10 1846	Jan 10 1846	49	55								0
Mary Quaid	Jun 2 1806		Jan 26 1846	Jan 26 1846	49	39								0
Sarah Morris	Nov 6 1810		Jan 26 1846	Jan 26 1846	49	35								0

	husbands & wives	birth	death	marriage	sealing	marriage age: husb	marriage age: wife	in JS life: wives	in JS life: children	> JS death: wives	> JS death: children	> Nauvoo: wives	> Nauvoo: children	total: wives	total: children
	Sarah Baldwin (Smith)[135]	May 15 1794		Jan 30 1846	Jan 30 1846	49	51								0
81	**Herriman, Henry**	**Jun 9 1804**	**May 17 1891**					**1**	**0**	**1**	**0**	**1**	**9**	**3**	**9**
	Clarissa Boynton	Sep 12 1807	Dec 30 1885	Apr 26 1827	Jan 16 1846	22	19								0
	Eliza Elizabeth Jones	Jan 5 1830	Sep 28 1909	Jan 16 1846	Jan 16 1846	41	16								9
	Sarah Loving (Perkins)	Oct 14 1825		1853		49	28								
82	**Hewitt, Wilkinson**	**Mar 20 1812**						**0**		**2**		**1**		**3**	**0**
	Sarah Ann Robinson	May 9 1816	1897	Jan 31 1846	Jan 31 1846	33	29								
	Julia Ann Jaquis	Nov 20 1823		Feb 6 1846	Feb 6 1846	33	22								
	Margaret Calhoun	Aug 16 1825		May 19 1848		36	22								
83	**Hickman, William Adams**	**Apr 16 1815**	**Aug 21 1883**					**1**	**7**	**1**	**0**	**8**	**32**	**10**	**39**
	Bernetta Burckhardt[136]	Aug 8 1812	Dec 27 1886	Apr 12 1832	Mar 8 1848	16	19								8
	Sarah Elizabeth Luce[137]	Sep 11 1828	Mar 29 1909	Jan 30 1846	Jan 30 1846	30	17								1
	Minerva Wade	Sep 2 1829	Dec 23 1918	May 1 1849	Oct 1 1849	34	19								8
	Sarah Basford Meacham	Oct 10 1834	Nov 29 1909	Aug 18 1850	Aug 18 1850	35	15								4
	Hannah Diantha Harr[137]	Aug 3 1836	Jul 27 1917	Sep 11 1853	Sep 11 1853	38	17								5
	Margaret (a Shoshone Indian)[138]	1820		Mar 28 1855		39	35								0
	Sarah Elizabeth (Virginia) Johnson[138]	Mar 7 1839		Mar 28 1855		39	16								5
	Mary Lucretia Harr	1835		Aug 30 1856	Aug 30 1856	41	21								2
	Martha Diana Case	Oct 8 1823	Mar 16 1872	Nov 2 1856	Nov 2 1856	41	33								4
	Mary Jane Hetherington	Mar 20 1840	May 29 1923	Jun 21 1859	May 5 1934	44	19								2

84	**Higbee, Isaac**	**Dec 23 1797**	**Feb 16 1874**					**1**	**1**	**1**	**1**	**5**	**4**	**7**	**6**
	Keziah String	Dec 25 1802	Nov 3 1841	Feb 11 1819	Jan 14 1846	21	16								10na
	Charlotte Woods (Carter)[139]	May 20 1814	Sep 21 1899	Apr 16 1842	Jan 30 1846	44	27								5
	Eliza Darling[140]	Feb 17 1814		Jan 14 1846	Jan 14 1846	48	31								1
	Elizabeth Nelson	ca. 1835		Apr 2 1856	Apr 2 1856	58	20								0
	Jane Nelson[141]	ca. 1844		Jul 29 1865	Jul 29 1865	67	20								0
	Sarah Crosby	ca. 1847		Oct 10 1868	Oct 10 1868	70	20								0
	Sophia Chlorinda	ca. 1847		Oct 10 1868	Oct 10 1868	70	20								0
	Margaret String	Apr 25 1811		Oct 10 1868	Oct 10 1868	70	57								0
85	**Hunt, Charles Jefferson**	**Jan 22 1804**	**May 11 1879**					**1**	**10**	**1**	**1**	**0**	**9**	**2**	**20**
	Celia Mounce[142]	Sep 18 1806	Jan 28 1897	Dec 1 1823	Feb 7 1846	19	17								11
	Matilda Neas	Jan 1 1828		Feb 7 1846	Feb 7 1846	42	18								9
86	**Hunter, Edward**	**Jun 22 1793**	**Oct 16 1883**					**1**	**2**	**2**	**0**	**1**	**11**	**4**	**13**
	Ann Standley[143]	Feb 16 1808	Nov 9 1855	Sep 30 1830	Jan 29 1846	37	22								2
	Laura Lovina Kaufman (Shimer)[144]	Mar 27 1827	Jul 16 1894	Dec 15 1845	Jan 29 1846	52	18								5
	Susanna Wann	Feb 18 1825	Dec 15 1885	Jan 29 1846	Jan 29 1846	52	20								3
	Henrietta Spencer	Mar 5 1839	Jan 1886	Nov 20 1856		63	17								3
87	**Hunter, Jesse Divined**	**Jul 5 1806**	**1882**					**1**	**5**	**1**	**0**	**0**	**2**	**2**	**7**
	Keziah Brown[145]	Dec 10 1810	Jan 12 1887	Dec 1827	Feb 2 1846	21	16								7
	Lydia Ann Edmunds	Jan 28 1824	Apr 27 1847	Feb 2 1846	Feb 2 1846	39	22								0
88	**Huntington, William Jr.**[146]	**Mar 28 1784**	**Aug 19 1846**					**1**	**0**	**2**	**0**	**0**	**0**	**3**	**0**
	Zina Dorcas Baker	May 2 1786	Jul 8 1839	Nov 28 1805	Jan 14 1846	21	19								9na

	husbands & wives	birth	death	marriage	sealing	marriage age husb	marriage age wife	in JS life wives	in JS life children	> JS death wives	> JS death children	> Nauvoo wives	> Nauvoo children	total wives	total children
	Lydia Clisbee (Partridge)[147]	Sep 26 1793	Jun 9 1878	Sep 27 1840	Jan 14 1846	56	47								0
	Mary Johnson	Apr 8 1792		Jan 24 1846	Jan 24 1846	61	53								0
	Mary Ann Armstrong	Sep 22 1784		Jan 24 1846	Jan 24 1846	61	61								0
89	**Huntington, William Dresser***	**Feb 28 1818**	**Mar 20 1881**					**2**	**0**	**1**	**1**	**0**	**6**	**3**	**7**
	Caroline Clark[148]	Sep 15 1819	Feb 28 1901	Sep 24 1839	Jan 16 1846	21	20								0
	Harriet Clark[149]	Aug 2 1825	Aug 2 1918	Feb 5 1843	Jan 16 1846	24	17								7
	Ann Maginn	Jun 20 1824		Jan 29 1846	Jan 29 1846	27	21								0
90	**Hyde, Orson***	**Jan 8 1805**	**Nov 28 1878**					**3**	**4**	**0**	**1**	**6**	**26**	**9**	**31**
	Marinda Nancy Johnson[150]	Jun 28 1815	Mar 24 1886	Sep 4 1834	Jan 11 1846	29	19								10
	Martha Rebecca Browett[151]	Jun 22 1818	Oct 30 1904	Feb/Mar 1843	Jan 11 1846	38	24								1
	Mary Ann Price[152]	Jun 5 1816	Jun 16 1900	Apr 1843	Jan 11 1846	38	26								0
	Charlotte S. Quindlin[153]	Aug 22 1802	Dec 3 1881	Nov 21 1852		47	50								0
	Ann Eliza Vickers	Jan 26 1841	May 4 1923	Mar 12 1857	Mar 12 1857	52	16								6
	Helen Melissa Winters	1841		1857		52	16								
	Julia Thomene Reinart	Jul 13 1842	May 19 1919	Aug 29 1863	Aug 29 1863	58	21								5
	Elizabeth Josephine Gallier	Feb 2 1844		1864		59	20								5
	Sophia Margaret Lyon	Feb 6 1847	Mar 25 1932	Oct 10 1865	Oct 10 1865	60	18								4
91	**Johnson, Aaron**	**Jun 22 1806**	**May 10 1877**					**1**	**4**	**3**	**0**	**8**	**47**	**12**	**51**
	Polly Zerviah Kelsey	Sep 14 1808	Jun 27 1850	Sep 13 1827	Jan 15 1846	21	18								4
	Sarah Mariah Johnson[154]	May 17 1824	Jul 3 1850	Dec 22 1844	Jan 15 1846	38	20								2

	Jane Scott[155]	Jul 10 1822	Feb 24 1880	Jul 12 1845	Jan 28 1846	39	23								6
	Mary Ann Johnson[156]	Aug 3 1831	Aug 14 1915	May 18 1846	Dec 28 1847	39	14								11
	Rachel Robinson Ford	Nov 10 1834	Feb 17 1878	Apr 25 1852	Apr 25 1852	45	17								4
	Harriet Fidelia Johnson	Aug 27 1837	Sep 20 1919	Dec 16 1852	Dec 16 1852	46	15								5
	Eunice Lucinda Johnson	Nov 2 1835	Apr 11 1873	Jun 14 1853	Jun 14 1853	46	17								0
	Margaret Jane Ford (Finley)	Apr 17 1831	Mar 23 1893	May 8 1854	May 8 1854	47	23								6
	Julia Maria Johnson	Sep 14 1842	Apr 6 1915	Mar 1 1857	Mar 1 1857	50	14								0
	Sarah James	Aug 13 1837	Jan 22 1922	Mar 1 1857	Mar 1 1857	50	19								5
	Cecelia Elmina Sanford	Aug 22 1841	May 20 1934	Mar 1 1857	Mar 1 1857	50	15								8
	Jemina Davis†[157]	Nov 4 1794	Nov 21 1863	Apr 6 1857		50	62								0
92	**Johnson, Benjamin Franklin***	**Jul 28 1818**	**Nov 18 1905**					**2**	**2**	**1**	**1**	**4**	**43**	**7**	**46**
	Melissa Bloomfield LeBaron[158]	Jan 28 1820	Sep 4 1860	Dec 25 1841	May 16 1843	23	21								9
	Mary Ann Hale[159]	Aug 11 1827	Dec 17 1910	May 17 1843	May 17 1843	24	15								5
	Flora Clarinda Gleason[160]	Aug 2 1819	Aug 13 1900	Feb 3 1846	Feb 3 1846	27	26								1
	Harriet Naomi Holman	Jan 28 1834	Aug 1 1914	Mar 17 1850	Mar 17 1850	31	16								8
	Sarah Melissa Holman	Nov 18 1838	Oct 5 1901	Feb 3 1856	Feb 3 1856	37	17								12
	Susan Adaline Holman	Oct 7 1841	Feb 5 1919	Feb 8 1857	Feb 8 1857	38	15								8
	Sarah Jane Spooner	Oct 1 1839	Nov 5 1911	Apr 5 1857	Apr 5 1857	38	17								3
93	**Johnson, Joel Hills**	**Mar 23 1802**	**Sep 24 1882**					**1**	**3**	**2**	**0**	**1**	**21**	**4**	**24**
	Anna Pixley	Aug 7 1800	Sep 11 1840	Nov 2 1826	Feb 3 1846	24	26								na
	Susan Bryant[161]	Aug 28 1812	Apr 7 1896	Oct 20 1840	Feb 3 1846	38	28								8
	Janet Fife	Feb 17 1828	Jun 18 1911	Oct 25 1845	Oct 25 1845	43	17								6

	husbands & wives	birth	death	marriage	sealing	marriage age husb	marriage age wife	in JS life wives	in JS life children	> JS death wives	> JS death children	> Nauvoo wives	> Nauvoo children	total wives	total children
	Lucinda Alzina Bascom[162]	Oct 26 1815	Oct 18 1885	Oct 25 1845	Mar 26 1993	43	29								1
	Margaret Threlkeld	Jul 22 1840	Dec 25 1914	Oct 11 1860	Oct 11 1860	58	20								9
94	**Kay, John Moburn**	**Oct 6 1817**	**Sep 27 1864**					**1**	**2**	**1**	**1**	**2**	**5**	**4**	**8**
	Ellen M. Cockcroft[163]	Feb 14 1814	Aug 11 1902	Jul 3 1836	Jan 27 1846	19	22								4
	Susannah Roberts	Jan 11 1811	Oct 6 1880	ca. 1846	Jan 27 1846	29	35								0
	Ellen Maria Partington Richards	Sep 14 1834	Oct 19 1903	Jun 19 1851	Jun 19 1851	33	16								4
	Martha Royle	Jan 1823	May 8 1852	Jun 19 1851	Jun 19 1851	33	28								0
95	**Kelly, Joseph**	**Feb 4 1806**	**Aug 9 1886**					**0**	**0**	**2**	**1**	**1**	**1**	**3**	**2**
	Lydia Morrison	Oct 8 1807	Feb 20 1836	Dec 24 1826	May 4 1939	20	19								na
	Abiah Huckins	Jan 6 1828	Aug 3 1854	Feb 7 1846	Feb 7 1846	40	18								2
	Matilda Hull	Aug 19 1817	Dec 20 1848	<Feb 7 1846	Feb 7 1846	40	28								0
	Elizabeth Potter	ca. 1810		Nov 24 1854	Nov 24 1854	48	44								0
96	**Kelsey, Eli Brazee**	**Oct 27 1819**	**Mar 27 1885**					**1**	**3**	**2**	**1**	**3**	**10**	**6**	**14**
	Letitia Sheets[164]	Oct 24 1817	Dec 10 1899	Jul 11 1837	Jan 20 1846	17	19								9
	Mary Forsythe	May 3 1790		Jan 20 1846	Jan 20 1846	26	55								0
	Jane Caldwell (Waite)[165]	Mar 27 1809	Sep 27 1891	Feb 7 1846	Feb 7 1846	26	36								0
	Mary Ann McIntyre	Jun 22 1827	Sep 11 1894	Nov 20 1852	Nov 20 1852	33	25								5
	Emma Boyce	ca. 1823		Dec 16 1852	Dec 16 1852	33	29								0
	Sarah Jane Morris	1819		May 31 1862	May 31 1862	42	43								0
97	**Kelting, Joseph Andrew***	**Oct 13 1811**	**ca. Sep 1903**					**3**	**2**	**0**	**0**	**0**	**0**	**3**	**2**

	Elizabeth Ann Martin	Apr 3 1817	May 1 1850	May 5 1832	Jan 20 1846	20	15								2
	Minerva Orrilla Woods[166]	Oct 18 1827	Jul 12 1896	spring 1844	spring 1844	32	16								0
	Lucy Matilda Johnson[167]	Mar 24 1827		spring 1844	spring 1844	32	17								0
98	**Kimball, Heber Chase***	**Jun 14 1801**	**Jun 22 1868**					**2**	**8**	**35**	**6**	**7**	**52**	**44**	**66**
	Vilate Murray[168]	Jun 1 1806	Oct 22 1867	Nov 7 1822	< 1842	21	16								10
	Sarah Peak (Noon)[169]	May 3 1811	Dec 3 1873	early 1842	1842	40	30								4
	Ruth Wellington	Mar 11 1809		Jul 23 1844	Jul 23 1844	43	35								0
	Rebecca Swain (Williams)†[170]	Aug 3 1798	Sep 25 1861	Sep 2 1844	Sep 2 1844	43	46								0
	Ann Alice Gheen[171]	Dec 20 1827	Oct 12 1879	Sep 10 1844	Sep 10 1844	43	16								5
	Mary Fielding (Smith)†[172]	Jul 21 1801	Sep 21 1852	Sep 14 1844	Sep 14 1844	43	43								0
	Sylvia Porter Sessions (Lyon Smith)†[173]	Jul 31 1818	Apr 12 1882	Sep 19 1844	Sep 19 1844	43	26								0
	Frances Jessie Swan[174]	Jun 20 1822		Sep 30 1844	Sep 30 1844	43	22								1
	Mary Ellen Able Harris[175]	Oct 5 1818	Oct 28 1902	Oct 1 1844	Oct 1 1844	43	25								1
	Charlotte Chase[176]	May 11 1825	Dec 15 1904	Oct 10 1844	Oct 10 1844	43	19								0
	Nancy Maria Winchester (Smith)†[177]	Aug 10 1828	Mar 17 1876	Oct 10 1844	Oct 10 1844	43	16								0
	Sarah Lawrence (Smith)†[178]	May 13 1826	Nov 28 1872	Oct 12 1844	Oct 12 1844	43	18								0
	Martha McBride (Knight Smith)†[179]	Mar 17 1805	Nov 20 1901	Oct 12 1844	Oct 12 1844	43	39								0
	Ellen Aagaat Sanders Ysteinsdatter[180]	Apr 11 1823	Nov 22 1871	Nov 5 1844	Nov 5 1844	43	21								5
	Lydia Kenyon (Carter)†[181]	Dec 11 1801	Dec 10 1866	ca. Dec 1844	Dec 1844	43	43								0
	Lucy Walker (Smith)†[182]	Apr 30 1826	Oct 1 1910	Feb 8 1845	Feb 8 1845	43	18								9
	Clarissa Cressy Cutler[183]	Dec 23 1824	1852	Feb 29 1845	Feb 29 1845	43	20								1
	Sarah Ann Whitney (Smith Kingsbury)†[184]	Mar 22 1825	Sep 4 1873	Mar 17 1845	Mar 17 1845	43	19								7

husbands & wives	birth	death	marriage	sealing	marriage age: husb	marriage age: wife	in JS life: wives	in JS life: children	> JS death: wives	> JS death: children	> Nauvoo: wives	> Nauvoo: children	total: wives	total: children
Presendia Lathrop Huntington (Buell Smith)†[185]	Sep 7 1810	Feb 1 1892	ca. Sep 1845	1845	44	35								2
Amanda Trimble Gheen[186]	Jan 18 1830	Nov 4 1904	Dec 1 1845	Dec 1 1845	44	15								4
Emily Trask Cutler[187]	Feb 23 1828	1852	Dec 1845	Dec 1845	44	17								1
Martha Abigail Pitkin[188]	Jul 17 1797	May 15 1847	Jan 7 1846	Jan 7 1846	44	48								0
Harriet Helga Sanders Ysteinsdatter[180]	Dec 7 1824	Sep 5 1896	Jan 26 1846	Jan 26 1846	44	21								3
Hulda Barnes	Oct 1 1806	Sep 2 1898	Feb 3 1846	Feb 3 1846	44	39								0
Christeen Golden[189]	Sep 20 1822	Jan 30 1896	Feb 3 1846	Feb 3 1846	44	23								4
Sophronia Melinda Harmon	Apr 5 1824	Jan 26 1847	Feb 3 1846	Feb 3 1846	44	21								0
Mary Huston (Smith)†[190]	Sep 11 1818	Dec 24 1896	Feb 3 1846	Feb 3 1846	44	27								0
Theresa Arathusa Morley[191]	Jul 18 1826	Oct 7 1855	Feb 3 1846	Feb 3 1846	44	19								0
Ruth L. Pierce (Cazier)[192]	Feb 11 1818	Nov 28 1907	Feb 3 1846	Feb 3 1846	44	27								0
Laura Pitkin[188]	Sep 10 1790	Nov 16 1866	Feb 3 1846	Feb 3 1846	44	55								0
Ruth Amelia Reese	May 10 1817	Nov 26 1902	Feb 3 1846	Feb 3 1846	44	28								3
Sarah Scott (Mulholland Smith)†[193]	Oct 25 1816	Dec 25 1878	Feb 3 1846	Feb 3 1846	44	29								0
Sarah Stiles (Granger)	Mar 5 1793	1899	Feb 3 1846	Feb 3 1846	44	52								0
Mary Ann Shefflin[194]	Oct 31 1815	Sep 26 1869	Feb 4 1846	Feb 4 1846	44	30								1
Abigail Buchanan	Jan 9 1802		Feb 7 1846	Feb 7 1846	44	44								0
Elizabeth Hereford[195]	Jul 1789		Feb 7 1846	Feb 7 1846	44	56								0
Sarah Shuler (Buckwalter)†[196]	May 15 1801	Jan 25 1879	Feb 7 1846	Feb 7 1846	44	44								0
Margaret Worrell McMinn	Apr 7 1829	Aug 5 1910	ca. 1847	ca. 1847	46	18								0

	Mary Whiting Duell	Nov 23 1807	Jul 12 1873	May 21 1848	May 21 1848	46	40								0
	Dorothy Moon	Feb 9 1804		Mar 14 1856	Mar 14 1856	54	52								0
	Hannah Moon	May 29 1802	Dec 4 1877	Mar 14 1856	Mar 14 1856	54	53								0
	Eliza Doty (Cravath Murray Brown)†[197]	Apr 29 1808	Jan 21 1889	Apr 11 1856	Apr 11 1856	54	47								0
	Adelia Almira Wilcox (Hatton Brown)	Mar 29 1828	Oct 19 1896	Oct 9 1856	Oct 9 1856	55	28								0
	Mary Smithies	Oct 7 1837	Jun 8 1880	Jan 25 1857	Jan 25 1857	55	19								5
99	**Kingsbury, Joseph Corrodon**	**May 2 1812**	**Oct 15 1898**					**1**	**0**	**2**	**0**	**2**	**17**	**5**	**17**
	Caroline Whitney[198]	Mar 10 1816	Oct 16 1842	Feb 3 1836	Mar 23 1843	23	19								na
	Sarah Ann Whitney (Smith)[184]	Mar 22 1825	Sep 4 1873	Apr 29 1843		30	18								0
	Dorcas Adelia Moore[199]	Jan 22 1828	Dec 27 1869	Mar 4 1845	Mar 4 1845	32	17								10
	Louisa Loenza Alcina Pond	Feb 15 1830	Jun 15 1853	Jan 26 1846	Jan 26 1846	33	15								3
	Mahala Dorcas Eggleston Higley (Moore)[442]	Feb 26 1806	Oct 27 1905	May 18 1870	May 18 1870	58	64								
	Eliza Mary Partridge	Mar 3 1842	Dec 13 1913	Sep 26 1870	Sep 26 1870	58	28								4
100	**Knight, Vinson***[200]	**Mar 14 1804**	**Jul 31 1842**					**2**	**7**	**0**	**0**	**0**	**0**	**2**	**7**
	Martha McBride[201]	Mar 17 1805	Nov 20 1901	Jul 6 1826		22	21								7
	Philinda Clark Eldredge (Myrick)[202]	Aug 2 1809	Jul 22 1852	<Jul 31 1842	<Jul 31 1842	38	32								0
101	**Langley, George Washington**	**Sep 20 1818**	**Feb 17 1850**					**1**	**0**	**1**	**0**	**0**	**2**	**2**	**2**
	Mary Turner	Apr 23 1820		ca. 1842	Jan 20 1846	24	22								0
	Martha McKinney Frost (Akes)[203]	Oct 7 1825	Aug 26 1902	Jan 20 1846	Jan 20 1846	27	20								2
102	**Lathrop, Asahel Albert**	**Dec 24 1810**	**1871**					**1**	**0**	**1**	**0**	**1**	**0**	**3**	**0**
	Cynthia Jackson[204]	1813	ca. Nov 1838	ca. 1835	Jan 21 1846	24	22								na
	Jane Peacock[205]	Nov 12 1820		Jul 29 1841	Jan 21 1846	30	20								0

	husbands & wives	birth	death	marriage	sealing	marriage age husb	marriage age wife	in JS life wives	in JS life children	> JS death wives	> JS death children	> Nauvoo wives	> Nauvoo children	total wives	total children
	Hannah Peacock[205]	Dec 25 1823		Jan 21 1846	Jan 21 1846	35	22								0
	Sarah Peacock[206]	Mar 16 1828		ca. 1847	ca. 1847	36	19								
103	**Lee, John Doyle**[207]	**Sep 6 1812**	**Mar 23 1877**					**1**	**6**	**10**	**2**	**8**	**51**	**19**	**59**
	Agatha Ann Woolsey[208]	Jan 18 1814	Jun 4 1866	Jul 24 1833	Jan 14 1846	20	19								11
	Nancy Bean (Williams)[209]	Dec 14 1826	Mar 3 1903	Feb 5 1845	Dec 23 1845	32	18								1
	Louisa Free[210]	Aug 9 1824	Jun 18 1886	Apr 19 1845	Dec 23 1845	32	20								1
	Sarah Caroline Williams[210]	Nov 24 1830	Feb 16 1907	Apr 19 1845	Dec 23 1845	32	14								11
	Abigail Schaeffer (Woolsey)[211]	Sep 13 1785	Sep 3 1848	May 3 1845	Dec 23 1845	32	59								0
	Rachel Andora Woolsey[210]	Aug 5 1825	Jul 7 1912	May 3 1845	Dec 23 1845	32	19								8
	Martha Elizabeth Berry	Nov 22 1826	Jun 18 1885	sum/fall 1845	Jan 29 1846	33	18								4
	Polly Ann Workman	May 11 1829		fall 1845	Jan 31 1846	33	16								0
	Delethea Morris	Nov 26 1825		fall/win 1845	Feb 7 1846	33	20								0
	Nancy Ann Vance	Sep 29 1824	Oct 30 1851	fall 1845	Mar 20 1847	33	21								1
	Emoline Vaughn Woolsey	Jan 4 1830		Dec 21 1846	Dec 21 1846	34	16								0
	Nancy Gibbons Armstrong[212]	Jan 7 1799	Aug 1847	Feb 27 1847	Feb 27 1847	34	48								0
	Lavina Young	Sep 25 1820	Jul 4 1883	Feb 27 1847	Mar 20 1857	34	26								3
	Mary Vance Young	Nov 10 1817	Jun 5 1890	Feb 27 1847	Mar 20 1847	34	29								3
	Mary Leah Groves	Oct 30 1836	Jul 12 1912	Dec 2 1852	Mar 20 1857	40	16								7
	Mary Ann Williams[213]	Sep 11 1844	Feb 8 1882	1856	1856	43	12								0
	Emma B. Batchelor[214]	Apr 21 1836	Nov 16 1897	Jan 7 1858		45	21								6

No.	Name	Born	Died	Date 1	Date 2	Age	Age								
	Terressa Morse (Bridges Chamberlain)	Oct 20 1813	Mar 20 1862	Mar 18 1859		46	45								0
	Ann Gordge	May 30 1849		Jun 10 1865	Jun 10 1865	52	16								3
104	**Lewis, Lemuel**	**Mar 19 1801**	**>1857**					**1**	**5**	**1**	**0**	**0**	**0**	**2**	**5**
	Weighty Stanton	Jun 11 1807	>1846	ca. 1832	Jan 13 1846	31	25								5
	Olive Matilda Stowe	Apr 29 1809	>1850	Jan 13 1846	Jan 13 1846	44	36								0
105	**Lott, Cornelius Peter**	**Sep 22 1798**	**Jul 6 1850**					**1**	**9**	**4**	**1**	**2**	**2**	**7**	**12**
	Permelia Darrow[215]	Dec 15 1804	Jan 6 1882	Apr 27 1823	Sep 20 1843	24	18								11
	Narcissus Rebecca Faucett	Mar 12 1829	Apr 19 1884	Jan 22 1846	Jan 22 1846	47	16								1
	Charity Dickinson (Pratt)[216]	Feb 24 1776	May 20 1849	Jan 22 1846	Jan 22 1846	47	69								0
	Eliz. J. Davis (G. B. Durfee Smith)†[101]	Mar 11 1791	Dec 16 1876	Jan 22 1846	Jan 22 1846	47	54								0
	Jane Rodger	Mar 5 1829		Feb 7 1846	Feb 7 1846	47	16								0
	Eleanor Wayman[217]	May 25 1792		Mar 30 1847	Mar 30 1847	48	54								0
	Phebe Crosby Peck (Knight)†[218]	Mar 21 1800	ca. 1850	Mar 30 1847	Mar 30 1847	48	47								0
106	**Loveland, Chester**	**Dec 30 1817**	**Mar 5 1886**					**1**	**3**	**1**	**0**	**4**	**32**	**6**	**35**
	Fanny Call[219]	May 11 1815	Nov 20 1898	Feb 15 1838	Jan 31 1846	20	22								8
	Rosannah Elvira Winters	Dec 6 1825	Apr 13 1896	Jan 15 1846	Feb 5 1846	28	20								6
	Celia Leanora Simmons	Apr 4 1835	Sep 25 1889	Jan 21 1854	Jan 21 1854	36	18								9
	Elizabeth White	Nov 5 1813	May 3 1884	Dec 16 1861	May 28 1866	43	48								0
	Rosetta Adaline Snow	Nov 7 1846	Jan 1 1933	Nov 17 1866	Nov 17 1866	48	20								5
	Louisa Faulkner	Sep 6 1847	May 2 1932	Sep 5 1868	Sep 5 1868	50	20								7
107	**Loveless, John**	**Jun 24 1807**	**Dec 6 1880**					**1**	**9**	**1**	**1**	**2**	**6**	**4**	**16**
	Rachel Mahala Anderson[220]	Aug 26 1805	Oct 25 1891	Jan 25 1826	Jan 28 1846	18	20								12

	husbands & wives	birth	death	marriage	sealing	marriage age husb	marriage age wife	in JS life wives	in JS life children	> JS death wives	> JS death children	> Nauvoo wives	> Nauvoo children	total wives	total children
	Sarah Elmer (Sweat)[221]	Sep 20 1813	Aug 20 1889	Feb 2 1846	Feb 2 1846	38	32								1
	Rhoda Sanford (Lawrence)†[222]	Jun 16 1812	Aug 23 1896	Nov 21 1847	Nov 21 1847	40	35								1
	Mary Pippard Gange[223]	Jul 16 1832	Jul 22 1869	Feb 18 1865	<Feb 18 1865	57	32								2
108	**Luddington, Elam**	**Nov 23 1806**	**Mar 3 1893**					**1**	**1**	**1**	**2**	**3**	**1**	**5**	**4**
	Mary Elizabeth Clark[224]	Jul 24 1824	Jan 24 1851	May 16 1841	Jan 17 1846	34	16								4
	Jane Tibbets†[225]	Aug 27 1804		Jan 17 1846	Jan 17 1846	39	41								0
	Susanne Eliza Gee[226]	Jan 31 1828	Aug 2 1860	Dec 16 1849	Dec 16 1849	43	21								0
	Mariah Moss	Oct 20 1840		Feb 8 1857	Feb 8 1857	50	16								
	Charlotte Buvelot	Dec 15 1806	Mar 10 1886	May 15 1876	May 15 1876	69	69								0
109	**Lyman, Amasa Mason**[227]	**Mar 30 1813**	**Feb 4 1877**					**1**	**3**	**7**	**1**	**1**	**33**	**9**	**37**
	Maria Louisa Tanner[228]	Nov 28 1818	May 3 1906	Jun 10 1835	Apr 18 1845	22	16								8
	Caroline Ely Partridge[229]	Jan 8 1827	May 5 1908	Sep 6 1844	Sep 6 1844	31	17								5
	Eliza Maria Partridge (Smith)[230]	Apr 20 1820	Mar 2 1886	Sep 28 1844	Sep 28 1844	31	24								5
	Cornelia Eliza Leavitt	Jan 5 1825	Dec 14 1864	Nov 14 1844	Nov 14 1844	31	19								2
	Dionitia Walker (Whitney)[231]	Mar 10 1816	Jul 11 1894	Jul 1845	Jul 1845	32	29								0
	Paulina Eliza Phelps	Mar 20 1827	Oct 11 1912	Jan 16 1846	Jan 16 1846	32	18								7
	Priscilla Rebecca Turley	Jun 1 1829	Sep 21 1904	Jan 16 1846	Jan 16 1846	32	16								6
	Laura Lucinda Reed[232]	May 22 1829	Nov 22 1903	Jan 28 1846	Jan 28 1846	32	16								0
	Lydia Partridge[233]	May 8 1830	Jan 16 1875	Feb 7 1853	Feb 7 1853	39	22								4
110	**Lyon, Windsor Palmer**	**Feb 8 1809**	**Jan 1849**					**1**	**4**	**1**	**0**	**0**	**3**	**2**	**7**

	Sylvia Porter Sessions[173]	Jul 31 1818	Apr 12 1882	Apr 21 1838		29	19								6
	Susanne Eliza Gee[234]	Jan 31 1828	Aug 2 1860	ca. Feb 1846		37	18								1
111	**Markham, Stephen**	**Feb 9 1800**	**Mar 10 1878**					**1**	**4**	**1**	**0**	**6**	**13**	**8**	**17**
	Hannah Hogaboom	Apr 1 1804	Jan 31 1892	Feb 1824	Jan 30 1846	24	19								3
	Prudence Fenner (Kinyon Fairchild)	Mar 25 1799	Sep 5 1895	Jan 30 1846	Jan 30 1846	45	46								0
	Mary Lucy Curtis (Houghton)[†235]	Nov 15 1832	Oct 6 1900	Oct 5 1850	Oct 5 1850	50	17								13
	Lydia Maria MacComber (Luce)	Aug 7 1798	Jun 30 1875	Apr 12 1852		52	53								0
	Martha Jane Boice (Wyott)	Mar 2 1836	Dec 26 1913	Oct 11 1852	Oct 11 1852	52	16								1
	Anna Matthews	Apr 20 1803	Jun 1892	Oct 11 1852	Oct 11 1852	52	49								0
	Lucy Ann Bellows	Oct 11 1838		Apr 22 1856	Apr 22 1856	56	17								0
	Eliza Jane Adamson	Aug 31 1822	Aug 12 1897	Nov 30 1867		67	45								0
112	**McArthur, Duncan**	**May 22 1796**	**Oct 20 1865**					**1**	**12**	**1**	**1**	**1**	**5**	**3**	**18**
	Susan McKeen[236]	Oct 10 1801	Nov 16 1866	Jan 1 1818	Jan 17 1846	21	16								14
	Cynthia Nickols	Apr 2 1800		Jan 29 1846	Jan 29 1846	49	45								0
	Eliza Rebecca Scoville	Feb 14 1841		Oct 23 1857	Oct 23 1857	61	16								4
113	**McGinnis, Benjamin**	**May 3 1803**	**Apr 6 1870**					**1**	**9**	**1**	**1**	**0**	**8**	**2**	**18**
	Sarah Johnston	Sep 4 1802	Nov 1849	ca. 1825	Feb 5 1846	22	23								10
	Mary Ann Brooks	Dec 8 1821		ca. 1846	Feb 5 1846	43	25								8
114	**Meacham, Joseph**[237]	**Feb 1 1806**	**Mar 6 1894**					**1**	**1**	**1**	**0**	**2**	**20**	**4**	**21**
	Hanna Ladd Tyler[238]	Feb 10 1808	Dec 7 1846	Feb 10 1827	Jan 22 1846	21	19								2
	Ann Elizabeth Bovee	Apr 18 1827	Oct 17 1869	Jan 9 1845	Jan 22 1846	38	17								11
	Sarah Maria Tuttle	Jan 25 1825	Feb 24 1880	Jan 5 1853	Sep 14 1867	46	27								7

	husbands & wives	birth	death	marriage	sealing	marriage age husb	marriage age wife	in JS life wives	in JS life children	> JS death wives	> JS death children	> Nauvoo wives	> Nauvoo children	total wives	total children
	Mary Catherine Green (Marius)	Sep 29 1827	Mar 15 1912	Aug 19 1855	Aug 19 1855	49	27								1
115	**Merkley, Christopher**	**Dec 18 1808**	**May 2 1893**					**1**	**1**	**1**	**0**	**1**	**9**	**3**	**10**
	Sarah Davis[239]	May 19 1810	May 7 1893	Feb 18 1828	Jan 24 1846	19	17								2
	Minerva Stowell	Apr 23 1824	Sep 12 1883	Jan 24 1846	Jan 24 1846	37	21								0
	Xarissa Fairbanks	Oct 29 1838	Nov 29 1904	Jan 17 1858	Jan 17 1858	49	19								8
116	**Miller, George***	**Nov 25 1794**	**1856**					**2**	**6**	**2**	**0**	**0**	**0**	**4**	**6**
	Mary Catherine Fry[240]	Jan 29 1801		Jun 25 1822	Aug 15 1844	27	21								2
	Julia Ann Chapman	Aug 20 1824		Jul 20 1843		48	18								
	Elizabeth Bouton[241]	Apr 2 1817		Jan 25 1846	Jan 25 1846	51	28								4
	Sophia Wallace	Apr 5 1800		Jan 25 1846	Jan 25 1846	51	45								0
117	**Miller, Reuben**	**Sep 4 1811**	**Jul 22 1882**					**1**	**3**	**2**	**1**	**2**	**26**	**5**	**30**
	Rhoda Ann Letts[242]	Nov 25 1814	Aug 2 1883	Apr 17 1836	Jan 27 1846	24	21								10
	Orice Burnham[243]	Nov 20 1815	Feb 14 1890	Dec 15 1845	Dec 15 1845	34	30								3
	Louisa Sanger (Smith)†[244]	Mar 26 1812		Jan 27 1846	Jan 27 1846	34	33								0
	Ann Crainer	Jul 15 1838	Apr 25 1906	Nov 22 1856	Nov 22 1856	45	18								11
	Jane Hughes	Jan 21 1849	Sep 25 1893	Jan 11 1869	Jan 11 1869	57	19								6
118	**Miller, William**	**Jan 8 1814**	**Aug 7 1875**					**1**	**2**	**3**	**0**	**3**	**1**	**7**	**3**
	Eliza Hasmer Scott[245]	1811	< 1834	< 1834	Jan 19 1846	20	23								na
	Phoebe Scott[246]	Aug 19 1816	Dec 13 1857	May 4 1834	Jan 19 1846	20	17								2
	Lucretia Marilla Johnson[247]	Oct 12 1830	Jan 3 1848	Dec 22 1845	Dec 22 1845	31	15								1

	Mary Ann Turner[248]	Mar 30 1827	Dec 16 1867	Jan 23 1846	Jan 23 1846	32	18								0
	Rhoda Emeline Potter	May 18 1828	Jul 19 1909	Feb 7 1846	Feb 7 1846	32	17								0
	Sarah Curtis[249]	Jun 16 1840	Mar 17 1925	Feb 17 1858	Feb 17 1858	44	17								
	Annie Lewis			Sep 8 1859	Sep 8 1859	45									0
	Jane Lewis			Oct 22 1864	Oct 22 1864	50									0
119	**Mitchell, Benjamin Thomas**	**Jan 12 1816**	**Mar 9 1880**					**1**	**0**	**1**	**2**	**4**	**45**	**6**	**47**
	Sarah Jane Fracebuck[250]	Jun 9 1817	Aug 21 1843	Apr 26 1835	Jan 17 1846	19	17								na
	Lovina Buckwater	Jan 28 1821	Mar 21 1874	Oct 8 1843	Jan 17 1846	27	22								8
	Caroline Conrad	Sep 18 1828	Aug 18 1851	Jan 7 1845	Jan 17 1846	28	16								2
	Lois Judd	Sep 15 1825	Jun 9 1912	Jan 9 1848	Jan 9 1848	31	22								8
	Maria (Lydia Mariah) Day	Jun 1 1833	Apr 8 1886	Jun 30 1851	Jun 30 1851	35	18								11
	Katrine Frederikke Marcussen Jensen	May 11 1837	Apr 21 1917	Dec 21 1856	Dec 21 1856	40	19								10
	Susannah Houston	Feb 11 1826	May 6 1900	Mar 6 1857	Mar 6 1857	41	31								8
120	**Morley, Isaac***[251]	**Mar 11 1786**	**Jun 24 1865**					**3**	**10**	**5**	**1**	**2**	**2**	**10**	**13**
	Lucy Gunn	Jan 24 1786	Jan 3 1848	Jun 20 1812	Feb 26 1844	26	26								10
	Abigail Leonora Snow (Leavitt)[252]	Aug 23 1801	Aug 17 1884	Dec 19 1843	Dec 19 1843	57	42								0
	Hannah Blakeslee Finch (Merriam)[253]	Mar 19 1811	Apr 16 1874	Jan 14 1844	Jan 14 1844	57	32								3
	Hannah Knight Libby	Oct 9 1786	Nov 17 1867	Jan 22 1846	Jan 22 1846	59	59								0
	Harriet Lucinda Cox	Jan 20 1823	Jul 23 1854	Jan 22 1846	Jan 22 1846	59	23								0
	Nancy Ann Bach (Buchanan)[254]	Feb 25 1791	Aug 17 1884	Jan 22 1846	Jan 22 1846	59	54								0
	Eleanor Mills	Dec 11 1800	Dec 7 1877	Jan 22 1846	Jan 22 1846	59	45								
	Betsy Bradford (Pinkham)†[255]	Dec 12 1788	> 1861	Jan 27 1846	Jan 27 1846	59	57								

	husbands & wives	birth	death	marriage	sealing	marriage age husb	marriage age wife	in JS life wives	in JS life children	> JS death wives	> JS death children	> Nauvoo wives	> Nauvoo children	total wives	total children
	Ann Dayer[256]	1812	> 1860	Mar 11 1856	Mar 11 1856	70	44								
	Sarah Scott[257]			Aug 23 1862	Aug 23 1862	76									
121	**Murray, William Ellis**	**Oct 4 1802**	**May 1847**					**1**	**4**	**1**	**0**	**0**	**0**	**2**	**4**
	Helen E. Sarvis	1805	< 1828	< 1825	Feb 3 1846	22	20								1na
	Mary Spring[258]	Sep 29 1811	> 1849	< 1828	Feb 3 1846	25	16								4
	Eliza Doty (Cravath)[259]	Apr 29 1808	Jan 21 1889	Feb 3 1846	Feb 3 1846	43	37								0
122	**Nickerson, Freeman**[260]	**Feb 5 1779**	**Jan 12 1847**					**1**	**9**	**2**	**0**	**0**	**0**	**3**	**9**
	Huldah Chapman[261]	Aug 16 1780	Mar 22 1860	Jan 19 1800	Jan 9 1846	20	19								9
	Huldah Howes (Hamblin)	Aug 16 1786	Sep 8 1846	Aug 1845	Jan 9 1846	66	58								0
	Eliza Kent	ca. 1783		1846		67	63								0
123	**Noble, Joseph Bates***[262]	**Jan 14 1810**	**Aug 17 1900**					**3**	**8**	**0**	**0**	**8**	**23**	**11**	**31**
	Mary Adeline Beaman[263]	Oct 19 1810	Feb 14 1851	Sep 11 1834	Jan 23 1846	24	23								9
	Sarah B. Alley[264]	Oct 17 1819	Dec 28 1846	Apr 5 1843	Apr 5 1843	33	23								1
	Mary Ann Washburn	Nov 18 1827	Oct 10 1882	Jun 28 1843	Jun 28 1843	33	15								5
	Susan Hammond (Ashby)†	Aug 28 1808	May 15 1851	Mar 3 1847	Mar 3 1847	37	38								1
	Millicent London	Dec 22 1805	ca. 1905	Jun 12 1853	Jun 12 1853	43	47								0
	Julia Rosetta Thurston	Nov 21 1841	Dec 20 1916	Jan 18 1857	Jan 18 1857	47	15								4
	Loretta Sylvia Meacham	Jan 4 1838	Jul 2 1913	Jan 18 1857	Jan 18 1857	47	19								11
	Jane Wallace	ca 1812		Jun 27 1867	Jun 27 1867	57	55								0
	Hannah Kerr	ca 1812		Nov 23 1870	Nov 23 1870	60	58								0

Catherine Wallace	ca 1812		Nov 23 1870	Nov 23 1870	60	58								0
Sarah Wallace	ca 1812		Nov 23 1870	Nov 23 1870	60	58								0
124 Pack, John[265]	**May 20 1809**	**Apr 4 1885**					**1**	**4**	**3**	**1**	**4**	**38**	**8**	**43**
Julia Ives[266]	Mar 8 1817	Jun 23 1903	Oct 10 1832	Aug 1843	23	15								11
Ruth Mosher[267]	Apr 12 1824	Sep 10 1914	Mar 1845	Mar 1845	35	20								9
Nancy Aurelia Boothe	Apr 11 1826	Aug 14 1853	Jan 21 1846	Jan 21 1846	36	19								2
Eliza Jane Graham	Nov 6 1825	Sep 1 1887	Jan 21 1846	Jan 21 1846	36	20								0
Mary Jane Walker	Apr 3 1835	Apr 5 1908	Sep 15 1852	Sep 15 1852	43	17								11
Jessie Bell Stirling	Sep 26 1845	Dec 27 1925	Jan 16 1864	Jan 16 1864	54	18								7
Lucy Jane Giles	Jun 13 1848	Jun 26 1918	May 2 1868	May 2 1868	58	19								3
Jane Robison (Pack Ackerly)[†268]	Feb 17 1828	Mar 2 1898	Jul 20 1870	Jul 20 1870	61	42								0
125 Page, John Edward[*269]	**Feb 25 1799**	**Oct 14 1867**					**2**	**2**	**2**	**3**	**0**	**4**	**4**	**9**
Betsey Thompson	ca. 1810	Oct 1 1833	Jul 1 1831		32	21								1na
Lorain Stevens	1804	Oct 14 1838	Dec 26 1833		34	29								4na
Mary Judd[270]	Nov 26 1818	Mar 6 1907	ca. Jan 1839	<Jun 27 1844	40	20								8
Nancy Bliss[271]			<Jun 27 1844	<Jun 27 1844	45									0
Rachel Judd[272]	Sep 15 1821	Feb 18 1865	ca. 1845		46	24								0
Lois Judd	Sep 15 1825	Jun 9 1912	ca. 1845		46	20								1
126 Parker, John Davis	**Nov 22 1799**	**Feb 27 1891**					**1**	**0**	**2**	**0**	**0**	**9**	**3**	**9**
Harriet Sherwood[273]	ca. 1818	ca. 1856	ca. 1837	Feb 3 1846	38	19								0
Almeda Sophia Roundy[274]	Mar 7 1829	Sep 25 1912	Feb 3 1846	Feb 3 1846	46	16								9
Samantha Roundy	Jun 2 1824	Jul 12 1906	Feb 3 1846	Feb 3 1846	46	21								0

	husbands & wives	birth	death	marriage	sealing	marriage age husb	marriage age wife	in JS life wives	in JS life children	> JS death wives	> JS death children	> Nauvoo wives	> Nauvoo children	total wives	total children
127	**Patten, Charles Wetherby**[275]	**Nov 4 1811**						**1**		**1**		**0**		**2**	**0**
	Peggy Campbell	Dec 11 1812		1831	Jan 24 1846	19	18								0
	Caroline Pope	Oct 2 1804		Jan 24 1846	Jan 24 1846	34	41								
128	**Peck, Hezekiah**	**Jan 19 1782**	**Aug 25 1850**					**1**	**0**	**1**	**0**	**0**	**0**	**2**	**0**
	Martha Long[276]	Mar 13 1789	Aug 25 1850	<Jun 28 1830	Jan 19 1846	48	41								0
	Mary Lemon (Bell)†[277]	Dec 1 1807	Aug 1846	Feb 4 1846	Feb 4 1846	64	38								0
129	**Peck, Martin Horton**[278]	**May 27 1806**	**Jun 17 1884**					**1**	**0**	**1**	**1**	**2**	**21**	**4**	**22**
	Susan Caroline Clough[279]	Jan 2 1804	Nov 6 1843	Jun 18 1827	Jan 13 1846	21	23								7na
	Mary Thorn[280]	Feb 14 1816	Jan 31 1908	Mar 30 1844	Jan 13 1846	37	28								5
	Arlytia Long Carter	May 18 1829	Jun 4 1854	Jan 20 1846	Jan 20 1846	39	16								4
	Charlotte Amelia Van Orden (West)†[281]	Jan 13 1828	Sep 13 1895	Dec 2 1851	Dec 2 1851	45	23								7
	Esther Lewis	Feb 20 1841	Sep 3 1924	Mar 27 1857	Mar 27 1857	50	16								6
130	**Phelps, William Wines**	**Feb 17 1792**	**Mar 7 1872**					**1**	**10**	**2**	**0**	**3**	**1**	**6**	**11**
	Sally Waterman[282]	Jul 24 1797	Jan 2 1874	Apr 28 1815	Feb 2 1844	23	17								10
	Laura Stowell[283]	Jul 7 1825		Feb 2 1846	Feb 2 1846	53	20								0
	Elizabeth Dunn[283]	Jul 4 1828		Feb 2 1846	Feb 2 1846	53	17								0
	Sarah Betsy Gleason	Sep 29 1828	Feb 4 1916	Dec 22 1847	Dec 22 1847	55	19								1
	Mary Jones	ca. 1796	Sep 22 1886	Apr 3 1853		61	56								0
	Harriet Schrader	Aug 10 1809	Jan 24 1892	Sep 8 1856	Sep 8 1856	64	47								0
131	**Pratt, Orson**	**Sep 19 1811**	**Oct 3 1881**					**1**	**3**	**4**	**2**	**5**	**40**	**10**	**45**

	Sarah Marinda Bates[284]	Feb 5 1817	Dec 25 1888	Jul 4 1836	Nov 22 1844	24	19								12
	Charlotte Bishop[285]	Mar 19 1823		Dec 13 1844	Dec 13 1844	33	21								0
	Adelia Ann Bishop[285]	Nov 5 1825	Dec 29 1913	Dec 13 1844	Dec 13 1844	33	19								6
	Mary Ann Merrill[286]	Jun 2 1819	Dec 12 1903	Mar 27 1845	Mar 27 1845	33	25								5
	Louisa Chandler	Mar 12 1822	Jun 12 1846	Jan 17 1846	Jan 17 1846	34	23								0
	Marian Ross	Jun 9 1829	Jul 19 1901	Feb 19 1852	Feb 19 1852	40	22								6
	Sarah Louisa Lewis	Jul 7 1831	Sep 27 1855	Jun 21 1853	Jun 21 1853	41	21								1
	Juliet Ann Phelps	Apr 19 1839	Mar 13 1919	Dec 14 1855	Dec 14 1855	44	16								7
	Eliza Crooks	Jul 1829	Jan 9 1869	Jul 24 1857	Jul 24 1857	45	28								5
	Margaret Graham	Jan 20 1852	Mar 31 1907	Dec 28 1868	Dec 28 1868	57	16								3
132	**Pratt, Parley Parker***	**Apr 12 1807**	**May 13 1857**					**2**	**3**	**5**	**3**	**4**	**25**	**11**	**31**
	Thankful Halsey[287]	Mar 18 1797	Mar 25 1837	Sep 9 1827	Jul 24 1843	20	30								1na
	Mary Ann Frost (Stearns)[†288]	Jan 14 1809	Aug 24 1891	May 9 1837	Jun 23 1843	30	28								4
	Elizabeth Brotherton[289]	Mar 27 1816	May 9 1897	Jul 24 1843	Jul 24 1843	36	27								1
	Mary Wood[290]	Jun 1 1818	Mar 5 1898	Sep 9 1844	Sep 9 1844	37	26								4
	Hannahette Snively[291]	Oct 22 1812	Feb 21 1898	Nov 2 1844	Nov 2 1844	37	32								3
	Belinda B. Marden (Hilton)[292]	Dec 24 1820	Feb 19 1894	Nov 20 1844	Nov 20 1844	37	23								5
	Sarah Huston[293]	Aug 3 1822	May 22 1886	Oct 15 1845	Oct 15 1845	38	23								4
	Phoebe E. Sopher[294]	Jul 8 1823	Sep 17 1887	Oct 15 1845	Oct 15 1845	38	22								3
	Martha Monks[295]	Apr 28 1825		Apr 28 1847	Apr 28 1847	40	22								1
	Ann Agatha Walker	Jun 11 1829	Jun 25 1908	Apr 28 1847	Apr 28 1847	40	17								5
	Keziah Downs	May 10 1812	Jan 11 1877	Dec 27 1853	Dec 27 1853	46	41								0

	husbands & wives	birth	death	marriage	sealing	marriage age: husb	marriage age: wife	in JS life: wives	in JS life: children	> JS death: wives	> JS death: children	> Nauvoo: wives	> Nauvoo: children	total: wives	total: children
	Eleanor Jane McComb (McLean)	Dec 29 1817	Oct 24 1874	Nov 14 1855	Nov 14 1855	48	37								1
133	**Redding, Return Jackson**	**Sep 26 1817**	**Aug 30 1891**					**0**	**0**	**2**	**0**	**2**	**10**	**4**	**10**
	Laura Louisa Trask	Mar 15 1818	ca. 1843	Feb 16 1841	Jan 24 1846	23	22								2na
	Martha Marie Hurlbutt[296]	Aug 27 1814	Mar 15 1847	<Jan 24 1846	Jan 24 1846	28	31								0
	Jane Fidelia Whiting	Feb 29 1824		Jan 24 1846	Jan 24 1846	28	21								0
	Naomi Eliza Murray	Jul 9 1830	Mar 11 1868	Feb 16 1847	Feb 16 1847	29	16								10
	Elizabeth Diana Harris[297]			Feb 23 1870	Oct 10 1870	52									
134	**Rich, Charles Coulson**	**Aug 21 1809**	**Nov 17 1883**					**1**	**3**	**4**	**2**	**1**	**46**	**6**	**51**
	Sarah De Armon Pea[298]	Sep 23 1814	Dec 12 1893	Feb 11 1838	Jan 15 1846	28	23								9
	Eliza Ann Graves[299]	Jun 3 1811	Jun 2 1879	Jan 6 1845	Jan 6 1845	35	33								3
	Mary Ann Phelps[300]	Aug 6 1829	Apr 17 1912	Jan 6 1845	Jan 6 1845	35	15								10
	Sarah Jane Peck[301]	Sep 15 1825	Nov 29 1893	Jan 9 1845	Jan 9 1845	35	19								11
	Emeline Grover[302]	Jul 30 1831	May 4 1917	Feb 3 1846	Feb 3 1846	36	14								8
	Harriet Sargent	Oct 23 1832	Jul 18 1915	Mar 28 1847	Mar 28 1847	37	14								10
135	**Richards, Franklin Dewey**	**Apr 2 1821**	**Dec 9 1899**					**1**	**1**	**1**	**0**	**10**	**21**	**12**	**22**
	Jane Snyder[303]	Jan 31 1823	Nov 17 1912	Dec 18 1842	Jan 23 1846	21	19								6
	Elizabeth McFate	Oct 28 1829	Mar 29 1847	Jan 31 1846	Jan 31 1846	24	16								0
	Sarah Snyder	Apr 11 1813	Oct 4 1894	Oct 13 1849	Oct 13 1849	28	36								2
	Charlotte Fox	Mar 8 1826	Nov 28 1918	Oct 13 1849	Oct 13 1849	28	23								0
	Susan Sanford Peirson	Dec 13 1831	Mar 2 1878	Jun 26 1853	Jun 26 1853	32	21								3

No.	Name	Birth	Death	Sealing	Marriage	Age	Age								
	Laura Altha Snyder	Feb 14 1836	Mar 11 1878	Mar 29 1854	Mar 29 1854	32	18								0
	Susannah Bayliss (Richards)†[304]	May 31 1812	Apr 17 1891	Mar 6 1857	Mar 6 1857	35	44								0
	Rhoda Harriet Foss (Richards)†[304]	Apr 19 1830	Nov 19 1881	Mar 6 1857	Mar 6 1857	35	26								4
	Nanny Longstroth (Richards)†[304]	Apr 15 1828	Jan 7 1911	Mar 6 1857	Mar 6 1857	35	28								3
	Mary Thompson (Richards)†[304]	Oct 21 1827	Sep 10 1905	Mar 6 1857	Mar 6 1857	35	29								4
	Josephine de la Harpe[305]	ca. 1832		Mar 6 1857	Mar 6 1857	35	24								0
	Ann Davis Dally	Mar 31 1791		Mar 19 1857	Mar 19 1857	35	65								0
136	**Richards, Levi**	**Apr 14 1799**	**Jun 18 1876**					**1**	**0**	**1**	**1**	**0**	**0**	**2**	**1**
	Sarah Griffith[306]	Dec 26 1802	Jun 7 1892	Dec 25 1843	Jan 27 1846	44	40								1
	Persis Goodall (Young)[307]	Mar 15 1806	Sep 16 1894	Jan 27 1846	Jan 27 1846	46	39								0
137	**Richards, Phineas Howe**	**Nov 5 1788**	**Nov 25 1874**					**1**	**6**	**1**	**0**	**5**	**0**	**7**	**6**
	Wealthy Dewey	Sep 6 1786	Oct 18 1853	Feb 24 1818	Jan 22 1846	29	31								6
	Mary Vail Morse[308]	Dec 8 1809		Feb 8 1846		57	36								0
	Martha Allen	Mar 15 1803	May 4 1860	Nov 26 1847	Nov 26 1847	59	44								0
	Margaret Phillips (Fullmer)[309]	May 26 1800	1890	Feb 29 1848	Feb 29 1848	59	47								0
	Emily Northrop	ca. 1790		Mar 24 1852	Mar 24 1852	63	61								0
	Ann Emerson	Apr 24 1822		Feb 14 1856	Mar 9 1979	67	33								0
	Jane McBride	ca. 1790	1874	Jun 22 1871	Jun 22 1871	82	80								0
138	**Richards, Willard***[310]	**Jun 24 1804**	**Mar 11 1854**					**4**	**2**	**5**	**0**	**2**	**12**	**11**	**14**
	Jennetta Richards[311]	Aug 21 1817	Jul 9 1845	Sep 24 1838	May 29 1843	34	21								2
	Sarah Longstroth[312]	Feb 19 1826	Jan 26 1858	Jan 18 1843	Jan 18 1843	38	16								4
	Nanny Longstroth[312]	Apr 15 1828	Jan 7 1911	Jan 18 1843	Jan 18 1843	38	14								3

husbands & wives	birth	death	marriage	sealing	marriage age: husb	marriage age: wife	in JS life: wives	in JS life: children	> JS death: wives	> JS death: children	> Nauvoo: wives	> Nauvoo: children	total: wives	total: children
Susannah Lee Liptrot[313]	May 19 1809	Dec 27 1872	Jun 12 1843	Jun 12 1843	38	34								0
Amelia Elizabeth Peirson[314]	Apr 16 1825	Feb 23 1851	Dec 22 1845	Dec 22 1845	41	20								1
Alice Longstroth[315]	Jan 28 1824	Nov 21 1909	Dec 23 1845	Dec 23 1845	41	21								0
Mary Thompson[316]	Oct 21 1827	Sep 10 1905	Jan 27 1846	Jan 27 1846	41	18								2
Jane Hall	Feb 18 1826	Dec 10 1849	Jan 31 1846	Jan 31 1846	41	19								0
Ann Reed Braddock	Mar 5 1794	Apr 18 1872	Feb 6 1846	Feb 6 1846	41	51								0
Susannah Bayliss[316]	May 31 1812	Apr 17 1891	Dec 22 1847	Dec 22 1847	43	35								1
Rhoda Harriet Foss[316]	Apr 19 1830	Nov 19 1881	Nov 30 1851	Nov 30 1851	47	21								1
139 Richardson, Ebenezer Clawson*	**Aug 7 1815**	**Sep 25 1874**					**2**	**5**	**0**	**1**	**2**	**29**	**4**	**35**
Angeline King[317]	Nov 25 1813	Apr 10 1880	1833	Feb 27 1848	18	19								12
Polly Ann Childs	Jul 20 1821	Jan 19 1905	Nov 1843	Feb 27 1848	28	22								6
Phebe Wooster Childs	Jan 17 1833	May 21 1917	May 14 1848	May 14 1848	32	15								11
Elizabeth Gilson	Jan 24 1843	Oct 7 1919	Nov 30 1860	Nov 30 1860	45	17								6
140 Robinson, Joseph Lee	**Feb 18 1811**	**Jan 1 1893**					**1**	**4**	**1**	**1**	**4**	**27**	**6**	**32**
Maria Wood[318]	Jan 5 1806	Dec 1 1872	Jul 23 1832	Jan 13 1846	21	26								7
Susan McCord	Dec 14 1808	Apr 19 1876	Jan 31 1846	Jan 31 1846	34	37								3
Laurinda Maria Atwood (Pinkham)	May 3 1821	Mar 1 1895	Mar 21 1847	Mar 21 1847	36	25								8
Lydia Foster	Jan 9 1831	Sep 25 1872	Feb 16 1853	Feb 16 1853	41	22								6
Mary Taylor (Upton Simmons)	Nov 6 1835	Mar 20 1899	Feb 2 1867		55	31								4
Minerva Wood[319]	1778			Sep 14 1870										4

141	**Rockwell, Orrin Porter**	**Jun 28 1813**	**Jun 9 1878**					**1**	**5**	**1**	**0**	**2**	**9**	**4**	**14**
	Luana Beebe	Oct 3 1814	Mar 6 1897	Feb 16 1832		18	17								5
	Mrs. Amos Davis			ca. Dec 1845		32									0
	Mary Ann Neff	Aug 5 1829	Sep 28 1866	May 3 1854	May 3 1854	40	24								6
	Christine Olsen	ca. 1836	Apr 14 1911	ca. 1870		57	34								3
142	**Rockwood, Albert Perry**	**Jun 9 1805**	**Nov 26 1879**					**1**	**6**	**2**	**0**	**2**	**16**	**5**	**22**
	Nancy Haven	Jun 13 1805	Jan 23 1876	Apr 4 1827	Jan 17 1846	21	21								6
	Angeline Hodgkins (Horne)[†320]	Feb 19 1820	Dec 21 1902	Jan 21 1846	Jan 21 1846	40	25								2
	Elvira Teeples (Wheeler)[†321]	Nov 11 1819	Dec 2 1886	Jan 21 1846	Jan 21 1846	40	26								2
	Juliane Sophie Olsen	Nov 3 1836	Feb 7 1914	Apr 11 1863	Apr 11 1863	57	26								8
	Susannah Cornwall	Oct 14 1841	Jan 5 1897	Jan 6 1870	Jan 6 1870	64	28								4
143	**Russell, Samuel Jr.**	**Sep 25 1812**						**1**	**0**	**2**	**0**	**0**	**1**	**3**	**1**
	Esther Hill	Mar 21 1816		ca. 1833	Jan 20 1846	21	17								0
	Frances Maria Stillman	May 29 1830	Sep 13 1903	Jan 20 1846	Jan 20 1846	33	15								0
	Mary Abigail Thorn	Apr 2 1821	Mar 7 1904	Jan 20 1846	Jan 20 1846	33	24								1
144	**Sagers, William Henry Harrison***	**May 3 1814**	**Jun 19 1886**					**2**	**0**	**3**	**0**	**5**	**19**	**10**	**19**
	Lucinda Madison[322]	1819		Dec 22 1834		20	15								
	Phoebe Madison[322]	ca. 1819		ca. Dec 1843		29	24								
	Olive Amanda Wheaton	Jan 26 1813	ca. 1849	Jan 22 1846	Jan 22 1846	31	32								0
	Sarah Lorene Bailey	Dec 3 1826		Jan 22 1846	Jan 22 1846	31	19								0
	Harriet Emeline Barney[323]	Oct 13 1830	Feb 14 1911	Mar 18 1846	<Mar 18 1846	31	15								3
	Ruth Adelia Wheaton	Sep 20 1832	Mar 12 1871	Jun 10 1851	Jun 10 1851	37	18								4

	husbands & wives	birth	death	marriage	sealing	marriage age husb	marriage age wife	in JS life wives	in JS life children	> JS death wives	> JS death children	> Nauvoo wives	> Nauvoo children	total wives	total children
	Lucy Marilla Wheaton	Apr 29 1831		Jun 10 1851	Jun 10 1851	37	20								3
	Frances Camelia Adams[324]	Jul 24 1835	Feb 23 1901	Dec 3 1852	Apr 9 1853	38	17								0
	Marion Browning Smith	Apr 15 1837	Aug 31 1879	Jun 5 1858	Jun 5 1858	44	21								5
	Elizabeth Mary Casto[325]	Jan 7 1853	Jul 20 1922	May 1 1873		58	20								4
145	**Sanders, Ellis Mendenhall**	**Dec 5 1808**	**Jan 15 1873**					**1**	**6**	**1**	**0**	**0**	**2**	**2**	**8**
	Rachel Broome Roberts[326]	Sep 14 1807	May 16 1892	Nov 9 1830	May 2 1845	21	23								8
	Esther Ann Peirce (Gheen)[†327]	Dec 24 1801	Sep 2 1858	Feb 2 1846	Feb 2 1846	37	44								0
146	**Scott, John**	**May 6 1811**	**Dec 16 1876**					**1**	**4**	**2**	**1**	**2**	**33**	**5**	**38**
	Elizabeth Menerey[328]	Sep 10 1815	Dec 24 1886	Apr 15 1836	Jan 23 1846	24	20								12
	Mary Pugh[329]	Nov 10 1821	Jan 5 1905	Mar 2 1845	Jan 23 1846	33	23								5
	Sarah Ann Willis	Feb 4 1825	Oct 30 1890	Mar 24 1846	Apr 11 1860	34	21								10
	Esther Yeates	Apr 4 1843	Apr 21 1920	Feb 18 1860	Feb 18 1860	48	16								7
	Roxey Angeline Keller	Apr 29 1851	Mar 19 1924	Apr 11 1868	Apr 11 1868	56	16								4
147	**Scovil, Lucius Nelson**	**Mar 18 1806**	**Feb 14 1889**					**1**	**5**	**1**	**5**	**5**	**18**	**7**	**28**
	Lura Snow[330]	Mar 11 1807	Jan 27 1846	Jun 18 1828	Oct 16 1844	22	21								9
	Alice Graves Hurst (Wallwork)[331]	Feb 18 1819	Apr 5 1885	Oct 16 1844	Jan 31 1846	38	25								9
	Emma Whaley	Apr 12 1823		Nov 8 1847	Nov 8 1847	41	24								0
	Elizabeth Turner	Oct 6 1826		Nov 8 1847	Nov 8 1847	41	21								0
	Jane Hobs Fales[332]	1833		Sep 7 1854	Sep 7 1854	48	21								0
	Hannah Maria Marsden	Nov 22 1839	Jul 1 1907	Jun 17 1856	Jun 17 1856	50	16								7

	Sarah Elizabeth McArthur (Fuller)[†333]	Feb 28 1827	Aug 7 1908	Oct 28 1857	Oct 28 1857	51	30								3
148	**Sessions, David**	**Apr 4 1790**	**Aug 11 1850**					**1**	**9**	**1**	**0**	**1**	**1**	**3**	**10**
	Patty Bartlett[334]	Feb 4 1795	Dec 14 1892	Jun 28 1812		22	17								9
	Rosilla Cowen[335]	Nov 8 1814		Oct 3 1845	Oct 3 1845	55	30								0
	Harriet Elvira Teeples (Wixom)[336]	Oct 15 1830	Oct 6 1911	Jan 13 1850	Jan 13 1850	59	19								1
149	**Sessions, Peregrine [Perrigrine]**	**Jun 15 1814**	**Jun 3 1893**					**0**	**0**	**3**	**0**	**5**	**51**	**8**	**51**
	Julia Ann Killgore	Aug 24 1815	Jan 25 1845	Sep 21 1834	Feb 6 1846	20	19								na
	Mary Call	Feb 21 1824	Nov 25 1865	Jun 28 1845	Jun 28 1845	31	21								5
	Lucina Call	Sep 29 1819	Jun 29 1904	Jun 28 1845	Jun 28 1845	31	25								4
	Rosannah Walton Virgin	Apr 1 1820	Nov 3 1877	Feb 2 1846	Feb 2 1846	31	25								
	Fanny Emorrett Loveland[337]	Dec 13 1838	May 14 1917	Sep 13 1852	Sep 13 1852	38	13								11
	Sarah Crossley	Jan 29 1843	Jan 24 1906	Mar 2 1861	Mar 2 1861	46	18								10
	Elizabeth Betsy Birdenow	Mar 6 1827	Oct 8 1903	Mar 25 1865	Mar 25 1865	50	38								0
	Sarah Ann Bryson	May 21 1850	Dec 23 1934	Sep 29 1866	Sep 29 1866	52	16								11
	Esther Mabey	Jul 4 1850	May 22 1930	Nov 22 1868	Nov 22 1868	54	18								10
150	**Sherwood, Henry Garlic**	**Apr 20 1785**	**ca. 1862**					**0**		**2**		**0**		**2**	**0**
	Marcia Abbott	Nov 26 1811		Jan 21 1846	Jan 21 1846	60	34								
	Jane McManagle (Stoddard Judd)	Feb 16 1804	ca. 1882	Jan 21 1846	Jan 21 1846	60	41								
151	**Shumway, Charles**	**Aug 1 1808**	**May 21 1898**					**1**	**3**	**1**	**1**	**3**	**31**	**5**	**35**
	Julia Ann Hooker[338]	Nov 28 1807	Nov 14 1846	Mar 26 1832	Jan 21 1846	23	24								5
	Louisa Minnerly	Jan 8 1824	Feb 28 1890	Aug 5 1845	Jan 21 1846	37	21								7
	Henrietta Bird	Jun 7 1833	May 3 1910	Jan 24 1852	Jan 24 1852	43	18								10

no.	husbands & wives	birth	death	marriage	sealing	marriage age husb	marriage age wife	in JS life wives	in JS life children	> JS death wives	> JS death children	> Nauvoo wives	> Nauvoo children	total wives	total children
	Adliza L. Truman	Jan 6 1815		Apr 5 1856	Apr 5 1856	47	41								0
	Elizabeth Jardine	Jan 25 1847	May 26 1935	Mar 29 1862	Mar 29 1862	53	15								13
152	**Smith, George Albert**	**Jun 26 1817**	**Sep 1 1875**					**1**	**2**	**7**	**3**	**3**	**15**	**11**	**20**
	Bathsheba Wilson Bigler[339]	May 3 1822	Sep 20 1910	Jul 25 1841	Jan 20 1844	24	19								3
	Lucy Meserve Smith[340]	Feb 9 1817	Oct 5 1892	Nov 29 1844	Nov 29 1844	27	27								2
	Nancy Clement[341]	Oct 31 1815	Mar 26 1847	Feb 1 1845	Feb 1 1845	27	29								1
	Zilpha Stark[342]	Jul 3 1818	Sep 19 1887	Mar 28 1845	Mar 28 1845	27	26								3
	Sarah Ann Libby[381]	May 7 1818	Jun 12 1851	Nov 20 1845	Nov 20 1845	28	27								1
	Hannah Mariah Libby[382]	Jun 29 1828	Sep 21 1906	Nov 20 1845	Jan 26 1846	28	17								5
	Agnes Moulton Coolbrith (Smith Smith)†[343]	Jul 9 1808	Dec 26 1876	Jan 28 1846	Jan 28 1846	28	37								0
	Susanna Ogden (Bigler)†[344]	Oct 11 1785		Feb 7 1846	Feb 7 1846	28	60								0
	Mary Jane Smith (Gee)†[345]	Apr 29 1812	Mar 1 1878	Jan 31 1852	Jan 31 1852	34	39								0
	Susan Elizabeth West	Dec 4 1833		Oct 28 1857	Oct 28 1857	40	23								5
	Elizabeth Boardman Smith (Wilson)	Jan 2 1817	Sep 25 1893	Apr 11 1868	Apr 11 1868	50	51								0
153	**Smith, Hyrum***[346]	**Feb 9 1800**	**Jun 27 1844**					**5**	**2**	**0**	**0**	**0**	**0**	**5**	**2**
	Jerusha Barden	Feb 15 1805	Oct 13 1837	Nov 2 1826	May 29 1843	26	21								6na
	Mary Fielding[172]	Jul 21 1801	Sep 21 1852	Dec 24 1837	May 29 1843	37	36								2
	Mercy Rachel Fielding (Thompson)†[347]	Jun 15 1807	Sep 15 1893	Aug 11 1843	Aug 11 1843	43	36								0
	Catharine Phillips[348]	Aug 1 1819	Sep 26 1905	Aug 1843	Aug 1843	43	24								0
	Lydia Dibble (Granger)[349]	Apr 5 1790	Sep 2 1861	ca. Aug 1843	1843	43	53								0

	Louisa Sanger[350]	Mar 26 1812		<Sep 17 1843	Sep 17 1843	43	31								
154	**Smith, John***	**Jul 16 1781**	**May 23 1854**					**3**	**4**	**5**	**0**	**0**	**0**	**8**	**4**
	Clarissa Lyman[351]	Jun 27 1790	Feb 14 1854	Sep 11 1815	Feb 26 1844	34	25								4
	Mary Aikens (Smith)[352]	Aug 13 1797	Apr 27 1877	Aug 13 1843	Aug 13 1843	62	46								0
	Julia Ellis Hills (Johnson)[353]	Sep 26 1783	May 30 1853	<Oct 21 1843	<Oct 21 1843	62	60								0
	Ann Carr (Fore Brimhall)[354]	Feb 28 1790		Jan 15 1846	Jan 15 1846	64	55								0
	Miranda Jones (Davis)	Nov 16 1784		Jan 15 1846	Jan 15 1846	64	61								0
	Sarah M. Kingsley (Howe Cleveland Smith)†355	Oct 20 1788	Apr 21 1856	Jan 15 1846	Jan 15 1846	64	57								0
	Asenath Hurlbut (Sherman)	Aug 2 1780		Jan 24 1846	Jan 24 1846	64	65								0
	Rebecca Smith	Apr 29 1788		Jan 24 1846	Jan 24 1846	64	57								0
155	**Smith, Joseph Jr.***356	**Dec 23 1805**	**Jun 27 1844**					**38**	**4**	**0**	**2**	**0**	**0**	**38**	**6**
	Emma Hale[357]	Jul 10 1804	Apr 30 1879	Jan 18 1827	May 28 1843	21	22								5
	Louisa Be[a]man[358]	Feb 7 1815	May 15 1850	Apr 5 1841	Apr 5 1841	35	26								0
	Mrs. Zina Diantha Huntington (Jacobs)[359]	Jan 31 1821	Aug 27 1901	Oct 27 1841	Oct 27 1841	35	20								0
	Mrs. Presendia Lathrop Huntington (Buell)[185]	Sep 7 1810	Feb 1 1892	Dec 11 1841	Dec 11 1841	35	31								0
	Agnes Moulton Coolbrith (Smith)†343	Jul 11 1811	Dec 26 1876	Jan 6 1842	Jan 6 1842	36	30								0
	Mrs. Lucinda Pendleton (Morgan Harris)[360]	Sep 27 1801	> 1860	< Jan 17 1842	< Jan 17 1842	36	40								0
	Mrs. Mary Elizabeth Rollins (Lightner)[361]	Apr 9 1818	Dec 17 1913	Feb 1842	Feb 1842	36	23								0
	Mrs. Sylvia Porter Sessions (Lyon)[173]	Jul 31 1818	Apr 12 1882	Feb 8 1842	Feb 8 1842	36	23								1
	Mrs. Patty Bartlett (Sessions)[362]	Feb 4 1795	Dec 14 1892	Mar 9 1842	Mar 9 1842	36	47								0
	Mrs. Sarah M. Kingsley (Howe Cleveland)[355]	Oct 20 1788	Apr 20 1856	< Mar 1842	< Mar 1842	36	53								0
	Mrs. Elizabeth Davis (G. Brackenbury Durfee)[101]	Mar 11 1791	Dec 16 1876	< Mar 1842	< Mar 1842	36	50								0

husbands & wives	birth	death	marriage	sealing	marriage age husb	marriage age wife	in JS life wives	in JS life children	> JS death wives	> JS death children	> Nauvoo wives	> Nauvoo children	total wives	total children
Mrs. Marinda Nancy Johnson (Hyde)[150]	Jun 28 1815	Mar 24 1886	Apr 1842	Apr 1842	36	26								0
Delcena Diadamia Johnson (Sherman)[†363]	Nov 19 1806	Oct 21 1854	ca. Jun 1842	ca. Jun 1842	36	35								0
Eliza Roxcy Snow[364]	Jan 21 1804	Dec 5 1887	Jun 29 1842	Jun 29 1842	36	38								0
Mrs. Sarah Rapson (Poulterer)[365]	Mar 27 1793	Aug 20 1879	< Jul 1842	1842	36	49								0
Sarah Ann Whitney[184]	Mar 22 1825	Sep 4 1873	Jul 27 1842	Jul 27 1842	36	17								0
Martha McBride (Knight)[179]	Mar 17 1805	Nov 20 1901	<Aug 5 1842	<Aug 5 1842	36	37								0
Mrs. Ruth Daggett Vose (Sayers)[366]	Feb 26 1808	Aug 18 1884	Feb 1843	Feb 1843	37	35								0
Flora Ann Woodworth[367]	Nov 14 1826	ca. 1851	Mar 4 1843	Mar 4 1843	37	16								0
Emily Dow Partridge[368]	Feb 28 1824	Dec 9 1899	Mar 4 1843	Mar 4 1843	37	19								0
Eliza Maria Partridge[230]	Apr 20 1820	Mar 2 1886	Mar 8 1843	Mar 8 1843	37	22								0
Almera Wood[w]ard Johnson[369]	Oct 22 1813	Mar 4 1896	< Apr 25 1843	< Apr 25 1843	37	29								0
Lucy Walker[182]	Apr 30 1826	Oct 1 1910	May 1 1843	May 1 1843	37	17								0
Sarah Lawrence[178]	May 13 1826	Nov 28 1872	May 11 1843	May 11 1843	37	16								0
Maria Lawrence[16]	Dec 18 1823	1847	ca. May 1843	ca. May 1843	37	19								0
Helen Mar Kimball[370]	Aug 25 1828	Nov 15 1896	ca. May 1843	ca. May 1843	37	14								0
Mrs. Elvira Anna Cowles (Holmes)[371]	Nov 23 1813	Mar 10 1871	Jun 1 1843	Jun 1 1843	37	29								0
Rhoda Richards[372]	Aug 8 1784	Jan 17 1879	Jun 12 1843	Jun 12 1843	37	58								0
Hannah S. Ells[373]	Mar 4 1813	1845	mid-1843	mid-1843	37	30								0
Mrs. Mary Ann Frost (Stearns Pratt)[374]	Jan 14 1809	Aug 24 1891	Jul 24 1843	Jul 24 1843	37	34								0
Olive Grey Frost[375]	Jul 24 1816	Oct 6 1845	ca. Jul 1843	mid-1843	37	27								0

	Nancy Maria Winchester[177]	Aug 10 1828	Mar 17 1876	ca. Jul 1843	< mid-1843	37	14								0
	Desdemona Catlin Wadsworth Fullmer[30]	Oct 6 1809	Feb 9 1886	< Jul 1843	< Jul 1843	37	33								0
	Melissa Lott[41]	Jan 9 1824	Jul 13 1898	Sep 20 1843	Sep 20 1843	37	19								0
	Sarah Scott (Mulholland)[193]	Oct 25 1816	Dec 15 1878	< Oct 25 1843	< Oct 25 1843	37	26								0
	Mrs. Phebe Watrous (Woodworth)[376]	Oct 1 1805	Oct 25 1887	< Oct 29 1843	< Oct 29 1843	37	38								0
	Mary Huston[190]	Sep 11 1818	Dec 24 1896	ca. Oct 1843	< Jun 27 1844	37	25								0
	Fanny Young (Carr Murray)[377]	Nov 8 1787	Jun 11 1859	Nov 2 1843	Nov 2 1843	37	55								0
156	**Smith, William***[378]	**Mar 13 1811**	**Nov 13 1893**					**2**	**2**	**10**	**0**	**3**	**5**	**15**	**7**
	Caroline Amanda Grant[379]	Jan 22 1814	May 22 1845	Feb 14 1833		21	19								2
	Mary Ann Covington (Sheffield)[380]	Mar 31 1815	Oct 5 1908	< Fall 1843	1845	32	28								0
	Sarah Ann Libby[381]	May 7 1818	Jun 12 1851	ca. 1844	ca. 1845	33	26								0
	Hannah Mariah Libby[382]	Jun 29 1828	Sep 21 1906	ca. 1844	ca. 1845	33	16								0
	Susan M. Cooney (Clark)[383]			1844		33									
	Mary Jane Rollins[384]	Feb 14 1823	1860	Jun 22 1845		34	22								0
	Henriette Rice[385]	1831		Aug 8 1845	Aug 8 1845	34	14								
	Priscilla Mogridge[386]	Mar 11 1822		ca.Aug 1845	ca.Aug 1845	34	23								0
	Mary Jones	ca. 1828		ca.Aug 1845	ca.Aug 1845	34	17								
	Elizabeth Weston[387]			1845		34									
	Rhoda Alkire	Sep 30 1830	Jan 21 1915	Dec 3 1846		35	16								
	Abeanade E. Archer[388]			1846		35									
	Roxie Ann (Rosanna) Grant[389]	Mar 16 1825	Mar 30 1900	May 18 1847		36	22								2
	Eliza Elsie Sanborn	Apr 16 1827	Mar 7 1889	Nov 12 1857		46	30								3

	husbands & wives	birth	death	marriage	sealing	marriage age husb	marriage age wife	in JS life wives	in JS life children	> JS death wives	> JS death children	> Nauvoo wives	> Nauvoo children	total wives	total children
	Rosella Goyette (Surprise)[389]	May 16 1830	Apr 6 1923	Dec 21 1889		78	59								0
157	**Smoot, Abraham Owen**	**Feb 17 1815**	**Mar 6 1895**					**1**	**1**	**2**	**0**	**3**	**24**	**6**	**25**
	Margaret Thompson McMeans (Adkinson)	Apr 16 1809	Sep 1 1884	Nov 11 1838	Jan 9 1846	23	29								1
	Sarah Gibbens[390]	Oct 20 1800		ca. 1845	Jan 9 1846	30	44								0
	Emily Hill (Harris)[391]	Nov 25 1815	Mar 20 1882	Jan 20 1846	Jan 20 1846	30	30								4
	Diana Tanner Eldredge[392]	Mar 28 1837	Jan 29 1914	May 6 1855	May 6 1855	40	18								13
	Anne Kirstine Mauritzen	Dec 19 1833	Jan 20 1894	Feb 17 1856	Feb 17 1856	41	22								7
	Hannah Caroline Rogers (Daniels)	Mar 20 1827	Mar 14 1915	Mar 11 1886		71	58								0
158	**Snow, Erastus***	**Nov 9 1818**	**May 27 1888**					**2**	**3**	**2**	**1**	**10**	**32**	**14**	**36**
	Artemisia Beaman[393]	Mar 3 1819	Dec 21 1882	Dec 13 1838	Feb 15 1844	20	19								11
	Minerva White[394]	Mar 22 1822	Apr 1 1896	Apr 2 1844	Apr 2 1844	25	22								9
	Achsah Wing (White)[395]	Mar 15 1788	Sep 18 1868	Jan 30 1846	Jan 30 1846	27	57								0
	Louisa Wing (Aldridge)[396]	Apr 9 1809	Jul 16 1891	Jan 30 1846	Jan 30 1846	27	36								0
	Elizabeth Rebecca Ashby	May 17 1831	Jun 12 1915	Dec 19 1847	Dec 19 1847	29	16								10
	Julia Josephine Spencer	Apr 9 1837	Oct 31 1909	Apr 11 1856	Apr 11 1856	37	19								6
	Mary Jane Farley	ca. 1820		Apr 14 1866	Apr 14 1866	47	46								0
	Ann McMenemy (Mousley)	Feb 11 1799	Jun 2 1882	Oct 15 1867	Oct 15 1867	48	68								0
	Ane Hansen Beckstrom	Apr 1 1825	Oct 12 1911	May 9 1870	May 9 1870	51	45								0
	Margaret Earl[397]	Nov 30 1820		Mar 28 1877	Mar 28 1877	58	56								0
	Rebecca Abigail Farley	ca. 1820		Jun 18 1880	Jun 18 1880	61	60								0

	Name	Birth	Death												
	Frances Fanny Porter	Jun 17 1814	May 13 1887	Feb 1 1882	Feb 1 1882	63	67								0
	Matilda Wells (Streeper Wadsworth)	ca. 1820		Nov 16 1882	Nov 16 1882	64	62								0
	Inger Nielsen (Andersen)	Apr 29 1827	Apr 13 1909	Jul 16 1884	Jul 16 1884	65	57								0
159	**Snow, Lorenzo**[398]	**Apr 3 1814**	**Oct 10 1901**					**0**	**0**	**4**	**0**	**5**	**42**	**9**	**42**
	Charlotte Squires	Nov 19 1825	Sep 25 1850	Apr 1845	Jan 17 1846	31	19								2
	Mary Adeline Goddard[399]	Mar 8 1812	Dec 28 1898	Apr 1845	Jan 17 1846	31	33								3
	Sarah Ann Prichard	Nov 29 1826		Apr 21 1845	Jan 17 1846	31	18								5
	Harriet Amelia Squires	Sep 13 1819	May 12 1890	Jan 17 1846	Jan 17 1846	31	26								5
	Eleanor Houtz	Aug 14 1831	Sep 13 1896	Jan 19 1848	Jun 1 1848	33	16								8
	Caroline Horton	Dec 25 1824	Feb 24 1857	Oct 9 1853	Oct 9 1853	39	28								3
	Mary Elizabeth Houtz	May 19 1840	Mar 31 1906	Mar 5 1857	Mar 5 1857	42	16								6
	Phoebe Amelia Woodruff	Mar 4 1842	Feb 15 1919	Mar 4 1859	Mar 4 1859	44	17								5
	Sarah E. Minnie Jensen	Oct 10 1855	Jan 2 1908	Jun 12 1871	Jun 12 1871	57	15								5
160	**Snow, Willard Trowbridge**	**May 16 1811**	**Aug 21 1853**					**1**	**4**	**1**	**1**	**1**	**4**	**3**	**9**
	Melvina Harvey[400]	Dec 16 1811	Oct 24 1882	May 14 1837	Jan 12 1846	25	25								9
	Susan Harvey	Mar 12 1808	Jan 25 1848	May 14 1846	1846	34	38								0
	Mary Bingham (Freeman)†[401]	Apr 1 1820	Sep 25 1893	Jan 16 1849	Jan 16 1849	37	28								0
161	**Snow, William**	**Dec 14 1806**	**May 19 1879**					**1**	**1**	**1**	**1**	**3**	**23**	**5**	**25**
	Hannah Miles	Jan 31 1810	Mar 30 1841	Sep 21 1832	Jan 16 1846	25	22								3na
	Lydia Leavitt[402]	Jul 4 1823	Jan 9 1847	Aug 2 1842	Jan 16 1846	35	19								2
	Sally Adams[403]	May 29 1825	Feb 13 1905	Jan 1845	Jan 1845	38	19								8
	Jane Maria Shearer (Wines)	Feb 12 1819	Nov 14 1910	Oct 17 1850	Oct 17 1850	43	31								5

	husbands & wives	birth	death	marriage	sealing	marriage age husb	marriage age wife	in JS life wives	in JS life children	> JS death wives	> JS death children	> Nauvoo wives	> Nauvoo children	total wives	total children
	Roxanna Leavitt (Fletcher Huntsman)	Dec 15 1818	Jun 16 1881	Mar 12 1853	Mar 12 1853	46	34								2
	Ann Rogers	Dec 30 1834	Mar 11 1928	Mar 13 1853	Mar 13 1853	46	18								8
162	**Spencer, Daniel**	**Jul 20 1794**	**Dec 8 1868**					**1**	**4**	**1**	**1**	**6**	**19**	**8**	**24**
	Sophronia Eliza Pomeroy	Jun 21 1806	Oct 5 1832	Jan 16 1823	Jan 16 1846	28	16								1na
	Sarah Lester (Van Schoonover)	Jan 3 1805	Oct 1 1845	Jun 30 1834	Jan 16 1846	39	29								4
	Mary Spencer[404]	Apr 12 1824	Aug 6 1846	Dec 1845	1845	51	21								1
	Emily Slafter Thompson (Spencer)[†405]	Aug 13 1819	Mar 15 1895	Jan 25 1847	Jan 25 1847	52	27								6
	Mary Woollerton	Jun 7 1837		Sep 10 1850	Sep 10 1850	56	13								
	Mary Jane Cutliffe	Jul 5 1835	Jun 28 1909	Dec 27 1856	Dec 27 1856	62	21								4
	Elizabeth Funnell	May 24 1833	Sep 21 1920	Dec 27 1856	Dec 27 1856	62	23								5
	Sarah Jane Gray	Jul 6 1842	May 10 1914	Dec 27 1856	Dec 27 1856	62	14								4
	Sarah McConckie	Apr 13 1814		Feb 13 1857	Feb 13 1857	62	42								0
163	**Spencer, Orson**	**Mar 14 1802**	**Oct 15 1855**					**1**	**7**	**1**	**1**	**4**	**5**	**6**	**13**
	Catherine Cannon Curtis	Mar 21 1811	Mar 12 1846	Apr 13 1830	Jan 15 1846	28	19								8
	Eliza Ann Dibble	Aug 18 1829	May 14 1891	Jan 15 1846	Jan 15 1846	43	16								0
	Martha Knight[406]	May 18 1826	Apr 1848	Apr 1847	Oct 13 1849	45	20								4
	Margaret Ann Miller[407]	Feb 22 1830	Mar 31 1915	Oct 13 1849	Oct 13 1849	47	19								0
	Jane T. Davis	Feb 14 1835		Feb 16 1852	Feb 16 1852	49	17								1
	Mary Hill (Bullock)	Aug 22 1812	Jan 1 1871	Sep 12 1852	Sep 12 1852	50	40								0
164	**Stewart, Levi**	**Apr 28 1812**	**Jun 14 1878**					**1**	**5**	**1**	**0**	**4**	**22**	**6**	**27**

	Melinda Howard[408]	Nov 7 1816	Nov 24 1853	Feb 7 1833	Jan 14 1846	20	16								9
	Charity Holdaway[409]	May 26 1824	May 31 1896	Jan 13 1846	Jan 20 1846	33	21								0
	Margery Wilkerson	Nov 16 1832	Dec 14 1870	Dec 13 1852	Dec 13 1852	40	20								8
	Artimacy Wilkerson	Oct 5 1834	Dec 2 1914	Dec 23 1854	Dec 23 1854	42	20								10
	Susan Elizabeth Edgar	Feb 11 1860	Sep 28 1900	Oct 26 1874		62	14								0
	Rebecca Llewyllen	1812													0
165	**Stiles, George Philander**[410]	**Jul 19 1816**						**1**		**2**		**0**		**3**	**0**
	Sophia J. Scofield			Feb 4 1842		25									
	Stephanie Williamson	Dec 17 1814		< Jan 19 1846	Jan 19 1846	29	32								
	Isabelle Keziah Hollister[411]	Aug 20 1825	Mar 9 1884	Jan 19 1846	Jan 19 1846	29	20								
166	**Stout, Hosea**	**Sep 18 1810**	**Mar 2 1889**					**1**	**2**	**2**	**1**	**2**	**16**	**5**	**19**
	Samantha Peck	Oct 12 1821	Nov 29 1839	Jan 7 1838	ca. 1845	27	16								na
	Louisa Bome Taylor[412]	Oct 19 1819	Jan 11 1853	Nov 29 1840	ca. 1845	30	21								8
	Lucretia Fisher[413]	Mar 13 1830		Apr 20 1845	Apr 20 1845	34	15								0
	Marinda Bennett	Aug 26 1826	Sep 26 1846	Jun 30 1845	Jun 30 1845	34	18								0
	Elvira Wilson	Apr 21 1834	Mar 20 1910	Jul 19 1855	Jul 19 1855	44	21								11
	Sarah Cox (Jones)†	Feb 28 1832	May 27 1885	May 23 1868	May 23 1868	57	36								0
167	**Taylor, John***	**Nov 1 1808**	**Jul 25 1887**					**6**	**4**	**7**	**1**	**5**	**30**	**18**	**35**
	Leonora Agnes Cannon[414]	Oct 6 1796	Dec 9 1868	Jan 28 1833	Jan 30 1844	24	36								4
	Elizabeth Kaighan[415]	Sep 11 1811	Aug 31 1895	Dec 12 1843	Dec 12 1843	35	32								3
	Mary Cook[416]			Jan 1 1844		35									
	Ann Vowles[417]			Feb 3 1844		35									

husbands & wives	birth	death	marriage	sealing	marriage age husb	marriage age wife	in JS life wives	in JS life children	> JS death wives	> JS death children	> Nauvoo wives	> Nauvoo children	total wives	total children
Jane Ballantyne[418]	Apr 11 1813	Dec 26 1900	Feb 25 1844	Feb 25 1844	35	30								3
Annie Ballantyne[419]	Sep 2 1819	Mar 10 1908	1844	1844	35	24								0
Mercy Rachel Fielding (Thompson Smith)[†347]	Jun 15 1807	Sep 15 1893	1845	1845	36	37								0
Mary Ann DeGroot Oakley[420]	Mar 20 1826	Aug 21 1911	Apr 1845	Apr 1845	36	19								5
Ann Hughlings (Pitchforth)[421]	Jun 30 1801	Oct 26 1846	Jan 7 1846	Jan 7 1846	37	44								0
Mary Amanda Utley	Nov 7 1821		Jan 17 1846	Jan 17 1846	37	24								0
Mary Ramsbottom	Jul 15 1826		Jan 23 1846	Jan 23 1846	37	19								0
Lydia Dibble (Granger Smith)[†349]	Apr 5 1790	Sep 2 1861	Jan 30 1846	Jan 30 1846	37	55								0
Sarah Thornton (Coleman)	Jun 11 1807	Mar 1 1892	<Jan 30 1846	Jan 30 1846	37	38								0
Sophia Whitaker	Apr 21 1825	Feb 27 1887	Apr 23 1847	Apr 23 1847	38	22								8
Harriet Whitaker	Jul 30 1816	Jul 16 1882	Dec 4 1847	Dec 4 1847	39	31								3
Caroline Hooper Saunders (Gilliam)	Jan 3 1813	Feb 7 1874	Dec 9 1852	Dec 9 1852	39	39								0
Margaret Young	Apr 24 1837	May 3 1919	Sep 27 1856	Sep 27 1856	47	19								9
Josephine Elizabeth Roueche	Mar 3 1860	Nov 27 1943	Dec 19 1886	Dec 19 1886	78	26								0
168 Tippets, Alvah Lewis	**Mar 12 1809**	**Oct 24 1847**					**1**	**0**	**1**	**1**	**0**	**2**	**2**	**3**
Abigail Tippets[422]	May 12 1815	< Jul 31 1842	Sep 1834	Jan 15 1846	25	19								na
Caroline Beard	Jan 15 1826	Sep 26 1906	Sep 19 1843	Jan 15 1846	34	17								2
Elizabeth Beard[423]	Jun 7 1830	Aug 31 1915	ca. 1846	Mar 12 1853	37	16								1
169 Tippets, John Harvey	**Sep 5 1810**	**Feb 14 1890**					**1**	**2**	**2**	**0**	**1**	**7**	**4**	**9**
Abigail Jane Smith[424]	May 10 1814	Mar 16 1840	Oct 1834	Jan 24 1846	24	20								2na

	Caroline Fidelia Calkins (Pew)	Jul 24 1808	Jul 15 1882	Sep 25 1840	Jan 26 1846	30	32								3
	Nancy Calkins	Dec 30 1800		Jan 28 1846	Jan 28 1846	35	45								0
	Abigail Sprague[424]	Aug 4 1812	Jan 16 1879	Jan 28 1846	Jan 28 1846	35	33								
	Eleanor Wise	Jul 20 1840	Oct 26 1920	Dec 26 1863	Dec 26 1863	53	23								6
170	**Turley, Theodore** *[425]	**Apr 10 1801**	**Aug 12 1871**					**4**	**11**	**0**	**6**	**1**	**5**	**5**	**22**
	Frances Amelia Kimberly[426]	Jun 22 1800	Aug 30 1847	Nov 26 1821	Dec 20 1845	20	21								10
	Mary Clift[427]	Jun 16 1815	Mar 30 1850	Mar 6 1844	Feb 2 1846	42	28								4
	Eliza Clift[428]	Jul 2 1813		Mar 6 1844	Feb 2 1846	42	30								2
	Sarah Ellen Clift[429]	May 3 1817	May 4 1847	Apr 26 1844	Dec 25 1845	43	26								3
	Ruth Jane Giles[430]	Jun 29 1812	Dec 28 1880	Jun 18 1850	Jun 18 1850	49	37								3
171	**Tuttle, Edward**	**Jul 1 1792**	**Aug 17 1847**					**1**	**9**	**1**	**0**	**1**	**0**	**3**	**9**
	Catherine Vanever Geyer	Aug 3 1796	May 24 1878	Nov 12 1815	Jan 29 1846	23	19								9
	Susan Ivers (Smith)†[431]	Apr 14 1789		Jan 29 1846	Jan 29 1846	53	56								0
	Mary Smith	ca. 1792													0
172	**Webb, Chauncey Griswold**	**Oct 24 1811**	**Jan 21 1903**					**1**	**2**	**1**	**1**	**4**	**20**	**6**	**23**
	Eliza Jane Churchill[432]	May 4 1817	Aug 16 1884	Sep 16 1834	Jan 21 1846	22	17								3
	Elizabeth Lydia Taft	Dec 6 1827	Feb 22 1909	Jan 21 1846	Jan 21 1846	34	18								12
	Elizabeth Moyle	Feb 12 1837	Mar 16 1861	Jan 12 1856		44	18								0
	Louisa Goodley	Dec 21 1825		Feb 13 1857		45	31								0
	Eliza Price	Nov 20 1838	Apr 12 1879	Mar 1 1857	Dec 3 1867	45	18								8
	Elizabeth Brown	Mar 7 1830	Dec 14 1870	Apr 7 1868		56	38								0
173	**Webb, Edward Milo**	**Aug 17 1815**	**Jul 31 1852**					**1**		**1**		**0**		**2**	**0**

	husbands & wives	birth	death	marriage	sealing	marriage age husb	marriage age wife	in JS life wives	in JS life children	> JS death wives	> JS death children	> Nauvoo wives	> Nauvoo children	total wives	total children
	Caroline Amelia Owens[433]	Jul 9 1821	Sep 1 1895	Dec 21 1839	Jan 21 1846	24	18								
	Ann Mathews	May 12 1828		< Jan 29 1846	Jan 29 1846	30	17								
174	**Weeks, Allen**	**Jan 24 1813**	**Sep 17 1884**					**1**	**2**	**2**	**1**	**0**	**6**	**3**	**9**
	Frances Elmira Strickland	Jun 17 1813	Dec 5 1841	Aug 17 1835		22	22								na
	Sarah Jane Bennett[434]	Oct 26 1814	Apr 6 1884	May 4 1842	Feb 7 1846	29	27								7
	Melissa Bennett	Dec 27 1828	Jun 4 1849	Feb 7 1846	Feb 7 1846	33	17								2
	Mary Bell	Dec 9 1786	Apr 12 1856	Feb 7 1846	Feb 7 1846	33	59								0
175	**West, Nathan Ayres**	**Apr 10 1808**						**1**		**2**		**0**		**3**	**0**
	Mary Smith Hulet[435]	Dec 15 1804	Sep 5 1831	Oct 11 1828	Jan 15 1846	20	23								
	Adeline Louisa Follett[436]	Dec 21 1816		Jan 15 1846	Jan 15 1846	37	29								
	Louisa Turner[437]	Aug 3 1798		Jan 15 1846	Jan 15 1846	37	47								
176	**Whiting, Edwin**	**Sep 9 1809**	**Dec 8 1890**					**1**	**7**	**2**	**4**	**2**	**23**	**5**	**34**
	Elizabeth Partridge Tillotson[438]	Apr 15 1814	Feb 4 1892	Sep 21 1833	Jan 27 1846	24	19								11
	Almira M. Meacham	May 13 1824	Oct 1 1898	Jan 3 1845	Jan 27 1846	35	20								7
	Mary Elizabeth Cox	Dec 15 1826	Jul 5 1912	Jan 27 1846	Jan 27 1846	36	19								9
	Hannah Haines Brown	Jul 21 1834	Dec 31 1896	Oct 8 1856	Oct 8 1856	47	22								5
	Mary Ann Washburn (Noble)	Nov 18 1828	Oct 10 1882	Apr 14 1857	Apr 20 1857	47	28								2
177	**Whitney, Clark Lyman**	**May 6 1808**						**1**	**0**	**2**	**0**	**0**	**0**	**3**	**0**
	Rhoda Ann Ballard	Jul 10 1822	Mar 30 1901	1839	Jan 30 1846	30	16								0
	Adeline Elizabeth Ballard	Mar 22 1824		Jan 30 1846	Jan 30 1846	37	21								0

	Nancy Richardson	Sep 27 1784	Aug 29 1864	Jan 30 1846	Jan 30 1846	37	61								0
178	**Whitney, Newel Kimball**	**Feb 5 1795**	**Sep 23 1850**					**1**	**10**	**7**	**0**	**0**	**4**	**8**	**14**
	Elizabeth Ann Smith[439]	Dec 26 1800	Feb 14 1882	Oct 20 1822	Aug 21 1842	27	21								11
	Olive Maria Bishop	Mar 17 1807	Aug 3 1874	Sep 10 1844	Sep 10 1844	49	37								0
	Elizabeth Almira Pond[440]	May 2 1827	May 12 1899	Feb 18 1845	Feb 18 1845	50	17								0
	Emmeline Blanche Woodward (Harris)[441]	Feb 29 1828	Apr 25 1921	Feb 24 1845	Feb 24 1845	50	16								2
	Abigail Augusta Pond	Jul 14 1828	Dec 7 1846	May 8 1845	May 8 1845	50	16								0
	Elizabeth Mahala Moore[442]	Sep 13 1826		Jul 25 1845	Jul 25 1845	50	18								0
	Anna Houston	May 8 1821	1848	Jan 7 1846	Jan 7 1846	50	24								1
	Henrietta Keys (Whitney)[†443]	Dec 25 1821	Feb 12 1901	Jan 26 1846	Jan 26 1846	50	24								0
179	**Wight, Lyman***	**May 9 1796**	**Mar 21 1858**					**4**	**6**	**0**	**5**	**0**	**1**	**4**	**12**
	Harriet Benton[444]	Mar 19 1801	Feb 26 1889	Jan 5 1823	< Jun 27 1844	26	21								6
	Jane Margaret Ballantyne[444]	Aug 27 1819	Aug 31 1884	< Jun 27 1844	< Jun 27 1844	48	24								1
	Mary Hawley[444]	Sep 1 1823	Jan 1852	< Jun 27 1844	< Jun 27 1844	48	20								2
	Mary Ann Hobart[444]	Oct 16 1828	Feb 17 1897	< Jun 27 1844	< Jun 27 1844	48	15								3
180	**Wight, Orange Lysander**[445]	**Nov 29 1823**	**Jun 20 1907**					**1**	**0**	**1**	**1**	**1**	**13**	**3**	**14**
	Matilda Carter[446]	1824	Apr 7 1879	Feb 6 1844	1954	20	20								10
	Sarah Hadfield[447]	Mar 15 1827	1864	Feb 7 1845		21	17								4
	Rosilla Milla Carter (Coolidge)[86]	Feb 22 1825		1849		25	24								0
181	**Willey, Jeremiah**[448]	**Nov 6 1804**	**May 21 1868**					**1**	**2**	**1**	**2**	**0**	**6**	**2**	**10**
	Bathsheba Stevens	ca. 1804	Sep 3 1838	Nov 29 1827	Jan 28 1846	23	22								na
	Hannah Pressey				Jan 28 1846										na

	husbands & wives	birth	death	marriage	sealing	marriage age husb	marriage age wife	in JS life wives	in JS life children	> JS death wives	> JS death children	> Nauvoo wives	> Nauvoo children	total wives	total children
	Samantha Call[449]	Nov 15 1814	Nov 13 1905	Apr 28 1839	Jan 28 1846	34	24								9
	Sarah Ann Ward (Saunders)[450]	May 16 1810	May 26 1886	<Apr 28 1845	1845	40	34								1
182	**Williams, Alexander**	**Oct 10 1803**	**Oct 5 1876**					**1**	**9**	**1**	**3**	**3**	**9**	**5**	**21**
	Isabel Gill[451]	Sep 11 1805	Apr 5 1862	Sep 30 1824	Jan 31 1846	20	19								12
	Jane Ortrey	1801		ca. 1845	Jan 31 1846	42	44								0
	Eliza Crosby (Terrill)[452]	Apr 8 1810	1891	<Feb 16 1852	Feb 16 1852	48	41								0
	Sarah Ann Dudley	Jan 17 1842	Nov 18 1923	Feb 8 1857	Feb 8 1857	53	15								0
	Elizabeth Jane Dack	Jun 24 1838	Jul 14 1935	Mar 2 1857	Mar 2 1857	53	18								9
183	**Wilson, Guy Carlton**[453]	**Aug 31 1801**	**Sep 17 1846**					**1**	**8**	**3**	**0**	**0**	**0**	**4**	**8**
	Mary Eliza Hunter[454]	Sep 26 1803	Mar 27 1878	Feb 27 1827	Feb 27 1853	25	23								8
	Amelia Granger[455]	ca. 1806		< 1846		45	40								0
	Jerusha Granger[455]	ca. 1806		< 1846		45	40								0
	Kate King Granger[455]	ca. 1806		< 1846		45	40								0
184	**Wilson, Lewis Dunbar**	**Jun 2 1805**	**Mar 11 1856**					**1**	**7**	**1**	**1**	**2**	**4**	**4**	**12**
	Nancy Ann Wagoner[456]	Jul 10 1810	Jul 19 1851	Jun 11 1830	Jan 20 1846	25	19								11
	Patsey M. Reynolds	Feb 3 1829		Feb 3 1846	Feb 3 1846	40	17								0
	Sarah E. Waldo	Dec 14 1819	Nov 1857	Sep 29 1851		46	31								1
	Nancy A. Cossett	Dec 27 1802	Aug 31 1874	Feb 12 1854	Apr 11 1854	48	51								0
185	**Winchester, Stephen**	**May 8 1795**	**Jan 1 1873**					**1**	**6**	**2**	**0**	**1**	**0**	**4**	**6**
	Nancy Case	May 21 1795	Nov 21 1878	Jul 31 1816	Jan 30 1846	21	21								6

	Caroline Fulton	Aug 15 1821		Feb 6 1846	Feb 6 1846	50	24								0
	Phylena Hastings Fulton†	Apr 24 1797		Feb 6 1846	Feb 6 1846	50	48								0
	Martha Pulham			Aug 13 1865	Aug 13 1865	70									
186	**Wood, Daniel**[457]	**Oct 16 1800**	**Apr 25 1892**					**1**	**6**	**2**	**0**	**8**	**24**	**11**	**30**
	Mary Elizabeth Snider	Nov 25 1803	Oct 7 1873	Mar 19 1824	Jan 27 1846	23	20								6
	Penina Shropshire Cotten	Mar 12 1827	May 28 1879	Jan 27 1846	Jan 27 1846	45	18								7
	Nancy Ann Boice[458]	Aug 12 1808		Feb 6 1846	Feb 6 1846	45	37								
	Lydia Ann Gibbs	Aug 9 1817	Jul 27 1893	Jul 22 1851	Jul 22 1851	50	33								2
	Sarah Grace (Mariner)	Jun 6 1815	Dec 29 1886	Jan 14 1852	Jan 14 1852	51	36								1
	Theodosia Hulda Parrish	Mar 25 1808	ca. 1894	Jan 4 1853	Jan 4 1853	52	44								0
	Emma Maria Ellis	Jul 12 1824	Sep 23 1888	Nov 22 1853	Nov 22 1853	53	29								6
	Margaret Morris	Sep 11 1839	Oct 1917	Mar 3 1857	Mar 3 1857	56	17								8
	Eliza Hundy	Apr 16 1810	Nov 3 1881	May 24 1859	May 24 1859	58	49								0
	Clara Aurora Matilda Roydberg	Jun 2 1828		Dec 14 1868	Dec 14 1868	68	40								0
	Maria Anning	Dec 1 1787		Jul 6 1869		68	81								0
187	**Woodruff, Wilford**	**Mar 1 1807**	**Sep 2 1898**					**1**	**4**	**3**	**1**	**6**	**30**	**10**	**35**
	Phoebe Whittemore Carter[459]	Mar 8 1807	Nov 10 1885	Apr 13 1837	Nov 11 1843	30	30								9
	Mary Ann Jackson[460]	Feb 18 1818	Oct 25 1894	Apr 15 1846	Apr 15 1846	39	28								1
	Mary Caroline Barton[460]	1829	1876	Aug 2 1846	Aug 2 1846	39	17								0
	Sarah Elinor (Eleanor) Brown[460]	Aug 22 1827	Dec 25 1915	Aug 2 1846	Aug 2 1846	39	18								0
	Mary Giles (Meeks, Webster)	Sep 6 1803	Oct 3 1852	Mar 28 1852	Mar 28 1852	45	48								0
	Clarissa Hardy	Nov 20 1834	Sep 3 1903	Apr 20 1852		45	17								0

husbands & wives	birth	death	marriage	sealing	marriage age: husb	marriage age: wife	in JS life: wives	in JS life: children	> JS death: wives	> JS death: children	> Nauvoo: wives	> Nauvoo: children	total: wives	total: children
Sarah Brown	Jan 1 1834	May 9 1909	Mar 13 1853	Mar 13 1853	46	19								8
Emma Smoot Smith	Mar 1 1838	Mar 4 1912	Mar 13 1853	Mar 13 1853	46	15								8
Sarah Delight Stocking[461]	Jun 26 1838	May 28 1906	Jul 31 1857	Jul 31 1857	50	19								9
Eudora Lovina Young	May 12 1852	Nov 21 1922	Mar 10 1877	Mar 10 1877	70	24								0
188 Woodworth, Lucien	**Apr 3 1799**	**Nov 20 1867**					**1**	**3**	**4**	**0**	**0**	**0**	**5**	**3**
Phebe Watrous†[462]	Oct 1 1805	> 1874	ca. 1825	Jan 17 1846	26	20								3
Charlotte Fox	Nov 6 1801	Sep 13 1846	Jan 19 1846	Jan 19 1846	46	44								0
Arminta Maria Williams	Sep 20 1815	1870	Jan 19 1846	Jan 19 1846	46	30								0
Margaret Johnston	Dec 16 1819		Jan 19 1846	Jan 19 1846	46	26								0
Rachel Thompson Kingsley	Jul 6 1805		Jan 19 1846	Jan 19 1846	46	40								0
189 Woolley, Edwin Dilworth*[463]	**Jun 28 1807**	**Oct 14 1881**					**3**	**4**	**0**	**4**	**3**	**18**	**6**	**26**
Mary Wickersham[464]	Nov 4 1808	Mar 29 1859	Mar 24 1831	Feb 6 1846	23	22								8
Ellen Wilding[465]	Apr 8 1822	Oct 5 1913	Dec 28 1843	Feb 6 1846	36	21								5
Louisa Chapin Gordon (Rising)[466]	Feb 28 1820	Apr 29 1847	1843	Feb 6 1846	36	23								1
Mary Ann Olpin[467]	May 8 1825	Sep 30 1894	Nov 10 1850	Nov 10 1850	43	25								11
Betsy Ann Fitzrandolph (Jackman)	Oct 7 1815	Jul 25 1908	Feb 11 1857	Feb 11 1857	49	41								1
Elizabeth Ann Jackman	Jan 31 1837	Jul 25 1908	Feb 11 1857		49	20								0
190 Woolsey, Thomas	**Nov 3 1806**	**Jan 5 1897**					**1**	**7**	**2**	**1**	**3**	**19**	**6**	**27**
Mary Burrell[468]	Apr 11 1812	1859	Apr 29 1829	Jan 24 1846	22	17								13
Julia Ann Mitchell	Mar 4 1829	Jan 10 1896	Jan 28 1846	Jan 28 1846	39	16								11

	Elizabeth Ann Holdaway	Jul 7 1829		Jan 28 1846	Jan 28 1846	39	16								0
	Mary Lane[469]	Aug 18 1827		Apr 13 1847	Apr 13 1847	40	19								0
	Catherine Lukittus Hickerson (Miles)[470]	Feb 2 1816	Apr 2 1897	Jul 18 1863		56	47								0
	Maria Catherine Miles[470]	Oct 28 1851	Oct 5 1916	Jun 1865	Nov 15 1867	58	13								3
191	**Yearsley, David Dutton**	**Mar 3 1808**	**1849**					**1**	**6**	**1**	**2**	**0**	**0**	**2**	**8**
	Mary Ann Hoopes[471]	Jan 8 1811	Nov 22 1903	Sep 11 1830	Jan 21 1846	22	19								8
	Harriet Wollerton Dilworth (Caulflesh)[472]	Feb 24 1824	Nov 19 1896	Feb 7 1846	Feb 7 1846	37	21								0
192	**Young, Brigham***	**Jun 1 1801**	**Aug 29 1877**					**5**	**5**	**35**	**6**	**15**	**44**	**55**	**55**
	Miriam Works[473]	Jun 7 1806	Sep 8 1832	Oct 8 1824	May 29 1843	23	18								2na
	Mary Ann Angell[474]	Jun 8 1808	Jun 27 1882	Feb 10 1834	May 29 1843	32	25								6
	Lucy Ann Decker (Seeley)[475]	May 17 1822	Jan 24 1891	Jun 14 1842	Jun 14 1842	41	20								7
	Augusta Adams (Cobb)	Dec 7 1802	Feb 3 1886	Nov 2 1843	Jan 30 1846	42	40								0
	Harriett Elizabeth Cook	Nov 7 1824	Nov 5 1898	Nov 2 1843	Nov 2 1843	42	18								1
	Clarissa Caroline Decker[476]	Jul 22 1828	Jan 5 1889	May 8 1844	May 8 1844	42	15								5
	Clarissa Chase Ross	Jun 16 1814	Oct 10 1857	Sep 10 1844	Sep 10 1844	43	30								4
	Louisa Beaman (Smith)[358]	Feb 7 1815	May 15 1850	Sep 19 1844	Sep 19 1844	43	29								5
	Emily Dow Partridge (Smith)[368]	Feb 28 1824	Dec 9 1899	Sep 1844	Jan 14 1846	43	20								7
	Zina D. Huntington (Jacobs Smith)[†359]	Jan 31 1821	Aug 27 1901	Sep 1844	Feb 2 1846	43	23								1
	Eliza Roxcy Snow (Smith)[†364]	Jan 21 1804	Dec 5 1887	Oct 3 1844	Oct 3 1844	43	40								0
	Elizabeth "Betsy" Fairchild	Mar 6 1828	Jun 10 1910	Oct 3 1844	Jan 30 1846	43	16								0
	Clarissa Blake (Homiston)	Oct 28 1796	Mar 13 1863	Oct 8 1844	Oct 8 1844	43	47								0
	Rebecca Greenleaf Holman	Feb 20 1824	Jul 11 1849	Oct 9 1844	Oct 9 1844	43	20								0

husbands & wives	birth	death	marriage	sealing	marriage age: husb	marriage age: wife	in JS life: wives	in JS life: children	> JS death: wives	> JS death: children	> Nauvoo: wives	> Nauvoo: children	total: wives	total: children
Diana Severance Chase	Jul 25 1827	Sep 6 1886	Oct 10 1844	Oct 10 1844	43	17								0
Maria Lawrence (Smith)†16	Dec 18 1823	1847	<Oct 12 1844	<Oct 12 1844	43	21								0
Susannah Snively	Oct 30 1815	Nov 20 1892	Oct 31 1844	Oct 31 1844	43	29								0
Olive Grey Frost (Smith)†375	Jul 24 1816	Oct 6 1845	Nov 7 1844	Jan 14 1846	43	28								0
Mary Ann Clark (Powers)	Dec 28 1816		Jan 15 1845	Jan 15 1845	43	28								0
Margaret Peirce (Whitesides)†	Apr 19 1823	Jan 16 1907	Jan 16 1845	Jan 16 1845	43	21								1
Mary Harvey Peirce	Nov 29 1821	Mar 17 1847	Jan 16 1845	Jan 16 1845	43	23								0
Emmeline Free	Apr 28 1826	Jul 17 1875	Apr 30 1845	Apr 30 1845	43	19								10
Mary Elizabeth Rollins (Lightner Smith)†361	Apr 9 1818	Dec 17 1913	May 22 1845	May 22 1845	43	27								0
Margaret Maria Alley	Dec 19 1825	Nov 26 1852	Jan 14 1846	Jan 14 1846	44	20								2
Olive Andrews (Smith?)†356	Sep 24 1818	Jan 2 1858	Jan 15 1846	Jan 15 1846	44	27								0
Emily Haws (Whitmarsh)	Jul 22 1823		Jan 15 1846	Jan 15 1846	44	22								0
Ellen Ackland Rockwood	Mar 23 1829	Jan 6 1866	Jan 21 1846	Jan 21 1846	44	16								0
Martha Bowker	Jan 24 1822	Sep 26 1890	Jan 21 1846	Jan 21 1846	44	23								0
Jemima Angell (Young)	Oct 5 1803	Jul 13 1869	Jan 28 1846	Jan 28 1846	44	42								0
Abigail Marks (Works)477	Nov 6 1781	Jul 14 1846	Jan 28 1846	Jan 28 1846	44	64								0
Phebe Morton (Angell)478	Mar 28 1786	Nov 15 1854	Jan 28 1846	Jan 28 1846	44	59								0
Cynthia Porter (Weston)	Feb 2 1783	Jan 4 1861	Jan 28 1846	Jan 28 1846	44	62								0
Mary Eliza Nelson (Greene)†	Nov 24 1812	Dec 28 1886	Jan 31 1846	Jan 31 1846	44	33								0
Rhoda Richards (Smith)†372	Aug 8 1784	Jan 17 1879	Jan 31 1846	Jan 31 1846	44	61								0

Amy Cecilia Cooper (Aldrich)	Jun 30 1804	Jul 13 1852	Feb 3 1846	Feb 3 1846	44	41				0
Mary Ellen de la Montague (Woodward)	May 2 1803		Feb 3 1846	Feb 3 1846	44	42				0
Julia Foster (Hampton)†	Oct 11 1811	Jan 17 1891	Feb 3 1846	Feb 3 1846	44	34				0
Abigail Harback (Hall)	Sep 20 1790	Mar 25 1849	Feb 3 1846	Feb 3 1846	44	55				0
Mary Ann Turley	Jul 13 1827	Dec 24 1904	Feb 3 1846	Feb 3 1846	44	18				0
Naamah K. J. Carter (Twiss)†[479]	Mar 20 1821	Aug 6 1909	Feb 6 1846	Feb 6 1846	44	24				0
Nancy Cressy (Walker)†[480]	Jan 20 1780	Dec 17 1871	Feb 6 1846		44	66				0
Lucy Bigelow	Oct 3 1830	Feb 3 1905	Mar 20 1847	Mar 20 1847	45	16				3
Mary Jane Bigelow	Oct 15 1827	Sep 26 1868	Mar 20 1847	Mar 20 1847	45	19				0
Sarah Malin	Jan 10 1804	Mar 20 1858	Apr 18 1848	Apr 18 1848	46	44				0
Amanda Barnes (Smith)	Feb 22 1809	Jun 30 1886	Jan 19 1852	Jan 19 1852	50	42				0
Eliza Burgess[481]	Dec 8 1827	Aug 20 1915	Oct 3 1852	Oct 3 1852	51	24				1
Mary Oldfield (Kelsey)	1793	Sep 24 1875	Dec 16 1852	Dec 16 1852	51	59				0
Eliza Babcock	Oct 8 1828	Jul 12 1874	< 1853		51	24				0
Catherine Reese (Clawson Egan)	Jan 27 1804	Nov 7 1860	Jun 10 1855	Jun 10 1855	54	51				0
Harriet Emeline Barney (Sagers)	Oct 13 1830	Feb 14 1911	Mar 14 1856	Mar 14 1856	54	25				1
Harriet Amelia Folsom	Aug 23 1838	Dec 11 1910	Jan 24 1863	1863	61	24				0
Mary Van Cott (Cobb)	Feb 2 1844	Jan 15 1884	Jan 8 1865	Jan 8 1865	63	20				1
Ann Eliza Webb (Dee)	Sep 13 1844		Apr 7 1868	Apr 7 1868	66	23				0
Elizabeth Jones (Lewis Jones)	Apr 6 1812	May 6 1895	Jul 3 1869	Jul 3 1869	68	57				0
Lydia Farnsworth (Mayhew)	Feb 5 1808	Feb 5 1896	May 8 1870		68	62				0
Hannah Tapfield (King)	Mar 16 1807	Sep 25 1886	Dec 8 1872	Dec 8 1872	71	65				0

husbands & wives	birth	death	marriage	sealing	marriage age: husb	marriage age: wife	in JS life: wives	in JS life: children	> JS death: wives	> JS death: children	> Nauvoo: wives	> Nauvoo: children	total: wives	total: children
193 Young, Joseph	**Apr 7 1797**	**Jul 16 1881**					**1**	**5**	**3**	**2**	**2**	**6**	**6**	**13**
Jane Adeline Bicknell[482]	Aug 14 1814	Jan 15 1913	Feb 18 1834	Jan 12 1845	36	19								11
Lydia Caroline Hagar (Fleming)†[483]	Oct 13 1817	ca. 1881	Jul 1845	Jul 1845	48	27								0
Lucinda Allen	Jun 2 1824	Jul 16 1881	Jan 16 1846	Jan 16 1846	48	21								0
Mary Ann Huntley (Burnham)†[484]	Mar 14 1816	Nov 10 1903	Feb 6 1846	Feb 6 1846	48	29								2
Elizabeth Stevens	ca. 1799		Nov 28 1866	Nov 28 1866	69	67								0
Sarah Jane Snow (Kinsman)†	Oct 30 1838	Nov 11 1910	Apr 7 1868	Apr 7 1868	71	29								0
194 Young, Lorenzo Dow*[485]	**Oct 19 1807**	**Nov 21 1895**					**2**	**9**	**1**	**3**	**5**	**13**	**8**	**25**
Persis Goodall[307]	Mar 15 1806	Sep 16 1894	Jun 26 1826	Apr 7 1904	18	20								11
Harriet Page Wheeler (Decker)[98]	Sep 7 1803	12 23 1871	Mar 9 1843	Mar 9 1843	35	39								2
Susan Ann Ashby	Feb 1 1830	Apr 28 1896	Jan 26 1846	Jan 26 1846	38	15								0
Electa Jane Lee[486]	ca. 1807		Nov 22 1855	Nov 22 1855	48	48								0
Ida Hannah Hewitt	Jun 11 1839	Sep 20 1888	Apr 29 1856	Apr 29 1856	48	16								5
Eleanor Jones	Nov 16 1830	Feb 3 1912	Nov 24 1856	Nov 24 1856	49	26								4
Christiana Nelson	ca. 1842		Sep 13 1862	Sep 13 1862	54	20								0
Johanna Larsen	Aug 24 1843	May 8 1925	Apr 18 1863	Apr 18 1863	55	19								3
195 Young, Phineas Howe[487]	**Feb 16 1799**	**Oct 10 1879**					**1**	**2**	**5**	**0**	**3**	**17**	**9**	**19**
Clarissa Hamilton	Oct 3 1799	ca. 1834	Sep 28 1818	Jan 18 1846	19	18								5na
Lucy Pearce Cowdery	Jun 3 1814	Nov 29 1898	Sep 28 1834	Jan 28 1846	35	20								3
Mary Elvira Beecher (Lincoln)†[488]	Jun 8 1820		Jan 18 1846	Jan 18 1846	46	25								0

	Levira Clark (Smith)[489]	Aug 30 1815		Jan 21 1846	Jan 21 1846	46	30								0
	Sarah Ann Hollister	Feb 7 1827	Aug 18 1913	Jan 22 1846	Jan 22 1846	46	18								0
	Constantia E. C. Langdon	Oct 14 1817	Dec 1 1863	ca. Feb 1846	ca. Feb 1846	46	28								1
	Harriet Amelia Decker (Little)†[490]	ca. 1801		Sep 18 1846	Sep 18 1846	47	45								0
	Phebe Groombridge Clark	Sep 15 1830	Dec 20 1901	Nov 1853	Nov 1853	54	23								9
	Maria Eleanor James	Mar 27 1828	Jul 26 1897	Apr 1 1856	Apr 1 1856	57	28								6
	Elizabeth Rea	ca. 1801		May 18 1868	May 18 1868	69	67								0
196	**Zundel, John**	**Apr 15 1792**	**Nov 12 1852**					**1**	**8**	**1**	**2**	**0**	**2**	**2**	**12**
	Christiana Lautenschlager[491]	Jul 31 1811	Feb 7 1901	1831 or 1832	Jan 31 1846	40	21								12
	Hannah B. Ricken (Baumeister)†[492]	Mar 25 1793		Jan 31 1846	Jan 31 1846	53	52								
	Total							**274**	**714**	**443**	**160**	**417**	**2,306**	**1,134**	**3,180**

— NOTES —

Abbreviations

AF	ancestral files available at www.familysearch.org
BD	birth date
BE	Andrew Jenson, *Latter Day Saint Biographical Encyclopedia,* 1920
BP	Book of Proxey, an 1846 record of Nauvoo temple ordinances where a living person acted as proxy for a deceased person in solemnizing a marriage with a living spouse.
Brown	Lisle G Brown, *Nauvoo Sealings, Adoptions, and Anointings,* 2006
Compton	Todd Compton, *In Sacred Loneliness: The Plural Wives of Joseph Smith,* 1997
DD	death date
DUP	*Pioneer Women of Faith and Fortitude*, 4 vols. (Salt Lake City: Daughters of Utah Pioneers, 1998).
Hierarchy-1	D. Michael Quinn, *The Mormon Hierarchy: Origins of Power*, 1994
HR	Andrew Jenson, *Historical Record*
MD	marriage date
NDM	Lyndon W. Cook, *Nauvoo Deaths and Marriages: 1839-1845,* 1994
NMPS	*Lyndon W. Cook, Nauvoo Marriages, Proxy Sealings: 1843-1846,* 2004
Quorum	Devery S. Anderson and Gary James Bergera, *Joseph Smith's Quorum of the Anointed, 1842-1845,* 2005
SAB	Smith Affidavit Book, Joseph F. Smith Collection, LDS Archives
SB	"Nauvoo Sealings & Adoptions, 1846," Book A, LDS Archives
SD	sealing date
Succession	B. H. Roberts, *Succession in the Presidency of the Church of Jesus Christ of Latter Day Saints,* 2nd ed., 1900
WQ	Winter Quarters, Nebraska

1. One month after his plural marriage to Roxena Rachel Repshire, Adams died of cholera in Nauvoo (Hogan, "James Adams"). One indication that Adams was part of the inner circle of polygamists is that he participated in a plural sealing of Eliza Partridge to Joseph Smith on May 11, 1843 (SAB 2:33, 3:33; *HR* 6:233).

2. Denton was sealed to Adams on the same date Emma Smith was sealed to Joseph Smith in 1843; Adams performed the polygamous marriages of Smith to Emily D. and Eliza M. Partridge, witnessed by Emma (*Hierarchy-1,* 494).

3. On Oct. 13, 1869, in Salt Lake City, Roxena Rachel Adams affirmed that on July 11, 1843, she was married to James Adams by Joseph Smith "for time and all eternity," James Adams already having one wife (SAB 1:86; 4:88; Bachman, "Study of the Mormon Practice of Plural Marriage," 351). An AF has SD 1847, perhaps a resealing (see also Bergera, "Identifying the Earliest Mormon Polygamists").

4. Childbirth years 1836-61, overlapping with date of subsequent marriage in SB, which confirms the marriages were polygamous.

5. DUP has BD Jan. 1, 1801.

6. Childbirth years 1833-57.

7. Elizabeth had a son named Isaac Allred.

8. Rulon C. Allred, *The Allred Family in America,* 1965, 1:2-9, has MD July 28, 1841, same day of month as SB although earlier than Joseph Smith's first recorded sealing. An AF has 1846.

9. Elisha's MD to stepdaughter Sarah Jane Witt same as SD to deceased first wife, Dorcas. SB has SD to Cherizade same month. An AF has brother Elijah married to Cherizade since Feb. 9, 1830, children by him after 1846. SB adoption record has Elisha's name next to "Sarah Jane Averett," Elijah's next to "Cherrizada Averett," both women sealed to Elisha. SB has Elisha two years older than brother; AF has same BD, making them twins, each married to Cherizade. SB does not contain sealing record for Elijah.

10. An AF has Dorcas giving birth after she died; she probably married Robert Witt in 1825 and had children, including Sarah Jane, from 1827 to 1835. Witt died in 1837; she married Elisha the next year, children 1839-43, died in childbirth Feb. 6, 1843.

11. In spite of bearing children, 1830-65, Cherizade was recorded as having married her husband's brother in 1846 (see note 9).

12. The Heber City Cemetery Record has BD 1821 (*NMPS,* 90); BD 1831 in SB conforms with mother's MD in 1825, age 15.

13. An AF has BD Oct. 1, 1813; SB has BD Oct. 9, 1812; original member of Smith's "anointed quorum."

14. SB has BD 1809.

15. Marriage for time, Almon proxy for sealing to Lyman Sherman; SB has BD Nov. 19, 1807.

16. Marriage to Brigham Young for time, Oct. 12, 1844; Brigham proxy for sealing to Joseph Smith. Divorced by 1845 (*NMPS,* 47n2, citing Heber Kimball diary, Oct. 12, 1844). Marriage to Almon Babbitt for time, Jan. 24, 1846; Almon proxy for sealing to Joseph Smith (SB). Lawrence sisters replaced Partridge sisters as wives whom Emma acknowledged, Maria likely on date of Sarah's known marriage in 1843 (Quinn, *Mormon Hierarchy: Extensions,* 499). Her marriage to Brigham denied by Benjamin Johnson; marriage ended before sealing to Almon Jan. 24, 1846, according to Young family (Compton, 477, 744n for undocumented Jan. 24, 1846, marriage to Brigham; Jeff Johnson & Dean Jessee dispute her marriage to Young).

17. Divorced sometime after last childbirth Dec. 1839, possibly responding to Bair's 1843 plural marriage to Lucinda Owen.

18. Childbirth years 1844-59. Some AFs have BD 1812 and name "Owens."

19. Childbirth years 1841-54.

20. Data derived from biographical sketch of Barlow family, LDS Archives; Barlow, *Israel Barlow Story,* 1968, 224, has MD Jan. 28, 1846, yet earlier 1843-45 call to enter polygamy.

21. Childbirth years 1830-49, overlapping SD of subsequent spouse.

22. *NDM,* 103; an AF shows a christening date Dec. 5, 1819.

23. Childbirth years 1836-57.

24. Childbirth year 1847.

25. SB gives name, date, place of birth; an AF shows "Nancy C." Aber, but without definite date or place of birth.

26. SB has BD, place of birth; an AF has Eliza Jane married to Rufus; other AF has Elizabeth J. without BD married to Rufus.

27. AFs show approximate BD 1800 and MDs Elizabeth Holmes about 1841, Charlotte Spencer 1842, Mary Dart 1843.

28. Childbirth years up to 1851. Resealed Jan. 16, 1846. An AF has MD Dec. 11, 1831, for "Pamela Andrews." DUP confirms Jan. 1, 1832 (cf. Alder and Alder, *Benson Family,* 38); Evans and Anderson, *Ezra T. Benson,* 355, show MD Jan. 1, 1831 (cf. SAB 2:42, 2:44).

29. Following sister Pamelia, Adeline married Ezra, "he already having one wife" (SAB 2:42, 2:44); resealed Jan. 16, 1846.

30. Initial MD to Joseph Smith unclear, but Clayton has her with 1841-42 wives, Jenson in 1842 as "one of the first." Marriage to Ezra Benson for time, 1846; Ezra proxy for sealing to Joseph Smith. Divorced Sept. 21, 1852.

31. *BE* 1:368 identifies first wife as Mary Hilbourne (Kilburn in AF), daughter of Rev. Joseph

Hilbourne, with four children, DD after Samuel was whipped 1836, before his subsequent move to Far West, MO.

32. Samuel was proxy for Lettis's sealing to Palmer.

33. Sealing canceled Dec. 20, 1893, by Wilford Woodruff.

34. Sealing canceled Oct. 27, 1893, by Wilford Woodruff.

35. Samuel proxy for Vina's sealing to John Hollister.

36. Samuel proxy for Polly's sealing to Hyrum Smith.

37. Naomi had children by prior marriage up to 1837 (DUP), apparently married to Samuel between 1837-46 since he left Nauvoo Feb. 6, 1846, and died in Aug. 1846.

38. First husband, William Van Orden, died July 1844; civil marriage to John Bernhisel 1845. Easily confused with sister-in-law, Julia Ann Van Orden (1811-69). Divorced 1893, sealing canceled.

39. Elizabeth was a daughter of sister wife Catherine; an AF has MD Jan. 20, 1846. Elizabeth was proxy for John's sealing to over 100 deceased women, 1868-69.

40. *NMPS,* 22, has church divorce, 1851.

41. Marriage for time, John Bernhisel standing as proxy for Melissa's sealing to Joseph Smith. Divorced 1849.

42. Childbirth years 1835-48.

43. Some AFs have MD Jan. 6, 1848, in Nauvoo, but child in WQ Feb. 18, 1847, suggests probable MD Jan. 6, 1846, as indicated by some files.

44. Marriage for time, William standing as proxy for Catharine's sealing to John Stephenson. An AF has "Bamford," BP has BD Mar. 1770.

45. Family journal has DD >1847. Daughter Ellen, by first husband Charles Merritt, joined Rebecca in mother-daughter polygamous marriage to Curtis, 1846.

46. Kate B. Carter, *Treasures of Pioneer History,* 1952-57, 3:485 (cf. Will Bagley, *Scoundrel's Tale: The Samuel Brannan Papers,* 1999, 49n3); Brannan's MD to Corwin was before June 1844, since Brannan's paper, *The Prophet,* would have mentioned it if contemporary (Bagley correspondence).

47. Marriage cited in Wilford Woodruff to Brigham Young, Oct. 9, Dec. 3, 1844. Brannan disfellowshipped Apr. 1845 for plural marriage performed by William Smith in New York, reinstated May 24, 1845 (*Hierarchy-1*, 214-15, 426n155, 427n161; Roberts, *History of the Church,* 7:395; Bagley dates MD Sept. 1844, personal correspondence).

48. Susan died three months before James married Esther Jones.

49. Childbirth years 1843-49. Esther served as proxy for two previous wives. There was a Nauvoo civil marriage (*NDM,* 102). *BE* 2:283-84 gives her name as Rapier; Cook has Raper/Roper, perhaps anglicized (an AF has Roper). After church divorce, Esther married Samuel Harrison Bailey Smith and was sealed to Joseph Smith Jr.

50. James's first polygamous wife, Sarah, would bear one child in 1846. Her first husband died in the 1830s. She left James by 1849 and married a Sprague.

51. Abigail's first spouse, Stephen J. Abbott, died Oct. 17, 1843. She divorced James Brown in 1850 when he married her daughter, Phoebe, age nineteen.

52. This was a possible proxy marriage (Gladys Brown White, "A History of Captain James Brown," LDS Archives) to George Black, who died Aug. 18-25, 1845. *NMPS,* 59, identifies SD as July 18 at Missouri River "for time only," resealed for time Mar. 27, 1857, in Endowment House, Salt Lake City. DUP has James's sixth wife, Mary McRee, but a July 1846 date which, along with an AF, suggests Council Bluffs, Iowa, not Nauvoo.

53. Childbirth years 1839-59.

54. MD from family biography. *BE* 2:599 has marriage three years earlier in 1843. An AF has SD Jan. 23, 1843, predating their May 31, 1843, arrival from England.

55. Childbirth years 1831-54; MD confirmed by DUP, not AFs.

56. An alternate SD of Nov. 12, 1843, in Brown, 47 (cf. *Quorum*).

57. An AF and DUP have MD ca.1842; childbirth years 1843-50.

58. SB shows BD Oct. 21; an AF suggests ca. 1794.

59. DD from *Deseret Evening News,* Apr. 7, 1893; Stella Cahoon Shurtleff and Brent Farrington Cahoon, *Reynolds Cahoon and His Stalwart Sons,* 1960, 79 ff. By contrast, *BE* 4:688 has DD 1883.

60. Childbirth years 1837-61.

61. William served as proxy for Mary's sealing to James Casson.

62. An AF has MD to Caroline Smith, Aug. 1845, Helen Clark, Dec. 1845; confirmed in "Important Incidents in the Life of Thomas Callister," LDS Archives; absent from SB, *NDM.*

63. Resealed Nov. 20, 1849, in Salt Lake City. Canfield married Louisa's sister Clarissa, 1844.

64. Marriage for time, William standing as proxy for Mary's sealing to Robert P. Wilson.

65. Childbirth years 1840-65.

66. Mary Ann is listed in the 1850 census as part of the family.

67. An AF has MD May 11, while a Carter family history has May 21, 1828 (Arthur D. Coleman, *Carter Pioneers of Provo, Utah,* 1966, 93.)

68. Childbirth years 1843-66. Divorced by Oct. 1845; married John Snider Nov. 3, 1855; SD Feb. 16, 1867 (Coleman, *Carter Pioneers*).

69. Carter's handwritten diary, 1843-45, says "Mary Durfee joined the grand Lodge on the 26 of January 1845," and "Sophronia Babcock joined the grand Lodge on November the 15, 1845" (Coleman, *Carter Pioneers*, 90, with MD to "Sylvia" Babcock Dec. 1838, Mary Durfee Jan. 1 or 2, 1844). An AF has Durfee MD 1844 and 13 children, 1848-72, with a MD for Sophronia of Feb. 9, 1868, twenty years after her DD.

70. MD from an AF, with Manti as location for sealing (no SD), but not possible in Manti on MD. At age seventeen, Eliza was six years younger than Sophronia.

71. AFs show alternate MDs 1850s/60s.

72. An AF has MD 1847/48 in Washington, Utah; Andrew F. Ehat, "The Nauvoo Journal of Joseph Fielding," *BYU Studies,* 1979, has 1846/47. The marriage appears to be post-Nauvoo.

73. Childbirth years 1843-55.

74. Childbirth years 1847-56. An AF has marriage 1846/56 in Nauvoo. Born in Wayne County, Illinois, four years after sister Mary Eliza, both sealed to Alexander in WQ, deaths in Utah.

75. William L. Clapp to North Carolina Mailing List (BrickChurchNC), Apr. 24, 2000 (ancestry.com) regarding 1830 marriage to Mary Shultz plus ten children; Quinn *Hierarchy-1*, 542; eleventh child, see *NDM*, 15, incl. an 1842 child.

76. Childbirth years 1837-57; resealed Jan. 26, 1846.

77. Resealed Jan. 26, 1846.

78. Alice married Austin Sturgess Nov. 3, 1844, within two months of marriage to Clayton. After Austin's death, Alice had four children by Clayton, 1852-57. Divorced Dec. 13, 1858 (Smith, *Intimate Chronicle,* 1991, lxviii, 149n112; *NMPS,* 31n3).

79. The *NDM,* 109, has MD to William Whitehead Feb. 8, 1844.

80. Divorced 1871 (Smith, *Intimate Chronicle,* lxviii).

81. Marriage for time, Zebedee serving as proxy for Sarah's sealing to Jeremiah Mackley.

82. Marriage for time, Zebedee serving as proxy for Hannah's sealing to Eliphas Marsh.

83. Lavina and Zebedee later divorced.

84. Childbirth years 1835-56.

85. For MD, see Bergera, "Identifying the Earliest Mormon Polygamists."

86. SB has Rosilla Milla Carter; her brother, Gideon Carter, called her "Rizilla" and said she married Orange L. Wight in 1849 in Texas (*Succession,* 122-25).

87. Childbirth years 1830-49.

88. One AF has MD Feb. 28, 1863.

89. Childbirth years 1837-43.

90. Name also spelled "Shimer" in an AF.

91. Childbirth years 1836-63; MDs, SDs for first three wives from "Fred W. Cox and His Family," n.d., LDS Archives.

92. Marriage for time, and to Joseph Smith for eternity. A sixteen-page autobiography, Mar. 17, 1909 (photocopy, L. Tom Perry Special Collections, BYU), tells of Smith's invitation to marry, which she refused, but was sealed to him Jan. 27, 1846, after encouragement from his "intimate friends" (*NMPS,* 140).

93. Alternately Chrisman, Crisman.

94. Childbirth years 1831-56.

95. Lois was present in the temple Dec. 1845-Jan. 1846 (Smith, *Intimate Chronicle*), with a likely initial SD at time of second anointing, Nov. 15, 1843.

96. Marriage for time, Charles standing as proxy for Susan's sealing to Nathaniel Thomas.

97. Childbirth years 1824-41. In SB, AFs, name spelled "Pamela."

98. Harriet left her husband, Isaac, in 1841 and married Lorenzo Dow Young on Mar. 9, 1843. She was resealed to Lorenzo on Jan. 26, 1846 (*Quorum,* 220-21). The DD from *Quorum,* AFs, versus Lorenzo's diary in the *Utah Historical Quarterly,* 1846, with DD Dec. 22 and *BE,* 743, with Sept. 22, 1871; cf. Marguerite L. Sinclair (USHS) to Frank M. Young, June 21, 1847, Lorenzo Dow Young Papers, A 1108-3, Utah State Historical Society.

99. Elizabeth's first child, Henry, by first husband, Haggerty, not included in count of polygamous children.

100. Marriage for time, William standing as proxy for Martha's sealing to Edward Weaver.

101. Two of Elizabeth's previous husbands, Gilbert Goldsmith and Joseph Brackenbury, had died before she married Jabez Durfee, with whom she lived in Nauvoo simultaneously with Joseph Smith, whom she married in 1842; she separated from Durfee and on Jan. 22, 1846, was resealed "for eternity" to Joseph Smith and to Cornelius Lott for time. In Bennett's *History of the Saints,* 256, she was identified ("Mrs. D*****") as one of Smith's wives. Jabez married Magdalena Pickle in 1846.

102. Marriage for time, Magdalena's maiden name alternately spelled "Pickett," but probably derived from "Pickle." Her father, John Pickle Jr., married Magdalena Saltzmann in 1778. Magdalena the daughter (alternate BD June 6) was one of fourteen children. An AF has her marrying Edmond Durfee in 1809 and his brother, Jabez, in 1846; SB has Laura Pickett marrying Jabez in 1846 and sealed to her deceased husband, Edmond, with Jabez serving as proxy. Since the AFs do not have a Laura Pickett, perhaps "Laney" was mistakenly recorded in SB as "Laura." AF variants have Magdalena Pickle/Laura P. Durfee as separate wives of Jabez, while *BE* 4:551 has Edmond Durfee with "Lancy Pickle" and child, Jabez, 1828.

103. This incomplete data comes from the 1860 Iowa census, as reported in Compton, 265.

104. There are no known vital statistics for Mary. An AF suggests a marriage ca. 1839, which would have been too early for a plural marriage.

105. An "Eliz. Allred," age forty, and William Edwards, age forty, were present in the 1850 census.

106. Childbirth years 1840-61. SB has BD 1824; Lee, *Mormonism Unveiled,* 288, has 1825.

107. Catherine was the widow of Zephaniah Clawson (1798-1838/41). Lee, *Mormonism Unveiled,* said Howard was "sealed to Mrs. Clawson."

108. Olive's brother, Isaac Freeman, married Winslow's sister, Lydia, 1817. Olive was resealed to Winslow Jan. 22, 1846. Isaac married Roxana Porter 1829 and died in 1843; Winslow served as proxy for Roxana's sealing to Isaac Jan. 22, 1846, and married Roxana for time on same date (*NMPS,* 110) or Feb. 22 (SB).

109. Childbirth years 1827-51.

110. Childbirth years 1837-51.

111. Marriage by July 1845 (Black, *Annotated Record*; Brown, 100; *Quorum,* 222); first child Mar. 22, 1846 (Ehat, "Nauvoo Journal," 160).

112. Nancy has an alternate BD, same day and month but different year (1811) in DUP. The AF has children 1825 and 1832; DUP 1832, 1835, and 1840. The AF shows a former spouse Henry Whiteman/Whitemore.

113. An AF has a divorce June 1846.

114. Childbirth years 1839-50. Divorced Oct. 29, 1851, sealing canceled (*NMPS,* 79).

115. DUP has BD May 16, 1805.

116. SB has Lucien sealed to Harriet and Mary, both deceased, with Ann as proxy, then married and sealed to Maria.

117. Childbirth years 1823-48.

118. Childbirth years 1833-61; see "Brief Sketch."

119. Margaret was Sarah Oysterbanks's mother (Nilson, "Fullmer Family," 8).

120. Childbirth years 1838-56.

121. Childbirth years 1838-61.

122. Amanda died in childbirth, delivering her second child, Rozelia, in 1848 (Swanson, *Sagers Clan,* 1980; Ehat, "Nauvoo Journal," 87-88). An AF has Rozelia as a child of Theresa Bowley.

123. An AF shows an 1846 Nauvoo marriage. The 1850 WQ SD appears to be original, not a resealing.

124. The MD and SD likely the same; an AF has Feb. 12, 1850, seemingly mimicking the Bowley marriage.

125. SB shows BD Sept. 14.

126. Childbirth years 1825-Apr. 1846.

127. Childbirth years 1841-46; divorced after SD 1846.

128. Childbirth years Feb. 1847-69.

129. Childbirth years Mar. 1847-71.

130. Fanny and Levi separated, and Fanny married Paul E. Kofford, July 29, 1849 (*Hierarchy-1,* 550).

131. An AF records a child, Rebecca Harris, born Dec. 24, 1845, about two weeks before marriage, SD same month and day but two years later, 1848, which is unusual but still possible. The online *Harris Family News* has 1846 MD. No SD in Brown or *NDM;* Black, *Annotated Record,* reports an 1846 sealing, but possibly based on MD.

132. Childbirth years 1847-53.

133. Lucy received her endowment Dec. 29, 1845, preceding her marriage.

134. Lucinda later married Douglas David.

135. This was a marriage for time, Peter standing as proxy for Sarah's sealing to Joshua Smith.

136. Childbirth years 1833-47.

137. Both Sarah Elizabeth and Hanna Diantha later divorced William.

138. Hope Hilton, *"Wild Bill" Hickman and the Mormon Frontier,* 1988, 51-52, has Hickman marrying two women in one day: 26-year-old Sarah Elizabeth, a daughter of Bill's friend Luke Johnson, and "Margaret," a Shoshone Indian servant of Brigham Young. Both ceremonies were performed by Young in the Endowment House. The BD for Sarah Elizabeth is from an AF, ten years younger than her reported age of twenty-six when married.

139. Childbirth years 1843-51; marriage for time, Isaac serving as proxy for Charlotte's sealing to Gideon Carter. An AF has MD Apr. 30; *NDM* Apr. 16; *NMPS* Apr. 16/30.

140. Eliza was proxy for Isaac's sealing to his first wife, Keziah. AF, SB and *NMPS* have SD Jan. 14; an AF has MD Jan. 12.

141. Jane was proxy for Isaac's sealing to Elizabeth McClelland, July 1865; *NMPS* has MD Feb. 1, 1852, making her eight years old if BD 1844 as in an AF.

142. DUP BD Sept. 19, 1805.

143. Ann is listed in the 1850 census.

144. Laura was known as Laura Shimer after her maternal grandparents who helped raise her. Her BD comes from SB, AFs, and James Smith, "Nauvoo Social History Project"; MD from AF; alter-

nate BD Mar. 23, 1825, MD 1844 in William E. Hunter, *Edward Hunter: Faithful Steward,* 1970.

145. Childbirth years 1832-43, plus two later children of unknown BDs; died in Los Angeles. BD from SB; alternate BD 1808 in an AF, Ehat, "Nauvoo Journal."

146. Son of William Sr. (b. 1757) and Presendia Lathrope, William Jr. has an alternate MD to Zina Baker Dec. 28, 1806 (Brown, 148; *NMPS,* 63, 64). Two of Zina's daughters, Zina and Presendia, were widows of Joseph Smith. William had no children by other wives. One wife, Lydia, was a widow and mother of two other Smith widows, Emily and Eliza Partridge. William's last wife is identified in *NMPS,* 63, as Mary Anna Thorn Armstrong.

147. Lydia and William were married for time, Lydia serving as proxy for William's sealing to Zina Baker.

148. Caroline's washing and anointing were performed Dec. 20, 1845; she was listed in the 1850 census.

149. Childbirth years 1845-70.

150. Childbirth years 1835-58, during which time Marinda married Joseph Smith, Apr. 1842. Her May 1, 1869, affidavit states a May 1843 SD to Smith. Sealed to Orson Jan. 11, 1846, to children Jan. 12; resealed to Smith July 31, 1857, Orson as proxy. Divorced 1870 (Barron, *Orson Hyde*).

151. Martha and Orson divorced in 1850. MD 1843 (Myrtle Stevens Hyde, *Orson Hyde: The Olive Branch of Israel,* 2000, 497, citing Orson's Sept. 15, 1869 affidavit).

152. The Orson Hyde affidavit of Sept. 15, 1869, has the marriage in April 1843; Mary Ann's autobiography says "spring 1843"; and Thomas Bullock has, in Joseph Smith's 1843 journal, "July 20 M[arinda]. P[ratt]. to O Hyde" (Faulring, *American Prophet's Record,* 396). "Probably sealed" Dec. 17, 1845, before temple completed (Weston N. Nordgren to Mrs. Ralph E. Woolley, Mar. 14, 1949, LDS Archives).

153. Charlotte and Orson later separated (Hyde, *Orson Hyde,* 499).

154. A list of Aaron's wives (Utah State Historical Society Archives) has Sarah Maria MD Mar. 1, 1857, and death "on plains (no children)," otherwise confirming data except for omission of Jemina Davis.

155. Childbirth years 1847-63.

156. AF indicate marriage in Nauvoo, or in Garden Grove, Iowa, en route to Salt Lake Valley, sealing in WQ 1847 (alternately May 18, 1846).

157. Jemina was sealed to Aaron's brother, Huntington, on Jan. 21, 1846, and married to Aaron for time in 1857.

158. Childbirth years 1842-60. For SD by Joseph Smith, see Johnson, *My Life's Review,* 95-96; cf. Smith, *Intimate Chronicle,* 123. SB has repeat sealing Feb. 3, 1846, and BD 1820; an AF has BD 1817.

159. The addenda to Johnson, *My Life's Review,* 389, confirms MD. Clayton records May 16-17, 1843, visit to Johnson where Smith gave "instructions on priesthood" (plural marriage). *HR* has resealing Nov. 14, 1844; SB has another resealing Feb. 3, 1846.

160. The AFs have Flora and Benjamin divorcing and having their sealing canceled.

161. Susan was proxy for Joel's sealing to his first wife, Anna, who died one month before Susan's marriage.

162. For SD, an AF has 1993; *NMPS,* 181, has "date and place unknown."

163. *BE* 3:663 has John marrying at age nineteen, between Oct. 1836 and 1837, and Ellen bearing six children, three of whom died in infancy or crossing the plains.

164. Childbirth years 1838-60.

165. SB has BD 1808, same day and month. When Eli left on mission, Jane separated and married Simeon Adams Dunn in WQ May 1846; she divorced Simeon 1848 and rejoined Eli when he returned in 1852, traveling to Salt Lake City with him.

166. An AF has a variant, Minerva Hunt, probably due to a later marriage. SB has Woods, though hard to read. Resealed Jan. 20, 1846.

167. MD comes from Joseph Kelting affidavit, Mar. 1, 1894 (*Succession,* 119-20). Resealed to Lucy Feb. 6, 1846.

168. Childbirth years 1823-50.

169. Childbirth years 1842/3-49/50. Kimball family has Sarah's marriage at age thirty-one, after May 3, 1842, but conception in Jan.-Mar. suggests earlier date (Kimball, *Heber C. Kimball,* 95; Kimball, "Heber C. Kimball," 467). An AF has MD to William Spencer Noon Feb. 12, 1829, at age seventeen. Resealed to Heber Jan. 15, 1846.

170. Marriage for time, Heber standing as proxy for Rebecca's sealing to Frederick Granger Williams; resealed Feb. 7, 1846.

171. Childbirth years 1851-61; resealed Feb. 2, 1846.

172. Resealed to Hyrum Smith Jan. 15, 1846, Heber proxy for Mary's sealing to Hyrum; marriage to Heber for time.

173. Sylvia affirmed that her MD to Joseph Smith was Feb. 8, 1842, while she remained married to Windsor P. Lyon, MD Apr. 21,1838 (SAB). *HR* 6:234 has SD 1842. On Sept. 19, 1844, she married Heber for time while he stood proxy for a resealing to Smith, repeated Jan. 26, 1846, even as she lived with Windsor. On Jan. 1, 1850, after Windsor died (1849), Sylvia separated from Heber and married Ezekiel Clark, resulting in three children. One of six prior children with Lyon, Josephine was said to be a daughter of Joseph Smith (SAB).

174. Frances separated from Heber in 1851 and married Ezekiel Clark.

175. Resealed Jan. 26, 1846.

176. Resealed Feb. 7, 1846. Charlotte was separated from Heber by 1849 and married Thadews Constatine Hicks/Hix Oct. 15, 1850.

177. Nancy and Heber married for time; they were resealed Feb. 3, 1846, and divorced in 1865 (Whitney, *Life of Heber C. Kimball*).

178. Marriage to Heber Kimball for time, Heber standing as proxy for Sarah's sealing to Joseph Smith; resealed Jan. 26, 1846. Heber and Sarah divorced in June 1851.

179. Married Heber for time among seven of Joseph's widows (Whitney, *Life of Heber C. Kimball,* 418-20). Martha affirmed her sealing to Joseph Smith in summer 1842; obituary said August, 1842 "in the Nauvoo temple" (Compton, 724). Heber proxy for Martha's resealing to Joseph on Jan. 26, 1846.

180. Ellen and sister Harriet Sanders emigrated from Denmark. They were the daughters of Aagaat Ystein Sondresen and Aase Olsdatter Rommerasen Bakka. Ellen was resealed Jan. 12, 1846.

181. Married for time, Heber standing as proxy for Lydia's sealing to Joseph Smith (Compton, 8, 632); she and Heber later divorced. An Endowment House record has Lydia later married to James Goff.

182. Married to Heber for time; resealed Jan. 15, 1846, Heber standing as proxy for Lucy's sealing to Joseph Smith (Whitney, *Life of Heber C. Kimball*).

183. MD comes from Compton and Hatch, *Widow's Tale,* 40; an AF has alternate MD Dec. 29, 1845. A son, Abraham Alonzo Kimball, was born Apr. 16, 1846. Resealed Feb. 2, 1846.

184. MD to Joseph Smith July 27, 1842; civil marriage to Joseph Kingsbury for appearance sake, Apr. 29, 1843 (*NDM,* 104); married to Heber for time, he was proxy for Sarah Ann's resealings to Joseph Smith in Mar. 1845 and on Jan. 12, 1846.

185. Presendia married Norman Buell, Joseph Smith, and Heber Kimball. Heber served as proxy for her sealing to Smith ca. 1845 (*NMPS,* 33; *Hierarchy-1,* 557; Compton, 125, "after March 17"; Brown, 171n130). She was resealed to Smith, Kimball for time, Feb. 4, 1846. Her brother Dimick said he married her to Joseph Smith Dec. 11, and sister Zina Oct. 27, 1841, witnessed by Fanny Maria Huntington (SAB, May 1, 1869).

186. Amanda was the younger sister of Heber's fifth wife, Ann Alice Gheen. Resealed Feb. 2, 1846.

187. Resealed Feb. 2, 1846.

188. Martha and Laura Pitkin were older "spinsters" who "came from Quincy to live with Vilate." Martha was resealed Feb. 3, 1846, divorced. She died in WQ (Kimball, *Heber C. Kimball,* 76, 95, 230, 312).

189. BD comes from Compton and Hatch, *Widow's Tale,* 41; an AF has alternate BD Sept. 12, 1823.

190. Among Joseph's widows, Mary Huston married Heber Kimball for time (Whitney, *Life of Heber C. Kimball*).

191. Theresa and Heber separated in Mar. 1852.

192. Ruth soon separated from Heber.

193. Married for time to Heber Kimball, who was proxy for Sarah's sealing to James Mulholland.

194. Mary Ann and Heber divorced in 1850.

195. Elizabeth and Heber separated in 1850.

196. Sarah and Heber were separated by 1847.

197. Eliza was the mother of Mary Cravath (1838-95), who married Heber's son-in-law, Horace Whitney, Dec. 1, 1856, making Helen Mar Kimball and Mary Cravath sister wives.

198. Caroline was sealed to Joseph Kingsbury three times after her death: in Mar. 1843, Mar. 4, 1845, and Jan. 26, 1846.

199. At her 1845 sealing to Joseph Kingsbury, Dorcas also served as proxy for Joseph's sealing to his first wife, Caroline; she was resealed to Joseph Jan. 26, 1846.

200. Vinson's first wife, Martha, married Joseph Smith Aug. 1842. No MD for Vinson and Philinda Clark, but prior to his death (Compton, 369-70). An AF has Martha's sealing to Joseph, Aug. 1842.

201. There are variant MDs of July 26 (Compton, 365; DUP; Bachman, "Study of the Mormon Practice of Plural Marriage"); June 26 (Kimball, *Heber C. Kimball,* 310); and Mar. 14 (*Quorum,* 225; Holzapfel and Cottle, *Old Mormon Nauvoo*). Martha's obituary has sealing to Joseph Smith August 1842 "in the Nauvoo temple" (Compton, 724). Married Heber Kimball Oct. 12, 1844, for time; Heber stood as proxy for Martha's sealing to Smith, Jan. 26, 1846.

202. Vinson's first wife, Martha, gave consent for him to marry "Mrs. Levi Myrick," a Haun's Mill widow (Belnap, "Martha McBride Knight").

203. George served as proxy for Martha's sealing to Harmon Jackson Akes.

204. Probably married 1830s; second wife, Jane, served as proxy for Cynthia's sealing to Asahel. An AF applies Jane's marriage date to Cynthia, which is unlikely. Asahel's affidavit, Apr. 9, 1839, has Cynthia's DD ca. Nov. 1838 (*NMPS,* 102).

205. Jane's MD comes from *NDM,* 93, and AF; Jane and Hannah washed and anointed respectively on Dec. 19 and 18, 1845, prior to 1846 sealing.

206. The third Peacock sister was "possibly sealed" to their common husband about 1847 (*NMPS,* 101-02).

207. There are variations in names and order of wives in Lee, *Mormonism Unveiled* (1877 and 1880 editions); Brooks, *John Doyle Lee,* 1984; and AFs.

208. Childbirth years 1834-57.

209. MD comes from family records (Brooks, *John Doyle Lee,* 381); cf. DUP Nov. 4, 1844; AF Feb. 4, 1844. Resealed Jan. 14, 1846 (Brooks, 72-73).

210. John D. Lee was "eager to have the wives who had been previously married to him" sealed to him in the temple in Dec. 1845; the sealings were re-solemnized on Jan. 20, 1846 (Brooks, *John Doyle Lee,* 72-73).

211. Abigail was the mother of two of John's other wives, Agatha Ann and Rachel Andora Woolsey. John said he married Abigail "for her soul's sake, for her salvation in the eternal state" (Lee, *Mormonism Unveiled,* 289). Resealed Jan. 20, 1846 (Brooks, *John Doyle Lee,* 72-73).

212. John said Nancy had "left her husband in Tennessee, in order to be with the Mormon people" (Lee, *Mormonism Unveiled,* 289).

213. An AF has Mary Ann's divorce from John and marriage to his son, John Alma Lee, Jan. 18, 1859; alternately Aug. 23, 1857. John gives his own MD as 1856 (Brooks, *John Doyle Lee,* 383); DUP has "1856/58" and undated marriage to son.

214. Brigham Young said John D. Lee and Isaac Haight needed "some young women to renew our vitality, so he gave us both a dashing young bride" (Lee, *Mormonism Unveiled,* 289).

215. Childbirth years 1824-48. SD comes from the family Bible; resealed Feb. 4, 1844; Jan. 22, 1846. *NMPS,* 105, has Lott marrying an unidentified wife Apr. 27, 1845. Daughter, Melissa, married Joseph Smith.

216. Charity was the mother of Orson and Parley Pratt; her husband, Jared (MD July 7, 1799), died Nov. 5, 1839.

217. Eleanor and Cornelius divorced on Mar. 17, 1848 (*NMPS,* 106).

218. Marriage for time, Cornelius standing as proxy for Phebe's sealing to Joseph Knight.

219. Childbirth years 1838-61.

220. Childbirth years 1827-50.

221. Marriage for time, John serving as proxy for Sarah's sealing to Luther Sweat; John and Sarah were later divorced.

222. Marriage for time, John serving as proxy for Rhoda's sealing to John Lawrence (b. June 23, 1803).

223. MD comes from an AF. *NMPS,* 179, has SD June 3, 1865; AF shows SD Nov. 21, 1847, likely confused with that of Rhoda Sanford.

224. Mary Elizabeth and Elam divorced in Kanesville, Iowa.

225. Jane was the mother of Elam's first wife, Mary Elizabeth. Jane's marriage to Elam was for time; she was said to have been sealed to Joseph Smith "during the Prophet's lifetime" (*NMPS,* 82).

226. Susanne and Elam married after Susanne's first husband, Windsor Lyon, died Jan. 1849; she was sealed to Elam in WQ. Her name was alternately spelled "Susan."

227. Amasa has been credited with two other marriages because he was sealed, Jan. 28, 1846, to Harriet Pamelia Partridge and Esther Gleason; but Harriet, sister of Amasa's wife, Eliza Partridge, had died in 1840; Esther had died in 1845, making these posthumous sealings.

228. Childbirth years 1836-57. SD comes from *Quorum,* 227.

229. Caroline and Amasa separated 1867, then divorced and had their sealing canceled.

230. Marriage for time, Amasa Lyman proxy for Eliza's sealing to Joseph Smith; Eliza and Amasa separated in 1867.

231. Under "Diontha," an AF has MD 1843, but under "Dionitia," another AF has 1843 and 1845. DUP shows 1845 but age twenty-seven, indicating 1843. Compton, 434, has 1845, making her the fifth wife. SB spells her name "Dianitia."

232. Laura and Amasa divorced in 1853.

233. Lydia and Amasa divorced in 1867.

234. Family tradition has Susanne marrying Windsor Jan. or Feb. 1846 and having a child, Charles W. Lyon (Compton, 186). Windsor died Jan. 1849 and Susanne married Elam Luddington in December; no temple record for an 1846 sealing for Susanne and Windsor.

235. Marriage for time, Stephen serving as proxy for Mary's sealing to Ornan Houghton.

236. Childbirth years 1818-46.

237. *NDM,* 111, has an 1844 civil marriage for Joseph Meacham's father, also Joseph "Mecham," to Lucina Harmon Mecham, widow of Joseph Sr.'s deceased brother, Joshua Mecham.

238. Hanna had two (AF) or ten (DUP) children. Daughter Loretta Sylvia Meacham, BD Jan. 4, 1838, married Joseph Bates Noble, 1857.

239. Childbirth years 1828-48.

240. Mary Catherine and George were sealed at the time of their second anointing (*Quorum,* 228); resealed Jan. 13, 1846.

241. An AF shows MD same as SD in SB, but children suggested in 1830s discredits an 1846 MD.

242. Childbirth years 1837-56.

243. Resealed Jan. 27, 1846.

244. Marriage for time, Reuben Miller standing as proxy for Louisa's sealing to Hyrum Smith.

245. Civil MD unknown (*NMPS,* 93), but it had to occur before William's 1834 marriage to Eliza's sister, Phoebe.

246. Phoebe acted as proxy for her sister, William's first wife, Eliza (*NMPS,* 93; *BE* 1:481-82).

247. Vital statistics come from *BE* 1:482; resealed Jan. 19, 1846.

248. Mary Ann and William were separated by Apr. 18, 1850, when Mary Ann married Robert Thomas.

249. Sarah and William were separated by Jan. 8, 1865, when Sarah married William Wimmer.

250. Sarah Jane and Benjamin Thomas were married in 1835 in Akron, Ohio; alternative spelling Trusback (*NMPS,* 81); AFs give Triesback, Triesbeck, Treasbaugh. Benjamin's second wife, Lovina, was proxy for the sealing.

251. Isaac was sealed to a plural wife in Dec. 1843, another in Jan. 1844, four on Jan. 22, 1846, and one more five days later (*Quorum,* 229).

252. Abigail was Eliza Snow's sister, and Eliza refers to her (*Biography and Family Record*) in an Aug. 1843 setting as "Mrs. Morley." Beecher, *Personal Writings of Eliza Roxcy Snow,* 273, notes that in Dec. 1843 Eliza made a copy of her sister's patriarchal blessing and identified her as "Morley," indicating an awareness of the marriage by that date. See also *Quorum,* 229.

253. *NMPS,* 143; *Quorum,* 229.

254. SB has BD 1791; an AF indicates 1790.

255. Betsy and Isaac separated in July 1861 (*NMPS,* 143, citing diary of J. D. T. McAllister).

256. Ann's last-known residence was in Santaquin, Utah, on Aug. 19, 1860 (AF; *NMPS,* 143).

257. SD from AF and *NMPS,* 143.

258. Mary served as proxy for Helen's sealing to William. An AF has "Springer," BD ca. 1802. Sealed to Isaac Chauncy Haight, May 16, 1849, in Salt Lake City.

259. Marriage for time, William standing as proxy for Eliza's sealing to A. Cravath.

260. Freeman's two wives named Huldah were first cousins. Their mothers, Abigail and Huldah Chase, were sisters—daughters of Richard and Thankful Chase of Yarmouth, Maine. *BE* 4:690 has Freeman's BD Feb. 5, 1778; DD Jan. 22, 1847.

261. She received her temple washing and anointing Dec. 15, 1845.

262. Information on Joseph's sealing to Mary Adeline, coinciding with their second anointing, and SDs for first two plural wives comes from *Quorum,* 230. Beginning with Mary Beaman, Noble left Nauvoo with three wives.

263. Childbirth years 1835-49. *BE* 4:691 and *HR* have MD 1837, same month and day; the Joseph Bates Noble diary (LDS Archives) has 1834.

264. SB does not have an 1846 resealing for Sarah.

265. John Pack was proxy for his parents' sealing to each other in Aug. 1843 (Bergera, "John C. Bennett"), with a repeat sealing Feb. 3, 1846 (*NMPS,* 19). John was sealed to eleven women on Apr. 4, 1870, and Oct. 4, 1876, who were deceased and had not been his wives.

266. Childbirth years 1834-60. *NMPS,* 19, has SD Aug. 1843; resealing Jan. 21, 1846.

267. Resealing Jan. 21, 1846. An AF and DUP show BD 1824; SB has 1827.

268. Jane was the widow of John's brother, Rufus (married 1847). After John died in 1885, Jane married John Ackerly. Born in Onondaga, New York, Jane died in Millard, Utah (*NMPS,* 19-20).

269. Mary Judd Eaton "gave her husband, John E. Page, other wives ... [because] well, he wanted them," as she told Joseph F. Smith in Aug. 1904 (Smith, *Blood Atonement,* 50). When this statement was published in the *Deseret News,* Mary "denied it all" (Minutes of the Quorum of the Twelve, May 5, 1954, 4, Alma Sonne Collection, LDS Archives). John's three plural marriages were transacted before his excommunication March 1846, the year he joined James J. Strang's church. His plural wives all separated from him. It is possible that, upon his excommunication, the sealings were erased; it is uncertain whether he was sealed to Rachel and Lois Judd, his last two wives.

270. An AF has Mary's MD Dec. 26, 1835, but the month and day repeat the MD for Lorraine Stevens; sources suggest an 1839 marriage, after Lorraine's death, while Quinn suggests 1838 (*Hierarchy-1,* 567). In *Quorum, 230,* Mary's SD is shown to be prior to Joseph Smith's death.

271. If Mary Judd gave her husband plural wives "in the days of Joseph Smith," it implies a MD earlier than June 1844 (Smith, *Blood Atonement,* 50). However, Quinn finds that Rachel and Lois Judd married John Page in 1845 and separated from him in 1846 (*Hierarchy-1,* 567).

272. Rachel was Mary's younger sister and widow of James Madison Henderson, who had died on Apr. 12, 1845, the year Quinn gives as Rachel's marriage to John (*Hierarchy-1,* 567). Although prominent in the LDS hierarchy, John was disciplined by a church court in February 1846 and excommunicated on Mar. 1, again on June 26 (*Quorum,* 230). Quinn says Rachel left John in 1846 and married Jacob Hamblin in Council Bluffs in 1849. If she was sealed to Henderson or Page, the records have been voided.

273. Harriet gave birth to a baby which died at ten months of age in Sept. 1839, suggesting a marriage around 1837 when Harriet was about nineteen years of age (*NDM,* 59, citing *Times and Seasons,* Dec. 1839).

274. Childbirth years 1847-71.

275. SB has BD but no other information.

276. Martha married Hezekiah in Bainbridge, New York, sometime before their 1830 baptisms in Colesville, New York. SD from SB; DD from AF looks like a copy of her husband's data.

277. Marriage for time, Hezekiah standing as proxy for Mary's sealing to her deceased husband, James Bell. Mary also served as proxy for her deceased daughter, Elizabeth Bell (Sawyer),

whom she gave to Hezekiah even though her daughter had already been civilly married to Levi Sawyer on May 11, 1845, in Nauvoo, and sealed to him in June, two days before he died. The 1846 proxy sealing overrode the earlier ceremony (*NMPS,* 194-95). Six months later, Mary, herself, died.

278. In addition to having five living wives, Martin was sealed in the 1870s to six women who were deceased (*NMPS,* 62).

279. A little more than two years after Susan's death, she was sealed to Martin in Jan. 1846, his second wife, Mary, acting as proxy.

280. The MD, SD come from *NDM,* 98. Mary was proxy for Martin's sealing to Susan.

281. Charlotte and Martin married for time only; Charlotte was the widow of Ira Enos West.

282. Sally was sealed to W. W. Phelps on the same day she and William received their second anointing, again on Jan. 15, 1846.

283. The MDs for Laura and Elizabeth are conjectures based on sealing dates. They received the endowment on Feb. 2 and Jan. 23, 1846, respectively.

284. Childbirth years 1837-58. SD from Orson's "Pratt Family Record" (*Quorum,* 231-32); resealed Jan. 8, 1846.

285. MDs from T. Edgar Lyon, "Orson Pratt: Early Mormon Leader," M.A. thesis, University of Chicago, 1932, 171 (cf. England, *Life and Thought of Orson Pratt,* 97: "latter months of 1844"). Charlotte and Adelia Ann were twenty- and seventeen-year-old sisters from Crown Point, New York, at time of double marriage to Orson (cf. Van Wagoner, "Sarah M. Pratt," 83-84, who has marriages separate and sealings together). Charlotte left Orson in 1845 and married a Mr. Tyler. Adelia Ann was resealed to Orson in the temple on Jan. 13, 1846.

286. Resealed Jan. 13, 1846.

287. Mary Ann Frost Stearns served as proxy for Thankful's sealing to Parley on July 24, 1843. Elizabeth Brotherton was proxy for her Jan. 10, 1846, resealing to Parley.

288. Childbirth years 1838-44. SD June 1843 soon after Parley had just returned from mission to England; but Joseph Smith canceled the sealing and married Mary Ann himself a month later, July 24, the same date Parley was sealed to his deceased first wife and to Elizabeth, his first plural wife, as well as apparently for time to Mary Ann. On Feb. 6, 1846, Parley acted as proxy for Mary Ann's resealing to Joseph Smith. LDS Archives record four children in connection with both Pratt and Smith, Fawn Brodie suggesting the fourth, Moroni Llewellyn (b. Dec. 7, 1844), might have been Smith's (*No Man Knows,* 461). Mary Ann and Parley divorced in 1853.

289. Resealed to Parley Jan. 10, 1846.

290. Resealed Jan. 10, 1846.

291. Resealed Jan. 21, 1846.

292. Resealed Jan. 12, 1846.

293. Resealed Jan. 28, 1846.

294. MD comes from Proctor and Proctor, *Autobiography of Parley P. Pratt*, 589n5 (cf. 1985 edition of Pratt's autobiography, MD Feb. 8, 1846; but the Proctors found the temple was closed that day). No 1846 resealing (*NMPS,* 16, asserts a Feb. 8 ceremony).

295. Martha and Parley divorced in 1849 (*Hierarchy-1,* 571). No known DD (Proctor and Proctor, *Autobiography of Parley P. Pratt,* 590).

296. Martha served as proxy for Return's sealing to his deceased first wife, Laura Trask.

297. An AF has an Elizabeth Simon, but little information.

298. Childbirth years 1839-59.

299. Arrington, *Charles C. Rich,* 86, has MD Jan. 3. Eliza and Charles were resealed Jan. 15, 1846.

300. MD comes from Arrington, *Charles C. Rich.* Mary Ann and Charles were resealed Jan. 15, 1846.

301. MD comes from Arrington, *Charles C. Rich.* Sarah Jane and Charles were resealed Jan. 15, 1846.

302. Arrington *Charles C. Rich,* has MD, SD Feb. 2, as do an AF and DUP.

303. Childbirth years 1843-59.

304. Three years after Franklin's uncle, Willard Richards, died in 1854, Franklin married four of his widows for time only: Susannah, Rhoda, Nanny, and Mary.

305. Josephine's surname, de la Harpe, might be in reference to La Harpe, Illinois, a town not far from Nauvoo. Josephine and Franklin eventually divorced.

306. Sarah's and Levi's 1843 civil marriage is documented in *NDM,* 96.

307. Most AFs have Persis marrying her first husband, Lorenzo Dow Young, on June 26, 1826, alternatively on June 6 (DUP). Her childbearing years were 1827-45. She left her twenty-year husband in 1846, the day after he took a third wife, fifteen-year-old Susan Ann Ashby, and she married forty-six-year-old Levi; she was thirty-nine (*NMPS,* 143). Apparently she continued to be known as Mrs. Lorenzo Dow Young.

308. An AF has the marriage in 1846 but no SD. Mary and Phineas were later divorced.

309. Margaret's marriage and sealing in 1846 to her first husband, David Fullmer, were revoked, according to Nilson, "The Fullmer Family."

310. Willard married eleven wives. Three years after his 1854 death, four of them (Nanny, Mary, Rhoda, and Susannah Bayliss) married his nephew Franklin. An additional three women were sealed to Willard after his death: Martha Falder, 1857; Sarah Edna Hinman, 1893; and Ann

Elizabeth Fox, 1901; some AFs suggest that he and Ann Elizabeth may have married in 1829 or 1836; one shows a Jan. 16, 1901, posthumous ceremony.

311. Resealed Jan. 22, 1846.

312. Sarah and Nanny became Willard's wives at ages sixteen and fourteen respectively (*Quorum,* 233). Sarah was resealed to him Oct. 3, 1845 (*NMPS,* 112), and again Jan. 22, 1846. Nanny was resealed Jan. 25, 1846. A great-granddaughter, Ann Richards Martin, suggests that the marriages were not consummated until after the 1846 sealings (Stevenson, *Richards Family History,* 279).

313. Susannah and Willard were sealed in "Josephs Store [in] Nauvoo" (Willard Richards Diary, 1836-52; Wilford Woodruff, "Historian's Private Journal," 1858-78; *Hierarchy-1,* 519). They were resealed Feb. 6, 1846.

314. Amelia and Willard were resealed Jan. 22, 1846; Amelia acted as proxy for Willard's resealing to his deceased first wife, Jenetta, on same date.

315. Without a formal ceremony, Alice and Willard "mutually acknowledge[d] each other husband & wife, in a covenant not to be broken in time or Eternity … as though the seal of the covenant had been placed upon us" (Willard Richards Diary). *Quorum* accepts the 1845 event a the SD; *NMPS,* 112, calls it a "self-performed" sealing, an "illegal ordinance." Alice left Willard and was not sealed to him in the temple in 1846; an AF shows her marriage to Moses Whitaker, who died in 1851, and to George D. Watt two years later.

316. Three years after Willard's death, Mary, Susannah, Rhoda, and Nanny were all sealed to his nephew, Franklin D. Richards, Mar. 6, 1857, in the Endowment House in Salt Lake City.

317. Childbirth years 1834-56.

318. Childbirth years 1833-49.

319. Minerva was the aunt of Joseph's first wife, Maria. AFs have two variants, showing Minerva's husband, Joseph Lee Robinson, born 1774 and Maria's MD 1836.

320. Marriage for time, Albert serving as proxy for Angeline's sealing to her first husband, Moses Horne, who was killed in a temple construction accident.

321. Elvira and Albert divorced in 1851 (*Hierarchy-1,* 578).

322. In testimony to the high council, Nov. 25, 1843, Lucinda accused her husband of seducing her sister, Phoebe (Nauvoo High Council Minute Book, LDS Archives, where William's name is spelled "Sagars"). The council acquitted William, again five months later (cf. Swanson, *Sagers Clan,* 35, 61, 65-66). In 1869, Nathan Tanner affirmed that he had heard Sagers discussing "celestial marriage or plurality of wives" with Joseph Smith in Montrose, Iowa, in the spring of 1844 (SAB), lending credence to Lucinda's suspicion that "the abominable doctrine of Spiritual wives" was behind the council's indifference toward her sister's moral welfare.

323. Most AFs have MD of Mar. 1846. Harriet left William 1855, reportedly displeased with his 1852 marriage to Frances; Harriet became Brigham Young's forty-seventh wife Mar. 14, 1856, and bore third child Nov. 28, 1855, after she and William divorced. No record of children sealed to Young, although they acquired his name (Swanson, *Sagers Clan,* 91-95; Wayne D. Stout, *Genealogy of the Sagers, Fisk, and Stout Families,* 1960, 414).

324. Frances divorced William and the sealing was canceled on Aug. 23, 1855 (Swanson, *Sagers Clan,* 91.)

325. Elizabeth married Richard M. Hunt on Mar. 3, 1887, in Blackfoot, Idaho, one year after William's death in the same town (AF). William bequeathed a sixty-acre farm to Elizabeth and her four children, but since the "Sagers" name disappears from Bingham County the children probably acquired Hunt's name. The 1870 census has a thirty-four-year-old Mary Sagers, seventeen years older than Elizabeth Mary, in Tooele County, Utah; Stout, *Genealogy of the Sagers,* 416-17, includes this Mary as an eighth wife married ca. 1861, with four children (cf. Stout, *History of Tooele County,* 1961, 570).

326. Childbirth years 1832-65. Rachel was resealed to Ellis on Jan. 21, 1846.

327. Esther married Ellis for time, and Ellis was proxy for her sealing to William Atkins Gheen.

328. Childbirth years 1837-59.

329. Resealed Jan. 23, 1846.

330. Resealed Jan. 31, 1846. Lura's name also given as "Lucy" (*NDM,* 68); "Lury" and "Lura" are found in AFs.

331. At the resealing in 1846, Alice served as proxy for Lucius's first wife, Lura.

332. AFs also have a Jane Fales, born "about 1810," and Jane Hobs, born "about 1808," married to Lucius on same date as to Jane Hobs Fales.

333. Sarah Elizabeth was sealed to her first husband, Thomas Eldredge Fuller, Jan. 26, 1846 (SB, *NMPS,* 167); she was resealed to him in 1857, her second husband, Lucius, serving as proxy.

334. Patty was sealed to Joseph Smith in 1842, although not resealed to him in 1846 as was her daughter, Sylvia (Compton, 683). After David's death in 1850, Patty married John Parry, Dec. 14, 1851, and was sealed to him for time. She died 1892/3 in Bountiful, formerly Sessions Settlement, Utah, where her daughter and son Peregrine lived.

335. MD comes from Patty Sessions diary (Smart, *Mormon Midwife,* 142, 276). The ceremony was performed by Brigham Young.

336. Harriet Elvira Teeples should not be confused with her aunt, Elvira Teeples, born eleven years earlier in 1819. The aunt, born in Rochester, New York, to Jacob Teeples and Rhoda Bentley, married Albert Perry Rockwood 1846. David's wife was born in Pontiac, Michigan, to George Bentley Teeples and wife, Hulda. The AFs also confuse David Sessions, born 1790, with his name-

sake son, born 1823. Patty's diary (Dec. 1, 1849) mentioned that her fifty-nine-year-old husband told her of his plans to marry the nineteen-year-old Harriet Teeples and that on Jan. 13, 1850, "Hariet [was] sealed to Mr Sessions" (Smart, *Mormon Midwife,* 139, 142).

337. Patty served as proxy for her son's sealing on Nov. 6, 1871, to a woman named Velora Emory who had died the year before. The similarity between Emory and Emorrett suggests a typographical error or the possibility that Velora may have been a sister of Fanny, as just one interpretation (*NMPS,* 205).

338. Childbirth years 1833-46.

339. Childbirth years 1842-47; resealed Jan. 13, 1846. Bathsheba's MD comes from *NDM,* 92.

340. Lucy remembered her MD as Nov. 23 (Lucy Meserve Smith, "Historical Narrative," Special Collections, J. Willard Marriott Library, University of Utah). George wrote that his first wife, Bathsheba, gave him five wives "before leaving the Temple of Nauvoo" (George A. Smith Family Papers, Marriott Library). Hannah Mariah had apparently separated from William Smith in 1845 but remained sealed to him until 1846 when George was resealed to his first wife and four plural wives and sealed for the first time to Hannah Mariah and two additional women.

341. The MD is confirmed in the George Albert Smith Papers, Marriott Library. AFs have MD of Nov. 29, 1844, same as Lucy, and use an alternate spelling of the surname: "Clements."

342. Zora Smith Jarvis, "Sketch of Zilpha Stark Smith's Life," LDS Archives, has MD Mar. 26; the George Albert Smith Papers, Marriott Library, have Mar. 8.

343. Agnes was the widow of Don Carlos Smith, who first married her deceased husband's brother, Joseph Smith, then George A. Smith for time as George stood proxy for Don Carlos (Brigham Young Diary; Compton, 674, citing Gideon Tibbetts Ridlon, *Saco Valley Settlements and Families,* 1984).

344. Marriage for time, George A. serving as proxy for Susanna's sealing to Mark Bigler (proxy record 187 has "for time"); sealing record 501 omits this qualification); sealing canceled by Wilford Woodruff, Mar. 16, 1894.

345. Mary Jane and George A. were first cousins. She was the daughter of Asael Smith Jr., George A.'s and Joseph Smith's uncle. She married her first husband, George Washington Gee, Feb. 5, 1837, in Kirtland, Ohio, and George A. (for time) ten years after Gee's death.

346. In addition to the women listed here, two others may have been wives: a Mrs. Derbot and someone named Perry (*Hierarchy-1,* 583-84). Hyrum was also sealed posthumously to Susan Ivers and Polly Miller, Jan. 1846.

347. After her husband's death, Mercy was married for time, first to Hyrum Smith on Aug. 11, 1843, as decreed "by direct revelation from Heaven through Brother Joseph the Prophet," then to John Taylor in 1845. Three months before her marriage to Hyrum, on May 29, 1843, Hyrum served as proxy for Mercy's sealing to her deceased husband, Robert B. Thompson (*Quorum,* 239; Mercy R. Thompson to "oldest female descender of Robert Taylor …," Dec. 20, 1880, LDS Archives; MD also found in AF and DUP). Other evidence hints at an earlier date: she said they were married "a few weeks" before Hyrum read Joseph's revelation on marriage to the High Council, Aug. 12, 1843 (*Deseret Evening News,* Feb. 6, 1886). An entry in Joseph Smith's diary, May 29, 1843, stated that "Hyrum, Brigham, Willard, and Sis[ter] Thompson <were married> and Heber and Newel K. [Whitney] [were] present" (Faulring, *American Prophet's Record,* 381). The year after Hyrum's death, she married John Taylor who then stood proxy for her sealing to the deceased Thompson. They divorced in 1847, the year of Taylor's fifteenth marriage (*Hierarchy-1,* 597; Brown, 308; *NMPS,* 119).

348. Catherine said "the prophet Joseph Smith himself" performed her marriage to Hyrum "in the brick office building belonging to my husband" (*Deseret Evening News,* Sept. 27, 1905, 2).

349. Resealed to Hyrum Smith Jan. 30, 1846, John Taylor acting as proxy.

350. Apparently Joseph H. Jackson, *Narrative of the Adventures and Experience,* 30, referred to Louisa when he wrote that Joseph Smith offered his brother "one of his spiritual girls, whom Hyrum loved dearly, a Miss S.," in consideration for Joseph's alleged interest in Hyrum's daughter, Lovina. Louisa received her patriarchal blessing coincident with these events on Sept. 17.

351. Clarissa was resealed to John on Jan. 15, 1846.

352. Married for time, followed by Mary's Jan. 15, 1846, sealing to Silas Smith, John serving as proxy (Irene M. Bates, "Uncle John Smith, 1781-1854: Patriarchal Bridge," *Dialogue,* Fall 1987, 86, citing Jesse N. Smith's journal; cf. Jesse N. Smith Family Association, *Journal of Jesse Nathaniel Smith,* 1953, 7).

353. Julia's son, Benjamin Johnson, noted in *My Life's Review* and Mar. 4, 1870, affidavit that marital arrangements were made during Joseph Smith's Oct. 19-21, 1843, visit (*HR* 6:222), implying that the ceremony was performed at the time or soon after on a subsequent visit.

354. Ann and John divorced in 1850.

355. Marriage for time, John acting as proxy for Sarah's sealing to Joseph Smith.

356. The DUP includes only one of Joseph Smith's plural wives under the Smith name. This was Desdemona Fullmer, who had adopted the Smith surname later in life. Twelve other wives of Smith's are included under the names of other husbands. Emma is not profiled at all among Utah pioneers since she did not settle in Utah. In Appendix B, "Mrs." in front of a wife's name indicates a living husband in addition to Joseph at the time he married her. Resealings of these women to the deceased prophet are identified in Table 3.1, pp. 223-24; an additional six "women of interest" are discussed on pp. 221-24 and listed in Table 3.2. Of these possible wives of Joseph, Jane Tibbets is affirmed by Cook (82) as having been "sealed husband and wife … during the Prophet's lifetime" even though "the precise date is unknown." Such women were among those sealed (or resealed) to Smith after his death.

357. When Emma eloped with Joseph in Jan. 1827, she may not have anticipated how plural wives would define the church he would found. In the 1830s she became aware of Joseph's relationship with Fanny Alger, and she confronted Eliza Snow and Emily and Eliza Partridge about their connections to her husband. She was also aware of the legal action initiated by family friends over Joseph's romantic connection to and fiduciary neglect of the Lawrence sisters. After Joseph's death in 1844, Emma refused to acknowledge that her husband had ever married other women.

358. Louisa Beaman's 1841 marriage to Joseph was confirmed by her brother-in-law, Joseph B. Noble, and reported in *HR* 6:233. On Jan. 14, 1846, she married Brigham Young for time, while he served as proxy for her resealing to Joseph. In her last six years, she bore five children to Brigham, and all died in the years of their birth.

359. Zina married her first husband, Henry Bailey Jacobs, on Mar. 7, 1841 (*NDM,* 92), became pregnant with her first child in April, and married Joseph Smith that fall. Her brother Dimick affirmed on May 1, 1869, that he had performed her marriage to Joseph, a ceremony witnessed by Fanny Maria Huntington (SAB). In Sept. 1844, Zina married Brigham Young (Compton, 661; *Hierarchy-1*, 607), then remarried him Feb. 2, 1846, when she was pregnant with her second child by Jacobs; she was resealed to Joseph at the same time. A daughter by Brigham named Zina was considered Joseph's offspring for the eternities.

360. Lucinda married two Freemasons: William Morgan, who was kidnapped and reportedly murdered when he published a Masonic exposé in 1826, and George Harris four years later. In 1834 the Harrises converted to Mormonism and moved to Missouri, then Illinois. While still living with George, Lucinda married Joseph sometime before Jan. 1842. She was resealed to him on Jan. 22, 1846, George acting as proxy for Joseph (SB).

361. Mary Elizabeth reported that she had a romantic relationship with Joseph Smith beginning in 1831 at age thirteen, although she did not marry him until 1842 when she was twenty-three and married. She was still living with her husband, Adam Lightner, when she married Brigham Young for time on May 22, 1845, Brigham serving as proxy for her resealing to Joseph; repeat sealing in 1846.

362. While married to David Sessions, Patty recorded in her journal that she was united to Joseph Mar. 9, 1842, by Willard Richards "in Newel K. Whitneys chamber," her daughter Sylvia witnessing the marriage. Sylvia had also polyandrously married Joseph the previous month and remained Windsor Lyon's wife (Compton, 179). See note 173.

363. Delcena's husband, Lyman Sherman, died Feb. 15, 1839, in Far West, Missouri. Her brother Benjamin returned from a mission to Canada in early July 1842 to find her married to Joseph Smith (Zimmerman, *I Knew the Prophets,* 45). Joseph probably wed her before his June 29 marriage to Eliza Snow. On Jan. 24, 1846, Delcena was married for time to Almon W. Babbitt, who acted as proxy for her eternal sealing to Lyman Sherman.

364. After marrying Joseph Smith and moving into his household in the summer of 1842, Eliza clashed with Emma and was forced to depart from the household on Feb. 11, 1843. About three months after Joseph's death, Eliza was resealed to Joseph and married for time to Brigham Young, who stood as Joseph's proxy.

365. Sarah Rapson seems to have been mistakenly referred to as Sarah B***** by Bennett in his 1842 *History of the Saints*. The name "Sarah Bapson" was nevertheless incorporated into church sealing records in 1899, along with a note that a sealing had presumably been performed "during the lifetime of the Prophet Joseph but there is no record thereof." On that assumption, "Bapson" was resealed on Apr. 4, 1899. For Sarah Rapson, there is no MD, only an assumption that it must have occurred before Bennett's departure in July 1842. Archival sources indicate that Sarah's full name was Sarah Rapson Poulterer. Her patriarchal blessing gives a BD of Mar. 7, 1791, Sussex, England (Patriarchal Blessings, Book 3, LDS Archives); she seems to have married Thomas Poulterer Sept. 26, 1814. After migrating to Utah in the 1850s, she died in Salt Lake City in 1879 (*Deseret Evening News,* Aug. 20, 1879).

366. Ruth married Edward Sayers Jan. 23, 1841 (*NDM,* 91) and continued to live with him after her 1843 marriage to Joseph. There is no record of an 1846 sealing (SB).

367. Compton, 389-91, finds Mar. 4, 1843, a feasible MD. Joseph Smith inserts "Woodsworth" in his Mar. 4 diary entry (Faulring, *American Prophet's Record*, 327). Quinn (research notes) interprets a possible Clayton anagram as evidence for a June 1 marriage. On May 2 and June 1, Flora went on pleasure rides with Joseph in a carriage (Smith, *Intimate Chronicle,* 100, 118-19).

368. A year and a half after her initial marriage to Joseph Smith in Mar. 1843 (a second ceremony was said to have been performed on May 11), Emily married Brigham Young for time as he stood as proxy for her sealing to Joseph for eternity.

369. It is thought that Almera's marriage to Joseph occurred at or about the time of his visits to see her on Apr. 2 and May 16, 1843 (Zimmerman, *I Knew the Prophets,* 41-43; Faulring, *American Prophet's Record,* 333; Smith, *Intimate Chronicle,* 101).

370. Helen Mar was pressured to marry Joseph Smith when she was a young girl in love with Horace Whitney. She married Horace (Feb. 3, 1846) after Joseph's death but was considered a "proxy wife" being cared for in her first husband's absence, her nine children by Horace belonging to Joseph in the eternities. Horace stood proxy for Helen's sealing to Joseph at the same time Horace married her for time (Compton and Hatch, *Widow's Tale,* introduction; Whitney, *Life of Heber C. Kimball,* 1945, 37). In the 1850s, Horace himself married two plural wives: Lucy Bloxham in 1850 and Mary Cravath in 1856.

371. Elvira affirmed on Aug. 28, 1869, that Heber Kimball had sealed her to Joseph on June 1, 1843.

372. Rhoda was a sister of Joseph Smith's apostle and scribe, Willard Richards. At age

fifty-eight when she married Joseph, she was the prophet's oldest wife; on Jan. 31, 1846, she married Brigham Young for time, Brigham serving as proxy for her sealing to Joseph.

373. Compton, 537, identifies Hannah's parents as Thompson and Hannah Ells; BD Mar. 4, 1806, Lewis, England; and notes that she married Joseph in the first half of 1843. The DUP identifies her as Hannah Ann Dubois, daughter of Richard and Ann Dubois; BD July 31, 1808, in Salem, New Jersey; mother of two children, Mary Jane Smith (b. July 27, 1833) and Peter Aker Smith (b. May 24, 1835), possibly fathered by Joseph. An AF specifies that Hannah's parents were Thomas Ells & Hannah Smart, hence her initial "S." John Benbow stated that when Hannah was boarding with him in the summer of 1843, Joseph frequently visited her and talked about plural marriage (affidavit, Aug. 28, 1869).

374. Quinn disputes whether Mary Ann was married to Joseph during his lifetime (*Hierarchy-1,* 399); for more on this, see note 288. An AF has alternate BD 1808, same day and month.

375. Just over a year after Olive married Joseph Smith in summer 1843, she married Brigham Young for time, Nov. 7, 1844, Brigham acting as proxy for her resealing to Smith.

376. Phebe was a member of Joseph's Quorum of the Anointed and was sealed to him instead of to her civil husband, himself a polygamist, after Joseph's death (SB). But Compton is unconvinced that this implies a temporal relationship; Quinn, too, considers it "only a possibility" that she married Joseph during his lifetime (*Hierarchy-1,* 399).

377. Two witnesses to Fanny's marriage, Harriet Cook Young and Augusta Adams Young, signed affidavits in Mar. 1870 and July 1869. Fanny was resealed to Joseph Apr. 4, 1899. The sealing record from 1899 assumes she was one of Joseph's wives during his lifetime.

378. Some AFs have "William B. Smith," the name he used in the Illinois infantry, 1864-65, or "William Francis Smith," an alias for a bigamous marriage, Feb. 21, 1889, to someone allegedly named Rosanna B. Jewitt Surprise (see note 389). He was publicly identified as a polygamist in 1844 after marrying Samuel Brannan to a second wife (*Hierarchy-1,* 214, 594-95) and 1845 when he delivered a speech saying he, for one, "was not in favor of making any secret of the matter" (Irene M. Bates, "William Smith, 1811-93: Problematic Patriarch," *Dialogue,* summer 1983, 16-17, 19). He later denied polygamy (Launius, *Joseph Smith III,* 208).

379. Caroline Amanda was a sister of Jedediah M. Grant, a future member of the LDS First Presidency and father of church president Heber J. Grant.

380. Mary Ann was born in Bedford, England. She separated from her husband, James Sheffield, and married William by the fall of 1843 (Brown, 288). In 1845 she separated from William (*Hierarchy-1,* 594). She married Joseph Stratton in Dec. 1846 in St. Louis and was sealed to him. They moved to Salt Lake City, where he died in 1850. Mary Ann married C. W. West the next year; C. W. stood as proxy for her sealing to Joseph Stratton. C. W. died in 1871, and Mary Ann died in Oct. 1908 in Ogden.

381. Sarah Ann and her younger sister, Hannah Mariah Libby, both married William in 1844 and both separated from him in 1845. Remaining together, the sisters both married George A. Smith on Nov. 20, 1845; they were resealed to him on Jan. 26, 1846 (George A. Smith Family Papers; *Hierarchy-1,* 581, 594; Compton, 156). *NMPS,* 149, confirms Sarah Ann's 1845 sealing to George A. without mentioning Hannah. It also gives Sarah Ann's repeat sealing on Jan. 26, 1846, the same date Hannah was sealed to George A., but does not connect the two or mention William. Brown, 277, 289, has Sarah Ann's MD to William "about 1845," while an AF claims to have a complete SD for William.

382. See note 381. An AF shows a MD Jan. 26, 1846 to "William B. Smith."

383. Susan and William married and then separated within the same year (*Hierarchy-1,* 594).

384. Mary Jane was born in Wiltshire, England, in 1823. She married William one month after William's first wife, Caroline, died (*Nauvoo Neighbor,* July 2, 1845). Mary Jane and William separated within two months and formally divorced in 1847 (*Hierarchy-1,* 594).

385. At fourteen, Henriette was William's youngest polygamous bride (Brigham Young Diary, Aug. 8, 1845; Eva A. Rice and Loretta C. Rice, *Footprints of Ira Rice,* 1973, 11). Henriette separated from William the same year they were married (Quinn, *Hierarchy-1,* 594).

386. About the same time William gave "a full declaration of his belief in the doctrine of a plurality of wives &c" in Aug. 1845, he gave patriarchal blessings to plural wives Priscilla and Mary Ann (William Smith Patriarchal Blessing Book, 108, Community of Christ Library-Archives, Independence, Missouri; William Smith Patriarchal Blessing Book, 72-73, Theodore Schroeder Collection, State Historical Society Library, Madison, Wisconsin).

387. In a consistent trend, Elizabeth and William married and separated the same year (*Hierarchy-1,* 594).

388. William and Abeanade married in 1846 and separated in 1847 (*Hierarchy-1,* 594).

389. Where William was said to have married another woman in 1889 named Rosanna B. Jewitt Surprise, the name is probably a conflation of Rosanna Grant and Rosella Goyette Surprise.

390. Various AFs have MDs spanning 1840-48.

391. Emily married her first husband, Zachariah Harris, Mar. 6, 1834. He died in 1839. After an 1846 SD, some AFs show an 1856 MD (resealing) to Abraham; childbirth years 1847-59.

392. The full name comes from DUP.

393. Resealed Jan. 23, 1846. Childbirth years 1841-63.

394. Resealed Jan. 23, 1846, and in proxy ceremony for Louisa Wing White, Jan. 30, 1846.

395. Achsah married Alden White on Mar. 12, 1809. He died Aug. 16, 1830, after fathering six children, including Erastus's second wife, Minerva. Two years later, Minerva's mother and Aunt Louisa became her sister wives. That same year, Erastus was married to Achsah's deceased daugh-

ter, Louisa (b. 1818), by proxy. An AF has a namesake daughter, Achsah, born "about 1820," who is also said to have married Erastus in 1846.

396. Louisa was born in Worcester, Massachusetts. On Nov. 17, 1826, she married Levi Aldrich, who died in 1868. She married Erastus in a double wedding with her sister, Achsah, two years after her niece, Minerva, had married the same husband.

397. Margaret Earl, born in Ontario in 1820, married Erastus in 1877 at age 56 in St. George, Utah. Cook identifies her as Margaret Earl Loudenbach, whose ancestral files have her born in Ohio in 1818 and married in 1836 to Reuben Loudenbach in Indiana, then living in Iowa where she and her husand die some years later. If this were Snow's wife, she would have to have left her first husband in the Midwest, married Erastus in St. George, Utah, then returned to the Midwest where she and her former husband would live out their lives together in the same town of Earlham, Iowa. Little is known about the woman from Ontario, even the identity of her parents, except that her appearance in St. George is a better match for a wife of a Mormon apostle than the woman who lived in Earlham.

398. Lorenzo's marriage history follows Smith, *Biography and Family Record;* Sorenson, "Harriet Amelia Squires Snow"; and Bray, "Eleanor Houtz Snow."

399. Contrary to Eliza Snow Smith, *Biography and Family Record,* who suggested a MD in April 1845, an AF asserts the MD was Jan. 17, 1845. It has been said without corroborating evidence that Mary's sister, Hannah Maria Goddard (1828-1919), married Lorenzo in 1845.

400. Childbirth years 1838-52.

401. Married for time, Willard serving as proxy for Mary's sealing to Elijah Freeman.

402. Childbirth years to 1846.

403. Sally was endowed on Dec. 24, 1845, using Snow's surname, suggesting that the marriage had taken place (Brown, 291n431). They were resealed on Jan. 24, 1846.

404. Mary married her uncle Daniel, her father Hiram Spencer's brother.

405. Emily's husband, Hiram Spencer, died Aug. 12, 1846; in a levirate ceremony on Jan. 24, 1847, his brother Daniel acted as proxy for her resealing to Hiram; she then married Daniel for time (*NMPS,* 75-76; AF has MD Jan. 25, 1847).

406. Soon after giving birth to her daughter, Martha Emma Spencer, on Jan. 30, 1848, Martha Knight died in April. She was sealed to Orson the next year, her sister-wife Margaret serving as proxy. Children attributed to her in 1850, 1851, and 1854 were eventually shown belonging to someone else.

407. WQ Sealing Record has an alternate BD for Margaret Ann of Feb. 28.

408. Childbirth years 1834-53.

409. There is disagreement about whether Charity and Levi were married Jan. 13 (AF) and sealed Jan. 20 (SB; Black, *Annotated Record*) or if both events occurred on the twentieth.

410. George was born in Watertown, New York. After converting to Mormonism, he became an alternate city councilman in Nauvoo and, after becoming disaffected from the LDS Church in Utah, a territorial judge, appointed in 1854 by U.S. President Franklin Pierce. In December 1856, in a church proceeding, Brigham Young charged Stiles with adultery (Stiles refused to participate) resulting in his excommunication. A week later, vandals broke into Stiles's office, burned his books, and threw his papers into the privy. In 1860 he was living in Ohio; he died in Texas (Jessee, *Papers of Joseph Smith,* 2:597; William P. MacKinnon, *At Sword's Point: A Documentary History of the Utah War to 1858,* 2008, 60, 61, 110).

411. All three of George's wives are in the SB.

412. Childbirth years 1841-52; Louisa was also proxy in sealing Hosea's first wife to him.

413. *BE* 3:532 indicates that Lucretia left Hosea by 1847.

414. Resealed Jan. 7, 1846.

415. The sealing was repeated Jan. 14, 1846.

416. Mary Cook's marriage was noted in the Nauvoo Marriage Record on Feb. 2, 1844 (*NDM,* 109).

417. The marriage ceremony was performed by Hyrum Smith (*NDM,* 109).

418. The Nauvoo Social History Project has BD Sep. 11, 1813. Resealed Jan. 14, 1846.

419. Annie and John separated in 1845 and received a church divorce Nov. 9, 1852 (*Hierarchy-1,* 597; Brown, 308; *NMPS,* 119).

420. Mary Ann was raised in Brooklyn and no doubt helped her father, Ezra, with his store in Manhattan. After the family moved to Nauvoo in 1841, Ezra opened another successful mercantile establishment. Mildred P. M. Fontano, "Ezra Oakley and Elizabeth DeGroot" (online at *The Pioneer Ancestors of Norman & Rebecca McClellan*), writes with pride about her ancestor's marriage to John Taylor but without explicitly mentioning polygamy.

421. Ann married Solomon Pitchforth in Halifax, England, June 13, 1824. An AF has MD to John Taylor Jan. 7 and SD Jan. 30; SB has only the latter.

422. Abigail died sometime between June 15 and July 31 (*NDM,* 78).

423. Caroline and Elizabeth Beard were sisters. Elizabeth married Alvah at age fifteen in 1845/46 (AF), but she is not in *NDM* (1839-45), so they were probably married in 1846. She bore a child in WQ, 1846/47. An AF has MD and SD 1853.

424. The BP, entry no. 86, has an 1846 sealing to a deceased Abigail Jane Smith, BD 1812, but probably a mistake carried over from the entry for Abigail Sprague, another of John's wives.

425. As early as 1841, Turley was charged with maintaining a "second female" and "sleeping with two females." Joseph Smith told the Nauvoo High Council, Feb. 6, 1841, to forgive

Turley as long as he confessed "that he had acted unwisely, unjustly, imprudently, and" in a way that was "unbecoming" a church member (Quinn, *Mormon Hierarchy: Extensions,* 632).

426. Childbirth years 1822-Sep. 1842.

427. Childbirth years Oct. 1842-1850. Mary was an unwed mother when she gave birth to a baby in Oct. 1842 that died a year later. The father was Gustavus Hills, who was ordered by the Nauvoo Municipal Court to pay alimony (Newell K. Whitney Papers, Perry Special Collections). The church disfellowshipped Gustavus for "illicit intercourse" and bigamy since he was already married to Elizabeth Ann Mansfield (Nauvoo High Council Minutes). Mary confirmed in an Aug. 29 affidavit that Hills had urged her to remove to Columbus, Ohio, until she gave birth (Journal History of the Church, Aug. 29, 1842). It is presumed that Theodore's marriage to Mary was a condition for marrying her sister, Eliza, in 1844. Turley family members antedated the marriage to 1842 to give Mary's son a legitimate father (AF, Turley and Turley, *Theodore Turley Family Book,* 1978).

428. Childbirth years 1845-47. Resealed Feb. 3, 1846; Feb. 2 in Turley and Turley, *Turley Family Book*.

429. Childbirth years July 1845-55. Resealed a second time, Jan. 19, 1846.

430. Childbirth years 1845-55.

431. Marriage for time, Edward standing as proxy for Susan's sealing to Hyrum Smith.

432. Childbirth years 1836-44.

433. An AF has an alternate BD of July 6. Caroline's 1855 marriage to Alexander McRae sets the limit for estimating when she and Edward separated.

434. Childbirth years 1842-54. An AF has an alternate BD of Nov. 26, as does Brown, 327.

435. Jessee, *John Taylor Nauvoo Journal*, and *NMPS,* 68, have DD Sept. 5/6, 1835. When Mary was sealed to Nathan in 1846, Adeline stood as proxy.

436. After a civil marriage about 1838, Adeline and Nathan were sealed in Jan. 1846, Adeline also acting as proxy for Nathan's deceased wife, Mary Hulet.

437. Louisa was Adeline's mother and widow of King Follett, a man remembered in LDS history for the theological wonderment his death elicited, as expounded by Joseph Smith in the eulogy at Follett's funeral.

438. Childbirth years 1834-53.

439. Childbirth years 1823-47. Elizabeth Ann and Newel were resealed in the temple Jan. 7, 1846.

440. Elizabeth Almira divorced Newel in 1848.

441. Emmeline's middle name is sometimes given as "Belos" (Madsen, "Emmeline B. Wells: 'Am I Not a Woman and a Sister?'"; Larry N. Poulsen, "The Life and Contributions of Newell Kimball Whitney," M.A. thesis, BYU, 1966; cf. Vicky Burgess-Olson, *Sister Saints,* 1978, for "Blanche"). She and Newel were resealed Jan. 26, 1846. *NMPS,* 36, and Brown, 333, report an earlier SD of Feb. 14, 1845.

442. Elizabeth divorced Newel in 1848. Her father, Thomas Moore, left the Mormon faith and died in 1868, after which Elizabeth's mother, Mahala, canceled her sealing to Thomas and married Joseph Kingsbury in 1870. Kingsbury had been the front husband for Sarah Ann Whitney, who had secretly married Joseph Smith in 1843. Through these convoluted relationships, Sarah Ann was, in effect, both Elizabeth's aunt and stepdaughter.

443. Marriage for time, Newel as proxy for Henrietta's sealing to Alonzo W. Whitney.

444. Lyman may have been sealed to four wives on May 14, 1844, when he was initiated into the Quorum of the Anointed (*Quorum,* 241). Wight, *Wild Ram of the Mountain,* 236, 441, has Wight surrounded by four wives at the church wood lots in Wisconsin in September 1844 at a time when Harriet was "old enough to be the other wives' mother." Mary Ann was just seventeen; Mary Hawley, from Vermont, was twenty-two; and young Jane was "expecting a child in late winter." Plural marriages ceased for a while after Joseph Smith's death, so Lyman's marriages must have been performed before June 27. AFs show Harriet Benton and Mary Hawley each a year younger than the biography indicates for Sept. 1844. Jane's expectation of a child in late winter would coincide with a marriage in June. AFs have Mary Ann's name alternately as Mary Ann Otis, her father's first name. She is said to have been born Oct. 1828, making her fifteen years old in Sept. 1844. The AFs also have her subsequent husband, Ralph Jenkins, marrying both a Mary Ann Otis and Mary Ann Hobart on same date in 1865 (cf. *Succession,* 122-25). Lyman's first three wives were resealed to him on Jan. 28, 1846, his fourth wife on Jan. 30.

445. Wight, *Wild Ram,* 500-01; Roberts, *Succession,* 122-25.

446. Childbirth years 1844-66. Matilda is the younger sister of Orange's wife, Rosilla Carter.

447. Matilda's brother, Gideon Carter, recalled that Orange married "a young lady" in the fall of 1844/45 "to whom he had been engaged before marrying my sister." Orange's father performed the ceremony (*Succession,* 123). That young lady was Sarah Hadfield, for whom an AF suggests a MD of Feb. 6, 1844. Wight, *Wild Ram,* 239, 442-47, 501, clarifies that this was Matilda's marriage date and that Sarah married the following year on Feb. 7. Orange recalled that "at first the Doctrine [of plural marriage] was taught in private. The first I knew about it was in John Hig[be]e[']s family[;] he lived close to us and being well a[c]quainted with him and family I discovered he had two wives" (untitled reminiscence). Sarah's childbirth years were 1847-54.

448. In Jeremiah Willey's autobiography (Family History Library, Salt Lake City), he recounts his 1804 birth in New Hampshire; his 1827 marriage to Bathsheba and her 1838 death near Indianapolis; his 1839 marriage to Samantha, who bore him nine children and was sealed to him in 1846; his mustering with the Mormon Battalion; and farming in Bountiful, Utah, to his 1868 death. He avoids explicit acknowledgment of his plural wives but mentions a son born in 1859,

"apparently by Samantha Willey," suggesting other possibilities. When Samantha was sealed to him, she was also proxy for his sealing to a Hannah (*NMPS,* 153). On the same date, he was sealed to Sarah Ann, following what an AF indicates was the birth of their child, John Alphonzo Willey, Oct. 23, 1845. Following Jeremiah's death, he was sealed on Nov. 15, 1871, to Elvira Burnham, Emma Jane Call (twenty-five years his junior), Lucia Irene Call, and Electa Parker (AFs).

449. Childbirth years 1840-59.

450. Sarah Ann married John Saunders in 1841.

451. Childbirth years 1825-51.

452. Eliza was sealed to Elizier Terrill in 1846 and apparently married Alexander in 1852. An AF indicates a sealing to Alexander, evidently for time, and resealing by proxy to Elizier. The AF has her as Elisa (cf. SB Eliza), with the possibility that a scribe allowed the "z" from her first husband's name (Elizier) to migrate to her name.

453. Guy married three Grangers, all sisters, apparently during the Nauvoo period.

454. Childbirth years 1831-43.

455. AFs show BD variances 1801-06 for each sister.

456. Childbirth years 1831-51. An AF for Nancy Ann has a DD July 19, and a typescript in Church Archives uses July 20, perhaps a burial date.

457. SB appears to have BD of Oct. 11, although 16 in AF may be correct. He and his first wife, Mary Elizabeth, had six children, 1826-42.

458. An AF has her father's name Benjamin Boyce Buys, which could be correct. Her DD June 4, 1833/35, is incorrect because Nancy Ann was present at her sealing to Daniel in 1846. Some AFs also have Nancy Ann improbably married to three different men simultaneously.

459. Childbirth years 1838-53.

460. Wilford referred to Mary Ann, Mary Caroline, and Sarah Elinor as "members of my family" and said that Mary Caroline and Sarah Elinor "had been lead away" by "young men" who spent their "nights in fiddleing & dancing And afterwards ... folley[,] evil & wickedness" (Kenney, *Wilford Woodruff's Journal,* 3:71). Two days after Wilford arrived in Nauvoo from England on Apr. 13, 1846, he went to the temple (3:39), the date of his marriage to Mary Ann (AF), who was again at the temple on May 1 (3:42). On Aug. 2 he made oblique reference to his young wives when he wrote that Brigham Young explained "the principal of sealing" to "Phoebe W. Woodruff[,] [Mary] Caroline Barton[,] [Sarah Elinor] Brown[,] [and] Mary [Ann] Jackson" (3:64-65).

461. Kenney, *Wilford Woodruff's Journals,* 1:208, 5:70, has Sarah Delight's BD July 26, 1838. Matthias F. Cowley, *Wilford Woodruff, Fourth President of the Church,* 1909, has her DD 1907, same day and month as AF.

462. Phebe was sealed to Lucien for time, and he served as Joseph Smith's proxy for her sealing to him. She lived about twenty-eight years beyond her sealing (Newell G. Bringhurst, *Reconsidering* No Man Knows My History: *Fawn M. Brodie and Joseph Smith in Retrospect,* 1996, 185; Compton, 395; *NMPS,* 85, specifying a DD later than 1872).

463. Edwin's vital statistics come from Arrington, *From Quaker to Latter-Day Saint,* 110-15, 489-90.

464. Childbirth years 1831-54.

465. Ellen gave birth in 1845, a year she may have been sealed, with a resealing in 1846 (Arrington, *From Quaker to Latter-Day Saint,* 489).

466. Childbirth years 1847-58.

467. Mary's BD comes from the WQ sealing records; Arrington has a BD Mar. 24, 1824 (*From Quaker to Latter-Day Saint*); AFs have BDs Mar. 8 and 24, 1824.

468. Childbirth years 1831-58. Mary's BD is from SB and James Smith, "Nauvoo Social History Project" (cf. AF, Apr. 11, 1813).

469. An AF gives a BD for Mary that is approximately the same as for Thomas.

470. Both Catherine Miles and her daughter, Maria Catherine Miles, married Thomas and lived with him in the remote Utah town of Kanosh until they both eventually divorced him, although they continued living in Kanosh. Maria married Noah Avery on Sept. 12, 1875. Thomas died in 1897. AFs mention a Susan Maria Miles not connected to Catherine. They also show an alternate MD for Catherine of July 29, 1865; DUP has MD Jan. 22, 1859.

471. Childbirth years 1831-48, plus a child of unknown BD.

472. Marriage for time, David serving as proxy for Harriet's sealing to William Caulflesh.

473. Resealed Jan. 7, 1846.

474. Childbirth years 1834-44; resealed Jan. 7, 1846.

475. Joseph Smith sealed Lucy Ann to Brigham; she was resealed to Brigham on Jan. 14, 1846. Her MD is from her affidavit in SAB; DUP has June 15; AFs have both dates.

476. The MD is confirmed by Johnson, "Determining and Defining 'Wife,'" (also AFs, DUP). *BE* 3:804 has an alternative MD of 1843, same day and month; Orson F. Whitney ("Three Pioneer Women," *History of Utah,* 1904, 4:63-67) reports May 8,1843.

477. Abigail was the mother of Brigham's first wife, Miriam.

478. Phebe was the mother of Brigham's wives, Mary Ann and Jemima Angell.

479. Marriage for time, Brigham serving as proxy for Naamah's sealing to John Saunders Twiss.

480. Marriage for time, Brigham acting as proxy for Nancy's sealing to Oliver Walker.

481. An alternate 1850 MD from AFs perpetuate a supposed typographical error in "Pre-

Endowment House and Endowment House Sealings," carried over into Crockwell, *Pictures and Biographies* (Johnson, "Determining and Defining 'Wife,'" 68n45).

482. Childbirth years 1834-56.

483. Marriage for time, Joseph acting as proxy for Lydia's sealing to Isaac Fleming.

484. Marriage for time, Joseph acting as proxy for Mary Ann's sealing to James L. Burnham.

485. SB has Lorenzo's Oct. 17 BD, as does James Smith, "Nauvoo Social History Project" (cf. AF; Compton, 611).

486. An AF estimates a BD about the same time as Lorenzo's.

487. *NMPS* identifies two wives named Maria James—an Eleanor Maria James (as opposed to Maria Eleanor James of the AFs), MD 1854, and Maria James, a daughter, MD Apr. 15, 1856. Phineas is also credited, on similarly sparse evidence, with having married a Fanny Smith in 1851, a Loisa Jones in 1853, and a Sarah Preece in 1856.

488. Marriage for time, Phineas serving as proxy for Mary's sealing to Ira Elisha Lincoln and Mary serving as proxy for Phineas's sealing to his first wife, Clarissa.

489. Levira, a widow of Samuel Harrison Smith, divorced Phineas before 1851 (*NMPS,* 88).

490. Various AFs have widely diverging MDs for Harriet, ranging from 1822 to 1858. *NMPS,* 88, has Harriet and Phineas marrying in WQ, which would be later than their 1847 divorce.

491. Childbirth years 1833-52.

492. Marriage for time, John serving as proxy for Hannah's sealing to her deceased husband, Henry Andrew Bauermaister. Hannah, John, and Henry were all from Germany.

Bibliography

Addams, R. Jean. "The Church of Christ (Temple Lot): Its Emergence, Struggles, and Early Schisms." In *Scattering of the Saints: Schism within Mormonism,* eds. Newell G. Bringhurst and John C. Hamer. Independence, Mo.: John Whitmer Books, 2007.

Affidavits and Certificates Disproving the Statements and Affidavits Contained in John C. Bennett's Letters. Nauvoo, Aug. 31, 1842.

Alder, Donald B., and Elsie L. Alder. *The Benson Family: The Ancestry and Descendants of Ezra T. Benson.* Salt Lake City: Ezra T. Benson Genealogical Society, 1979.

Alexander, Thomas G. *Things in Heaven and Earth: The Life and Times of Wilford Woodruff, a Mormon Prophet.* Salt Lake City: Signature Books, 1991.

Allen, James B., and Malcolm R. Thorp. "The Mission of the Twelve to England, 1840-41: Mormon Apostles and the Working Classes." *BYU Studies* 15 (Summer 1975): 499-526.

Allred, James. Affidavit, Oct. 2, 1869. "40 Affidavits on Celestial Marriage," 1869. LDS Archives.

ancestral files, *Family Search,* online at www.familysearch.org.

Anderson, Devery S., and Gary James Bergera, eds. *Joseph Smith's Quorum of the Anointed, 1842-1845: A Documentary History.* Salt Lake City: Signature Books, 2005.

__________. *The Nauvoo Endowment Companies, 1845-1846: A Documentary History.* Salt Lake City: Signature Books, 2005.

Anderson, Lavina Fielding, ed. *Lucy's Book: A Critical Edition of Lucy Mack Smith's Family Memoir.* Salt Lake City: Signature Books, 2001.

Anderson, Mary Audentia Smith, ed. *Joseph Smith III and the Restoration.* Independence, Mo.: Herald House, 1952.

Anderson, Rodger I. *Joseph Smith's New York Reputation Reexamined.* Salt Lake City: Signature Books, 1990.

Anonymous. "The Cochran Fanaticism in York County [Maine]," Aug. 3, 1867. In *Maine Historical Quarterly* 20 (Summer 1980): 23-39.

Arrington, Leonard J. "The Writing of Latter-day Saint History: Problems, Accomplishments, and Admonitions." *Dialogue: A Journal of Mormon Thought* 14 (Autumn 1981): 119-129.

———. *Brigham Young: American Moses.* Urbana: University of Illinois Press, 1986.

———. *Charles C. Rich: Mormon General and Western Frontiersman.* Provo: Brigham Young University Press, 1974.

———, ed. *From Quaker to Latter-day Saint: Bishop Edwin D. Woolley.* Salt Lake City: Deseret Book, 1976.

———, and Davis Bitton. *The Mormon Experience.* New York: Alfred A. Knopf, 1979.

Bachman, Danel W. "New Light on an Old Hypothesis: The Ohio Origins of the Revelation on Eternal Marriage." *Journal of Mormon History* 5 (1978): 19-32.

———. "A Study of the Mormon Practice of Plural Marriage before the Death of Joseph Smith," M.A. thesis, Purdue University, 1975.

Backman, Milton V., Jr. *Joseph Smith's First Vision.* Salt Lake City: Bookcraft, 1971.

Bagley, Will. *Blood of the Prophets: Brigham Young and the Massacre at Mountain Meadows.* Norman: University of Oklahoma Press, 2002.

Bailey, Alice M. "Last Wife of Chief Kanosh." *Frontier Times,* Mar. 1980.

Baker, James R. *Women's Rights in Old Testament Times.* Salt Lake City: Signature Books, 1992.

Bancroft, Hubert Howe. *History of Utah, 1540-1886.* San Francisco: The History Company, 1889.

Bancroft, Matilda G. "The Inner Facts of Social Life in Utah," an interview with Jane Snyder Richards, San Francisco, 1880, Bancroft Library.

Barlow, Ora H. *The Israel Barlow Story and Mormon Mores.* Salt Lake City: By the Author, 1968.

Barron, Howard H. *Orson Hyde.* Salt Lake City: Horizon, 1977.

Bartholomew, Rebecca. *Audacious Women: Early British Mormon Immigrants.* Salt Lake City: Signature Books, 1995.

Barton, Almira W. Johnson Smith. Affidavit, Aug. 1, 1883. "Affidavits [on Celestial Marriage], 1869-1915." LDS Archives.

Baskin, Robert N. *Reminiscences of Early Utah.* Salt Lake City: Signature Books, 2006.

Bax, E. Belfort. *The Rise and Fall of the Anabaptists.* 1903; New York: A. M. Kelley, 1970; online at *Marxists Internet Library*, www.marxist.org.

Beecher, Maureen Ursenbach. "Eliza R. Snow's Nauvoo Journal." *BYU Studies* 15 (Summer 1975): 391-416.

———, ed. *The Personal Writings of Eliza Roxcy Snow.* Logan: Utah State University Press, 2000.

———, Linda King Newell, and Valeen Tippetts Avery. "Emma and Eliza and the Stairs." *BYU Studies* 22 (Winter 1982): 87-96.

Belnap, Della. "Martha McBride Knight," typescript. LDS Archives.

Belnap, Hyrum. Journal, July 24, 1908.

Benbow, John. Affidavit, Aug. 28, 1869. "40 Affidavits on Celestial Marriage," 1869. LDS Archives.

Bender, Mary E. "The Sixteenth-Century Anabaptists as a Theme in Twentieth-Century German Literature," Ph.D. diss. abstract, Indiana University, 1959, in *Mennonite Quarterly Review* 42 (July 1968): 226-27.

Bennett, John C. *The History of the Saints: Or an Exposé of Joe Smith and Mormonism.* 1842; Urbana: University of Illinois Press, 2000.

Bennett, Richard E. *Mormons at the Missouri, 1846-1852.* Norman: University of Oklahoma Press, 1987.

Bennion, Lowell. "The Incidence of Mormon Polygamy in 1880: 'Dixie' versus Davis Stake." *Journal of Mormon History* 11 (1984): 27-42.

Bergera, Gary James. "Identifying the Earliest Mormon Polygamists, 1841-44." *Dialogue: A Journal of Mormon Thought* 38 (Fall 2005): 1-74.

———. "John C. Bennett, Joseph Smith, and the Beginnings of Mormon Plural Marriage in Nauvoo." *John Whitmer Historical Journal* 25 (2005): 53-92.

———. "'Illicit Intercourse,' Plural Marriage, and the Nauvoo Stake High Council, 1840-44." *John Whitmer Historical Journal* 23 (2003): 59-90.

———. "Buckeye's Laments: Two Early Insider Exposés of Mormon Polygamy and Their Authorship." *Journal of the Illinois State Historical Society* 95 (Winter 2003): 350-90.

———. "The Earliest Eternal Sealings for Civilly Married Couples Living and Dead." *Dialogue: A Journal of Mormon Thought* 35 (Fall 2002): 41-66.

———. *Conflict in the Quorum: Orson Pratt, Brigham Young, Joseph Smith.* Salt Lake City: Signature Books, 2002.

Berrett, William E. *The Restored Church.* Salt Lake City: Deseret Book, 1940.

Bitton, Davis. "Ten Years in Camelot: A Personal Memoir." *Dialogue: A Journal of Mormon Thought* 16 (Autumn 1983): 9-20.

———, and Maureen Ursenbach Beecher. *New Views of Mormon History: A*

Collection of Essays in Honor of Leonard J. Arrington. Salt Lake City: University of Utah Press, 1987.

Black, Susan Easton. *Annotated Record of Baptisms for the Dead, 1840-1845*. Provo: Brigham Young University Press, 2002.

Bolton, Andrew. "Learning from Anabaptism: A Major Peace Tradition." *Restoration Studies,* 5 vols. Independence, Mo.: Herald Publishing House, 1993.

The Book of Mormon, an Account Written by the Hand of Mormon upon Plates Taken from the Plates of Nephi, Translated by Joseph Smith, Jun. 1830; Salt Lake City: The Church of Jesus Christ of Latter-day Saints, 1951.

"A Book of Proxey [Sealings]." L. Tom Perry Special Collections, Harold B. Lee Library, Brigham Young University, Provo, Utah.

"A Book of Records Containing the Proceedings of the Female Relief Society of Nauvoo." Joseph Smith Collection.

"Book of Sealings. (Living)—Wives to Husbands," Book A. LDS Archives.

Boyack, Hazel Noble. *A Nobleman in Israel: A Biographical Sketch of Joseph Bates Noble*. Cheyenne: Pioneer Print Co., 1962.

Bradley, Martha Sonntag. *Pedestals & Podiums: Utah Women, Religious Authority, and Equal Rights*. Salt Lake City: Signature Books, 2005.

———, to author, May 1, 2004.

———. "Changed Faces: The Official LDS Position on Polygamy, 1890-1990." *Sunstone* 14 (Feb. 1990): 26-33.

———, and Mary Brown Firmage Woodward. *Four Zinas: A Story of Mothers and Daughters on the Mormon Frontier*. Salt Lake City: Signature Books and Smith Research Associates, 2000.

Bray, Mildred H. "Eleanor Houtz Snow, 5th Wife of Pres. L. Snow," typescript, 2-3. LDS Archives.

Brewer, Fanny. Affidavit, Sept. 13, 1842, in John C. Bennett, *History of the Saints*. Boston: Leland & Whiting, 1842.

"A Brief Sketch of the Life & History of Margaret Thompson Smoot." LDS Archives.

"A Brief Sketch of the Life of Rhoda Ann Marvin Fullmer." LDS Archives.

Bringhurst, Newel G. *Brigham Young and the Expanding American Frontier*. Boston: Little Brown, 1986.

__________, and John Hamer, eds. *Scattering of the Saints: Schism within Mormonism*. Independence, Mo.: John Whitmer Books, 2007.

Broadhurst, Dale R. "Crisis at Kirtland." *Oliver Cowdery Memorial Home Page—D. P. Hurlbut,* online at http://olivercowdery.com.

Brodie, Fawn M. *No Man Knows My History: The Life of Joseph Smith,* 2nd ed. New York: Alfred A. Knopf, 1971.

Brooke, John L. *The Refiner's Fire: The Making of Mormon Cosmology, 1644-1844.* Cambridge: Cambridge University Press, 1994.

Brooks, Juanita. *John Doyle Lee: Zealot, Pioneer Builder, Scapegoat.* Salt Lake City: Howe Brothers, 1984.

———. *The Mountain Meadows Massacre.* Stanford, Calif.: Stanford University Press, 1950.

———, ed. *On the Mormon Frontier: The Diary of Hosea Stout, 1844-1861,* 2 vols. Salt Lake City: University of Utah Press and Utah State Historical Society, 1964.

Brown, Lisle G, comp. *Nauvoo Sealings, Adoptions, and Anointings: A Comprehensive Register of Persons Receiving LDS Temple Ordinances, 1841-1846.* Salt Lake City: Smith-Pettit Foundation, 2006.

Brundage, James A. *Law, Sex, and Christian Society in Medieval Europe.* Chicago: University of Chicago Press, 1987.

Buchanan, Frederick S. "Mormons Meet the Mennonites: A View from 1884." *Mennonite Quarterly Review* 62 (Apr. 1988): 159-66.

Buchholz, Stephan. *Recht, Religion und Ehe.* Frankfurt: Klostermann, 1988.

———. *Political Implications and Perspectives.* Frankfurt: Mohnhaupt and Klostermann, 1987.

Buerger, David John. "'The Fulness of the Priesthood': The Second Anointing in Latter-day Saint Theology and Practice." *Dialogue: A Journal of Mormon Thought* 16 (Spring 1983): 10-44.

———. *Mysteries of Godliness.* San Francisco: Smith Research Associates, 2002.

Bullock, Thomas. *Conference Report,* Apr. 8, 1844, 30-33. LDS Archives.

Bullough, Vern L., and James A. Brundage. *Sexual Practices and the Medieval Church.* Buffalo, N.Y.: Prometheus Books, 1982.

Bush, Lester E. "Mormonism's Negro Doctrine: An Historical Overview." *Dialogue: A Journal of Mormon Thought* 8 (Spring 1973), 11-68.

———, and Armand L. Mauss. *Neither White nor Black: Mormon Scholars Confront the Race Issue in a Universal Church.* Midvale: Signature Books, 1984.

Bushman, Richard L. *Joseph Smith and the Beginnings of Mormonism.* Urbana: University of Illinois Press, 1984.

———, and Jed Woodworth. *Joseph Smith: Rough Stone Rolling.* New York: Alfred A. Knopf, 2005.

Butler, John L. Autobiography. LDS Archives.

Callister, Helen Mar Clark. Statement. LDS Archives.

Callister, Thomas. "Important Incidents in the Life of Thomas Callister." LDS Archives.

Campbell, Alexander. *Delusions: An Analysis of the Book of Mormon.* Boston: Benjamin H. Green, 1832.

Campbell, Douglas. "'White' or 'Pure': Five Vignettes." *Dialogue: A Journal of Mormon Thought* 29 (Winter 1996): 119-35.

Campbell, Eugene E. *Establishing Zion: The Mormon Church in the American West, 1847-1869.* Salt Lake City: Signature Books, 1988.

Cannon, Donald Q., and Lyndon W. Cook, eds. *Far West Record: Minutes of the Church of Jesus Christ of Latter-day Saints, 1830-1844.* Salt Lake City: Deseret Book, 1983.

Cannon, Kenneth L. "Mountain Common Law: The Extralegal Punishment of Seducers in Early Utah." *Utah's Lawless Fringe: Stories of True Crime*, ed. Stanford J. Layton. Salt Lake City: Signature Books, 2001.

Cannon, Oa Jacobs. "History of Henry Bailey Jacobs." LDS Archives.

Carrott, Richard G. *The Egyptian Revival: Its Sources, Monuments, and Meaning, 1805-1858.* Berkeley: University of California Press, 1978.

Carter, John, and Percy H. Muir, eds. *Printing and the Mind of Man: A Descriptive Catalogue.* London: Cassell and Co., 1967.

Carter, Kate B. *Brigham Young: His Wives and Family.* Salt Lake City: Daughters of Utah Pioneers, 1967.

———. *Our Pioneer Heritage.* 20 vols. Salt Lake City: Daughters of Utah Pioneers, 1960, 1965.

———. comp. *Heart Throbs of the West*, 12 vols. Salt Lake City: Daughters of Utah Pioneers, 1939-51.

Carter, Verna Seely. "When I Die, Let It Be with My Boots On," online at www.Rootsweb.com.

"Cemetery Burials Database." *Utah State History*, online at http://history.utah.gov.

Charles, Melodie Moench. "The Mormon Christianizing of the Old Testament." *Sunstone* (Nov.-Dec. 1980): 35-39.

"Christian History and Biography." *Christianity Today*, www.christianitytoday.com.

Church History in the Fullness of Times: Religion 341-43, 2nd ed. Salt Lake City: Intellectual Reserve, 2003.

Clark, David L. *Joseph Bates Noble: Polygamy and the Temple Lot Case.* Salt Lake City: University of Utah Press, 2009.

Claus-Peter, Clasen. "Anabaptist Sects in the Sixteenth Century: A Research Report." *Mennonite Quarterly Review* 46 (July 1972): 256-79.

Clayton, William. Affidavit, Feb. 16, 1874. "Affidavits [on Celestial Marriage], 1869-1915." LDS Archives.

———, to Madison M. Scott, Nov. 11, 1871. William Clayton Letterbooks. Special Collections, J. Willard Marriott Library, University of Utah, Salt Lake City.

———, to Robert Clayton, a nephew, Nov. 7, 1869. William Clayton Letterbook, Bancroft Library, University of California, Berkeley.

Clerk's Report of Brigham Young's Interview with Horace Greeley, July 13, 1859. LDS Archives.

Cleveland, Sarah, to Augusta Lyman, 1847. John Lyman Smith Collection, L. Tom Perry Special Collections, Harold B. Lee Library, Brigham Young University, Provo, Utah.

Compton, Todd, to the Editor, *Journal of Mormon History* 25 (Fall 1999): x.

———, to the Editor, *Journal of Mormon History* 23 (Fall 1997): vi-vii.

———. *In Sacred Loneliness: The Plural Wives of Joseph Smith.* Salt Lake City: Signature Books, 1997.

———, and Charles M. Hatch, eds. *A Widow's Tale: The 1884-1896 Diary of Helen Mar Kimball Whitney.* Logan: Utah State University Press, 2004.

Conference Reports of the Church of Jesus Christ of Latter-day Saints. Salt Lake City, Deseret Press, 1890.

Cook, Lyndon W. *Nauvoo Marriages, Proxy Sealings: 1843-1846.* Provo, Utah: Grandin Book, 2004.

———. *William Law: Biographical Essay, Nauvoo Diary, Correspondence, Interview.* Orem, Utah: Grandin Book, 1994.

———, comp. *Nauvoo Deaths and Marriages.* Orem, Utah: Grandin Book, 1994.

———. *Joseph C. Kingsbury: A Biography.* Provo, Utah: Grandin Books, 1985.

———. *Revelations of the Prophet Joseph Smith: A Historical and Biographical Commentary of the Doctrine and Covenants.* Provo: Seventy's Bookstore, 1981.

———. "Lyman Sherman—Man of God, Would-Be Apostle." *BYU Studies* 19 (Fall 1978): 121-24.

Coolidge, Lowell W., ed. *Complete Prose Works of John Milton,* vol. 2, gen. ed. New Haven, Conn. 1959.

Cooper, Robert P. "Martha Jane Knowlton Coray and the History of Joseph Smith by His Mother," 1965, an eighteen-page typescript, photocopy in possession of Lavina Fielding Anderson.

Coray, Howard. Affidavit, June 12, 1882, in "Affidavits [on Celestial Marriage]," 1869-1915. LDS Archives.

Cornelius, Carl Adolf. *Historische Arbeiten vornehmlich zur Reformationsgeschichte.* Leipzig: Duncker and Humboldt, 1899.

Council of the Twelve, minutes, May 5, 1954. Alma Sonne Collection, Msf, 678, #2, bx 3, fd 5. LDS Archives.

Cowles, Austin. Affidavit, May 4, 1844. *Nauvoo Expositor,* June 7, 1844.

Cox, Cordelia Morley. Autobiographical statement, Mar. 17, 1909, L. Tom Perry Special Collections, Harold B. Lee Library, Brigham Young University, Provo, Utah.

———. Autobiography, MS 6105. LDS Archives.

Crockwell, James H. *Pictures and Biographies of Brigham Young and His Wives.* Salt Lake City: Cannon & Sons, 1877.

Cross, Whitney R. *The Burned-over District: The Social and Intellectual History of Enthusiastic Religion in Western New York, 1800-1850.* Ithaca: Cornell University Press, 1950.

Cumberlege, Geoffrey, ed. *Complete Prose Works of John Milton,* vol. 6, gen. ed. Don M. Wolfe. New Haven: Yale University Press, 1980.

"Cut and Recut: New Emma Smith Film Skirts Polygamy." *Sunstone* (July 2008): 76-77.

Dahl, Paul E. *William Clayton: Missionary, Pioneer, and Public Servant.* Cedar City, Utah: Dahl, 1959.

Daughters of the American Revolution Collection, 17:101. LDS Family History Library, Salt Lake City.

David Rumsey Historical Map Collection, online at www.davidrumsey.com.

Davis, David Brion. "The New England Origins of Mormonism." *New England Quarterly* 26 (June 1953): 148-65.

Daynes, Kathryn M. *More Wives than One: Transformation of the Mormon Marriage System 1840-1910.* Urbana and Chicago: University of Illinois Press, 2004.

de Las Cases, Emmanuel. *Le Mémorial de Sainte Hélène.* Paris, 1951.

De Voto, Bernard. *The Year of Decision, 1846.* Boston: Little, Brown and Company, 1943.

Denton, Sally. *American Massacre: The Tragedy at Mountain Meadows, September 1857.* New York: Alfred A. Knopf, 2003.

Dick, Thomas. *The Philosophy of a Future State,* 2nd American ed. Brookfield, Mass.: n.p., 1830.

Doctrine and Covenants of the Church of Latter Day Saints. Kirtland, Ohio: F. G. Williams & Co., 1835.

Dr. Miner's Defense, Being a Concise Relation of the Church's Charge against Him, for Professing the Doctrine of Polygamy, or the Lawfulness of Having a Plurality of Wives. Hartford: Hudson and Goodwin, 1781.

Driggs, Ken. "The Prosecutions Begin: Defining Cohabitation in 1885." *Dialogue: A Journal of Mormon Thought* 21 (Spring 1988): 109-25.

Dunford, C. Kent. "The Contributions of George A. Smith to the Establishment of the Mormon Society in the Territory of Utah," Ph.D. diss., Brigham Young University, 1970.

Edwards, Paul M. "William B. Smith: The Persistent Pretender." *Dialogue: A Journal of Mormon Thought* 18 (Summer 1985): 128-39.

Egan, William M., ed. *Pioneering the West, 1846-1878: Major Howard Egan's Diary.* Richmond, Utah: H. R. Egan Estate, 1917.

Ehat, Andrew F. "Joseph Smith's Introduction of Temple Ordinances and the 1844 Mormon Succession Question." M.A. thesis, Brigham Young University, 1982.

———, and Lyndon W. Cook, eds. *The Words of Joseph Smith.* Provo: Brigham Young University, 1980.

Eichler, Margrit. "Charismatic Prophets and Charismatic Saviors." *Mennonite Quarterly Review* 55 (Jan. 1981): 45-61, citing Otthein Rammstedt's *Sekte und soziale Bewegung: Sociologische Analyse der Täufer in Münster,* 1966.

Elders Quorum Record, Nov. 23, 1837. Archives, Community of Christ, Independence, Missouri.

Ellsworth, S. George, ed. *The Journals of Addison Pratt.* Salt Lake City: University of Utah Press, 1990.

England, Breck. *Life and Thought of Orson Pratt.* Salt Lake City: University of Utah Press, 1985.

Erickson, Dan. *"As a Thief in the Night": The Mormon Quest for Millennial Deliverance.* Salt Lake City: Signature Books, 1998.

Essholm, Frank Ellwood. *Pioneers and Prominent Men of Utah.* Salt Lake City: Utah Pioneers Book Publishing, 1913.

Estep, William R. *The Anabaptist Story.* Grand Rapids: Eerdmans, 1974.

Evans, John H., and Minnie E. Anderson. *Ezra T. Benson: Pioneer, Statesman, Saint.* Salt Lake City: Deseret News Press, 1947.

Evans, John Henry. *Charles Coulson Rich: Pioneer Builder of the West.* New York: MacMillan, 1936.

Faulkner, John Alfred. "Luther and the Bigamous Marriage of Philip of Hesse." *American Journal of Theology* 17 (April 1913): 206-31.

Faulring, Scott H., ed. *An American Prophet's Record: The Diaries of Joseph*

Smith. Salt Lake City: Signature Books and Smith Research Associates, 1987.

Female Relief Society of Nauvoo, Minutes. LDS Archives.

Ferris, Cornelia Woodcock. *The Mormons at Home.* New York: Dix & Edwards, 1856.

Fielding, Amos. Affidavit, August 24, 1869. "40 Affidavits on Celestial Marriage," 1869. LDS Archives.

Fielding, Joseph. Journal, 1832-59. LDS Archives.

Fifteen Years among the Mormons, ed. Nelson Winch Green. New York: Scribner, 1858.

Firmage, Edwin Brown, and Richard Collin Mangrum. *Zion in the Courts: A Legal History of the Church of Jesus Christ of Latter-day Saints, 1830-1900.* Urbana: University of Illinois Press, 1988.

Fisher, Josephine E. "Josephine Rosetta Lyon Fisher," online at *Bountiful Historical Museum,* www.bountifulutah.gov.

Fisher, Josephine R. Affidavit, Feb. 24, 1915. "Affidavits [on Celestial Marriage], 1869-1915." LDS Archives.

Flanders, Robert Bruce. *Kingdom on the Mississippi Revisited: Nauvoo in Mormon History.* Urbana: University of Illinois Press, 1996.

———. *Nauvoo: Kingdom on the Mississippi.* Urbana: University of Illinois Press, 1965.

Ford, Thomas. *A History of Illinois from Its Commencement as a State in 1818 to 1847.* 1854; Chicago: Lakeside Press, 1945.

Foster, Lawrence. *Women, Family, and Utopia: Communal Experiments of the Shakers, the Oneida Community, and the Mormons.* Syracuse, N.Y.: Syracuse University Press, 1991.

———. *Religion and Sexuality: Three American Communal Experiments of the Nineteenth Century.* New York: Oxford University Press, 1981.

———. "A Little-Known Defense of Polygamy from the Mormon Press in 1842." *Dialogue: A Journal of Mormon Thought* 9 (Winter 1974): 21-34.

Fraser, Antonia. *The Wives of Henry VIII.* New York: Knopf, 1992.

Fullmer, David. Affidavit, June 15, 1869. "40 Affidavits on Celestial Marriage," 1869. LDS Archives.

———, et al. Affidavit, Oct. 10, 1869. "[Affidavits] Book No. 2," 1869-1870. LDS Archives.

Gates, Susa Young. *Unique Story—President Brigham Young.* Salt Lake City: Daughters of Utah Pioneers, 1990.

———. "Brigham Young and His Nineteen Wives." Susa Young Gates Papers, 1852-1932, bx 12, fd 2, Utah State Historical Society, Salt Lake City.

———, and Mabel Young Sanborn. "Brigham Young Genealogy." *Utah Genealogical and Historical Magazine,* July 1920, 131.

Geisberg, Max, comp., *Die Wiedertäufer in Münster: Bildwiedergaben ausgewälter Urkunden und Akten zur Geschichte Westfalens,* 12 Bd. Velen, Westfallen: Archivbildstelle, 1930.

Godfrey, Kenneth W. "A Note on the Nauvoo Library and Literary Institute." *BYU Studies* 14 (Spring 1974): 386-89.

———. "Causes of Non-Mormon Conflict in Hancock County, Illinois, 1839-1846," Ph.D. diss., 1967.

Goldberger, Michelle. *Kingdom Coming: The Rise of Christian Nationalism.* New York: W. W. Norton, 2007.

Goodwin, Doris Kearns. *Team of Rivals: The Political Genius of Abraham Lincoln.* New York: Simon and Schuster, 2005.

Grant, Heber J., to Ray O. Wyland, Dec. 12, 1936. LDS Archives.

Grotius, Hugo. *De Jure Belli ac Pacis, 1625,* 1.2.6; 2.5.5, 9; trans. A. C. Campbell, *On the Law of War and Peace,* London, 1814.

Grover, Thomas. Affidavit, July 6, 1869. "40 Affidavits on Celestial Marriage," 1869. LDS Archives.

Hallwas, John E., and Roger D. Launius. *Cultures in Conflict: A Documentary History of the Mormon War in Illinois.* Logan: Utah State University Press, 1995.

Hansen, Klaus J. "The Metamorphosis of the Kingdom of God." *Dialogue: A Journal of Mormon Thought* 1 (Autumn 1966): 63-83.

———. "The World and the Prophet," review of *Nauvoo: Kingdom on the Mississippi* by Robert Bruce Flanders. *Dialogue: A Journal of Mormon Thought* 1 (Summer 1966): 103-7.

Hardy, B. Carmon. *Solemn Covenant: The Mormon Polygamous Passage.* Urbana: University of Illinois Press, 1992.

Harwell, William S., ed. *Manuscript History of Brigham Young, 1847-1850.* Salt Lake City: Collier's Publishing Co., 1997.

Heath, Harvard S., ed. *In the World: The Diaries of Reed Smoot.* Salt Lake City: Signature Books and Smith Research Associates, 1997.

Hill, Christopher. *World Turned Upside Down: Radical Ideas during the English Revolution.* New York: Viking, 1972.

———. *Puritanism and Revolution: Studies in Interpretation of the English Revolution of the Seventeenth Century.* London: Secker and Warburg, 1965.

Hill, Marvin S. "Counter-Revolution: The Mormon Reaction to the Coming of American Democracy." *Sunstone* (June 1989): 24-32.

———. *Quest for Refuge*. Salt Lake City: Signature Books, 1989.

Hillman, Eugene. *Polygamy Reconsidered: African Plural Marriage and the Christian Churches*. Maryknoll, New York: Orbis Books, 1975.

Hinckley, Gordon B., interviewed by Larry King, CNN broadcast, Sept. 8, 1998, qtd. in "On the Record: 'We Stand for Something,'" *Sunstone* (Dec. 1998): 70-72.

Hirshson, Stanley P. *The Lion of the Lord: A Biography of Brigham Young*. New York: Knopf, 1969.

History of the Church of Jesus Christ of Latter-day Saints, ed. B. H. Roberts, 2nd ed. rev., 7 vols. Salt Lake City: Deseret Book, 1963.

Hogan, Mervin B. "James Adams and the Founding of the Grand Lodge of Illinois." LDS Archives.

Holmes, Elvira A. C. Affidavit, Aug. 28, 1869. "40 Affidavits on Celestial Marriage," 1869. LDS Archives.

Holzapfel, Jeni B., and Richard N. Holzapfel, eds. *A Woman's View: Helen Mar Whitney's Reminiscences of Early Church History*. Provo: BYU Religious Studies Center, 1997.

Holzapfel, Richard N., and T. Jeffery Cottle. *Old Mormon Nauvoo and Southeastern Iowa: Historic Photographs and Guide*. Santa Ana, Calif.: Fieldbrook Productions, 1991.

Homer, Michael W. "The Waldensian Valleys: Seeking 'Primitive Christianity' in Italy." *Journal of Mormon History* 31 (Summer 2005): 134-87.

Horne, Mary Isabella Hales. "Migration and Settlement of the Latter Day Saints." Utah State Historical Society, from 42-page holograph, Bancroft Library.

Howard, Richard P. "The Changing RLDS Response to Mormon Polygamy: A Preliminary Analysis." *John Whitmer Historical Journal* 3 (1983): 14-29.

Howe, Eber D. *Mormonism Unvailed*. 1834; New York: AMS Press, 1977.

Hume, David. *Essays: Moral, Political, and Literary*. 1741; London: Grant Richards, 1903.

Huntington, Oliver. Journal, Nov. 14, 1884. Utah State Historical Society.

Hyde, Marinda Nancy Johnson. Affidavit, May 1, 1869. "40 Affidavits on Celestial Marriage," 1869. LDS Archives.

Hyde, Mary Ann Price. Autobiography. Bancroft Library.

Ivins, Stanley Snow. "Notes on Mormon Polygamy." *Western Humanities Review* 10 (Summer 1956), 3:229-39, rpt. in *The New Mormon History: Revi-*

sionist Essays on the Past, ed. D. Michael Quinn. Salt Lake City: Signature Books, 1992.

———. "Notes on Mormon Polygamy." *Utah Historical Quarterly* 35 (Fall 1967): 309-21.

———, to Israel Smith, Sept. 17, 1956. Stanley Snow Ivins Papers. Utah State Historical Society.

Jencks, E. N. *The History and Philosophy of Marriage.* Boston: James Campbell, 1869, microfilm, New York Public Library, ZAN T 3340: R336, no. 2900, 78 ff, 224.

Jensen, Richard L., and Malcolm R. Thorp, eds. *Mormons in Early Victorian Britain.* Salt Lake City: University of Utah Press, 1989.

Jenson, Andrew, comp. *The Historical Record: A Monthly Periodical Devoted Exclusively to Historical, Biographical, Chronological, and Statistical Matters,* 9 vols. Salt Lake City: Andrew Jenson, 1887.

Jessee, Dean C. "Brigham Young's Family: The Wilderness Years." *BYU Studies* 19 (1978-79), 474-500; online at *GospeLink,* http://gospelink .com.

———. "Joseph Knight's Recollection of Early Mormon History." *BYU Studies* 17 (1976): 29-39.

———. "A Comparative Study and Evaluation of Latter-day Saint and 'Fundamentalist' Views Pertaining to the Practice of Plural Marriage." M.A. thesis, Brigham Young University, 1959.

———, ed. "The John Taylor Nauvoo Journal, January 1845-September 1845." *BYU Studies* 23 (Summer 1983): 1-105.

———, ed. *The Personal Writings of Joseph Smith,* rev. ed. Salt Lake City: Deseret Book, 2002.

———, ed. *John Taylor Nauvoo Journal.* Provo: Grandin Book, 1996.

———, ed. *The Essential Joseph Smith.* Salt Lake City: Signature Books, 1995.

———, ed. *The Papers of Joseph Smith,* 2 vols. Salt Lake City: Deseret Book, 1992.

Johnson, Benjamin F. "A Life Review." LDS Archives.

———. *My Life's Review.* 1947; Mesa, Ariz.: 21st Century Printing, 1992.

———, to George F. Gibbs, Apr.-Oct. 1903. LDS Archives.

———. "Open Letter to the President of the United States." Jan. 15, 1886. LDS Archives.

———. Affidavit, Mar. 4, 1870, in "[Affidavits] Book No. 2," 1869-1870. LDS Archives.

Johnson, Jeffery O. "Determining and Defining 'Wife.'" *Dialogue: A Journal of Mormon Thought* 20 (Fall 1987), 57-70.

Johnson, Paul E. *A Shopkeeper's Millennium: Society and Revivals in Rochester, New York, 1815-1837.* New York: Hill and Wang, 1990.

Journal of Discourses, 26 vols. London: Latter-day Saint's Book Depot, 1854-86.

Journal History of the Church of Jesus Christ of Latter-day Saints, Oct. 9, 1845. LDS Archives.

Juhnke, William E. "Anabaptism and Mormonism: A Study in Comparative History." *John Whitmer Historical Journal* 2 (1982): 38-46; *Mennonite Life* 40 (Dec. 1985): 22-25.

Kelly, Henry Ansgar. *The Matrimonial Trials of Henry VIII.* Eugene, Ore.: Wipf and Stock, 2004.

Kelting, Joseph Andrew. Affidavit, March 1, 1894. "Affidavits [on Celestial Marriage], 1869-1915." LDS Archives.

Kendall, Edward A. "Account of the Writing Rock." *Memoirs of the American Academy of Arts & Sciences* 3 (1809): 165-91.

Kenney, Scott G., ed. *Wilford Woodruff's Journal, 1833-1898.* 9 vols. Midvale, Utah: Signature Books, 1983-85.

Kimball, Heber C., to wives Ann, Amanda, Lucy, and Sarah Ann Kimball, Dec. 31, 1855. LDS Archives.

———. Diary, Dec. 12, 1844. LDS Archives.

———. Blessing to His Daughter Helen Mar Kimball, May 28, 1843. Helen Mar Whitney Papers.

Kimball, Helen Mar. "Helen Mar Kimball's Retrospection about Her Introduction to the Doctrine and Practices of Plural Marriage in Nauvoo at Age 15," Mar. 30, 1881. Helen Mar Whitney Papers. LDS Archives.

Kimball, Lucy Walker. Statement, n.d. Bancroft Library, University of California, holograph and typescript at LDS Archives.

Kimball, Lucy Walker Smith. Affidavit, Dec. 17, 1902. "Affidavits [on Celestial Marriage], 1869-1915." LDS Archives.

Kimball, Mary Ellen Able. "Sketch of Pioneer History." LDS Archives.

———. 1818-1902, MS 42182. LDS Archives.

Kimball, Presenda Lathrop Huntington. Affidavit, May 1, 1869. "40 Affidavits on Celestial Marriage," 1869. LDS Archives.

———. Autobiographical Sketch. LDS Archives.

Kimball, Sarah Ann. Affidavit, June 19, 1869. "40 Affidavits on Celestial Marriage," 1869. LDS Archives.

Kimball, Sarah Perry Peak. Affidavit, September 7, 1869. "40 Affidavits on Celestial Marriage," 1869. LDS Archives.

Kimball, Stanley B. *Heber C. Kimball: Mormon Patriarch and Pioneer.* Urbana: University of Illinois Press, 1981.

———. "Heber C. Kimball and Family: The Nauvoo Years." *BYU Studies* 15 (1975): 447-79.

———, ed. *On the Potter's Wheel: The Diaries of Heber C. Kimball.* Salt Lake City: Signature Books and Smith Research Associates, 1987.

Kimball, Tom, to author, Feb. 4, 2008.

Kimball, Vilate, to Heber C. Kimball. June 29, 1843. LDS Archives.

King of the Last Days (*König der letzten Tage*). Aired on German television in 1993.

Kingsbury, Joseph C. Autobiography, 1812-1864. Special Collections, Marriott Library.

———. "History of Joseph Kingsbury, Written by His Own Hand, 1846, 1849, 1850." Utah State Historical Society, photocopy, original holograph and typescript at Marriott Library.

Kingsley, Sarah Maryetta. Biography. LDS Archives.

Kirche Jesu Christi der Heiligen der letzten Tage, www.kirche-jesu-christi.org.

Kirchhoff, Karl-Heinz, to the author, April 20, 2008.

———. "Das Phänomen des Täuferreichs zu Münster, 1534/35," in *Der Raum Westfalen,* Hrsg. Franz Petri u.a., 6 Bd Münster: Aschendorff, 1989.

———. "Die Täufer im Münsterland: Verbreitung und Verfolgung des Täufertums im Stift Münster, 1533-1550." *Westfälische Zeitschrift,* 113 (1963).

———. "Die Belagerung und Eroberung Münsters, 1534/35." *Westfälische Zeitschrift* 112. 1962.

———. "Was There a Peaceful Anabaptist Congregation in Münster in 1534?" trans. Elizabeth H. Bender, *Mennonite Quarterly Review* 44 (Oct. 1970): 357-70, a translation of Kirchhoff's "Gab es eine friedliche Täufergemeinde in Münster?" *Jahrbuch des Vereins für westfälische Kirchengeschichte* 55/56 [1962/1963].

Klötzer, Ralf. *Täuferherrschaft von Münster: Stadtreformation und Welterneuerung.* Münster: Aschendorff Verlag, 1992.

Knowlton, Minerva E. Richards. "Nanny Langstroth," in *Richards Family History,* ed. Joseph Grant Stevenson. Provo: Stevenson's Genealogical Center, 1991.

Krahn, Cornelius. *Dutch Anabaptism: Origin, Spread, Life, and Thought, 1450-1600.* 1968; Scottdale, Penn.: Herald Press, 1981.

Larsen, Herbert R. "Familism in Mormon Social Structure," Ph.D. diss., University of Utah, 1954.

Larson, Andrew Karl. *Erastus Snow: The Life of a Missionary and Pioneer for the Early Mormon Church.* Salt Lake City: University of Utah Press, 1971.

———, and Katharine Miles Larson, eds. *The Diary of Charles Lowell Walker.* Logan, Utah: Utah State University Press, 1980.

Larson, Gustive O. *The Americanization of Utah for Statehood.* San Marino, Calif.: Huntington Library, 1971.

Larson, Stan, ed. *Prisoner for Polygamy: The Memoirs and Letters of Rudger Clawson at the Utah Territorial Penitentiary, 1884-87.* Urbana: University of Illinois Press, 1993.

———, and Samuel J. Passey, eds. *The William E. McLellin Papers, 1854-1880.* Salt Lake City: Signature Books, 2007.

Laubach, Ernst. "Das Täuferreich zu Münster." *Westfälische Zeitschrift* 141 (1991): 123-24.

———. "Die Täuferherrschaft in Münster." *Geschichte in Wissenschaft und Unterricht* 45 (1994): 503.

Launius, Roger D. *Joseph Smith III: Pragmatic Prophet.* Urbana: University of Illinois Press, 1988.

Lavender, David. *The Great West.* Boston: Houghton Mifflin, 1965.

Law, William. Affidavit, July 17, 1885, reprinted in Cook, *William Law.*

———, to Isaac Hill, July 20, 1844, in Cook, *William Law,* 88-89.

———, to Isaac Russell, Nov. 29, 1840. LDS Archives.

LeBaron, Verlan M. *The LeBaron Story.* Lubbock, Tex.: Keels & Co., 1981.

Lee, John D. *Mormonism Unveiled: Or the Life and Confessions of the Late Mormon Bishop, John D. Lee.* St. Louis: Bryan, Brand, 1877.

Leonard, Glen M. *Nauvoo: A Place of Peace, a People of Promise.* Salt Lake City: Deseret Book, 2002.

LeSueur, Stephen C. *The 1838 Mormon War in Missouri.* Columbia: University of Missouri Press, 1987.

Lewis, Catherine. *Narrative of Some Proceedings of the Mormons.* Lynn, Mass.: n.p., 1848.

Lewis, Hyrum S. "Kanosh and Ute Identity in Territorial Utah." *Utah Historical Quarterly* 71 (Fall 2003): 332-47.

Leyser, Johannes. *Polygamia Triumphatrix.* Frankfurt, 1676.

Lightner, Mary Elizabeth Rollins. *The Life & Testimony of Mary Lightner.* Salt Lake City: Kraut's Pioneer Press, n.d.

———. Autobiography. Utah State Historical Society Library, Salt Lake City.

———. "Testimony: As Delivered at Brigham Young University." L. Tom Perry Special Collections, Harold B. Lee Library, Brigham Young University, Provo, Utah.

———. Statement, Feb. 8, 1902. LDS Archives.

Linn, William Alexander. *The Story of the Mormons: From the Date of Their Origin to the Year 1901.* New York: Macmillan, 1923.

Littell, Franklin Hamlin. *The Anabaptist View of the Church: An Introduction to Sectarian Protestantism.* Chicago: American Society of Church History, 1952.

Littlefield, Lyman O. *Reminiscences of Latter-day Saints.* Logan: Utah Journal Co., 1888.

Löffler, Klemens. *Die Wiedertäufer zu Münster, 1534-35: Berichte, Aussagen, und AktenstÜcke von Augenzeugen und Zeitgenossen.* Jena: Eugen Diederichs, 1923.

Lott, Melissa. Affidavit, Aug. 4, 1893, in Stanley Ivins Papers, Utah State Historical Society.

Lott Family Bible. LDS Archives.

Luther, Martin. Vorrede, *Neue Zeitung von den Widertäufern zu Münster,* 1535, in Stupperich, *Schriften von evangelischer Seite,* 51-55.

Lyman, Albert R. *Amasa Mason Lyman: Trailblazer and Pioneer from the Atlantic to the Pacific.* Delta, Utah: Melvin A. Lyman, 1957.

Lyman, Eliza Maria Partridge (Smith). "Autobiography and Diary of Eliza Maria Partridge (Smith) Lyman," 1846-85. LDS Archives.

———. "Life and Journal of Eliza Maria Partridge (Smith) Lyman." Special Collections, J. Willard Marriott Library, University of Utah.

———. Diary. LDS Archives.

———. Affidavit, July 1, 1869. "[Affidavits] Book No. 2," 1869-1870. LDS Archives.

MacCulloch, Diarmaid. *Reformation: A History.* New York: Viking, 2004.

MacKinnon, William P. *At Sword's Point: A Documentary History of the Utah War to 1858.* Norman, Okla., University of Oklahoma Press, 2008.

Madan, Martin. *Thelyphthora; or, A Treatise on Female Ruin, in its Causes, Affects, Consequences, Prevention, and Remedy; Considered on the Basis of the Divine Law; under the Following Heads, viz Marriage, Whoredom, and Fornication, Adultery, Polygamy, Divorce, with Many Other Incidental Matters.* London, 1781.

Madsen, Carol Cornwall. *In Their Own Words: Women and the Story of Nauvoo.* Salt Lake City: Deseret Book, 1994.

———. "Emmeline B. Wells: Romantic Rebel," in *Supporting Saints: Life*

Stories of Nineteenth-Century Mormons. Provo: Religious Studies Center, Brigham Young University, 1985.

Madsen, Carol Cornwall. "Emmeline B. Wells: 'Am I Not a Woman and a Sister?'" *BYU Studies* 22 (Spring 1982): 161-78.

Madsen, Gordon. "The Lawrence Estate Revisited: Joseph Smith and Illinois Law regarding Guardianships." Nauvoo Symposium, Sept. 21, 1989, Brigham Young University, copy in possession of Todd Compton.

Madsen, Truman G. *The Heritage of Heber J. Grant.* Salt Lake City: By the author, 1969.

Manuscript History of the Church. LDS Archives.

Margulis, Lynn, and Dorion Sagan. *Mystery Dance: On the Evolution of Human Sexuality.* New York: Summit Books, 1991.

Markham, Olive Amanda Smith. Biographical sketch. LDS Archives.

Marquardt, H. Michael. *The Rise of Mormonism: 1816-1844.* Longwood, Fla.: Xulon Press, 2005.

———, and Wesley P. Walters. *Inventing Mormonism: Tradition and the Historical Record.* San Francisco: Smith Research Associates, 1994.

Marx, Karl, and Friedrich Engels, *Communist Manifesto.* 1848; New York: Bantam, 1992.

McCormick, John S., and John R. Sillito. "Henry W. Lawrence: A Life in Dissent," in *Differing Visions: Dissenters in Mormon History,* eds. Roger D. Launius and Linda Thatcher. Urbana: University of Illinois Press, 1994.

McLellin, William E., to Joseph Smith III, July 1872. Community of Christ Library-Archives, Independence, Missouri.

"Memoirs of Matthias the Prophet, Prepared for the *New York Sun.*" Stanley S. Ivins Collection, USHS. In Richard S. Van Wagoner. *Mormon Polygamy: A History.* Salt Lake City: Signature Books, 1989.

Merritt, Timothy. *Anabaptism Disapproved, and the Validity and Sufficiency of Infant Baptism Asserted: In Two Letters from a Minister to His Friend.* New York: Methodist Episcopal Church, 1818.

Mikat, Paul. *Die Polygamiefrage in der frühen Neuzeit.* Opladen: Westdeutscher Verlag, 1988.

Miller, David E., and Della S. Miller. *Nauvoo: The City of Joseph.* Santa Barbara: Peregrine Smith, 1974.

Miller, Leo. *John Milton among the Polygamophiles.* New York: Loewenthal Press, 1974.

Minutes, LDS Council of Twelve, May 5, 1954. Alma Sonne Collection, Msf 678 #2, bx 3, fd 5. LDS Archives.

Minutes of the High Council of the Church of Jesus Christ of Nauvoo, Illinois, Nov. 21, 1843, Book No. 3, p. 21. LDS Archives, from a typescript prepared by Lyndon W. Cook, 1978.

Moffitt, John Clifton, and Frederick Walter Cox. "Frontiersman of the American West." LDS Archives.

Morgan, Dale L. *The State of Deseret.* Logan: Utah State University Press with the Utah State Historical Society, 1987.

———. *The Great Salt Lake.* Albuquerque: University of New Mexico Press, 1973.

Morris, Rob. *William Morgan: Or Political Anti-Masonry.* New York: Robert Macoy, 1883.

Murdock, George Peter. *Atlas of World Cultures.* Pittsburgh: Pittsburgh Press, 1980.

———. *Ethnographic Atlas.* Pittsburgh: University of Pittsburgh Press, 1967.

———, and D. R. White, "Ethnographic Atlas Codebook." *World Cultures* 10 (1998): 86-136.

———, and Douglas R. White. "Standard Cross-Cultural Sample." *Ethnology* 8 (Oct. 1969): 329-69.

A Narrative of the Adventures and Experience of Joseph H. Jackson. Warsaw, Ill.: Signal Office, 1846, available online at *Joseph Smith's History Vault,* www.olivercowdery.com.

Nauvoo City Council Minutes. LDS Archives.

Nauvoo High Council minutes. LDS Archives.

Nauvoo Stake High Council Minutes. LDS Archives.

Nelson, James G. *The Sublime Puritan: Milton and the Victorians.* Madison: University of Wisconsin Press, 1963.

Nelson, Stephen F., and Jean Rott. "Strasbourg: The Anabaptist City in the Sixteenth Century." *Mennonite Quarterly Review* 58 (July 1984): 3:230-40.

Newell, Linda King. "Women's Reaction to Early Mormon Polygamy, 1841-45." LDS Archives.

———. "Gifts of the Spirit: Women's Share." In *Sisters in Spirit: Mormon Women in Historical and Cultural Perspective,* eds. Maureen Ursenbach Beecher and Lavina Fielding Anderson. Urbana: University of Illinois Press, 1987.

———, and Valeen Tippetts Avery. *Mormon Enigma: Emma Hale Smith,*

Prophet's Wife, "Elect Lady," Polygamy's Foe, 1804-1879. Garden City, N.Y.: Doubleday, 1984.

Nibley, Preston. *Brigham Young: The Man and His Work.* Salt Lake City: Deseret Book, 1937.

Niesert, Johann Heinrich Joseph. *Beiträge zu einem Münsterischen Urkundenbuche aus vaterländischen Archiven.* Münster: Coppenrath, 1823.

Noble, Joseph Bates. Affidavit, June 26, 1869. "40 Affidavits on Celestial Marriage," 1869. LDS Archives.

———. Autobiography, 1810-1834, typescript, MSS 968, L. Tom Perry Special Collections, Harold B. Lee Library, Brigham Young University, Provo, Utah. See also online at "Diaries, Journals, and Histories of Some Early Mormons." *Book of Abraham Project,* www.boap.org.

———. Journal. LDS Archives.

Noble, Mary A. Autobiography, in Vogel, *Early Mormon Documents,* 3:308-10.

Oaks, Dallin H. "The Suppression of the *Nauvoo Expositor.*" *Utah Law Review* 9 (Winter 1965): 862-903.

'Omar, Amatul Ra<u>h</u>mân, and 'Abdul Mannân 'Omar, trans. *The Holy Qur'an: Arabic Text—English Translation.* Hockessin, Del.: Noor Foundation, 2000.

Oyer, John S. "The Strasbourg Conferences of the Anabaptists, 1554-1607." *Mennonite Quarterly Review* 58 (1984): 218-29.

Page, John E., to Brigham Young, July 13, 1845. Brigham Young Collection, d1234, bx 41, fd 2. LDS Archives.

Page, Justin E. Letters to P. A. Watts, Mar. 16, 1936, and Wilford Poulson, Mar. 20, June 11, Sept. 12, 1936. Wilford Poulson Papers, L. Tom Perry Special Collections, Harold B. Lee Library, Brigham Young University, Provo, Utah.

Parkin, Max H. "The Nature and Cause of Internal and External Conflict of the Mormons in Ohio between 1830 and 1838," M.A. thesis, Brigham Young University, 1966.

Parley P. Pratt Family Record, copy in author's possession.

Parrinder, E. Geoffrey. *The Bible and Polygamy: A Study of Hebrew and Christian Teachings.* London: Society for Promoting Christian Knowledge, 1950.

Partridge, Emily Dow, to Lula Clawson Young, June 27, 1897. LDS Archives.

Patrick, John R. "The School of the Prophets: Its Development and Influence in Utah Territory." M.A. thesis, Brigham Young University, June 1970.

Paul, Robert. "Joseph Smith and the Manchester (New York) Library." *BYU Studies* 22 (Summer 1982): 333-56.

Paulos, Michael Harold, ed. *The Mormon Church on Trial: Transcripts of the Reed Smoot Hearings.* Salt Lake City: Signature Books, 2008.

Pelikan, Jaroslav J. *The Christian Tradition: A History of the Development of Doctrine.* Chicago: University of Chicago Press, 1973.

———, and Helmut T. Lehman, eds. *Luther's Works,* 55 vols. St. Louis: Concordia Publishing and Fortress Press, 1955-86; available on CD-ROM from Augsburg Fortress, 1999.

Perego, Ugo A., Natalie M. Myres, and Scott R. Woodward. "Reconstructing the Y-Chromosome of Joseph Smith, Jr.: Genealogical Applications." *Journal of Mormon History* 31 (Summer 2005): 70-88.

Perrin, William Henry, ed. *History of Cass County, Illinois.* Chicago: O. L. Baskin & Co., 1882.

Petersen, LaMar. *Problems in Mormon Text: A Brief Study of Changes in Important Latter-day Saint Publications.* Salt Lake City: By the author, 1957.

Phelps, W. W., to Brigham Young, Aug. 12, 1861. LDS Archives.

———, to Sally Phelps, Sept. 9, 1835, paraphrasing 1 Cor. 11:8, 9, 11. LDS Archives.

Pioneer Women of Faith and Fortitude, 4 vols. Salt Lake City: Daughters of Utah Pioneers, 1998.

Pitzer, Donald E., ed. *America's Communal Utopias.* Chapel Hill: University of North Carolina Press, 1997.

Poll, Richard D., ed. *Utah's History.* Provo: Brigham Young University Press, 1978.

Pratt, Mary Ann. Affidavit, Sept. 3, 1869. "[Affidavits] Book No. 2," 1869-1870. LDS Archives.

Pratt, Orson. *The Essential Orson Pratt.* Salt Lake City: Signature Books, 1991.

Pratt, Orson, Mrs. "Workings of Mormonism Related by Mrs. Orson Pratt." LDS Archives.

Pratt, Parley P. *A Voice of Warning and Instruction to All People.* 1837; Liverpool: Brigham Young Jr., 1866.

Pratt, Parley P., Jr., ed. *Autobiography of Parley P. Pratt.* Salt Lake City: Deseret Book, 1961.

Price, Richard, and Pamela Price. "Joseph Smith Fought Polygamy." Online at http://restorationbookstore.org.

Prince, Gregory A. *Power from on High.* Salt Lake City: Signature Books, 1995.

Proctor, Scott F., and Maurine J. Proctor. *Autobiography of Parley P. Pratt,* rev. 1874; Salt Lake City: Deseret Book, 2000.

Public Broadcasting Service. *Apocalypse! The Evolution of Apocalyptic Belief and How It Shaped the Western World,* a production of *Frontline*, 2000, at www.pbs.org.

Pulsipher, Juanita Leavitt, ed. "Autobiography of Sarah S. Leavitt, from Her History." Utah State Historical Society Library, Salt Lake City.

Pusey, Merlo J. *Builders of the Kingdom: George A. Smith, John Henry Smith, George Albert Smith.* Provo: Brigham Young University Press, 1981.

Quinn, D. Michael, *The Mormon Hierarchy: Extensions of Power.* Salt Lake City: Signature Books and Smith Research Associates, 1997.

———. *The Mormon Hierarchy: Origins of Power.* Salt Lake City: Signature Books and Smith Research Associates, 1994.

———. "Remarkable Book about Memorable Polygamy," a review of *Mormon Polygamous Families: Life in the Principle* by Jessie L. Embry. *Sunstone* (Nov. 1988): 47-48.

———. *Early Mormonism and the Magic World View.* Salt Lake City: Signature Books, 1987.

———. "LDS Church Authority and New Plural Marriages, 1890-1904." *Dialogue: A Journal of Mormon Thought* 18 (Spring 1985): 9-105.

Rathbone, Timothy. "Brigham Young's Masonic Connection and Nauvoo Plural Marriages," 1996. LDS Archives.

Raymond, E. Nilson, comp. "The Fullmer Family," typescript. LDS Archives.

"A Record of the Organization, and Proceedings of the Female Relief Society of Nauvoo." Joseph Smith Collection.

Reichling, D. *Johannes Murmellius: Sein Leben und seine Werke* (Nieuwkoop, 1963).

"Reminiscences of Mrs. F[ranklin]. D. Richards [Jane Snyder Richards]." San Francisco, 1880, Bancroft Library, University of California, Berkeley.

Reorganized Church of Jesus Christ of Latter Day Saints v. Church of Christ of Independence, Missouri, et al. 60 F. 937 (W. D. Mo. 1894), deposition testimony, electronic copy prepared by Richard D. Ouellette.

Revised Laws of Illinois 1833 and Revised Statutes of the State of Illinois 1845. University of Chicago Law Library.

Rhodehamel, Josephine DeWitt, and Raymund Francis Wood. *Ina Coolbrith:*

Librarian and Laureate of California. Provo: Brigham Young University Press, 1973.

Rich, Charles C. Affidavit, July 12, 1869. "40 Affidavits on Celestial Marriage," 1869. LDS Archives.

Rich, Mary Phelps. "Autobiographical Sketch," cited in Evans, *Charles Coulson Rich,* 110.

Rich, Sarah DeArmon Pea. Autobiography. LDS Archives.

Richards, Franklin D. Journal, Jan. 22, 1869. LDS Archives.

Richards, Levi. Journal, 1840-1853. LDS Archives.

Richards, Rhoda. Affidavit, May 1, 1869. "40 Affidavits on Celestial Marriage," 1869. LDS Archives.

Richards, Samuel W., to Mary Richards, Apr. 25, 1852. LDS Archives.

Richards, Willard. "History of Willard Richards." LDS Archives.

———. Diary, 1836-1852, 19 vols. LDS Archives, holograph 1490, microfilm 309.

Ridlon, Gideon Tibbetts, *Saco Valley Settlements and Families.* Somersworth, N.H.: New England History Press, 1984.

Rigdon, John W. Affidavit, July 28, 1905, in "Affidavits [on Celestial Marriage]," 1869-1915. LDS Archives.

Riggs, Michael S., and John E. Thompson. "Joseph Smith, Jr., and 'The Notorious Case of Aaron Lyon': Evidence of Earlier Doctrinal Development of Salvation for the Dead and a Trigger for the Practice of Polyandry?" *John Whitmer Historical Journal* 26 (2006): 101-19.

Roberts, Brigham Henry. *Successions in the Presidency of the Church of Jesus Christ of Latter-day Saints.* 2nd ed. Salt Lake City: George Q. Cannon & Sons, 1900.

———. *The Life of John Taylor.* Salt Lake City: Bookcraft, 1963.

———. *A Comprehensive History of the Church of Jesus Christ of Latter-day Saints.* 6 vols. Salt Lake City: The Church of Jesus Christ of Latter-day Saints, 1930.

Robinson, Ebenezer, to Jason W. Briggs, Jan. 28, 1880. LDS Archives.

Robinson, George W., to James Arlington Bennet, July 27, 1842. LDS Archives.

Robinson, Joseph Lee. Diary. L. Tom Perry Special Collections, Harold B. Lee Library, Brigham Young University, Provo, Utah.

———. Journal. Utah State Historical Society Library.

Rodgers, Robert. "An Introduction to Anabaptism." *Evangelical Quarterly* 54 (Jan.-Feb. 1982): 46-54.

Rogers, Jedediah S., ed. *In the President's Office: The Diaries of L. John Nuttall,*

1879-1892. Salt Lake City: Signature Books and the Smith-Pettit Foundation, 2007.

Roper, Lyndal. "Sexual Utopianism in the German Reformation." *Journal of Ecclesiastical History* 42 (July 1991): 398-400.

Rothmann, Bernhard. *Eyne Restitution edder Eine wedderstellinge rechter unde gesunder Christlicher leer gelovens unde levens.* Münster, 1534., in Robert Stupperich, ed. *Schriften von evangelischer Seite gegen die Täufer,* vol. 3 in the *Schriften der münsterischen Täufer und ihrer Gegner* series. Münster: Aschendorff, 1983, 172-83

Russell, Bertrand. *History of Western Philosophy.* New York: Simon & Schuster, 1946.

Rust, Val D. *Radical Origins: Early Mormon Converts and Their Colonial Ancestors.* Urbana: University of Illinois Press, 2004.

Sanborn, Mabel Young. *Brigham Young's Wives, Children, and Grandchildren.* Salt Lake City: By the author, 1940.

Schindler, Harold. *Orrin Porter Rockwell: Man of God, Son of Thunder.* Salt Lake City: University of Utah Press, 1966.

Schopenhauer, Arthur. *Parerega und Paralipomena.* Wiesbaden, 1947.

"Scope and Content." *The Stanley Snow Ivins Papers, 1850-1968,* online at http://history.utah.gov.

Scott, James Wesley. "The Jacob and Sarah Warnock Scott Family, 1779-1910," June 2002, www.scottcorner.org.

Séguy, Jean. "The French Anabaptists: Four and One-Half Centuries of History." *Mennonite Quarterly Review* 58 (July 1984): 206-17.

Seifert, Thomas. *Die Täufer zu Münster.* Münster: Agenda Verlag, 1993.

Sessions, Patty. *Woman's Exponent* 13 (Nov. 15, 1884): 95.

———. Diary, *Woman's Exponent* 13 (Nov. 1, 1884): 86.

Sessions, Perrigrine. Diary, Nov. 3, 1852. LDS Archives.

Shook, Charles A. *The True Origin of Mormon Polygamy.* Cincinnati: Standard Publishing, 1914.

Sinclair, Marguerite L., to Frank M. Young, June 21, 1947. Lorenzo Dow Young Papers, Utah State Historical Society, Salt Lake City.

"A Sketch of the Life of Nancy Naomi Tracy." Utah State Historical Society.

Smart, Donna Toland, ed. *Mormon Midwife: The 1846-1888 Diaries of Patty Bartlett Sessions.* Logan: Utah State University Press, 1997.

Smith, Andrew F. *The Saintly Scoundrel: The Life and Times of Dr. John Cook Bennett.* Urbana: University of Illinois Press, 1997.

Smith, Bathsheba W. Affidavit, Nov. 19, 1903. "[Affidavits] Book No. 2," 1869-1870. LDS Archives.

———. Autobiography, 13. LDS Archives.

Smith, Desdemona Fullmer. Affidavit, June 17, 1869. "40 Affidavits on Celestial Marriage," 1869. LDS Archives.

———. Statement, June 7, 1868. Desdemona Wadsworth Fullmer Papers. LDS Archives.

Smith, Eliza R. Snow. *Biography and Family Record of Lorenzo Snow.* Salt Lake City: Deseret News, 1884.

———. Affidavit, June 7, 1869. "40 Affidavits on Celestial Marriage," 1869. LDS Archives.

Smith, Ethan. *A View of the Hebrews.* Poultney, Vt.: Smith & Shute, 1825.

Smith, George A., to Joseph Smith III, Oct. 9, 1869. Joseph Smith III Papers, Library-Archives of the Community of Christ, Independence, Missouri.

Smith, George D. "Nauvoo Roots of Mormon Polygamy." *Dialogue: A Journal of Mormon Thought* 27 (Spring 1994): 1-72.

———. "'Is There No Way to Escape These Difficulties?' The Book of Mormon Studies of B. H. Roberts." *Dialogue: A Journal of Mormon Thought* 17 (Summer 1984): 95-111.

———. "Joseph Smith and the Book of Mormon." *Free Inquiry* 4 (Winter 1983-84): 21-31.

———, ed. *An Intimate Chronicle: The Journals of William Clayton,* 2nd ed. Salt Lake City: Signature Books and Smith Research Associates, 1995.

Smith, Joseph, to Emma Smith, June 27, 1844. Community of Christ Library-Archives, Independence, Missouri.

———, to Thomas Ford, June 14, 1844. In *History of the Church,* 6:466-67.

———, to Jennetta Richards, June 23, 1842. In *History of the Church,* 5:40-41.

———, Letter to "Brother and Sister [Newel K.] Whitney, and &c.," Nauvoo, Illinois, Aug. 18, 1842. LDS Church Archives, Salt Lake City. Photocopy in George Albert Smith Papers, Special Collections, Marriott Library.

———, to Presendia Huntington Buell, Mar. 15, 1839. In Jessee, *Personal Writings.*

———. Letter Book 1, Joseph Smith Papers. LDS Archives.

———, et al. *History of the Church of Jesus Christ of Latter-day Saints,* ed. B. H. Roberts, 2nd ed. rev., 7 vols. Salt Lake City: Deseret Book, 1963.

Smith, Joseph F., to Orson Pratt, Sr., July 19, 1875. Joseph F. Smith Letterbooks, Joseph F. Smith Collection, LDS Archives; from notes by Scott G. Kenney, with permission.

Smith, Joseph F. Diary. LDS Archives.

Smith, Joseph Fielding. *Essentials of Church History.* Salt Lake City: Deseret News Press, 1922.

———. *Blood Atonement and the Origin of Plural Marriage: A Discussion.* Salt Lake City: Deseret News Press, 1905.

Smith, Joseph, III, ed. "Last Testimony of Sister Emma." *Saints' Advocate,* Oct. 1879, 49-52.

Smith, Mary Elizabeth Rollins Lightner, to Emmeline B. Wells. Summer 1905. Lightner Collection.

Snow, Eliza Roxcy. *The Personal Writings of Eliza Roxcy Snow,* ed. Maureen Ursenbach Beecher. Logan: Utah State University Press, 2000.

———, to John Taylor, Dec. 12, 1886. Eliza Snow Letter File. LDS Archives.

———. "Sketch of My Life," Apr. 13, 1885, 13, 17. Bancroft Library, Berkeley, California.

Snow, Erastus, to Eliza [Snow], Aug. 7, 1887. LDS Archives.

Snow, Lorenzo. Affidavit, August 28, 1869, in "[Affidavits] Book No. 2," 1869-1870. LDS Archives.

Soby, Leonard. Affidavit, Mar. 23, 1886. "Affidavits [on Celestial Marriage]," 1869-1915. LDS Archives.

Sorenson, Maude R. "Harriet Amelia Squires Snow," typescript. LDS Archives.

Speek, Vickie Cleverley. *"God Has Made Us a Kingdom": James Strang and the Midwest Mormons.* Salt Lake City: Signature Books, 2006.

Stanley, Reva. *A Biography of Parley P. Pratt: The Archer of Paradise.* Caldwell, Idaho: Caxton Printers, 1937.

Stayer, James M. "Vielweiberei als 'innerweltliche Askese': Neue Eheauffassungen in der Reformationszeit." *Mennonitische Geschichtsblätter* 37 (1980), translated for the author by Henry L. Miner.

———. *Anabaptists and the Sword.* 2nd ed. Lawrence, Kans.: Coronado Press, 1976.

Stegner, Wallace. *Mormon Country.* Lincoln: University of Nebraska Press, 1981.

Stenhouse, T. B. H. *The Rocky Mountain Saints.* New York: D. Appleton and Co., 1873.

———, to Brigham Young, June 7, 1863. LDS Archives.

Stout, Wayne. *Hosea Stout: Utah's Pioneer Statesman.* Salt Lake City: By the author, 1953.

Stupperich, Robert, ed. *Die Schriften Bernhard Rothmanns,* vol. 1 in *Die Schriften der münsterischen Täufer und ihrer Gegner* series. Münster: Aschendorff Verlag, 1971.

Sumner, Charles. *A Treatise on Christian Doctrine.* Cambridge, Eng.: Cambridge University Press, 1825; Boston: Cummings, Hilliard and Co., 1825.

Swanson, Ellis Sagers. *The Sagers Clan: William Henry Harrison Sagers and His Descendants.* Tucson, Ariz.: n.p., 1980.

Swedenborg, Emanuel. *Heaven and Hell,* trans. George F. Dole. West Chester, Pa.: Swedenborg Foundation, 2002.

Thomasius, Christian. *De Crimine Bigamiae.* Halle, 1685.

Thompson, D[aniel]. P. *May Martin, or The Money Diggers: A Green Mountain Tale, 1835.* Montpelier, Vt.: E. P. Walton and Son, 1835.

Thompson, John E. "The Mormon Baptism of William Morgan." *Mormon Temples,* online at www.lds-mormon.com.

Thompson, Mercy Rachel Fielding Smith. Untitled autobiographical sketch. LDS Archives.

Tinney, Thomas Milton. *Royal Family of the Prophet Joseph Smith Jr.* Salt Lake City: Tinney-Green Family Organization, 1973.

Tolk, Norman, Lynn Travers, George D. Smith, and F. Charles Graves. "The Facsimile Found: The Recovery of Joseph Smith's Papyrus Manuscripts." *Dialogue: A Journal of Mormon Thought* 2 (Winter 1967): 51-64.

Tullidge, Edward. *The Women of Mormondom.* New York: Tullidge & Crandall, 1877.

Turley, Ella Mae. "Theodore Turley Biography and Autobiography," MS 7661. LDS Archives.

Turley, Nancy R., and Lawrence E. Turley. *The Theodore Turley Family Book.* Mesa, Ariz.: By the authors, 1978.

Underwood, Grant. *The Millenarian World of Early Mormonism.* Urbana: University of Illinois Press, 1993.

Unruh, John D., Jr., *The Plains Across: The Overland Emigrants and the Trans-Mississippi West, 1840-60.* Urbana: University of Illinois Press, 1982.

Van Wagoner, Richard S. *Sidney Rigdon: A Portrait of Religious Excess.* Salt Lake City: Signature Books, 1994.

———. "Sarah M. Pratt: The Shaping of an Apostate." *Dialogue: A Journal of Mormon Thought* 19 (Summer 1986): 69-99.

———. *Mormon Polygamy: A History.* Salt Lake City: Signature Books, 1986.

———, and Steven C. Walker. *A Book of Mormons*. Salt Lake City: Signature Books, 1982.

———, and Steven Walker. "Joseph Smith: 'The Gift of Seeing,'" *Dialogue: A Journal of Mormon Thought* 15 (Summer 1982): 48-68.

Verduin, Leonard. *The Reformers and Their Stepchildren*. Grand Rapids: Eerdmans, 1964.

Vetterli, Richard. *Mormonism, Americanism, and Politics*. Salt Lake City: Ensign Publishing, 1961.

Vogel, Dan. *Indian Origins and the Book of Mormon*. Salt Lake City: Signature Books, 1986.

———. *Joseph Smith: The Making of a Prophet*. Salt Lake City: Signature Books, 2004.

———, ed. *Early Mormon Documents*, 5 vols. Salt Lake City: Signature Books, 1996.

Vogel, Ursula. "Political Philosophers and the Trouble with Polygamy: Patriarchal Reasoning in Modern Natural Law." *History of Political Thought* 12 (Summer 1991): 229-51.

Vogt, Lorna, host, with Mary Batchelor, Doe Daughtery, Richard Dutcher, and Anne Wilde. *RadioActive*, KRCL FM 90.9, Salt Lake City, Mar. 15, 2006.

von Kerssenbroch, Hermann. *Anabaptistici Furoris Narratio*. Münster, 1899.

Wadsworth, Nelson B. *Set in Stone, Fixed in Glass: The Mormons, the West, and Their Photographers*. Salt Lake City: Signature Books, 1992.

Waite, Gary K. "From Apocalyptic Crusaders to Anabaptist Terrorists: Anabaptist Radicalism after Münster, 1535-1544." *Archiv für Reformationsgeschichte* 80 (1989): 173-93.

———. "Post Munster Melchiorite Debate on Marriage: David Joris Response to Johannes Eisenburg, 1537. *Mennonite Quarterly Review* 63 (1989): 367-99.

Walgren, Kent, to Gary Bergera, Oct. 13, 2001, copy in author's possession.

Walker, Kyle R. "William Smith's Quest for Ecclesiastical Station: A Schismatic Odyssey, 1848-93." In *Scattering of the Saints: Schism within Mormonism*, eds. Newel G. Bringhurst and John C. Hamer. Independence: John Whitmer Books, 2007.

Walker, Ronald W. "Joseph Smith, the Palmyra Seer." *BYU Studies* 24 (Fall 1984): 461-72.

———. "Rachel R. Grant: The Continuing Legacy of the Feminine Ideal." *Dialogue: A Journal of Mormon Thought* 15 (Autumn 1982): 105-23.

———, et al. *Massacre at Mountain Meadows.* New York: University of Oxford Press, 2008.

Walters, Wesley P. *Joseph Smith's Bainbridge, N.Y., Court Trials.* Salt Lake City: Modern Microfilm, n.d., reprinted from *Westminster Theological Journal* 36 (Winter 1974): 123-55.

Wappler, Paul. *Die Täuferbewegung in Thüringen von 1526-1584.* Jena: Verein für Reformationsgeschichte, 1913.

———. *Die Stellung Kursachsens und des Landgrafen Philipp von Hessen zur Täuferbewegung,* 1910.

Ward, Maureen Carr. "'This Institution Is a Good One': The Female Relief Society of Nauvoo, 17 March 1842 to 16 March 1844." *Mormon Historical Studies* 3 (2002): 86-203.

Watson, Elden J. *Manuscript History of Brigham Young, 1801-1844.* Salt Lake City: By the author, 1968.

Wells, Emmeline B., to Mary Elizabeth Rollins Lightner, Feb. 10, 1887. LDS Archives.

———. "Ruth Sayers." *Woman's Exponent* 13 (Sept. 15, 1884): 61.

———. Diary. L. Tom Perry Special Collections, Harold B. Lee Library, Brigham Young University, Provo, Utah.

West, Franklin L. *Life of Franklin D. Richards.* Salt Lake City: Deseret News Press, 1924.

White, Jean Bickmore, ed. *Church, State, and Politics: The Diaries of John Henry Smith.* Salt Lake City: Signature Books and Smith Research Associates, 1990.

Whitmer, David. *An Address to All Believers in Christ.* Richmond, Mo.: By the author, 1887.

Whitney, Elizabeth Ann. "A Leaf from an Autobiography." *Woman's Exponent* 7 (Dec. 15, 1878): 105; 7 (Jan 1, 1879): 115; 7 (Feb. 15, 1879): 191.

———. Affidavit, Aug. 30, 1869. "40 Affidavits on Celestial Marriage," 1869. LDS Archives.

Whitney, Helen Mar. "Scenes and Incidents in Nauvoo." *Woman's Exponent,* 1881-1883.

———. "Scenes in Nauvoo." *Woman's Exponent* 11 (Mar. 1, 1883), 146.

———. "Scenes and Incidents." *Woman's Exponent* 11 (June 1, 1882): 2.

Whitney, Helen Mar Kimball Smith, to her children, Mar. 30, 1881. Helen Mar Whitney Papers.

Whitney, Newel K. Papers. L. Tom Perry Special Collections, Harold B. Lee Library, Brigham Young University, Provo, Utah.

Whitney, Orson F. *The Life of Heber C. Kimball.* 1945; Salt Lake City: Bookcraft, 1977.

Whittaker, David J. "The Bone in the Throat: Orson Pratt and the Public Announcement of Plural Marriage." *Western Historical Quarterly* 18 (July 1987): 293-314.

Die Wiedertäufer in Münster, a catalog for the opening exhibit of the Münster City Museum, October 1, 1982, 2nd enlarged ed. Münster: Aschendorff Verlag, 1986.

Wight, Jermy Benton. *The Wild Ram of the Mountain: The Story of Lyman Wight.* Bedford, Wyo.: Star Valley Llama, 1996.

Wight, Orange Lysander. "Recollections," 1903, typescript, L. Tom Perry Special Collections, Harold B. Lee Library, Brigham Young University, Provo, Utah; original in LDS Archives.

———. Untitled Reminiscence, 1903. LDS Archives.

Wilde, Anne. "Fundamentalist Mormonism: Its History, Diversity, and Stereotypes, 1886-Present." In *Scattering of the Saints: Schism within Mormonism,* edited by Newell G. Bringhurst and John C. Hamer. Independence, Mo.: John Whitmer Books, 2007.

Williams, George Huntston. *The Radical Reformation,* 3rd ed. Kirksville, Mo.: Truman State University Press, 2000.

Williamson, Darren T. "'For the Honor of God and to Fulfill His Will': The Role of Polygamy in Anabaptist Münster." *Restoration Quarterly* 42 (2000): 27-38.

Willis, Delta. *The Hominid Gang.* New York: Viking, 1989.

Witte, John Jr. *From Sacrament to Contract: Marriage, Religion, and Law in the Western Tradition.* Louisville, Ky.: Westminster John Knox Press, 1997.

Wolfe, Don M., ed. *Complete Prose Works of John Milton,* vol. 1. New Haven: Yale University Press, 1980.

Woodruff, Abraham Owen. Diary. LDS Archives.

Woodruff, Wilford, to Andrew Jenson, Aug. 6, 1887.

———, to George A. Smith, Apr. 1, 1857. Journal History of the Church of Jesus Christ of Latter-day Saints.

Woolley, Edwin Gordon. Autobiography, 1845-98, typescript, 2-3. LDS Archives.

Wyl, W. (pseud. Wilhelm Ritter von Wymetal). *Mormon Portraits: Or the Truth about the Mormon Leaders.* Salt Lake City: Tribune Printing and Publishing, 1886.

Yeats, William Butler. "The Second Coming." In *The New Oxford Book of*

English Verse, 1250-1950, ed. Helen Gardner. New York: Oxford University Press, 1984.

Young, Ann Eliza. *Wife No. 19 or the Story of a Life in Bondage.* Hartford: Dustin, Gilman & Co., 1876.

Young, Augusta A. Affidavit, July 12, 1869. "40 Affidavits on Celestial Marriage," 1869. LDS Archives.

Young, Brigham. Address, Oct. 8, 1866, unpublished typescript. LDS Archives.

———. "A Few Words of Doctrine," Oct. 8, 1861. LDS Archives.

———. Diary. LDS Archives.

———. Journal. LDS Archives.

———. Manuscript History, Feb. 16, 1849. LDS Archives.

Young, Emily Dow Partridge. "Incidents in the Life of a Mormon Girl." LDS Archives.

———, to Mr. W. Collins, Jan. 27, 1899. LDS Archives.

———. "Diary and Reminiscences, 1874-1899." L. Tom Perry Special Collections, Harold B. Lee Library, Brigham Young University, Provo, Utah.

———. "What I Remember." LDS Archives.

———, to Mary Elizabeth Lightner, Apr. 28, 1886. Lightner Collection, 1865-1957; original at L. Tom Perry Special Collections, Harold B. Lee Library, Brigham Young University, Provo, Utah.

———. "Autobiography." *Woman's Exponent*, Dec. 1884-Aug. 1885.

Young, Harriet Cook. Affidavit, Mar. 4, 1870. "[Affidavits] Book No. 2," 1869-1870. LDS Archives.

Young, John Ray, to Vesta P. Crawford, Apr. 1931. LDS Archives.

———. Scrapbook, 1928-30.

Young, Lorenzo Dow. Diary. *Utah Historical Quarterly* 14 (1946): 25-132.

———. Family Record. LDS Archives.

Young, Lucy Ann Decker. Affidavit, July 10, 1869. "40 Affidavits on Celestial Marriage," 1869. LDS Archives.

Young, Margaret Peirce. Journal, 1903, MS 5716. LDS Archives.

Young, S. Dilworth. *Here Is Brigham: Brigham Young, the Years to 1844.* Salt Lake City: Bookcraft, 1964.

Young, Thomas. *An Account of Some Recent Discoveries in Hieroglyphic Literature and Egyptian Antiquities.* London: John Murray, 1823.

Young, Zina D. H. Family Papers and Photographs, 1876-1898. L. Tom Perry Special Collections, Harold B. Lee Library, Brigham Young University, Provo, Utah.

———, to Mary Elizabeth Lightner, June 27, 1886. Lightner Collection, 1865-1957; original at L. Tom Perry Special Collections, Harold B. Lee Library, Brigham Young University, Provo, Utah.

———. Journal, 1844. Zina Card Brown Collection.

———. Autobiography 2. Zina D. H. Young Collection, LDS Archives.

Ziff, Larzer, ed. *The Portable Benjamin Franklin.* New York: Penguin Books, 2005.

Zimmerman, Dean R., ed. *I Knew the Prophets: An Analysis of the Letter of Benjamin F. Johnson to George F. Gibbs.* Bountiful, Utah: Horizon Publishers, 1976.

Index

About the author

George D. Smith is a graduate of Stanford and New York University. He is the editor of the landmark frontier diaries of one of the most prominent Mormon pioneers, *An Intimate Chronicle: The Journals of William Clayton*, and of *Religion, Feminism, and Freedom of Conscience*. He has published in *Dialogue: A Journal of Mormon Thought*, *Free Inquiry*, the *John Whitmer Historical Journal*, *Journal of Mormon History*, *Restoration Studies*, and *Sunstone*. He has served on the boards of the Graduate Theological Union in Berkeley, the *Kenyon Review*, the Leakey Foundation, and National Public Radio.

PRAISE FOR **NAUVOO POLYGAMY**

"[Here is] a portal to understanding where some contemporary Utah polygamists found inspiration for their way of life. From child brides and secret ceremonies to a defiance of marriage laws, the narrative in *Nauvoo Polygamy* illustrates the development and breadth of polygamy as first practiced in the 1840s by members of the LDS Church living in Illinois. ... It uniquely chronicles Illinois marriages between 196 Mormon men and 717 women—about four wives to each man."

—Jennifer Dobner, Associated Press

"The origins of Judaism, Christianity, and Islam are hidden by the sands of time. ... In Mormonism, we are close enough to the origins of the fourth Abrahamic religion ... so that an accurate account of its historical beginnings is available. ... Contributing to that history is this meticulously researched and well documented book."

—Paul Kurtz, editor in chief, *Free Inquiry*

"I was astonished to learn that ... Joseph Smith had married an average of one new wife a month between April 1841 and November 1843 and that he personally launched at least thirty-three plural marriages among his closest friends ... to share the 'favors and privileges of polygamy.' ... The author reads between the lines of diaries, autobiographies, letters, affidavits, Church records, and the authorized *History of the Church* ... to show how Joseph Smith went about secretly courting and marrying women ... This was publicly denied during Smith's lifetime and kept secret for eight years after his death."

—Vickie Cleverley Speek, *Association for Mormon Letters Online Reviews*

"Through exhaustive research and documentation, George Smith has chronicled the definitive account of polygamy in early Mormonism ... with encyclopedic detail."

—William D. Morain, *John Whitmer Historical Journal*

"George D. Smith, long a student of Mormon polygamy, offers the most detailed and sophisticated analysis of polygamy's origins and practice during the life of the prophet."

—Roger D. Launius, *Journal of Illinois History*

"In his ambitious new book, ... George D. Smith adds a square to the patchwork portrait that remains a work in progress some 164 years after the death of the charismatic founder of the LDS Church. ... *Nauvoo Polygamy* is a hefty tome that draws on diaries, letters, marriage records, affidavits, and Church records."

—Brooke Adams, *The Salt Lake Tribune*

"This book significantly broadens our understanding of plural marriage as practiced during the 1840s. In order to get a complete picture and understanding of Joseph Smith, I see this book as absolutely essential reading."

—Newell Bringhurst, co-editor, *The Persistence of Polygamy: Joseph Smith and the Origins of Mormon Polygamy*

"Impressive, meticulous, insightful, detailed, and documented historical scholarship by a noted Mormon historian ... highly recommended reading."

—*Midwest Book Review*

"*Nauvoo Polygamy* changes our understanding of a plurality of wives. It provides indisputable, quantifiable evidence that the scope of plural marriage was more broad and deep than we had imagined. It was all laid out in Nauvoo. The book's view on plural marriage in its earliest and subterranean years suggest that underage marriage has always been a part of the story."

—Martha Sonntag Bradley, author, *Four Zinas: A Story of Mothers and Daughters on the Mormon Frontier*

"On a scale of 1 to 10, I give this book a 9.78."

—Richard Howard, Church Historian Emeritus, Community of Christ (formerly the Reorganized Church of Jesus Christ of Latter Day Saints)

"George D. Smith has done some of the best work on early polygamy and Nauvoo. He tries very hard to say it like it is."

—B. Carmon Hardy, author, *Doing the Works of Abraham: Mormon Polygamy, Its Origin, Practice, and Demise*

"The author traces the origins and establishment of Joseph Smith's vision of 'spiritual wives' before it ever stepped foot in Utah. ... He places a human face on the men and women who struggled with their strange lives in a new religion. ... Whether you are a history buff, ... or just waiting for the new season of *Big Love* to start, *Nauvoo Polygamy* should be on your reading list."

—Dallas Robbins, *Salt Lake Weekly*